TEACHER'S EDITION

MAGRUDER'S AMERICAN GOVERNMENT

Daniel M. Shea

PEARSON

Boston, Massachusetts   Chandler, Arizona   Glenview, Illinois   New York, New York

Cover Images: The Ronald Reagan Presidential Library and Museum. Buttons, badges, and watches from the Reagan-Bush presidential campaign in the 80's are on display at the Ronald Reagan Presidential Library and Museum. Ruaridh Stewart/ZUMA/Corbis. Vintage American patriotic and political pins. Comstock/Stockbyte/Getty Images.

PEARSON

ISBN-13: 978-0-13-330710-8
ISBN-10: 0-13-330710-7

Authors, Consultants, Partners

[Authors]

Daniel M. Shea

Daniel M. Shea is a Professor of Political Science and Director of the Goldfarb Center for Public Affairs and Civic Engagement at Colby College. He earned his Ph.D. from the University of Albany, State University of New York. An award-winning teacher, Shea has spearheaded numerous initiatives at Colby and other institutions designed to help young Americans better appreciate their potential to affect democratic change. The author or editor of nearly twenty books and dozens of articles and chapters on the American political process, Shea's research focuses on campaigns and elections, political parties, the politics of scandal, and grassroots activism. His coauthored volume *The Fountain of Youth* (2007) garnered national attention for its findings on how local party organizations often neglect young citizens. His work on civility and compromise led to the publication of a co-edited volume, *Can We Talk? The Rise of Rude, Nasty, Stubborn Politics* (2012). Other works authored by Shea include *Let's Vote: The Essentials of the American Electoral Process* and the college text *Living Democracy*.

Magruder's American Government, first published in 1917, is a testament to the authors' faith in American ideals and American institutions. Frank Abbott Magruder's life and work serve as an outstanding example of American patriotism. After Magruder's death in 1949, his student, Bill McClenaghan, authored the text for the next sixty years and poured his own passion for American government into his work. The torch has now been passed to a new author, but the legacies of the previous authors live on through all the students and future readers of *Magruder's American Government*.

[Program Consultant]

Dr. Kathy Swan is an Associate Professor of Curriculum and Instruction at the University of Kentucky. Her research focuses on standards-based technology integration, authentic intellectual work, and documentary-making in the social studies classroom. Swan has been a four-time recipient of the National Technology Leadership Award in Social Studies Education. She is also the advisor for the Social Studies Assessment, Curriculum, and Instruction Collaborative (SSACI) at CCSSO.

[Program Partners]

NBC Learn, the educational arm of NBC News, develops original stories for use in the classroom and makes archival NBC News stories, images, and primary source documents available on demand to teachers, students, and parents. NBC Learn partnered with Pearson to produce the myStory videos that support this program.

Constitutional Rights Foundation is a nonprofit, nonpartisan organization focused on educating students about the importance of civic participation in a democratic society. Constitutional Rights Foundation is the lead contributor to the development of the Civic Discussion Topic Inquiries for this program. Constitutional Rights Foundation is also the provider of the Civic Action Project (CAP) for the *Economics* and *Magruder's American Government* programs. CAP is a project-based learning model for civics, government, and economics courses.

Reviewers & Academic Consultants

Pearson Magruder's American Government was developed especially for you and your students. The story of its creation began with a three-day Innovation Lab in which teachers, historians, students, and authors came together to imagine our ideal Social Studies teaching and learning experiences. We refined the plan with a series of teacher roundtables that shaped this new approach to ensure your students' mastery of content and skills. A dedicated team, made up of Pearson authors, content experts, and social studies teachers, worked to bring our collective vision into reality. Kathy Swan, Professor of Education and architect of the new College, Career, and Civic Life (C3) Framework, served as our expert advisor on curriculum and instruction.

Pearson would like to extend a special thank you to all of the teachers who helped guide the development of this program. We gratefully acknowledge your efforts to realize Next Generation Social Studies teaching and learning that will prepare American students for college, careers, and active citizenship.

[Program Advisors]

Campaign for the Civic Mission of Schools is a coalition of over 70 national civic learning, education, civic engagement, and business groups committed to improving the quality and quantity of civic learning in American schools. The Campaign served as an advisor on this program.

Buck Institute for Education is a nonprofit organization dedicated to helping teachers implement the effective use of Project-Based Learning in their classrooms. Buck Institute staff consulted on the Project-Based Learning Topic Inquiries for this program.

[Program Academic Consultants]

Barbara Brown
Director of Outreach
College of Arts and Sciences
African Studies Center
Boston University
Boston, Massachusetts

William Childs
Professor of History Emeritus
The Ohio State University
Columbus, Ohio

Jennifer Giglielmo
Associate Professor of History
Smith College
Northhampton, Massachusetts

Joanne Connor Green
Professor, Department Chair
Political Science
Texas Christian University
Fort Worth, Texas

Ramdas Lamb, Ph.D.
Associate Professor of Religion
University of Hawaii at Manoa
Honolulu, Hawaii

Huping Ling
Changjiang Scholar Chair Professor
Professor of History
Truman State University
Kirksville, Missouri

Jeffery Long, Ph.D.
Professor of Religion and Asian Studies
Elizabethtown College
Elizabethtown, Pennsylvania

Gordon Newby
Professor of Islamic, Jewish and
    Comparative Studies
Department of Middle Eastern and South
    Asian Studies
Emory University
Atlanta, Georgia

Mark Peterson
Associate Professor
Department of Asian and Near Eastern
    Languages
Brigham Young University
Provo, Utah

William Pitts
Professor, Department of Religion
Baylor University
Waco, Texas

Benjamin Ravid
Professor Emeritus of Jewish History
Department of Near Eastern and Judaic
    Studies
Brandeis University
Waltham, Massachusetts

Harpreet Singh
College Fellow
Department of South Asian Studies
Harvard University
Cambridge, Massachusetts

Christopher E. Smith, J.D., Ph.D.
Professor
Michigan State University
MSU School of Criminal Justice
East Lansing, Michigan

John Voll
Professor of Islamic History
Georgetown University
Washington, D.C.

Michael R. Wolf
Associate Professor
Department of Political Science
Indiana University-Purdue University Fort
    Wayne
Fort Wayne, Indiana

Realize Results. Social studies is more than dots on a map or dates on a timeline. It's where we've been and where we're going. It's stories from the past and our stories today. And in today's fast-paced, interconnected world, it's essential.

Instruction Your Way!

Comprehensive teaching support is available in two different formats:

- **Teacher's Edition:** Designed like a "T.V. Guide," teaching suggestions are paired with preview images of digital resources.

- **Teaching Support Online:** Teaching suggestions, answer keys, blackline masters, and other resources are provided at point-of-use online in Realize.

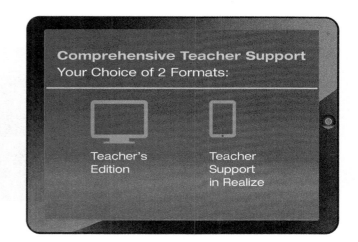

Comprehensive Teacher Support
Your Choice of 2 Formats:

Teacher's Edition

Teacher Support in Realize

Pearson Mastery System

This complete system for teaching and learning uses best practices, technology, and a four-part framework—Connect, Investigate, Synthesize, and Demonstrate—to prepare students to be college-and-career ready.

- Higher-level content that gives students support to access complex text, acquire skills and tackle rigorous questions.

- Inquiry-focused Projects, Civic Discussions, and Document-Based Questions that prepare students for real-world challenges;

- Digital content on Pearson Realize that is dynamic, flexible, and uses the power of technology to bring social studies to life.

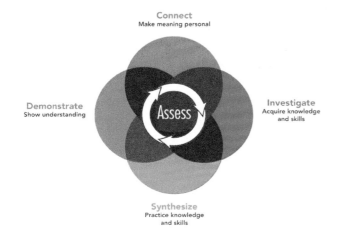

Table of Contents for Today's Learners

Today's learners research new information by using a search engine and browsing by topic. Breaking out of a book metaphor of "chapters," this table of contents is organized by:

- **Topic:** As you decide what you want to teach, you search first for the topic.

- **Lesson:** Within each topic are several lessons where you will find a variety of diverse resources to support teaching and learning.

- **Text:** Each lesson contains chunked information called Texts. This is the same informational text that appears in the print Student Edition.

This organization saves time, improves pacing, and makes it easy to rearrange content.

» Go online to learn more and see the program overview video.

PEARSON
realize™

CONNECT! Begin the Pearson Mastery System by engaging in the topic story and connecting it to your own lives.

Preview—Each Topic opens with the Enduring Understandings section, allowing you to preview expected learning outcomes.

>> Instruction begins with an **Essential Question**. These thought-provoking questions engage students and introduce the Topic.

[**ESSENTIAL QUESTION**] What Should Governments Do?

6 The Executive Branch at Work

Watch the My Story Video to learn more about independent agencies by exploring NASA's role in advancements in technology.

Developed in partnership with NBCLearn, the **My Story** videos help students connect to the Topic content by hearing the personal story of an individual whose life is related to the content students are about to learn.

INVESTIGATE! Step two of the Mastery System allows you to investigate the topic story through a number of engaging features as you learn the content.

>> **Active Classroom Strategies** integrated in the daily lesson plans help to increase in-class participation, raise energy levels and attentiveness, all while engaging in the story. These 5-15 minute activities have you use what you have learned to draw, write, speak, and decide.

>> **Interactive Primary Source Galleries:** Use primary source image galleries throughout the lesson to see, analyze, and interact with images that tie to the topic story content.

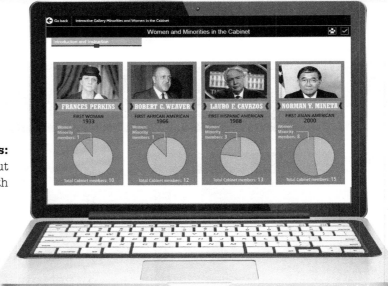

Investigate

>> Feel like you are a part of the story with **interactive 3-D models**.

>> Continue to investigate the topic story through **dynamic interactive charts, graphs, and timelines**. Build skills while covering the essential standards.

>> Learn content by reading narrative text online or in a printed Student Edition.

Synthesize: Practice Knowledge and Skills

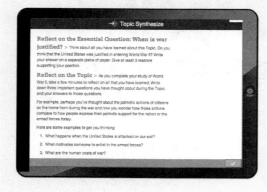

SYNTHESIZE!

In step three of the Mastery System, pause to reflect on what you learn and revisit an essential question.

DEMONSTRATE! The final step of the Mastery System is to demonstrate understanding of the text.

PEARSON realize™

>> The digital course on Realize! The program's digital course on Realize puts engaging content, embedded assessments, instant data, and flexible tools at your fingertips.

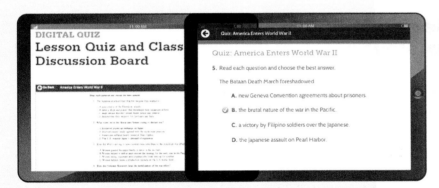

>> Assessment. At the end of each lesson and topic, demonstrate understanding through Lesson Quizzes, Topic Tests, and Topic Inquiry performance assessments. The System provides remediation and enrichment recommendations based on your individual performance towards mastery.

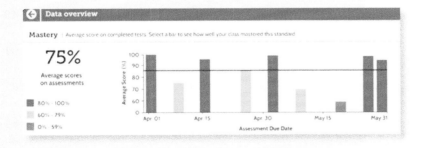

>> Class and Data features on Realize make it easy to see your mastery data.

Digital Course Content

Digital Course Content

Digital Course Content

Many types of digital resources help you investigate the topics in this course. You'll find biographies, primary sources, maps, and more. These resources will help bring the topics to life.

Core Concepts

 Culture

- What Is Culture?
- Families and Societies
- Language
- Religion
- The Arts
- Cultural Diffusion and Change
- Science and Technology

 Economics

- Economics Basics
- Economic Process
- Economic Systems
- Economic Development
- Trade
- Money Management

 Geography

- The Study of Earth
- Geography's Five Themes
- Ways to Show Earth's Surface
- Understanding Maps

- Earth in Space
- Time and Earth's Rotation
- Forces on Earth's Surface
- Forces Inside Earth
- Climate and Weather
- Temperature
- Water and Climate
- Air Circulation and Precipitation
- Types of Climate
- Ecosystems
- Environment and Resources
- Land Use
- People's Impact on the Environment
- Population
- Migration
- Urbanization

 Government and Civics

- Foundations of Government
- Political Systems
- Political Structures
- Conflict and Cooperation
- Citizenship

 History

- How Do Historians Study History?
- Measuring Time
- Historical Sources
- Archaeology and Other Sources
- Historical Maps

 Personal Finance

- Your Fiscal Fitness: An Introduction
- Budgeting
- Checking
- Investments
- Savings and Retirement
- Credit and Debt
- Risk Management
- Consumer Smarts
- After High School
- Taxes and Income

Landmark Supreme Court Cases

- *Korematsu* v. *United States*
- *Marbury* v. *Madison*
- *McCulloch* v. *Maryland*
- *Gibbons* v. *Ogden*
- *Worcester* v. *Georgia*
- *Dred Scott* v. *Sandford*
- *Plessy* v. *Ferguson*
- *Schenck* v. *United States*
- *Brown* v. *Board of Education*
- *Engel* v. *Vitale*

- *Sweatt* v. *Painter*
- *Mapp* v. *Ohio*
- *Hernandez* v. *Texas*
- *Gideon* v. *Wainwright*
- *Wisconsin* v. *Yoder*
- *Miranda* v. *Arizona*
- *White* v. *Regester*
- *Tinker* v. *Des Moines School District*
- *Roe* v. *Wade*

- *Baker* v. *Carr*
- *Grutter* v. *Bollinger*
- *Edgewood* v. *Kirby*
- *Texas* v. *Johnson*
- *National Federation of Independent Businesses et al.* v. *Sebelius et al.*
- *Mendez* v. *Westminster* and *Delgado* v. *Bastrop*

Digital Resources

 Interactive Primary Sources

- Code of Hammurabi
- Psalm 23
- The Republic, Plato
- Politics, Aristotle
- Edicts, Asoka
- Analects, Confucius
- First Letter to the Corinthians, Paul
- The Quran
- The Magna Carta
- Travels, Ibn Battuta
- The Destruction of the Indies, Bartolomé de Las Casas
- Mayflower Compact
- English Petition of Right
- English Bill of Rights
- Two Treatises of Government, John Locke
- The Spirit of Laws, Baron de Montesquieu
- The Social Contract, Jean-Jacques Rousseau
- The Interesting Narrative of the Life of Olaudah Equiano
- "Give Me Liberty or Give Me Death," Patrick Henry
- "Remember the Ladies," Abigail Adams
- Common Sense, Thomas Paine
- Declaration of Independence
- Virginia Declaration of Rights
- Virginia Statute for Religious Freedom, Thomas Jefferson
- "To His Excellency, General Washington," Phillis Wheatley
- Articles of Confederation
- Anti-Federalist Papers
- The Federalist No. 10, James Madison
- The Federalist No. 39, James Madison
- The Federalist No. 51
- The Federalist No. 78, Alexander Hamilton
- Northwest Ordinance
- Iroquois Constitution
- Declaration of the Rights of Man and the Citizen
- Farewell Address, George Washington
- Mexican Federal Constitution of 1824
- State Colonization Law of 1825
- Law of April 6, 1830
- Debate Over Nullification, Webster and Calhoun
- Turtle Bayou Resolutions
- Democracy in America, Alexis de Tocqueville
- 1836 Victory or Death Letter from the Alamo, Travis
- Texas Declaration of Independence
- Declaration of Sentiments and Resolutions
- "Ain't I a Woman?," Sojourner Truth
- Uncle Tom's Cabin, Harriet Beecher Stowe
- "A House Divided," Abraham Lincoln
- First Inaugural Address, Abraham Lincoln
- Declaration of Causes: February 2, 1861
- Emancipation Proclamation, Abraham Lincoln
- Gettysburg Address, Abraham Lincoln
- Second Inaugural Address, Abraham Lincoln
- "I Will Fight No More Forever," Chief Joseph
- How the Other Half Lives, Jacob Riis
- The Pledge of Allegiance
- Preamble to the Platform of the Populist Party
- Atlanta Exposition Address, Booker T. Washington
- The Jungle, Upton Sinclair
- Hind Swaraj, Mohandas Gandhi
- The Fourteen Points, Woodrow Wilson
- Two Poems, Langston Hughes
- Four Freedoms, Franklin D. Roosevelt
- Anne Frank: The Diary of a Young Girl, Anne Frank
- Charter of the United Nations
- Universal Declaration of Human Rights
- Autobiography, Kwame Nkrumah
- Inaugural Address, John F. Kennedy
- Silent Spring, Rachel Carson
- "I Have a Dream," Martin Luther King, Jr.
- "Letter From Birmingham Jail," Martin Luther King, Jr.
- "Tear Down This Wall," Ronald Reagan
- "Freedom From Fear," Aung San Suu Kyi
- "Glory and Hope," Nelson Mandela

Biographies

- Abigail Adams
- John Adams
- John Quincy Adams
- Samuel Adams
- James Armistead
- Crispus Attucks
- Moses Austin
- Stephen F. Austin
- James A. Baker III
- William Blackstone
- Simón Bolívar
- Napoleon Bonaparte
- Chief Bowles
- Omar Bradley
- John C. Calhoun
- César Chávez
- Wentworth Cheswell
- George Childress
- Winston Churchill
- Henry Clay
- Bill Clinton
- Jefferson Davis
- Martin De León
- Green DeWitt
- Dwight Eisenhower
- James Fannin
- James L. Farmer, Jr.
- Benjamin Franklin
- Milton Friedman
- Betty Friedan
- Bernardo de Gálvez
- Hector P. Garcia
- John Nance Garner
- King George III
- Henry B. González
- Raul A. Gonzalez, Jr.
- Mikhail Gorbachev
- William Goyens

- Ulysses S. Grant
- José Gutiérrez de Lara
- Alexander Hamilton
- Hammurabi
- Warren Harding
- Friedrich Hayek
- Jack Coffee Hays
- Patrick Henry
- Adolf Hitler
- Oveta Culp Hobby
- James Hogg
- Sam Houston
- Kay Bailey Hutchison
- Andrew Jackson
- John Jay
- Thomas Jefferson
- Lyndon B. Johnson
- Anson Jones
- Barbara Jordan
- Justinian
- John F. Kennedy
- John Maynard Keynes
- Martin Luther King, Jr.
- Marquis de Lafayette
- Mirabeau B. Lamar
- Robert E. Lee
- Abraham Lincoln
- John Locke
- James Madison
- John Marshall
- George Marshall
- Karl Marx
- George Mason
- Mary Maverick
- Jane McCallum
- Joseph McCarthy
- James Monroe
- Charles de Montesquieu

- Edwin W. Moore
- Moses
- Benito Mussolini
- José Antonio Navarro
- Chester A. Nimitz
- Richard M. Nixon
- Barack Obama
- Sandra Day O'Connor
- Thomas Paine
- Quanah Parker
- Rosa Parks
- George Patton
- John J. Pershing
- John Paul II
- Sam Rayburn
- Ronald Reagan
- Hiram Rhodes Revels
- Franklin D. Roosevelt
- Theodore Roosevelt
- Lawrence Sullivan Ross
- Haym Soloman
- Antonio Lopez de Santa Anna
- Phyllis Schlafly
- Erasmo Seguín
- Juan N. Seguín
- Roger Sherman
- Adam Smith
- Joseph Stalin
- Raymond L. Telles
- Alexis de Tocqueville
- Hideki Tojo
- William B. Travis
- Harry Truman
- Lech Walesa
- Mercy Otis Warren
- George Washington
- Daniel Webster

- Lulu Belle Madison White
- William Wilberforce
- James Wilson
- Woodrow Wilson
- Lorenzo de Zavala
- Mao Zedong

Digital Resources

21st Century Skills

- Identify Main Ideas and Details
- Set a Purpose for Reading
- Use Context Clues
- Analyze Cause and Effect
- Categorize
- Compare and Contrast
- Draw Conclusions
- Draw Inferences
- Generalize
- Make Decisions
- Make Predictions
- Sequence
- Solve Problems
- Summarize
- Analyze Media Content
- Analyze Primary and Secondary Sources
- Compare Viewpoints
- Distinguish Between Fact and Opinion
- Identify Bias
- Analyze Data and Models

- Analyze Images
- Analyze Political Cartoons
- Create Charts and Maps
- Create Databases
- Read Charts, Graphs, and Tables
- Read Physical Maps
- Read Political Maps
- Read Special-Purpose Maps
- Use Parts of a Map
- Ask Questions
- Avoid Plagiarism
- Create a Research Hypothesis
- Evaluate Web Sites
- Identify Evidence
- Identify Trends
- Interpret Sources
- Search for Information on the Internet
- Synthesize
- Take Effective Notes
- Develop a Clear Thesis
- Organize Your Ideas

- Support Ideas With Evidence
- Evaluate Existing Arguments
- Consider & Counter Opposing Arguments
- Give an Effective Presentation
- Participate in a Discussion or Debate
- Publish Your Work
- Write a Journal Entry
- Write an Essay
- Share Responsibility
- Compromise
- Develop Cultural Awareness
- Generate New Ideas
- Innovate
- Make a Difference
- Work in Teams
- Being an Informed Citizen
- Paying Taxes
- Political Participation
- Serving on a Jury
- Voting

Atlas

- United States: Political
- United States: Physical
- World Political
- World Physical
- World Climate
- World Ecosystems
- World Population Density
- World Land Use
- North Africa and Southwest Asia: Political
- North Africa and Southwest Asia: Physical
- Sub-Saharan Africa: Political
- Sub-Saharan Africa: Physical
- South Asia: Political
- South Asia: Physical
- East Asia: Political

- East Asia: Physical
- Southeast Asia: Political
- Southeast Asia: Physical
- Europe: Political
- Europe: Physical
- Russia, Central Asia, and the Caucasus: Political
- Russia, Central Asia, and the Caucasus: Physical
- North America: Political
- North America: Physical
- Central America and the Caribbean: Political
- Central America and the Caribbean: Physical
- South America: Political
- South America: Physical
- Australia and the Pacific: Political
- Australia and the Pacific: Physical

Creating an Active Classroom

This Social Studies program places a strong emphasis on

Inquiry in the form of

- Document-Based Questions
- Project-Based Learning
- Civic Discussions

Each inquiry strand requires students to formulate their own arguments based on evidence. To support this learning approach, the program integrates **Active Classroom strategies** throughout each lesson. These strategies encourage students to begin building their own arguments and collecting evidence about the past and present at even the earliest stages of a lesson.

You can use these strategies to help students participate in their own learning as you call upon them to

- draw
- write
- speak
- decide

You'll find a rich variety of these strategy suggestions throughout both the Teacher's Edition and online **Teacher Support** for each lesson.

Creating an Active Classroom

ACTIVE CLASSROOM STRATEGIES

ACTIVITY NAME	HOW TO ACTIVATE
Quickdraw	· Pair students and give them 30 seconds to share what they know about a concept or Key Term by creating a symbol or drawing.
Graffiti Concepts	· Ask students to reflect on the meaning of a concept or idea and create a visual image and/or written phrase that represents that concept. Allow approximately 3–5 minutes. · Next ask students to post their "graffiti" on the board or on chart paper and ask students to look at all the various responses. · Next discuss similarities and differences in the responses as a group.
Word Wall	· Ask students to chose one of the Key Terms for the lesson and create a visual image with a text definition. Allow approximately 3–5 minutes. · Ask students to post their words on the board or on chart paper and ask students to look at all the various responses. · Discuss similarities and differences in the responses as a group. · Pick a few favorites and post them on the cvlass "Word Wall" for the year.
Cartoon It	· Ask students to make a quick drawing of one compelling image from this lesson on a piece of paper. · Next ask students to turn their drawing into a political cartoon that illustrates a key concept or main idea from the lesson by adding a text caption or text "bubbles." · Ask students to share their cartoons with a partner or within small groups.
Wallpaper	· Ask students to review information they have learned in a topic and design a piece of "wallpaper" that encapsulates key learnings. · Then have students post their wallpaper and take a "gallery" walk noting what others have written and illustrated in their samples.
Quick Write	· Ask students to write what they know about a key idea or term in 30 seconds.
Make Headlines	· Have students write a headline that captures the key idea in a map, photo, timeline, or reading. · Ask students to share their headline with a partner.
Circle Write	· Break into groups and provide a writing prompt or key question. · Have students write as much as they can in response to the question or prompt for 1 minute. · Next have students give their response to the person on their right. That person should improve or elaborate on the response where the other person left off. · Continue to pass each response to the right until the original response comes back to the first person. · Each group then reviews all the responses and decides which is the best composition and shares that with the larger group.
Write 1-Get 3 (or Write 5-Get 4)	· Ask a question with multiple answers, such as: What are 4 key characteristics of _____ (a dictator)? What are the 5 key causes of _____? · Have students write down 1 response and then go around the room asking for 3 other responses. If they think a response is correct, ask them to write it down. · Have students keep asking and writing until they have 3 more responses on their page. · Have students share and discuss responses with the class.

ACTIVE CLASSROOM STRATEGIES

ACTIVITY NAME	HOW TO ACTIVATE
Sticky Notes	· Ask students to spend three minutes jotting down their response to a critical thinking question on a sticky note. · Ask students to work in pairs and share their responses. · Next ssk students to post their sticky notes on the board or on chart paper and read all the notes. · Discuss similarities and differences in the responses as a group.
Connect Two	· Select 10 to 12 words or phrases you think are important for students to know prior to reading a selection. · List the words on the board. · Ask students to "Connect Two" or choose two words they think might belong together, and state the reason. "I would connect _____ and _____ because _____." Consider posting their Connect Two statements on the board. · As students read the text they should look for evidence to support or refute their Connect Two statements.
Conversation With History	· Ask students to choose one of the people mentioned or pictured in the text and write down a question they would like to ask that person if they could. · Next ask students to write what they think that person would say in response and then what they would say in response to that.
Walking Tour	· Post passages from a reading around the room. · Ask small groups to tour the room and discuss each passage. · Summarize each passage as a class. · Alternatively, assign each small group to a passage and have them summarize that passage for the rest of the class.
Audio Tour	· Ask students to work in pairs. Have the first student give the second a verbal "tour" of a map or graph or infographic. · Have the second student give the first an explanation of what the graphic shows.
My Metaphor	· Post the following metaphor on the board: This (map, timeline, image, primary source) shows that _____ is like _____ because _____. · Ask students to fill in the metaphor prompt based on their understanding of the source.
Act It Out	· Choose an image in the lesson and ask students to think about one of the following questions as appropriate to the image: · What may have happened next in this image? · What may have happened just before this image? · What do you think the people in this image are thinking? · What do you think the people in this image are saying to each other?
If Photos/Images/Art Could Talk	· Ask the following questions about an image in the course: What do you think the person in this photo would say if they could talk? What's your evidence?

Creating an Active Classroom

ACTIVE CLASSROOM STRATEGIES

ACTIVITY NAME	HOW TO ACTIVATE
See-Think-Wonder	· Ask students to work in pairs. · Ask them to look at an image, map, or graph and answer these questions: · What do you see? · What does that make you think? · What are you wondering about now that you've seen this? · Have students share their answers with the class.
A Closer Look	· Project a map or image on the board and divide it into four numbered quadrants. · Have students count off from 1 to 4 into four small groups. Have each group look closely at the part of the image in their quadrant. · Have each small group report on what they observed and learned as a result of their focus on this part of the image.
Take a Stand	· Ask students to take a stand on a yes-or-no or agree/disagree critical thinking question. · Ask students to divide into two groups based on their answer and move to separate areas of the classroom. · Ask students to talk with each other to compare their reasons for answering yes or no. · Ask a representative from each side to present and defend the group's point of view. · Note: you can adapt this activity to have students take their place on a continuum line from 1 to 10 depending on how strongly they agree or disagree.
Rank It	· List a group of items/concepts/steps/causes/events on the board. · Ask students to rank the items/steps . . . according to X criteria (which is most important, which had the greatest impact . . . most influential, essential, changed, affected). · Ask students to provide a justification for the ranking decisions they made. · Then ask students to work in pairs to share their rankings and justifications. · Poll the class to see if there is agreement on the ranking. OR · Place stickies on the board with key events from the lesson or topic. · Break students into small groups and ask each group to go up and choose the sticky with what they think is the most significant event. · Ask the group to discuss among themselves why they think it is most significant. · Ask one person from each group to explain why the group chose that event.
Sequence It	· Place key events from a lesson or topic on sticky notes on the board. · Ask students to place the events in chronological order. · You could do this activity with multiple groups in different parts of the classroom.
PMI Plus/Minus/Interesting	· Place students in groups and give each group a 3-column organizer with headings Plus/Minus/Interesting for recording responses. · Ask students to analyze a text or examine an issue and then answer these three questions in their organizer: · What was positive about this text/issue? · What was negative about this text/issue? · What was interesting about this text/issue?

Celebrate Freedom

Objective 1: Analyze and evaluate the importance of the Declaration of Independence and the U.S. Constitution; **2:** Identify the full text of the first three paragraphs of the Declaration of Independence.

Quick Instruction

Using these materials, students can prepare for Celebrate Freedom Week by thinking about the importance of the Declaration of Independence and the U.S. Constitution. Have students read the first three paragraphs of the Declaration of Independence. Then ask them to recite the "social contract" section. The materials will help you make links between Celebrate Freedom Week and your course of study.

Aa Vocabulary Development: Before students recite the words of the Declaration of Independence, review key terms such as *self-evident, endowed, unalienable* and *consent*. Ask students to compose a sentence using each word. Then have students paraphrase the excerpt from the Declaration, putting the ideas into their own words.

Have students recite the Declaration to each other or as a whole class.

During the school year, remember to help students look back to the ideas expressed in the Declaration, especially if your course includes topics like: the American Revolution, writing of the U.S. Constitution, Abolitionist Movement, Emancipation Proclamation, Women's Suffrage Movement, and immigration and American diversity.

Identify Central Ideas *an agreement between the people and the government; the people benefit because they control the government, which is created by the people to ensure that they will have their rights protected.*

Contrast *In a monarchy, all rights come from the royal power; rights are not created or determined by the people. In a dictatorship, power is concentrated in the hands of one person; the people have few or any rights.*

Apply Information *Answers will vary, but might include ideas such as: local and state governments provide police protection to ensure everyone's safety. The federal government protects against discrimination based on characteristics like race, gender, national background, or disabilities.*

Further Instruction

Constitution Day Assembly Help students organize and carry out a Constitution Day assembly.

Organize Students may need help getting organized. Ask them to consider additional questions such as these:

1. What activities will keep students of different grade levels interested?

2. Should you hang posters around the school or get permission to make announcements about the assembly?

3. How can you make this year's Celebrate Freedom Week special?

Plan After the discussion, divide the class into committees that will work on various aspects of the assembly. Depending on how much time you have and the skills and interests of your students, you might suggest committees such as these:

- Administrative Committee: prepares a proposal for the school administration, explaining the purpose of the assembly and what will be needed. The Administrative Committee also organizes the final assembly.

- Advertising Committee: publicizes the assembly in the school and community. This may include creating posters, using social media and other online resources, and contacting local media outlets.

- Activity Committees: plan and execute the individual parts of the program.

Communicate After the assembly, ask some students to publish photos taken during the assembly or to write a letter to the local newspaper about the assembly. If you invited guest speakers, others should send thank-you notes to the speakers. Have students write a thank-you note to the school administrator for allowing them to present the assembly.

Foundations of Government

TOPIC 1 ORGANIZER	PACING: APPROX. 1 PERIOD, .5 BLOCKS
	PACING
Connect	1 period
MY STORY VIDEO **John Locke, Natural Rights**	10 min.
DIGITAL ESSENTIAL QUESTION ACTIVITY **What Should Governments Do?**	10 min.
DIGITAL OVERVIEW ACTIVITY **Five Concepts of U.S. Government**	10 min.
TOPIC INQUIRY: CIVIC ACTION PROJECT **Constitutional Rights Foundation**	20 min.
Investigate	2–4 periods
TOPIC INQUIRY: CIVIC ACTION PROJECT **Constitutional Rights Foundation**	Ongoing
LESSON 1 Principles of Government	30–40 min.
LESSON 2 Types of Government	30–40 min.
LESSON 3 Origins of the Modern Democratic State	30–40 min.
LESSON 4 The Basics of Democracy	30–40 min.
Synthesize	1 period
DIGITAL ACTIVITY **Reflecting on What Governments Should Do**	10 min.
TOPIC INQUIRY: CIVIC ACTION PROJECT **Constitutional Rights Foundation**	20 min.
Demonstrate	1–2 periods
DIGITAL TOPIC REVIEW AND ASSESSMENT **Foundations of Government**	10 min.
TOPIC INQUIRY: CIVIC ACTION PROJECT **Constitutional Rights Foundation**	20 min.

 **TOPIC INQUIRY:**

Civic Action Project

For this topic's Inquiry, you may choose to do a Civic Action Project with your students by using the materials found at the Constitutional Rights Foundation's CAP website: http://www.crfcap.org. Civic Action Project (CAP) is a project-based learning model for government and economics courses. It offers a practicum for high school students in effective and engaged citizenship and uses blended learning to engage students in civic activities both in the traditional U.S. government and economics classrooms.

Constitutional
Rights
Foundation
Educate. Participate.

THE TEACHER'S ROLE

THE CAP TEACHER coaches and guides students through the civic action process as they select a problem or issue, research it, determine and take civic actions, and report and document the experience. The teacher motivates, challenges, critiques, and assesses student progress. Through a blended learning approach, teachers can let students take the reins of their civic learning, guiding them along the way.

[You can create your CAP classroom in three easy steps]

[**STEP 1**
Register yourself for the CAP website]

[**STEP 2**
Enroll your students]

[**STEP 3**
Engage your students in the CAP process and its many resources]

THE STUDENT'S ROLE

CAP ALLOWS STUDENTS to create projects on issues they care about for their school or community. They see the connection between their civic actions and public policy and can share ideas for civics projects with each other and other CAP students nationwide. Students also see how the content of government and economics courses can apply to the real world. By taking civic actions, they practice what real citizens do when they go about trying to solve real policy-related problems. CAP fulfills best-practices in service-learning with an emphasis on public policy.

The CAP student is accountable for completing the civic action process, just as with a science project or term paper. The CAP Planner, a set of documents that guide students through the process, provides teachers with assessment information as well as a way to manage multiple student projects. While the teacher introduces and monitors the CAP, it is important that students take the lead in completing their civic actions. By using web-based technology and civics-based instruction and activities, students exercise important 21st century skills in digital literacy, critical thinking, collaboration, self-direction, and learning to be engaged and effective citizens.

CIVIC ACTIONS CAP challenges students to work on an actual problem, issue, or policy by taking civic actions. Civic actions build upon classroom civics issues, service-learning, and other proven practices of effective civic education. These actions can be many and varied, including:

- getting informed about a public issue or problem
- thinking critically about the issue or problem
- discovering how government is involved with the problem
- learning how government makes decisions
- developing a position
- engaging in civic dialogue
- building constituencies
- working together toward a common goal
- doing civic writing
- making presentations
- advocating for and defending positions
- meeting with officials

Brainstorming

Brainstorming is a method for generating ideas. It can be done by individuals or in small or large

Rules for Brainst

Pose a question to a

Set a time limit on th more ideas out.

Work as fast as you

Handout Lesson 5B
Civic Action Project

G R A D E
CAP Policy Analysis Tool

AS CITIZENS IN A DEMOCRACY, YOU'LL BE CONFRONTED WITH POLICY QUESTIONS. IS A TAX PROPOSAL A GOOD IDEA? SHOULD YOU VOTE FOR A PARTICULAR BALLOT INITIATIVE? GOVERNMENT POLICIES CAN PROFOUNDLY AFFECT OUR NATION AND YOUR LIFE. IN A DEMOCRACY, YOU HAVE A SAY ON GOVERNMENT POLICIES AND PROPOSED POLICIES. IT'S IMPORTANT THAT YOU TAKE A CRITICAL LOOK AT THEM. USE THE FOLLOWING GRADE TESTS TO EVALUATE A POLICY:

G OAL. WHAT IS THE GOAL OF THE POLICY? IF YOU DON'T KNOW WHAT IT'S SUPPOSED TO DO, YOU CAN'T MEASURE ITS SUCCESS OR FAILURE. POLICIES ARE DESIGNED TO ADDRESS PROBLEMS. WHAT PROBLEM OR PROBLEMS IS

OLICY? WHO MIGHT (OR DOES) YOU UNDERSTAND WHO THE ICY FAVORS SPECIAL CES FOR INFORMATION, BUT

ITS? WHAT IS GOOD ABOUT THE SES OR EFFECTS OF THE VED) ITS GOAL? WILL IT NSIVE? DOES IT PROTECT E'S LIBERTIES?

OSTS? WHAT IS BAD ABOUT THE THE CAUSES OR EFFECTS OF THE ? DOES IT CAUSE HARM? DOES RE ANY POTENTIAL

E DISADVANTAGES. ARE THERE TO DO NOTHING. MOST SERIOUS EVALUATE THEM. LOOK AT ES.

© 2012 Constitutional Rights Foundation

Conducting Meetings

Your meetings should be organized, to-the-point, and fun.

Decide how you're going to make decisions. If you are a small group, try deciding by whole-group consensus or by a two-thirds vote. A simple-majority decision may lead to bad feelings and resentment.

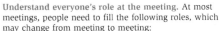

Understand everyone's role at the meeting. At most meetings, people need to fill the following roles, which may change from meeting to meeting:

- Leader or facilitator runs the meeting, follows the agenda item by item, and watches the time allotted for each. The leader helps participants focus on the task and makes sure everyone has a chance to participate.
- Recorder takes minutes, which include date and time of meeting, the persons attending, and notes on each agenda item.
- Treasurer.
- Group members contribute agenda items, discuss topics, make decisions, and take responsibility for various tasks.
- Adviser is an adult whose role is to give advice—not to run the group.
- Guests may participate in group discussions, but usually do not participate in final decision making.

Have an agenda. This is a list of things to be dealt with at a meeting. All members should be encouraged to put topics on the agenda. After the recorder reads the minutes of the previous meeting and they are approved, the members approve the agenda. Agenda items are considered in the following order:

- Old business—ongoing and follow-up items.

© 2012. Constitutional Rights Foundation
and Close Up Foundation

Constitutional
Rights
Foundation
Educate. Participate.

Guardian of Democracy: The Civic Mission of Schools
Released September, 2011, *Guardian of Democracy: The Civic Mission of Schools report* builds on the findings of the seminal 2003 Civic Mission of Schools report. CAP has been designed to support the promising approaches described in these reports.

Foundations of Government

Government is commonly considered a necessary part of society. Because of this, almost all states have governments. Many governments share common features and purposes. The types of government, though, can vary greatly, from dictatorships to democracies. In addition, not all governments effectively perform the services required of them. Why do governments exist? What should governments do?

▊ CONNECT

MY STORY VIDEO
John Locke, Natural Rights

Watch a video that introduces students to the principles that helped inspire American independence.

Identify Central Issues What did Locke think was "the great question" of all ages? *("Who shall have the power?")*

Apply Concepts How did Locke's ideas help inspire the American Revolution? *(He said that if rulers did not have the consent of the governed, people had the right to rebel.)*

> **⚑ FLIP IT!**
>
> Assign the My Story video

DIGITAL ESSENTIAL QUESTION ACTIVITY
What Should Governments Do?

Ask students to think about the Essential Question for this Topic: What Should Governments Do? Government is considered by many to be a necessary part of society. What needs do governments fulfill?

Conduct a class discussion, in which you ask volunteers to answer the Essential Question. Write responses on the board and then discuss the responses with the class.

Infer The Preamble of the U.S. Constitution states: "We the People of the United States, in Order to form a more perfect Union, establish Justice, insure domestic Tranquility, provide for the common defence, promote the General Welfare, and secure the Blessings of Liberty . . ." What does this statement suggest about what governments should do? *(help to unify countries; make sure that people are treated fairly; protect citizens from enemies; and protect people's rights)*

Paraphrase What does "insure domestic tranquility" mean? Write the answer in your own words without using a dictionary. *(Possible answer: make sure that people's daily lives are peaceful; make sure that people are not afraid of violent acts in their daily lives)*

DIGITAL OVERVIEW ACTIVITY
Five Concepts of U.S. Government

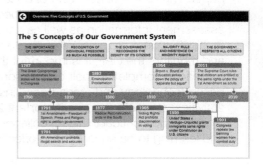

Display the timeline showing major events in the development of the U.S. government. These events provide examples of the five concepts of the U.S. government.

ⅅ Differentiate: Extra Support How many years are there between when Radical Reconstruction ended in the South and when the Voting Rights Act was passed? *(88 years; Radical Reconstruction ended in 1877; Voting Rights Act passed in 1965)*

Check Understanding What events show the U.S. government supporting the recognition of individual freedoms? *(1st Amendment, United States v. Verdugo-Urquidez)*

Draw Conclusions Based on the timeline, do you think the U.S. government always insisted on minority rights? Explain. *(Possible answer: No; legislation that supported minority rights is first listed in 1965. This late date indicates that perhaps the United States did not always insist on minority rights.)*

Topic Inquiry
Launch the Topic Inquiry with students after introducing the Topic.

Principles of Government

Supporting English Language Learners

Use with Digital Text 1, **Government–We the People.**

Learning Strategies
Have students look at images in the text which represent the word *government*. Ask students to provide information about other symbols of government.

Beginning Tell students that all of the images are related to the word *government*. Define the word for the students. Guide students to label each picture.

Intermediate Based on their prior knowledge about government, have partners with similar language abilities find two images that have something in common. Discuss the definition and purposes of government with students. Have students tell what their two images have in common.

Advanced Ask students to select an image that is familiar to them. Have partners with similar language abilities share their prior knowledge about the images. After a class discussion about the definition and purpose of government, have partners discuss new knowledge they have about the images.

Advanced High Have students discuss their prior knowledge about the images. Discuss the definition and purpose of government and the characteristics of a state. Have students select an image and write about how it relates to the discussion topic.

Use with Digital Text 4, **What Government Does.**

Reading
Read the preamble to the Constitution with students and point out examples of language structure. Explain that the language structure tells students why the Preamble was written the way it was written.

Beginning Guide students to read the language structure of the Preamble. Have students complete the following sentence frame: *The _____ tells the people of the _____ what the purpose is of the Constitution.*

Intermediate In addition to language examples, provide examples of comprehension questions. Ask students to read and label each example as *language* or *question*.

Advanced Have partners find other examples of language structure and questions in the text. Create a class chart of the examples students find.

Advanced High Have partners write two sentences using language structure similar to the Preamble and two questions. Have students read their examples to the class.

▷ Differentiate Instruction

Use the Differentiated Instruction notes throughout the lesson plan to support the varied skill sets, levels of readiness, and interests in the mixed-ability classroom.

Challenge These notes include suggestions for expanding the activity for advanced students.

On-Level These notes include suggestions for modifying the activity to address different interests or learning styles.

Extra Support These notes include ideas for providing more scaffolding or reading spuport.

Special Needs These notes provide ideas for adapting instruction to support the needs of various special needs students.

■ NOTES

Principles of Government

Objectives

Objective 1: Define government and the basic powers every government holds.

Objective 2: Describe the four defining characteristics of a state.

Objective 3: Identify the four theories that attempt to explain the origin of the state.

Objective 4: Understand the purpose of government in the United States and other countries.

LESSON 1 ORGANIZER		PACING: APPROX. 1 PERIOD, .5 BLOCKS			
		OBJECTIVES	PACING	RESOURCES	
				Online	Print
Connect					
DIGITAL START UP ACTIVITY **Government and You**			5 min.	●	
Investigate					
DIGITAL TEXT 1 **Government–We The People**		Objective 1	10 min.	●	●
INTERACTIVE CHART **The Three Branches of Government**			10 min.	●	
DIGITAL TEXT 2 **The State**		Objective 2	10 min.	●	●
INTERACTIVE MAP **Four Characteristics of a State**			10 min.	●	
DIGITAL TEXT 3 **How States Arose**		Objective 3	10 min.	●	●
DIGITAL TEXT 4 **What Government Does**		Objective 4	10 min.	●	●
Synthesize					
DIGITAL SYNTHESIZE ACTIVITY **Revisiting Government and You**			5 min.	●	
Demonstrate					
DIGITAL QUIZ **Lesson Quiz and Class Discussion Board**			10 min.	●	

PEARSON
realize ™
www.PearsonRealize.com

Go online to access additional resources including:
Primary Sources • Biographies • Supreme Court cases •
21st Century Skill Tutorials • Maps • Graphic Organizers.

■ CONNECT

DIGITAL START UP ACTIVITY
Government and You

Project the Start Up Activity As students get settled in the classroom, ask them to answer the following question: What have you done recently that involved government *(Sample response: rode on a public bus; obeyed street signs; attended a public school)*

Identify What do you think is the most important function of the government? Explain. *(Sample response: Forming just laws. If people did not have laws to live by, then our society would be too chaotic.)*

Tell students that in this lesson they will be learning about the powers and purposes of government, the characteristics of states, and how states are formed.

Aa Vocabulary Development: Use the Interactive Reading Notepad to preview the Key Terms and Academic Vocabulary in this Lesson with students.

ℕ FLIP IT!

Assign the Flipped Video for this lesson.

■ STUDENT EDITION PRINT
PAGES: 4–11

■ INVESTIGATE

DIGITAL TEXT 1
Government–We The People

Objective 1: Define government and the basic powers every government holds.

Quick Instruction

The Three Branches of Government: Interactive Chart Project the chart on the whiteboard and point out the three branches and the list of various actions. Introduce the chart activity by telling students that every government has three branches. Each branch of government has the power to do certain things. Explain that each one of the actions listed corresponds with a branch of government.

📷 ACTIVE CLASSROOM

Have students spend three minutes jotting down their responses to the following question on sticky notes: Why do you think the Framers of the Constitution separated these powers? *(Possible Answer: to ensure that one branch did not gain too much power)* When they are finished, have students post their sticky notes on the board, noting similarities and differences in the responses.

D Differentiate: Challenge Have students write a short speech that tries to convince the people in a small community that they need a local government. Tell students to think of the benefits that governments offer and the drawbacks if a government is not set up.

ELL Use the ELL activity described in the ELL chart.

INTERACTIVE CHART
The Three Branches of Government

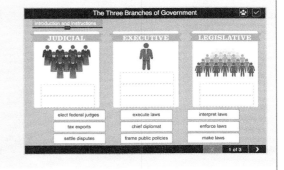

Further Instruction

Editable Presentation Use the Editable Presentation to present the main ideas for this Core Reading.

Government–We the People: Core Reading and Interactive Reading Notepad Project and discuss the Interactive Reading Notepad questions, including the graphic organizer asking students to think of examples that show the three powers of government in action. Encourage students to use some examples from daily life. Review the examples with the class and fill in the graphic organizer on the whiteboard as you go. *(Sample response: legislative power: tax regulations, rules of the road, the structure of corporations; executive powers: declaring war on another nation; implementing disaster relief; judicial powers: settling a dispute; setting a precedent for interpreting the law)*

Interpret Aristotle stated the following idea: "Man is by nature a political animal." Why do you think Aristotle believed that being political is in a person's nature? *(Sample response: I think Aristotle saw that his society and all the societies he knew about had governments. This means that people have a natural tendency to engage in the political process, which decides how a society will be governed.)*

Principles of Government

DIGITAL TEXT 2
The State

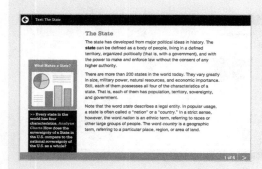

INTERACTIVE MAP
Four Characteristics of a State

DIGITAL TEXT 3
How States Arose

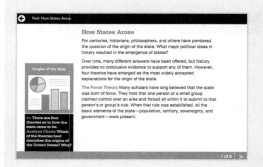

Objective 2: Describe the four defining characteristics of a state.

Quick Instruction

Interactive Map: Four Characteristics of a State Project the map on the whiteboard. Introduce the map activity by telling students that all states have sovereignty. However, political areas within a state do not have sovereignty. Point to a hotspot on the map and ask if it has sovereignty. Ask for a show of hands for "yes" and "no." Then click the hotspot to reveal the correct answer, and explain why this area does or does not have sovereignty. Do the same for all the hotspots on the map.

👥 ACTIVE CLASSROOM

Have students use a Circle Write to describe the population of the United States. Break the class into groups and provide the following writing prompt: "In one minute, describe the population of the United States." *(Sample response: The population of the United States is huge. It consists of millions of people. There are people from many ethnic backgrounds. Also, the income level of people varies greatly, depending on the type of work they do.)*

Further Instruction
Go through the Interactive Reading Notepad questions and discuss the answers with the class.

Compare and Contrast Have students compare and contrast the population, territory, sovereignty, and government of the following: London, Vatican City, and the United States. *(Sample response: London is a city that has a large dense population. Its territory is larger than Vatican City, but much smaller than the United States. London does not have sovereignty, but the United States and Vatican City do have sovereignty. London has a democratic government that is part of a larger democratic government. The United States also has a democratic government. The Vatican City does not have a democratic government, but instead is ruled by the pope and other officials.)*

Draw Inferences Most Americans think of themselves as "just Americans." What effect might this way of thinking have on how people perform the responsibilities, duties, and obligations of citizenship? *(Sample response: The United States includes people of many ethnicities and backgrounds, and they all think of themselves as part of the same political entity. Therefore, they are less likely to be at odds with each other and more likely to observe laws, do things that serve the public good, pay attention to civic affairs, or serve in the military.)*

Identify Cause and Effect Read the discussion of Thomas Hobbes' ideas about why states need government. Explain why Thomas Hobbes considered government necessary. Use the text to support your answer. *(Sample response: Hobbes thought that without government people's lives would be "solitary, poor, nasty, brutish, and short." Having a government would result in people's lives being better.)*

Objective 3: Identify four theories that attempt to explain the origin of the state.

Quick Instruction

Origins of the State Chart Display the Historical Theories of the Origins of the State chart and point out the four theories and the list of characteristics. Tell students that four theories have emerged as the most widely accepted explanations for the origin of the state. Each theory has certain characteristics. Have students discuss the major differences between the four theories.

Ⓓ Differentiate: Extra Support Help students form a connection between the social contract theory and the formation of democracy. Tell students to list three important traits of the social contract theory. Then ask students: Why do you think these traits encouraged the development of democracies?

Further Instruction

Editable Presentation Use the Editable Presentation to present the main ideas for this Core Reading.

How States Arose: Core Reading and Interactive Reading Notepad Project and discuss the Interactive Reading Notepad questions.

DIGITAL TEXT 4

What Government Does

Text: What Government Does

What Government Does

What does government do? You can find a very meaningful answer to that question in the Constitution of the United States. The American system of government was created to serve the purposes set out there.

We the People of the United States, in Order to form a more perfect Union, establish Justice, insure domestic Tranquility, provide for the common defence, promote the general Welfare, and secure the Blessings of Liberty to ourselves and our Posterity, do ordain and establish this Constitution for the United States of America.
— Preamble to the Constitution

>> The Preamble to the Constitution spells out the purpose of the U.S. Constitution and identifies the values and principles of the government.

1 of 8 >

The Declaration of Independence begins with the following statement: "When in the Course of human events, it becomes necessary for one people to dissolve the political bands which have connected them with another, and to assume among the powers of the earth, the separate and equal station to which the Laws of Nature and of Nature's God entitle them, a decent respect to the opinions of mankind requires that they should declare the causes which impel them to the separation."

Hypothesize According to the Declaration of Independence, what rights do you think "Nature and Nature's God" entitles people? *(Sample response: The right for a people to choose a government that represents their will and not the will of a king.)*

Contrast How do the ideas expressed in the above excerpt differ from the force theory? *(Sample response: The excerpt supports the idea that people have the right to dissolve a government and form another government. However, the force theory claims that governments are formed when one group forces a people to accept the group's government.)*

Infer What two theories on the origins of government do you think are presented as opposing viewpoints in the Declaration of Independence? *(the divine right of kings theory and the social contract theory)*

Objective 4: Understand the purpose of government in the United States and other countries.

Quick Instruction

Under British rule, Americans suffered many injustices, including unfair taxation and little representation in government. After Americans gained independence from Britain, they continued to have grievances because the United States had an inadequate governmental system. To address these problems, the United States wrote a constitution.

Write the seven purposes of government set forth in the Preamble to the U.S. Constitution on the board. Ask students: How do you think each of these purposes addressed grievances suffered by Americans under British rule and after Americans gained independence? Do you think these purposes of government remain important in today's world? Why or why not?

ELL Use the ELL activity described in the ELL chart.

Further Instruction

Editable Presentation Use the Editable Presentation to present the main ideas for this Core Reading.

What Government Does: Core Reading and Interactive Reading Notepad Project and discuss the Interactive Reading Notepad questions.

Check Understanding What are three important characteristics of good citizenship? *(Sample response: serving the public good, being well informed about civic affairs, observing the laws, serving in the military)*

Evaluate Sources The lawyer Clarence Darrow stated: "You can only be free if I am free." What do you think he meant by this? *(Sample response: Freedom is based on relationships between people. If a person acts in a way that denies the freedom of other people, then this person is not supporting a free society.)*

Analyze How does James Madison explain the principles of the American constitutional system in *The Federalist* No. 51? *(Sample response: Madison said that "no government would be necessary" if people behaved perfectly. He knew that government was in fact a necessary principle of the nation because people do not act perfectly all of the time.)*

Topic Inquiry

Launch the Topic Inquiry with students after introducing the Topic.

Principles of Government

SYNTHESIZE

Revisiting Government and You

Ask students to recall the Topic Essential Question, "What Should Governments Do?" Then have students revisit their lists of services that the U.S. government provides for its citizens. Students should revise their lists based on what they learned in this lesson. For each item on their lists, students should explain why they decided to include this government service.

Then have students form pairs. Ask the question: Do you think it is appropriate for the government to provide the services you listed? Explain your answer. Have students share their answers with their partners. Encourage students to ask questions about and offer suggestions for their partner's answer. Then ask volunteers to share their answers with the class.

Discuss Ask students to consider what they thought was the most important function of the U.S. government at the beginning of this Topic. Ask: Would you change your answer? Why or why not? *(Sample response: I thought that the most important function of government was to defend its country from attack. Now I think the most important function is for the government to form and enforce just laws. Laws forms the basis that allows a people to thrive and live peacefully with each other.)*

DEMONSTRATE

Lesson Quiz and Class Discussion Board

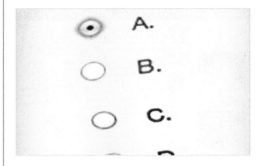

Assign the online Lesson Quiz for this lesson if you haven't already done so. Students will be offered automatic remediation or enrichment based on their score.

Pose this question to the class on the Discussion Board:

In "Principles of Government" you read about the purposes of the United States government as expressed in its constitution. This government is a democracy. However, you also learned about other types of government, including dictatorships.

Hypothesize Do you think the purposes of a dictatorship would be different from the purposes of a democracy? Why or why not? *(Sample response: I think the purposes of a democracy and dictatorship would be similar and different. Both types of government would want to unify their countries, insure domestic tranquility, and provide for the defense of the country. However, dictatorships would not be concerned about establishing justice, promoting general welfare, and securing liberty for all citizens. In a dictatorship, a few citizens would reap the benefit of these services, but many citizens would not receive these benefits. Both types of government would promote patriotism, but would have a different definition of patriotism.)*

Topic Inquiry

Have students continue their investigations for the Topic Inquiry.

PEARSON realize www.PearsonRealize.com
Access your Digital Lesson

Types of Government

Supporting English Language Learners

Use with Digital Text 2, **Who Can Participate?**

Learning Strategies
Explain how one way of classifying governments is by who is allowed to participate in the process. Define the words *democracy* and *dictatorship*. Discuss how, just like in government, many people participate in making decisions for schools, such as the principal. Ask students to think about other leaders they know and if these leaders make decisions by themselves or with the input of others. (*Examples of leaders can include parents, coaches, clergy, and club leaders.*) Tell students that thinking about their experiences with leaders will help them understand different kinds of government. Ask them to think about their experiences as they fill in graphic organizers.

Beginning Help the class complete two web graphic organizers, one for the topic *democracy* and one for *dictatorship*. Allow students to use words, pictures, or symbols to fill in the graphic organizer.

Intermediate Guide students to complete a web graphic organizer for the topic *democracy* or *dictatorship*. Have students talk about their webs with a partner using the sentence frames: *An example of a democracy is _____ because _____. An example of a dictatorship is _____ because _____.*

Advanced Have student pairs complete web graphic organizers for *democracy* and *dictatorship*. Ask students to discuss their graphic organizers.

Advanced High After student pairs complete web graphic organizers for *democracy* and *dictatorship*, have them individually write a paragraph defining each term and giving examples. Have them read their paragraphs to a partner.

Use with Digital Text 3, **Geographic Distribution of Power.**

Reading
Write the words Unitary, Federal, and Confederate, and ask the students to read the words aloud. Tell the students that these are the three basic forms of government. Show students that these systems are also headings in the text. Create an outline of the text with the three systems. Provide a list of other terms found in the reading, such as *centralized government, alliance of independent states,* and *confederate states*. Tell students that these terms will be among the subheadings for each of the three main topics of the outline. Explain that the graphic organizer will help them understand what they read.

Beginning Help the class refer to the text in order to complete the outline by placing the subheadings under the correct topic. Read the text aloud as the students follow along.

Intermediate Have small groups refer to the text in order to complete the outline by placing the subheadings under the main topics. Read text aloud. Review the definitions of the words on the outline.

Advanced Have student partners complete the outline with words on the word list. As they read the text, ask them to jot down a brief definition next to the words on the outline.

Advanced High Have students use the word list to complete the outline. As they read the text, ask them to jot down a short sentence explaining the words on the outline.

D Differentiate Instruction

Use the Differentiated Instruction notes throughout the lesson plan to support the varied skill sets, levels of readiness, and interests in the mixed-ability classroom.

Challenge These notes include suggestions for expanding the activity for advanced students.

On-Level These notes include suggestions for modifying the activity to address different interests or learning styles.

Extra Support These notes include ideas for providing more scaffolding or reading spuport.

Special Needs These notes provide ideas for adapting instruction to support the needs of various special needs students.

NOTES

Types of Government

Objectives

Objective 1: Classify governments according to three sets of characteristics.

Objective 2: Define systems of government based on who can participate.

Objective 3: Identify ways that power can be distributed, geographically, within a state.

Objective 4: Describe a government by the distribution of power between the legislative branch and executive branch.

LESSON 2 ORGANIZER	OBJECTIVES	PACING	RESOURCES Online	RESOURCES Print
Connect				
DIGITAL START UP ACTIVITY **Compare Forms of Government**		5 min.	●	
Investigate				
DIGITAL TEXT 1 **Classifying Governments**	Objective 1	10 min.	●	●
DIGITAL TEXT 2 **Who Can Participate?**	Objective 2	10 min.	●	●
INTERACTIVE MAP **Forms of Government Among Countries of the World**		10 min.	●	
DIGITAL TEXT 3 **Geographic Distribution of Power**	Objective 3	10 min.	●	●
DIGITAL TEXT 4 **Legislative and Executive Branches**	Objective 4	10 min.	●	●
INTERACTIVE 3D MODEL **The Capitol: A Working Symbol of Representative Democracy**		10 min.	●	
INTERACTIVE CHART **Choosing a Chief Executive**		10 min.	●	
Synthesize				
DIGITAL SYNTHESIZE ACTIVITY **Reflect on Democracy**		5 min.	●	
Demonstrate				
DIGITAL QUIZ **Lesson Quiz and Class Board Discussion**		10 min.	●	

PACING: APPROX. 1 PERIOD, .5 BLOCKS

PEARSON
realize™
www.PearsonRealize.com

Go online to access additional resources including:
Primary Sources • Biographies • Supreme Court cases •
21st Century Skill Tutorials • Maps • Graphic Organizers.

■ CONNECT

DIGITAL START UP ACTIVITY
Compare Forms of Government

Project the Start Up Activity Introduce the activity by telling students that many people have expressed strong opinions about various forms of government.

Tell students to read the quotation from Sir Winston Churchill. Then ask students to answer the following question:

Compare What are some of the positive and negative ways democracy compares with other forms of government? *(Possible answer: Dictatorships and oligarchies involve the rule of a few people. Democracy involves the rule of all the people.)*

Tell students that in this lesson they will be learning how governments are classified and the different ways power is distributed.

Aa **Vocabulary Development:** Use the Interactive Reading Notepad to preview the Key Terms and Academic Vocabulary in this Lesson with students.

> **⇅ FLIP IT!**
> Assign the Flipped Video for this lesson.

■ STUDENT EDITION PRINT
PAGES: 12–18

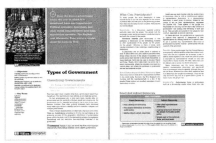

■ INVESTIGATE

DIGITAL TEXT 1
Classifying Governments

Objective 1: Classify governments according to three sets of characteristics.

Quick Instruction
Three Classifications of Government Tell students that all governments can be divided into the three classifications: (1) who can participate, (2) the geographic distribution of governmental power within the state, and (3) the relationship between the legislative and executive branches of the government. Then have students form pairs and ask them the following:

- Who participates in the governing process in the U.S. government?

- How is power distributed within the U.S. government? Does the power lie with one group of officials or with several groups?

- How do the legislative and executive branches of the U.S. government relate?

Have pairs discuss their responses and then ask volunteers to share their answers with the class. Write responses on the board and discuss them as a class.

ELL Use the ELL activity described in the ELL chart.

Further Instruction
Go through the Interactive Reading Notepad questions and discuss the answers with the class.

Draw Inferences Why is geographical distribution of power important in the United States? *(Possible answer: In the United States, the national government has specific powers, and the 50 states have other powers. This division of power was established by the Constitution. It requires the national government to make and enforce laws that affect all U.S. citizens, no matter where they live, and the state governments to make and enforce laws specific to people living within the specific states. Neither the national government nor any of the state governments can change this on their own.)*

Draw Conclusions Why is the relationship between the executive and legislative branches a useful way to classify governments? *(Possible answer: Understanding the relationship between the executive and legislative branches of governments helps one to know how much power is held by a chief executive and how much power is held by a law-making body. Knowing this enables citizens of a state to know who yields the most influence, or controls the government.)*

Project the following quote by Alexander Pope on the whiteboard: "For Forms of Government let fools contest; Whate'er is best administer'd is best . . . ." Read this quote aloud and then ask the following:

Evaluate Sources Do you agree with this quote? Why or why not? *(Possible answer: Yes; all forms of government have problems. The way a government is administered or put into effect is the most important factor.)*

Types of Government

DIGITAL TEXT 2

Who Can Participate?

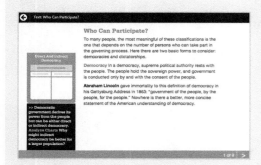

INTERACTIVE MAP

Forms of Government Among Countries of the World

Objective 2: Define systems of government based on who can participate.

Quick Instruction

Interactive Map: Forms of Government Among Countries of the World Project the map on the whiteboard. Introduce the activity by telling students that the five countries are color-coded based on each country's form of government. Click through some of the forms of government on the key. Tell students to study the map and click on more forms of government. Then ask students the following:

Analyze Maps Based on the map, which highlighted country do you think the United States conflicts with the most? Explain your answer. *(Sample response: North Korea: This country is a dictatorship run by one person. Also, it seems isolated from many other countries, including the United States. Because North Korea's government is very different from the U.S. government and other democracies, it probably has many conflicts with these countries.)*

🖳 ACTIVE CLASSROOM

Have students participate in a Word Wall for the forms of government. Ask students to choose one form of government and create a visual image that represents this government, including its definition. If only a few students take a certain form of government, assign other students to this government.

After students complete their images and definition, have them post their work on the board or on chart paper. Ask students to look at all the various responses and then discuss similarities and differences. Students can pick a favorite for each form of government and post it on the Class Word Wall for the year.

D Differentiate: Extra Support Help students to compare and contrast an authoritarian dictatorship and an autocracy. Tell students to list three traits for each form of government. Then ask students: How are the traits of these governments similar? How are they different?

ELL Use the ELL activity described in the ELL chart.

Further Instruction

Editable Presentation Use the Editable Presentation to present the main ideas for this Core Reading.

Who Can Participate?: Core Reading and Interactive Reading Notepad Project and discuss the Interactive Reading Notepad questions. Then project the Direct and Indirect Democracy chart. After students study this graphic, ask the following questions:

Compare How are direct democracy and indirect democracy similar? *(Sample response: In both forms of government, people participate in the government and have a voice in their government.)*

Contrast How are direct democracy and indirect democracy different? *(Sample response: In direct democracy, the people have a direct say in their government. In indirect democracy, people vote for representatives. These representatives will directly influence the government.)*

Ask a student to read aloud the information about theocracy and tribal and other republics in the Core Reading. Then ask the following:

Compare and Contrast How is the theocracy of Iran similar to and different from the government of the United States? *(Possible answer: Both Iran and the United States hold elections for governmental posts. However, Iran has a Supreme Leader who has the final say in all matters. This leader must be Muslim. The U.S. President, though, does not have the final say on all matters. Also, religious affiliation does not determine the acceptability of a candidate for the presidency. In Iran, all law must be compatible with Muslim law. In the U.S. government, the law does not have to be compatible with any religious code.)*

DIGITAL TEXT 3

Geographic Distribution of Power

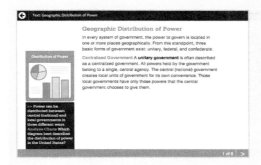

Explain What is the main characteristic of tribal government? Contrast this with other republics and the government of the United States. *(Possible answer: Tribal governments had a central chief who was elected for life and held all religious and military responsibilities. This form of government was replaced by a monarchy that allowed a royal family to take leadership. The U.S. government has a President at its head who is elected for up to eight years.)*

Objective 3: **Identify different ways that power can be distributed, geographically, within a state.**

Quick Instruction

Tell students that three basic forms of government exist: unitary, federal, and confederate. Describe each system to students, explaining how each differs on where the power is located geographically.

ELL Use the ELL activity described in the ELL chart.

Further Instruction

Editable Presentation Use the Editable Presentation to present the main ideas for this Core Reading.

3 Ways to Distribute Governmental Power Project and discuss the Interactive Reading Notepad questions, including the graphic organizer asking students to analyze the advantages and disadvantages of the federal, confederate, and unitary systems of government. Review the advantages and disadvantages with the class and fill in the table on the whiteboard as you go. *(Sample Response: Federal: Advantages: 1. Local officials are answerable to local people. 2. Federal government can deal with national and foreign policy; local or state government can deal with local or state issues. 3. More input for making policy decisions in areas such as education, public health, and safety. Disadvantages: 1. Greater chance of both kinds of government providing the same or similar services. 2. Legal or social services might be very different from region to region. 3. Conflict over which laws take precedence. Unitary: Advantages: 1. More uniform government throughout the state. 2. Fewer conflicts between central and subsidiary units of government. 3. Better coordination of government services. Disadvantages: 1. Central government might become out of touch with local issues. 2. Delay in meeting local needs. 3. Might marginalize some parts of the population. Confederate: Advantages: 1. Power at local level can check the growth of a central government. 2. Sets of independent states could cooperate on regional issues. 3. Independent states can be more individual in their character and issues. Disadvantages: 1. Could be more difficult to enforce national laws. 2. Tax collection might be affected. 3. More variety and potential conflicts with laws from place to place.)*

Hypothesize Why do you think the European Union uses the confederation system rather than the unitary or federal systems? *(Sample response: The European Union consists of many nations, each with their own government. These countries would probably resist having one government body that makes the laws for all of them. Also, they would have difficulty electing executive and legislative branches that would deal with the concerns of all the countries. Countries might complain about giving up their national identities and not being justly represented.)*

Types of Government

DIGITAL TEXT 4
Legislative and Executive Branches

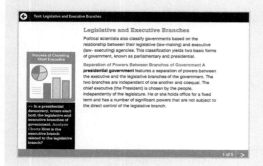

INTERACTIVE 3D MODEL
The Capitol: A Working Symbol of Representative Democracy

INTERACTIVE CHART
Choosing a Chief Executive

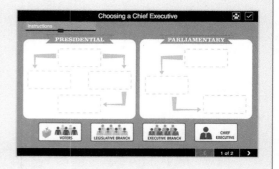

Objective 4: Describe a government by the distribution of power between the executive branch and legislative branch.

Quick Instruction

Interactive 3D Model: The Capitol: A Working Symbol of Representative Democracy Project the 3D Model. Explain that members of the legislative branch of the U.S. government work together in the Capitol to make laws for the nation. Click on the hotspots with students to explore the functions of the different rooms in the Capitol.

◆ ACTIVE CLASSROOM

Have students complete an Act It Out activity, in which they act out elected representatives in the House Chamber of the Capitol. Tell them to read through the related hotspot on the flipbook, and then reenact a House Chamber in session.

Interactive Chart: Choosing a Chief Executive Project the chart on the whiteboard and point out the two ways to structure democracies and the group of tiles. Introduce the chart activity by explaining that scholars often divide democracies into two types: Presidential and Parliamentary. Each form follows a certain process to select a chief executive. Have students drag the tiles to the correct areas to show the presidential and parliamentary processes.

◆ ACTIVE CLASSROOM

Ask students to Take a Stand on the following question: What form of government is better, the presidential or the parliamentary? Students break into two groups based on their answer. If a group is not represented or only has a few members, then some students from the other group should be moved into the group with few or no members. Have students in each group compare reasons for their answers. Then have a student from each group present and defend the group's point of view.

D Differentiate: Challenge Have students write a letter to a friend in Great Britain that explains how the presidential system works. Also, students should include what they like and dislike about this system. After this, students should write the response from the friend in Great Britain. This response should explain the parliamentary system and what the writer likes and dislikes about this system.

Further Instruction

Go through the Interactive Reading Notepad and discuss the answers with the class.

Determine Central Ideas How is the executive branch related to the legislative branch in a presidential government? *(Sample response: The two branches are independent of one another and coequal.)*

Analyze Analyze the advantages and disadvantages of parliamentary systems of government. *(Sample response: Advantage: Parliamentary government avoids the prolonged conflict and deadlock between the executive and legislative branches that can plague a presidential system. Disadvantage: Parliamentary governments do not feature strong checks and balances between the executive and legislative branches of government.)*

Ask a student to read aloud the first paragraph under the heading "Separation of Powers Between Branches of Government." Then ask another student to read the first paragraph under the heading "Parliamentary Government." After this, ask students to answer the following question:

Analyze Information Who do you think has more power, the president of a presidential government or the prime minister of a parliamentary government? *(Sample response: A president has more power because he or she is not under the control of a legislature, while a prime minister is under the control of a legislature.)*

SYNTHESIZE

DEMONSTRATE

DIGITAL SYNTHESIZE ACTIVITY

Reflect on Democracy

DIGITAL QUIZ

Lesson Quiz and Class Board Discussion

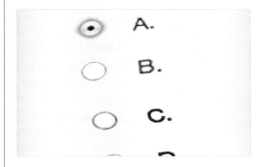

Ask students to recall the Topic Essential Question, "What Should Governments Do?" Have them reflect on what they have learned about democracy as a form of government, as well as the three ways government can be classified (the number of people who can participate in the governing process, how power is geographically distributed, and the relationship between the executive and legislative branches). After this, have students write a brief essay to answer the following questions.

- In which area does democracy as it is practiced in the United States best meet the needs and interests of the American people?

- What should the U.S. government do to improve the democratic system in the United States?

Assign the online Lesson Quiz for this lesson if you haven't already done so. Students will be offered automatic remediation or enrichment based on their score.

In "Types of Government" you read about classifications of governments, who can participate in governments, the geographic distribution of power in governments, and legislative and executive branches of government.

Identify Patterns What pattern do you see concerning the types of governments that nations are adopting? Why do you think this pattern is happening? *(Sample response: More and more nations seem to be adopting democratic governments with a parliamentary system. One-person dictatorships were once common, but have become less common in today's world. People want more freedom and, because of this, are striving for more democratic governments.)*

Making Predictions Do you think every nation of the world will eventually have one form of government? Why or why not? *(Sample response: No; the peoples of the world have different problems and backgrounds. Also, powerful minorities in countries will always strive to maintain or obtain power in their country. Because of this, forms of dictatorship will always be present in the world. However, democracies will always be present as well.)*

Topic Inquiry

Have students continue their investigations for the Topic Inquiry.

Origins of the Modern Democratic State

Supporting English Language Learners

Use with Digital Text 1, **American Government–Building on the Past.**

Learning Strategies

Find images in the text representative of the governments of Greece, Rome, and the feudal system of the Middle Ages. Use the images to support a discussion before reading the text, and ask students to predict characteristics of each of these forms of government. After reading the text, provide students with opportunities to monitor and self-correct their oral language production by discussing the images. Whenever possible, provide feedback by modeling correct speech.

Beginning Using the images, ask students simple questions about what they see and what they can tell about the subject based on clues from the pictures. Model more sophisticated answers and encourage students to repeat after you.

Intermediate Ask students simple questions about the images that require short answers. Help students to monitor their oral language with prompts such as *Tell me more.* or *Can you say it another way?*

Advanced Have students select several images. Ask them open-ended questions such as *What are the pictures about? What do the pictures tell us about government?* As students make errors, provide opportunities to self-correct by using prompts such as *Can you explain that again?* Use the following sentence frame to model correct oral language: *Let me make sure I understand. What you are saying is _____.*

Advanced High Have students prepare brief oral presentations based on several images. Encourage students to self-correct their oral language while they practice with a partner. After the presentation, ask students to self-evaluate their presentations.

Use with Digital Texts 3 and 4, **Power, Authority, and Legitimacy and European Colonialism.**

Reading

Write lesson vocabulary words from the two readings on the board. Show students that these words are boldfaced or hyperlinked in the text. Tell students that these words are hyperlinked in order to provide extra support to help them understand what they read.

Beginning Help students to read the list of words. Show them how to find the definition for each word. Guide students to read the definitions. If possible, provide visuals as support.

Intermediate Help students locate the definitions for each word on the list. Have them read each word and definition with a partner. Ask them to restate the definitions in their own words.

Advanced Have partners read and discuss the definitions for each word on the list. Have them find the word in the text and discuss the meaning of the sentence where each word appears.

Advanced High Ask partners to read the definitions for each word. Have partners look in the text for the sentences with each word. Tell students to rewrite the sentences in their own words, using the definitions for help.

▣ Differentiate Instruction

Use the Differentiated Instruction notes throughout the lesson plan to support the varied skill sets, levels of readiness, and interests in the mixed-ability classroom.

Challenge These notes include suggestions for expanding the activity for advanced students.

On-Level These notes include suggestions for modifying the activity to address different interests or learning styles.

Extra Support These notes include ideas for providing more scaffolding or reading spuport.

Special Needs These notes provide ideas for adapting instruction to support the needs of various special needs students.

▣ NOTES

PEARSON ⋯
realize™
www.PearsonRealize.com

Go online to access additional resources including:
Primary Sources • Biographies • Supreme Court cases •
21st Century Skill Tutorials • Maps • Graphic Organizers.

Objectives

Objective 1: Identify the ancient foundations of the state in Athens, in Rome and in the Feudal system.

Objective 2: Analyze the rise of sovereign states.

Objective 3: Explain how governments can achieve legitimacy.

Objective 4: Understand why European nations turned to colonialism.

Objective 5: Understand how Enlightenment ideas helped influence the expansion of popular sovereignty.

LESSON 3 ORGANIZER		PACING: APPROX. 1 PERIOD, .5 BLOCKS			
				RESOURCES	
		OBJECTIVES	**PACING**	**Online**	**Print**
Connect					
DIGITAL START UP ACTIVITY **What Makes Governments Legitimate?**			5 min.	●	
Investigate					
DIGITAL TEXT 1 **American Government–Building on the Past**		Objective 1	10 min.	●	●
DIGITAL TEXT 2 **Nations and Kings**		Objective 2	10 min.	●	●
INTERACTIVE GALLERY **The Beginning of Monarchy**			10 min.	●	
DIGITAL TEXT 3 **Power, Authority, and Legitimacy**		Objectives 3, 4	10 min.	●	●
DIGITAL TEXT 4 **European Colonialism**			10 min.	●	●
DIGITAL TEXT 5 **Power Comes from the People**		Objective 5	10 min.	●	●
INTERACTIVE GALLERY **Great Thinkers of the Enlightenment Age**			10 min.	●	
Synthesize					
DIGITAL SYNTHESIZE ACTIVITY **Ancient Governments Shape Modern Ones**			5 min.	●	
Demonstrate					
LESSON QUIZ **Lesson Quiz and Class Discussion Board**			10 min.	●	

Origins of the Modern Democratic State

CONNECT

DIGITAL START UP ACTIVITY

What Makes Governments Legitimate?

Project the Start Up Activity Have students look at the painting. Ask: What is shown in the painting? *(The painting shows Henry IV being crowned king.)*

Discuss Point out to students that the Church had great legitimacy in the eyes of most people at this time. Because of that, the Church's support for Henry IV would have helped him gain legitimacy as well.

Tell students that in this lesson they will be learning about the origins of the modern democratic state.

Aa Vocabulary Development: Use the Interactive Reading Notepad to preview the Key Terms and Academic Vocabulary in this Lesson with students.

↥ FLIP IT!

Assign the Flipped Video for this lesson.

STUDENT EDITION PRINT PAGES: 19–26

INVESTIGATE

DIGITAL TEXT 1

American Government– Building on the Past

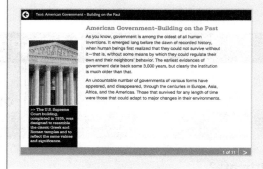

Objective 1: Identify the ancient foundations of the state in Athens, in Rome, and in the fuedal system.

Quick Instruction

The roots of democratic government in today's world—including government in the United States—lie deep in human history. Ancient Greece was the home of the first direct democracy, where the people made governmental decisions. Ancient Rome was the home of a republic, where people were elected to represent others in government. After that, feudalism was implemented in Europe. The Black Plague and the rise of towns changed Europe. Monarchs, supported by the people and money of the towns, rose in power.

ELL Use the ELL activity described in the ELL chart.

Further Instruction

Editable Presentation Use the Editable Presentation to present the main ideas for this Core Reading.

American Government–Building on the Past and Interactive Reading Notepad Project and discuss the Interactive Reading Notepad questions.

The United States of America was founded on many political traditions, including democracy and republicanism. Ask students to find evidence of these political traditions in American government today. *(Possible answer: Democracy is rule by the people. In the Roman Republic, senators were elected, beginning the idea of representative government rather than direct participation.)*

Compare Compare the U.S. constitutional republic to the classical republic founded by the Romans. *(Possible answer: The Romans introduced the concept of representation and held elections.)*

Analyze Data Why might the founders have thought feudalism was not a good model for a government? *(Feudalism was a makeshift form of government open to conflict.)*

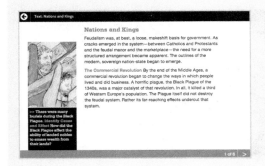

DIGITAL TEXT 2

Nations and Kings

DIGITAL TEXT 2

Nations and Kings

INTERACTIVE GALLERY

The Beginning of Monarchy

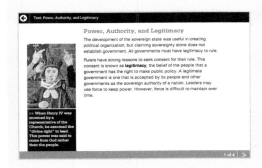

DIGITAL TEXT 3

Power, Authority, and Legitimacy

Objective 2: Analyze the rise of sovereign states.

Quick Instruction

The Beginning of Monarchy: Interactive Gallery Rule of the people, or democracy, can arise from monarchies. Project the first slide of the image gallery. Name all the countries for students. Then project each subsequent slide. Name the rulers shown.

🗣 ACTIVE CLASSROOM

Have students review each slide. Using a Sticky Note strategy, have students respond to the following question: How did this monarch create a large national entity from multiple, small city states? Then use the sticky notes to make a generalization. What made single, organized governments more functional than multiple, small city states? *(Possible answer: Pooling resources and governments allowed for more functionality.)*

D Differentiate: **Challenge/Gifted** Have students compare two of the countries on the map. Ask them to create a 2-column chart showing the similarities and differences between the two nations and the monarchs who ruled them. Tell them to use the text or other sources to complete the chart. Then have students share their charts with the class.

Further Instruction

Draw Conclusions Why were monarchs an outgrowth of feudalism? What problems did absolute monarchy create? *(Monarchs existed within the feudal system. They were the strongest rulers who could protect the most people and collect the most wealth. Everyone was subordinate to one person's authority. Only that person would make laws, wield authority, and maintain order.)*

Analyze How are absolute monarchies different from the constitutional republic of the United States? *(Possible answer: Monarchs had absolute power and could ignore representative assemblies if desired. Everyone under their rule was subordinate to the power of the monarch's authority. In a constitutional republic, leaders do not have absolute power and depend on "rule by the people.")*

Objectives 3: Explain how governments can achieve legitimacy; 4: Understand why European nations turned to colonialism.

Quick Instruction

Legitimacy and Colonialism The founders of the United States of America used previous forms of government as they created the new country. To understand why they chose the elements they did, it is important to understand the issues of absolute monarchy and the impact colonialism had on wealth distribution.

ELL Use the ELL activity described in the ELL chart.

Further Instruction

Governments gain legitimacy through charisma, tradition, and rule of law. Ask students to explain each method of finding legitimacy. *(Charisma is the power of personality, where a person with strong leadership skills can convince people to follow him or her. Tradition is the idea that people have always done something in a certain way. Rule of law is the idea that consent comes from fair and just law.)*

Colonialism is the idea that a central government rules lands far away from itself. During the 1400s and 1500s, Europe spread ideas, people, and goods between colonies and capitals. Trade routes created by the monarch led to the expansion of mercantilism. Ask students to define mercantilism and its relationship to absolute monarchy and colonial

Origins of the Modern Democratic State

DIGITAL TEXT 4
European Colonialism

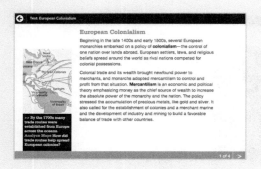

DIGITAL TEXT 5
Power Comes from the People

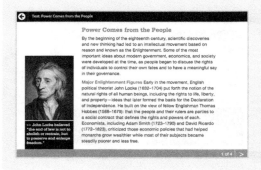

INTERACTIVE GALLERY
Great Thinkers of the Enlightenment Age

trade. *(Mercantilism emphasizes money as the chief source of wealth used to increase the power of the monarchy and nation. Related policies allowed monarchs to set up trade routes that brought money from the colonies to the capitals, further cementing power through wealth.)*

Identify Central Issues Why do governments need legitimacy? *(Legitimacy is consent. Without consent, governments would find it very hard to rule.)* Before mercantilism, what is the chief source of wealth for the ruling classes? *(land)*

Draw Inferences How would state taxation policies on goods from the colonies be impacted by a policy of mercantilism? *(Possible answer: Mercantilism means that the state is heavily invested in economic policy. Therefore, a state might tax goods from the colonies more to fund more ventures into the colonies.)*

Predict Consequences List two consequences of colonialism for monarchy and mercantilism. *(Possible answer: As people move farther away from capitals, it will be harder for one person to rule a wider area. More people will gain wealth so it will not be as concentrated in the monarchy, signaling the end of mercantilism. People will want to change their governments so that they rule themselves.)*

Objective 5: Understand how Enlightenment ideas helped influence the expansion of popular sovereignty.

Quick Instruction

Remind students that the founders of the United States used several different philosophies as they thought about rights and responsibilities of individuals. Some of those ideas arose from the Enlightenment period of thinking.

Interactive Gallery: Great Thinkers of the Enlightenment Age Project the slideshow. Look at each image individually. Identify each person, and discuss as a class how each thinker impacted the development of American government.

⬛ ACTIVE CLASSROOM

For each image, ask the following question using the Sticky Note strategy: How did this figure embody the Enlightenment Age?

D **Differentiate: Extra Support** After asking students to identify each person, allow students five minutes to reread the section on the Enlightenment. Tell them to note what the reading says about the person's contribution to the Enlightenment.

Further Instruction

Go through the Interactive Reading Notepad questions and discuss answers with the class.

The founders of the United States of America relied on the thinkers of the Enlightenment. Voltaire, a pen name for Francois-Marie Arouet, advocated reason, freedom of religion, the importance of scientific observation, and the idea of human progress. Baron de Montesquieu advocated a separation of the powers of government, so that the different branches might check and balance one another. William Blackstone, an English jurist, believed strongly in "common law"—the idea that legal decisions should be made on the basis of similar decisions made in the past. All of these thinkers influenced the men who wrote the Constitution and therefore the document itself.

Identify Cause and Effect How did the monarchs lose legitimacy? What replaced it? *(Reason and thought began to supercede religion. Monarchs who had gained legitimacy through tradition, or divine rule, began to lose it. Popular sovereignty or consent of the governed became more important.)*

Interpret Why would a group of political theorists and economists be the strongest voices against mercantilism? *(Possible answer: Mercantilism is an economic theory relating concentrated power and wealth. People who study government and economics would understand best the issues with the theory.)*

SYNTHESIZE

Ancient Governments Shape Modern Ones

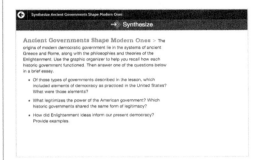

Ask students to recall the Topic Essential Question, "What Should Governments Do?" Have students use the Think Pair Share strategy to answer the questions in the essay-writing activity. Ask them to take five minutes to write down some brief answers, and then share their answers with a talking partner.

Have students think about the following question: On what political traditions and ideas was modern government founded? Ask them to take five minutes to write down a brief summary. Then have them organize their answers to the previous questions from the activity into an essay using the summary as an introduction.

DEMONSTRATE

Lesson Quiz and Class Discussion Board

Assign the online Lesson Quiz for this lesson if you haven't already done so. Students will be offered automatic remediation or enrichment based on their score.

In "Origins of the Modern Democratic State," you read about how modern governments were built on both traditional and new ideas. Pose these questions to the class on the Discussion Board:

Compare and Contrast Compare and contrast one traditional and one new idea. How did the new ideas of the Enlightenment compare to traditional ideas of government?

Draw Inferences Governments are often created to solve problems faced by the population. What problems might a government with popular sovereignty find easy to solve? What problems might it find not easy to solve?

Topic Inquiry

Have students continue their investigations for the Topic Inquiry.

The Basics of Democracy

Supporting English Language Learners

Use with Digital Text 1, **Foundations of Democracy.**

Learning Strategies
Have students look at the image in this section of citizens showing their patriotism. Tell students they are going to write about this image. Help them brainstorm ideas about how the image is related to the concept of democracy.

Beginning Guide students to complete cloze sentences or write short sentences about the image. Help students to review and revise their work. Have them read their work to a partner.

Intermediate Have students write short sentences about the image. Guide students as they self-correct their writing. Have partners read their work aloud as a way to check their writing. If possible, provide an editing checklist.

Advanced Have students write a paragraph for the image explaining how it is related to the concept of democracy. Guide students to review and revise their work and make necessary edits. If possible, provide an editing checklist.

Advanced High Ask students to write a summary of the different concepts of democracy represented by the image. Have students self-correct their work using an editing checklist, if possible. Have them read their work to a partner of the same language ability and make additional edits as needed.

Use with Digital Text 3, **Democracy and the Free Enterprise System.**

Reading
Have students look at the visuals in the reading and read the captions. Discuss how the visuals relate to the concepts of democracy. Tell students that the visuals can help understanding of the text.

Beginning After students discuss the visuals, have students read the related paragraphs. Help students to make connections between words in the text and the visuals.

Intermediate Guide students to select two words from the list and read the related paragraphs aloud. Have partners discuss how each visual is related to the text.

Advanced Ask partners to read the text. Have them identify parts of the text that correspond with each visual.

Advanced High Have students read the text independently. Ask students to identify parts of the text that are supported by visuals. Have partners discuss how the visual helps them understand what they read.

▷ Differentiate Instruction

Use the Differentiated Instruction notes throughout the lesson plan to support the varied skill sets, levels of readiness, and interests in the mixed-ability classroom.

Challenge These notes include suggestions for expanding the activity for advanced students.

On-Level These notes include suggestions for modifying the activity to address different interests or learning styles.

Extra Support These notes include ideas for providing more scaffolding or reading spuport.

Special Needs These notes provide ideas for adapting instruction to support the needs of various special needs students.

■ NOTES

PEARSON
realize.™
www.PearsonRealize.com

Go online to access additional resources including:
Primary Sources • Biographies • Supreme Court cases •
21st Century Skill Tutorials • Maps • Graphic Organizers.

Objectives

Objective 1: Understand the foundations of democracy.

Objective 2: Analyze the connections between democracy and the free enterprise system.

LESSON 4 ORGANIZER		OBJECTIVES	PACING	RESOURCES	
				Online	Print
Connect					
DIGITAL START UP ACTIVITY **What Makes a Democracy?**			5 min.	●	
Investigate					
DIGITAL TEXT 1 **Foundations of Democracy**		Objective 1	10 min.	●	●
INTERACTIVE GALLERY **Expanding Democratic Rights**			10 min.	●	
DIGITAL TEXT 2 **Responsibilities, Duties, and Obligations of Citizenship**		Objective 1	10 min.	●	●
INTERACTIVE CHART **Duties and Responsibilities of Citizenship**			10 min.	●	
DIGITAL TEXT 3 **Democracy and the Free Enterprise System**		Objective 2	10 min.	●	●
Synthesize					
DIGITAL SYNTHESIZE ACTIVITY **Democratic Concepts**			5 min.	●	
Demonstrate					
DIGITAL QUIZ **Lesson Quiz and Class Discussion Board**			10 min.	●	

PACING: APPROX. 1 PERIOD, .5 BLOCKS

The Basics of Democracy

CONNECT

DIGITAL START UP ACTIVITY
What Makes a Democracy?

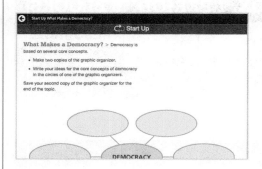

Project the Start Up Activity Ask students to copy the graphic organizer and fill in the circles as they enter and get settled. Then have them share their ideas with another student, either in class or through a chat or blog space.

Discuss If you were to describe democracy to someone who lived where there was no government, what would you say? What are its most important elements? What examples of how it works would you offer?

Tell students that in this lesson they will understand the foundations of democracy, including the duties and responsibilities of citizens, and analyze the connections between democracy and the free enterprise system.

Aa Vocabulary Development: Use the Interactive Reading Notepad to preview the Key Terms and Academic Vocabulary in this Lesson with students.

⚡ FLIP IT!

Assign the Flipped Video for this lesson.

■ STUDENT EDITION PRINT PAGES: 27–32

INVESTIGATE

DIGITAL TEXT 1
Foundations of Democracy

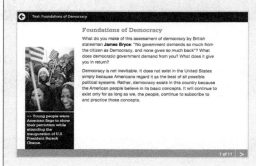

Objective 1: Understand the foundations of democracy.

Quick Instruction
Remind students that the American concept of democracy rests on five basic notions: Each person has worth and dignity; respect for the equality of all persons; a majority makes the rules while respecting minority rights; compromise is necessary; and there should be a wide degree of individual freedom.

Interactive Gallery: Expanding Democratic Rights Project the image gallery on the whiteboard. Look at each image individually and then the collection of images as a whole.

Analyze Images Which image do you find to be most persuasive that a change is needed? What image do you find least effective? Explain your answer. *(Possible answer: The image of the poor working conditions is most effective, because people can empathize with those conditions. Images of marches are least effective, because they don't explain how the change will impact people.)*

👥 ACTIVE CLASSROOM

Ask the following question using the Sticky Note strategy: Viewed together, how do these images support the five basic notions of democracy? Gather the sticky notes and post them on the board alongside a written list of the five basic notions of democracy.

INTERACTIVE GALLERY
Expanding Democratic Rights

D Differentiate: Extra Support Name each image for students. Have them describe what is happening in each image. Link the image to the event, giving extra support. Have students connect what is happening in the image to how the United States is different today. For example, women can vote, children can't work until age 16, and schools are no longer segregated.

ELL Use the ELL activity described in the ELL chart.

Further Instruction
Go through the Interactive Reading Notepad questions and discuss the answers with the class.

Democracy can only thrive when paired with a belief in individual freedom. The five elements of democracy show how democracy achieves this balance.

Support Ideas with Evidence Explain the following John F. Kennedy quotation using the five elements of democracy: "The rights of every man are diminished when the rights of one man are threatened." *(Possible answer: The quotation speaks to the worth and dignity of every person and shows how minority rights must be respected by the majority.)*

Predict Consequences What would happen to democracy if complete individual freedom was achieved? *(Possible answer: Democracy would not succeed because one person's decisions would infringe on another person. One example are the accidents that would occur if people in cities decided to ignore all speed limits.)*

Evaluate Arguments Most Americans think that democracy is the best form of government. Evaluate this argument using what you understand about the responsibilities of citizens in a democracy. *(Possible answer: Democracy is the best form of government because it is the best compromise between individual freedom and respect for the minority and majority.)*

DIGITAL TEXT 2

Responsibilities, Duties, and Obligations of Citizenship

Objective 1: Understand the foundations of democracy.

Quick Instruction

Citizenship requires duties and responsibilities. This is especially true in the United States. Duties revolve around observing the laws. Responsibilities are the things citizens must do to support the democracy.

Understanding Duties and Responsibilities of Citizenship: Interactive Chart Project the chart on the whiteboard. Click through the tiles, and explain to students that they will decide whether each civic activity is a duty or a responsibility.

👥 ACTIVE CLASSROOM

Use the Ranking Strategy to go through each civic activity on the tiles and decide which ones they think are most important to society as a whole. Ask students to provide a justification for the ranking decisions they made. Then ask students to work in pairs to share their rankings and justifications.

D Differentiate: Challenge Have students analyze the poll. For each image where not everybody answered the same, have students think about an image that might more clearly illustrate the duty or responsibility. Then have students defend the new image using examples of duties and responsibilities.

INTERACTIVE CHART

Duties and Responsibilities of Citizenship

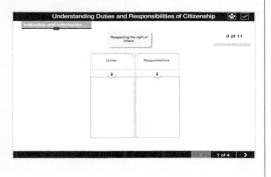

Further Instruction

Go through the Interactive Reading Notepad questions and discuss the answers with the class.

Citizenship carries duties and responsibilities. These include being well informed about civic affairs, serving in the military, voting, serving on a jury, observing the laws, paying taxes, and serving the public good.

Connect How are the rights and responsibilities of citizens connected to the five basic tenets of democracy? *(Possible answer: Citizens must obey the law and support the democracy. Then the government will protect them if they are in the minority and support their individual freedom.)*

Compare What is the difference between personal and civic responsibilities? *(Personal responsibilities involve taking care of yourself, such as being considerate of others. On the other hand, civic responsibilities involve your role as a citizen of a larger community, including paying taxes and obeying the law.)*

From Reform to Revolution

DIGITAL TEXT 3

Democracy and the Free Enterprise System

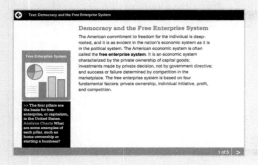

Objective 2: Analyze the connections between democracy and the free enterprise system.

Quick Instruction

The American economic system is the free enterprise system. It is characterized by the private ownership of capital goods; investments made by private decision, not by government directive; and success or failure determined by competition in the marketplace. Government's role in the system is to protect the public and private enterprise.

ELL Use the ELL activity described in the ELL chart.

Further Instruction

Editable Presentation Use the Editable Presentation to present the main ideas for this Core Reading.

Go through the Interactive Reading Notepad questions and discuss the answers with the class.

Both democracy and free enterprise rely on individual freedom.

Make Decisions How much should government participate, regulate, promote, police, and serve? Use evidence from the topic in your answer. *(Possible answer: Government should regulate and police only to protect its citizens. It should take care to balance public and private enterprise.)*

Explain Explain how the following Abraham Lincoln quote shows the struggle between balancing democracy and free enterprise: "The legitimate object of government, is to do for a community of people, whatever they need to have done, but can not do, at all, or can not, so well do, for themselves—in their separate, and individual capacities." *(Possible answer: It is important in democracy to support free enterprise because it is one way citizens express their freedom. However, the government steps in to ensure that companies don't grow too big just as they write laws to protect minority rights.)*

Connect How is the political-economic system of monarchy-mercantilism similar to and different from the political-economic system of democracy-free enterprise? *(Both systems are related to making the government stronger. Mercantilism supports one person, the monarch, while free enterprise can support many and the government through taxes.)*

SYNTHESIZE

Democratic Concepts

Ask students to recall the Start Up activity where they completed a graphic organizer titled "What is Democracy." Ask them to complete the organizer again. Then have them compare the two organizers. Ask students to summarize what they learned about democracy and their rights and responsibilities as citizens.

Using a Think Pair Share activity, have students discuss how their understanding of democracy changed.

Discuss Who has a greater responsibility in a democracy: the government or the people? Students should explain their answers using examples from the topic.

DEMONSTRATE

Lesson Quiz and Class Discussion Board

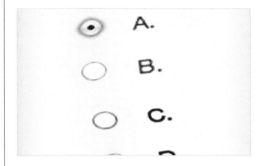

Assign the online Lesson Quiz for this lesson if you haven't already done so. Students will be offered automatic remediation or enrichment based on their score.

In "Basics of Democracy" you read about the rights and responsibilities of citizenship. Pose these questions to the class on the Discussion Board:

Make Decisions Which responsibility do you think is most important for the government and for the people? Why?

Draw Inferences What is your responsibility as a citizen if you think that the government is not living up to its own responsibilities? What can you do?

Topic Inquiry

Have students continue their investigations for the Topic Inquiry.

Foundations of Government and Citizenship

▌SYNTHESIZE

DIGITAL ACTIVITY

Reflecting on What Governments Should Do

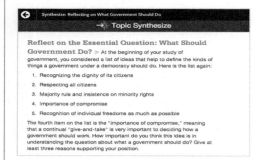

First ask students to reconsider the Essential Question for the Topic: What should governments do? Remind students of the services of government they considered at the start of the Topic. For example,

- to establish laws
- to enforce laws
- to settle legal disputes fairly
- to defend the country
- to maintain public works
- to provide education

Ask students, "Do you think the U.S. government fulfills all the services listed?" Then ask, "What are some services of the U.S. government that you would add to, or take away from, the list?" Discuss their answers as a class or ask students to post their answers to the Class Discussion Board.

Next ask students to reflect on the Topic as a whole and jot down 1–3 questions they've thought about during the Topic. Share these examples if students need help getting started:

- Do governments influence the economy of a country? If so, how?
- Do governments ever misuse their authority? If so, how?
- Do the purposes of governments vary depending on the characteristics of the people and region they serve?

You may ask students to share their questions and answers on the Class Discussion Board.

Have students complete Step 3 of the Topic Inquiry.

▌DEMONSTRATE

DIGITAL TOPIC REVIEW AND ASSESSMENT

Foundations of Government and Citizenship

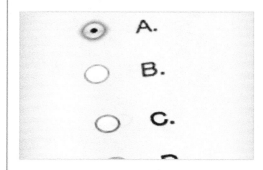

Students can prepare for the Topic Test by answering the questions in the Topic Review and Assessment online or the Assessment questions in the Print Student text. They can also prepare by reviewing their answers to the Interactive Reading Notepad questions or reviewing their notes in the Reading and Notetaking Study Guide.

TOPIC TEST

Assign the Topic Test to assess students' understanding of topic content.

DIGITAL TOPIC TEST

Foundations of Government and Citizenship

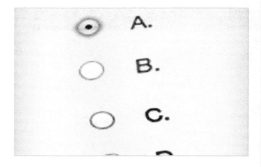

BENCHMARK TESTS

Assign these benchmark tests as you complete the relevant topics to monitor student progress toward mastering the course content and as preparation for the End-of-Course Test.

Benchmark Test 1: Topics 1–4

Benchmark Test 2: Topics 5–8

Benchmark Test 3: Topics 9–11

Benchmark Test 4: Topics 12–14

Topic 2

The Beginnings of American Government

PEARSON **realize**™ www.PearsonRealize.com Access your Digital Lesson

TOPIC 2 ORGANIZER	PACING: APPROX. 1 PERIOD, .5 BLOCKS
	PACING
Connect	**1 period**
MY STORY VIDEO **James Madison,** *The Federalist Papers*	10 min.
DIGITAL ESSENTIAL QUESTION ACTIVITY **How Much Power Should a Government Have?**	10 min.
DIGITAL OVERVIEW ACTIVITY **The Road to Independence**	10 min.
TOPIC INQUIRY: DOCUMENT-BASED QUESTION **Should the Constitution Be Ratified?**	20 min.
Investigate	**2–4 periods**
TOPIC INQUIRY: DOCUMENT-BASED QUESTION **Should the Constitution Be Ratified?**	Ongoing
LESSON 1 Origins of American Political Ideals	30–40 min.
LESSON 2 Independence	30–40 min.
LESSON 3 First Steps	30–40 min.
LESSON 4 Creating and Ratifying the Constitution	30–40 min.
Synthesize	**1 period**
DIGITAL ACTIVITY **Reflecting on How Much Power Government Should Have**	10 min.
TOPIC INQUIRY: DOCUMENT-BASED QUESTION **Should the Constitution Be Ratified?**	20 min.
Demonstrate	**1–2 periods**
DIGITAL TOPIC REVIEW AND ASSESSMENT **The Beginnings of American Government**	10 min.
TOPIC INQUIRY: DOCUMENT-BASED QUESTION **Should the Constitution Be Ratified?**	20 min.

TOPIC INQUIRY: DOCUMENT-BASED QUESTION

Should the Constitution Be Ratified?

In this Document Based Question activity, students will work independently to analyze and evaluate the validity of information, arguments, and counterarguments from several primary and secondary sources for point of view and frame of reference. They will use these documents to form an opinion in answer to the question: Should the Constitution Be Ratified? Examining the debates that impacted the creation of the Constitution will contribute to students' understanding of the Topic Essential Question: How Much Power Should a Government Have?

STEP 1: CONNECT
Develop Questions and Plan the Investigation

Launch the Project and Generate Questions
Display and discuss the assignment. Build background knowledge about the United States Constitution. Have students list some of the compromises and debates they know went into the creation of the Constitution. Tell students that they will mostly be working independently on this project.

Suggestion: Some students might be more successful if they work in pairs. For example you might want to pair a more and less fluent reader.

Review the Infographic
Display the infographic "Two Sides of Ratification." Have students read the quotations and then summarize the positions of the Federalists and Anti-Federalists with regard to the ratification of the Constitution.

Suggestion: To ensure that students gain a complete understanding, you may wish to assign students a particular State or position to take notes on as they read. Then have students present their notes before the discussion in Step 2.

Resources
- Project Launch
- Project Contract
- Infographic: "Two Sides of Ratification"
- Student Instructions
- DBQ Essay Rubric

STEP 2: INVESTIGATE
Apply Disciplinary Concepts and Tools

Discuss the Infographic
Review the bulleted points and the quotations from the infographic with students. Ask students to identify which group favored ratification and which group opposed ratification.

Suggestion: If time is an issue, combine Steps One and Two. This might also help support student understanding.

Resources
- Infographic: "Two Sides of Ratification"
- Information Organizer

⏻ PROFESSIONAL DEVELOPMENT

Document-Based Question
Be sure to view the Document-Based Question Professional Development resources in the online course.

STEP 3: SYNTHESIZE
Evaluate Sources and Use
Evidence to Formulate Conclusions

Introduce the Documents

Explain that students will now begin their review of primary and secondary sources from both sides of the question: Should the Constitution Be Ratified? Project each document and read the introductions together.

Suggestion: If time is short, you may wish to assign students one or two documents and then have students present the information they found to the entire class. You may also wish to reduce the number of primary and secondary sources. Documents A, B, E, and F provide students enough information to answer the question.

Analyze the Documents

Have students identify which documents are primary and which are secondary sources. Then have them analyze each document using the following questions: *Which point of view does this support? Compare the viewpoint and the person's job or position and the time period in which he or she lived (frame of reference).* Does the author present examples or facts to support his point of view? In what way has the author's frame of reference influenced his point of view? What qualifications does the author have with regard to ratification? Do residents of the same State have similar viewpoints?

Have students analyze and evaluate the validity of each document's point of view and frame of reference. Point out that some documents present counterarguments. Create a two-column chart in which students list arguments in one column and the corresponding counterarguments in the other.

Resources
- Document A "All Men Are Born Equal and Free"
- Document B *Federalist No. 10*
- Document C Speech from Jonathan Smith
- Document D Speech by Amos Singletary
- Document E "Letter V"
- Document F *A Pennsylvania Farmer*
- Document G An Historian Considers Both Sides
- Document H "The Anti-Federalists Were Right"

STEP 4: DEMONSTRATE
Communicate Conclusions
and Take Informed Action

Write Your Essay

Have students read the assignment. Remind students that they will introduce evidence to support two points of view and frames of reference: that of a person living in current times and that of a person living during the debate over ratification. Students should use quotations to support their ideas.

Project the rubric for the essay and discuss each point. Discuss the steps of writing: prewrite, draft, revise, edit, and publish. Be sure that students use social studies terminology correctly and use standard grammar, spelling, sentence structure, and punctuation.

Suggestion: Provide students with instructions for how to quote from a primary souce and cite the references they use. This may be in the form of a link to an outside university writing center or a document produced by your school.

Reflect on the Project

After students have finished their essays, help them go over what they thought went well and what did not, so they can be even more effective in the future.

Resources
- Essay Rubric
- Self Assessment

The Beginnings of American Government

The English colonists who settled in North America brought a strong tradition of representative government with them. When Parliament and the king began to threaten their rights as English citizens, the colonists rebelled and formed their own country. The government they chose for that country borrowed from centuries of political history and Enlightenment ideas. But it also established a system of governing that had never yet been tried before.

CONNECT

MY STORY VIDEO
James Madison, *The Federalist Papers*

Watch a video that introduces students to one of the most important political thinkers in U.S. history.

Identify Central Issues Why did Madison, Hamilton, and Jay write the Federalist Papers? (To explain political ideas and promote the ratification of the new Constitution.)

Cite Evidence Explain why Madison was so important in creating the new U.S. government. *(Possible answers: He explained political ideas such as checks and balances, was important in debate at Constitutional Convention, helped ensure ratification, served as Secretary of State and then President.)*

FLIP IT!
Assign the My Story video.

DIGITAL ESSENTIAL QUESTION ACTIVITY
How Much Power Should a Government Have?

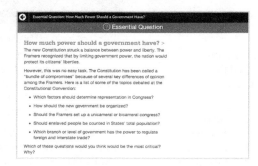

Ask students to think about the Essential Question for this Topic: How Much Power Should a Government Have?

If students have not already done so, ask them to respond to the poll. Then go over the results as a class.

Support a Point of View with Evidence Why did you rate this reason as most critical? *(Possible answer: Representation in Congress is most important because it strikes at the heart of democratic government—that is, it is the mechanism through which the people are heard and through which the will of the people is translated into public policy.)*

Make Connections You have learned that there are different types of government, such as democracy, autocracy, and theocracy. What are some of the basic notions of a democracy? Name at least two. *(each person has worth and dignity, respect for the equality of all persons, majority rule, minority rights, compromise is necessary, wide degree of individual freedom)*

DIGITAL OVERVIEW ACTIVITY
The Road to Independence

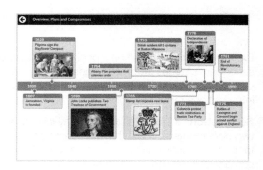

The roots of American democracy can be found in the basic concepts of government brought to North American by the earliest English settlers. Those ideas flourished in the colonies, and as a result, the British met with resistance when they tried to impose stricter policies.

Make Connections How did the events of 1765 –1773 lead to those of 1775 and 1776? *(The Stamp Act, Boston Massacre, and Boston Tea Party are examples of the growing tension between the colonies and Great Britain. That tension finally erupted in war with the Battles of Lexington and Concord, and with the colonies declaring independence.)*

Topic Inquiry
Launch the Topic Inquiry with students after introducing the Topic.

Origins of American Political Ideals

Supporting English Language Learners

Use with Digital Text 2, **Influential Documents and Ideas.**

Learning Strategies

Read the text, emphasizing the important documents discussed, such as the Magna Carta, the Petition of Right, and the English Bill of Rights. Read the glossary to learn more about these landmark documents. Have students use the strategic learning technique of creating concept maps.

Beginning Read aloud the text, using visuals as support. Provide a list of key words related to one of the documents. Guide the class to create a concept map using these words. Have students copy the map and read it to each other. Repeat the strategy for each important document.

Intermediate Have partners read the text. As a group, create a list of words describing two of the documents. Guide students to create a concept map for each document, using words from the list they created.

Advanced Have students read the text. Have partners create concept maps for two documents of their choice, using short phrases. Have students share their concept maps with each other.

Advanced High After reading the text, have students create concept maps for two documents of their choice, using short sentences. Have students share their concept maps with the class.

Use with Digital Text 1, **Origins of American Constitutional Government.**

Reading

Have students identify the three concepts of government. Guide them to use the chart, "Basic Concepts of Government," and context support in the reading to enhance and confirm their understanding of these concepts.

Beginning Define the words *ordered, limited,* and *representative*. Direct students' attention to the chart, "Basic Concepts of Government," and have them read each entry aloud. Point out context clues, such as the words *regulates, order, restricted,* and *the people.*

Intermediate Help students define the words *ordered, limited,* and *representative*. Provide a list of words or phrases from the text that help explain the meanings of these words, such as the words *regulates, order, restricted,* and *the people.* Have students read the sections on ordered, limited, and represenative government. Ask partners to discuss how words and phrases on the list help them understand the three concepts of government.

Advanced Have students read the text on ordered, limited, and represenative government. Ask them to use the text to create a list of words that are context clues to help them understand each concept of government. Have them share and explain their words with one another.

Advanced High Ask students to read the text on ordered, limited, and represenative government. Have them choose two context words from each section that they feel provide the most help in understanding each concept of government. Have them discuss their choices with a partner.

▣ Differentiate Instruction

Use the Differentiated Instruction notes throughout the lesson plan to support the varied skill sets, levels of readiness, and interests in the mixed-ability classroom.

Challenge These notes include suggestions for expanding the activity for advanced students.

On-Level These notes include suggestions for modifying the activity to address different interests or learning styles.

Extra Support These notes include ideas for providing more scaffolding or reading spuport.

Special Needs These notes provide ideas for adapting instruction to support the needs of various special needs students.

■ NOTES

Origins of American Political Ideals

Objectives

Objective 1: Explain how constitutional government in the United States has been influenced by centuries of political ideas and traditions from England and elsewhere.

Objective 2: Analyze the significance of three landmark historical documents to the American system of government.

Objective 3: Describe the three types of colonies that the English established in North America and explain why they are important to the study of American government.

LESSON 1 ORGANIZER		PACING: APPROX. 1 PERIOD, .5 BLOCKS		
			RESOURCES	
	OBJECTIVES	**PACING**	**Online**	**Print**
Connect				
DIGITAL START UP ACTIVITY **Establishing a New Government**		5 min.	●	
Investigate				
DIGITAL TEXT 1 **Origins of American Constitutional Government**	Objective 1	10 min.	●	●
DIGITAL TEXT 2 **Influential Documents and Ideas**	Objective 2	10 min.	●	●
INTERACTIVE TIMELINE **Foundations of American Rights**		10 min.	●	
DIGITAL TEXT 3 **Three Types of Colonies**	Objective 3	10 min.	●	●
INTERACTIVE MAP **The Thirteen Colonies in 1775**		10 min.	●	
Synthesize				
DIGITAL SYNTHESIZE ACTIVITY **Influences on American Constitutional Government**		5 min.	●	
Demonstrate				
DIGITAL QUIZ **Lesson Quiz and Class Discussion Board**		10 min.	●	

CONNECT

DIGITAL START UP ACTIVITY
Establishing a New Government

Project the Start Up Activity Ask students to answer the question as they enter and get settled. Then have them share their ideas with another student, either in class or through a chat or blog space.

Discuss If you were establishing a new system of government, what laws, customs, and institutions from our political system would you implement? As students share, you may wish to keep a list of answers. Then take a poll to see how many students agree with each category of answer.

Aa Vocabulary Development: Use the Interactive Reading Notepad to preview the Key Terms and Academic Vocabulary in this Lesson with students.

↯ FLIP IT!
Assign the Flipped Video for this lesson.

■ STUDENT EDITION PRINT
PAGES: 40–45

INVESTIGATE

DIGITAL TEXT 1
Origins of American Constitutional Government

Objective 1: Identify how constitutional government in the United States has been influenced by key ideas about government that were developed over centuries in England and elsewhere.

Quick Instruction

When they settled in North America, the English settlers of the thirteen colonies brought along ideas of government that had developed over centuries. English common law—unwritten, judge-made law developed over centuries—was part of that system. So, too, was English constitutionalism, the notion that government leaders are subject to the limitations of the law. Judeo-Christian traditions, and especially biblical law, were also a central part of English culture. The concept of the rule of law, for example, can be traced back at least as far as the Hebrew Bible. The rule of law is the idea that government is always subject to, never above, the law.

Basic Concepts of Government The English settlers brought three basic concepts of government to the colonies: ordered, limited, and representative government. Explain the role of limited government in the protection of individual rights—that is, this concept keeps government from becoming too powerful and thus destroying individual rights.

ELL Use the ELL activity described in the ELL chart.

Further Instruction

Basic Principles of Government: Core Reading and Interactive Reading Notepad Project and discuss the Interactive Reading Notepad questions.

Be sure that students understand that the three notions of government are broad categories. They encompass some of the major Enlightenment ideas that later influenced the colonists, such as the notion that all people are created equal and have certain rights that government cannot take away, which Thomas Jefferson called the "laws of nature and of nature's God," and "unalienable Rights."

Compare Which concepts of government are present in today's government? *(Possible answer: Ordered government regulates relationships. Today, we have local and State governments to regulate those relationships. Limited government restricts what government can do. Today, the police need a warrant to enter homes or arrest people. Representative governments serve the will of the people. Today, representatives and senators are elected by the people to govern them.)*

Analyze Interactions Which elements proposed by Enlightenment thinkers are similar to the basic notions of ordered, limited, and representative government? *(Possible answer: Separation of powers is linked to limited and ordered government. Legal decisions based on past decisions (precedent) are linked to ordered government. Natural rights are linked to representative and limited government.)*

Origins of American Political Ideals

DIGITAL TEXT 2

Influential Documents and Ideas

INTERACTIVE TIMELINE

Foundations of American Rights

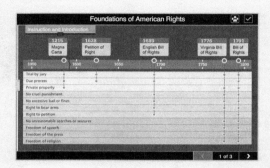

Objective 2: Explain the significance of three landmark English documents.

Quick Instruction

The basic notions of government can be traced back to several English documents that were written hundreds of years ago. These include the Magna Carta, the Petition of Right, and the English Bill of Rights. Point out to students that these documents reflect major political ideas in history, including the rights of resistance to illegimate government. When the English barons and Parliament were unhappy with the rule of King John and Charles I, they resisted by forcing those monarchs to sign the Magna Carta and later, the Petititon of Right. Note, too, that all of these documents challenged the divine right of kings, because by forcing the king to sign them, the barons and Parliament were rejecting the idea that the king had a divine right to rule given to them from God.

Interactive Timeline: Foundations of American Rights Project the timeline. Look at each image individually, and then view the timeline as a whole.

ACTIVE CLASSROOM

Use the Ranking Strategy to have students go through the events in the timeline, and rank which ones had the greatest influence on the constitutional government in the United States.

D Differentiate: Extra Support Step through each image with students. Have them identify each document and explain why it is important. Help students link each one to an important idea in democracy or the United States. Then continue with the activity.

ELL Use the ELL activity described in the ELL chart.

Further Instruction

Landmark Historical Documents: Core Reading and Interactive Reading Notepad Project and discuss the Interactive Reading Notepad questions.

Magna Carta and English Bill of Rights The landmark documents in English history include the Magna Carta, the Petition of Right, and the English Bill of Rights. The Magna Carta limited the power of the king and guaranteed trial by jury and due process. The Petition of Right guaranteed judgment by peers, limited martial law and required consent to shelter king's troops, and required an act of Parliment to tax people. These two documents supported the idea that the monarchy's power was not absolute, and that even monarchs must obey laws. The English Bill of Rights provided for the right of petition, free elections, and prohibited having a standing army during peacetime.

Project the Magna Carta and the English Bill of Rights. Have students find where the documents guarantee rights and discuss which rights they are.

Mayflower Compact Project the Mayflower Compact and give students time to read it. Discuss what rights the document guarantees.

Analyze Interactions Think about what you know about the present-day constitutional government in the United States. Describe how the historical English documents have influenced modern government. *(Possible answer: Many of the rights that are protected by government today are influenced by those expressed in the historical English documents. For example, the Petition of Right said that leaders had to obey the law of the land, which is an idea that is present in our government today.)*

Make Decisions The Mayflower Compact is a social contract. The signers agreed to follow laws to ensure their survival. Did they create a government? Is a social contract the same as a government? *(Possible answer: Yes, a social contract is a government. People agree to obey a certain structure that protects them.)*

DIGITAL TEXT 3

Three Types of Colonies

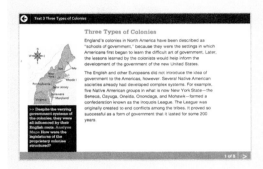

INTERACTIVE MAP

The Thirteen Colonies in 1775

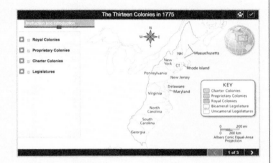

Objective 3: Describe the three types of colonies that the English established in the American colonies.

Quick Instruction

Remind students that the colonies were settled by mostly English settlers who brought their own forms of hard-won government with them.

Interactive Map: The Thirteen Colonies in 1775 Step through the Interactive Map with students. Point out that it shows how the colonies grew. Note how populations changed. Note the governmental types for each colony.

> ### 📷 ACTIVE CLASSROOM
>
> Have students use the Think Pair Share Strategy to relate the government for each colony to how each colony was established. Have students summarize the links they found, and display their summaries on a student blog or on the whiteboard.

D Differentiate: **Extra Support** Pair a less experienced student with a more experienced student. Give each pair two or three colonies to explore. Provide explicit questions. For example: *How was this colony established? Who named or elected the governor? What kind of legislature did each colony have?*

ELL Use the ELL activity described in the ELL chart.

Further Instruction

Three Types of Colonies: Core Reading and Interactive Reading Notepad Project and discuss the Interactive Reading Notepad questions, including the graphic organizer that asks students to chart the three types of colonies. Review the three types of colonies and fill in the graphic organizer on the whiteboard as you go.

Remind students of the similarities among the colonies: each was established on the basis of a charter and each was shaped by English origins.

Make Inferences Why might giving all colonies the same freedoms and self-government that were allowed in Connecticut and Rhode Island have possibly prevented the American Revolution? *(If all of the colonists had enjoyed the same freedoms and self-government, then they would have had no reason to revolt against the British. There would have been no reason to fight for equal rights.)*

Predict Consequences Settlers often thought of themselves as still English, even though they had crossed an ocean and resided in a colony. As time went on, each colony, and later State, began to have its own idea of autonomy. How might identifying with a colony or a State instead of a country as a whole be problematic in forming a new government? *(Possible answer: It might be hard to get people to agree to consider the good of the entire nation, rather than just one's State.)*

Origins of American Political Ideals

■ SYNTHESIZE

DIGITAL SYNTHESIZE ACTIVITY

Influences on American Constitutional Government

Ask students to recall the Topic Essential Question: "How Much Power Should the Government Have?" Have them use the Think Pair Share strategy to answer the questions in Influences on our Government. Ask them to take five minutes to write down some brief answers to the questions below, then share their answers with a talking partner.

Have partners think about the following question: What are three ideas, documents, or types of colonial government that you believe made the greatest impact on our constitutional government? Have pairs share their answers with the class.

Discuss Project these terms: ordered government, limited government, representative government, Magna Carta, Petition of Right, English Bill of Rights, Royal Colonies, Proprietary Colonies, and Charter Colonies. Call on students to define each term. Explain that how much power a government has often depends on how well the citizens believe the government wields that power.

■ DEMONSTRATE

DIGITAL QUIZ

Lesson Quiz and Class Discussion Board

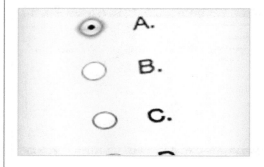

Assign the online Lesson Quiz for this lesson if you haven't already done so. Students will be offered automatic remediation or enrichment based on their scores.

In "Origins of American Political Ideals" you read about the origins of constitutional government: the English system of government, Enlightenment thought, and the experiences of the colonists in creating and governing the colonies.

Pose these questions to the class on the Discussion Board:

Analyze Main Idea The English Bill of Rights and Mayflower Compact build upon the ideas in the Magna Carta. Which main ideas of the Magna Carta were preserved in the other documents? What elements were added?

Make Decisions The title of this text is "Origins of American Political Ideals." Why is the creation of a government idealistic?

Topic Inquiry
Have students continue their investigations for the Topic Inquiry.

Independence

Supporting English Language Learners

Use with Digital Text 5, **The Declaration of Independence.**

Learning Strategies
Read the text, focusing on the section *Debates and Compromises*. Guide students to speak about these debates and compromises using the requesting assistance learning strategy.

Beginning Tell students that it is important to request assistance when they don't understand something. Provide students with a list of sentence frames they can use to ask for assistance such as: *Can you repeat that, please? What does _____ mean? Can you say that using other words?* Review the list with the class. Discuss the text. Prompt students to request assistance using a sentence frame from the list.

Intermediate Remind students that they can request assistance when they don't understand something. Model several sentences students can use such as: *Could you speak more slowly? Can you give an example?* Have partners generate one or two more questions and share them with the class. Discuss the text. Have students request assistance using the sentences that were discussed.

Advanced Point out to students that requesting assistance to clarify a concept or definition can improve understanding of difficult ideas. Provide sentence frames for requesting assistance such as: *Why did _____ happen? What does _____ mean?* Choose difficult terms or concepts from the text and guide students to use the sentence frames to request assistance.

Advanced High Model and explain requesting assistance for the students. Provide students with challenging concepts or terms from the text, and have partners take turns requesting assistance to better understand them.

Use with Digital Text 5, **The Declaration of Independence.**

Reading
Choose words from the text that show how American beliefs and principles are reflected in the Declaration of Independence, such as *natural rights, revolt, unalienable, consent.* Help students find context clues that help them understand these words.

Beginning Explain the meaning of each word. Have students copy each word and write their own definition for each. Direct them to where the words are used in the text and have them read these sentences. Point out context clues, such as the phrase "rights that the government could not take away."

Intermediate Define each word. Have students copy the definitions, read the text to find the words, and write a short sentence or phrase using each word.

Advanced Using short sections of the text, point out the vocabulary words and the context clues that help students understand them. Have partners read the sections and use the context clues to figure out the meaning of the words.

Advanced High Have students read the text and find the vocabulary words. Ask them to write a definition for each word, then direct them to identify the context clues that helped them figure out the meaning of the words.

▣ Differentiate Instruction

Use the Differentiated Instruction notes throughout the lesson plan to support the varied skill sets, levels of readiness, and interests in the mixed-ability classroom.

Challenge These notes include suggestions for expanding the activity for advanced students.

On-Level These notes include suggestions for modifying the activity to address different interests or learning styles.

Extra Support These notes include ideas for providing more scaffolding or reading spuport.

Special Needs These notes provide ideas for adapting instruction to support the needs of various special needs students.

▆ NOTES

Independence

Objectives

Objective 1: Explain how Britain's colonial policies contributed to the growth of self-government in the colonies.

Objective 2: Identify the major steps that led to growing feelings of colonial unity.

Objective 3: Consider the ways the colonists organized to protest British policies, and the contributions of significant individuals, including Thomas Jefferson, Samuel Adams, John Adams, Roger Sherman, John Jay, and George Washington.

Objective 4: Examine the debates and compromises that impacted the creation of the Declaration of Independence.

Objective 5: Understand the major ideas of the Declaration of Independence, including unalienable rights, the social contract theory, and the right of resistance to illegitimate government.

Objective 6: Summarize the common features of the first State constitutions and how they were related to documents such as the Declaration of Independence, the Articles of Confederation, and the U.S. Constitution.

LESSON 2 ORGANIZER		PACING: APPROX. 1 PERIOD, .5 BLOCKS			
				RESOURCES	
		OBJECTIVES	PACING	Online	Print
Connect					
DIGITAL START UP ACTIVITY **Speaking Up for Change**			5 min.	●	
Investigate					
DIGITAL TEXT 1 **Britain's Colonial Policies**		Objective 1	10 min.	●	●
DIGITAL TEXT 2 **Growing Colonial Unity**		Objective 2	10 min.	●	●
INTERACTIVE GALLERY **Analyzing Political Cartoons**			10 min.	●	
DIGITAL TEXT 3 **First Continental Congress**		Objective 3	10 min.	●	●
DIGITAL TEXT 4 **Second Continental Congress**		Objective 4	10 min.	●	●
DIGITAL TEXT 5 **The Declaration of Independence**		Objectives 4, 5	10 min.	●	●
INTERACTIVE TIMELINE **The Road to Independence**		Objective 3	10 min.	●	
DIGITAL TEXT 6 **The First State Constitutions**		Objective 6	10 min.	●	●
Synthesize					
DIGITAL SYNTHESIZE ACTIVITY **Revolt!**			5 min.	●	
Demonstrate					
DIGITAL QUIZ **Lesson Quiz and Class Discussion Board**			10 min.	●	

PEARSON realize™
www.PearsonRealize.com

Go online to access additional resources including:
Primary Sources • Biographies • Supreme Court cases •
21st Century Skill Tutorials • Maps • Graphic Organizers.

CONNECT

DIGITAL START UP ACTIVITY

Speaking Up for Change

Project the Start Up Activity Ask students to answer the questions. Then have them share their ideas with another student, either in class or through a chat or blog space.

Discuss Why do you think the colonists objected to this new tax? *(Possible answer: They were not able to vote on taxes levied upon them.)*

Tell students that in this lesson they will learn about how and why colonists fought against British policies, and the results of their actions.

Aa Vocabulary Development: Use the Interactive Reading Notepad to preview the Key Terms and Academic Vocabulary in this Lesson with students.

⇧ FLIP IT!

Assign the Flipped Video for this lesson.

▮ STUDENT EDITION PRINT PAGES: 46–54

▮ INVESTIGATE

DIGITAL TEXT 1

Britain's Colonial Policies

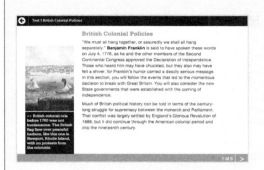

Objective 1: Explain how Britain's colonial policies contributed to the growth of self-government in the colonies.

Quick Instruction

The colonies were controlled by the king for a century and a half. They were mostly autonomous, creating their own colonial governments. After the French and Indian War in the mid-18th century, Britain would begin to assert more control, levying more taxes and restricting trade. British troops stayed on American soil even after the war had been won by the Crown.

Further Instruction

Britain's Colonial Policies: Core Reading and Interactive Reading Notepad Project and discuss the Interactive Reading Notepad questions.

The colonists considered themselves to be British, but took exception to British policies that taxed them and impeded trade. They also objected to the continued presence of British soldiers on colonial soil.

Make Inferences Benjamin Franklin said, "We must all hang together, or assuredly we shall all hang separately." Why might it have been so difficult to support colonial independence? *(Possible answer: Failure meant death. The colonists still considered themselves British.)*

Cause and Effect The French and Indian War forced the French out of the colonies. Why is understanding what happened during this war important to understanding what happened in the 1760s? *(The cost of the war directly impacted the taxes levied on the colonists. The soldiers remained in the colonies even though they were no longer fighting.)*

Independence

Growing Colonial Unity

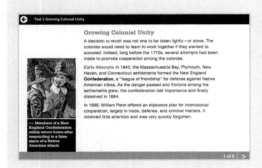

Analyzing Political Cartoons

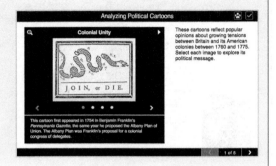

First Continental Congress

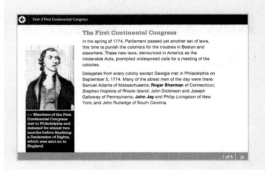

Objective 2: **Identify the major steps that led to growing feelings of colonial unity.**

Quick Instruction

Colonies needed to work together if they were to oppose Britain. Confederations were formed between colonies that shared geography. William Penn and Benjamin Franklin proposed plans for intercolonial cooperation. The Stamp Act Congress was a meeting of delegates from nine of the thirteen colonies to protest British policies. Committees of Correspondence, began in Massachusetts by Samuel Adams, spread throughout the colonies and provided a continuing network for cooperation and the exchange of information.

Interactive Gallery: Analyzing Political Cartoons Remind students that media is one way of getting one's point across. Project each political cartoon, and discuss the main point of each cartoon.

🖥 ACTIVE CLASSROOM

Use a Write 1 Get 3 strategy to answer the following question: What are four key characteristics of an effective political cartoon? Collect answers on the whiteboard.

🄳 Differentiate: Extra Support Explain that cartoons use common representations to illustrate a point. Point to the representation in each cartoon and have students explain what connections they make to the image. Then explain the main idea of the cartoon. Have students discuss whether or not the cartoonist did an effective job of illustrating his main idea. Then continue with the group activity.

Analyze Why might a political cartoon be more effective than a printed explanation of one side of an argument? *(Art can be clearer and more pointed than a printed explanation. It can appeal to emotions in a different way than print.)*

Further Instruction

Growing Colonial Unity: Core Reading and Interactive Reading Notepad Project and discuss the Interactive Reading Notepad questions.

Cooperation among the colonies succeeded because the colonists had similar ideas of the role of government. Their response of ignoring new laws and policies showed their belief in the right of resistance to illegitimate government.

Draw Conclusions Why was Franklin's Albany Plan of Union ahead of its time? *(Some elements of the plan would be reflected in the Constitution.)*

Objective 3: **Consider the ways that the colonists organized against British policies, and the contributions of significant individuals, including Thomas Jefferson, Samuel Adams. John Adams, Roger Sherman, John Jay, and George Washington.**

Quick Instruction

The Intolerable Acts, the name for a group of laws passed by Parliament to punish the colonists, prompted calls for a meeting of the colonies. This meeting was the First Continental Congress. At the meeting, leaders prepared a Declaration of Rights, which they sent to King George III.

Further Instruction

First Continental Congress: Core Reading and Interactive Reading Notepad Project and discuss the Interactive Reading Notepad questions.

The First Continental Congress included several significant individuals: Samuel Adams and John Adams of Massachusetts; Roger Sherman of Connecticut; Stephen Hopkins of Rhode Island; John Dickinson, James Wilson, and Joseph Galloway of Pennsylvania; John Jay and Philip Livingston of New York; George Washington, Richard Henry Lee, and Patrick Henry of Virginia; and John Rutledge of South Carolina. Some of the contributions of the political philosophies of these men on the development of the U.S. government were:

DIGITAL TEXT 4

Second Continental Congress

Text 4 Second Continental Congress

The Second Continental Congress

During the fall and winter of 1774–1775, the British government continued to refuse to compromise, let alone reverse, its colonial policies. It reacted to the Declaration of Rights as it had to other expressions of colonial discontent—with even stricter and more repressive measures.

The Second Continental Congress met in Philadelphia on May 10, 1775. By then, the Revolution had begun. The "shot heard 'round the world" had been fired. The battles of Lexington and Concord had been fought three weeks earlier, on April 19. With this bloodshed, many delegates believed that compromise with Great Britain was no longer possible.

>> The Second Continental Congress met just weeks after the battles of Lexington and Concord. One of their first tasks was to appoint George Washington as commander in chief of the new army.

1 of 4   >

George Washington Washington, former colonel of Virginia troops in the French and Indian War, served as a Virginia legislator. He had voted against British policies, then defied royal orders for the legislature to stop meeting. After helping to organize a boycott of British trade in Virginia, he helped pass a boycott at the First Continental Congress.

John Adams Adams, a rising lawyer in Boston, was also present. Adams strongly opposed British colonial policies. By the time of the First Continental Congress, he was a staunch supporter of independence and was well known as a brilliant political analyst. Therefore, his ideas carried great weight with the other delegates.

James Wilson Wilson, a lawyer from Pennsylvania, circulated a pamphlet, *Considerations on the Nature and Extent of the Legislative Authority of the British Parliament*, which proposed the idea that the British government had no authority to govern the colonies.

Make Inferences All thirteen colonial legislatures gave their support to the actions of the First Continental Congress. Why do you think that was? *(Possible answers: The men meeting were from a diverse set of colonies and supported the resolutions in their various legislatures. Even though the colonies were diverse, they all felt punished by the laws passed by Parliament.)*

Objective 4: **Examine the debates and compromises that impacted the creation of the Declaration of Independence and its major ideas, including those of unalienable rights, the social contract theory, and the right of resistance to illegitimate government.**

Quick Instruction

The Second Continental Congress met after the Revolution had begun. Each colony sent representatives. The Congress resolved several issues. First, it created an army with George Washington as it's commander-in-chief. Second, it created a final petition to make peace. John Jay of New York favored this move, and he drafted the Olive Branch petition himself. The petition was rejected by King George III. The Congress, supported by public opinion and practical necessity, served as the first government of the United States.

Further Instruction

Second Continental Congress: Core Reading and Interactive Reading Notepad Project and discuss the Interactive Reading Notepad questions.

The Second Continental Congress served as the first government for five years. It fought a war, raised armies and a navy, borrowed funds, bought supplies, created a money system, made treaties with foreign powers, and did other things that any government would have had to do in those circumstances. It also exercised both legislative powers, with each colony or state having one vote, and executive powers, handled by committees of delegates.

Cause and Effect The Second Continental Congress was thought by Britain to be an unlawful den of traitors. Why do you think they held that opinion? *(Possible answer: These men were deliberately defying the British government.)*

Draw Conclusions Why do you think the Olive Branch petition was not received by King George III? *(Possible answer: He was angry that the colonists had already revolted.)*

Independence

DIGITAL TEXT 5

The Declaration of Independence

INTERACTIVE TIMELINE

The Road to Independence

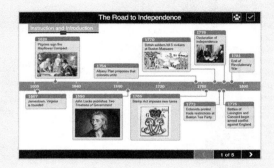

Objectives 3: **Consider the ways the colonists organized to protest British policies, and the contributions of significant individuals, including Thomas Jefferson, Samuel Adams, John Adams, Roger Sherman, John Jay, and George Washington; 4: Examine the debates and compromises that impacted the creation of the Declaration of Independence and its major ideas, including those of unalienable rights, the social contract theory, and the right of resistance to illegitimate government; 5: Understand the major ideas of the Declaration of Independence, including unalienable rights, the social contract theory, and the right of resistance to illegitimate government.**

Quick Instruction

The Second Continental Congress named a committee to write a Declaration of Independence from Great Britain. Jefferson, influenced by the ideas of the English political theorist John Locke and other Enlightenment ideas of liberty, rights, and responsibilities of individuals, did most of the work on the Declaration. Jefferson based his work on the idea that governments are responsible to their citizens to act in their best interests and that all people have certain unalienable rights. These are God-given rights that people are entitled to simply by the natural order of things—in Jefferson's words, because of "the laws of nature and nature's God." The idea of unalienable rights is a central concept in the theories of natural rights and the social contract theory put forth by

Enlightenment-era thinkers. Remind students that the social contract theory holds that the state exists only to serve the will of the people, and they are the sole source of its power.

Interactive Timeline: The Road to Independence Project the timeline. Remind students that these events are related and show some of the most important steps leading up to the formation of the United States of America. Discuss each event and its causes. Some causes might not be shown on the timeline.

▣ ACTIVE CLASSROOM

Have students form an Opinion Line to answer the following question: Was the American Revolution inevitable? Yes or no? *(Possible answer: No; with more time and political energy, the colonists could have gotten representation and addressed the issues of equality and taxation.)*

D Differentiate: **Extra Support** After asking students to take a stand, allow students five minutes to think about the question individually. Tell them to write down their response (*Yes* or *No*) and two reasons why they answered that way. Then continue with the group activity.

ELL Use the ELL activity described in the ELL chart.

Further Instruction

Declaration of Independence: Core Reading and Interactive Reading Notepad Project and discuss the Interactive Reading Notepad questions.

Debates and Compromises Explain that during the months leading to the American Declaration of Independence, the delegates to the Second Continental Congress debated many issues and came to compromises so they could move forward. Review some of those debates and compromises with students, including the debate over the merits of declaring independence and the debates and compromises over various specific items in the Declaration (criticisms of the English people and the condemnation of the slave trade).

Unalienable Rights The American political system was founded on the notion that the people should rule instead of be ruled and on the idea that every person is important as an individual, "created equal," and endowed with "certain unalienable rights." The term *unalienable* means that the government could not take away these rights. Jefferson identified these as the right to life, liberty, and the pursuit of happiness. The Declaration was founded on the concept of "the consent of the governed," rather than divine right of kings as the basis of power. The colonists rejected the idea that kings were given power to rule from God. Also central to this concept was the notion of the right of resistance to illegitimate government—that is, the people's right to rebel against any government that abuses its power.

Make Inferences Point out to students that Roger Sherman, like several other colonists, had been part of colonial resistance to British policies, beginning with the First Continental Congress. He also served on the committee assigned to draft a Declaration of Independence. Ask: How did Sherman's political philosophies contribute to the development of U.S. government? *(Sherman*

DIGITAL TEXT 6

The First State Constitutions

The First State Constitutions

In January 1776, New Hampshire adopted a constitution to replace its royal charter. Less than three months later, South Carolina followed suit. Then, on May 10, nearly two months before the adoption of the Declaration of Independence, the Congress urged each of the colonies to adopt "such governments as shall, in the opinion of the representatives of the people, best conduce to the happiness and safety of their constituents."

Drafting State Constitutions In 1776 and 1777, most of the States adopted written constitutions—bodies of fundamental laws setting out the principles, structures, and processes of their governments. Assemblies or conventions were commonly used to draft and then adopt these new documents.

>> The Massachusetts constitution, written by John Adams (above) and ratified on June 15, 1780, was a model for the U.S. Constitution, which wasn't completed until September 17, 1787.

1 of 5 >

---

originally hoped for reconciliation with Great Britain and he signed the Olive Branch petition in hopes that this could be accomplished. However, when King George rejected the petition, he became a strong supporter of independence. These viewpoints contributed to the development of the U.S. government, because they were part of both the initial effort to find a peaceful solution and the growing movement toward independence.)

Draw Conclusions Why might having the ability to build a brand new government allow for such a radical notion of rule? (Possible answer: Governments in the past were changed and the same people kept in power like King John and the Magna Carta. If Britain was defeated, there would be no government to come in and take over. The founders had the ability to use what they thought were the best ideas to create what they thought was the best government.)

Identify How do the beliefs and principles reflected in the Declaration of Independence contribute to both a national and a federal identity? How are these beliefs and principles embodies in the United States today? (Possible answer: The ideals present in the Declaration of Independence, such as the belief that certain rights would be protected by the national government and others by the State governments, were groundbreaking at the time. They are still embodied in the United States today and can be seen through American principles such as representative government, federalism, limited government, and popular sovereignty.)

Objective 6: Summarize the common features of the first State constitutions.

Quick Instruction

Colonies began to adopt State constitutions to replace their charters, beginning with New Hampshire. Here, the political philosophies of some of the Founding Fathers were in evidence. John Adams wrote the Massachusetts constitution of 1780, for example, and John Jay helped draft New York's State constitution. These documents had a profound effect on the development of the U.S. government and the protection of individual rights. Their most common features were the principles of popular sovereignty (a government that exists only with the consent of the governed), limited government, civil rights and liberties, separation of powers, and checks and balances.

Further Instruction

The First State Constitutions: Core Reading and Interactive Reading Notepad Project and discuss the Interactive Reading Notepad questions, including the graphic organizer asking students to chart the common features of state constitutions. Review the common features with the class and fill in the graphic organizer on the whiteboard as you go.

Draw Conclusions The elements of the state constitutions were very similar. Why did each one adopt its own instead of just using one for all? (Possible answer: The people in each State were citizens of that State, as well as citizens of a new country.)

Independence

SYNTHESIZE

DIGITAL SYNTHESIZE ACTIVITY
Revolt!

Ask students to recall the Essential Question: How Much Power Should the Government Have? Then read aloud the introduction to the Synthesize activity. Students should understand that the answer to what led to a major shift in thinking directly relates to how much power people believed the government should have.

Using a Think Pair Share strategy, have students respond to one of the questions. Provide five minutes for students to think before sharing with their talking partner. Have one partner record the pair's thinking. Then have students move on to a different screen. Post responses to the whiteboard.

Discuss Ask students to think about the poll they took at the beginning of this lesson. Ask if they would change any of their responses now that they have learned more about the road to independence.

DEMONSTRATE

LESSON QUIZ
Lesson Quiz and Class Discussion Board

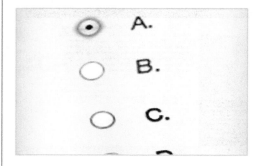

Assign the online Lesson Quiz for this lesson if you haven't already done so. Students will be offered automatic remediation or enrichment based on their score.

In "Independence" you read about America's road to independence: the beginning of self-rule in the colonies within a royal framework, the increasingly harsh laws passed by Parliament and objected to by the colonists, the two Continental Congresses that resolved to become independent, and the states' development of their own constitutions.

Pose these questions to the class on the Discussion Board:

Identify Cause and Effect What led to a revolutionary war and American independence?

Identify Which person do you think had the most influence in the movement for independence? Why?

Evaluate Sources You are a delegate at the Second Continental Congress. Would you vote for or against Lee's Resolution? Why?

Topic Inquiry
Have students continue their investigations for the Topic Inquiry.

First Steps

PEARSON realize™

www.PearsonRealize.com
Access your Digital Lesson

Supporting English Language Learners

Use with Digital Text 1, **The Articles of Confederation.**

Reading

Examine the debates and compromises that took place during the Second Continental Congress that impacted the creation of the Articles of Confederation. These included how the Federal Government should be organized and how much money each State should pay into a common treasury. How were these issues settled? Then discuss the weaknesses of the Articles of Confederation and the effects of these weaknesses. Provide a cause-and-effect graphic organizer. Tell students that using a graphic organizer and reading carefully will help them understand how the constitutional government has been influenced by ideas, people, and historical documents such as the Articles of Confederation. An example cause and effect is provided: *Cause: The Congress did not have the power to tax. Effect: It could raise money only by borrowing and by asking the States for funds.*

Beginning Using visuals and gestures as support, review a completed graphic organizer with students. Emphasize how the graphic organizer supports understanding. Have students copy or add to the graphic organizer.

Intermediate Provide students with sentences from the text to use in completing the graphic organizer. Guide the group to complete the graphic organizer.

Advanced After reading the text, have partners complete the graphic organizer. Discuss how students identified the cause and the effect.

Advanced High Have students read the text and complete the graphic organizer. Ask students to discuss their graphic organizers with a partner.

Use with Digital Text 3, **A Demand for Stronger Government.**

Learning Strategies

Based on the language levels of your students, identify basic academic vocabulary words, including *instability, negotiations,* and *delegates.* Use these words in the following speaking activities in order for students to build concept and language attainment.

Beginning Write the words on the board and define them for students. Guide partners to use the words in sentence stems, such as *Instability means _____.*

Intermediate Guide students to read the words as you write them on the board. Encourage students to use the words in longer sentences by providing sentence stems. For example: *Instability, meaning _____, was seen under the Articles of Confederation in relation to _____.*

Advanced Ask partners to find the selected words in the text and to read the relevant paragraphs. Have partners discuss the meaning of the words and then share their ideas with the group.

Advanced High Provide students with a list of the selected words. Have the group discuss the meanings of the words. After reading the text, ask the students whether their definitions made sense with the way the words were used in the reading. Discuss any adjustments to the definitions that students need to make.

Ⅾ Differentiate Instruction

Use the Differentiated Instruction notes throughout the lesson plan to support the varied skill sets, levels of readiness, and interests in the mixed-ability classroom.

Challenge These notes include suggestions for expanding the activity for advanced students.

On-Level These notes include suggestions for modifying the activity to address different interests or learning styles.

Extra Support These notes include ideas for providing more scaffolding or reading spuport.

Special Needs These notes provide ideas for adapting instruction to support the needs of various special needs students.

■ NOTES

Topic ② Lesson 3

First Steps

Objectives

Objective 1: Describe the debates that impacted the creation of the Articles of Confederation, the structure of the government set up under the Articles, and how that government was influenced by ideas, people, and historical documents.

Objective 2: Explain why the weaknesses of the Articles led to a critical period for the country in the 1780s.

Objective 3: Describe how a growing need for a stronger national government led to plans for a Constitutional Convention.

LESSON 3 ORGANIZER		PACING: APPROX. 1 PERIOD, .5 BLOCKS		
			RESOURCES	
	OBJECTIVES	PACING	Online	Print
Connect				
DIGITAL START UP ACTIVITY **A Plan of Confederation**		5 min.	●	
Investigate				
DIGITAL TEXT 1 **The Articles of Confederation**	Objective 1	10 min.	●	●
INTERACTIVE CHART **The Government Created by the Articles**		10 min.	●	
DIGITAL TEXT 2 **A Time of Troubles, the 1780s**	Objective 2	10 min.	●	●
INTERACTIVE CHART **Articles of Confederation**		10 min.	●	
DIGITAL TEXT 3 **A Demand for a Stronger Government**	Objective 3	10 min.	●	●
Synthesize				
DIGITAL SYNTHESIZE ACTIVITY **Reflect on a Plan of Confederation**		5 min.	●	
Demonstrate				
DIGITAL QUIZ **Lesson Quiz and Class Discussion Board**		10 min.	●	

PEARSON
realize™
www.PearsonRealize.com

Go online to access additional resources including:
Primary Sources • Biographies • Supreme Court cases •
21st Century Skill Tutorials • Maps • Graphic Organizers.

■ CONNECT

DIGITAL START UP ACTIVITY
A Plan of Confederation

Project the Start Up Activity Ask students to answer the questions as they enter and get settled. Then have them jot down their ideas on a sheet of paper.

Predict In 1776 and 1777, most of the States adopted written constitutions centered on popular sovereignty and limited government. What predictions can you make about the powers and responsibilities that would be given to the new Federal Government? *(Answers may vary, but will likely include establishing what duties the government should take over, defining local responsibilities, and encouraging unity.)*

Aa Vocabulary Development: Use the Interactive Reading Notepad to preview the Key Terms and Academic Vocabulary in this Lesson with students.

> **↕ FLIP IT!**
> Assign the Flipped Video for the lesson.

■ STUDENT EDITION PRINT PAGES: 55–59

■ INVESTIGATE

DIGITAL TEXT 1
The Articles of Confederation

Objective 1: Describe the debates that impacted the creation of the Articles of Confederation, the structure of the government set up under the Articles, and how that government was influenced by ideas, people, and historical documents.

Quick Instruction
During the Second Continental Congress, delegates debated the best structure for the new national government, as well as specific issues such as how much money each State would owe the treasury and how much voting power each State would have in Congress. The historical document that developed from these debates became the Articles of Confederation. The Articles handled the respective roles of the National and State governments by limiting the powers of the National Government and putting a great deal of power in the hands of the individual States.

The Government Created by the Articles of Confederation: Interactive Chart Arrange students into small groups. Project the chart on a digital whiteboard. Have students make a list of what they think the answers to the chart are based on what they know about government's duties and responsibilities. Students should then jot these answers down. Appoint scorekeepers responsible for one or more groups. As you reveal the answers in the chart, have the scorekeeper note each group's correct answers. The team with the most correct answers wins.

INTERACTIVE CHART
The Government Created by the Articles

🗣 ACTIVE CLASSROOM
Break the class into small groups. Tell each group that they need to come up with a possible scenario that illustrates an action related to each governmental power set up by the Articles of Confederation. (For instance, a powerful earthquake strikes Boston, destroying homes and businesses. The Navy is drafted to deliver needed supplies to the stricken area; the Massachusetts delegate recruits volunteers to notify family members of the deceased through the mail; a dispute arises with a local Native American tribe whose village is suddenly inhabited by homeless survivors. The delegate negotiates a treaty with the tribe and pays them for the use of their homes and supplies for the survivors.) Have students develop their group's scenario by starting with one student. That student should write as much as they can for one minute, then switch with the person on their right. The next person tries to improve or elaborate the response where the other person left off. Continue to switch until the paper comes back to the first person. The group then adds in any information that has been left out and shares that with the larger group.

First Steps

DIGITAL TEXT 2

A Time of Troubles, the 1780s

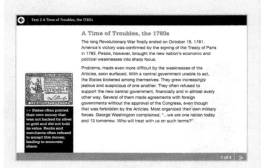

INTERACTIVE CHART

Articles of Confederation

D Differentiate: Extra Support Pair students who need more support with students who are more adept. Have pairs discuss the scenario before writing. Project the chart for the discussion so students can focus on the governmental elements of the Articles.

ELL Use the ELL activity described in the ELL chart.

Further Instruction

Editable Presentation Use the Editable Presentation to present the main ideas for this Core Reading.

Articles of Confederation: Core Reading and Interactive Reading Notepad Project and discuss the Interactive Reading Notepad questions, including the graphic organizer asking students to explain the effects of the weaknesses of the Articles of Confederation. Review the causes and effects with the class and fill in the graphic organizer on the whiteboard as you go. Be sure students understand that the debates over specific issues in the Articles led to the calling of the Constitutional Convention. Discuss whether the Constitution could have been written before the Articles of Confederation.

Make Decisions Which decisions made by the writers of the Articles caused problems among the States? Why? *(Possible answer: One problem created by the writers was the fact that States could tax goods from other States, which was detrimental to interstate commerce.)*

Objective 2: Explain why the weaknesses of the Articles led to a critical period for the country in the 1780s.

Quick Instruction

Government in the new United States was influenced by ideas, people, and historical documents. Weaknesses in the Articles of Confederation caused confusion and conflict among the States. The States began to print their own money, banned each other's goods, made agreements with foreign countries, and even organized their own military forces. Under the Articles, the central government had little power to address these issues. Shays' Rebellion was a series of incidents in response to small property holders losing their land and possessions for lack of payment on taxes and other debts.

Interactive Chart: Articles of Confederation Display the interactive chart on the whiteboard. Step through each weakness and its effect and read the questions with students.

🖵 ACTIVE CLASSROOM

Using a Write One strategy, have students explain the weaknesses of the Articles of Confederation. One student should write all he or she can and then pass the paper to another member of the group. You may wish to give students particular topics to write on or invite them to think about all the weaknesses. Have students discuss what they wrote as a team. You may wish to ask the following questions to guide the discussion: *Why did the writers of the Articles create a weak government? Which element of the government was weakest? Which element was the strongest?* Circulate and ask questions that encourage students to use information from the text, chart, and their writings in their discussions.

D Differentiate: Challenge Have students create their own Constitutional Convention using the answers to their questions. Have them debate whether or not the Articles should continue or if they should create a new government.

DIGITAL TEXT 3

A Demand for a Stronger Government

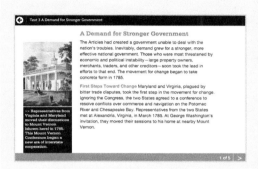

>> Representatives from Virginia and Maryland moved their discussions to Mount Vernon (shown here) in 1785. This Mount Vernon Conference began a new era of interstate cooperation.

Further Instruction

Go through the Interactive Reading Notepad questions and discuss the answers with the class.

The Articles of Confederation provided for a friendship between the States and national government. However, distrust caused the States to act in their own interests. Economic chaos followed.

Draw Conclusions The Articles of Confederation said that States needed to look out for the welfare of their own citizens. How does Shays' Rebellion demonstrate a breakdown of this expectation? *(Shays' Rebellion showed that States, for a variety of reasons, could not pay their citizens what they were owed.)*

Predict Consequences How might States respond to a change in government? How might the citizens of those States respond? *(Possible answer: People who are involved with trade or who are owed money by the States will be interested in the change. States might be wary of the change because their own sovereignty will be changed.)*

Objective 3: Describe how a growing need for a stronger national government led to plans for a Constitutional Convention.

Quick Instruction

Two States began negotiations over commerce and trade. This meeting between Maryland and Virginia was the first step in addressing the issues of the Articles of Confederation and the developing constitutional government. Two meetings, first in Annapolis and next in Philadelphia, brought more and more States together to discuss economic issues. The meeting in Philadelphia began as a debate of how to change the Articles, but soon became a meeting to create a new national government. The meeting in Philadelphia is now called the Constitutional Convention.

ELL Use the ELL activity described in the ELL chart.

Further Instruction

Some of the Founding Fathers believed that the Articles' plan for the respective roles of the National and State governments was not working. They believed that plan had resulted in a central government that was so weak the very existence of the United States was threatened and that the nation needed a stronger, more effective National Government. This political philosophy was a major contribution to the development of the U.S. government, because these men advocated for meetings among the States to revise the Articles of Confederation. George Washington invited Maryland and Virginia to his home, Mount Vernon. James Madison and Alexander Hamilton invited States to send delegates to a meeting in Annapolis. When only five came, they persuaded the Annapolis meeting to invite delegates to the Philadelphia meeting.

Make Generalizations Why might Hamilton, Washington, and Madison have worked so hard to bridge the differences among the States? *(Possible answer: They believed that the new country would only survive if all the States worked together to effect change.)*

Draw Conclusions Why might the States have been reluctant to send delegates to the meetings? *(Possible answer: States might be worried that their concerns would not be addressed. They could also have been wary about losing power to the National Government.)*

First Steps

■ SYNTHESIZE

DIGITAL SYNTHESIZE ACTIVITY
Reflect on a Plan of Confederation

At the beginning of this lesson, you made some predictions about the powers and responsibilities that the Continental Congress would give to the new government. Look back at your predictions, and for each prediction you made, cite evidence in the lesson that supported or contradicted your position.

Discuss Ask students to think about the new government. In groups have students use their predictions to discuss how well the new government met the needs of the new country. Then have them compare the current government with the government created by the Articles of Confederation. Discuss what elements seem similar and why that might be.

■ DEMONSTRATE

DIGITAL QUIZ
Lesson Quiz and Class Discussion Board

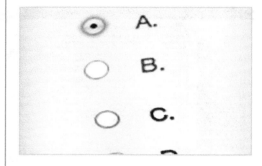

Assign the online Lesson Quiz for this lesson if you haven't already done so. Students will be offered automatic remediation or enrichment based on their score.

Pose these questions to the class on the Discussion Board:

In "The Critical Period," you read about the creation of the first set of guidelines that governed the States and the issues that arose with a weak central government.

Make Generalizations What were the main issues that the writers of the Articles of Confederation were trying to address with their document?

Make Decisions Were the Articles of Confederation destined to fail? Why or why not?

Topic Inquiry
Have students continue their investigations for the Topic Inquiry.

Creating and Ratifying the Constitution

Supporting English Language Learners

Use with Digital Text 1, **The Framers Meet.**

Learning Strategies
Based on the language levels of your students, choose basic vocabulary words that they will encounter in the text. Select words that can be supported by images in the text or images that can be easily provided. Use these words in the following writing activities in order for students to build concept and language attainment as they identify the contributions of the Framers.

Beginning Using images for support, write the words on the board and discuss each one with the class. Create a word web with the selected words, with the *The Framers* in the center. Have the students copy the web.

Intermediate Using images for support, explain each selected word to the students. After reading the text aloud, guide students to create a word web about the Framers using the selected words. Help the class to write a short sentence for each word.

Advanced Discuss the selected words with students. Have partners read the text. Ask partners to create a word web using the selected words, then write a short paragraph using the words.

Advanced High Provide students with a list of the selected words. After reading the text, have them create a word web and write a short paragraph using the words. Ask students to read their paragraphs to a partner.

Use with Digital Text 4, **Debates and Compromises.**

Reading
Ask students to look at the map titled "Slavery in the United States, 1790" and read the caption. Use this visual support to give students background knowledge about the situation that led to some of the debates and compromises of the Constitutional Convention. Have them read about the compromises.

Beginning Have students read the caption for the map. Have students complete the following sentence frame: *This map shows that _____.* Ask students to read their completed sentences to the class and then have them read about the Three-Fifths Compromise. Explain that the map shows the reason why the southern States wanted enslaved people counted in their populations.

Intermediate Have students read the caption for the map and then ask them to explain what the colors on the map represent. Then have students read about the Three-Fifths Compromise and then complete the following sentence: *Southern States wanted the enslaved counted in their populations because _____.*

Advanced Have students look at the map and read the caption, then read about the Three-Fifths Compromise. Have them write a few sentences to respond to the following question: *Why did the southern States want the enslaved to be counted as part of their populations?*

Advanced High Have students look at the map and read the caption, then read about the Three-Fifths Compromise. Have them write a few sentences to respond to the following question: *What is the connection between the data in this map and the Three-Fifths Compromise?*

D Differentiate Instruction

Use the Differentiated Instruction notes throughout the lesson plan to support the varied skill sets, levels of readiness, and interests in the mixed-ability classroom.

Challenge These notes include suggestions for expanding the activity for advanced students.

On-Level These notes include suggestions for modifying the activity to address different interests or learning styles.

Extra Support These notes include ideas for providing more scaffolding or reading spuport.

Special Needs These notes provide ideas for adapting instruction to support the needs of various special needs students.

■ NOTES

Creating and Ratifying the Constitution

Objectives

Objective 1: Identify the Framers of the Constitution, the individuals, principals, and ideas that influenced them, how they organized the Constitutional Convention, and their contributions to the creation of the United States Constitution.

Objective 2: Compare and contrast the Virginia and New Jersey plans for the new government.

Objective 3: Examine the convention's major debates and compromises.

Objective 4: Identify the opposing sides in the fight for ratification and describe the major arguments for and against the proposed Constitution.

Objective 5: Describe the inauguration of the new government of the United States of America.

LESSON 4 ORGANIZER		PACING: APPROX. 1 PERIOD, .5 BLOCKS			
				RESOURCES	
		OBJECTIVES	**PACING**	**Online**	**Print**
Connect					
DIGITAL START UP ACTIVITY **"My Esteemed Colleagues . . ."**			5 min.	●	
Investigate					
DIGITAL TEXT 1 **The Framers Meet**		Objective 1	10 min.	●	●
INTERACTIVE ILLUSTRATION **The Framers and Their Political Philosophies**			10 min.	●	
DIGITAL TEXT 2 **The Delegates Adopt Rules of Procedure**		Objective 1	10 min.	●	●
DIGITAL TEXT 3 **Two Plans of Government**		Objective 2	10 min.	●	●
DIGITAL TEXT 4 **Debates and Compromises**		Objective 3	10 min.	●	●
INTERACTIVE CHART **The Connecticut Compromise**			10 min.	●	
DIGITAL TEXT 5 **The Fight for Ratification**		Objectives 4, 5	10 min.	●	●
Synthesize					
DIGITAL SYNTHESIZE ACTIVITY **Solving the Problems of the Articles**			5 min.	●	
Demonstrate					
DIGITAL QUIZ **Lesson Quiz and Class Discussion Board**			10 min.	●	

PEARSON
realize™
www.PearsonRealize.com

Go online to access additional resources including:
Primary Sources • Biographies • Supreme Court cases •
21st Century Skill Tutorials • Maps • Graphic Organizers.

■ CONNECT

DIGITAL START UP ACTIVITY
"My Esteemed Colleagues . . ."

Project the Start Up Activity Ask students to answer the questions as they enter and get settled. Then have them share their ideas with another student, either in class or through a chat or blog space.

Discuss If you were a delegate to the Constitutional Convention, what major concerns would you have wanted the convention to address? *(Possible answer: My main concern woulld be that the people of my State would have all the freedoms originally sought in breaking from Britain.)*

Tell students that in this lesson they will learn about the creation and ratification of the Constitution.

Aa Vocabulary Development: Use the Interactive Reading Notepad to preview the Key Terms and Academic Vocabulary in this Lesson with students.

⚡ FLIP IT!
Assign the Flipped Video for this lesson.

■ STUDENT EDITION PRINT PAGES: 60–71

■ INVESTIGATE

DIGITAL TEXT 1
The Framers Meet

Objective 1: Identify the Framers of the Constitution and the individuals, principals, and ideas that influenced them, how they organized the Philadelphia Convention, and their contributions.

Quick Instruction
The Framers of the Constitution met in Philadelphia in May 1787. Delegates from twelve of the thirteen States gathered to write an historical document that would meet the needs of a new nation. The Framers of the Constitution were all men, all educated in major philosophical ideas, including the Enlightenment, and many had been involved in some form of public service, whether in the military or in State government. James Madison was the most influential delegate, because he not only devised much of the plan of government on which the Constitution was based, he also kept careful notes of the proceedings. Later, he would play a critical role in the ratification process.

ELL Use the ELL activity described in the ELL chart.

Interactive Illustration: The Framers and Their Politcal Philosophies Click on the hotspots and name each of the Framers. Call on students to identify contributions of the political philosophies of Alexander Hamilton, James Madison, George Washington, and James Wilson on the development of the U.S. government.

INTERACTIVE ILLUSTRATION
The Framers and Their Political Philosophies

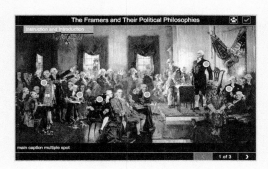

📖 ACTIVE CLASSROOM
Define with students the opposing philosophies of the Federalists and Anti-Federalists. Have students use a Sticky Note strategy to answer the following question for each man: *Am I a Federalist or an Anti-Federalist?* For each person, then have the student note how the quotation shows each man's philosophy.

D Differentiate: Extra Support Post the following statement: *The Articles of Confederation should change.* Then have students find at least one person who agrees with this statement. Continue with the following statements: *I think there should be a strong federal, or National, government. I think States should be more powerful than the Federal Government.*

Further Instruction
The Framers Meet: Core Reading and Interactive Reading Notepad Project and discuss the Interactive Reading Notepad questions.

Creating and Ratifying the Constitution

The Delegates Adopt Rules of Procedure

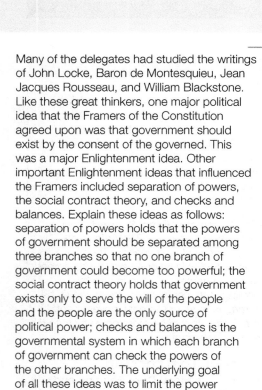

Text 2 The Delegates Adopt Rules of Procedure

The Delegates Adopt Rules of Procedure

The Framers met in the Pennsylvania State House (now Independence Hall), probably in the same room in which the Declaration of Independence had been signed 11 years earlier. Not enough States were represented on the date Congress had set, May 14, to begin the meeting. The delegates who were present met until the 25th, when a **quorum** of the States was finally on hand.

On that date, the delegates unanimously elected George Washington president of the convention. Then, and at the second session on Monday, May 28, they adopted several rules of procedure. A majority of the States would be needed to conduct business. Each State delegation was to have one vote on all matters, and a majority of the votes cast would carry any proposal.

>> Independence Hall, often referred to as the birthplace of the United States, was originally home to all three branches of Pennsylvania's colonial government.

1 of 4 >

Many of the delegates had studied the writings of John Locke, Baron de Montesquieu, Jean Jacques Rousseau, and William Blackstone. Like these great thinkers, one major political idea that the Framers of the Constitution agreed upon was that government should exist by the consent of the governed. This was a major Enlightenment idea. Other important Enlightenment ideas that influenced the Framers included separation of powers, the social contract theory, and checks and balances. Explain these ideas as follows: separation of powers holds that the powers of government should be separated among three branches so that no one branch of government could become too powerful; the social contract theory holds that government exists only to serve the will of the people and the people are the only source of political power; checks and balances is the governmental system in which each branch of government can check the powers of the other branches. The underlying goal of all these ideas was to limit the power of government.

Make Decisions Why were the Framers compared to demi-gods? *(Possible answer: The Framers were leading men of their day. Their work at the Constitutional Convention was brilliant and incorporated all the most important elements of the era's political philosophy.)*

Draw Conclusions The Framers believed in the consent of the governed. Did they consider themselves "the governed"? How might that have impacted the writing of the Constitution? *(Possible answer: They did consider themselves "the governed." They wrote a set of laws that would be conducive to their own freedom and self-government.)*

Objective 1: Identify the Framers of the Constitution and the individuals, principals, and ideas that influenced them, how they organized the Philadelphia Convention, and their contributions.

Quick Instruction

At the Constitutional Convention, the delegates elected George Washington, who had been significant in the field of government and politics since the First Continental Congress, as president of the convention. Because he was so admired and respected, Washington's presence at the convention gave the entire proceeding respectability.

Further Instruction

The Delegates Adopt Rules of Procedure: Core Reading and Interactive Reading Notepad Project and discuss the Interactive Reading Notepad questions.

A quorum of States arrived on May 25, 1787, to begin the convention. Rules were adopted at the second meeting. Their final meeting was on September 17. While the purpose of the convention was to recommend revisions to the Articles of Confederation, they adopted a proposal on May 30 that expressed "a national Government ought to be established consisting of a supreme Legislative, Executive and Judiciary." This was the beginning of writing the U.S. Constitution.

Make Inferences Why did the Framers decide to begin writing a new document instead of revising the Articles? *(Possible answers: The weak central government was a big flaw of the Articles and a stronger central government as described in the proposal was a better idea. The Framers wanted their government to reflect a balance of powers.)*

Two Plans of Government

Debates and Compromises

Objective 2: Compare and contrast the Virginia and the New Jersey plans.

Quick Instruction

One major debate the delegates had to resolve was how to organize the new government. The Virginia Plan, which favored the larger States, proposed a government of three branches: legislative, executive, and judicial. A bicameral Congress would be based on proportional representation among the States.

The Virginia Plan's major support came from the three most populous States. The New Jersey Plan, supported by the smaller States, proposed a unicameral Congress where each State was equally represented.

Further Instruction

Two Plans of Government: Core Reading and Interactive Reading Notepad Project and discuss the Interactive Reading Notepad questions.

The New Jersey Plan closely limited the powers of the Congress to tax and regulate trade between the States. Under the Virginia Plan, the structure of the government gave Congress all the powers it had in the Articles of Confederation. Additionally it would have the power to legislate between States, to make States follow national laws, and to veto State laws that did not follow national laws. These very principles are reflected in the U.S. Constitution and are embodied in the United States today.

The two plans also differed on the executive and judicial branches, which impacted the creation of the founding documents.

Draw Conclusions Look at each plan and the States that supported it. How does each plan benefit its supporters? Why are they worried the other plan will be chosen? *(The smaller States fear they will lose power if representation in Congress is based on population. The larger States fear they will lose power if representation is the same for all States.)*

Connect The Articles of Confederation were supposed to be revised at the convention. While they weren't revised, they weren't scrapped either. What elements of the Articles are still found in the Constitution? *(The Virginia Plan kept intact all of Congress's powers.)*

Objective 3: Examine the convention's major debates and compromises and the effects of those decisions.

Quick Instruction

The Framers of the Constitution knew that democracy was built on compromise. Several key compromises were agreed to during the convention. The Connecticut Compromise, largely devised by Connecticut delegate Roger Sherman, proposed that the structure of Congress should be made up of two houses. States would be equally represented in the Senate. In the House of Representatives, representation would be based on population. Sherman's compromise was important because this dispute had threatened to derail the entire convention.

Interactive Chart: The Conneticut Compromise Read through the differences of the two plans with students. Drag tiles from each plan into the center to review which elements became part of the Conneticut Compromise. Point out to students that the bicameral Congress would have the power to make laws for the nation, but a bill would have to pass both houses to become law.

ELL Use the ELL activity described in the ELL chart.

Topic ② Lesson 4

Creating and Ratifying the Constitution

The Connecticut Compromise

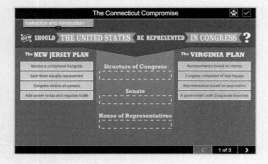

The Fight for Ratification

🗣 ACTIVE CLASSROOM

Review the flow chart. Using a Sticky Note strategy, have students note the most important parts of the Virginia Plan, New Jersey Plan, and the Connecticut Compromise. Then have students use their notes to create a summary of each plan, including the most important details for each plan. Summaries should include why each plan got its name and people important to the process in their summaries: Adams, Madison, Mason, and Sherman. In the summary for the Connecticut Compromise, encourage students to include which elements came from the other plans.

D Differentiate: Extra Support Have students focus on one plan at a time. Then have students find the most important element of each structure. Using a different color sticky note or ink color, have them note which people support or suggested the plan. Then have students share their notes with others. Provide students enough time to ask each other questions to determine the who, what, and why for each plan. Then have students continue with the activity and create their summaries.

Further Instruction

Debates and Compromises: Core Text and Interactive Reading Notepad Project and discuss the Interactive Reading Notepad questions.

The Framers had several other compromises that impacted the creation of the founding documents. The Three-Fifths Compromise allowed that each "free person" should be counted and "three fifths of all other persons." The Commerce and Slave Trade Compromise forbade Congress from taxing exported goods from States and acting on the slave trade for 20 years.

Even with these compromises, the Framers agreed on most issues. They agreed that a new, stronger Federal Government had to be created to deal with social and economic problems. They believed in the consent of the governed, limited and representative government, separation of powers, and checks and balances.

Evaluate Impact How did the wealth concentrated in the South frame the debate at the convention? *(There were debates about how slaves would be counted and taxed. There were debates about the difference in the economies and how Congress would regulate or support the agricultural South versus the manufacturing North.)*

Make Decisions Do you agree with Franklin's thought, "Sir, I agree with this Constitution with all its faults, if they are such; because I think a general Government necessary for us . . . I doubt . . . whether any other Convention we can obtain, may be able to make a better Constitution." Why or why not? *(Possible answer: The Constitution has lasted for over 200 years. It has been changed, but the basic tenets of government have not been.)*

Objectives 4: Identify the opposing sides in the fight for ratification and describe the major arguments for and against the proposed Constitution; 5: Describe the inauguration of the new government of the United States of America.

Quick Instruction

Article VII of the Constitution states that nine States needed to ratify the Constitution for it to become law. The Federalists, those who were for ratification, argued that the Constitution was a superior plan to the Articles. The Anti-Federalists, those against ratification, were unhappy with the new plan. Among other concerns, they argued that unanimous consent should be needed for ratification and that the executive could become too powerful. Anti-Federalists also wanted a Bill of Rights, which Federalists promised to add after ratification. Over the course of the struggle for ratification, a collection of essays titled *The Federalist: A Commentary on the Constitution of the United States*, was written by Alexander Hamilton, James Madison, and John Jay. These essays were influential in convincing many people to support the proposed Constitution and are still read by people today.

SYNTHESIZE

DIGITAL SYNTHESIZE ACTIVITY

Solving the Problems of the Articles

Ask students to recall two examples of problems that arose under the Articles of Confederation. Remind students that there were problems between States, such as trade or money issues, and within States, such as collection of debts and taxes.

Project the two problems on the whiteboard. Make sure students remember the problems outlined and why they were problems. Using a Think Pair Share strategy, have students work on finding an answer to each problem.

DEMONSTRATE

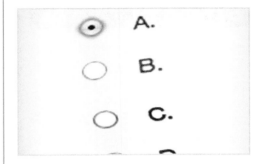

DIGITAL QUIZ

Lesson Quiz and Class Discussion Board

Assign the online Lesson Quiz for this lesson if you haven't already done so. Students will be offered automatic remediation or enrichment based on their scores.

Pose these questions to the class on the Discussion Board:

In "Creating and Ratifying the Constitution" you read about the process of fashioning a new government.

Identify Identify the Framers of the Constitution and the individuals, principles, and ideas that influenced them.

Examine Causes and Effects What were the major compromises and debates of the convention? What were the effects of those compromises?

Topic Inquiry

Have students continue their investigations for the Topic Inquiry.

Further Instruction

The Fight for Ratification: Core Reading and Interactive Reading Notepad Project and discuss the Interactive Reading Notepad questions.

The fight for ratification was close in many States. In Virginia, George Mason had refused to sign the Constitution and he fought against its ratification. Supporting the new plan of government, however, were James Madison, John Marshall, and Governor Edmund Randolph. Thomas Jefferson was eventually persuaded to the Federalist side. His support was critical to ratification in Virginia and to the ultimate success of the new national government, because Virginia's support was critical to that success.

Compare How were the President and Vice President elected under the new plan of government? *(The States chose presidential electors who voted for the President and Vice President.)*

The Beginnings of American Government

■ SYNTHESIZE

DIGITAL ACTIVITY
Reflecting on How Much Power Government Should Have

First ask students to reconsider the Essential Question for the Topic: How much power should a government have?

Ask students "Do you think the strengthening of the Federal Government in the Constitution was a good thing?" Ask them to give at least three reasons to support their positions. Discuss their answers as a class or ask students to post their answers on the Class Discussion Board.

Next ask students to reflect on the Topic as a whole and jot down 1–3 questions they've thought about during the Topic. Share these examples if students need help getting started:

- What influenced the writers of the Articles of Confederation and the Constitution?

- Why did the Framers choose to create a new government instead of revising the Articles?

- What issues did the Anti-Federalists have with the Constitution? Were those issues ever addressed?

- How can States with different economic philosophies, populations, and influences come together to form a government?

You may ask students to share their questions and answers on the Class Discussion Board.

Topic Inquiry
Have students complete Step 3 of the Topic Inquiry.

■ DEMONSTRATE

DIGITAL TOPIC REVIEW AND ASSESSMENT
The Beginnings of American Government

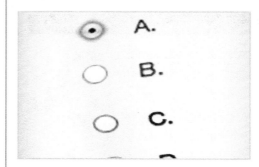

Students can prepare for the Topic Test by answering the questions in the Topic Review and Assessment online or the Assessment questions in the Print Student text. They can also prepare by reviewing their answers to the Interactive Reading Notepad questions or reviewing their notes in the Reading and Notetaking Study Guide.

TOPIC TEST
Assign the Topic Test to assess students' understanding of topic content.

DIGITAL TOPIC TEST
The Beginnings of American Government

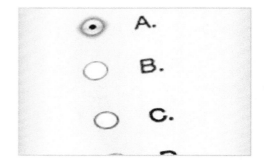

BENCHMARK TESTS
Assign these benchmark tests as you complete the relevant topics to monitor student progress toward mastering the course content and as preparation for the End-of-Course Test.

Benchmark Test 1: Topics 1–4

Benchmark Test 2: Topics 5–8

Benchmark Test 3: Topics 9–11

Benchmark Test 4: Topics 12–14

The Constitution

TOPIC 3 ORGANIZER	PACING: APPROX. 1 PERIOD, .5 BLOCKS
	PACING
Connect	1 period
MY STORY VIDEO **The Fight for Suffrage**	10 min.
DIGITAL ESSENTIAL QUESTION ACTIVITY **What Is the Right Balance of Power in Good Government?**	10 min.
DIGITAL OVERVIEW ACTIVITY **The Bill of Rights**	10 min.
TOPIC INQUIRY: CIVIC ACTION PROJECT **Constitutional Rights Foundation**	20 min.
Investigate	2–4 periods
TOPIC INQUIRY: CIVIC ACTION PROJECT **Constitutional Rights Foundation**	Ongoing
LESSON 1 An Overview of the Constitution	30–40 min.
LESSON 2 Amending the Constitution	30–40 min.
LESSON 3 Federalism: Powers Divided	30–40 min.
LESSON 4 The National Government and the States	30–40 min.
Synthesize	1 period
DIGITAL ACTIVITY **Reflect on the Essential Question**	10 min.
TOPIC INQUIRY: CIVIC ACTION PROJECT **Constitutional Rights Foundation**	20 min.
Demonstrate	1–2 periods
DIGITAL TOPIC REVIEW AND ASSESSMENT **The Constitution**	10 min.
TOPIC INQUIRY: CIVIC ACTION PROJECT **Constitutional Rights Foundation**	20 min.

Civic Action Project

For this topic's Inquiry, you may choose to do a Civic Action Project with your students by using the materials found at the Constitutional Rights Foundation's CAP website: http://www.crfcap.org. Civic Action Project (CAP) is a project-based learning model for government and economics courses. It offers a practicum for high school students in effective and engaged citizenship and uses blended learning to engage students in civic activities both in the traditional U.S. government and economics classrooms.

Constitutional
Rights
Foundation
Educate. Participate.

THE TEACHER'S ROLE

THE CAP TEACHER coaches and guides students through the civic action process as they select a problem or issue, research it, determine and take civic actions, and report and document the experience. The teacher motivates, challenges, critiques, and assesses student progress. Through a blended learning approach, teachers can let students take the reins of their civic learning, guiding them along the way.

You can create your CAP classroom in three easy steps

STEP 1
Register yourself for the CAP website

STEP 2
Enroll your students

STEP 3
Engage your students in the CAP process and its many resources

THE STUDENT'S ROLE

CAP ALLOWS STUDENTS to create projects on issues they care about for their school or community. They see the connection between their civic actions and public policy and can share ideas for civics projects with each other and other CAP students nationwide. Students also see how the content of government and economics courses can apply to the real world. By taking civic actions, they practice what real citizens do when they go about trying to solve real policy-related problems. CAP fulfills best-practices in service-learning with an emphasis on public policy.

The CAP student is accountable for completing the civic action process, just as with a science project or term paper. The CAP Planner, a set of documents that guide students through the process, provides teachers with assessment information as well as a way to manage multiple student projects. While the teacher introduces and monitors the CAP, it is important that students take the lead in completing their civic actions. By using web-based technology and civics-based instruction and activities, students exercise important 21st century skills in digital literacy, critical thinking, collaboration, self-direction, and learning to be engaged and effective citizens.

CIVIC ACTIONS CAP challenges students to work on an actual problem, issue, or policy by taking civic actions. Civic actions build upon classroom civics issues, service-learning, and other proven practices of effective civic education. These actions can be many and varied, including:

- getting informed about a public issue or problem
- thinking critically about the issue or problem
- discovering how government is involved with the problem
- learning how government makes decisions
- developing a position
- engaging in civic dialogue
- building constituencies
- working together toward a common goal
- doing civic writing
- making presentations
- advocating for and defending positions
- meeting with officials

Brainstorming

Brainstorming is a method for generating ideas. It can be done by individuals or in small or large

Rules for Brainst

Pose a question to an

Set a time limit on th more ideas out.

Work as fast as you

Conducting Meetings

Your meetings should be organized, to-the-point, and fun.

Decide how you're going to make decisions. If you are a small group, try deciding by whole-group consensus or by a two-thirds vote. A simple-majority decision may lead to bad feelings and resentment.

Understand everyone's role at the meeting. At most meetings, people need to fill the following roles, which may change from meeting to meeting:

- Leader or facilitator runs the meeting, follows the agenda item by item, and watches the time allotted for each. The leader helps participants focus on the task and makes sure everyone has a chance to participate.
- Recorder takes minutes, which include date and time of meeting, the persons attending, and notes on each agenda item.
- Treasurer.
- Group members contribute agenda items, discuss topics, make decisions, and take responsibility for various tasks.
- Adviser is an adult whose role is to give advice—not to run the group.
- Guests may participate in group discussions, but usually do not participate in final decision making.

Have an agenda. This is a list of things to be dealt with at a meeting. All members should be encouraged to put topics on the agenda. After the recorder reads the minutes of the previous meeting and they are approved, the members approve the agenda. Agenda items are considered in the following order:

- Old business—ongoing and follow-up items.

© 2012, Constitutional Rights Foundation and Close Up Foundation

Handout Lesson 5B
Civic Action Project

GRADE
CAP Policy Analysis Tool

AS CITIZENS IN A DEMOCRACY, YOU'LL BE CONFRONTED WITH POLICY QUESTIONS. IS A TAX PROPOSAL A GOOD IDEA? SHOULD YOU VOTE FOR A PARTICULAR BALLOT INITIATIVE? GOVERNMENT POLICIES CAN PROFOUNDLY AFFECT OUR NATION AND YOUR LIFE. IN A DEMOCRACY, YOU HAVE A SAY ON GOVERNMENT POLICIES AND PROPOSED POLICIES. IT'S IMPORTANT THAT YOU TAKE A CRITICAL LOOK AT THEM. USE THE FOLLOWING GRADE TESTS TO EVALUATE A POLICY:

G OAL. WHAT IS THE GOAL OF THE POLICY? IF YOU DON'T KNOW WHAT IT'S SUPPOSED TO DO, YOU CAN'T MEASURE ITS SUCCESS OR FAILURE. POLICIES ARE DESIGNED TO ADDRESS PROBLEMS. WHAT PROBLEM OR PROBLEMS IS

© 2012 Constitutional Rights Foundation

Constitutional Rights Foundation
Educate. Participate.

Guardian of Democracy: The Civic Mission of Schools
Released September, 2011, *Guardian of Democracy: The Civic Mission of Schools* report builds on the findings of the seminal 2003 Civic Mission of Schools report. CAP has been designed to support the promising approaches described in these reports.

INTRODUCTION

The Constitution

The Framers of the Constitution set out six basic principles to define how the newly-formed American government would be organized and operated. Over the years, many amendments have been added to the Constitution to allow it to grow with the changing nation. How has the Constitution changed since its creation?

■ CONNECT

MY STORY VIDEO
The Fight for Suffrage

Watch a video that introduces students to the long battle to win the right to vote for American women.

Hypothesize Why, do you think, didn't the Framers include the right to vote for everyone in the Constitution? *(Possible answer: Women had few political rights of any kind at the time.)*

Draw Conclusions Why did it take 70 years for women to gain the right to vote? *(Possible answer: Many people, both men and women, did not think women should be a part of public life or politics.)*

⇅ FLIP IT!
Assign the My Story video

DIGITAL ESSENTIAL QUESTION ACTIVITY
What Is the Right Balance of Power in Good Government?

Tell students that the United States Constitution set out six basic principles, which defined in very broad terms how the newly formed American government was to be organized and operated. Even as the nation has grown and changed, these six principles have held steady.

Then have students look at the list, and think what each of these principles might mean for the working of our limited government. Have students pick the principle they think is the most important and then complete the prompt for the principle.

- Popular sovereignty is the most important principle because . . .
- Limited government is the most important principle because . . .
- Separation of powers is the most important principle because . . .
- Checks and balances is the most important principle because . . .
- Judicial review is the most important principle because . . .
- Federalism is the most important principle because . . .

DIGITAL OVERVIEW ACTIVITY
The Bill of Rights

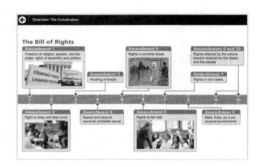

Display the timeline showing the Bill of Rights. During this Topic students will learn more about the challenging task of putting together the Constitution. This timeline will provide a framework into which they can see how changes to the Constitution have coincided with the needs of a changing nation.

D Differentiate: Challenge Tell students to write a short essay about which amendment they feel is most important as an individual's right. Essays should include evidence to support students' reasoning.

Analyze Charts How does the Bill of Rights reflect a commitment to personal freedom that reflects America's colonial past? *(The Bill of Rights specified individual rights which the colonists had fought to preserve and protect through the Revolutionary War.)*

Topic Inquiry
Launch the Topic Inquiry with students after introducing the Topic.

An Overview of the Constitution

Supporting English Language Learners

Use with Digital Texts 5 and 6, **Basic Principles** and **More Basic Principles.**

Learning Strategies

Teach students the six basic principles of the Constitution: *popular sovereignty, limited government, separation of powers, checks and balances, judicial review,* and *federalism.* Provide visuals as support. Use these terms in the following speaking activities in order to for students to build concept and language attainment.

Beginning Write the words on the board and use images and gestures to help define them. Have students make sketches of the terms. Have students use the words to describe their sketches to a partner.

Intermediate Guide students to read the words as you write them on the board. Help clarify the meaning of the words by using images. Ask students to name and/or describe the images using the selected terms. Encourage students to speak in longer sentences by providing sentence stems. Example: *Popular sovereignty is _____ and _____.*

Advanced Ask partners to find the terms in the text and to read the relevant paragraphs. Have partners discuss the meaning of the terms and then share their ideas with the class.

Advanced High Provide students with a list of the terms. Have the class discuss their meanings. After reading the text, ask the students how their definitions were the same or different from the ones in the text.

Use with Digital Texts 5 and 6, **Basic Principles** and **More Basic Principles.**

Learning Strategies

Read the sections on the six basic principles of the Constitution: *popular sovereignty, limited government, separation of powers, checks and balances, judicial review,* and *federalism.* Use these terms in the following writing activities in order for students to build concept and language attainment.

Beginning With the class, create word webs for each of the terms. Then use the word webs to write simple sentences. Have students copy the word webs and the sentences and read them to each other.

Intermediate With the class, create word webs for each of the terms. Have students use the word webs to help them complete sentence stems. Example: *People have the _____ (power) under popular sovereignty.*

Advanced Have partners create word webs for each of the terms. Have students write sentences for each of the terms and read them to each other.

Advanced High Have students create word webs for each of the terms. Have students choose one of the terms and write a paragraph about it. Ask students to read their paragraphs to the class.

▣ Differentiate Instruction

Use the Differentiated Instruction notes throughout the lesson plan to support the varied skill sets, levels of readiness, and interests in the mixed-ability classroom.

Challenge These notes include suggestions for expanding the activity for advanced students.

On-Level These notes include suggestions for modifying the activity to address different interests or learning styles.

Extra Support These notes include ideas for providing more scaffolding or reading spuport.

Special Needs These notes provide ideas for adapting instruction to support the needs of various special needs students.

■ NOTES

An Overview of the Constitution

Objectives

Objective 1: Understand the basic outline of the Constitution.

Objective 2: Understand the basic principles of the Constitution: popular sovereignty, limited government, and separation of powers.

Objective 3: Understand the basic principles of the Constitution: checks and balances, judicial review, and federalism.

LESSON 1 ORGANIZER	OBJECTIVES	PACING	RESOURCES Online	Print
Connect				
DIGITAL START UP ACTIVITY **We the People**		5 min.	●	
Investigate				
DIGITAL TEXTS 1–4 **An Outline of the U.S. Constitution; Article I; Article II; Article III**	Objective 1	10 min.	●	●
DIGITAL TEXT 5 **Basic Principles**	Objective 2	10 min.	●	●
INTERACTIVE CARTOON **Limited Government**		10 min.	●	
DIGITAL TEXT 6 **More Basic Principles**	Objective 3	10 min.	●	●
INTERACTIVE CHART **Checks and Balances**		10 min.	●	
Synthesize				
DIGITAL SYNTHESIZE ACTIVITY **The Basic Principles Today**		5 min.	●	
Demonstrate				
DIGITAL QUIZ **Lesson Quiz and Class Discussion Board**		10 min.	●	

PACING: APPROX. 1 PERIOD, .5 BLOCKS

PEARSON realize™
www.PearsonRealize.com

Go online to access additional resources including:
Primary Sources • Biographies • Supreme Court cases •
21st Century Skill Tutorials • Maps • Graphic Organizers.

■ CONNECT

We the People

Have students read the Preamble from the Constitution. As they read, have them understand why the American beliefs and principles reflected in the introduction to the Constitution are significant and how they might paraphrase it for someone who lives in another country but is curious about our form of government.

Paraphrase Rewrite the Preamble in your own words, using simple language. *(Possible answer: The people of the United States established a Constitution because they wanted to form a unified, just, and peaceful country. Also, they wanted to promote the general good for all citizens and provide the qualities of liberty for themselves and for future generations.)*

Aa Vocabulary Development: Use the Interactive Reading Notepad to preview the Key Terms and Academic Vocabulary in this Lesson with students.

⇅ FLIP IT!

Assign the Flipped Video for this lesson.

■ STUDENT EDITION PRINT
PAGES: 78–89

■ INVESTIGATE

An Outline of the U.S. Constitution

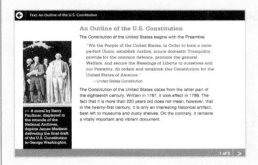

Objective 1: **Understand the basic outline of the Constitution.**

Quick Instruction

Review the articles of the U.S. Constitution and write a brief summary of each one on the board. The first article deals with establishing a bicameral legislature, which means a legislature made up of two houses. Ask students: Why do you think the Framers made this article the first one? Why do you think the Executive Article and Judiciary Article were second and third instead of being among the four to seven articles?

Further Instruction

Editable Presentation Use the Editable Presentation to present the main ideas for this Core Reading.

Outline of the Constitution, Article I, Article II, and Article III: Close Reading and Interactive Reading Notepad Project and discuss the Interactive Reading Notepad questions including the graphic organizers.

Be sure students understand the reasons for creating each article of the Constitution. Ask the following:

Draw Conclusions Analyze the structure of the legislative branch in your State. Do you think your State would benefit by equal representation in the Senate? Explain your answer. *(Possible answer: Yes, my State covers a large area, but has a low population compared to many other States. Because of this, my State benefits from equal representation in the Senate because it ensures that people in my State will have*

Article I

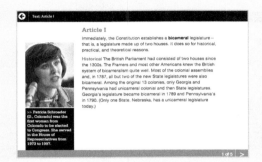

an equal voice in the government despite having a low population.)

Support a Point of View with Evidence Do you think the Constitution allows the executive branch of government to have too much power? Support your answer with evidence. *(Possible answer: Yes, the Constitution allows the U.S. President to command the armed forces. Many leaders with this power have misused it. For example, some leaders have used the military to take control of the government.)*

Infer The vast majority of court cases are heard in local and State courts. In comparison, very few cases come before the federal court system. Do you think it is necessary to have a Supreme Court? Why or why not? *(Possible answer: Yes, there has to be a court that has final say in legal matters. If not, some cases could be argued indefinitely. Also, decisions of the Supreme Court apply to all the States. States cannot pick and choose which Supreme Court rulings to follow. In addition, the decisions of the Supreme Court set a precedent that other courts can use to decide later cases.)*

An Overview of the Constitution

DIGITAL TEXT 3
Article II

DIGITAL TEXT 4
Article III

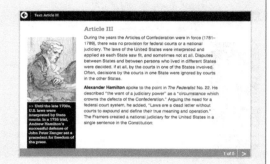

DIGITAL TEXT 5
Basic Principles

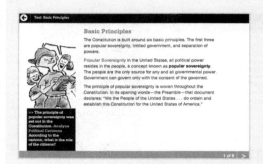

Objective 2: Understand the basic principles of the Constitution: popular sovereignty, limited government, and separation of powers.

Quick Instruction

Interactive Cartoon: Limited Government Introduce the cartoon activity by telling students that limited government holds that the national government may do only those things that the people have given it the power to do. Project the cartoon about Limited Government on the whiteboard. Have students study the cartoon and click through the hotspots.

> **ACTIVE CLASSROOM**
>
> Use a Quick Write to have students write in one minute what they know about the following constitutional provisions for limiting the role of government: popular sovereignty, checks and balances, and separation of powers. After this, discuss these concepts with the class, asking volunteers to share their Quick Writes.

D Differentiate: **Extra Support** Point out to students that voting for political candidates shows popular sovereignty in action. Ask students to write a brief paragraph to explain how voting for a political candidate shows popular sovereignty.

ELL Use the ELL activity described in the ELL chart.

INTERACTIVE CARTOON

Limited Government

DIGITAL TEXT 6

More Basic Principles

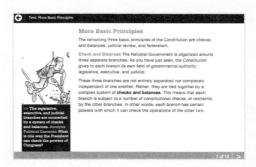

INTERACTIVE CHART

Checks and Balances

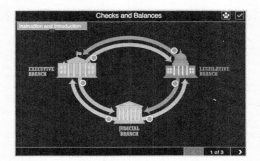

Further Instruction

Go through the Interactive Reading Notepad questions and discuss the answers with the class.

For further discussion, ask the following questions:

Analyze Cartoons Study the cartoon that deals with limited government. What judgment is this cartoon making about President Obama's leadership? *(Possible answer: The cartoon suggests that Obama has had a difficult time figuring out how to weigh all of the different factors that must be considered in effective leadership.)*

Evaluate Sources Read the James Madison quotation from the *The Federalist*, No. 47. Why do you think he says that combining the legislative, executive, and judiciary powers can lead to tyranny? *(Possible answer: The person or group who holds the combined power of three branches of government would have no group to check this power. This person or group could do whatever they wanted and refuse to serve the will of the people.)*

Draw Conclusions How does limited government play a role in the protection of individual rights? *(The Constitution's guarantee of freedom of expression prohibits the power of government and protects individual rights by guaranteeing freedoms vital to a democratic government.)*

Objective 3: Understand the basic principles of the Constitution: checks and balances, judicial review, and federalism.

Quick Instruction

Interactive Chart: Checks and Balances
Introduce the chart activity by telling students that the U.S. government uses a checks and balances system to control the power of the government. Project the chart on the whiteboard. Then have students click on the hotspots to learn more about how the powers of one branch check the powers of another.

🖳 ACTIVE CLASSROOM

Use a Quick Write to have students write in one minute what they know about the following constitutional provisions for limiting the role of government: checks and balances, judicial review, and federalism. After this, discuss these concepts with the class, asking volunteers to share their Quick Writes.

D **Differentiate: Challenge** Does Congress have too much power? Have students write brief essays that answer this question. Tell students that their answers should be supported by reasons. Students should consider the system of checks and balances in their essays.

ELL Use the ELL activity described in the ELL chart.

Further Instruction

Go through the Interactive Reading Notepad questions and discuss the answers with the class. For further discussion, ask the following questions:

Paraphrase James Madison referred to judicial review as an auxiliary precaution. Write in your own words what he meant by this. *(Possible answer: Judicial review is an extra safeguard to prevent a branch of government from controlling the entire government.)*

Draw Conclusions How do the principles of checks and balances, judicial review, and federalism relate to the principle of limited government? *(Checks and balances, judicial review, and federalism all limit government. Checks and balances limits the power of the government by having branches of the government check or restrain each other. Judicial review holds that the courts have the power to declare a government action unconstitutional, which limits the power of the government. By dividing the U.S. government into federal and regional governments, federalism limits the power of the National Government.)*

Topic Inquiry

Launch the Topic Inquiry with students after introducing the Topic.

An Overview of the Constitution

SYNTHESIZE

DIGITAL SYNTHESIZE ACTIVITY

The Basic Principles Today

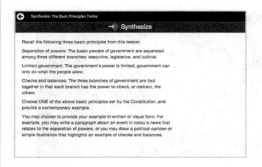

Ask students to recall the Topic Essential Question, "What is the right balance of power in good government?"

After this, have students recall the following three basic principles from this lesson:

- Separation of powers: The basic powers of government are separated among three different branches: executive, legislative, and judicial.
- Limited government: The government's power is limited; government can only do what the people allow.
- Checks and balances: The three branches of government are tied together in that each branch has power to check, or restrain, the others.

Have students choose ONE of the above basic principles set by the Constitution and provide a contemporary example. In their example, students should identify how the American beliefs reflected in the document are embodied in the United States today.

Students may choose to provide their examples in written or visual form. For example, a student may write a paragraph about an event in today's news that relates to the separation of powers, or may draw a political cartoon or simple illustration that highlights an example of checks and balances.

DEMONSTRATE

DIGITAL QUIZ

Lesson Quiz and Class Discussion Board

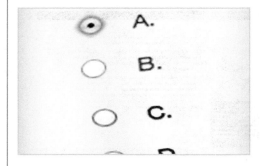

Assign the online Lesson Quiz for this lesson if you haven't already done so. Students will be offered automatic remediation or enrichment based on their score.

In "An Overview of the Constitution" students read about the basic outline of the Constitution and the six basic principles of the Constitution.

Pose these questions to the class on the Discussion Board:

Determine Author's Purpose Why do you think the Framers of the Constitution made the document so brief and imprecise?

Hypothesize If a U.S. president wanted to take control of the government and become a tyrant, what are the main roadblocks that would stand in his or her way?

Topic Inquiry

Have students continue their investigations for the Topic Inquiry.

PEARSON realize™

www.PearsonRealize.com
Access your Digital Lesson

Amending the Constitution

Supporting English Language Learners

Use with Digital Text 1, **Formal Amendment Process.**

Learning Strategies
Have students read the section *Formal Amendment Process*. Guide students to identify accessible language that helps them learn new and essential language related to the process of making amendments to the Constitution.

Beginning In the text, help the class identify and underline words they know. Guide them to understand how these words relate to process of creating new amendments. Create a chart for the process of amending the Constitution with each step at the top and the accessible words below. Have students copy the charts.

Intermediate Have partners create a graphic organizer for the amendment process. For each step, have them copy the accessible words on the organizer. Have them share their work with the class.

Advanced Have partners read the text. For each step of the amendment process, have them copy the accessible words on a graphic organizer. Have them write a sentence describing each step in their own words.

Advanced High After reading the process for amendments, have students copy the accessible words on a graphic organizer. Have students write a short paragraph describing each step.

Use with Digital Text 3, **Proposing an Amendment.**

Reading
Tell students the word *amend* means *to change*. Discuss what the title of the section *Proposing an Amendment* means. Remind students that their classmates and the teacher can help them read the text.

Beginning Read the captions of the images in the text. Guide students in a discussion that allows both the teacher and students to respond to questions.

Intermediate Have partners read the captions of the images in the text. Ask them to think of questions they have about the text. Have them pose these questions to the class for a response.

Advanced Have partners read and discuss the text. Ask them to create a short list of questions about the text. Have them ask their questions to the teacher or their classmates.

Advanced High Ask students to read the text and jot down their questions. Have them think about which questions they will ask the teacher and which they will ask their peers. Have students ask their questions.

▣ Differentiate Instruction

Use the Differentiated Instruction notes throughout the lesson plan to support the varied skill sets, levels of readiness, and interests in the mixed-ability classroom.

Challenge These notes include suggestions for expanding the activity for advanced students.

On-Level These notes include suggestions for modifying the activity to address different interests or learning styles.

Extra Support These notes include ideas for providing more scaffolding or reading spuport.

Special Needs These notes provide ideas for adapting instruction to support the needs of various special needs students.

■ NOTES

Amending the Constitution

Objectives

Objective 1: Describe the constitutionally prescribed procedures by which the Constitution may be formally changed.

Objective 2: Explain how the formal amendment process illustrates the principles of federalism and popular sovereignty.

Objective 3: Understand the 27 amendments that have been added to the Constitution, and that several amendments have been proposed but not ratified.

Objective 4: Identify how basic legislation has added to our understanding of the Constitution over time.

Objective 5: Analyze how interpretation of the Constitution has changed over the years through the actions of the executive and judicial branches, and by party practices and customs.

LESSON 2 ORGANIZER		PACING: APPROX. 1 PERIOD, .5 BLOCKS			
				RESOURCES	
		OBJECTIVES	PACING	Online	Print
Connect					
DIGITAL START UP ACTIVITY **Write Your Own Amendment**			5 min.	●	
Investigate					
DIGITAL TEXT 1 **Formal Amendment Process**		Objective 1	10 min.	●	●
DIGITAL TEXT 2 **Federalism and Popular Sovereignty**			10 min.	●	●
INTERACTIVE GALLERY **The 18th and 21st Amendments**			10 min.	●	
DIGITAL TEXT 3 **Proposing an Amendment**		Objective 2	10 min.	●	●
DIGITAL TEXT 4 **The 27 Amendments**		Objective 3	10 min.	●	●
INTERACTIVE TIMELINE **The Bill of Rights**			10 min.	●	
DIGITAL TEXT 5 **Change by Other Means**		Objectives 4, 5	10 min.	●	●
Synthesize					
DIGITAL SYNTHESIZE ACTIVITY **Revisit Your Amendment**			5 min.	●	
Demonstrate					
DIGITAL QUIZ **Lesson Quiz and Class Discussion Board**			10 min.	●	

PEARSON
realize™
www.PearsonRealize.com

Go online to access additional resources including:
Primary Sources • Biographies • Supreme Court cases •
21st Century Skill Tutorials • Maps • Graphic Organizers.

◼ CONNECT

DIGITAL START UP ACTIVITY

Write Your Own Amendment

Inform students that even though the Constitution was written in 1787, it has lived through the years because it is a flexible document that can be changed, or amended, to address issues or problems not foreseen by the Framers. For example, after Franklin Delano Roosevelt served four terms in office for a total of sixteen years, an amendment was passed limiting the number of terms a President may serve to two.

Then have students consider some of the problems facing our nation today and choose one that could be solved with an amendment to the Constitution. Have students write a description of their proposed amendment along with a justification that tells why the amendment is needed and should be passed.

Aa Vocabulary Development: Use the Interactive Reading Notepad to preview the Key Terms and Academic Vocabulary in this Lesson with students.

⇅ FLIP IT!

Assign the Flipped Video for this lesson.

◼ STUDENT EDITION PRINT PAGES: 90–98

◼ INVESTIGATE

DIGITAL TEXT 1

Formal Amendment Process

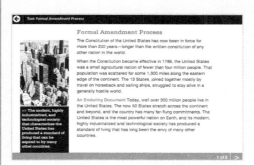

Objective 1: Describe the constitutionally prescribed procedures by which the Constitution may be formally changed.

Quick Instruction

Interactive Timeline: The 18th and 21st Amendments Project the timeline. Click the various images and discuss the details of each. Then have students write down the similarities and differences between the ratification of the 18th Amendment and the ratification of the 21st Amendment.

Contrast What do you think is the most important difference between the two methods of ratification? *(Possible answer: The convention method involves the direct vote of the people living in each State. The legislature method involves Federal and State government representatives acting on the people's behalf.)*

💬 ACTIVE CLASSROOM

Have students use the Make Headlines activity to analyze the ratification of the 18th and 21st amendments. Tell students they should write a headline for the ratification of the 18th Amendment that captures the most important aspect of ratification by State legislatures. Then have students write a headline for the ratification of the 21st Amendment that captures the most important aspect of ratification by conventions.

DIGITAL TEXT 2

Federalism and Popular Sovereignty

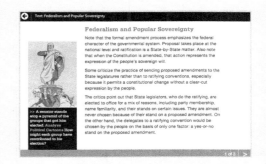

D Differentiate: Extra Support Help students understand the most common amendment process. Ask students: How are most amendments proposed? How are most amendments ratified? What is the most common amendment process? What role does the amendment process play in our constitutional government?

ELL Use the ELL activity described in the ELL chart.

Further Instruction

Editable Presentation Use the Editable Presentation to present the main ideas for this Core Reading.

Formal Amendment Process and Proposing an Amendment: Core Reading and Interactive Reading Notepad Project and discuss the Interactive Reading Notepad questions, including the graphic organizer. For further discussion, ask the following questions:

Infer Do you think the method used to adopt the Constitution is often used to propose amendments? Explain. *(No, the most common method to propose amendments is through Congress. The Constitution was proposed by a convention.)*

Analyze Information Why do you think the legislative method is used much more often than the convention method to propose and ratify amendments? *(Possible answer: The convention method involves voting for convention delegates and setting up conventions. However, the legislative method uses government bodies that have already been set up. The convention method, therefore, seems more time consuming and perhaps more expensive than the legislative method.)*

Amending the Constitution

INTERACTIVE GALLERY

The 18th and 21st Amendments

DIGITAL TEXT 3

Proposing an Amendment

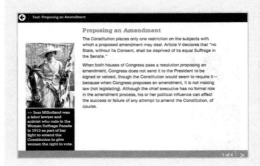

Draw Conclusions Why do you think so few of the 12,000 proposed amendments have actually been ratified? *(Possible answer: The States are very hesitant to alter a long-standing document like the Constitution, and it is not common that all lawmakers will agree on an issue in order to ratify it.)*

Objective 2: Explain how the formal amendment process illustrates the principles of federalism and popular sovereignty.

Quick Instruction

Have a class discussion about whether ratification of an amendment by State legislatures is a fair process. Ask students: Do you think it is more fair to ratify amendments by State legislatures or by conventions? Why? Why do you think the U.S. government almost always uses the ratification by State legislatures method?

> **ELL** Use the ELL activity described in the ELL chart.

Further Instruction

Go through the Interactive Reading Notepad questions and discuss the answers with the class.

The method of ratifying amendments by State legislatures has many critics. For further discussion, ask the following questions:

Check Understanding What is the main argument of the people who criticize the ratification of amendments by State legislatures? *(The critics point out that State legislators are elected to office for a mix of reasons. They are almost never chosen because of their stand on a proposed amendment. However, the delegates to a ratifying convention would be chosen by the people solely based on their stand on the proposed amendment.)*

Draw Conclusions Why do you think the Supreme Court decided that a State cannot require that an amendment proposed by Congress be approved by a vote of the people of the State? *(Possible answer: The Supreme Court probably wanted to make sure that the same method was used for all the states for ratifying an amendment. Differences between states concerning ratification could lead to disputes about the amendment.)*

DIGITAL TEXT 4

The 27 Amendments

INTERACTIVE TIMELINE

The Bill of Rights

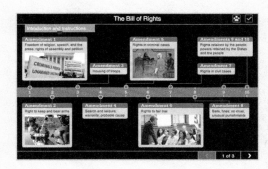

Objective 3: **Understand the 27 amendments that have been added to the Constitution, and that several amendments have been proposed but not ratified.**

Quick Instruction

Throughout U.S. history, amendments have been proposed as an attempt to solve problems. In fact, the first 10 amendments arose out of the controversy surrounding the ratification of the Constitution. In total, 27 amendments have been proposed and ratified.

Interactive Timeline: The Bill of Rights

Project the timeline. Look at each amendment in chronological order, and have students identify the freedoms and rights guaranteed by each. Ask students: What do all of these amendments have in common? *(Possible answers: They were all ratified by the legislative method; they all came about to solve problems.)* Discuss various answers.

🖳 ACTIVE CLASSROOM

Have students use the Word Wall to analyze why amendments have been added to the Constitution. Ask students to choose an amendment from the timeline. Make sure that all the amendments have been chosen. Then tell students to draw a visual image that depicts the problem that the amendment attempts to solve. Also, students should write a summary of the problem to accompany the image. However, students should NOT identify the amendment that they have chosen.

After this, have students post their images and summaries on the board or on chart paper. Tell students to look at all the responses. Ask students to identify the amendments that correspond to the images and summaries. Then discuss similarities and differences in the responses as a group.

D Differentiate: **Challenge** Have students draw a picture that depicts either the 13th, 18th, 22nd, or 26th amendments. Tell students that the pictures can show examples of these amendments in action.

Further Instruction

Project and discuss the Interactive Reading Notepad questions, including the graphic organizer asking students to write the subject of each amendment. Review the amendments and fill in the graphic organizer on the whiteboard as you go.

For further discussion, ask the following questions:

Identify Cause and Effect Why do you think the vast majority of amendments sent by Congress to the States have been ratified? *(Possible answer: For an amendment to be sent to the States, it needs to have strong support from U.S. senators and representatives. This support reflects the will of the people. The will of the people also influences State governments. As a result, most amendments approved by Congress and sent to the States are ratified.)*

Hypothesize Do you think the Constitution would have survived so long if the Bill of Rights had not been adopted? *(Possible answer: No, if the Bill of Rights were not adopted, the government and political leaders could more easily abuse their power. As a result, there would have been more internal conflict in the United States, which might have caused the Constitution to be abolished or replaced.)*

Amending the Constitution

DIGITAL TEXT 5
Change by Other Means

Objectives 4: Identify how basic legislation has added to our understanding of the Constitution over time; 5: Analyze how interpretation of the Constitution has changed over the years through the actions of the executive and judicial branches, and by party practices and customs.

Quick Instruction
Tell students that over the years Congress has passed basic legislation to fill out the Constitution. By doing this, Congress has applied the principles of the Constitution to situations that the government faces everyday. As an example, tell students they are given the task to bake a cake. If they have no idea how to bake a cake, can they accomplish this goal? Why or why not? However, if they are given a detailed recipe on how to bake a cake, does this make the task more doable? Why or why not?

The Constitution provides basic goals or principles for the government to follow, such as to regulate foreign commerce. However, for the government to effectively do this, it needs more detailed laws to accomplish the task. Basic legislation provides these laws.

Further Instruction
Go through the Interactive Reading Notepad questions and discuss the answers with the class.

For further discussion, ask the following questions:

Summarize How has basic legislation changed the judicial system as described in the Constitution? *(The Constitution established one Supreme Court. Basic legislation has created all of the other courts in the United States.)*

Analyze Maps Study the map of the Louisiana Purchase. How did President Jefferson justify buying this land? *(Jefferson decided that the phrase "executive power" in the Constitution gave him the power to acquire territory.)*

Do you think President Jefferson's interpretation of the constitution regarding the Louisiana Purchase was justified? *(Possible answer: Yes, the Louisiana Purchase significantly increased the size and wealth of the United States. Considering this, his liberal interpretation of the Constitution was correct.)*

Evaluate Sources President Wilson once referred to the Supreme Court as "a constitutional convention in continuous session." What did Wilson mean by this statement? *(Wilson meant that the Supreme Court is constantly interpreting the Constitution. Therefore, like a constitutional convention, the Supreme Court constantly changes the way the Constitution is applied in American society.)*

Topic Inquiry
Launch the Topic Inquiry with students after introducing the Topic.

SYNTHESIZE

DIGITAL ACTIVITY
Revisit Your Amendment

Ask students to recall the Topic Essential Question, "What is the right balance of power in good government?"

After this, have students look back at the proposed amendment you described in the Connect activity.

Now that students understand the procedures by which the Constitution can be changed, would they still propose the amendment? Are there ways you would change the amendment to ensure its passage? Explain why or why not, and describe any changes you would make.

DEMONSTRATE

DIGITAL QUIZ
Lesson Quiz and Class Discussion Board

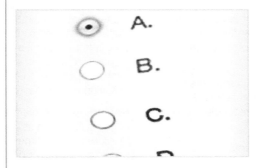

Assign the online Lesson Quiz for this lesson if you haven't already done so. Students will be offered automatic remediation or enrichment based on their score.

In "Amending the Constitution" students read about procedures for changing the Constitution, the 27 amendments that have been added to the Constitution, and how the interpretation of the Constitution has changed over the years.

Pose these questions to the class on the Discussion Board:

Compare and Contrast How are the amendments in the Bill of Rights similar to and different from later amendments?

Make Predictions Consider the amendments proposed by Congress that were not ratified by the States. Which one do you think will most likely be ratified in the future? Why?

Topic Inquiry
Have students continue their investigations for the Topic Inquiry.

Federalism: Powers Divided

Supporting English Language Learners

Use with Digital Text 3, **Three Types of Federal Powers.**

Learning Strategies
Using visuals as support while reading the section *Three Types of Federal Powers*, compare the structures, functions, and processes of the three types of powers of the Federal Government. Create a three-column chart with the headings *Expressed Powers*, *Implied Powers*, and *Inherent Powers*. Tell students that they will support each other to complete the chart.

Beginning Create a list of key words from the text. Have students read the words aloud using support from their peers and the teacher. Guide students to work together to place the words in the correct columns on the chart.

Intermediate Have partners read the text. Guide students to create a list of key words related to the three types of powers. Have partners fill in the chart using the key words.

Advanced Have partners read the text in chunks and fill in the chart using the key words. Ask them to share their chart with other students and discuss similarities and differences.

Advanced High Have students read the text and create a list of key words or phrases related to the three types of powers. Ask them to compare their lists of words with a partner. Have partners discuss and choose the most appropriate words and use these to complete a chart.

Use with Digital Texts 4 and 5, **Powers Denied to the Federal Government** and **Powers of the Fifty States.**

Reading
Based on the language levels of your students, choose words from the text that will help them understand the limits on the National and State Governments in the U.S. federal system of government. Provide visuals from the text as support. Tell the class that each of them will be responsible for teaching at least one word to the rest of the class. Provide each student with a list of all the vocabulary words with space to write a definition next to each word.

Beginning Assign a pair of students to be the "expert" for one word from the list. Have students draw and/or write a definition for their word. Provide students time to teach each other their assigned words. Students should then write and/or draw definitions for all of the words.

Intermediate Have students read and find the words in the text. Assign each student to be the "expert" for one wordfrom the list. Divide the class into pairs. Have students write a short definition for their word and teach it to the other student in their pair. Have each pair teach their words to the class. Ask students to write the definitions for all of the words.

Advanced Assign each student to be the "expert" for one or more words. Have the students read the text and find the definition for their words using a dictionary or glossary. Have students write a definition for their words and share the definition with the other students. Ask students to write the definitions for all of the words.

Advanced High Assign each student to be the "expert" for one or more words. Have the students read the text and find the definition for their words using a dictionary or glossary. Have students write a definition for their words and share the definition with the other students. Ask students to write the definitions for all of the words. Have them work together to write sentences for each word.

◘ Differentiate Instruction

Use the Differentiated Instruction notes throughout the lesson plan to support the varied skill sets, levels of readiness, and interests in the mixed-ability classroom.

Challenge These notes include suggestions for expanding the activity for advanced students.

On-Level These notes include suggestions for modifying the activity to address different interests or learning styles.

Extra Support These notes include ideas for providing more scaffolding or reading spuport.

Special Needs These notes provide ideas for adapting instruction to support the needs of various special needs students.

■ NOTES

PEARSON
realize™
www.PearsonRealize.com

Go online to access additional resources including:
Primary Sources • Biographies • Supreme Court cases •
21st Century Skill Tutorials • Maps • Graphic Organizers.

Objectives

Objective 1: Define federalism and explain why the Framers adopted a federal system instead of a unitary system.

Objective 2: Categorize powers delegated to and denied to the National Government, and powers reserved for and denied to the States, and the difference between exclusive and concurrent powers.

Objective 3: Summarize the obligations that the Constitution, as the "the supreme Law of the Land," places on the National Government with regard to the States.

LESSON 3 ORGANIZER		PACING: APPROX. 1 PERIOD, .5 BLOCKS			
				RESOURCES	
		OBJECTIVES	PACING	Online	Print
Connect					
DIGITAL START UP ACTIVITY **Who Does What?**			5 min.	●	
Investigate					
DIGITAL TEXT 1 **The Founders Choose Federalism**			10 min.	●	●
DIGITAL TEXT 2 **What is Federalism?**		Objective 1	10 min.	●	●
INTERACTIVE CHART **Division of Power**			10 min.	●	
DIGITAL TEXT 3 **Three Types of Federal Powers**			10 min.	●	●
DIGITAL TEXT 4 **Power Denied to the Federal Government**			10 min.	●	●
DIGITAL TEXT 5 **Powers of the 50 States**		Objective 2	10 min.	●	●
DIGITAL TEXT 6 **The Exclusive and the Concurrent Powers**			10 min.	●	●
INTERACTIVE GALLERY **Powers Reserved to the State**			10 min.	●	
DIGITAL TEXT 7 **The Constitution Reigns Supreme**		Objective 3	10 min.	●	●
Synthesize					
DIGITAL ACTIVITY **The Supremacy Clause**			5 min.	●	
Demonstrate					
DIGITAL QUIZ **Lesson Quiz and Class Discussion Board**			10 min.	●	

Federalism: Powers Divided

CONNECT

DIGITAL START UP ACTIVITY
Who Does What?

Have students compare the functions of National, State, and local governments in the U.S. federal system. List on the board some of the governmental activities suggested by students. Tell students that the National Government has the power to do some of the things they thought of, while the State and local governments do others. Still other governmental powers, like collecting taxes, are shared by both.

After this, have students list six activities performed by government and catergorize which activities they think are performed by the National Government, the State government, or both.

Aa **Vocabulary Development:** Use the Interactive Reading Notepad to preview the Key Terms and Academic Vocabulary in this Lesson with students.

↻ FLIP IT!
Assign the Flipped Video for this lesson.

STUDENT EDITION PRINT PAGES: 99–108

INVESTIGATE

DIGITAL TEXT 1
The Founders Choose Federalism

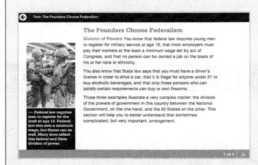

Objective 1: Define federalism and explain why the Framers adopted a federal system instead of a unitary system.

Quick Instruction
The concept of federalism is a form of government that divides power between the National Government and the State governments. Have students think about why the Founding Fathers created a distinctly new form of federalism and adopted a federal system of government instead of a unitary system. Ask students: How do you think the British Empire and American Revolution influenced the decision to set up a federal system of government in the United States? Do you think federalism accomplished what the Framers of the Constitution wanted? Why or why not?

ELL Use the ELL activity described in the ELL chart.

DIGITAL TEXT 2
What is Federalism?

Further Instruction
Go through the Interactive Reading Notepad questions and discuss the answers with the class.

For further discussion, ask the following questions:

Infer What types of problems do you think the Federal Government faced under the Articles of Confederation? *(Possible answer: Under the Articles of Confederation, the Federal Government probably faced many disputes among States, including States with different currencies and some States taking military action against others.)*

Draw Conclusions How did federalism both strengthen and limit the National and State governments? *(Possible answer: Federalism gave the National Government certain powers over State governments. However, State governments have certain powers that the National Government does not have.)*

INTERACTIVE CHART
Division of Power

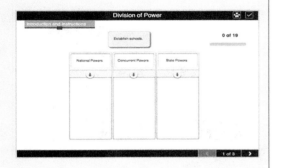

DIGITAL TEXT 3
Three Types of Federal Powers

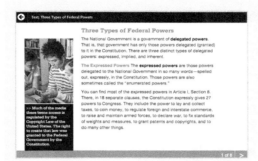

DIGITAL TEXT 4
Power Denied to the Federal Government

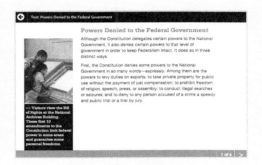

Support Ideas with Evidence Compare how National and State Governments function in response to disaster relief. Is this structure of shared power between the National and State Governments typical in the U.S. federal system? Why or why not? *(Possible answer: The government of the State where a disaster hits provides relief. The Federal Government also provides relief and can order the mobilization of aid from other States. This is not typical of Federalism because the National Government often handles concerns that affect the entire country, while State governments handle local concerns. However, in certain situations the National and State Governments unite.)*

Objective 2: Categorize powers delegated to and denied to the National Government, and powers reserved for and denied to the States, and the difference between exclusive and concurrent powers.

Quick Instruction
Interactive Chart: Division of Power
Project the diagram and point out the list of powers. Tell students that in the Federal system, power is divided between National and State governments. The National Government has some powers and the States have other powers. Also, some powers are shared, or concurrent, for both the National and States governments. For this activity, students should place the power in the correct category.

Interactive Gallery: Powers Reserved to the State Next project the gallery on the whiteboard and click through the various images. Introduce the gallery activity by telling students that the States have reserved powers. These are powers that the Constitution does not grant to the Federal Government and does not deny State governments. Have students review the images and accompanying text and then answer the questions.

ACTIVE CLASSROOM

Have students use a Circle Write activity to review the powers denied to the National and State Governments. Have students break into groups and then ask: How are the National and State Governments limited? Have students write as much as they can for one minute and then pass the paper to the person on their right. The next person tries to improve or elaborate the response where the other person left off. Students should continue to switch until the paper comes back to the first person. The group then decides which is the best response and shares it with the class.

Federalism: Powers Divided

DIGITAL TEXT 5
Powers of the 50 States

DIGITAL TEXT 6
The Exclusive and the Concurrent Powers

INTERACTIVE GALLERY
Powers Reserved to the State

D Differentiate: Extra Support Ask students to write a definition of the word *concurrent* in their own words without referring to the lesson or using a dictionary. After this, have students check their definition with the definition in a dictionary. Tell them to make any needed changes to their definition, based on the dictionary's definition.

ELL Use the ELL activity described in the ELL chart.

Further Instruction
Go through the Interactive Reading Notepad questions and discuss the answers with the class, including the graphic organizer asking students to categorize the powers of the Federal Government. For further instruction, ask the following:

Contrast What is the difference between inherent powers and implied powers for the Federal Government? *(Possible answer: Implied powers are not directly stated in the Constitution, but they are suggested. Inherent powers are not directly stated or implied by the Constitution. However, they are powers that belong to the National Government because it is the national government of a sovereign state. They are powers that all national governments possess.)*

Infer Why do you think the States are denied the power to coin money? *(Possible answer: If States could coin money, they could increase the supply of money as needed in a given State. As a result, some States would have access to more money than other States, thereby creating unequal money supplies and throwing the national economy into turmoil. This could also hinder economic relations among the States. Also, the type of money coined could be different, thereby causing economic confusion.)*

Draw Conclusions Why do you think the power to levy and collect taxes is a concurrent power? *(Possible answer: Both the National and State governments need money to operate and to provide services to citizens. Also, each State government knows the specific financial needs of its State. Because of these reasons, it makes sense for taxes to be levied at both the national and State levels. The power to tax is a critical power for a government at any level to have. Without it, as was discovered under the Articles of Confederation, the government has no means to raise necessary funds.)*

DIGITAL TEXT 7

The Constitution Reigns Supreme

Objective 3: Summarize the obligations that the Constitution, as "the supreme Law of the Land," places on the National Government with regard to the States.

Quick Instruction

The Constitution ranks above all other forms of law in the United States. This aspect of the Constitution is often referred to as the Supremacy Clause. Ask students: How do you think the history of the United States would be different without the Supremacy Clause? Have students form pairs. Students should then discuss a response to the question with their partners. After this, have volunteers share their responses, and then conduct a class discussion.

Further Instruction

Go through the Interactive Reading Notepad questions and discuss the answers with the class.

John Marshall, a significant individual in the field of government, believed strongly that the Supreme Court was a force in determining the law of the land. The Supreme Court has used the Supremacy Clause to declare some State laws as being unconstitutional in both historical and contemporary conflicts.

Hypothesize Why do you think "unconstitutional" State laws became laws to begin with? *(Possible answer: The interpretation of the Constitution changes throughout history. Because of this, a State could pass a law that is generally viewed as constitutional. However, several years later, this same law could be seen by the Supreme Court as being unconstitutional because the interpretation of the Constitution changed.)*

Evaluate Sources In the text, review the quotation from Justice Oliver Wendell Holmes. Do you agree with this statement? Why or why not? *(Possible answer: I agree. If the Supreme Court could not declare the laws of States void, then States could pass unconstitutional laws, which would empower these States to break away from the Union.)*

Federalism: Powers Divided

SYNTHESIZE

DIGITAL ACTIVITY

The Supremacy Clause

Ask students to recall the Topic Essential Question, "What Is the Right Balance of Power in Government?" Have them use the Think Pair Share strategy to complete the Supremacy Clause activity. Ask them to take ten minutes to complete the activity, and then share their answer with a talking partner.

Project the two quotations on the whiteboard. Ask students to study them and then, in a short paragraph, explain how the Supremacy Clause is used to reconcile these very different points of view.

DEMONSTRATE

DIGITAL QUIZ

Lesson Quiz and Class Discussion Board

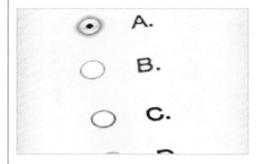

Assign the online Lesson Quiz for this lesson if you haven't already done so. Students will be offered automatic remediation or enrichment based on their score.

In "Federalism: Powers Divided" students read about the federal system of government, the powers of the National and State Governments, and the powers denied these governments. Also students learned about the obligations that the Constitution places on the National Government concerning the States.

Pose these questions to the class on the Discussion Board:

Identify Cause and Effect Why do you think certain powers have been denied to the States? *(Possible answer: The National Government wants to make sure that a State does not attempt to break away from the Union and form its own nation. Because of this, States are not allowed to enter into any treaty or alliance or to print or coin money.)*

Draw Conclusions How does the Supremacy Clause safeguard the rights of U.S. citizens in all 50 States? *(Possible answer: This clause declares that the States have no power to stop or impede the constitutional laws enacted by Congress. These laws include the Bill of Rights.)*

Topic Inquiry
Have students continue their investigations for the Topic Inquiry.

The National Government and the States

Supporting English Language Learners

Use with Digital Texts 1 and 2, **The Nation's Obligations Under the Constitution.**

Listening

Tell students that *main points* are the most important ideas of something you read or hear. Ask students to listen for the main points as you read aloud the section *Making War, Keeping Peace*. Tell them that this section will help them compare the functions and processes of the National, State and local governments in the U.S. federal system.

Beginning As you read the section aloud, provide visuals as support. Read the text again, one paragraph at a time. Guide students to identify the main points of each paragraph by asking questions that require yes/no or one- or two-word responses. Write a list of the main points on the board.

Intermediate Provide visuals as support as your read the section aloud twice. During the second reading, stop periodically to ask questions about the main points. Use the question frame *Is the main point _____ or _____?* Write a list of the main points on the board.

Advanced After reading the section aloud, have partners discuss and write down the main points. Read the section aloud again and have partners discuss if they want to add to or change their responses.

Advanced High Read the section aloud twice. During the second reading, have students take notes. After the reading, ask partners to discuss their notes and determine the main points of the section.

Use with Digital Text 2, **Admitting New States.**

Listening

Tell students that an *important detail* is specific information that adds to the general ideas and main points of something you read or hear. On the board, write the headings *Admitting New States, Congress and New States, Admission Procedure,* and *Conditions for Admission.* Ask students to listen for important details for each of these topics as you read these sections aloud. Tell students that these sections will help them categorize governmental powers as National, State, or shared.

Beginning As you read aloud, provide visuals as support. Read the text again, one paragraph at a time. Guide students to identify the important details of each paragraph by asking questions that require yes/no or one- or two-word responses. Write a list of the important details on the board.

Intermediate Provide visuals as support as your read the sections aloud twice. During the second reading, stop after each section to ask questions about the important details. Use the question frame *Which is an important detail: _____ or _____?* Write a list of the important details on the board.

Advanced After reading the sections aloud, have partners discuss and write down the important details. Read the sections aloud again and have partners discuss if they want to add to or change their responses.

Advanced High Read the sections aloud twice. During the second reading, have students take notes. After the reading, ask partners to discuss their notes and determine the important details of each section.

▶ Differentiate Instruction

Use the Differentiated Instruction notes throughout the lesson plan to support the varied skill sets, levels of readiness, and interests in the mixed-ability classroom.

Challenge These notes include suggestions for expanding the activity for advanced students.

On-Level These notes include suggestions for modifying the activity to address different interests or learning styles.

Extra Support These notes include ideas for providing more scaffolding or reading spuport.

Special Needs These notes provide ideas for adapting instruction to support the needs of various special needs students.

▮ NOTES

The National Government and the States

Objectives

Objective 1: Explain the process for admitting new States to the Union.

Objective 2: Examine the many and growing areas of cooperative federalism.

Objective 3: Explain why States make interstate compacts.

Objective 4: Understand the purpose of the Full Faith and Credit Clause, the Extradition Clause, and the Privileges and Immunities Clause.

LESSON 4 ORGANIZER		PACING: APPROX. 1 PERIOD, .5 BLOCKS			
				RESOURCES	
		OBJECTIVES	**PACING**	**Online**	**Print**
Connect					
DIGITAL START UP ACTIVITY **How the United States Functions**			5 min.	●	
Investigate					
DIGITAL TEXTS 1 AND 2 **The Nation's Obligations Under the Constitution, Admitting New States**			10 min.	●	●
INTERACTIVE MAP **Territorial Expansion 1787–1898**		Objective 1	10 min.	●	
INTERACTIVE CARTOON **Repairing the Union**			10 min.	●	
DIGITAL TEXT 3 **States and Federal Government Sharing Resources**		Objective 2	10 min.	●	●
DIGITAL TEXT 4 **Agreements Among States**		Objective 3	10 min.	●	●
DIGITAL TEXT 5 **How the Law Crosses State Lines**			10 min.	●	●
DIGITAL TEXT 6 **Extradition**		Objective 4	10 min.	●	●
DIGITAL TEXT 7 **Priviliges and Immunities**			10 min.	●	●
Synthesize					
DIGITAL SYNTHESIZE ACTIVITY **Federal Grants to States**			5 min.	●	
Demonstrate					
DIGITAL QUIZ **Lesson Quiz and Class Discussion Board**			10 min.	●	

PEARSON

realize.™

www.PearsonRealize.com

Go online to access additional resources including:
Primary Sources • Biographies • Supreme Court cases •
21st Century Skill Tutorials • Maps • Graphic Organizers.

CONNECT

DIGITAL START UP ACTIVITY

How the United States Functions

Project the Start Up Activity Ask students to answer the questions as they enter and get settled. Then have them share their ideas with another student, either in class or through a chat or blog space.

Discuss Many countries have names related to their culture, language, or even geography. What does the name the *United States of America* tell you about the way in which American government functions? *(Possible answer: The words "United States" suggest a group of sovereign entities united together for a particular purpose.)*

Aa Vocabulary Development: Use the Interactive Reading Notepad to preview the Key Terms and Academic Vocabulary in this Lesson with students.

⚡ FLIP IT!

Assign the Flipped Video for this lesson.

■ STUDENT EDITION PRINT PAGES: 109–120

INVESTIGATE

DIGITAL TEXT 1

The Nation's Obligations Under the Constitution

Objective 1: Explain the process for admitting new States to the Union.

Quick Instruction

Territorial Expansion 1787–1898: Interactive Map Project the map on the whiteboard and click through the hot spots on the map. Introduce the map activity by explaining how geography influences U.S. political divisions and policies. Tell students that the United States expanded its territory by various means, including war, purchase, and request to be admitted to the United States. After students review the map, ask them: What method of adding territory to the United States was used most often?

📷 ACTIVE CLASSROOM

Have students use a Sequence It activity to list the steps involved in statehood admission. Ask students to form groups of five. Give each student in a group a slip of paper with one of the following written on it: *territorial convention prepares constitution, act of admission, voter approval, request for admission,* and *enabling act.* Each student in a group should have a different step of the State admission process.

Then have students in each group arrange themselves in a line that reflects the correct order of steps involved for a territory to obtain statehood. The student with step one should be at the front of the line, the student with step two should be second in line, and so on. After the line is formed, each student in line should read their step from front to back.

DIGITAL TEXT 2

Admitting New States

D Differentiate: Challenge/Gifted Ask students to write speeches that attempt to convince Congress to add a territory to the United States. Possible territories could include Puerto Rico, Guam, or the Virgin Islands.

Repairing the Union After the Civil War: Interactive Cartoon Project the cartoon on the whiteboard and click through the hot spots on the cartoon. Introduce the cartoon activity by telling students that after the Civil War, Abraham Lincoln and Andrew Johnson were significant in the field of politics, and faced the difficult task of bringing the southern States back into the Union and mending relations between northern and southern States.

📷 ACTIVE CLASSROOM

Have students use a Rank It activity to analyze historical and contemporary reasons for the use of federal assistance within a State. List the following on the board: *U.S. Army subdues riot in Detroit, federal troops end rioting during the Pullman Strike, federal troops halt the unlawful obstruction of school integration,* and *Federal Goverment aids area stricken by flood.*

Ask students to rank the events based on which was the most justified use of federal assistance, to which was the least justified use of federal assistance. Have students provide reasons for the ranking decisions they made. Then ask students to work in pairs to share their rankings and reasons. Poll the class to see if there is agreement on the rankings.

ELL Use the ELL activity described in the ELL chart.

The National Government and the States

INTERACTIVE MAP
Territorial Expansion 1787–1898

INTERACTIVE CARTOON
Repairing the Union

DIGITAL TEXT 3
States and Federal Government Sharing Resources

Further Instruction

Go through the Interactive Reading Notepad questions and discuss the answers with the class.

Analyze Maps Study the interactive map of the United States from 1776 to 1783 and from 1791 to 1842. How did State boundaries change? How can geography influence U.S. political divisions? *(Possible answers: The States of North Carolina and Virginia had new boundaries on the western side. Massachusetts had a new boundary to the north. The U.S. Government decided to break up these States. As a result, the new States of Kentucky, Tennessee, and Maine formed from land that belonged to Virginia, North Carolina, and Massachusetts respectively.)*

Infer Why do you think the U.S. Government makes certain conditions for the admission of some States? *(Possible answer: The territory asking to be admitted as a State might have a unique practice that the U.S. Government views as unfair or wrong.)*

Objective 2: Examine the many and growing areas of cooperative federalism.

Quick Instruction

Tell students that States often share resources through grants. There are three types of grants that the Federal Government gives to States: categorical grants, block grants, and project grants. Have students write a brief definition for each type of grant without using a dictionary or referring to the text. Then ask volunteers to share their definitions.

Further Instruction

Editable Presentation Use the Editable Presentation to present the main ideas for this Core Reading.

States and Federal Governments Sharing Resources: Core Reading and Interactive Reading Notepad Project and discuss the Interactive Reading Notepad questions, including the graphic organizer asking students to place examples of grants-in-aid in the correct category.

Compare and Contrast Compare the functions of categorical grants and project grants. *(Possible answer: Both types of grants are used for specific purposes. However, categorical grants apply to programs within a specific category and come with many strings attached. Project grants, on the otherhand, apply to specific projects such as cancer research, and do not have as many strings attached as categorical grants.)*

Support Ideas with Examples Provide a hypothetical example of how grants-in-aid can be used by the Federal Government to influence public policy. *(Possible answer: The Federal Government can provide grants-in-aid to a State for education with the understanding that this State will support an certain educational policy.)*

DIGITAL TEXT 4

Agreements Among States

Objective 3: Explain why States make interstate compacts.

Quick Instruction

Tell students that States can enter into interstate compacts, or agreements among themselves. For example, States often form such agreements with regard to law enforcement. Ask students: Why would States form interstate compacts concerning natural resources? Have volunteers answer, and list these answers on the board. Then have the class discuss this issue.

Further Instruction

Go through the Interactive Reading Notepad questions and discuss the answers with the class.

Identify Patterns What pattern do you see with the type of issues that States make interstate compacts about? *(Possible answer: States seem to make interstate compacts about issues that overlap States. For example, two States might make an interstate compact about wildlife because wildlife roams from one State to the other and back again with no regard for boundaries.)*

DIGITAL TEXT 5

How the Law Crosses State Lines

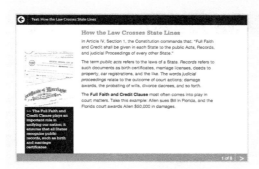

Objective 4: Understand the purpose of the Full Faith and Credit Clause, the Extradition Clause, and the Privileges and Immunities Clause.

Quick Instruction

In Article IV, Section 1, the Constitution commands that: "Full Faith and Credit shall be given in each State to the public Acts, Records, and judicial Proceedings of every other State." The Full Faith and Credit Clause most often comes into play in court matters.

Further Instruction

Go through the Interactive Reading Notepad question concerning how the law crosses State lines and discuss the answers with the class.

Check Understanding How did "quickie" divorces misuse the exception granted divorces concerning the Full Faith and Credit Clause? *(Possible answer: One State must recognize another State's divorce laws. Because of this, some people went to Nevada, obtained legal residency by living in this State for six weeks, and then obtained a divorce. However, these people were not actual permanent residents of Nevada. They were just taking advantage of the exception granted divorces concerning the Full Faith and Credit Clause.)*

D **Differentiate: Extra Support** Provide the following example to help students understand that divorce is an exception to the Full Faith and Credit Clause. Smith is a resident of Kansas, but was granted a divorce in Iowa. Can States other than Kansas refuse to

DIGITAL TEXT 6

Extradition

recognize this divorce? Why? Is this example an exception to the Full Faith and Credit Clause? Why?

Tell students that the law also crosses State lines with regard to extradition. Extradition is the legal process by which a fugitive from justice in one State can be returned to that State. Go through the Interactive Reading Notepad questions concerning extradition and discuss the answers with the class.

Draw Conclusions In *Kentucky* v. *Dennison* (1861), the Supreme Court held that the Constitution did not give the Federal Government any power with which to compel a governor to act in an extradition case. How do you think the conflict between the northern and southern States at that time influenced this decision? Do you think reversing this Supreme Court ruling was a good decision? *(Possible answer: In 1861, many slaves were escaping the South and taking refuge in northern States. This Supreme Court ruling took away the right of the Federal Government to force northern States to return slaves. The later reversal of this ruling was good because it prevented criminals from taking refuge in other States.)*

Next, go through the Interactive Reading Notepad question concerning the Privileges and Immunity Clause and discuss the answers with the class.

The National Government and the States

SYNTHESIZE

DEMONSTRATE

DIGITAL TEXT 7
Privileges and Immunities

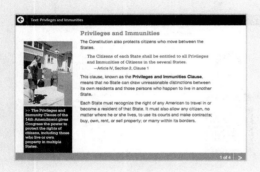

DIGITAL ACTIVITY
Federal Grants to States

Ask students to recall the Topic Essential Question, "What Is the Right Balance of Power in Government?"

Tell students that shared powers, or "cooperative federalism," help make it possible for States to support the Federal Government and vice versa. Grants-in-aid are an example of this.

Have students decide if they are for or against grants-in-aid. Student should choose one of the block grants, categorical grants, or project grants listed in the infographic to support their opinions. *(Possible answer: Grants-in-aid programs are a problem in our nation because they blur the line between the powers of National and State Governments. For example, when the National Government gives a State a categorical grant-in-aid to spend on a particular school program such as school lunches, it is operating in a policy area in which it would otherwise have no constitutional authority. Grants-in-aid programs should be carefully reviewed to ensure that they do not cross over the constitutionally-defined powers of National and State Governments.)*

DIGITAL QUIZ
Lesson Quiz and Class Discussion Board

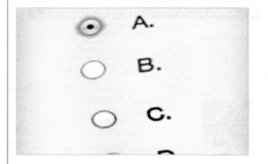

Assign the online Lesson Quiz for this lesson if you haven't already done so. Students will be offered automatic remediation or enrichment based on their score.

In "The Federal Government and the States," students read about the process of admitting new States to the Union, interstate compacts, and growing areas of cooperative federalism. Also, they examined the Full Faith and Credit Clause, the Extradition Clause, and the Privileges and Immunities Clause.

Pose these questions to the class on the Discussion Board:

Hypothesize If another State is admitted into the United States, where do you think this State would be located and why would it be admitted? *(Possible answer: The next State added to the United States would probably be Puerto Rico. Since this area already has close ties with the United States, many Puerto Ricans and Americans would support statehood.)*

Solve Problems What contemporary conflicts and political divisions will need to be solved concerning the Supreme Court ruling in the case of *United States* v. *Windsor*? *(Possible answer: Problems will need to solved concerning tax codes, healthcare, pensions, and many other issues that are indirectly associated with laws surrounding marriage. Some States have different laws than other States concerning these issues. These differences will need to be sorted out.)*

Topic Inquiry
Have students continue their investigations for the Topic Inquiry.

PEARSON
realize™

www.PearsonRealize.com
Access your Digital Lesson

The Constitution

■ SYNTHESIZE

DIGITAL ACTIVITY
Reflect on the Essential Question

Reflect on the Essential Question First ask students to reconsider the Essential Question for the Topic: What is the right balance of power in good government? Remind students of the six basic principles of the Constitution.

- Popular sovereignty
- Limited government
- Separation of powers
- Checks and balances
- Judicial review
- Federalism

Why is separation of powers so important in government? *(It prevents the abuse of power and stops one branch from being too powerful; it stops the states from taking too much power; and it helps each branch of government to remain independent.)*

Reflect on the Topic Ask students to write down three important questions they have thought about during the topic and their answers to those questions.

Topic Inquiry
Have students complete Step 3 of the Topic Inquiry.

■ DEMONSTRATE

DIGITAL TOPIC REVIEW AND ASSESSMENT
The Constitution

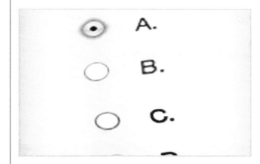

Students can prepare for the Topic Test by answering the questions in the Topic Review and Assessment online or the Assessment questions in the Print Student text. They can also prepare by reviewing their answers to the Interactive Reading Notepad questions or reviewing their notes in the Reading and Notetaking Study Guide.

DIGITAL TOPIC TEST
The Constitution

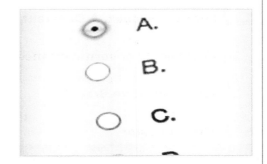

TOPIC TEST
Assign the Topic Test to assess students' understanding of topic content.

BENCHMARK TESTS
Assign these benchmark tests as you complete the relevant topics to monitor student progress toward mastering the course content and as preparation for the End-of-Course Test.

Benchmark Test 1: Topics 1–4
Benchmark Test 2: Topics 5–8
Benchmark Test 3: Topics 9–11
Benchmark Test 4: Topics 12–14

The Legislative Branch

		PACING
Connect		1 period
MY STORY VIDEO	**Loretta Sanchez, A Different Path to Office**	10 min.
DIGITAL ESSENTIAL QUESTION ACTIVITY	**How should government meet the needs of its people?**	10 min.
DIGITAL OVERVIEW ACTIVITY	**The Legislative Branch**	10 min.
TOPIC INQUIRY: CIVIC DISCUSSION	**The Filibuster**	20 min.
Investigate		3–6 periods
TOPIC INQUIRY: CIVIC DISCUSSION	**The Filibuster**	Ongoing
LESSON 1	National Legislature Overview	30–40 min.
LESSON 2	The Two Houses	30–40 min.
LESSON 3	The Expressed Powers	30–40 min.
LESSON 4	The Implied and Nonlegislative Powers	30–40 min.
LESSON 5	Congress at Work: Organization and Committees	30–40 min.
LESSON 6	Congress at Work–Making Law	30–40 min.
Synthesize		1 period
DIGITAL ACTIVITY	**Representatives' Approaches to Voting**	10 min.
TOPIC INQUIRY: CIVIC DISCUSSION	**The Filibuster**	20 min.
Demonstrate		1–2 periods
DIGITAL TOPIC REVIEW AND ASSESSMENT	**The Legislative Branch**	10 min.
TOPIC INQUIRY: CIVIC DISCUSSION	**The Filibuster**	20 min.

TOPIC INQUIRY: CIVIC DISCUSSION

The Filibuster

In this Topic Inquiry, students work in teams to examine different perspectives on this issue by analyzing several sources, arguing both sides of a Yes/No question, then developing and discussing their own point of view on the question: **Should the filibuster be abolished in the Senate?**

STEP 1: CONNECT
Develop Questions and Plan the Investigation

Launch the Civic Discussion

Divide the class into groups of four students. Students can access the materials they'll need in the online course or you can distribute copies to each student. Read the main question and introduction with the students.

Have students complete Step 1 by reading the Discussion Launch and filling in Step 1 of the Information Organizer. The Discussion Launch provides YES and NO arguments on the main question. Students should extract and paraphrase the arguments from the reading in Step 1 of their Information Organizers.

Next, students share within their groups the arguments and evidence they found to support the YES and NO positions. The group needs to agree on the major YES and NO points and each student should note those points in their Information Organizer.

Resources
- Student Instructions
- Information Organizer
- Discussion Launch

⏻ PROFESSIONAL DEVELOPMENT

Civic Discussion
Be sure to view the Civic Discussion Professional Development resources in the online course.

STEP 2: INVESTIGATE
Apply Disciplinary Concepts and Tools

Examine Sources and Perspectives

Students will examine sources with the goal of extracting information and perspectives on the main question. They analyze each source and describe the author's perspective on the main question and key evidence the author provides to support that viewpoint in Information Organizer Step 2.

Ask students to keep in mind:

- **Author/Creator:** Who created the source? An individual? Group? Government agency?
- **Audience:** For whom was the source created?
- **Date/Place:** Is there any information that reveals where and when the source was created?
- **Purpose:** Why was the source created? Discuss with students the importance of this question in identifying bias.
- **Relevance:** How does the source support one argument or another?

Suggestion: Reading the source documents and filling in Step 2 of the Information Organizer could be assigned as homework.

Resources
- Student Instructions
- Information Organizer
- Source documents

TOPIC INQUIRY: CIVIC DISCUSSION

The Filibuster *(continued)*

STEP 3: SYNTHESIZE
Use Evidence to Formulate Conclusions

Formulate Compelling Arguments with Evidence
Now students will apply perspectives and evidence they extracted from the sources to think more deeply about the main question by first arguing one side of the issue, then the other. In this way students become more prepared to formulate an evidence-based conclusion on their own.

Within each student group, assign half of the students to take the position of YES on the main question and the others to take the position of NO. Students will work with their partners to identify the strongest arguments and evidence to support their assigned YES or NO position.

Present Yes/No Positions
Within each group, those assigned the YES position share arguments and evidence first. As the YES students speak, those assigned NO should listen carefully, take notes to fill in the rest of the Compelling Arguments Chart (Step 3 in Information Organizer) and ask clarifying questions.

When the YES side is finished, students assigned the NO position present while those assigned YES should listen, take notes, and ask clarifying questions. Examples of clarifyin questions are:

- I think you just said [x]. Am I understanding you correctly?
- Can you tell me more about [x]?
- Can you repeat [x]? I am not sure I understand, yet.

Suggestion: You may want to set a 5 minute time limit for each side to present. Provide a two-minute warning so that students make their most compelling arguments within the time frame.

Switch Sides
The students will switch sides to argue the opposite point of view. To prepare to present the other position, partners who first argued YES will use the notes they took during the NO side's presentation, plus add any additional arguments and evidence from the reading and sources. The same for students who first argued the NO position.

STEP 4: DEMONSTRATE
Communicate Conclusions and Take Informed Action

Individual Points of View
Now the students will have the opportunity to discuss the main question from their own points of view. To help students prepare for this discussion, have them reflect on the YES/NO discussions they have participated in thus far and fill in Step 4 of their Information Organizers.

After all of the students have shared their points of view, each group should list points of agreement, filling the last portion of Step 4 on their Information Organizers.

Reflect on the Discussion
Ask students to reflect on the civic discussion thinking about:

- The value of having to argue both the YES and NO positions.
- If their individual views changed over the course of the discussion and why.
- What they learned from participating in the discussion.

Resources
- Student Instructions
- Information Organizer

The Legislative Branch

The Legislative Branch consists of the House of Representatives and the Senate. Their main function is to write and pass national laws. Additionally, through oversight and some explicit powers, they provide checks and balances on the other branches. Congress has created its own structure that assists in its primary function.

CONNECT

MY STORY VIDEO

Loretta Sanchez, A Different Path to Office

Watch a video that introduces students to a lawmaker with an unusual success story.

Identify Central Issues In ways did Rep. Sanchez take "a different path" to political office? *(She came from a non-political background, was successful in a different career, had no political ambitions, won a close and contested election, found herself on an unusual House committee.)*

Determine Point of View What motivated Sanchez to run for political office? *(She tried to reach her member of Congress about an issue but could not. She thought a legislator should be available to his or her constituents, so she decided to run for office and be the type of legislator she believes the people deserve.)*

FLIP IT!

Assign the My Story video.

DIGITAL ESSENTIAL QUESTION ACTIVITY

How should government meet the needs of its people?

Ask students to think about the Essential Question for this Topic: How should the government meet the needs of its people? There are several different approaches to lawmaking. Which approach best serves the people?

If students have not already done so, ask them to respond to the poll. Then go over the results as a class.

Support Reasons with Evidence Why did you rate this reason as most important? *(Answers will vary.)*

Cause and Effect What kind of law would make a lawmaker change his or her approach from a partisan to a delegate? *(Possible answer: He or she really believes in the law.)* from a trustee to a delegate? *(Possible answer: His or her constituents believe the law is important.)*

Make Inferences What makes a trustworthy lawmaker? *(Possible answers: a good listener, works well with others, has a vision for how things should be, has strong convictions)* What makes a trustworthy system of laws? *(Possible answers: supports all citizens, gives ways for citizens to get needs met, provides oversight, is overseen by other branches)*

DIGITAL OVERVIEW ACTIVITY

The Legislative Branch

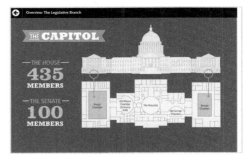

Project the activity and step through the images. Have students name the people they see. Assist as necessary. During this topic, students will learn about the roles these people play in the legislative process. This framework should get students thinking about what it means to represent a district or a State.

D Differentiate: Extra Support What are the two elements of the legislative branch? *(Senate and House of Representatives)*

Check Understanding How is Congress the face of the United States? *(Possible answer: Congress is meant to represent all the people in the country, regardless of race or creed.)*

Topic Inquiry

Launch the Topic Inquiry with students after introducing the Topic.

National Legislature Overview

Supporting English Language Learners

Use with Digital Text 1, **The Role of Congress in a Democracy.**

Learning Strategies
Explain the difference between formal and informal English. After reading the sections on the five major roles of Congress, guide students to summarize the concepts in informal English. Use visuals from the text as support.

Beginning Display a list of the five major roles of Congress written in formal English. Provide simple explanations of these roles in informal English. Guide students to match the formal English to its informal explanation.

Intermediate Have students look in the text to create a list of formal words that describe the roles of Congress. Have students describe the roles of Congress in informal English.

Advanced Have partners copy sentences from the text that describe the roles of Congress. Ask them to rewrite the descriptions in informal English.

Advanced High Have students write an informal description of the roles of Congress. Ask partners to share their work and discuss what makes their writing informal.

Use with the Lesson 1 readings.

Reading
Explain to students how the phrases *in addition* and *for example* are used when an idea or concept is described. Have students locate these phrases in the text and discuss their use in the context of how they are used in learning about and understanding government.

Beginning Display the paragraphs with these phrases. Highlight and discuss the sentences that are relevant to the phrase. Read the sentences aloud and have the students repeat.

Intermediate Guide partners to read the paragraphs with these phrases. Provide a list of concepts that are described by the phrases. Ask partners to identify the concept that is being described by the sentences that use each phrase.

Advanced Have students read the paragraphs independently. Guide partners to find the sentence that gives the concept and the sentence that describes the concept. Highlight the use of the phrases.

Advanced High Ask partners to identify the concept that is being described by the sentences that use each phrase.

▶ Differentiate Instruction

Use the Differentiated Instruction notes throughout the lesson plan to support the varied skill sets, levels of readiness, and interests in the mixed-ability classroom.

Challenge These notes include suggestions for expanding the activity for advanced students.

On-Level These notes include suggestions for modifying the activity to address different interests or learning styles.

Extra Support These notes include ideas for providing more scaffolding or reading spuport.

Special Needs These notes provide ideas for adapting instruction to support the needs of various special needs students.

■ NOTES

PEARSON
realize™
www.PearsonRealize.com

Go online to access additional resources including:
Primary Sources • Biographies • Supreme Court cases •
21st Century Skill Tutorials • Maps • Graphic Organizers.

Objectives

Objective 1: Explain why the Constitution provides for the bicameral structure of Congress.

Objective 2: Explain the difference between a term and a session of Congress.

Objective 3: Describe a situation in which the President may convene or end a session of Congress.

Objective 4: Identify the personal and political backgrounds of members of Congress.

Objective 5: Describe the duties performed by those who serve in Congress.

Objective 6: Describe the compensation and privileges of members of Congress.

LESSON 1 ORGANIZER		PACING: APPROX. 1 PERIOD, .5 BLOCKS			
				RESOURCES	
		OBJECTIVES	PACING	Online	Print
Connect					
DIGITAL START UP ACTIVITY **What Makes a Successful Congress?**			10 min.	●	
Investigate					
DIGITAL TEXT 1 **The Role of Congress in a Democracy**		Objective 1	10 min.	●	●
DIGITAL TEXT 2 **Congress: The Job**		Objectives 4, 5	10 min.	●	●
3-D MODEL **A Tour of the Capitol**			10 min.	●	
DIGITAL TEXT 3 **Terms and Sessions of Congress**		Objectives 2, 3	10 min.	●	●
DIGITAL TEXT 4 **Congressional Compensation**		Objective 6	10 min.	●	●
INTERACTIVE GALLERY **Congressional Pay and Benefits**			10 min.	●	
Synthesize					
DIGITAL SYNTHESIZE ACTIVITY **How Should Representatives Vote?**			10 min.	●	
Demonstrate					
DIGITAL QUIZ **Lesson Quiz and Discussion Board**			10 min.	●	

National Legislature Overview

■ CONNECT

DIGITAL START UP ACTIVITY
What Makes a Successful Congress?

Project the Start Up Activity Ask students to read the list and answer the question as they enter and get settled. Then have them share their ideas with another student, either in class or through a chat or blog space.

Discuss If you were a Founder, how would you balance the need to create laws on a national scale with ensuring representation for States and citizens? *(Possible answers: bicameral Congress with representation based on population in one house; a federal system of government; legislature with limited powers)*

Tell students that in this lesson they will be learning about the United States Congress.

Aa Vocabulary Development: Use the Interactive Reading Notepad to preview the Key Terms and Academic Vocabulary in this Lesson with students.

⇗ FLIP IT!
Assign the Flipped Video for this lesson.

■ STUDENT EDITION PRINT PAGES: 128–136

■ INVESTIGATE

DIGITAL TEXT 1
The Role of Congress in a Democracy

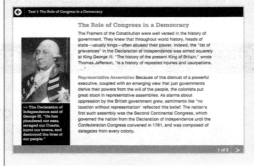

Objective 1: Explain why the Constitution provides for the bicameral structure of Congress.

Quick Instruction
The Framers worried about vesting too much power in a body chosen directly by the people. The average citizen can be overly passionate and driven by self-interest, they argued. So, they designed a National Government whose structure and functions couched the legislature's powers within both a broader system of checks and balances and a federal system where a good deal would be left to the States. It would be the job of each representative to "enlarge and refine the public will," as suggested by James Madison in *The Federalist* No. 10. That is, to help citizens look beyond their immediate interest to the national interest.

ELL Use the ELL activity described in the ELL chart.

Further Instruction
Editable Presentation Use the Editable Presentation to present the main ideas for this Core Reading.

The Role of Congress in a Democracy: Core Reading and Interactive Reading Notepad Project and discuss the Interactive Reading Notepad questions, including the graphic organizer. The colonists distrusted powerful executives. They believed that just governments derive their powers from the will of the people through representative assemblies. The nation's first such assembly was the Second Continental Congress, which governed the nation from the Declaration of Independence until the Confederation Congress convened in 1781. It was composed of delegates from every colony.

Draw Conclusions How did sentiments like "no taxation without representation" support the new ideas about assemblies? *(Colonists thought governments derived powers not from an executive, but rather through the will of the people. People should have a say in how many taxes they pay and what they are used for.)*

Cause and Effect Why did the Framers incorporate a system of checks and balances in the Constitution? *(Possible answer: Checks and balances prevent one branch of government from having too much power.)*

Congress: The Job

A Tour of the Capitol

Terms and Sessions of Congress

Objectives 4: Identify the personal and political backgrounds of members of Congress; 5: Describe the duties performed by those who serve in Congress.

Quick Instruction

Members of both houses of Congress have five major functions. They are most importantly (1) legislators and (2) representatives of their constituents. Beyond those roles, they are also (3) committee members, (4) servants of their constituents, and (5) politicians.

Interactive 3D Model: A Tour of the Capitol Project and step through the 3D model with students. Tell students that they will learn more about the places within the United States Capitol and the functions they serve.

ACTIVE CLASSROOM

Have students use a Cartoon It strategy to explain what happens in a chosen room in the Capitol. Post the cartoons and have students explain their images.

D Differentiate: **Extra Support** Ask students to name the two houses of Congress and post student answers. *(House of Representatives and Senate)* Discuss the five major roles of Congress. Then continue with the activity.

ELL Use the ELL activity described in the ELL chart.

Further Instruction

Editable Presentation Use the Editable Presentation to present the main ideas for this Core Reading.

Congress: the Job: Core Reading and Interactive Reading Notepad Project and discuss the Interactive Reading Notepad questions.

Backgrounds of Congress Take a class poll in which you tally the numbers of women, African Americans, Hispanic Americans, Asian Americans, Native Americans, and other groups. Does the composition of Congress reflect the ethnic and gender balance in your classroom? Discuss with students the implications of the nation's representative body not accurately representing the American population.

Make Judgments Which job function do you think is most important to a member of Congress? Why? *(Possible answer: Doing favors for constituents is most important because it builds relationships and ensures the member keeps his or her job.)*

Cause and Effect What is the impact of career legislators on the role of representatives of the people? *(They are more likely to vote as their constituents want them to as opposed to for themselves or for their own ideas.)*

Objectives 2: Explain the difference between a term and a session of Congress; 3: Describe a situation in which the President may convene or end a session of Congress.

Quick Instruction

Terms of Congress Explain to students that each term of Congress lasts for two years, and each of those two-year terms is numbered consecutively (Article I, Section 2, Clause 1). Congress began its first term on March 4, 1789. That term ended two years later, on March 3, 1791. The date for the start of each new term was changed by the 20th Amendment in 1933. The start of each new two-year term is now "noon of the 3d day of January" of every odd-numbered year.

Sessions of Congress A session of Congress is that period of time during which, each year, Congress assembles and conducts business. There are two sessions to each term of Congress—one session each year. The Constitution provides that: The Congress shall assemble at least once in every year, and such meeting shall begin at noon on the 3d day of January, unless they shall by law appoint a different day.

Special Sessions Only the President may call Congress into special session. Only 27 of these special joint sessions of Congress have ever been held. President Harry Truman called the most recent one in 1948, to consider anti-inflation and welfare measures in the aftermath of World War II.

National Legislature Overview

DIGITAL TEXT 4
Congressional Compensation

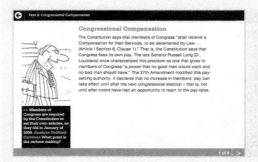

INTERACTIVE GALLERY
Congressional Pay and Benefits

Further Instruction

Editable Presentation Use the Editable Presentation to present the main ideas for this Core Reading.

Terms and Sessions of Congress: Core Reading and Interactive Reading Notepad Project and discuss the Interactive Reading Notepad questions.

Students should know that as part of outlining the structure and function of the Congress the Constitution explains that "Neither House . . . shall, without the Consent of the other, adjourn for more than three days, nor to any other Place than that in which the two Houses shall be sitting." —Article I, Section 5, Clause 4. Article II, Section 3 of the Constitution gives the President the power to prorogue a session, but only when the two houses cannot agree on a date for adjournment. No President has ever used that power.

Analyze Why does the structure of Congress require the consent of both houses to adjourn? *(It balances power between the houses. Neither can act without the other.)*

Cause and Effect What circumstances might force a President to end a session of Congress? *(The President may prorogue a session only if Congress can't agree on a date for adjournment.)*

Objective 6: Describe the compensation and privileges of members of Congress.

Quick Instruction

The Constitution says that members of Congress "shall receive a Compensation for their Services, to be ascertained by Law . . ." (Article I, Section 6, Clause 1). That is, the Constitution says that Congress fixes its own pay. The 27th Amendment declares that no increase in members' pay can take effect until after the next congressional election, meaning not until after voters have had an opportunity to react to the pay raise.

Salary and Compensation Today, senators and representatives are paid $174,000 per year. Each member has generous travel allowances for the cost of several round trips each year between home and Washington, get full medical care at any military hospital, and have a generous retirement plan.

Interactive Gallery: Congressional Pay and Benefits Project and step through the gallery with students, pointing out the many benefits received by members of Congress.

📷 ACTIVE CLASSROOM

Using a Ranking strategy, determine which compensation is most helpful as members of Congress assist constituents. Then determine which compensation is most likely to attract the best people for the job. Are they the same? Discuss why or why not.

D Differentiate: Extra Support Remind students that compensation is not just monetary. Discuss other compensation they might know, such as discounts at their workplaces, health insurance, or retirement.

Further Instruction

Editable Presentation Use the Editable Presentation to present the main ideas for this Core Reading.

Congressional Compensation: Core Reading and Interactive Reading Notepad Project and discuss the Interactive Reading Notepad questions.

Students should know that a few members of Congress are paid more. The Speaker of the House makes $223,500 per year. The Vice President makes $230,700 per year. The Senate's president pro tem and the floor leaders in both houses receive $193,400 per year.

Explain that members have perks that allow them to function as representatives, such as multiple offices, funds to hire staff, free parking at Washington's major airports, and resources at the Library of Congress. Then ask the following questions.

Analyze How do these perks allow Congress to function better? *(Possible answer: They facilitate members' trips home and their communications with constituents.)*

Draw Conclusions Why might members of Congress give themselves generous perks instead of increasing pay? *(Possible answer: Constituents might be frustrated if their members of Congress made significantly more money than they do.)*

■ SYNTHESIZE

How Should Representatives Vote?

Ask students to recall the Topic Essential Question, "How should the government meet the needs of its people?" Have them use the Think Pair Share strategy to analyze and discuss the quotation. Ask them to take five minutes to write down some brief answers to the questions below, then share their answers with a talking partner.

Have partners think about the following question: What factors do you think are most important for members of Congress to consider when casting their votes? Have pairs share their answers with the class.

Discuss Ask students to think about the checklist they filled out at the beginning of this Topic. Ask if they would change any of their responses, now that they have learned more about the functions and responsibilities of Congress.

■ DEMONSTRATE

Lesson Quiz and Discussion Board

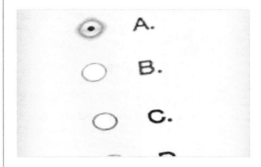

Assign the online Lesson Quiz for this lesson if you haven't already done so. Students will be offered automatic remediation or enrichment based on their score.

In "The National Legislature Overview" you read about the two houses of Congress. Pose these questions to the class on the Discussion Board:

Make Judgments Do you think having a diverse Congress is important? What would you do to ensure this diversity?

Compare What is the most important difference between the House of Representatives and the Senate?

Topic Inquiry

Have students continue their investigations for the Topic Inquiry.

The Two Houses

Supporting English Language Learners

Use with the Lesson 2 readings.

Learning Strategies
Give examples of situations where formal and informal English should be used. Have students give a summary of the text in formal or informal English depending on the situation.

Beginning Name a situation. Read a sentence about the text in formal English and another in informal English. Have students identify which sentence would be appropriate for the situation.

Intermediate Provide students with sentences about the text in formal and informal English. Guide them to read the sentences. Name a situation and ask students to identify a sentence that would be appropriate for the situation.

Advanced Provide students with 3 or 4 situations. Have partners identify which would require formal English and which would require informal English. Guide them to write brief summaries of the text in formal and informal English.

Advanced High Name a situation. Have students role play a conversation about the text in the given situation. Repeat with other situations.

Use with the Lesson 2 readings.

Reading
Preview the lesson "The Two Houses" by guiding students to look at the visuals in the text. Complete the K and W sections of a KWL chart to develop background knowledge about the bicameral structure of Congress. Complete the L section of the chart after reading and discussing the text.

Beginning Have the class complete the chart together. Provide a list of key words and have the students read them aloud with the teacher. Guide them to refer to the text as they fill in the chart with words and phrases.

Intermediate Have small groups work together to complete the chart. Guide them to read the text as they fill in the chart with phrases and short sentences.

Advanced Have partners work together to complete the chart, reading and using the text as needed for reference. Ask partners to share their charts with another pair of students.

Advanced High Have students read the text and complete their charts and discuss with another student. Encourage students to add to their charts after the discussion.

▣ Differentiate Instruction

Use the Differentiated Instruction notes throughout the lesson plan to support the varied skill sets, levels of readiness, and interests in the mixed-ability classroom.

Challenge These notes include suggestions for expanding the activity for advanced students.

On-Level These notes include suggestions for modifying the activity to address different interests or learning styles.

Extra Support These notes include ideas for providing more scaffolding or reading spuport.

Special Needs These notes provide ideas for adapting instruction to support the needs of various special needs students.

▪ NOTES

PEARSON
realize™
www.PearsonRealize.com

Go online to access additional resources including:
Primary Sources • Biographies • Supreme Court cases •
21st Century Skill Tutorials • Maps • Graphic Organizers.

Objectives

Objective 1: Explain how House seats are distributed and describe the length of a term in the House.

Objective 2: Explain how House seats are reapportioned among the States after each census.

Objective 3: Describe a typical congressional election and congressional district.

Objective 4: Analyze the formal and informal qualifications for election to the House and the Senate.

Objective 5: Compare the size of the Senate to the size of the House of Representatives.

Objective 6: Explain how and why a Senator's term differs from a representative's term.

LESSON 2 ORGANIZER		PACING: APPROX. 1 PERIOD, .5 BLOCKS			
				RESOURCES	
		OBJECTIVES	**PACING**	**Online**	**Print**
Connect					
DIGITAL START UP ACTIVITY **Who Represents You?**			10 min.	●	
Investigate					
DIGITAL TEXT 1 **The House**		Objective 1	10 min.	●	●
DIGITAL TEXT 2 **Reapportionment of Congress**			10 min.	●	●
INTERACTIVE MAP **Gerrymandering: Redistricting Voters**		Objective 2	10 min.	●	
INTERACTIVE CHART **Reapportionment of Congressional Districts**			10 min.	●	
DIGITAL TEXT 3 **House Elections**		Objective 3	10 min.	●	●
DIGITAL TEXT 4 **Qualifications for Office in the House**		Objective 4	10 min.	●	●
DIGITAL TEXT 5 **The Senate—Size, Election, and Terms**		Objectives 5, 6	10 min.	●	●
DIGITAL TEXT 6 **Qualifications for Office in the Senate**			10 min.	●	●
Synthesize					
DIGITAL SYNTHESIZE ACTIVITY **Gerrymandering and the Democratic Process**			10 min.	●	
Demonstrate					
DIGITAL QUIZ **Lesson Quiz and Discussion Board**			10 min.	●	

The Two Houses

CONNECT

DIGITAL START UP ACTIVITY
Who Represents You?

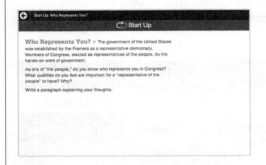

Project the Start Up Activity Ask students to read the statement and answer the questions as they enter and get settled. Then have them share their ideas with another student, either in class or through a chat or blog space.

Discuss Remind students of the overview they discussed. Would you rather be a senator or a representative? Why? *(Possible answers: A senator, because they have longer terms. A representative, because they are in charge of the budgeting process.)*

Tell students that in this lesson they will be learning about specifics of the House and Senate.

Aa Vocabulary Development: Use the Interactive Reading Notepad to preview the Key Terms and Academic Vocabulary in this Lesson with students.

⇅ FLIP IT!
Assign the Flipped Video for this lesson.

STUDENT EDITION PRINT
PAGES: 137–146

INVESTIGATE

DIGITAL TEXT 1
The House

Objective 1: Explain how House seats are distributed and describe the length of a term in the House.

Quick Instruction
Explain to students that the exact size of the House of Representatives—today, 435 members—is not fixed by the Constitution. Rather, it is set by Congress. The Constitution provides that the total number of seats in the House of Representatives shall be apportioned among the States on the basis of their respective populations (Article I, Clause 3). Each State is guaranteed at least one seat no matter what its population.

Article I, Section 2, Clause 1 of the Constitution provides that "Representatives shall be . . . chosen every second Year." That is, they are elected for two-year terms.

ELL Use the ELL activity described in the ELL chart.

Further Instruction
Editable Presentation Use the Editable Presentation to present the main ideas for this Core Reading.

The House: Core Reading and Interactive Reading Notepad Project and discuss the Interactive Reading Notepad questions.

Students should know that the House of Representatives includes officials who are not full members. These delegates represent various U.S. territories and the District of Columbia. They do not vote on bills. Full political power is distributed among States only.

Make Inferences Why might full political power not be granted to territories? *(Possible answer: States and the Federal Government share power. Territories don't have that sovereignty.)*

Predict Consequences In the 1990s, there were efforts to put term-limits on members of Congress. What might have happened if that effort had been successful? *(Possible answer: More people would get to be members of Congress.)*

Cause and Effect What is a negative result of having a two-year term for a representative? *(Representatives are constantly campaigning.)*

DIGITAL TEXT 2
Reapportionment of Congress

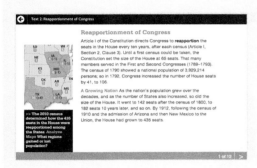

INTERACTIVE MAP
Gerrymandering: Redistricting Voters

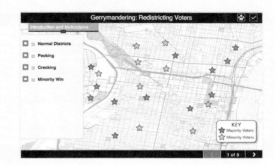

INTERACTIVE CHART
Reapportionment of Congressional Districts

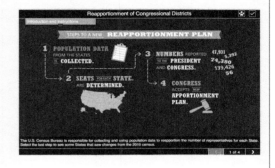

Objective 2: Explain how House seats are reapportioned among the States after each census.

Quick Instruction

Summarize for students as follows: Article I of the Constitution directs Congress to reapportion the seats in the House every ten years, after each census. Congress passed the Reapportionment Act of 1929. That law sets up what is often called an "automatic reapportionment." It provides: 1. The "permanent" size of the House is 435 members. (Today each of the 435 seats in the House represents an average of over 700,000 persons.) 2. Following each census, the Census Bureau is to determine the number of seats each State should have. 3. When the Bureau's plan is ready, the President must send it to Congress. 4. If, within 60 days of receiving it, neither house rejects the Census Bureau's plan, it becomes effective.

Interactive Map: Gerrymandering: Redistricting Voters Project and discuss the map with students. Before beginning the activity, review the definition of gerrymandering—the process of redrawing district lines to create a political advantage for the party that controls the State's legislature. Then select the squares to show the different methods of gerrymandering.

ACTIVE CLASSROOM

Using a Make Headlines strategy, have students summarize the impact of the gerrymandering that is shown in each example. Then have students share their headlines. Discuss similarities or differences.

D Differentiate: **Challenge** Have students look at the different methods and choose the one they think best allows for representation. Then have students write a paragraph that explains their position.

Interactive Chart: Reapportionment of Congressional Districts Project and step through the flow chart with students. Introduce the activity by telling students that all of the different interactives show the ways in which Congress has been reapportioned.

ACTIVE CLASSROOM

Have students use a Sticky Note strategy to examine political boundaries and summarize how new political divisions are crafted.

ELL Use the ELL activity described in the ELL chart.

Further Instruction

Editable Presentation Use the Editable Presentation to present the main ideas for this Core Reading.

Reapportionment of Congress: Core Reading and Interactive Reading Notepad Project and discuss the Interactive Reading Notepad questions. In a case from Georgia, *Wesberry* v. *Sanders*, the Supreme Court held that the Constitution demands that the States draw congressional districts of substantially equal populations. The Court's "one person, one vote" decision in *Wesberry* had an immediate and extraordinary impact on the makeup of the House, on the content of public policy, and on the shape of electoral politics in general.

Partisan Gerrymandering The Court has said that under some circumstances, which it has never spelled out, excessively partisan gerrymandering might be unconstitutional. It did so for the first time in a 1986 case, *Davis* v. *Bandemer*. In a 2006 decision, a bare majority of the Court ruled that neither the Constitution nor any act of Congress prevents a State from redrawing its district lines whenever the party in control of the legislature believes that it might be to its advantage to do so (*United Latin American Citizens* v. *Perry*).

Cause and Effect Before the Court's "one person, one vote" ruling, why were rural areas overrepresented in the House? *(Congressional districts were drawn so that rural areas, which had much lower populations, had as many or more representatives in the House than did much more populated urban areas.)*

Analyze Maps Explain how each slide of the Interactive Map uses political boundaries to alter the distribution of political power. *(Possible answer: By packing majority voters together into "safe" districts, a majority win is ensured in more districts.)*

The Two Houses

House Elections

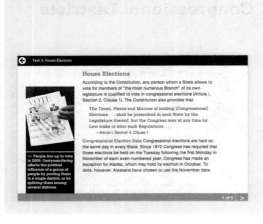

Qualifications for Office in the House

The Senate—Size, Election, and Terms

Objective 3: Describe a typical congressional election and congressional district.

Quick Instruction
According to the Constitution, any person whom a State allows to vote for members of "the most numerous Branch" of its own legislature is qualified to vote in congressional elections (Article I, Section 2, Clause 1). The Constitution also provides that "The Times, Places and Manner of holding [Congressional] Elections . . . shall be prescribed in each State by the Legislature thereof; but the Congress may at any time by Law make or alter such Regulations. . . ."

Further Instruction
Editable Presentation Use the Editable Presentation to present the main ideas for this Core Reading.

House Elections: Core Reading and Interactive Reading Notepad Project and discuss the Interactive Reading Notepad questions.

Explain to students that off-year elections occur between presidential elections. Often the party that holds the presidency loses Congressional seats in the off-year elections.

Make Connections Why do you think the party that holds the presidency often loses seats in the off-year elections? *(Possible answer: Fewer people vote in off year elections, and those who do are often voting because they are unhappy with the way things are going in the country.)*

Objective 4: Analyze the formal and informal qualifications for election to the House and the Senate.

Quick Instruction
The Constitution says that a member of the House must (1) be at least 25 years of age, (2) have been a citizen of the United States for at least seven years, and (3) be an inhabitant of the State from which he or she is elected. Customarily a representative must also live in the district he or she represents. Informal qualifications include electability.

Further Instruction
Editable Presentation Use the Editable Presentation to present the main ideas for this Core Reading.

Qualifications for Office in the House: Core Reading and Interactive Reading Notepad Project and discuss the Interactive Reading Notepad questions.

Article I, Section 5, Clause 1 makes the House "the Judge of the Elections, Returns and Qualifications of its own Members." Even though members are elected, the House may refuse to seat a member-elect if that person's qualifications are challenged and a majority votes to refuse to seat that person. These challenges are rarely successful.

Explain Why are there formal and informal qualifications in place for members elected to the House? *(Possible answer: The Constitution lays out the formal qualifications, but also gives Congress leeway to create their own informal qualifications. Also custom and constituencies provide for informal qualifications.)*

Objectives 5: Compare the size of the Senate to the size of the House of Representatives; **6:** Explain how and why a senator's term differs from a representative's term.

Quick Instruction
The Constitution says that the Senate "shall be composed of two Senators from each State," and so the Senate is a much smaller body than the House of Representatives (Article I, Section 3, Clause 1 and the 17th Amendment).

Originally, the Constitution provided that the members of the Senate were to be chosen by the State legislatures. Since the passage of the 17th Amendment in 1913, however, senators have been picked by the voters in each State at the regular November elections. Only one senator is elected from a State in any given election, except when the other seat has been vacated by death, resignation, or expulsion. Senators serve for six-year terms, three times the length of those for which members of the House are chosen (Article I, Section 3, Clause 1). The Constitution puts no limit on the number of terms any senator may serve.

A senator must meet a higher level of qualifications for office than those the Constitution sets for a member of the House. A senator must (1) be at least 30 years of age, (2) have been a citizen of the United States for at least nine years, and (3) be an inhabitant of the State from which he or she is elected (Article I, Section 3, Clause 3). Senators must satisfy a number of informal qualifications for office—various extralegal yardsticks based on

SYNTHESIZE

DEMONSTRATE

DIGITAL TEXT 6

Qualifications for Office in the Senate

DIGITAL SYNTHESIZE ACTIVITY

Gerrymandering and the Democratic Process

DIGITAL QUIZ

Lesson Quiz and Discussion Board

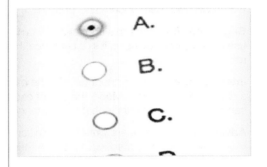

such factors as party, name familiarity, gender, ethnic characteristics, and political experience. Both incumbency and a talent for fundraising are also major assets in Senate races.

ELL Use the ELL activity described in the ELL chart.

Further Instruction

Editable Presentation Use the Editable Presentation to present the main ideas for this Core Reading.

The Senate: Core Reading and Interactive Reading Notepad Project and discuss the Interactive Reading Notepad questions. The Framers hoped that the smaller Senate would be a more enlightened and responsible body than the House. Many of them thought that the House would be too often swayed by the immediate impact of events and by the passions of the moment, mostly because of the short term of office for members of the lower chamber. They reinforced that hope by giving senators a longer term of office and by setting the qualifications for membership in the Senate a cut above those they set for the House.

Draw Conclusions Why do you think the Framers wanted to have a body that was swayed by popular events as well as a more staid, slower body? *(Possible answer: They would balance each other and provide checks on power.)*

Compare How are the Senate and House qualifications similar? *(Possible answer: They both have informal qualifications related to electability.)*

Ask students to recall the Topic Essential Question, "How should the government meet the needs of its people?" Have them use the Think Pair Share strategy to analyze what they have learned in this lesson about gerrymandering. Ask them to take five minutes to write down some brief answers to the questions below, then share their answers with a talking partner.

Have partners think about the following questions. How does being elected in a "safe" district affect the ways a representative acts and votes? Are they more or less likely to represent the views of those who live in their district? How and why does this affect the way Congress as a whole functions? Have pairs share their answers with the class.

Discuss Ask students to think about the question from the beginning of this Topic about the most important qualities of their representatives. Ask if their opinions have changed after reading this lesson. Then ask what questions they would ask their representatives now that they have learned more about the differences between the two houses.

Assign the online Lesson Quiz for this lesson if you haven't already done so. Students will be offered automatic remediation or enrichment based on their score.

In "The Two Houses," you read about the House and the Senate, how members of Congress are elected, and the qualifications for each house. Pose these questions to the class on the Discussion Board:

Draw Conclusions How does the 17th Amendment to directly elect Senators reflect the ideals of the Founders?

Compare Compare how Senators and Representatives get elected.

Make Inferences How does gerrymandering demonstrate how political power is distributed?

Topic Inquiry

Have students continue their investigations for the Topic Inquiry.

The Expressed Powers

Supporting English Language Learners

Use with Digital Text 1, **Types of Congressional Powers.**

Learning Strategies
Explain the meaning of the following words from the text: *inherent, implied, expressed.* Tell students that understanding base and related words will help them understand English.

Beginning Write the base and related words on the board. Model the use of each word by using it in a sentence. Have students copy and repeat the sentences.

Intermediate Guide partners to write the base and related words, using a dictionary as needed. Model the use of each word by using it in a sentence. Have students repeat the sentences and think of their own.

Advanced Have partners write the definition for the base words. Have them make a list of related words. Guide them to write sentences using the words.

Advanced High Have students make a list of the base and related words. Have the class sort the words into parts of speech such as verbs, nouns, and adjectives. Ask students to use the words in sentences.

Use with Digital Text 4, **Other Domestic Powers.**

Reading
Preview the reading about the other domestic powers of Congress with students. Read the text aloud to the students as they follow along. Stop as appropriate to check for understanding. Depending on the language level of your students, support comprehension in the following ways:

Beginning Preview the text with students by looking at the images, captions and headings. Stop during reading as appropriate to explain what has been read. Check for understanding by asking questions that require a yes/no or one- or two-word response.

Intermediate Preview the text with students. Ask questions that require phrases or short sentences as a response.

Advanced Have partners preview the text. Have partners discuss answers to *who, what, where,* and *why* questions.

Advanced High Have students preview the text. Ask students to summarize what has been read.

▣ Differentiate Instruction

Use the Differentiated Instruction notes throughout the lesson plan to support the varied skill sets, levels of readiness, and interests in the mixed-ability classroom.

Challenge These notes include suggestions for expanding the activity for advanced students.

On-Level These notes include suggestions for modifying the activity to address different interests or learning styles.

Extra Support These notes include ideas for providing more scaffolding or reading spuport.

Special Needs These notes provide ideas for adapting instruction to support the needs of various special needs students.

■ NOTES

PEARSON
realize.™
www.PearsonRealize.com

Go online to access additional resources including:
Primary Sources • Biographies • Supreme Court cases •
21st Century Skill Tutorials • Maps • Graphic Organizers.

Objectives

Objective 1: Describe the three types of powers delegated to Congress.

Objective 2: Understand the expressed powers of Congress, including the commerce, taxing, bankruptcy, and borrowing powers, and explain why the Framers gave Congress the power to issue currency.

Objective 3: Identify the key sources of the foreign relations powers of Congress.

Objective 4: Describe the power-sharing arrangement between Congress and the President on the issues of war and national defense.

Objective 5: List other key domestic powers exercised by Congress.

LESSON 3 ORGANIZER — PACING: APPROX. 1 PERIOD, .5 BLOCKS

		OBJECTIVES	PACING	RESOURCES Online	Print
Connect					
	DIGITAL START UP ACTIVITY **What Congress Can and Cannot Do**		10 min.	●	
Investigate					
	DIGITAL TEXT 1 **Types of Congressional Powers**	Objective 1	10 min.	●	●
	INTERACTIVE CHART **The Expressed Powers of Congress**		10 min.	●	
	DIGITAL TEXT 2 **The Commerce Power**	Objective 2	10 min.	●	●
	DIGITAL TEXT 3 **The Money Powers**		10 min.	●	●
	DIGITAL TEXT 4 **Other Domestic Powers**	Objective 5	10 min.	●	●
	INTERACTIVE GALLERY **A Case Study on Copyrights and Patents**		10 min.	●	
	DIGITAL TEXT 5 **Congress and Foreign Policy**	Objectives 3, 4	10 min.	●	●
	DIGITAL TEXT 6 **The War Powers**		10 min.	●	●
Synthesize					
	DIGITAL SYNTHESIZE ACTIVITY **Rank the Expressed Powers**		10 min.	●	
Demonstrate					
	DIGITAL QUIZ **Lesson Quiz and Discussion Board**		10 min.	●	

The Expressed Powers

■ CONNECT

DIGITAL START UP ACTIVITY
What Congress Can and Cannot Do

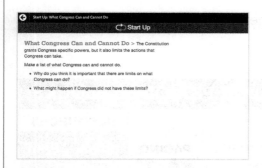

Project the Start Up Activity Ask students to read the statement and answer the questions as they enter and get settled. Then have them share their ideas with another student, either in class or through a chat or blog space.

Discuss Share background information about the structure and functions of the legislative branch. What do students know about the powers Congress has? What do they want to find out? Collect responses in a chart.

Tell students that in this lesson they will be learning about the expressed powers of Congress.

Aa Vocabulary Development: Use the Interactive Reading Notepad to preview the Key Terms and Academic Vocabulary in this Lesson with students.

ⓝ FLIP IT!

Assign the Flipped Video for this lesson.

■ STUDENT EDITION PRINT PAGES: 147–158

■ INVESTIGATE

DIGITAL TEXT 1
Types of Congressional Powers

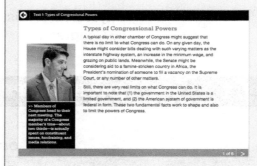

Objective 1: Describe the three types of powers delegated to Congress.

Quick Instruction
Congress has only those powers delegated to it by the Constitution. Large areas of power are denied to Congress (1) in so many words in the Constitution, (2) by the Constitution's silence on many matters, and (3) because the Constitution creates a federal system. The Constitution grants the legislative branch a number of specific powers—and, it delegates those powers in three different ways: (1) explicitly, in its specific wording—the expressed powers; (2) by reasonable deduction from the expressed powers—the implied powers; and (3) by creating a national government for the United States—the inherent powers.

Interactive Chart: The Expressed Powers of Congress Project the chart on the whiteboard. Introduce the activity by explaining that students will drag the tiles showing the powers of Congress to the correct category of expressed powers.

🎥 ACTIVE CLASSROOM

Use a Write 1 Get 3 strategy to answer the following question: What are the powers of Congress? Then use this information to write a paragraph about the five expressed powers and examples for each.

ⅾ Differentiate: Extra Support Have pairs create a chart of the five expressed powers. List examples for each of the powers from the interactive chart.

INTERACTIVE CHART
The Expressed Powers of Congress

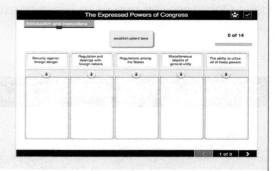

ELL Use the ELL activity described in the ELL chart.

Further Instruction
Editable Presentation Use the Editable Presentation to present the main ideas for this Core Reading.

Types of Congressional Powers: Core Reading and Interactive Reading Notepad Project and discuss the Interactive Reading Notepad questions. Students should know that most, but not all, of the expressed powers of Congress are found in Article I, Section 8 of the Constitution. There, in 18 separate clauses, 27 different powers are explicitly given to Congress.

Compare What is the difference between an inherent power and an expressed power? *(An expressed power is stated in the Constitution. An inherent power is one that is given because Congress is the legislative body of a sovereign state.)*

Draw Conclusions If a power is not stated specifically in the Constitution, does that necessarily mean that Congress can infer it? *(No, Congress needs to be careful that it doesn't infer powers that go against individual rights or infringe on the powers of other branches of the Federal Government.)*

DIGITAL TEXT 2

The Commerce Power

DIGITAL TEXT 3

The Money Powers

DIGITAL TEXT 4

Other Domestic Powers

Objective 2: Understand the expressed powers of Congress, including the commerce, taxing, bankruptcy, and borrowing powers, and explain why the Framers gave Congress the power to issue currency.

Quick Instruction

Congress has the power to regulate interstate and foreign trade. However, the Constitution places four explicit limits on the use of the commerce power. It cannot tax exports, favor the ports of one State over those of any other in the regulation of trade, require that "Vessels bound to, or from, one State, be obliged to enter, clear, or pay Duties in another," and cannot interfere with the slave trade, at least not until the year 1808. This last limitation has been a dead letter for more than two centuries.

Additionally, Congress has several expressed powers related to money, including the power to tax, the power to borrow, the power to establish laws on bankruptcy, and the power to coin money. The Commerce Clause and the Money Powers allowed for the building of a strong United States out of a weak confederation.

Further Instruction

Editable Presentation Use the Editable Presentation to present the main ideas for this Core Reading.

The Commerce Power, The Money Powers: Core Reading and Interactive Reading Notepad Project and discuss the Interactive Reading Notepad questions.

Students should know that the function of the legislative branch called the Commerce Clause is found in the list of powers in Article 1, Section 8 and explicit limits are found in Article 1, Section 9. However, in 1824 the Supreme Court case *Gibbons* v. *Ogden* provided the precedent for a broad reading of the clause. This broad reading has allowed Congress to increase competition by decreasing monopoly power. It is also the reason why businesses can't have separate but equal facilities.

Draw Conclusions Why did the Framers give Congress the power to coin money, rather than giving this power to the States? *(Possible answer: The Framers knew that while States needed to have power, they needed to be united. States with their own currencies made trade difficult during the period of the Articles of Confederation. A strong union could only happen if the money powers resided with one federal entity.)*

Make Judgments The current reading of the Commerce Clause has allowed the federal government to make laws that have a wide impact on life in the United States. Does this create a strong union or a weak union? Explain your thinking. *(Possible answer: This creates a stronger union because it allows the building of a strong economy.)*

Objective 5: List other key domestic powers exercised by Congress.

Quick Instruction

Article I, Section 8 also gives Congress explicit domestic powers. These include the power to create a process for copyright and patents, establish post offices and post roads, acquire and manage territory, fix standard weights and measures, set rules of naturalization, set up federal courts below the Supreme Court, and define federal crimes and appropriate punishments.

Interactive Gallery: A Case Study on Copyrights and Patents Project and step through the gallery with students. Explain that throughout history U.S. constitutional protections, such as patents, have fostered competition and entrepreneurship in the American economy. Point out that this interactive focuses on one example of this power: Elias Howe's sewing machine.

ACTIVE CLASSROOM

Using a Headline strategy, have students create headlines about the importance of congressional power over copyright and patent. Headlines should explain the key elements of the congressional power, what powers are explicitly and implicitly found in the Constitution, how this power helps strengthen the Union, and how the power is useful today. Have students present their headlines and choose the best ones to create a series of class blogposts about this power.

The Expressed Powers

INTERACTIVE GALLERY

A Case Study on Copyrights and Patents

DIGITAL TEXT 5

Congress and Foreign Policy

D Differentiate: **Extra Support** Ask: What is an explicit power? *(power defined in the Constitution)* What is an implied power? *(power not in the Constitution, but given other authority can logically be determined to belong to Congress)*

ELL Use the ELL activity described in the ELL chart.

Further Instruction

Editable Presentation Use the Editable Presentation to present the main ideas for this Core Reading.

Other Domestic Powers: Core Reading and Interactive Reading Notepad Project and discuss the Interactive Reading Notepad questions.

Explain that the reason for oversight of the process for copyright and patents is to foster competition and entrepreneurship. Patents give a person the sole right to manufacture, use, or sell a new and useful idea. Recently, pharmaceuticals and technology companies have protected their important ideas with patents. These companies gain competitive advantage through their patents. Giving people and companies a way to protect and make money from their ideas provides monetary incentives to pursue ideas and make important scientific discoveries that they might not otherwise pursue.

Analyze Why does the patent process give companies a competitive advantage? *(It allows protection for ideas and allows only the company holding the patent to manufacture, use, or make money on the idea.)*

Identify Central Ideas Which domestic power given to Congress is used to explain why the government can annex land to build a football stadium? *(power to acquire and manage territory)*

Compare Which explicit power gives Congress the power to declare that cookies cannot be sent through the mail? *(postal powers)* Which implicit power would set the punishment for that crime? *(Possible answer: postal powers or judicial powers)*

Objectives 3: **Identify the key sources of the foreign relations powers of Congress; 4:** **Describe the power-sharing arrangement between Congress and the President on the issues of war and national defense.**

Quick Instruction

The Constitution gives the President primary responsibility for the conduct of American foreign policy. However, Congress affects foreign policy through expressed powers, and because the United States is a sovereign state in the world community. As the lawmaking body of the sovereign United States, Congress has the inherent power to act on matters affecting the security of the nation.

Congressional War Powers Only Congress can declare war, raise and support armies, provide and maintain a navy, and make rules for the governing of the nation's military forces. Congress can call out the National Guard, and organize, arm, and discipline that force. Congress can also grant letters of marque and reprisal, and make rules concerning captures on land and water.

Further Instruction

Editable Presentation Use the Editable Presentation to present the main ideas for this Core Reading.

SYNTHESIZE

DEMONSTRATE

DIGITAL TEXT 6

The War Powers

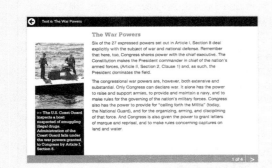

DIGITAL SYNTHESIZE ACTIVITY

Rank the Expressed Powers

DIGITAL QUIZ

Lesson Quiz and Discussion Board

Congress and Foreign Policy: Core Reading and Interactive Reading Notepad Project and discuss the Interactive Reading Notepad questions. Point out to students that these powers are checked and balanced by the executive branch. Congress does not have sole foreign authority. As the Supreme Court explained in *United States* v. *Curtiss-Wright Export Corp,* in 1936, the chief executive, or President, is "the sole organ of the Federal Government in the field of international relations."

Explain Why does the question of constitutionality of the War Powers Resolution have to wait until there is a dispute between Congress and the President over the statute? *(Possible answer: The Supreme Court weighs in on conflicts between branches, but only after one branch sues another.)*

Draw Conclusions Besides the explicit war power, where else does Congress derive its power over elements of foreign policy? *(It is part of the inherent power to act in the interest of national security as the lawmaking body of the sovereign United States.)*

Identify Central Ideas What powers does the Congress have regarding the military? How are those in conflict with the President's powers? *(Possible answer: The President commands the military, but needs approval from Congress to establish and pay for a military.)*

Ask students to recall the Topic Essential Question, "How should the government meet the needs of its people?" Have them use a Ranking Strategy to analyze each of the ten expressed powers. Have partners discuss their rankings and share their answers with the class. Determine a class ranking for the importance of each power.

Discuss Ask students to think about the question they discussed at the beginning of this Topic. Ask if they would change their responses now that they have learned more about the expressed powers of Congress.

Assign the online Lesson Quiz for this lesson if you haven't already done so. Students will be offered automatic remediation or enrichment based on their score.

In "The Expressed Powers," you read about the powers that were enumerated in the Constitution for Congress. Pose these questions to the class on the Discussion Board:

Evaluate Evidence Most of the congressional powers explicitly stated in Article I, Section 8 have at their heart the creation of a strong national economy. Do you agree or disagree with the statement? Explain your thinking.

Make Inferences Why are there only a few expressed powers?

Cause and Effect How have patents fostered competition and entrepreneurship?

Topic Inquiry

Have students continue their investigations for the Topic Inquiry.

The Implied and Nonlegislative Powers

Supporting English Language Learners

Use with the Lesson 4 readings.

Listening

Depending on the language levels of your students, choose words from the text related to the functions of the legislative branch that students have difficulty reading or pronouncing. Model correct pronunciation of the words. Encourage students to repeat, and accept their attempts without explicitly correcting their pronunciation.

Beginning Display the words. Read the words, emphasizing the letter sounds. Explain the meaning of the words. Provide visuals as support, if possible. Have students repeat and copy the words.

Intermediate Display phrases from the text and explain their meanings, using visuals as support. Read each phrase one at a time. As you read each phrase have students repeat and copy the phrase.

Advanced Display sentences from the text. Read each sentence and have students repeat. Have students read each sentence to each other.

Advanced High Display a short paragraph from the text. Read the paragraph aloud. Have the students read the paragraph to a partner. Have them identify words they need to practice.

Use with Digital Text 5, **Impeachment.**

Reading

Provide a graphic organizer for the main idea and supporting details. Have students read the sections on impeachment, Andrew Johnson, Bill Clinton and Richard Nixon. Guide them to fill in the graphic organizer and give a summary.

Beginning Read aloud one section. Reread the section to the class and complete the graphic organizer. After reading, guide the class to summarize the section using the graphic organizer as support, using the sentence frame: *President _____ was impeached because _____.*

Intermediate Read aloud one section. Have partners reread one section and complete the graphic organizer. Have them orally summarize the section using the graphic organizer as a guide.

Advanced Have partners read all four sections. Guide partners to complete the graphic organizer for one of the sections. Have them share an oral summary with another set of partners.

Advanced High Have students independently read all four sections and complete the graphic organizer for one of the sections. Have students share an oral summary with another student.

▯ Differentiate Instruction

Use the Differentiated Instruction notes throughout the lesson plan to support the varied skill sets, levels of readiness, and interests in the mixed-ability classroom.

Challenge These notes include suggestions for expanding the activity for advanced students.

On-Level These notes include suggestions for modifying the activity to address different interests or learning styles.

Extra Support These notes include ideas for providing more scaffolding or reading spuport.

Special Needs These notes provide ideas for adapting instruction to support the needs of various special needs students.

▮ NOTES

Objectives

Objective 1: Explain how the Necessary and Proper Clause gives Congress flexibility in lawmaking.

Objective 2: Compare the strict construction and liberal construction positions on the scope of congressional power.

Objective 3: Describe the ways in which the implied powers have been applied.

Objective 4: Describe the investigatory powers of Congress.

Objective 5: Identify the executive powers of Congress.

Objective 6: Describe the power of Congress to impeach, and summarize presidential impeachment cases.

Objective 7: Describe the role of Congress in amending the Constitution and its electoral duties.

LESSON 4 ORGANIZER		PACING: APPROX. 1 PERIOD, .5 BLOCKS			
				RESOURCES	
		OBJECTIVES	PACING	Online	Print
Connect					
DIGITAL START UP ACTIVITY **Congress and Changes in Society and Technology**			10 min.	●	
Investigate					
DIGITAL TEXT 1 **The Necessary and Proper Clause**		Objectives 1, 2	10 min.	●	●
DIGITAL TEXT 2 **The Doctrine in Practice**		Objective 3	10 min.	●	●
INTERACTIVE TIMELINE **The Necessary and Proper Clause in Education**				●	
DIGITAL TEXT 3 **The Power to Investigate**		Objective 4	10 min.	●	●
INTERACTIVE GALLERY **The Implied Power of Congressional Investigation**			10 min.	●	
DIGITAL TEXT 4 **Executive Powers**		Objective 5	10 min.	●	●
DIGITAL TEXT 5 **Impeachment**		Objective 6	10 min.	●	●
DIGITAL TEXT 6 **Other Powers**		Objective 7	10 min.	●	●
Synthesize					
DIGITAL SYNTHESIZE ACTIVITY **Strict vs. Liberal Constructionists**			10 min.	●	
Demonstrate					
DIGITAL QUIZ **Lesson Quiz and Discussion Board**			10 min.	●	

The Implied and Nonlegislative Powers

CONNECT

DIGITAL START UP ACTIVITY

Congress and Changes in Society and Technology

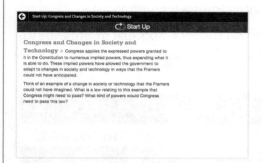

Project the Start Up Activity Ask students to read the statement and answer the questions as they enter and get settled. Then have them share their ideas with another student, either in class or through a chat or blog space.

Discuss Name the expressed powers. Discuss student ideas about what happens if Congress wants or needs a power not expressed in the Constitution.

Tell students that in this lesson they will be learning about the Implied Powers.

Aa Vocabulary Development: Use the Interactive Reading Notepad to preview the Key Terms and Academic Vocabulary in this Lesson with students.

⇅ FLIP IT!

Assign the Flipped Video for this lesson.

STUDENT EDITION PRINT PAGES: 159–169

INVESTIGATE

DIGITAL TEXT 1

The Necessary and Proper Clause

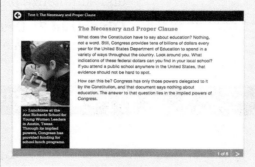

Objectives 1: Explain how the Necessary and Proper Clause gives Congress flexibility in lawmaking; 2: Compare the strict construction and liberal construction positions on the scope of congressional power.

Quick Instruction

Implied powers are drawn from the powers explicitly found in the Constitution. The Necessary and Proper Clause, the final clause in Article I, Section 8, gives Congress the expressed power "To make all Laws which shall be necessary and proper for carrying into Execution the foregoing Powers, and all other Powers vested by this Constitution in the Government of the United States, or in any Department or Officer thereof."

Strict vs Liberal Construction Strict constructionists, led by Thomas Jefferson, worried that giving more power to Congress meant taking that power from the States. Liberal constructionists, led by Alexander Hamilton, wanted Congress to have broad power, so that the new nation could be more flexible.

ELL Use the ELL activity described in the ELL chart.

Further Instruction

Editable Presentation Use the Editable Presentation to present the main ideas for this Core Reading.

The Necessary and Proper Clause: Core Reading and Interactive Reading Notepad Project and discuss the Interactive Reading Notepad questions.

Point out that the more liberal construction, as championed by Alexander Hamilton, is the one that prevailed.

Support for Growth in National Power Several factors, working together with the liberal construction of the Constitution, have been responsible for marked growth in national power. They have included wars, economic crises, and other national emergencies. Advances, especially in transportation and communication, have also had a real impact on the size and the scope of government. Equally important have been the demands of the people for more and more services from government. Congress, the President, and the Supreme Court have all looked favorably on increasing the power of the National Government.

Compare What is an example of an increase in national power that is beneficial to citizens? What is an example of an increase that might not be beneficial? *(Possible answers: Beneficial: Congress supplies money for education. Not Beneficial: Congress requires that all citizens have a national identification card.)*

Make Inferences How do you think Alexander Hamilton would view the increase in national power under the Necessary and Proper Clause? *(Possible answer: He would likely be surprised because it had gone much farther than he intended.)*

Draw Conclusions Why might Thomas Jefferson have believed that a constitutional amendment might be necessary to allow the Louisiana Purchase? Why might the Senate have approved the purchase without such an amendment? *(Possible answer: Jefferson believed he was authorized to use only those powers explicitly enumerated in the Constitution. The Senate, however, believed it had the power to increase the nation through the Necessary and Proper Clause and the territory power.)*

DIGITAL TEXT 2

The Doctrine in Practice

INTERACTIVE TIMELINE

The Necessary and Proper Clause in Education

Objective 3: Describe the ways in which the implied powers have been applied.

Quick Instruction

Every exercise of implied powers must be based on at least one of the expressed powers. Congress has most often found a basis for the exercise of implied powers in the commerce power, its power to tax and spend, or the war powers.

Interactive Timeline: The Necessary and Proper Clause in Education Project and step through the timeline with students. Explain how each use of the Necessary and Proper Clause shown on the timeline has improved education in the United States.

👥 ACTIVE CLASSROOM

Several of the Framers wanted a national education policy because of the special duties and responsibilities citizens in a democracy have. Using a Ranking strategy, have students rate how important each change was to the welfare of the democratic nation. Then have students write a paragraph explaining one of their rankings. They should explain why they think the Framers felt education might have been important to understanding the responsibilities a citizen has in a democracy.

D Differentiate: Extra Support Discuss explicit and implicit powers and have students define each one. Ask: Why does education policy fall under implicit powers? *(Power over education is not an explicit power in the Constitution.)* Discuss why Congress might have decided to pay for or implement a national education policy. Students should understand that the welfare of the nation is linked to its ability to educate its citizens.

ELL Use the ELL activity described in the ELL chart.

Further Instruction

Editable Presentation Use the Editable Presentation to present the main ideas for this Core Reading.

The Doctrine in Practice: Core Reading and Interactive Reading Notepad Project and discuss the Interactive Reading Notepad questions.

Students should know that *Gibbons* v. *Ogden* expands the Commerce Clause using the language in the Necessary and Proper Clause. The reliance on this clause has expanded the function of Congress to provide consumer protections, regulate air travel, and determine the minimum wage. The Supreme Court has found that the legislative branch cannot simply pass a law because it will promote "the general Welfare of the United States." It has, however, found that powers not found in the Commerce Clause can be found in the other explicit powers. For example, Social Security and Medicare can be provided because Congress can levy taxes and provide for the spending of tax dollars.

Explain Why does an increase in the interpretation of the Necessary and Proper Clause mean that there are fewer constitutional amendments? *(Congress uses the interpretation to meet the changing needs of the country in a quicker way than creating and passing amendments.)*

Make Inferences If Congress were to appropriate and distribute money for a new wireless system for the country, why would they derive their power from the Necessary and Proper Clause? *(It isn't explicitly in the Constitution to build wireless networks.)*

Draw Conclusions What is the check on the authority of the Congress under the Necessary and Proper Clause? *(Any power it asserts under the clause must be linked to an explicit power.)*

The Implied and Nonlegislative Powers

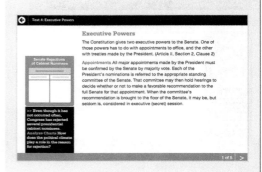

DIGITAL TEXT 3

The Power to Investigate

INTERACTIVE GALLERY

The Implied Power of Congressional Investigation

DIGITAL TEXT 4

Executive Powers

Objective 4: Describe the investigatory powers of Congress.

Quick Instruction

Congress has the implied power to investigate any matter that falls within the scope of its lawmaking authority based upon Article I, Section 1. Both the House and Senate exercise that power through the standing committees and their subcommittees and often through special committees, as well. Both houses may choose to conduct investigations for any one or a number of reasons. Inquiries are held to gather information necessary to the framing of legislation, oversee the operations of various agencies in the executive branch, focus public attention on some particular matter, expose the questionable activities of some public official or private person or group, and/or promote the particular interests of some members of Congress.

Interactive Gallery: The Implied Power of Congressional Investigation Project and step through the gallery with students. Guide students to compare the different results of the Congressional power of investigation. Ask, Have the outcomes all been positive?

📖 ACTIVE CLASSROOM

Using a Wallpaper strategy, have students explain what the investigations in the gallery learned. Explain elements of each investigation, including why congressional oversight was necessary in each case. Students should include questions they would have asked if they were on the congressional panel.

ELL Use the ELL activity described in the ELL chart.

Further Instruction

Editable Presentation Use the Editable Presentation to present the main ideas for this Core Reading.

The Power to Investigate: Core Reading and Interactive Reading Notepad Project and discuss the Interactive Reading Notepad questions.

Oversight Agencies The Congressional Budget Office explains issues around taxing, spending, and other budget-related matters. The Congressional Research Service, in the Library of Congress, provides members with factual information on virtually any subject. The Government Accountability Office has broad authority to monitor the work of the Federal Government and report its findings to Congress.

Cause and Effect Why are oversight agencies so important to congressional investigation? *(They allow Congress to get information quickly and from trusted sources.)*

Make Judgments Which is the most important reason for Congress' power to investigate? Explain your answer. *(Exposing questionable activities is the most important reason because corruption in the government is something that affects the nation and should always be dealt with immediately.)*

Objective 5: Identify the executive powers of Congress.

Quick Instruction

Two executive powers rest in the Senate. All major appointments made by the President must be confirmed by the Senate by majority vote. The Senate gives advice and consent to treaties negotiated by the President.

ELL Use the ELL activity described in the ELL chart.

Further Instruction

Editable Presentation Use the Editable Presentation to present the main ideas for this Core Reading.

Executive Powers: Core Reading and Interactive Reading Notepad Project and discuss the Interactive Reading Notepad questions. Students should know that the Senate has rejected both treaties and appointments. They should also know that the Senate does not negotiate treaties, but offers only its consent. However, it can accept or reject a treaty as it stands, or offer amendments, reservations, or understandings that would apply to it.

Make Connections The Constitution provides treaty powers only to the Senate. What is one way that the House of Representatives can be involved in treaties? *(The House controls the power of the purse.)*

DIGITAL TEXT 5

Impeachment

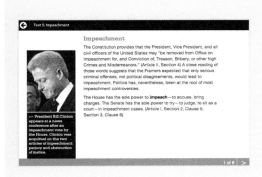

DIGITAL TEXT 6

Other Powers

Objective 6: Describe the power of Congress to impeach, and summarize presidential impeachment cases.

Quick Instruction

The Constitution provides that the President, Vice President, and all civil officers of the United States may "be removed from Office on Impeachment for, and Conviction of, Treason, Bribery, or other high Crimes and Misdemeanors." (Article II, Section 4) The House has the sole power to impeach, or to accuse or bring charges. The Senate has the sole power in impeachment cases to try, or to judge, to sit as a court. (Article I, Section 2, Clause 5; Section 3, Clause 6)

Two Presidents, Andrew Johnson and Bill Clinton, have been impeached by the House. Andrew Johnson was impeached for violation of the Tenure of Office Act. Bill Clinton was impeached for perjury and obstruction of justice regarding an "inappropriate relationship" with an intern. The Senate, in both instances, voted for acquittal. Richard Nixon resigned before he could be impeached by the House.

ELL Use the ELL activity described in the ELL chart.

Further Instruction

Editable Presentation Use the Editable Presentation to present the main ideas for this Core Reading.

Impeachment: Core Reading and Interactive Reading Notepad Project and discuss the Interactive Reading Notepad questions.

Impeachment Rules and Results Impeachment requires only a majority vote in the House; conviction requires a two-thirds vote in the Senate. The Chief Justice presides over the Senate when a President is to be tried. The penalty for conviction is removal from office. The Senate may also prohibit a convicted person from ever holding federal office again; and he or she can be tried in the regular courts for any crime involved in the events that led to the impeachment. To date, there have been 19 impeachments and 8 convictions; all 8 persons removed by the Senate were federal judges.

Cause and Effect Why might impeachment proceedings be partisan? *(Possible answer: They require only a majority vote in the House and they are a very visible way of showing displeasure with the President.)*

Objective 7: Describe the role of Congress in amending the Constitution and its electoral duties.

Quick Instruction

Besides legislative duties, Congress has a role in amending the Constitution and also has electoral duties. Article V says that Congress may propose amendments to the Constitution by a two-thirds vote in each house. All 27 of the amendments thus far added to the document have been proposed by Congress. The Constitution gives certain electoral duties to Congress, to be exercised only in very unusual circumstances. The House may be called on to elect a President, if no one candidate receives a majority of the electoral votes for President, the House, voting by States, is to decide the issue. The Senate must choose a Vice President if no candidate wins a majority of the electoral votes for that office. In that situation, the vote is by individual senators, with a majority of the full Senate necessary for election.

ELL Use the ELL activity described in the ELL chart.

Further Instruction

Editable Presentation Use the Editable Presentation to present the main ideas for this Core Reading.

Other Powers: Core Reading and Interactive Reading Notepad Project and discuss the Interactive Reading Notepad questions.

The Implied and Nonlegislative Powers

SYNTHESIZE

DEMONSTRATE

DIGITAL SYNTHESIZE ACTIVITY
Strict vs. Liberal Constructionists

DIGITAL QUIZ
Lesson Quiz and Discussion Board

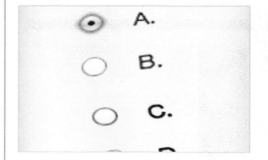

Students should know that as its electoral function was explained in the Constitution, the House has twice chosen a President: Thomas Jefferson in 1801 and John Quincy Adams in 1825. The Senate has only once chosen a Vice President: Richard M. Johnson in 1837. The 25th Amendment clarifies the functions of Congress in filling an unexpected vice presidential vacancy. The President nominates a successor and the function of Congress is to approve the nomination with a majority vote in each house. This process has been used twice: Gerald Ford in 1973 and Nelson Rockefeller in 1974.

Compare How is the vote taken by the House to elect a President similar to the way in which Presidential elections are currently run? *(Electors elect the President, voting by state.)*

Make Inferences Why might all the amendments have started in Congress instead of in the States as can also be done according to the Constitution? *(Possible answer: There are fewer people in the Congress, so it is easier to get them all to agree than to get two-thirds of all states to agree. Two-thirds of the states haven't, in recent memory chosen the same President.)*

Ask students to recall the Topic Essential Question, "How should the government meet the needs of its people?" Have them use the Think Pair Share strategy to answer the questions in the activity. Ask them to take five minutes to write down some brief answers to the questions below, then share their answers with a talking partner.

Have partners think about the following questions. What does it mean to be a strict constructionist or a liberal constructionist? Which Founder supported which construction? Have pairs share their answers with the class.

Discuss Ask students to think about what would have happened if a Supreme Court case overturned *McCulloch* v *Maryland.* What would be different about what Congress would see as its duties? What would be the same?

Assign the online Lesson Quiz for this lesson if you haven't already done so. Students will be offered automatic remediation or enrichment based on their score.

In "The Implied and Nonlegislative Powers," you read about the ways in which Congress exercises powers not explicitly in the Constitution. Pose these questions to the class on the Discussion Board:

Make Judgments Which is a better philosophy for a modern country: strict construction or liberal construction?

Explain What is the most important element of an implied power?

Topic Inquiry
Have students continue their investigations for the Topic Inquiry.

Congress at Work: Organization and Committees

Supporting English Language Learners

Use with Digital Text 1, **Congress Convenes.**

Listening
Tell students that intonation patterns are different for statements and questions. Read aloud the section "Congress Convenes." Discuss how the intonation of your voice provides information about the sentence.

Beginning Guide students to repeat after you. Have partners read the section to each other using proper intonation.

Intermediate After students repeat after you, have partners read the quote from Senator Sherrod Brown to each other.

Advanced Emphasize different words when reading aloud to the students. Discuss how this affects the meaning. Have partners read the quote from Senator Sherrod Brown while emphasizing different words.

Advanced High Have one partner read a passage emphasizing different words. Have the second partner tell how the intonation affected the meaning. Have partners switch roles.

Use with the Lesson 5 readings.

Reading
Help students demonstrate comprehension of increasingly complex English by responding to questions about the section *Congress Convenes*.

Beginning Read the text aloud. Guide students to look at the images and read the captions aloud to them. Ask questions that can be answered with a gesture, a one- or two-word response, or yes or no.

Intermediate Have students read the text aloud, helping with difficult words as needed. Emphasize the images and captions. Ask questions that can be answered with a phrase or a short sentence.

Advanced Have partners read the text. Have students answer questions in the text by helping each other locate the paragraphs where answers can be found.

Advanced High After students read independently, have partners work together to answer questions in the text.

▷ Differentiate Instruction

Use the Differentiated Instruction notes throughout the lesson plan to support the varied skill sets, levels of readiness, and interests in the mixed-ability classroom.

Challenge These notes include suggestions for expanding the activity for advanced students.

On-Level These notes include suggestions for modifying the activity to address different interests or learning styles.

Extra Support These notes include ideas for providing more scaffolding or reading spuport.

Special Needs These notes provide ideas for adapting instruction to support the needs of various special needs students.

■ NOTES

Congress at Work: Organization and Committees

Objectives

Objective 1: Describe how and when Congress convenes.

Objective 2: Compare the roles of the presiding officers in the Senate and the House.

Objective 3: Identify the duties of the party officers in each house.

Objective 4: Describe how committee chairman are chosen and explain their role in the legislative process.

Objective 5: Explain how standing committees function.

Objective 6: Describe the responsibilities and duties of the House Rules Committee.

Objective 7: Describe the role of select committees.

Objective 8: Compare the functions of joint and conference committees.

LESSON 5 ORGANIZER	OBJECTIVES	PACING	RESOURCES Online	RESOURCES Print
PACING: APPROX. 1 PERIOD, .5 blocks				
Connect				
DIGITAL START UP ACTIVITY **Working in Committees**		10 min.	●	
Investigate				
DIGITAL TEXT 1 **Congress Convenes**	Objective 1	10 min.	●	●
DIGITAL TEXT 2 **The Presiding Officers**	Objective 2	10 min.	●	●
INTERACTIVE CHART **Congressional Leadership**		10 min.	●	
DIGITAL TEXT 3 **Party Officers**	Objective 3	10 min.	●	●
INTERACTIVE MAP **State Representation in the 113th Congress**		10 min.	●	
DIGITAL TEXT 4 **Committee Chairs**	Objectives 4, 5, 6	10 min.	●	●
DIGITAL TEXT 5 **Standing Committees**		10 min.	●	●
DIGITAL TEXT 6 **Select Committees**	Objective 7	10 min.	●	●
DIGITAL TEXT 7 **Joint and Conference Committees**	Objective 8	10 min.	●	●
Synthesize				
DIGITAL SYNTHESIZE ACTIVITY **Revisiting Working in Committees**		10 min.	●	
Demonstrate				
DIGITAL QUIZ **Lesson Quiz and Discussion Board**		10 min.	●	

CONNECT

Working in Committees

Project the Start Up Activity Ask students to read the quotation and answer the questions as they enter and get settled. Then have them share their ideas with another student, either in class or through a chat or blog space.

Discuss Ask students to think about a professional sport they've watched recently. Use the following questions: How were the rules of the game enforced? If the officials did not agree on a call, what happened? How are the rules of the game decided on? Guide students to understand that committees help make rules.

Tell students that in this lesson they will be learning about the organization of Congress and its committees.

Aa Vocabulary Development: Use the Interactive Reading Notepad to preview the Key Terms and Academic Vocabulary in this Lesson with students.

⤵ FLIP IT!

Assign the Flipped Video for this lesson.

■ STUDENT EDITION PRINT
PAGES: 170–181

INVESTIGATE

Congress Convenes

Objective 1: Describe how and when Congress convenes.

Quick Instruction

Every other January, the 435 men and women who have been elected to the House come together at the Capitol to begin a new term. Because all 435 of its seats are up for election every 2 years, the House technically has no sworn members, no rules, and no organization until its opening day ceremonies are held.

The Senate is a continuous body. It has been organized without interruption since its first session in 1789. Because only one-third of the seats are up for election every two years, two-thirds of the Senate's membership is carried over from one term to the next. As a result, the Senate does not face large organizational problems at the beginning of a term. Its first-day session is nearly always fairly short and routine, even when the elections have brought a change in the majority party. Newly elected and reelected members must be sworn in, vacancies in Senate organization and on committees must be filled, and a few other details attended to.

ELL Use the ELL activity described in the ELL chart.

Further Instruction

Editable Presentation Use the Editable Presentation to present the main ideas for this Core Reading.

Congress Convenes: Core Reading and Interactive Reading Notepad Project and discuss the Interactive Reading Notepad questions. Students should know that the first order of business in the House is to elect leaders and adopt rules.

State of the Union When the Senate is notified that the House of Representatives is organized, a joint committee of the two chambers is appointed and instructed "to wait upon the President of the United States and inform him that a quorum of each House is assembled and that the Congress is ready to receive any communication he may be pleased to make." Within a few weeks the President delivers the annual State of the Union message to a joint session of Congress.

Support Conclusions with Evidence How does the fact that the Senate has been organized without interruption since 1789 support the conclusion that it is a more staid and deliberative body? *(Possible answer: Fewer new members are sworn in each term, which gives the Senate more continuity and stability than the House.)*

Congress at Work: Organization and Committees

DIGITAL TEXT 2
The Presiding Officers

INTERACTIVE CHART
Congressional Leadership

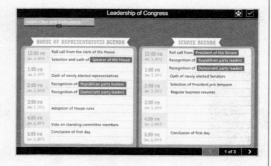

DIGITAL TEXT 3
Party Officers

Objective 2: Compare the roles of the presiding officers in the Senate and the House.

Quick Instruction

The Constitution provides for the presiding officers of each house of Congress—the Speaker of the House and the President of the Senate. Article I, Section 2, Clause 5 directs that "The House of Representatives shall choose their Speaker and other Officers. . . ." And Article I, Section 3, Clause 4 declares: "The Vice President of the United States shall be President of the Senate. . . ."

Interactive Chart: Leadership of Congress Project and step through the interactive with students. Tell students that the presiding officers and party leaders of each chamber provide leadership over other members of Congress. Have students explore the highlighted titles in the chart.

🎬 ACTIVE CLASSROOM

Have students use the information from the chart to write a persuasive email arguing that that person should run for a leadership role in Congress. Students should make assumptions about the person to whom they write, as long as they are supported by the requirements for the role. For example, if the role has an expectation of age, then the person will be assumed to have met that expectation. Students can present their emails to the class. The class can decide whether or not the person was persuasive.

D **Differentiate: Extra Support** Discuss what happens when Congress convenes. First, discuss the House of Representatives and then the Senate. For each, have students explain what happens on the convening day. Then continue with the activity.

Further Instruction

Editable Presentation Use the Editable Presentation to present the main ideas for this Core Reading.

The Presiding Officers: Core Reading and Interactive Reading Notepad Project and discuss the Interactive Reading Notepad questions.

Explain to students that the Senate President pro tempore is the longest serving member of the majority party.

Compare Presiding Officers Nearly all of the Speaker's powers revolve around two duties: to preside and to keep order. The Speaker interprets and applies the rules, refers bills to committee, rules on points of order (questions of procedure raised by members), puts motions to a vote, and decides the outcome of most votes taken on the floor of the House. The Speaker also names the members of all select and conference committees and must sign all bills and resolutions passed by the House. The president of the Senate has the usual powers of a presiding officer: to recognize members, put questions to a vote, and so on. However, the Vice President cannot take the floor to speak or debate and may vote only to break a tie.

Compare Which role is more powerful: the Speaker of the House or the Senate President? Why? *(Possible answer: The Speaker is more powerful because he or she makes rules and appoints people to committees.)*

Objective 3: Identify the duties of the party officers in each house.

Quick Instruction

The party caucus is a closed meeting of the members of each party in each house. The floor leaders are party officers, picked for their posts by their party colleagues. The floor leader of the party that holds the majority of seats in each house of Congress is known as the majority leader. The floor leader of the party that holds the minority of seats in each house is the minority leader. The two floor leaders in each house are assisted by party whips. The majority whip and the minority whip are, in effect, assistant floor leaders. Each of them is chosen at the party caucus, almost always at the floor leader's recommendation.

Interactive Map: State Representation in the 113th Congress Project and step through the map with students. Make sure students understand the map key, and which parties are represented by which color.

🎬 ACTIVE CLASSROOM

Using a Sticky Note strategy, have students make generalizations about the Congress. Some generalizations students make might revolve around regional differences in representation, comparing House and Senate parties, or the correlation between state size and population.

ELL Use the ELL activity described in the ELL chart.

INTERACTIVE MAP

State Representation in the 113th Congress

DIGITAL TEXT 4

Committee Chairs

DIGITAL TEXT 5

Standing Committees

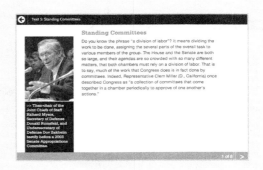

D Differentiate: **Challenge** Have students look at the difference between the House and Senate make-up across the nation and write a paragraph about whether or not the country is a liberal or conservative nation. Students should use examples and evidence from the interactive map in their paragraphs.

Further Instruction

Editable Presentation Use the Editable Presentation to present the main ideas for this Core Reading.

Party Officers: Core Reading and Interactive Reading Notepad Project and discuss the Interactive Reading Notepad questions.

Students should know that the whips assist in the functioning of Congress and are a vital part of the procedure for enacting laws. Whips act as a liaison between the leadership and the members. They count votes for a particular piece of legislation to make sure party members vote with the leadership. They also work to make sure members are present for key votes so that passing legislation will not be adversely affected.

Cause and Effect What is the role of the party whip if a member of Congress begins to vote against his or her party? *(The whip will try to convince that member to vote with the party or potentially lose his or her role in the party.)*

Objectives 4: Describe how committee chairmen are chosen and explain their role in the legislative process; 5: Explain how standing committees function; 6: Describe the responsibilities and duties of the House Rules Committee.

Quick Instruction

Summarize for students: Most bills receive their most thorough consideration in the House and Senate standing committees. Members of both houses regularly respect the decisions and follow the recommendations they make. Each committee is headed by a committee chair, who, by senority rule, is the longest serving member of Congress in the majority party. They have a major say in such matters as which bills a committee will consider and in what order and at what length, whether public hearings are to be held, and what witnesses the committee will call. When a committee's bill has been reported—approved for consideration—to the floor, the chairman usually manages the debate and tries to steer it to final passage. Standing parties can be served by subcommittees, which focus on one of the elements overseen by the standing committee.

House Rules Committee The Rules Committee exists in the House to control the flow of bills to the floor and set the conditions for their consideration there. Each bill that is voted on has been granted a rule, or scheduled for floor consideration.

ELL Use the ELL activity described in the ELL chart.

Further Instruction

Editable Presentation Use the Editable Presentation to present the main ideas for this Core Reading.

Committee Chairs and Standing Committees: Core Reading and Interactive Reading Notepad Project and discuss the Interactive Reading Notepad questions.

Students should know that when a bill is introduced in either house, the Speaker or the president of the Senate refers the measure to the appropriate standing committee. Thus, the Speaker sends all tax measures to the House Ways and Means Committee; in the Senate, tax measures go to the Finance Committee. A bill dealing with the creation of additional federal district judgeships will be sent to the Judiciary Committee in both chambers.

Explain What is the function of a committee chairman in terms of a bill's final vote? *(The chairman steers the bill towards passage and manages the floor debate.)*

Draw Conclusions Why might standing committees have subcommittees? *(Possible answer: It is impossible for the standing committees to handle all the work involved with the investigation and recommendations of bills. The subcommittees flesh out issues and concerns before bringing a bill or concern to the larger committee and then the full house.)*

Cause and Effect Why is the House Rules Committee considered to be such a powerful committee? *(It controls all the business that gets to the floor of the House, including which bills get voted on when.)*

Congress at Work: Organization and Committees

DIGITAL TEXT 6
Select Committees

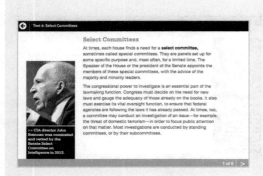

DIGITAL TEXT 7
Joint and Conference Committees

Objective 7: Describe the role of select committees.

Quick Instruction

At times, each house finds a need for a select committee, sometimes called special committees. They are panels set up for some specific purpose and, most often, for a limited time. The Speaker of the House or the President of the Senate appoints the members of these special committees, with the advice of the majority and minority leaders. Select committees are sometimes formed to investigate a current issue, as the Senate's Select Committee on Indian Affairs recently did. Other Select Committees have investigated the Watergate Scandal and the Iran-Contra Affair.

> **ELL** Use the ELL activity described in the ELL chart.

Further Instruction

Editable Presentation Use the Editable Presentation to present the main ideas for this Core Reading.

Select Committees: Core Reading and Interactive Reading Notepad Project and discuss the Interactive Reading Notepad questions.

Committees serve a vital role in the legislative branch, but sometimes their role is in oversight. Select committees are one way Congress can jointly oversee an investigation. This is especially important to ascertain whether laws that have been passed are carried out appropriately by federal agencies or to focus public attention on an issue. Students should understand that investigative authority resides most often in individual standing committees and subcommittees.

Compare How are select committees different from standing committees?
(They meet for only a short amount of time and have members from both houses.)

Objective 8: Compare the functions of joint and conference committees.

Quick Instruction

A joint committee is one composed of members of both houses. Some of these are select committees set up to serve some temporary purpose. Most are permanent groups that serve on a regular basis. Some joint committees are investigative in nature and issue periodic reports to the House and Senate. Most often, those committees perform more routine duties—for example, the Joint Committee on the Library oversees the administration of the Library of Congress.

Conference Committee Before a bill may be sent to the President, each house must pass it in identical form. Sometimes, the two houses pass differing versions, and the first house will not agree to the changes the other has made. When this happens, a conference committee—a temporary, joint body—is created to produce a compromise bill that both houses will accept.

> **ELL** Use the ELL activity described in the ELL chart.

Further Instruction

Editable Presentation Use the Editable Presentation to present the main ideas for this Core Reading.

SYNTHESIZE

DEMONSTRATE

DIGITAL SYNTHESIZE ACTIVITY

Revisiting Working in Committees

DIGITAL QUIZ

Lesson Quiz and Discussion Board

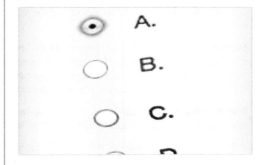

Joint and Conference Committees: Core Reading and Interactive Reading Notepad Project and discuss the Interactive Reading Notepad questions.

Point out the differences between select, joint, and conference committees. Select committees and conference committees are set up for a limited time. However, conference committees deal solely with creating legislative compromise for a particular bill so it can be passed and enacted. Joint committees, on the other hand, often last longer. Like select committees, they can investigate topics, but the topics often relate to a standing committee's particular responsibility, such as the federal tax system. Joint committees make periodic reports.

Compare How is a Joint Committee different from a Conference Committee? (*A Conference Committee is created solely to produce a compromise bill that both houses can agree on. A Joint Committee is a permanent committee that serves a specific function.*)

Analyze If standing committees in each house duplicate work, how might more joint committees reduce duplication? (*Joint committees are made up of members of both houses, so one committee would investigate issues that arose in both houses.*)

Ask students to recall the Topic Essential Question, "How should the government meet the needs of its people?" Have them use the Think Pair Share strategy to analyze and discuss the quotation. Remind students that they analyzed the Woodrow Wilson quotation at the beginning of the Topic. Ask them to take five minutes to write down some brief answers to the questions below, then share their answers with a talking partner.

Have partners think about the following questions. Why is committee work more important than floor work in Congress? What happens in committees? Have pairs share their answers with the class.

Discuss Ask students to share examples from the text that support Wilson's quotation. Compare the evidence that was found.

Assign the online Lesson Quiz for this lesson if you haven't already done so. Students will be offered automatic remediation or enrichment based on their score.

In "Congress at Work: Organization and Committees" you read about how Congress works to create laws. Pose these questions to the class on the Discussion Board:

Draw Conclusions What makes the party structure important in the legislating process?

Analyze Even though the House is seen as the more volatile part of Congress, it has rules and powers that make it very powerful. Is this a contradiction or a benefit? Why?

Explain What are the different committees that members of Congress can serve on?

Topic Inquiry

Have students continue their investigations for the Topic Inquiry.

Congress at Work–Making Law

Supporting English Language Learners

Use with the Lesson 6 readings.

Listening

Review vowels and the short and long vowel sounds with students using words from the text. Long vowels: *rules, role, labor*. Short vowels: *steps, bill, passage*. Help students recognize the vowel sounds in the following ways:

Beginning Display a list of one-syllable words from the text containing short and long vowel sounds. Say each word and have the students repeat. Have students raise a hand if they hear a long vowel and raise a fist if they hear a short vowel. Have students copy the words.

Intermediate Guide partners to find one-syllable words in the text with short and long vowel sounds. Create class lists of the words.

Advanced Display a list of two-syllable words from the text containing long and short vowel sounds. Help the students determine whether the syllables have short or long vowel sounds.

Advanced High Have students find two-syllable words in the text with short and long vowels. Have partners read their words to each other and identify the short and long vowel sounds.

Use with the Lesson 6 readings.

Reading

Read a section of the text aloud and model taking notes. Help students demonstrate comprehension of increasingly complex English through note taking.

Beginning Read another section of the text aloud. Provide a list of two short phrases related to the text and one phrase not related to the text. Ask students to choose the phrases that would make good notes.

Intermediate Read another section of the text aloud. Have students take notes on the section and share their notes with the other students in their group.

Advanced Guide partners to read sections of the text and take notes. Have them share their notes with another pair.

Advanced High Have students read sections of the text and take notes on the most important details. Have them compare notes with another student of their reading level.

▣ Differentiate Instruction

Use the Differentiated Instruction notes throughout the lesson plan to support the varied skill sets, levels of readiness, and interests in the mixed-ability classroom.

Challenge These notes include suggestions for expanding the activity for advanced students.

On-Level These notes include suggestions for modifying the activity to address different interests or learning styles.

Extra Support These notes include ideas for providing more scaffolding or reading spuport.

Special Needs These notes provide ideas for adapting instruction to support the needs of various special needs students.

■ NOTES

Objectives

Objectives 1 & 5: Identify how a bill is introduced in the House and the Senate.

Objective 2: Describe what happens to a bill once it is referred to a committee.

Objective 3: Explain how leaders schedule debate.

Objective 4: Explain what happens to a bill on the House floor, and identify the final step in the House.

Objective 6: Compare the Senate's rules for debate with those in the House.

Objective 7: Describe the role of conference committees in the legislative process.

Objective 8: Evaluate the actions the President can take after both houses have passed a bill.

LESSON 6 ORGANIZER		PACING: APPROX. 1 PERIOD, .5 BLOCKS			
				RESOURCES	
		OBJECTIVES	**PACING**	**Online**	**Print**
Connect					
DIGITAL START UP ACTIVITY **There Ought to be a Law**			10 min.	●	
Investigate					
DIGITAL TEXT 1 **The First Steps**		Objective 1	10 min.	●	●
INTERACTIVE CHART **Forms of Legislation**			10 min.	●	
DIGITAL TEXT 2 **The Bill in Committee**		Objective 2	10 min.	●	●
DIGITAL TEXT 3 **Scheduling Floor Debate**		Objective 3	10 min.	●	●
DIGITAL TEXT 4 **The Bill on the House Floor**			10 min.	●	●
DIGITAL TEXT 5 **The Bill on the Senate Floor**		Objectives 4, 5, 6	10 min.	●	●
INTERACTIVE CHART **Making Law—The Process**			10 min.	●	
DIGITAL TEXT 6 **House-Senate Conference Committees**		Objective 7	10 min.	●	●
DIGITAL TEXT 7 **The President Acts on a Bill**		Objective 8	10 min.	●	●
DIGITAL TEXT 8 **Unorthodox and Emergency Law Making**		Objectives 2, 7	10 min.	●	●
Synthesize					
DIGITAL SYNTHESIZE ACTIVITY **Turning an Idea into Law**			10 min.	●	
Demonstrate					
DIGITAL QUIZ **Lesson Quiz and Discussion Board**			10 min.	●	

Congress at Work–Making Law

■ CONNECT

DIGITAL START UP ACTIVITY
There Ought to Be a Law

Project the Start Up Activity Ask students to read the text as they enter and get settled. Then have them share their ideas with another student, either in class or through a chat or blog space.

Discuss What new laws do you think are needed in the country today? Why? What do you know about how lawmakers go about getting laws enacted?

Tell students that in this lesson they will be learning about how Congress makes laws.

Aa Vocabulary Development: Use the Interactive Reading Notepad to preview the Key Terms and Academic Vocabulary in this Lesson with students.

⇅ FLIP IT!

Assign the Flipped Video for this lesson.

■ STUDENT EDITION PRINT
PAGES: 182–194

■ INVESTIGATE

DIGITAL TEXT 1
The First Steps

INTERACTIVE CHART
Forms of Legislation

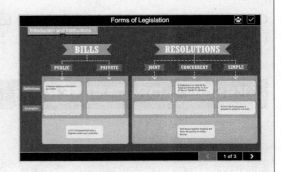

Objective 1:   Identify how a bill is introduced in the House and the Senate.

Quick Instruction

Only members can introduce bills in the House, and they do so by dropping them into the hopper, a box hanging on the edge of the clerk's desk. Often, before a member introduces a bill, he or she will circulate a letter informing other members about the measure and why its sponsor thinks it should become law. The clerk of the House numbers each bill as it is introduced and gives each bill a short title—a brief summary of its principal contents. Then the bill is entered in the House Journal and in the Congressional Record for the day. All bills are printed immediately after introduction and distributed to all members of the House.

Interactive Chart: Forms of Legislation Project and step through the chart with students. Explain that students will need to drag the tiles showing definitions and examples of legislation to match the corresponding type of legislation.

📹 ACTIVE CLASSROOM

Using a Sticky Note strategy, have students summarize the different forms of legislation. Then have students work in pairs to compare and contrast the different forms.

D Differentiate: Challenge Have students work together to think of new examples for each type of legislation. Have them create a game that tests their classmates' understanding of the types of legislation.

ELL Use the ELL activity described in the ELL chart.

Further Instruction

Editable Presentation Use the Editable Presentation to present the main ideas for this Core Reading.

The First Steps: Core Reading and Interactive Reading Notepad Project and discuss the Interactive Reading Notepad questions.

The Constitution calls out a particular legislative function for the House of Representatives. Article I, Section 7, Clause 1 explains "bills for raising Revenue shall originate in the House." Tax bills arise in the House, but both houses can write bills for spending tax dollars. Earmarks were often tacked onto appropriations measures. House Republican leaders passed a rule banning earmarks in 2011. It was renewed in 2013.

Identify Central Ideas What kind of bills must start in the House and then go to the Senate? (*tax bills*)

DIGITAL TEXT 2

The Bill in Committee

The Bill in Committee

The Constitution makes no mention of standing committees. These bodies do play an absolutely essential role in the lawmaking process, however—and in both houses of Congress. Indeed, their place is so pivotal that they are sometimes called "little legislatures."

The standing committees act as sieves. They sift through all of the many bills referred to them—rejecting most, considering and reporting only those they find to be worthy of floor consideration. In short, the fate of most bills is decided in these committees rather than on the floor of either house.

Most of the thousands of bills introduced in each session of Congress are **pigeonholed**. That is, they are buried; they die in committee. They are simply put away, never to be acted upon. The term comes from the old-fashioned rolltop desks with pigeonholes—slots into which papers were put and often soon forgotten. Most "by request" bills are routinely pigeonholed; they are the measures that members introduce but only because some constituent or some interest group has asked them to do so.

>> The term "pigeonholed" originally referred to the practice of shelving items in the pigeonholes of a desk.

DIGITAL TEXT 3

Scheduling Floor Debate

Scheduling Floor Debate

Before it goes to the floor for consideration, a bill reported by a standing committee is placed on one of several calendars in the House. A calendar is a schedule of the order in which bills will be taken up on the floor.

The Purpose of Five Calendars There are five calendars in the lower house. The *Calendar of the Committee of the Whole House on the State of the Union*, commonly known as the *Union Calendar*, is for all bills having to do with revenues, appropriations, or government property. The *House Calendar* is for all other public bills. The *Private Calendar* is for all private bills. The *Corrections Calendar* is for all bills from the Union or House Calendar taken out of order by unanimous consent of the House of Representatives. These are most often minor bills to which there is no opposition. The *Discharge Calendar* is for petitions to discharge bills from committee.

>> The House Appropriations Committee calendar for the 105th Congress as it hung on the wall in the Appropriations Committee office, ready to be filled in with scheduled meetings.

Objective 2: Describe what happens to a bill once it is referred to a committee.

Quick Instruction

Once a bill is referred to a committee, the chairman refers it to a subcommittee for review. After work on the bill is completed by the subcommittee, it goes to the full committee. The committee can then report the bill favorably, refuse to report the bill, report the bill in amended form, report the bill with an unfavorable recommendation, or report a committee bill.

ELL Use the ELL activity described in the ELL chart.

Further Instruction

Editable Presentation Use the Editable Presentation to present the main ideas for this Core Reading.

The Bill in Committee: Core Reading and Interactive Reading Notepad Project and discuss the Interactive Reading Notepad questions.

The subcommittee or committee may hold hearings on bills or visit areas affected by the bill. The minority party, or a group of members who disagree with the majority of house, can use a discharge petition to force the House to vote on a bill. This function of enacting law requires that the discharge be signed by a majority of members. This attempts to force the committee to report the bill. If the committee does not report it, a member who signed the petition can offer a motion to send the bill to the floor. If carried, rules require the House to vote on the bill. However, these motions are rarely tried.

Make Inferences Why are committees called "little legislatures"? *(Their actions are similar to the actions of the Congress, but on a smaller scale.)*

Predict Consequences What features does a successful bill need to have to allow it to leave the committee and not be pigeon-holed? *(Possible answer: It is supported by a majority of members and Americans.)*

Objective 3: Explain how leaders schedule debate.

Quick Instruction

House Rules Before it goes to the floor for consideration, a bill reported by a standing committee is placed on one of several calendars in the House. A calendar is a schedule of the order in which bills will be taken up on the floor. The House Rules Committee must also grant a rule for the bill.

Further Instruction

Editable Presentation Use the Editable Presentation to present the main ideas for this Core Reading.

Scheduling Floor Debate: Core Reading and Interactive Reading Notepad Project and discuss the Interactive Reading Notepad questions.

Students should know that the Rules Committee can effectively kill a bill. It can also grant a special rule, which sets a time limit on floor debate or prohibit amendments to certain, or even to any, of the bill's provisions. Then, too, certain bills are privileged. That is, they may be called up at almost any time, ahead of any other business before the House. The most privileged measures include major appropriations *(spending)* and general revenue *(tax)* bills, conference committee reports, and special rules granted by the Rules Committee.

Draw Conclusions The House uses five calendars to determine house business. Why are there so many calendars and rules about when to hear and vote on bills? *(It is a way to funnel business similar to sending and voting a bill out of committee.)*

Congress at Work–Making Law

DIGITAL TEXT 4

The Bill on the House Floor

DIGITAL TEXT 5

The Bill on the Senate Floor

INTERACTIVE CHART

Making Law—The Process in the House and Senate

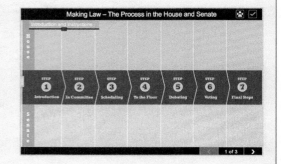

Objectives 4: Explain what happens to a bill on the House floor, and identify the final step in the House; 5: Identify how a bill is introduced in the House and the Senate; 6: Compare the Senate's rules for debate with those in the House.

Quick Instruction

House Rules Bills are read three times in the House. Rules impose limits on debate. Members can vote via voice vote, standing vote, teller vote, or roll call vote. After the second reading, the bill is engrossed. After the third reading and approval, an aide delivers the bill to the Senate.

Senate Rules The Senate allows free debate, with a few exceptions. Senators can only make two speeches in the same legislative day. They can also filibuster a bill to force a change to the bill being presented. Debate can be limited via cloture.

Interactive Chart: Making Law—The Process in the House and Senate Project and step through the slider with students. Introduce the activity by explaining that students will use the slider to compare and contrast the steps a bill goes through in both the House and Senate.

📷 ACTIVE CLASSROOM

Using a Write 1 Get 3 strategy, have students answer the following question: Compare and contrast how a bill goes through the House and Senate.

D Differentiate: Extra Support Use a specific example, such as a budget bill, to step through the process in each chamber. Then continue with the activity.

ELL Use the ELL activity described in the ELL chart.

Further Instruction

Editable Presentation Use the Editable Presentation to present the main ideas for this Core Reading.

The Bill on the Floors: Core Reading and Interactive Reading Notepad Project and discuss the Interactive Reading Notepad questions.

Students should understand that the chief differences in House and Senate procedures involve the consideration of measures on the floor. With introduction by a senator formally recognized for the purpose, a measure is given a number, read twice, and then referred to a standing committee, where it is dealt with much as are bills in the House. The Senate's proceedings are less formal and its rules less strict than those in the much larger lower house.

Draw Conclusions Why are there so many more procedures and rules for bill passage in the House than the Senate? *(The Senate has fewer members than the House.)*

DIGITAL TEXT 6

House-Senate Conference Committees

Objective 7: Describe the role of conference committees in the legislative process.

Quick Instruction

When the House and Senate pass different versions of the same bill, the first house usually concurs in the other's amendments, and congressional action is completed. When one house will not accept the other's version of a bill, the measure is sent to a conference committee—a temporary joint committee of the two chambers. It seeks to produce a compromise bill acceptable to both houses. Conferees—managers—are named by the respective presiding officers. Mostly, they are leading members of the standing committee that first handled the measure. Once the conferees agree, their report, the compromise bill, is submitted to both houses. It must be accepted or rejected without amendment.

ELL Use the ELL activity described in the ELL chart.

Further Instruction

Editable Presentation Use the Editable Presentation to present the main ideas for this Core Reading.

House-Senate Conference Committees: Core Reading and Interactive Reading Notepad Project and discuss the Interactive Reading Notepad questions.

Students should know that legislative bills must be passed in identical form. Further conference committees can only consider parts of the bill on which the two houses have a disagreement. Having leading members of each standing committee that introduced legislation allows for the conference committee to function and enact laws.

Analyze Why is the description "the third house of Congress" apt? *(Possible answer: The bill passed out of conference must be passed by both committees without amendment and only rarely does either house reject these bills.)*

Explain Why are bills reported out of conference rarely rejected? *(Possible answer: The members of the conference committee are often influential.)*

DIGITAL TEXT 7

The President Acts on a Bill

Objective 8: Evaluate the actions the President can take after both houses have passed a bill.

Quick Instruction

The Constitution requires that bills and resolutions be sent to the President after they have passed both houses of Congress. The President may sign the bill, and it then becomes law. The President may veto the bill. The President may allow the bill to become law without signing it—by not acting on it within 10 days, not counting Sundays, of receiving it. The fourth option is a variation of the third, called the pocket veto.

Further Instruction

Editable Presentation Use the Editable Presentation to present the main ideas for this Core Reading.

The President Acts on a Bill: Core Reading and Interactive Reading Notepad Project and discuss the Interactive Reading Notepad questions.

Students should know that the legislative branch can enact laws after a presidential veto, by a two-thirds vote of the full membership in each house. This represents an important balance to the President's power to enact law and a check on any President who wants to enact his or her own agenda without the legislative branch.

Evaluate Which result would a President use if he or she did not want to be have a signing ceremony, but did want the law to pass? *(allow the bill to become law without signing it, by not acting on it within ten days)*

Congress at Work–Making Law

DIGITAL TEXT 8
Unorthodox Law Making and Emergency Legislations

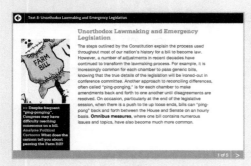

Objective 2: Describe what happens to a bill in committee;
Objective 7: Describe the role of conference committees

Quick Instruction
A number of adjustments in recent decades have continued to transform the lawmaking process. For example, it is increasingly common for each chamber to pass generic bills, knowing that the true details of the legislation will be ironed-out in conference committee. At other times each chamber makes amendments back and forth to one another until disagreements are resolved. Omnibus measures, where one bill contains numerous issues and topics, have also become much more common.

Emergencies arise during which the legislature is called upon to act quickly and to condense the process into a few days. With such events, Congress does not have the luxury to follow every step strictly by the book.

ELL Use the ELL activity described in the ELL chart.

Further Instruction
Editable Presentation Use the Editable Presentation to present the main ideas for this Core Reading.

Unorthodox Law Making and Emergency Legislations: Core Reading and Interactive Reading Notepad Project and discuss the Interactive Reading Notepad questions.

Point out the photograph of President George W. Bush signing the Patriot Act. Tell students that a Senate bill was passed by a vote of 96–1 on October 11, 2001, and the House passed its own version on October 12. On October 23, the House introduced a compromise bill which was passed the following day. The Senate adopted the House bill by an overwhelming majority and without amendment on October 25, and the following day President Bush signed the measure into law.

Apply Concepts Hold a class discussion about what other sorts of emergencies might result in a bill being pushed quickly through Congress. *(Possible answer: An economic emergency, such as occurred in 2008.)*

Predict Consequences In an attempt to slow the spending of federal money, the majority party in Congress has voted down a bill to appropriate money for a disaster in Oklahoma. What legislative actions do you think might happen as a result? *(Possible answer: House members from Oklahoma might refuse to vote in favor of appropriating money for federal disasters in other areas.)*

■ SYNTHESIZE

DIGITAL SYNTHESIZE ACTIVITY
Turning an Idea into Law

Ask students to recall the Topic Essential Question, "How should the government meet the needs of its people?" Ask them to take five minutes to write down some brief answers to the questions below, then share their answers with a talking partner.

Have partners think about the following question: How does a bill become law? Have pairs share their answers with the class.

Discuss Ask students to think about the law they wanted to enact at the beginning of the Topic. Have students discuss the reasons they thought the step would be the most difficult. Share ideas about how to get the bill through the difficult steps.

■ DEMONSTRATE

DIGITAL QUIZ
Lesson Quiz and Discussion Board

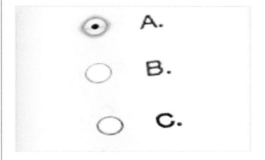

Assign the online Lesson Quiz for this lesson if you haven't already done so. Students will be offered automatic remediation or enrichment based on their score.

In "Congress at Work–Making Law" you read about how laws are made, passed, and enacted. Pose these questions to the class on the Discussion Board:

Explain Which elements of law-making show the importance the Founders placed on checks and balances?

Compare How do the Senate and House of Representatives differ in bringing bills to the floor to be voted on?

Analyze How does the committee structure support enacting laws even after the two houses have voted on a bill?

Topic Inquiry
Have students continue their investigations for the Topic Inquiry.

The Legislative Branch

▮ SYNTHESIZE

DIGITAL ACTIVITY

Representatives' Approaches to Voting

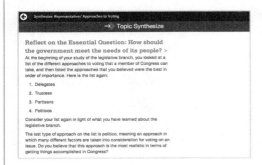

First ask students to reconsider the Essential Question for the Topic: How should the government meet the needs of its people? Remind students of the different approaches to voting that a member of Congress can take that they saw at the start of the Topic. For example,

- delegates
- trustees
- partisans
- politicos

Ask students: The last type of approach on the list is politico, meaning an approach in which many different factors are taken into consideration for voting on an issue. Do you believe that this approach is the most realistic in terms of getting things accomplished in Congress? Then ask them to give at least three reasons to support their position. Discuss their answers as a class or ask students to post their answers on the Class Discussion Board.

Next ask students to reflect on the Topic as a whole and jot down 1–3 questions they've thought about during the Topic. Share these examples if students need help getting started:

- What is the role of the legislative branch in the checks and balances of the other branches?
- How does Congress enact laws?
- What are the differences between the House of Representatives and the Senate?

You may ask students to share their questions and answers on the Class Discussion Board.

Topic Inquiry
Have students complete Step 3 of the Topic Inquiry.

▮ DEMONSTRATE

DIGITAL TOPIC REVIEW AND ASSESSMENT

The Legislative Branch

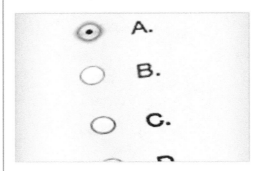

Students can prepare for the Topic Test by answering the questions in the Topic Review and Assessment online or the Assessment questions in the Print Student text. They can also prepare by reviewing their answers to the Interactive Reading Notepad questions or reviewing their notes in the Reading and Notetaking Study Guide.

DIGITAL TOPIC TEST

The Legislative Branch

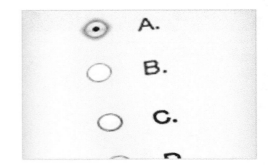

TOPIC TEST

Assign the Topic Test to assess students' understanding of topic content.

BENCHMARK TESTS

Assign these benchmark tests as you complete the relevant topics to monitor student progress toward mastering the course content and as preparation for the End-of-Course Test.

Benchmark Test 1: Topics 1–4
Benchmark Test 2: Topics 5–8
Benchmark Test 3: Topics 9–11
Benchmark Test 4: Topics 12–14

The Executive Branch: The Presidency and Vice Presidency

TOPIC 5 ORGANIZER	PACING: APPROX. 1 PERIOD, .5 BLOCKS	
		PACING
Connect		1 period
MY STORY VIDEO **Theodore Roosevelt and Ronald Reagan, Qualities of a President**		10 min.
DIGITAL ESSENTIAL QUESTION ACTIVITY **What Makes a Good Leader?**		10 min.
DIGITAL OVERVIEW ACTIVITY **Expanding Presidential Power**		10 min.
TOPIC INQUIRY: CIVIC ACTION PROJECT **Constitutional Rights Foundation**		20 min.
Investigate		2–4 periods
TOPIC INQUIRY: CIVIC ACTION PROJECT **Constitutional Rights Foundation**		Ongoing
LESSON 1 The Presidency—An Overview		30–40 min.
LESSON 2 The Vice President and the First Lady		30–40 min.
LESSON 3 The President's Domestic Powers		30–40 min.
LESSON 4 The President's Foreign Affairs Powers		30–40 min.
Synthesize		1 period
DIGITAL ACTIVITY **Reflect on the Essential Question**		10 min.
TOPIC INQUIRY: CIVIC ACTION PROJECT **Constitutional Rights Foundation**		20 min.
Demonstrate		1–2 periods
DIGITAL TOPIC REVIEW AND ASSESSMENT **The Executive Branch: The Presidency and Vice Presidency**		10 min.
TOPIC INQUIRY: CIVIC ACTION PROJECT **Constitutional Rights Foundation**		20 min.

TOPIC INQUIRY:

Civic Action Project

For this topic's Inquiry, you may choose to do a Civic Action Project with your students by using the materials found at the Constitutional Rights Foundation's CAP website: http://www.crfcap.org. Civic Action Project (CAP) is a project-based learning model for government and economics courses. It offers a practicum for high school students in effective and engaged citizenship and uses blended learning to engage students in civic activities both in the traditional U.S. government and economics classrooms.

Constitutional
Rights
Foundation
Educate. Participate.

THE TEACHER'S ROLE

THE CAP TEACHER coaches and guides students through the civic action process as they select a problem or issue, research it, determine and take civic actions, and report and document the experience. The teacher motivates, challenges, critiques, and assesses student progress. Through a blended learning approach, teachers can let students take the reins of their civic learning, guiding them along the way.

You can create your CAP classroom in three easy steps

STEP 1
Register yourself for the CAP website

STEP 2
Enroll your students

STEP 3
Engage your students in the CAP process and its many resources

Constitutional Rights Foundation

Pearson Magruder's American Government Students

Welcome to the Civic Action Project site

All of the information you're learning in your Government course will help you understand important Government policy issues that will be discussed and debated at the local, state, and national level throughout your lifetime.

Participating in a Civic Action Project (CAP) of your choosing will show you how you can use that knowledge as an engaged citizen in a democracy.

This CAP website will show you how to plan and carry out your project and give you lots of help along the way. Good luck!

Click on the logo to get started on your CAP!

THE STUDENT'S ROLE

CAP ALLOWS STUDENTS to create projects on issues they care about for their school or community. They see the connection between their civic actions and public policy and can share ideas for civics projects with each other and other CAP students nationwide. Students also see how the content of government and economics courses can apply to the real world. By taking civic actions, they practice what real citizens do when they go about trying to solve real policy-related problems. CAP fulfills best-practices in service-learning with an emphasis on public policy.

The CAP student is accountable for completing the civic action process, just as with a science project or term paper. The CAP Planner, a set of documents that guide students through the process, provides teachers with assessment information as well as a way to manage multiple student projects. While the teacher introduces and monitors the CAP, it is important that students take the lead in completing their civic actions. By using web-based technology and civics-based instruction and activities, students exercise important 21st century skills in digital literacy, critical thinking, collaboration, self-direction, and learning to be engaged and effective citizens.

CIVIC ACTIONS CAP challenges students to work on an actual problem, issue, or policy by taking civic actions. Civic actions build upon classroom civics issues, service-learning, and other proven practices of effective civic education. These actions can be many and varied, including:

· getting informed about a public issue or problem

· thinking critically about the issue or problem

· discovering how government is involved with the problem

· learning how government makes decisions

· developing a position

· engaging in civic dialogue

· building constituencies

· working together toward a common goal

· doing civic writing

· making presentations

· advocating for and defending positions

· meeting with officials

Brainstorming

Brainstorming is a method for generating ideas. It can be done by individuals or in small or large

Rules for Brainst

Pose a question to a

Set a time limit on th more ideas out.

Work as fast as you

GRADE
CAP Policy Analysis Tool

As citizens in a democracy, you'll be confronted with policy questions. Is a tax proposal a good idea? Should you vote for a particular ballot initiative? Government policies can profoundly affect our nation and your life. In a democracy, you have a say on government policies and proposed policies. It's important that you take a critical look at them. Use the following GRADE tests to evaluate a policy:

GOAL. What is the goal of the policy? If you don't know what it's supposed to do, you can't measure its success or failure. Policies are designed to address problems. What problem or problems is

© 2012 Constitutional Rights Foundation

Conducting Meetings

Your meetings should be organized, to-the-point, and fun.

Decide how you're going to make decisions. If you are a small group, try deciding by whole-group consensus or by a two-thirds vote. A simple-majority decision may lead to bad feelings and resentment.

Understand everyone's role at the meeting. At most meetings, people need to fill the following roles, which may change from meeting to meeting:

* Leader or facilitator runs the meeting, follows the agenda item by item, and watches the time allotted for each. The leader helps participants focus on the task and makes sure everyone has a chance to participate.
* Recorder takes minutes, which include date and time of meeting, the persons attending, and notes on each agenda item.
* Treasurer.
* Group members contribute agenda items, discuss topics, make decisions, and take responsibility for various tasks.
* Adviser is an adult whose role is to give advice—not to run the group.
* Guests may participate in group discussions, but usually do not participate in final decision making.

Have an agenda. This is a list of things to be dealt with at a meeting. All members should be encouraged to put topics on the agenda. After the recorder reads the minutes of the previous meeting and they are approved, the members approve the agenda. Agenda items are considered in the following order:

* Old business—ongoing and follow-up items.

© 2012, Constitutional Rights Foundation and Close Up Foundation

Constitutional Rights Foundation
Educate. Participate.

Guardian of Democracy: The Civic Mission of Schools Released September, 2011, *Guardian of Democracy: The Civic Mission of Schools report* builds on the findings of the seminal 2003 Civic Mission of Schools report. CAP has been designed to support the promising approaches described in these reports.

The Executive Branch: The Presidency and Vice Presidency

Any person wishing to be President must meet certain requirements and fulfill several important roles. Likewise, the Vice President and First Lady play important roles in support of the President.

■ CONNECT

MY STORY VIDEO

Theodore Roosevelt and Ronald Reagan, Qualities of a President

Watch a video that introduces students to two of America's most influential Presidents.

Compare and Contrast How did both Roosevelt and Reagan use the presidency as a "bully pulpit"? How were their methods different? *(Both used the office to put their ideas and philosophies into action. Reagan used personality and charm; Roosevelt was more forceful in using legislation.)*

Determine Point of View Would Teddy Roosevelt have agreed with Reagan that "government is the problem"? Why or why not? *(Probably not, since Roosevelt used government power to break up trusts and create government regulation.)*

N FLIP IT!

Assign the My Story video.

DIGITAL ESSENTIAL QUESTION ACTIVITY

What Makes a Good Leader?

Remind students that the President of the United States leads the world's richest, mightiest country. Because of this, the person who holds the presidency must be able to handle both vast power and massive pressure.

In this exercise, have students explore the qualities they think are most important in the making of a good leader.

To help students analyze this issue, ask the following:

Cause and Effect What factors contribute to the massive pressure that the current President faces? *(Possible answer: The current President faces challenges in dealing with Congress, with international issues, and with helping to improve the economy.)*

Analyze Choose one of the items from your list of leadership qualities. How has this quality been helpful to the current President in dealing with problems? *(Possible answer: The quality of being tough has helped the President because it has allowed him to stand his ground when dealing with difficult issues.)*

Identify Central Issues What do you think are some of the most difficult challenges that a President faces? *(Possible answers: whether to go to war; helping to bring the United States out of a depression; taking an unpopular stand on an issue)*

DIGITAL OVERVIEW ACTIVITY

Expanding Presidential Power

Display the cartoon, which deals with the dominence of the executive branch of the U.S. government. During this Topic students will learn that one of the responsibilities of the President is to be the director of the huge executive branch. This cartoon will provide a reference point that students can refer to as they read about the Presidency.

Analyze Cartoon What do you think this cartoon is saying about the power of the executive branch of the government? *(Possible answer: The executive branch has become so large and powerful that it has made the judicial and legislative branches useless. As a result, in the cartoon, the executive and legislative branches are being used as firewood.)*

Hyphothesize What do you think this cartoon is saying about the office of the U.S. President? *(Possible answers: Answers will vary. Since the office of the President is in charge of such a huge department, this office is extremely powerful and threatens to take control of the entire government.)*

D Differentiate: Challenge Have students write an editorial article for a newspaper about the office of the U.S. President that supports the viewpoint depicted in the cartoon.

Topic Inquiry

Launch the Topic Inquiry with students after introducing the Topic.

The Presidency—An Overview

Supporting English Language Learners

Use with Digital Text 1, **The President's Many Roles.**

Listening

Read the text and discuss the executive branch of government. Tell students that expressions are phrases that may not always mean exactly what the words say. Write the following phrases from the text and ask the students to listen as each is read aloud:

- He or she lives in an environment filled with constitutional *checks and balances* . . . .
- He or she *heads* one of the largest *governmental machines* the world has ever known.
- *In close concert* with the President's role in foreign affairs . . . .

Discuss and explain the italicized expressions in each sentence.

Beginning Guide partners to illustrate and label each expression. Have students listen to their partners as they read each expression aloud.

Intermediate Have students illustrate each expression and take turns reading them aloud. Guide them to write a short definition for each and to share their work with the group. Tell students to listen to others in the group as they read the expressions aloud.

Advanced Have partners write a sentence for each expression and ask them to illustrate one of their sentences. Have partners take turns listening as the sentences are read aloud.

Advanced High Ask students to write two sentences for each expression and have them illustrate one of their sentences. Have students listen to others in the group as they share their work aloud.

Use with Digital Texts 1 and 2, **The President's Many Roles** and **Qualifications for the Presidency.**

Reading

Preview the content of the text with the students by creating two lists: the roles of the President and the qualifications needed to be President. Tell students that when reading silently, they should focus on the meaning of the words rather than how to pronounce the words. This will help them understand what they read.

Beginning Read aloud as the students follow along. Stop after every paragraph and ask students to add details to the lists created during the preview of the text.

Intermediate Guide students to read the section on the roles of the President silently. Have students describe each role to a partner. Repeat with the section on the qualifications needed to be President.

Advanced Ask students to read the two sections silently. Have students ask each other questions about what they read. Repeat with remaining sections of the text.

Advanced High Have students read the text silently. Ask students to write questions about what they read. Have partners ask each other their questions.

▶ Differentiate Instruction

Use the Differentiated Instruction notes throughout the lesson plan to support the varied skill sets, levels of readiness, and interests in the mixed-ability classroom.

Challenge These notes include suggestions for expanding the activity for advanced students.

On-Level These notes include suggestions for modifying the activity to address different interests or learning styles.

Extra Support These notes include ideas for providing more scaffolding or reading spuport.

Special Needs These notes provide ideas for adapting instruction to support the needs of various special needs students.

■ NOTES

The Presidency—An Overview

Objectives

Objective 1: Describe the President's many roles.

Objective 2: Understand the formal qualifications necessary to become President.

Objective 3: Explain how the number of terms for which a President may serve has changed over time and the roles played by Presidents George Washington and Franklin D. Roosevelt in that evolution.

Objective 4: Describe the President's pay and benefits and how the role played by Congress in the setting of those compensations contributes to the system of checks and balances.

Objective 5: Understand the structure of presidential succession created by the U.S. Constitution.

Objective 6: Understand the constitutional provisions relating to presidential disability.

LESSON 1 ORGANIZER		PACING: APPROX. 1 PERIOD, .5 BLOCKS		RESOURCES	
	OBJECTIVES	PACING		Online	Print
Connect					
DIGITAL START UP ACTIVITY **The People's Office**		5 min.		●	
Investigate					
DIGITAL TEXT 1 **The President's Many Roles**	Objective 1	10 min.		●	●
INTERACTIVE CHART **The Many Roles of the President**		10 min.		●	
DIGITAL TEXT 2 **Qualifications for the Presidency**	Objective 2	10 min.		●	●
DIGITAL TEXT 3 **The Presidential Term of Office**	Objective 3	10 min.		●	●
INTERACTIVE GALLERY **Presidential Pay and Benefits**	Objective 4	10 min.		●	
DIGITAL TEXT 4 **Presidential Succession and Disability**	Objectives 5, 6	10 min.		●	●
Synthesize					
DIGITAL SYNTHESIZE ACTIVITY **How Long Should a President Serve?**		5 min.		●	
Demonstrate					
DIGITAL QUIZ **Lesson Quiz and Class Discussion Board**		10 min.		●	

PEARSON
realize™
www.PearsonRealize.com

Go online to access additional resources including:
Primary Sources • Biographies • Supreme Court cases •
21st Century Skill Tutorials • Maps • Graphic Organizers.

CONNECT

DIGITAL START UP ACTIVITY
The People's Office

Project the Start Up Activity Ask students to answer the questions as they enter and get settled. Then have them share their ideas with another student, either in class or through a chat or blog space.

Discuss Have students form pairs. Then ask students: In what way is the presidency "the people's office"? *(Possible answer: The President is a symbol of all of the people who live in the United States and acts as a respresentative of all citizens.)* What do you know about our current President? Have you seen news reports or magazine articles about the President?

Tell students that in this lesson they will be learning about the office of the President, and the types of roles a President must play.

Aa Vocabulary Development: Use the Interactive Reading Notepad to preview the Key Terms and Academic Vocabulary in this Lesson with students.

🕅 FLIP IT!
Assign the Flipped Video for this lesson.

■ STUDENT EDITION PRINT
PAGES: 200–206

INVESTIGATE

DIGITAL TEXT 1
The President's Many Roles

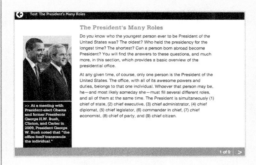

Objective 1: Describe the President's many roles.

Quick Instruction
The U.S. President heads the executive branch. As the President performs the functions described in the Constitution, he or she plays many different roles. As presidential power has grown, so have the roles.

Interactive Chart: The Many Roles of the President Introduce the activity by telling students that the job of the President is a difficult one. In fact, there are many roles the President must take on in order to succeed.

Then project the interactivity on the whiteboard. Tell students to drag the roles of the President from the left of the screen to match the corresponding activity on the President's daily planner.

Analyze Which presidential role do you think is followed most closely by those living in other countries? *(chief diplomat)* Why do you think it is necessary for the President to fulfill this role? *(Possible answer: The United States is interconnected with many other countries in the world, so it is important for the President to maintain good relations with other countries.)*

👥 ACTIVE CLASSROOM
Have students use a Rank It activity for the roles of the President. Ask students to rank these roles based on which they think is the most important. Tell students that they also need to justify their ranking decisions.

INTERACTIVE CHART
The Many Roles of the President

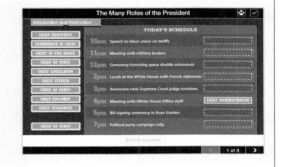

After this, ask students to work in pairs to share their rankings and justifications. Then poll the class to see if there is agreement on the ranking.

D Differentiate: Challenge Have students draw or describe a political cartoon that represents one of the nine roles of the President explained in this reading. Tell students to keep in mind the actions, symbols, and objects that best depict the role.

ELL Use the ELL activity described in the ELL chart.

Further Instruction
Editable Presentation Use the Editable Presentation to present the main ideas for this Core Reading.

The President's Many Roles: Core Reading and Interactive Reading Notepad Project and discuss the Interactive Reading Notepad questions, including the graphic organizer, asking students to keep track of the presidential roles and the responsibilities that each entails. Review the roles with the class and fill in the graphic organizer on the whiteboard as you go.

For further discussion, ask the following:

Connect Which presidential roles are also constitutional powers of the President—that is, which are mandated by the Constitution? *(The roles of chief of state, chief executive, chief administrator, chief diplomat, commander in chief, and chief legislator all come directly from the Constitution.)*

The Presidency—An Overview

DIGITAL TEXT 2
Qualifications for the Presidency

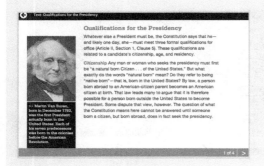

DIGITAL TEXT 3
The Presidential Term of Office

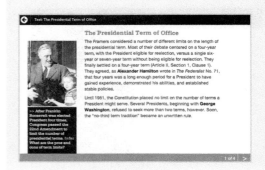

Objective 2: Understand the formal qualifications necessary to become President.

Quick Instruction

Tell students that anyone wishing to become President of the United States must meet certain basic criteria. These qualifications are related to citizenship, age, and residency. Then tell students to list three people they know who meet these basic qualifications. After this, ask: Which of these people do you think would make the best President? Does your answer have anything to do with the person meeting the basic qualifications? Discuss these questions with the class. Ask volunteers to share their answers.

Point out that Theodore Roosevelt was the youngest person to ever become President, while Ronald Reagan was the oldest.

Analyze Charts Review the chart showing the ages of the Presidents. Why might the 50s be considered an ideal time to run for the office of President? *(Possible answer: When candidates are in their 50s, they are old enough to have gained a good deal of the experience needed to be President but are not too old to be able to handle the rigors of the office.)*

ELL Use the ELL activity described in the ELL chart.

Further Instruction

Go through the Interactive Reading Notepad questions and discuss the answers with the class.

Point out that there is some dispute over the requirement that a President be "a natural born Citizen . . . of the United States." The words "natural born" could refer to a person born abroad to an American citizen parent. In this case, some argue that a person born a citizen, but born abroad, could in fact become a presidential candidate. For further discussion, ask the following:

Identify Supporting Details To become President, a person must have lived in the United States for 14 years. What evidence shows that these 14 years do not have to be consecutive? *(Sample response: Neither President Hoover nor President Eisenhower lived for 14 consecutive years in the United States before becoming President. The fourteen years, therefore, is interpreted as nonconsecutive.)*

Support Point of View with Evidence The President must be a "natural born Citizen" of the United States. Do you think this phrase means that the President must be born within the boundaries of the United States? Why or why not? *(Possible answer: No, the main qualification should be that the President is a citizen of the United States. Being born outside of the United States should make no difference as long as the person has lived for 14 years in the United States.)*

Objective 3: Explain how the number of terms for which a President may serve has changed over time, and the roles played by Presidents George Washington and Franklin D. Roosevelt in that evolution.

Quick Instruction

Inform students that the presidency is structured to allow Presidents to serve two terms of fours years each. Alexander Hamilton and other Framers believed that a four-year term with the possibility of being reelected was preferable to a longer term without the possibility of being reelected.

Analyze Images Why was the Constitution amended after Franklin D. Roosevelt was President? *(The 22nd amendment was added to the Constitution because Franklin D. Roosevelt served four terms, and Americans decided this was too long to serve as President.)*

Further Instruction

Remind students that George Washington began the "no-third-term" tradition in 1796, and it remained intact until Franklin D. Roosevelt won four terms during the Great Depression and World War II. Congress then passed the 22nd Amendment, limiting a President to two full terms. Explain that some Presidents, including Ronald Reagan, have tried to get this amendment repealed.

Editable Presentation Use the Editable Presentation to present the main ideas for this Core Reading.

INTERACTIVE GALLERY

Presidential Pay and Benefits

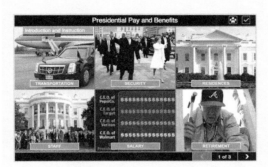

Objective 4: Describe the President's pay and benefits and how the role played by Congress in the setting of those compensations contributes to the system of checks and balances.

Quick Instruction

Explain to students that Congress sets the President's salary, which was originally $25,000 a year. To prevent members of Congress from using presidential pay to bend the chief executive to their will, the amount of the President's salary cannot be increased or decreased during a presidential term.

Interactive Gallery: Presidential Pay and Benefits
Project the gallery on the whiteboard and discuss the images. Introduce the gallery activity by telling students that the President has a set salary and benefits. These include staff, residences, retirement benefits, security, and vehicles. Ask students to review the gallery images and corresponding text. Then have them answer the questions at the end of the interactive.

🗣 ACTIVE CLASSROOM

Have students use a Conversation activity for this objective. Ask students to have a conversation with one of the people in the images of the interactive gallery. Have students write down a question they would like to ask and what the person might say in response. Students should also include a response to the person's response.

The Presidential Term of Office: Core Reading and Interactive Reading Notepad
Project and discuss the Interactive Reading Notepad questions.

Be sure students understand that the U.S. government did not specify the number of terms a President can serve until the 22nd Amendment was ratified in 1951. Before this time, most Presidents served two terms based on tradition. Also, point out that the number of terms and the length of each term that a President serves could be changed if the 22nd Amendment were to be repealed.

Infer Why do you think George Washington refused to serve more than two terms? *(Possible answer: The United States had recently gained independence from the tyrannical rule of Great Britain and its king. Washington wanted to make sure that the United States did not also establish a monarchy that could endanger the democratic rights of the people.)*

D Differentiate: **Extra Support** Help students analyze the benefits of the President's job. Ask students: What type of benefits do you think most jobs have? Then ask them: What benefits does the President receive? After this, ask: How are the benefits of the presidential office different from the benefits for most jobs?

Further Instruction

Today, the President's pay is set by Congress at $400,000. Presidential benefits include two residences (the White House and Camp David), the use of many vehicles, a large support staff, and more.)

Cite Evidence How do the President's pay and benefits contribute to the system of checks and balances? *(The legislative branch sets the President's pay, which provides a check on the President's power. The President does not have the power to choose whatever pay he or she desires.)*

Support Point of View with Evidence Do you think the President should live in the lavish surroundings provided by the White House and Camp David? *(Possible answer: Yes, the President as chief of state should live in residences that reflect his power and prestige. Also, these surroundings are necessary because the President has many interactions with foreign dignitaries.)*

The Presidency—An Overview

DIGITAL TEXT 4

Presidential Succession and Disability

Objectives 5: Understand the structure of presidential succession created by the U.S. Constitution; 6: Understand the constitutional provisions relating to presidential disability.

Quick Instruction

The Presidential Succession Act of 1947 identifies the method in which the office of the President would be filled in a situation in which both the President and Vice President are unable to serve. The 25th Amendment, on the other hand, details the method for filling the office of the presidency should the President become disabled. The amendment states that the Vice President will become Acting President if the President informs Congress that he or she is unable to perform his or her duties. The Cabinet also has a role to play in this process. The Vice President also becomes Acting President if the Vice President and a majority of the Cabinet inform Congress that the President is disabled.

Order of Succession Review the chart showing the order of presidential succession with students. Explain to students that Congress fixes the order and that it begins with the Vice President and then the leaders of the House and Senate. After that come the 15 executive department heads (the Cabinet). Ask: What does this order of succession tell you about the different heads that are listed? *(Possible answer: It shows which heads the Framers considered to be the most important or capable of filling the role of President.)*

Further Instruction

Go through the Interactive Reading Notepad questions and discuss the answers with the class.

Explain to students that, in a few instances, Presidents have chosen to transfer power to the Vice President on a temporary basis. This is one of the provisions of the 25th Amendment. Both Ronald Reagan and George W. Bush chose to transfer power while having medical procedures performed.

Compare and Contrast Presidents can come to power through election or by other methods. Compare the different methods of filling the office of President. *(One method of filling the office of President is through election by the people. Other methods come into play in the event that the President dies or is disabled while in office. In those cases, the Vice President becomes President or Acting President under the terms of the 25th Amendment. Should the Vice President also become disabled, the Presidential Succession Act is followed to determine who is next in line for the presidency.)*

Identify Cause and Effect Why do you think it was necessary for the disability gap to be filled, when it had existed for some 180 years? *(Possible answer: Since the provisions for filling the presidency were not spelled out, it was always possible that someone would challenge the Vice President for the position, or that the nation would end up without a President if the President was disabled but his or her replacement could not be agreed upon; to avoid having this happen, the 25th Amendment was passed in 1967.)*

Topic Inquiry

Launch the Topic Inquiry with students after introducing the Topic.

■ SYNTHESIZE

DIGITAL SYNTHESIZE ACTIVITY

How Long Should a President Serve?

Ask students to recall the Topic Essential Question, "What makes a good leader?" Have them use the Think-Pair-Share strategy to complete the 22nd Amendment Activity. Ask them to take ten minutes to complete this activity and then share their answer with a talking partner.

The 22nd Amendment helps flesh out the structure of the executive branch by establishing a limit of two full terms (or ten years at most) for any President to serve. As an alternative, several Presidents have suggested reconsidering one of the original Framers' ideas of a single six-year, nonrenewable term.

Support a Point of View with Evidence
Have students recollect what they have learned about a President's roles and responsibilities, and write an opinion about this proposal. Students should support their opinion with details from the lesson. *(Possible answers: I approve the proposal of a single, six-year nonrenewable term for the office of the President because most Presidents cannot get very much done in just four years. However, eight years is far too long for one individual to be influencing the government. OR I do not approve of the proposal because a single term, although six years, is not long enough for a President to accomplish many goals. Also, if a President's job performance is not satisfactory, a four-year term allows the voters to select a replacement sooner.)*

■ DEMONSTRATE

DIGITAL QUIZ

Lesson Quiz and Class Discussion Board

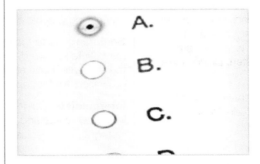

Assign the online Lesson Quiz for this lesson if you haven't already done so. Students will be offered automatic remediation or enrichment based on their score.

The President has many roles, including chief of state, chief executive, and chief administrator. To become President, a person must meet certain basic qualifications, which are part of the structure of the presidency established in the Constitution. The Constitution also gives Congress the power to set presidential pay and benefits, thus contributing to the system of checks and balances. Finally, the Constitution sets up a structure for presidential succession as well as provisions relating to presidential disability.

Pose this question to the class on the Discussion Board:

Support a Point of View with Evidence The many roles played by the President have grown as the powers of the office have grown. Do you think the power of the President should increase, remain the same, or decrease in the future? Support your answer with evidence.

Topic Inquiry

Have students continue their investigations for the Topic Inquiry.

The Vice President and the First Lady

Supporting English Language Learners

Use with Digital Text 1, **The Structure and Function of the Vice Presidency.**

Listening

Tell students that as they learn about the roles of the Vice President and First Lady, they will also learn some new basic vocabulary. Based on the language levels of your students, select basic vocabulary words from the text. Examples: *duties, position, formal, assign, vacancy*. Write them on the board and read the words aloud as the students listen. Discuss their meanings.

Beginning Read the words aloud as the students listen. Have them repeat each word. Read aloud the text and have the students raise their hands when they hear one of the words.

Intermediate Guide the students to read the words and copy them. Read the text together. Have students put a check mark next to a word each time they hear it.

Advanced After reading the text, ask students to write sentences using the words. Have them read the sentences aloud while a partner listens.

Advanced High Have one partner listen and create cloze sentences for the words as the other partner reads each word aloud. Have students give their sentences to their partners to complete and then take turns listening and reading the sentences aloud.

Use with the Lesson 2 readings.

Reading

Using images as support, guide students to read about the Vice President and the First Lady. Have them demonstrate English comprehension by completing graphic organizers.

Beginning Read the text aloud as the students follow along. As you read, write key words and phrases on the board and discuss these with the students. Have students use these words to complete web graphic organizers for the topics *Vice President* and *First Lady*.

Intermediate Guide students to read the text. Have the group create a list of key words and phrases. Have students use these words to complete web graphic organizers for the topics *Vice President* and *First Lady*.

Advanced Have partners read the text. Guide them to use phrases or sentences to complete web graphic organizers for the main ideas *How the Role of the Vice President Has Changed* and *How the Role of the First Lady Has Changed*.

Advanced High Have students read the text. Ask them to use sentences to complete web graphic organizers for the main ideas *How the Role of the Vice President Has Changed* and *How the Role of the First Lady Has Changed*. Have students share their work with the group.

⚙ Differentiate Instruction

Use the Differentiated Instruction notes throughout the lesson plan to support the varied skill sets, levels of readiness, and interests in the mixed-ability classroom.

Challenge These notes include suggestions for expanding the activity for advanced students.

On-Level These notes include suggestions for modifying the activity to address different interests or learning styles.

Extra Support These notes include ideas for providing more scaffolding or reading spuport.

Special Needs These notes provide ideas for adapting instruction to support the needs of various special needs students.

▮ NOTES

Objectives

Objective 1: Analyze the functions of the executive branch of government in terms of the formal duties the Constitution assigns to the Vice President.

Objective 2: Describe how the role of the Vice President has changed over time.

Objective 3: Explain the part played by First Ladies throughout the nation's history.

LESSON 2 ORGANIZER	PACING: APPROX. 1 PERIOD, .5 BLOCKS				
		OBJECTIVES	PACING	RESOURCES	
				Online	Print
Connect					
DIGITAL START UP ACTIVITY **How Important is the Vice President?**			5 min.	●	
Investigate					
DIGITAL TEXT 1 **The Structure and Function of the Vice Presidency**		Objectives 1, 2	10 min.	●	●
INTERACTIVE GALLERY **Balancing the Ticket**			10 min.	●	
DIGITAL TEXT 2 **The First Lady**		Objective 3	10 min.	●	●
INTERACTIVE GALLERY **A Closer Look–Six First Ladies**			10 min.	●	
Synthesize					
DIGITAL SYNTHESIZE ACTIVITY **The Functions of the Vice President**			5 min.	●	
Demonstrate					
DIGITAL QUIZ **Lesson Quiz and Class Discussion Board**			10 min.	●	

The Vice President and the First Lady

■ **CONNECT**

■ **INVESTIGATE**

DIGITAL START UP ACTIVITY

How Important is the Vice President?

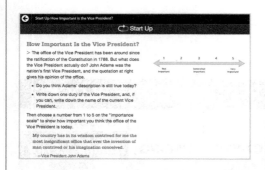

DIGITAL TEXT 1

The Structure and Function of the Vice Presidency

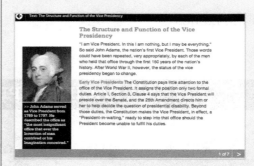

INTERACTIVE GALLERY

Balancing the Ticket

Project the Start Up Activity with the quotation Ask students to answer the questions as they enter and get settled. Then have them share their ideas with another student, either in class or through a chat or blog space.

Recall Have students write down one duty of the Vice President, and, if they can, the name of the current Vice President. Then have students choose a number from 1 to 5 on the "importance scale" to show how important they think the office of Vice President is today.

Aa Vocabulary Development: Use the Interactive Reading Notepad to preview the Key Terms and Academic Vocabulary in this Lesson with students.

⇅ FLIP IT!

Assign the Flipped Video for this lesson.

Objectives 1: Analyze the functions of the executive branch of government in terms of the formal duties the Constitution assigns to the Vice President; 2: Describe how the role of the Vice President has changed over time.

Quick Instruction

Interactive Gallery: Balancing the Ticket
Project the gallery on the whiteboard. Introduce the activity by telling students that the executive branch structure includes both a President and a Vice President, and that the Constitution makes the Vice President the president of the Senate. Explain that the vice presidency is filled by election, and that the President and Vice President appear on a "ticket," or ballot, together. Presidential candidates select their running mates carefully, often choosing someone who will increase votes and strengthen his or her chances of being elected.Inform students that in this activity they will choose the vice-presidential candidate who best balances the ticket for a particular presidential candidate.

📖 ACTIVE CLASSROOM

Have students use a Write 1-Get 3 activity to analyze the qualities that a Vice President should have in today's world. Ask the question: What are four important qualities that a Vice President should have? Have students take a piece of paper and fold it into quarters, write down one response in the first box, and then go around the room asking to hear other responses. If students think a response is correct, they should write it in one of their boxes until they have three more responses on their pages. Ask volunteers to share responses with the class.

D Differentiate: Extra Support Help students analyze the changing role of the Vice President. Ask students: What was the role of early Vice Presidents? What is the role of recent Vice Presidents? How did the role of the Vice President change?

ELL Use the ELL activity described in the ELL chart.

■ **STUDENT EDITION PRINT PAGES: 207–210**

DIGITAL TEXT 2
The First Lady

INTERACTIVE GALLERY
A Closer Look–Six First Ladies

Further Instruction

Editable Presentation Use the Editable Presentation to present the main ideas for this Core Reading.

The Structure and Function of the Vice Presidency: Core Reading and Interactive Reading Notepad Project and discuss the Interactive Reading Notepad questions, including the Venn diagram that asks students to compare and contrast the functions for the Vice President and First Lady. Review the functions of the Vice President and list these functions on the whiteboard as you go. The Venn diagram will be completed during the *First Ladies* reading.

Explain to students that the method for filling the office of the Vice President varies depending on circumstances. During a presidential election year, the Vice President is elected on a ticket with the President. Should the President die or become disabled during his or her term, however, the office is filled according to the terms of the 25th Amendment, which means the Vice President is appointed by the President and confirmed by Congress.

Compare and Contrast How were the functions of Vice President Gore and Vice President Biden both similar and different? *(Both Gore and Biden were given important responsibilities by the President. Gore studied the spending of the Federal Government, had full access to the President, and had one-on-one lunch meetings with him. Biden attends most strategy meetings and is a trusted advisor of the President.)*

Objective 3: Explain the role played by First Ladies throughout the nation's history.

Quick Instruction

Throughout U.S. history, First Ladies have played important roles in presidential administration. Although this role usually involved informal advice and supporting certain policies, the specific work that First Ladies have done has varied greatly. First Ladies take the duties, responsibilities, and obligations of citizenship seriously. Their work has ranged from advocating for particular causes to serving the public good through the arts and support of military families.

Serving the Public Good First Ladies have had a great impact on their husband's administrations as well as on the American public at large. As citizens, they often work to serve the public good and bring about political changes. For example, Laura Bush helped bring about education reform, and Michelle Obama has worked to promote healthier lifestyles, especially among children.

Interactive Gallery: A Closer Look–Six First Ladies Project the slideshow. Look at each image individually and read the accompanying text. Have students answer the questions at the end of the slideshow.

Analyze Images List three characteristics that describe the image of Eleanor Roosevelt. *(Possible answers: dignified, businesslike, intelligent)*

📷 ACTIVE CLASSROOM

Have students use a Conversation activity to help analyze the role of First Lady Michelle Obama. Ask students to study the image of Michelle Obama and think about having a conversation with her. Have them write down a question they would like to ask the First Lady and what she might say in response. Students can then write a response to Michelle Obama's answer. Ask volunteers to share their work.

D Differentiate: Challenge First Ladies often have special projects that they support. Ask students to write a short proposal for a special project for a First Lady. Tell students that these proposals should be backed by well-thought-out reasons.

ELL Use the ELL activity described in the ELL chart.

Further Instruction

Go through the Interactive Reading Notepad questions and discuss the answers with the class. Also, have students complete the Venn diagram that compares and contrasts the functions of the Vice President and First Lady.

Point out to students that the position of First Lady is not an elected position, or even an official part of the President's administration. Despite this fact, First Ladies throughout history have been able to raise awareness of particular social causes and bring about change. One example of this is First Lady Michelle Obama's *Let's Move!* campaign, which has resulted in healthier school lunch menus across the nation.

The Vice President and the First Lady

SYNTHESIZE

DIGITAL SYNTHESIZE ACTIVITY
The Functions of the Vice President

DEMONSTRATE

DIGITAL QUIZ
Lesson Quiz and Class Discussion Board

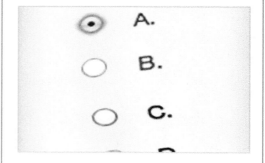

Make Predictions How do you think the role of the First Lady will change in the future? *(Possible answer: I think the First Lady will take on more responsibilities in the future. Because of this, the First Lady might become an official position in the executive branch of the government. Also, when a woman is elected President, the role of First Lady will change to First Gentleman.)*

Identify Cause and Effect What do you think caused the role of First Lady to change during the past 50 years? *(Possible answer: I think the feminist movement contributed to the expanding role of the First Lady. In society, women gained more professional positions in the workplace, such as doctors, lawyers, and business leaders. The role of the First Lady has reflected these changes in society.)*

Topic Inquiry
Launch the Topic Inquiry with students after introducing the Topic.

Ask students to recall the Topic Essential Question, "What makes for a good leader?" Have them use the Think Pair Share strategy to answer the questions below, then share their answers with a talking partner.

Discuss Have students discuss the ways in which their ratings about the importance of the vice presidency have changed after reading this lesson. Have a class discussion about this topic, asking students to list specific examples from the reading to support their beliefs.

Assign the online Lesson Quiz for this lesson if you haven't already done so. Students will be offered automatic remediation or enrichment based on their score.

Tell students that in "The Vice President and the First Lady" they learned about the roles of the Vice President and First Lady, how these roles changed over time, and key historical figures who helped to change these roles. Pose this question to the class on the Discussion Board:

Support a Point of View with Evidence What person do you think had the greatest impact on changing the role of Vice President? What person do you think had the greatest impact on changing the role of First Lady? Give reasons to support your point of view.

Topic Inquiry
Have students continue their investigations for the Topic Inquiry.

The President's Domestic Powers

Supporting English Language Learners

Use with the Lesson 3 readings.

Listening
Read the title of the lesson, *The President's Domestic Powers.* Tell students that *domestic* is an academic vocabulary word. Based on the language levels of your students, choose academic vocabulary words from the text. Examples: *expand, maintain, consist, invoke, domestic, restrain, impose.* Write the words on the board, then read the words as the students listen. Discuss their meanings.

Beginning Choose academic vocabulary words that can be supported with images, such as *expand, scores,* and *subordinates.* Use each word in a simple sentence as students listen. Then have the students repeat the sentences. Have students copy the words and read them aloud as a partner listens.

Intermediate Have students read the words. Provide cloze sentences for each word. Guide students to read and complete each sentence with the appropriate word. Have students copy the sentences and read them aloud while a partner listens.

Advanced Have students write one cloze sentence for each word. Guide partners to trade papers and read aloud each cloze sentence while their partner listens and supplies the appropriate word.

Advanced High Ask students to write a sentence for each word. Have students read their sentences aloud while a partner listens.

Use with Digital Texts 2 through 7.

Reading
Have students read carefully to identify the main ideas and supporting details of the text on the President's domestic powers and create graphic organizers reflecting this content.

Beginning Provide a list of the President's domestic powers and discuss what each one means: *power to execute the law, ordinance power, power of executive privilege, appointment power, removal power, powers of clemency, power to recommend legislation, message power, power to call special sessions and adjourn Congress, veto power.* Guide the group to complete a graphic organizer with words, phrases, or drawings that support the main idea *Presidential Powers.*

Intermediate Guide students to read and discuss the text. Help them create a list of the President's powers. Have them complete a graphic organizer with *Presidential Powers* as the main idea.

Advanced Have partners read the text. Ask them to identify the main idea of the entire text or for sections of the text. Ask them to complete a graphic organizer using phrases or sentences to show the supporting details.

Advanced High Ask students to read the text and identify the main idea. Have them complete a graphic organizer using complete sentences for the entire text or for sections of the text. Have them share their work with a partner.

⎆ Differentiate Instruction

Use the Differentiated Instruction notes throughout the lesson plan to support the varied skill sets, levels of readiness, and interests in the mixed-ability classroom.

Challenge These notes include suggestions for expanding the activity for advanced students.

On-Level These notes include suggestions for modifying the activity to address different interests or learning styles.

Extra Support These notes include ideas for providing more scaffolding or reading spuport.

Special Needs These notes provide ideas for adapting instruction to support the needs of various special needs students.

■ NOTES

The President's Domestic Powers

Objectives

Objective 1: List the reasons for the growth of presidential power and explain how the systems of checks and balances limits that growth.

Objective 2: Understand the constitutional powers of the President, including the President's power to execute the law and issue executive orders.

Objective 3: Explain how certain provisions of the Constitution provide for checks and balances among the three branches of government, including the appointment and removal powers of the President.

Objective 4: Examine the powers of executive privilege and clemency, and consider notable examples of their use over time.

Objective 5: Explain the legislative powers and how they are an important part of the system of checks and balances.

LESSON 3 ORGANIZER		PACING: APPROX. 1 PERIOD, .5 BLOCKS			
				RESOURCES	
		OBJECTIVES	PACING	Online	Print
Connect					
DIGITAL START UP ACTIVITY **What Powers Should the President Have?**			5 min.	●	
Investigate					
DIGITAL TEXT 1 **The Growth of Presidential Power**		Objective 1	10 min.	●	●
INTERACTIVE GALLERY **Examples of Expansions and Limitations of Presidential Powers**			10 min.	●	
DIGITAL TEXT 2 **The Power to Execute the Law**		Objectives 2, 4	10 min.	●	●
DIGITAL TEXT 3 **Executive Orders and Executive Privilege**			10 min.	●	●
DIGITAL TEXT 4 **The Powers of Appointment and Removal**		Objective 3	10 min.	●	●
INTERACTIVE CHART **The President's Domestic Powers**			10 min.	●	
DIGITAL TEXT 5 **The Powers of Clemency**		Objective 4	10 min.	●	●
DIGITAL TEXT 6 **The Power to Recommend Legislation**		Objective 5	10 min.	●	●
DIGITAL TEXT 7 **The Power of the Veto**			10 min.	●	●
Synthesize					
DIGITAL SYNTHESIZE ACTIVITY **Create a Presidential Dictionary**			5 min.	●	
Demonstrate					
DIGITAL QUIZ **Lesson Quiz and Class Discussion Board**			10 min.	●	

PEARSON
realize™
www.PearsonRealize.com

Go online to access additional resources including:
Primary Sources • Biographies • Supreme Court cases •
21st Century Skill Tutorials • Maps • Graphic Organizers.

■ CONNECT

DIGITAL START UP ACTIVITY

What Powers Should the President Have?

Project the Start Up Activity Ask students to answer the questions as they enter and get settled. Then have them share their ideas with another student, either in class or through a chat or blog space.

Discuss Suppose you were one of the Framers of the Constitution. What three powers would you give the President? *(Possible answer: The ability to oversee the military; the responsibility of overseeing that laws are executed; the ability to negotiate with other foreign leaders.)*

Tell students that in this lesson they will be learning about the President's domestic powers, as well as the checks and balances on the executive branch.

Aa Vocabulary Development: Use the Interactive Reading Notepad to preview the Key Terms and Academic Vocabulary in this Lesson with students.

⇅ FLIP IT!

Assign the Flipped Video for this lesson.

■ STUDENT EDITION PRINT PAGES 211–223

■ INVESTIGATE

DIGITAL TEXT 1

The Growth of Presidential Power

INTERACTIVE GALLERY

Examples of Expansions and Limitations of Presidential Powers

Objective 1: **List the reasons for the growth of presidential power and explain how the system of checks and balances limits that growth.**

Quick Instruction

Changes in Presidential Power The Framers settled on an executive branch with one person at its head. While some people worried that the President would become too powerful, the Constitution limited those powers by giving the legislative and judicial branches important checks and balances on the executive branch. The nation's first Presidents, such as George Washington and Thomas Jefferson, generally viewed the powers of the office in narrow terms, preferring to let Congress lead in policy matters. Later, the actions of certain Presidents, including Andrew Jackson, Abraham Lincoln, Theodore Roosevelt, and Franklin Roosevelt, led to the growth of presidential power.

Interactive Gallery: Examples of Expansions and Limitations of Presidential Power Project the gallery and discuss the examples. Students should be able to recognize and briefly describe each of the Presidents. Discuss briefly the roles of the President, both foreign and domestic. Explain that students will compare Presidents across time to understand the growth of presidential power in each area.

Analyze Images Have students answer these questions after viewing each President in the gallery: What makes a President weak or strong? Can a President be strong in both foreign and domestic areas? Why or why not?

🗨 ACTIVE CLASSROOM

Have students complete a Conversation with History activity. Ask them to choose a President from the gallery and determine how they think the President would answer the questions posed above. What follow-up questions would students ask the President?

Generalize Generalize about what factors check presidential power and why Presidents might want to expand their powers. *(Possible answers: Congress, elections, or public opinion. Congress isn't working fast enough, immediate action is needed.)*

D Differentiate: Extra Support Ask: Why were the Framers initially worried about having one person at the head of the executive branch? *(They worried he would have too much power.)* Then ask: What supports the idea of expanded power? *(People have decided that the Constitution explains what the branch cannot do.)* Then continue with the activity.

ELL Use the ELL activity described in the ELL chart.

Further Instruction

The Growth of Presidential Power: Core Reading and Interactive Reading Notepad Project and discuss the Interactive Reading Notepad questions, including the graphic organizer that asks students to explain the reasons for the expansion of presidential power. Review the reasons with the class and complete the graphic organizer on the whiteboard as you go.

Limits to Presidential Power Like other branches of government, the Framers gave the executive branch wide latitude in some

The President's Domestic Powers

The Power to Execute the Law

Executive Orders and Executive Privilege

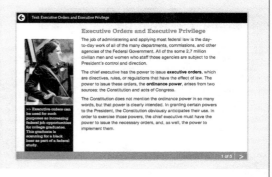

areas, but ensured it would also be checked by the other branches. The legislative branch can check the President's power through oversight to ensure that the President is following the laws of the land. Additionally, Congress approves all appointments made by the President, can override a presidential veto of a bill, and must consent to any treaties negotiated by the President. The judicial branch can also check the President's power by declaring executive acts unconstitutional.

Draw Conclusions Does presidential power ever decrease? What might make that happen? *(Possible answer: In general, presidential power has not decreased over time, but the President's power is checked more vigorously when an opposing party holds the majority of seats in Congress. A more formal reduction of presidential powers could only be accomplished by the passage of a constitutional amendment.)*

Make Decisions Review this quotation from President Taft: "My judgment is that the view of Mr. Roosevelt, ascribing an undefined residuum of power to the President, is an unsafe doctrine . . . . The true view of the Executive function is, as I conceive it, that the President can exercise no power which cannot be fairly and reasonably traced to some specific grant of power . . . . Such specific grant must be either in the Federal Constitution or in an act of Congress . . . . There is no undefined residuum of power which he can exercise because it seems to him to be in the public interest." Do you agree or disagree with this view of presidential power? Explain your thinking. *(Possible answer: I don't agree because the world today is constantly changing. The executive branch is the only branch that can act quickly to address those changes.)*

Objectives 2: **Understand the constitutional powers of the President, including the President's power to execute the law and the ordinance power; 4: Examine the powers of executive privilege, and consider notable examples of their use over time.**

Quick Instruction

Constitutional Powers The foremost constitutional power of the President is to execute the laws passed by Congress. Additionally, the Constitution implies a broad power to issue executive orders, which are directives, rules, or regulations that have the effect of law. The power to issue these orders is called the ordinance power. Executive privilege is not in the Constitution. It is the power to refuse to disclose certain information to Congress or to the federal courts. Presidents have argued that this is an inherent power in the Constitution.

Further Instruction

The Power to Execute the Law: Core Reading and Interactive Reading Notepad Project and discuss the Interactive Reading Notepad questions.

In executing the laws, Presidents have wide latitude to interpret them. The people whom Presidents appoint and the organizations within the executive branch must determine the minutiae of how laws should be enacted. However, Presidents must enact and faithfully execute all laws regardless of the President's personal views.

Executive Orders and Executive Privilege: Core Reading and Interactive Reading Notepad Project and discuss the Interactive Reading Notepad questions.

The Constitution does not mention the ordinance power in so many words, but that power is clearly intended. In granting certain powers to the President, the Constitution obviously anticipates their use. In order to exercise those powers, the chief executive must have the power to issue the necessary orders, and, as well, the power to implement them.

Congress has never recognized executive privilege and continues to try to compel members of the executive branch to defer to their oversight in all matters. The courts are reluctant to intercede between the branches. However they have decided that although the President might legitimately claim executive privilege in matters involving national security, that privilege cannot be used to prevent evidence from being heard in a criminal proceeding. The result of that court case was a key factor in the resignation of President Nixon.

Compare Ideas How is the ordinance power related to the expansion of presidential responsibilities? *(Possible answer: Issuing executive orders is one way for the President to execute the laws passed by Congress. As laws and the world have become more complex, presidential responsibilities have grown, and the use of the executive order has become more important.)*

Infer How do you think the power of executive privilege could be misused? *(Possible answer: Students might mention that a president could use the power of executive privilege to implement actions that are unconstitutional.)*

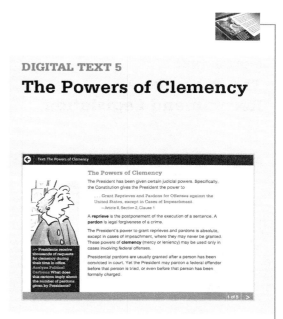

DIGITAL TEXT 4

The Powers of Appointment and Removal

INTERACTIVE CHART

The President's Domestic Powers

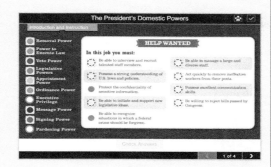

DIGITAL TEXT 5

The Powers of Clemency

Objective 3: Explain how certain provisions of the U.S. Constitution provide for checks and balances among the three branches of government, including the appointment and removal powers of the President.

Quick Instruction

While the President and Vice President are elected, other public offices at the national level are filled through the appointment process. The President has the power to appoint many of the people who work in the executive branch. The President also has the power to remove those people from office.

Interactive Chart: The President's Domestic Powers Project the help wanted advertisement, and point out the different types of presidential powers and what they mean. Tell students they will drag the colored circles from each power to the correct spot on the advertisement.

📷 ACTIVE CLASSROOM

Use a Ranking strategy to respond to the following question: What is the most important responsibility of the President? Have students defend their position. Then ask students to work in pairs to share their rankings and justifications.

D Differentiate: **Extra Support** Define each of the responsibilities of the domestic powers of the President outlined in the advertisement with students. If time, have students use a Sticky Note strategy and jot down a brief definition. Then continue with the activity.

ELL Use the ELL activity described in the ELL chart.

Further Instruction

The Powers of Appointment and Removal: Core Reading and Interactive Reading Notepad Project and discuss the Interactive Reading Notepad questions.

One important check on the President's power is that Congress must approve appointees. One contentious exception is recess appointments. In that case, the President appoints without approval during a time when the Congress is not in session. The power to remove appointed officials is as important as the power to approve them. Congress may not compel the President to fire an appointee, nor get in the way of the President firing an appointee. One exception is that Congress sets the conditions for firing for agencies and committees not solely under the executive branch, such as independent regulatory agencies.

Identify Cause and Effect Why are recess appointments considered a contentious issue? *(Recess appointments allow the President to bypass the Senate confirmation process.)*

Compare Points of View How has the Supreme Court placed limits on the President's power of removal? *(The Court has upheld laws that state that officials may be removed only if they are inefficient or neglectful, not just because they disagree with the President's views.)*

Objective 4: Examine the powers of clemency, and consider notable examples of their use over time.

Quick Instruction

Clemency is the power to change a decision made by a federal court regarding a specific person, except in the matter of impeachment. These changes take the form of reprieves and pardons. A reprieve is the postponement of the execution of a sentence. A pardon is legal forgiveness of a crime.

Further Instruction

The Powers of Clemency: Core Reading and Interactive Reading Notepad Project and discuss the Interactive Reading Notepad questions.

Be sure students understand that Presidents have the power to grant reprieves, or the postponement of the execution of a sentence, and pardons, or legal forgiveness of a crime. Discuss the reasons Presidents have had throughout history for enacting these powers.

Make Inferences Why do you think Gerald Ford gave "a full, free and absolute pardon" to Richard Nixon in 1974? *(Possible answer: Because Nixon served in the highest position in the country, Ford might have believed he deserved to be pardoned of his crimes during the Watergate scandal.)*

Make Judgments Do you think the power to grant clemency is an appropriate power for a President to have? Why? *(Possible answer: Yes because it allows for a check on the judicial branch. The President can use the power to ensure that people are treated fairly.)*

The President's Domestic Powers

DIGITAL TEXT 6

The Power to Recommend Legislation

DIGITAL TEXT 7

The Power of the Veto

Text: The Power to Recommend Legislation

The Power to Recommend Legislation

In *The Federalist* No. 51, **James Madison** analyzes the Constitution's elaborate system of checks and balances. Its "constant aim," he says, "is to divide and arrange the several [branches] in such a manner as that each may be a check on the other." And, he adds, "the great security against a gradual concentration of the several powers in the same department consists in giving to those who administer each department the necessary constitutional means and personal motives to resist encroachments of the others. . . ."

The Constitution gives the President certain legislative powers. They are, in Madison's phrase, "the constitutional means" that make it possible for the President to check the actions of Congress.

The President's legislative powers, exercised in combination with a skillful playing of the roles of chief of party and chief citizen, have made the President, in effect, the nation's chief legislator. It is the President who initiates, suggests, and demands that Congress enact much of the major legislation that it produces.

>> President James Madison praised the Constitution's system of checks and balances as a way of preventing any one branch of government from wielding too much power.

1 of 4

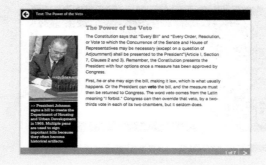

Text: The Power of the Veto

The Power of the Veto

The Constitution says that "Every Bill" and "Every Order, Resolution, or Vote to which the Concurrence of the Senate and House of Representatives may be necessary (except on a question of Adjournment) shall be presented to the President"(Article I, Section 7, Clauses 2 and 3). Remember, the Constitution presents the President with four options once a measure has been approved by Congress.

First, he or she may sign the bill, making it law, which is what usually happens. Or the President can **veto** the bill, and the measure must then be returned to Congress. The word veto comes from the Latin meaning "I forbid." Congress can then override that veto, by a two-thirds vote in each of its two chambers, but it seldom does.

>> President Johnson signs a bill to create the Department of Housing and Urban Development in 1965. Multiple pens are used to sign important bills because they often become historical artifacts.

1 of 7

Objective 5: **Explain the legislative powers and how they are an important part of the system of checks and balances.**

Quick Instruction

The President has two major legislative powers. First, the President must provide information to Congress regarding the state of the union. Second, the President has the power to veto any piece of legislation passed by Congress. This provision of the Constitution provides checks and balances to the lawmaking power of Congress.

ELL Use the ELL activity described in the ELL chart.

Further Instruction

The Power to Recommend Legislation: Core Reading and Interactive Reading Notepad Project and discuss the Interactive Reading Notepad questions.

The State of the Union address is required by the Constitution, as are presidential messages on the economy and the budget. Guide students in a discussion on the merits of providing these messages. Ask, Who is the intended audience? *(Possible answers: the American public, members of Congress, foreign leaders)* Be sure students understand the purpose of these legislative powers.

The Power of the Veto: Core Reading and Interactive Reading Notepad Project and discuss the Interactive Reading Notepad questions.

Review the four options the President has after a measure has been approved by Congress. Create a chart on the board to summarize these options: to sign the bill into law; to veto the bill; to neither sign nor veto the bill; and to use the pocket veto. Have students complete the chart with brief descriptions of each option.

Draw Conclusions Why might the Framers have wanted the President to make a State of the Union speech? *(It is a way for the President to balance the legislative branch by directing the formation of public policy.)*

Compare How is a signing statement like a line-item veto? *(It is a way for a President to choose not to enact parts of a law that the President has signed.)*

■ SYNTHESIZE

DIGITAL SYNTHESIZE ACTIVITY

Create a Presidential Dictionary

Project the following heads on the board. *executive powers, legislative powers,* and *judicial powers*.

Using a Sticky Note strategy, have students write examples of the President's domestic powers that fall into each category. Then, in pairs, have them create a dictionary of the answers they wrote.

You may wish to project a sample definition for xstudents.

Discuss Have students share their terms and how they categorized each term based on whether it describes the President's executive, judicial, or legislative responsibility. Students can share their entries by tweeting or creating a classroom blog.

■ DEMONSTRATE

DIGITAL QUIZ

Lesson Quiz and Class Discussion Board

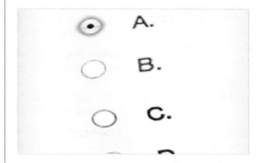

Assign the online Lesson Quiz for this lesson if you haven't already done so. Students will be offered automatic remediation or enrichment based on their score.

In "The President's Domestic Powers," you read about the domestic duties and responsibilities of the President.

Pose these questions to the class on the Discussion Board:

Analyze Arguments In the Federalist papers, James Madison used the following argument about checks and balances. Its "constant aim," he said, "is to divide and arrange the several [branches] in such a manner as that each may be a check on the other." And he adds, "the great security against a gradual concentration of the several powers in the same department consists in giving to those who administer each department the necessary constitutional means and personal motives to resist encroachments of the others . . . . " Do you agree that checks and balances as they are used today reflect Madison's view? Why or why not?

Make Connections Think about what you know about the size of the executive branch and all of its responsibilities. Do you think that the growth of presidential power was inevitable? Could the other branches do anything to stop it? Would that be a good or a bad thing?

Topic Inquiry

Have students continue their investigations for the Topic Inquiry.

The President's Foreign Affairs Powers

Supporting English Language Learners

Use with Digital Texts 1–2, **The President's Diplomatic Powers** and **Commander in Chief.**

Listening
Read and discuss the lesson "The President's Foreign Affairs Powers." Based on the language levels of the students, teach vocabulary from the lesson such as *foreign, treaty, recognition,* and *resolution.* Guide students to listen as the words and definitions are read aloud and monitor their understanding of spoken language as described below.

Beginning Have students copy the vocabulary words onto cards. As students listen to your instruction of lesson content, have them hold up the cards when they hear the word being used.

Intermediate Provide students with a list of the vocabulary words. As you discuss the words, have students put a mark next to each word, according to their level of understanding. * = I understand it well. + = I have a general idea of what it means. ? = I need more explanation. For words marked with a ?, have students pair up and listen while their partners speak each word and its definition and use it in a sentence. Then have partners trade roles.

Advanced Have the students listen as you summarize sections of the text, emphasizing the vocabulary words. Have them complete a two-column chart with the headings *Things I Understood* and *Questions I Have.* Discuss the charts with the group.

Advanced High Have the students listen as you summarize the text. Ask them to write three sentences telling what they have learned and three questions that they have about the topic. Have them discuss their work with a partner.

Use with the Lesson 4 readings.

Reading
Tell students they will be learning about the foreign affairs powers of the President. Have students look at the images in the text and read the captions and section headings. Ask them to make predictions about the text and read to find out whether their predictions were accurate.

Beginning After reading captions and section headings and discussing the images, guide students to predict by asking questions that require a yes/no or one- or two-word response. Examples: *Will this lesson provide information about the leaders of other countries? Will this lesson provide information about the military?*

Intermediate Ask students to describe the images in the text. Ask them to make predictions about the text. Have them read the text aloud and discuss whether their predictions were correct.

Advanced Have partners create a list of predictions about the text. Ask them to read the text to find out if their predictions were correct.

Advanced High Ask students to jot down their predictions. Have them share their predictions with a partner. Ask partners to read together to find out which predictions were correct.

▣ Differentiate Instruction

Use the Differentiated Instruction notes throughout the lesson plan to support the varied skill sets, levels of readiness, and interests in the mixed-ability classroom.

Challenge These notes include suggestions for expanding the activity for advanced students.

On-Level These notes include suggestions for modifying the activity to address different interests or learning styles.

Extra Support These notes include ideas for providing more scaffolding or reading spuport.

Special Needs These notes provide ideas for adapting instruction to support the needs of various special needs students.

■ NOTES

PEARSON
realize™
www.PearsonRealize.com

Go online to access additional resources including:
Primary Sources • Biographies • Supreme Court cases •
21st Century Skill Tutorials • Maps • Graphic Organizers.

Objectives

Objective 1: Explain how treaties are negotiated by the President, approved by the Senate, and ratified by the President under the system of checks and balances.

Objective 2: Explain why and how executive agreements are made.

Objective 3: Summarize how the power of recognition is used by the President.

Objective 4: Describe the President's constitutional powers as commander in chief.

LESSON 4 ORGANIZER		PACING: APPROX. 1 PERIOD, .5 BLOCKS			
				RESOURCES	
		OBJECTIVES	**PACING**	**Online**	**Print**
Connect					
DIGITAL START UP ACTIVITY **Analyze a Political Cartoon**			5 min.	●	
Investigate					
DIGITAL TEXT 1 **The President's Diplomatic Powers**		Objectives 1, 2, 3	10 min.	●	●
INTERACTIVE CHART **Comparing Treaties and Executive Agreements**			10 min.	●	
DIGITAL TEXT 2 **Commander in Chief**		Objective 4	10 min.	●	●
INTERACTIVE MAP **Examples of U.S. Military Interventions after World War II**			10 min.	●	
Synthesize					
DIGITAL SYNTHESIZE ACTIVITY **Diplomacy or War?**			5 min.	●	
Demonstrate					
DIGITAL QUIZ **Lesson Quiz and Class Discussion Board**			10 min.	●	

Topic ⑤ Lesson 4

The President's Foreign Affairs Powers

■ CONNECT

DIGITAL START UP ACTIVITY
Analyze a Political Cartoon

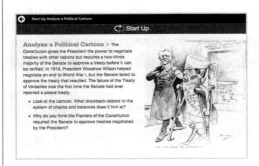

Project the Start Up Activity Ask students to answer the questions as they enter and get settled. Then have them share their ideas with another student, either in class or through a chat or blog space.

Make Inferences Why do you think the Framers of the Constitution required the Senate to approve treaties negotiated by the President? *(Possible answer: This is part of the system of a checks and balances between the executive and legislative branches, put in place to prevent the President from becoming too powerful.)*

Aa Vocabulary Development: Use the Interactive Reading Notepad to preview the Key Terms and Academic Vocabulary in this Lesson with students.

⇊ FLIP IT!

Assign the Flipped Video for this lesson.

■ STUDENT EDITION PRINT PAGES 224–229

■ INVESTIGATE

DIGITAL TEXT 1
The President's Diplomatic Powers

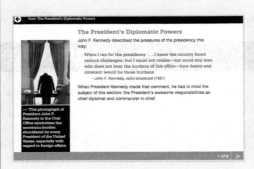

Objectives 1: Explain how treaties are negotiated by the President, approved by the Senate, and ratified by the President under the system of checks and balances; 2: Explain why and how executive agreements are made; 3: Summarize how the power of recognition is used.

Quick Instruction
As the chief diplomat, the President has the constitutional power to negotiate and make treaties. The Constitution has provided for checks and balances between the legislative and executive branches, however, by stipulating that the Senate must consent to treaties by a two-thirds majority. Presidents can also make executive agreements with the heads of other nations. These agreements do not need Senate consent. As such, they are not a permanent part of the law of the land and only remain in force as long as they are renewed by each succeeding President.

Interactive Chart: Comparing Treaties and Executive Agreements
Step through the interactive chart. Point out that it shows the steps the President takes to make a treaty and the steps the President takes to make an executive agreement.

INTERACTIVE CHART
Comparing Treaties and Executive Agreements

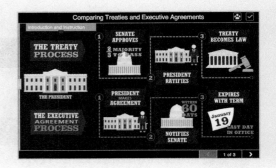

📖 ACTIVE CLASSROOM

Using the Sticky Note strategy, have students note the important steps in creating a treaty, including the roles of the executive and legislative branches. Then have students use the same strategy to note the important steps in creating an executive agreement. In pairs, have students compare the two processes, noting their similarities and differences. Discuss as a group.

D Differentiate: Challenge Have students research a recent treaty and then prepare a slide show that describes the treaty's content and the result of the Senate vote.

ELL Use the ELL activity described in the ELL chart.

Further Instruction
The President's Diplomatic Powers: Core Reading and Interactive Reading Notepad Project and discuss the Interactive Reading Notepad questions, including the graphic organizer asking students to compare treaties and executive agreements. Review the elements of each with the class and fill in the graphic organizer on the whiteboard as you go.

Remind students that one of the constitutional powers of the executive branch of government is the power to make treaties.

DIGITAL TEXT 2

Commander in Chief

INTERACTIVE MAP

Examples of U.S. Military Interventions after World War II

Make Inferences Why might the Framers have increased the number of senators needed to consent to a treaty from majority to two-thirds? *(Possible answer: It allows for a more measured approach to diplomacy because more people must be convinced that it is appropriate to the goals of the nation.)*

Evaluate Evidence Why is the power of recognition important on a world stage? Why might Presidents recognize heads of states with whom the United States does not agree? *(The power of recognition allows for the President to acknowledge the government of another. It gives that nation standing in the world. The President would recognize states without approval perhaps in an attempt to show good will or encourage them to give citizens more freedoms.)*

Objective 4: Describe the President's constitutional powers as commander in chief.

Quick Instruction

The President has the final authority over and responsibility for all military matters, and the most critical decisions are invariably made by the commander in chief. The Constitution provides for checks and balances between the legislative and executive branches in this area by giving Congress the ability to declare war, while making the President commander in chief. Review with students the military actions taken by Presidents Washington, Lincoln, Theodore Roosevelt, Franklin Roosevelt, and Reagan.

Interactive Map: Examples of U.S. Military Interventions after World War II Project the interactive map and step through the countries shown. Introduce the activity by explaining that the President's war powers are extensive and Congress is not always involved.

ACTIVE CLASSROOM

Using the Make Headlines strategy, have students choose a portion of the map and create a headline expressing which presidential war power was used and how the conflict ended. Have students use bias in their headline to clearly indicate how they feel about that particular war power as used. Students can present their headlines either as tweets or as part of a classroom blog.

D **Differentiate: Extra Support** Ask: What are the responsibilities of the commander in chief? *(The President oversees the operations of the military.)* Then ask, What is Congress's war responsibility? *(Congress declares war.)* Students should understand that there is a gulf between the war powers of Congress and the President. This gulf is why the President's war powers are extensive and Congress is not always involved. Then continue with the activity.

Further Instruction

Commander in Chief: Core Reading and Interactive Reading Notepad Project and discuss the Interactive Reading Notepad questions.

Undeclared War and Congressional Powers The Constitution divides military powers between the legislative and executive branches. In times of national emergency, however, when the nation's safety and interests are threatened, there has been a shift of power to the President. This fact has contributed to the growth of presidential power over time.

Draw Conclusions How do the President's war powers exemplify the growth of presidential power? Why are these powers described as "almost without limit"? *(As the commander in chief, the President can send the military anywhere neccesary, often without the agreement of Congress. There appears to be no check on this power as evidenced by how many undeclared wars and conflicts the United States has been a part of.)*

The President's Foreign Affairs Powers

■ SYNTHESIZE

DIGITAL SYNTHESIZE ACTIVITY
Diplomacy or War?

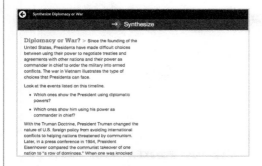

Project the first slide of the activity Remind students that Presidents have the responsibility to oversee many different aspects of national affairs. Sometimes events require that the President use those responsibilities in differing ways to achieve a particular goal.

Timeline After students have read and understood the first slide, project the timeline. Ask: Look at the events listed on this timeline. Which ones show the President using diplomatic powers? Which ones show him using his power as commander in chief? *(1947–diplomatic; 1954–diplomatic; 1964–commander in chief; 1969–commander in chief)*

Troops in Vietnam Ask: Why did President Johnson ask Congress to pass the Gulf of Tonkin Resolution instead of simply ordering troops overseas, as President Truman did in the Korean conflict in 1950? *(Possible answer: Johnson wanted congressional approval to show that he was not acting alone in sending U.S. troops into harm's way.)*

President Nixon Ask: Why did Congress need to pass a special War Powers Resolution to limit the President's powers as commander in chief when a system of checks and balances was already built into the Constitution? *(The Constitution gives Congress the power to declare war to check and balance the President's role as commander in chief, but Vietnam was an undeclared war. Congressional leaders wanted to rein in the power of the President as commander in chief because that power had become almost limitless in terms of committing the U.S. to a long, costly war in Vietnam.)*

■ DEMONSTRATE

DIGITAL QUIZ
Lesson Quiz and Class Discussion Board

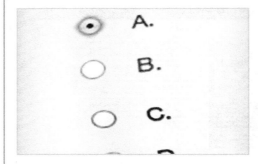

Assign the online Lesson Quiz for this lesson if you haven't already done so. Students will be offered automatic remediation or enrichment based on their score.

In "The President's Foreign Affairs Powers" you read about the President's responsibilities as chief diplomat and commander in chief. Pose these questions to the class on the Discussion Board:

Explain President Kennedy commented that the burdens of office were heavy and constant. Do you agree with that assessment based on what you know about the President's foreign affairs powers?

Make Decisions Do you agree with the statement in the text that "military force is the ultimate language of diplomacy"? Explain your thinking using what you know about the President's foreign affairs powers.

Topic Inquiry
Have students continue their investigations for the Topic Inquiry.

The Executive Branch: The Presidency and Vice Presidency

■ SYNTHESIZE

DIGITAL ACTIVITY
Reflect on the Essential Question

First, ask students to reconsider the Essential Question for the Topic: What makes a good leader? Remind students of the qualities they chose at the start of the Topic. For example,

- decisive
- ntelligent
- tough
- open minded
- cooperative

Have students consider the list again, in light of what they have learned about the presidency. One of the traits on the list is "tough," meaning that a president sometimes needs to take an unpopular stand or do something that others may not agree with. Ask students: Why do you think this quality is (or is not) important for a President?

Next ask students to reflect on the Topic as a whole and jot down 1–3 questions they've thought about during the Topic. Share these examples if students need help getting started:

- Is an imperial presidency the only type of presidency that works in modern times?
- What can a President do when working with a Congress that blocks his initiatives?

You may ask students to share their questions and answers on the Class Discussion Board.

Topic Inquiry
Have students complete Step 3 of the Topic Inquiry.

■ DEMONSTRATE

DIGITAL TOPIC REVIEW AND ASSESSMENT
The Executive Branch: The Presidency and Vice Presidency

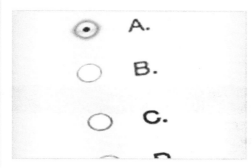

Students can prepare for the Topic Test by answering the questions in the Topic Review and Assessment online or the Assessment questions in the Print Student text. They can also prepare by reviewing their answers to the Interactive Reading Notepad questions or reviewing their notes in the Reading and Notetaking Study Guide.

DIGITAL TOPIC TEST
The Executive Branch: The Presidency and Vice Presidency

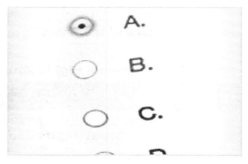

TOPIC TEST
Assign the Topic Test to assess students' understanding of topic content.

BENCHMARK TESTS
Assign these benchmark tests as you complete the relevant topics to monitor student progress toward mastering the course content and as preparation for the End-of-Course Test.

Benchmark Test 1: Topics 1–4
Benchmark Test 2: Topics 5–8
Benchmark Test 3: Topics 9–11
Benchmark Test 4: Topics 12–14

The Executive Branch at Work

TOPIC 6 ORGANIZER	PACING: APPROX. 1 PERIOD, .5 BLOCKS	
		PACING
Connect		1 period
MY STORY VIDEO **NASA, Independent Executive Agency**		10 min.
DIGITAL ESSENTIAL QUESTION ACTIVITY **What Should Governments Do?**		10 min.
DIGITAL OVERVIEW ACTIVITY **The Size of the Executive Branch**		10 min.
TOPIC INQUIRY: CIVIC ACTION PROJECT **Constitutional Rights Foundation**		20 min.
Investigate		3–6 periods
TOPIC INQUIRY: CIVIC ACTION PROJECT **Constitutional Rights Foundation**		Ongoing
LESSON 1 The Federal Bureaucracy		30–40 min.
LESSON 2 The EOP and the Executive Departments		30–40 min.
LESSON 3 The Independent Agencies		30–40 min.
LESSON 4 Foreign Policy Overview		30–40 min.
LESSON 5 Diplomacy		30–40 min.
LESSON 6 National Security		30–40 min.
Synthesize		1 period
DIGITAL ACTIVITY **Reflect on the Essential Question**		10 min.
TOPIC INQUIRY: CIVIC ACTION PROJECT **Constitutional Rights Foundation**		20 min.
Demonstrate		1–2 periods
DIGITAL TOPIC REVIEW AND ASSESSMENT **The Executive Branch at Work**		10 min.
TOPIC INQUIRY: CIVIC ACTION PROJECT **Constitutional Rights Foundation**		20 min.

Civic Action Project

For this topic's Inquiry, you may choose to do a Civic Action Project with your students by using the materials found at the Constitutional Rights Foundation's CAP website: http://www.crfcap.org. Civic Action Project (CAP) is a project-based learning model for government and economics courses. It offers a practicum for high school students in effective and engaged citizenship and uses blended learning to engage students in civic activities both in the traditional U.S. government and economics classrooms.

Constitutional
Rights
Foundation
Educate. Participate.

THE TEACHER'S ROLE

THE CAP TEACHER coaches and guides students through the civic action process as they select a problem or issue, research it, determine and take civic actions, and report and document the experience. The teacher motivates, challenges, critiques, and assesses student progress. Through a blended learning approach, teachers can let students take the reins of their civic learning, guiding them along the way.

You can create your CAP classroom in three easy steps

STEP 1
Register yourself for the CAP website

STEP 2
Enroll your students

STEP 3
Engage your students in the CAP process and its many resources

Constitutional Rights Foundation

Pearson Magruder's American Government Students

Welcome to the Civic Action Project site

All of the information you're l___ng __ __ur Government course will help you understand impor__t Govern___ policy issues that will be discussed and debated at __e lo_____ate, __d national level throughout your lifetime.

Participating in a Civic Action __ __P) of your choosing will show you how you can use that knowledge as an engaged citizen in a democracy.

This CAP website will show you how to plan and carry out your project and give you lots of help along the way. Good luck!

Click on the logo to get started on your CAP!

THE STUDENT'S ROLE

CAP ALLOWS STUDENTS to create projects on issues they care about for their school or community. They see the connection between their civic actions and public policy and can share ideas for civics projects with each other and other CAP students nationwide. Students also see how the content of government and economics courses can apply to the real world. By taking civic actions, they practice what real citizens do when they go about trying to solve real policy-related problems. CAP fulfills best-practices in service-learning with an emphasis on public policy.

The CAP student is accountable for completing the civic action process, just as with a science project or term paper. The CAP Planner, a set of documents that guide students through the process, provides teachers with assessment information as well as a way to manage multiple student projects. While the teacher introduces and monitors the CAP, it is important that students take the lead in completing their civic actions. By using web-based technology and civics-based instruction and activities, students exercise important 21st century skills in digital literacy, critical thinking, collaboration, self-direction, and learning to be engaged and effective citizens.

CIVIC ACTIONS CAP challenges students to work on an actual problem, issue, or policy by taking civic actions. Civic actions build upon classroom civics issues, service-learning, and other proven practices of effective civic education. These actions can be many and varied, including:

- getting informed about a public issue or problem

- thinking critically about the issue or problem

- discovering how government is involved with the problem

- learning how government makes decisions

- developing a position

- engaging in civic dialogue

- building constituencies

- working together toward a common goal

- doing civic writing

- making presentations

- advocating for and defending positions

- meeting with officials

Brainstorming

Brainstorming is a method for generating ideas. It can be done by individuals or in small or large

Handout Lesson 5B
Civic Action Project

GRADE
CAP Policy Analysis Tool

AS CITIZENS IN A DEMOCRACY, YOU'LL BE CONFRONTED WITH POLICY QUESTIONS. IS A TAX PROPOSAL A GOOD IDEA? SHOULD YOU VOTE FOR A PARTICULAR BALLOT INITIATIVE? GOVERNMENT POLICIES CAN PROFOUNDLY AFFECT OUR NATION AND YOUR LIFE. IN A DEMOCRACY, YOU HAVE A SAY ON GOVERNMENT POLICIES AND PROPOSED POLICIES. IT'S IMPORTANT THAT YOU TAKE A CRITICAL LOOK AT THEM. USE THE FOLLOWING GRADE TESTS TO EVALUATE A POLICY:

GOAL. WHAT IS THE GOAL OF THE POLICY? IF YOU DON'T KNOW WHAT IT'S SUPPOSED TO DO, YOU CAN'T MEASURE ITS SUCCESS OR FAILURE. POLICIES ARE DESIGNED TO ADDRESS PROBLEMS. WHAT PROBLEM OR PROBLEMS IS

Rules for Brainst

Pose a question to a

Set a time limit on t
more ideas out.

Work as fast as you

© 2012 Constitutional Rights Foundation

Conducting Meetings

Your meetings should be organized, to-the-point, and fun.

Decide how you're going to make decisions. If you are a small group, try deciding by whole-group consensus or by a two-thirds vote. A simple-majority decision may lead to bad feelings and resentment.

Understand everyone's role at the meeting. At most meetings, people need to fill the following roles, which may change from meeting to meeting:

- **Leader or facilitator** runs the meeting, follows the agenda item by item, and watches the time allotted for each. The leader helps participants focus on the task and makes sure everyone has a chance to participate.
- **Recorder** takes minutes, which include date and time of meeting, the persons attending, and notes on each agenda item.
- **Treasurer.**
- **Group members** contribute agenda items, discuss topics, make decisions, and take responsibility for various tasks.
- **Adviser** is an adult whose role is to give advice—not to run the group.
- **Guests** may participate in group discussions, but usually do not participate in final decision making.

Have an agenda. This is a list of things to be dealt with at a meeting. All members should be encouraged to put topics on the agenda. After the recorder reads the minutes of the previous meeting and they are approved, the members approve the agenda. Agenda items are considered in the following order:

- Old business—ongoing and follow-up items.

© 2012, Constitutional Rights Foundation
and Close Up Foundation

Constitutional Rights Foundation
Educate. Participate.

Guardian of Democracy: The Civic Mission of Schools
Released September, 2011, *Guardian of Democracy: The Civic Mission of Schools report* builds on the findings of the seminal 2003 Civic Mission of Schools report. CAP has been designed to support the promising approaches described in these reports.

The Executive Branch at Work

The President of the United States is often seen as the most powerful person in the world. Over the years, the President's powers have expanded, both in domestic and foreign affairs. However, the President is still subject to the limitations imposed by the Constitution and the checks and balances system of the Federal Government. The President is aided in the execution of his or her duties by numerous advisors and agencies, which make up the executive branch of the U.S. government. What are these entities and what sort of work do they do?

CONNECT

MY STORY VIDEO

NASA, Independent Executive Agency

Watch a video that shows the many programs and projects of NASA, the National Aeronautics and Space Administration, the government agency that conducts the US space program.

Determine Point of View What are the goals of NASA scientists and administrators? *(They carry on space research and technology, hoping to get public support and inspire the next generation to become scientists and explorers.)*

Apply Concepts From what you have seen of NASA's work, what aspects of the space program interest you most? Why? *(Possible answers: Space travel, the International Space Station, basic science, research on other planets. Student responses should show they have thought seriously about the possibilities.)*

FLIP IT!

Assign the My Story video.

DIGITAL ESSENTIAL QUESTION ACTIVITY

What Should Governments Do?

Ask students to think about the Essential Question for this Topic: What Should Governments Do?

If students have not already done so, ask them to respond to the poll. Then go over the results as a class.

The Federal Government has many responsibilities, both at home and in foreign policy, including national defense. As citizens, Americans need to be aware of what the government is doing, and decide whether its actions are appropriate. When, for example, should the United States involve itself in international affairs?

Have students review the scenarios and indicate whether they think the event requires Federal Government involvement by checking "Yes" or "No." Then ask them to write how they think the Federal Government should respond to each event.

Support a Point of View with Evidence Which scenarios do you think the Federal Government should get involved with? Why? Which scenarios do you think the Federal Government should NOT get involved with? Why not?

Infer How do you think the U.S. government could use economic resources in foreign policy for the earthquake in China?

DIGITAL OVERVIEW ACTIVITY

The Size of the Executive Branch

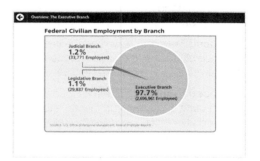

The executive branch of the Federal Government is much larger than either the legislative or judicial branches. That is because it is responsible for executing the nation's laws, a task that encompasses a dizzying array of policy areas, from regulating the money supply to protecting national security.

Project the chart on the whiteboard. Tell students that this chart shows the number of civilians employed in each branch of the Federal government. Also, the chart shows the percent of the total government workforce that each branch accounts for.

D Differentiate: Extra Support What percentage of government workers are employed by the executive branch? the legislative branch? the judicial branch? What branch is by far the largest? *(Answers: 97.7%, 1.1%, 1.2%. The executive branch is by far the largest.)*

Check Understanding Why do you think the executive branch is so much larger than the legislative and judicial branches?

Topic Inquiry

Launch the Topic Inquiry with students after introducing the Topic.

The Federal Bureaucracy

Supporting English Language Learners

Use with Digital Text 1, **What Is a Bureaucracy?**

Listening
Read aloud the sections on bureaucracy. As you review the reading in relation to the structure and functions of the executive branch of government, have students listen and then ask and answer questions to clarify their understanding.

Beginning Read aloud each of the three paragraphs under the heading **What Is a Bureaucracy?** as students listen. Have students ask for clarification after each paragraph, using sentence stems such as: *Please repeat that.* and *What does _____ mean?*

Intermediate Guide partners to take turns reading aloud and listening to each of the three paragraphs under the heading **What Is a Bureaucracy?** During discussion, have students ask one another for clarification using sentence stems such as: *The part I don't understand is _____. Can you give an example of _____?*

Advanced Have partners read the sections. During discussion, provide sentence stems that require the students to repeat what they heard: *Did you mean _____? I heard you say _____.*

Advanced High Have students read the sections independently. Form small groups and have students take turns asking for clarification using sentence stems such as: *Can you tell me more about _____? How do these ideas fit together? I don't understand the use of the word _____.* Remind students to listen as their questions are answered.

Use with the Lesson 1 readings.

Reading
Have students read the sections on bureaucracy. Have them use a graphic organizer such as a T-chart to respond to the following question from the text: *Explain how the defining features of a bureaucracy both help and hurt the effectiveness and efficiency of the Federal Government.*

Beginning Read aloud the text to students. Provide phrases that describe ways a bureaucracy helps and hurts the Federal Government. Have the class sort the phrases into the two categories on the graphic organizer.

Intermediate Guide partners to read the text. Provide phrases that describe ways a bureaucracy helps and hurts the Federal Government. Have partners copy the phrases onto the correct spots on the graphic organizer.

Advanced Have partners read the text. After a group discussion, have partners complete the graphic organizer.

Advanced High Have students read the text and complete the graphic organizer. Then have students discuss their graphic organizers with a classmate.

▷ Differentiate Instruction

Use the Differentiated Instruction notes throughout the lesson plan to support the varied skill sets, levels of readiness, and interests in the mixed-ability classroom.

Challenge These notes include suggestions for expanding the activity for advanced students.

On-Level These notes include suggestions for modifying the activity to address different interests or learning styles.

Extra Support These notes include ideas for providing more scaffolding or reading spuport.

Special Needs These notes provide ideas for adapting instruction to support the needs of various special needs students.

■ NOTES

PEARSON
realize™
www.PearsonRealize.com

Go online to access additional resources including:
Primary Sources • Biographies • Supreme Court cases •
21st Century Skill Tutorials • Maps • Graphic Organizers.

Objectives

Objective 1: Define a bureaucracy.

Objective 2: Identify the major elements of the federal bureaucracy.

Objective 3: Explain how groups within the federal bureaucracy are named.

Objective 4: Describe the difference between a staff agency and a line agency.

LESSON 1 ORGANIZER		PACING: APPROX. 1 PERIOD, .5 BLOCKS			
				RESOURCES	
		OBJECTIVES	**PACING**	Online	Print
Connect					
DIGITAL START UP ACTIVITY **Bureaucracies in Your Community**			10 min.	●	
Investigate					
DIGITAL TEXT 1 **What Is a Bureaucracy?**		Objective 1	10 min.	●	●
DIGITAL TEXT 2 **Executive Branch Bureaucracy**		Objective 2	10 min.	●	●
DIGITAL TEXT 3 **How Units Are Named**		Objective 3	10 min.	●	●
DIGITAL TEXT 4 **Staff and Line Agencies**		Objective 4	10 min.	●	●
INTERACTIVE CHART **Staff or Line Agency?**			10 min.	●	
Synthesize					
DIGITAL SYNTHESIZE ACTIVITY **Too Much Red Tape?**			10 min.	●	
Demonstrate					
DIGITAL QUIZ **Lesson Quiz and Class Board Discussion**			10 min.	●	

The Federal Bureaucracy

■ CONNECT

DIGITAL START UP ACTIVITY

Bureaucracies in Your Community

Bureaucracies in Your Community Start Up

↻ Start Up

Bureaucracies in Your Community > By definition, a **bureaucracy** is a large, complex administrative structure that handles the everyday business of an organization. Similarly, a **bureaucrat** is a person who works for a bureaucratic organization.

Think about your school as a bureaucratic organization and fill in the following information about your school bureaucracy and its bureaucrats:

Bureaucracy of _____ High School

Bureaucrats:
- Superintendent: _____
- Principal: _____
- Vice Principal: _____
- Guidance Counselor: _____
- Teacher: _____
- Teacher: _____
- Teacher: _____

Project the Start Up Activity Ask students to answer the questions as they enter and get settled. Then have them share their ideas with another student.

Discuss Have students think about their local community. What organizations fit this definition of bureaucracy? Who are each organization's bureaucrats? *(Possible answers: Students' responses might include the principal, vice principal, counselor, and teachers at the school.)*

Tell students that in this lesson they will be learning about the major elements of the federal bureaucracy.

Aa Vocabulary Development: Use the Interactive Reading Notepad to preview the Key Terms and Academic Vocabulary in this Lesson with students.

⇡ FLIP IT!

Assign the Flipped Video for this lesson.

■ STUDENT EDITION PRINT PAGES: 236–241

■ INVESTIGATE

DIGITAL TEXT 1

What Is a Bureaucracy?

Text 1 What Is a Bureaucracy?

What Is a Bureaucracy?

The Federal Government is an immense organization. Its employees deliver the mail, regulate business practices, collect taxes, defend the nation, administer Social Security programs, manage the national forests, explore outer space, and do dozens of other things every day. Indeed, you cannot live through a single day without somehow encountering the federal bureaucracy.

A **bureaucracy** is a large, complex administrative structure that handles the everyday business of an organization. To many Americans, the word *bureaucracy* suggests such things as waste, red tape, and delay. While that image is not altogether unfounded, it is quite lopsided. Basically, at its best, bureaucracy can be an efficient and effective way to organize people (bureaucrats) to do work.

>> A U.S. border patrol officer checks a driver's documents. He is one of more than 2.7 million people who work for the agencies and organizations that make up the federal bureaucracy.

1 of 6 >

Objective 1: Define a bureaucracy.

Quick Instruction

Project the quotation below from the *Federalist No. 51* on the whiteboard. Have students form pairs. Ask students to review the quotation and discuss what it means with their partner. Then tell pairs to analyze how the *Federalist No. 51* explains one principle of the American constitutional system of government. Ask volunteers to share their analysis with the class. *(Possible answer: This quotation explains why the Constitution uses a checks and balances system, which helps the government control itself and prevents any branch of the government from gaining too much power.)*

"In framing a government which is to be administered by men over men, the great difficulty lies in this: you must first enable the government to control the governed; and in the next place oblige it to control itself."

D Differentiate: Extra Support Help students understand the need for specialization in a bureaucracy by using the example of running a cafeteria. Ask students: What jobs need to be done to run a cafeteria? Have students think about supplying the food, distributing the food, and organizing the workers. Ask students: Do you think it would be effective to have each worker do all these jobs? Why or why not?

ELL Use the ELL activity described in the ELL chart.

Further Instruction

What Is a Bureaucracy?: Core Reading and Interactive Reading Notepad Go through the Interactive Reading Notepad questions and discuss the answers with the class. For further discussion, ask the following:

Analyze Information Why do you think hierarchies are structured as a pyramid? What do you think would happen if the structure was inverted to an upside-down pyramid? *(Possible answers: For a hierarchy to work, many people are needed to carry out the purpose of an organization. However, only a few people are needed to make decisions about what an organization should do and to tell various people to do it. Because of this, only a few people are at the top and many people are at the bottom. If the structure were reversed, there would not be enough people to put the organization's purpose into effect (i.e., carry out the day-to-day work of the organization). Also, too many people at the top could get confusing, because their decisions might conflict with one another.)*

Infer Most of the people who work in the bureaucracy of the Federal Government are not elected, including the heads of executive departments. Why do you think department heads of the Federal Government are not elected by the people? *(Possible answer: If the people had to elect every department head, elections would become too unwieldy.)*

DIGITAL TEXT 2

Executive Branch Bureaucracy

>> The Internal Revenue Service is part of the huge executive branch bureaucracy, responsible for processing all federal tax returns. The agency handles millions of pages of paperwork each year.

DIGITAL TEXT 3

How Units Are Named

>> Many government agencies are well known by their acronyms. **Analyze Political Cartoons** What point does the cartoon make about bureaucracies and their names?

Objective 2: Identify the major elements of the federal bureaucracy.

Quick Instruction

The structure of the federal bureaucracy consists of all the agencies, people, and procedures through which the Federal Government operates. Most of bureaucracy is located in the executive branch. The President is the chief administrator of the Federal Government. The President and Congress work with the administration to put policies into action around the country and the world.

ELL Use the ELL activity described in the ELL chart.

Further Instruction

Editable Presentation Use the Editable Presentation to present the main ideas for this Core Reading.

Executive Branch Bureaucracy: Core Reading and Interactive Reading Notepad Project and discuss the Interactive Reading Notepad questions, including the graphic organizer asking students to identify the structure of the executive branch of the Federal Government. Review this structure with the class and fill in the graphic organizer on the whiteboard as you go.

For further discussion, ask the following questions:

Hypothesize What do you think is the role of the Cabinet members in the executive branch of the Federal Government? *(Possible answers: The Cabinet members probably are in charge of important departments of the executive branch,*

such as education and defense. Also, the Cabinet members might advise the President.)

Analyze Images Have students look at the chart showing the major components of the executive branch. Ask them to analyze the structure of the executive branch of government, including the executive departments. For example, ask: What area of specialization is covered by the executive departments? *(The executive departments focus on broad policy areas, such as agriculture or transportation.)*

Objective 3: Explain how groups within the federal bureaucracy are named.

Quick Instruction

Tell students that a variety of names are used for sections of bureaucracies, including the executive branch of government. The term *agency* is often used to refer to any governmental body. It is sometimes used to identify a major unit headed by a single administrator of near-cabinet status, such as the Environmental Protection Agency. Ask students to think of names used for various sections of their school's bureaucracy. List names on the board and discuss why these names were chosen.

D Differentiate: **Challenge/Gifted** Have students think of an agency that they believe should be added to the executive branch of the Federal Government. Then tell students to name this agency and choose an acronym for it. Students should write a explanation about why this name and acronym were chosen.

Further Instruction

Go through the Interactive Reading Notepad questions and discuss the answers with the class. For further discussion, ask the following questions:

Support Point of View with Evidence Do you think it would have been better if the Federal Government established rules for the naming of sections of the government? Explain. *(Possible answers: Yes; by establishing naming rules, a person could tell what a section of the government does just by its name. With the present system, the names*

The Federal Bureaucracy

DIGITAL TEXT 4
Staff and Line Agencies

INTERACTIVE CHART
Staff or Line Agency?

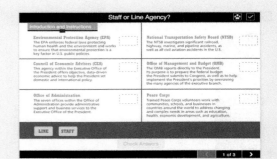

really have little connection with the function of the section. OR No; by not having rules, the names used for sections of the government is probably left up to the people organizing the section. These people should have the right to choose the name for their section.)

Recall What names are most often used for government agencies that conduct businesslike activities? *("corporation" and "authority")*

Objective 4: Describe the difference between a staff agency and a line agency.

Quick Instruction

Agencies and departments within the executive branch of the Federal Government can be classified as staff or line. Staff agencies function to support the work of the President and other administrators by offering advice and assistance. Line agencies perform the work for which the organization exists.

Interactive Chart: Staff or Line Agency? Project the interactive chart on the whiteboard. Tell students to read the description for each agency, and decide whether it is staff or line. Then tell students to drag the correct label to the agency.

📷 ACTIVE CLASSROOM

Use the Graffiti Concepts activity to have students reflect on the meaning of "staff agency." Then tell them to create a visual image that represents this term. After this, have them do the same for the term "line agency." Ask students to post their images on the board or on chart paper. Then have students look at all the various responses and discuss similarities and differences as a group.

Further Instruction

Go through the Interactive Reading Notepad questions and discuss the answers with the class. For further discussion, answer the following questions:

Compare and Contrast How are the functions of staff agencies and line agencies similar and different? *(Possible answer: Both staff and line agencies function in the executive branch of the Federal Government. Also, both focus on certain areas, such as education or commerce. Staff agencies, though, serve to support and advise administrators. On the other hand, line agencies perform the task for which an organization exists.)*

Draw Conclusions The President needs to respond to a hurricane that hit the southern United States. How could both line agencies and staff agencies help the President with this task? *(Possible answer: Line agencies could deliver emergency supplies or help clean up stricken areas. Staff agencies could gather information about the disaster, including the amount of damage, to help the President assess the situation.)*

SYNTHESIZE

DIGITAL SYNTHESIZE ACTIVITY
Too Much Red Tape?

Ask students to recall the Topic Essential Question, "What Should Governments Do?" Have them use the Think Pair Share strategy to complete the Red Tape Activity. Ask them to take ten minutes to complete this activity and then share their answers with a talking partner.

Historically, early bureaucrats in Europe used red cloth ribbons to hold together official records and documents, and this is where the phrase "red tape" originated. People often refer to bureaucracies as being messy and having too much red tape to accomplish anything quickly.

Support Point of View with Evidence Do you agree or disagree with the statement about bureaucracies being messy and having too much red tape? Defend your argument using evidence from your Federal Bureaucracy table.

DEMONSTRATE

DIGITAL QUIZ
Lesson Quiz and Class Board Discussion

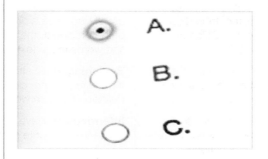

Assign the online Lesson Quiz for this lesson if you haven't already done so. Students will be offered automatic remediation or enrichment based on their score.

Bureaucracies are based on three principles: hierarchical authority, job specialization, and formalized rules. These principles make bureaucracies effective, but can also make them inefficient.

Support a Point of View with Evidence Which bureaucratic principle do you think is the main cause for the effectiveness of the Federal Government? Which principle is the main cause of the inefficiency of the government? *(Possible answer: I think that job specialization is the main reason why the Federal Government is efficient. Because of this principle, people with expertise in a certain area can focus on this area and thereby do a good job. I think formalized rules are the main cause of inefficiency in the U.S. government. A large number of rules can slow down the process of various departments.)*

Topic Inquiry
Have students continue their investigations for the Topic Inquiry.

The EOP and the Executive Departments

Supporting English Language Learners

Use with Digital Text 1, **Structure of the Executive Office of the President.**

Listening

Guide students to preview the text by looking at all the visuals and reading the captions. Read aloud the captions while students listen, then discuss how the visuals help the students understand the Executive Office of the President.

Beginning Have students listen as you read aloud one section of the text. Ask the students questions about the visuals that can be answered with gestures, yes or no, or one- and two-word responses.

Intermediate Have partners take turns listening and reading the text aloud. Ask students questions about the visuals that require short phrases as responses. Guide partners to find the answers to the questions.

Advanced Have partners take turns listening and reading the text aloud. Ask partners to select two visuals and discuss how the visuals help in understanding the content. Ask partners to share with another set of partners.

Advanced High Have partners read the text and select a visual that enhanced their understanding. Have them share the visual they selected with the group and read aloud the portion of the text that is supported by the visual while the rest of the group listens.

Use with the lesson 2 readings.

Writing

Teach students that "shun" can be spelled in three ways: *tion* , *cion* , *cian* . Explain that *tion* and *cion* often indicate an action or condition, while *cian* usually indicates a profession. As students read about the Executive Office of the President, the executive departments, and the Cabinet, have them find words in the text with these spellings.

Beginning Have students copy words from the text and sort them into three groups: *tion*, *cion*, and *cian*. Discuss and have students write a definition for each word.

Intermediate Have students practice reading the words to each other. Guide them to write sentences using these words.

Advanced Guide partners to write sentences using the words. Have them read the sentences to another set of partners.

Advanced High Have students write short paragraphs using these words. Guide them to think of other words that have the same spellings.

◖ Differentiate Instruction

Use the Differentiated Instruction notes throughout the lesson plan to support the varied skill sets, levels of readiness, and interests in the mixed-ability classroom.

Challenge These notes include suggestions for expanding the activity for advanced students.

On-Level These notes include suggestions for modifying the activity to address different interests or learning styles.

Extra Support These notes include ideas for providing more scaffolding or reading spuport.

Special Needs These notes provide ideas for adapting instruction to support the needs of various special needs students.

▮ NOTES

PEARSON
realize™
www.PearsonRealize.com

Go online to access additional resources including:
Primary Sources • Biographies • Supreme Court cases •
21st Century Skill Tutorials • Maps • Graphic Organizers.

Objectives

Objective 1: Analyze the structure and functions of the executive branch of government.

Objective 2: Describe the Executive Office of the President.

Objective 3: Explain the duties of the White House, the National Security Council, and the Office of Management and Budget.

Objective 4: Identify other agencies that make up the Executive Office of the President.

Objective 5: Describe the role of the Cabinet and executive departments in the executive branch.

LESSON 2 ORGANIZER		PACING: APPROX. 1 PERIOD, .5 BLOCKS			
		OBJECTIVES	PACING	**RESOURCES**	
				Online	Print
Connect					
DIGITAL START UP ACTIVITY **Choosing Your Cabinet**			10 min.	●	
Investigate					
DIGITAL TEXT 1 **Structure of the Executive Office of the President**		Objectives 1, 2, 3, 4	10 min.	●	●
INTERACTIVE 3-D MODEL **The White House West Wing**			10 min.	●	
DIGITAL TEXT 2 **The Executive Departments**		Objective 5	10 min.	●	●
INTERACTIVE TIMELINE **The Executive Departments**			10 min.	●	
DIGITAL TEXT 3 **The Cabinet and Its Function**		Objective 4	10 min.	●	●
INTERACTIVE GALLERY **Women and Minorities in the Cabinet**			10 min.	●	
Synthesize					
DIGITAL SYNTHESIZE ACTIVITY **Revisit Your Cabinet Pick**			10 min.	●	
Demonstrate					
DIGITAL QUIZ **Lesson Quiz and Class Discussion Board**			10 min.	●	

The EOP and the Executive Departments

■ CONNECT

DIGITAL START UP ACTIVITY

Choosing Your Cabinet

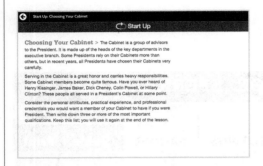

Tell students that President Franklin Roosevelt is responsible for persuading Congress to establish the administrative agency known as the Executive Office of the President. One key individual who works in the EOP is the White House chief of staff.

Ask students to consider the personal attributes, practical experience, and professional credentials they would want their chief of staff to have if they were President. Then tell students to write down at least three of the most important attributes they would look for when selecting a chief of staff.

Tell students that in this lesson they will be learning about the structure and function of the executive branch of government.

Aa Vocabulary Development: Use the Interactive Reading Notepad to preview the Key Terms and Academic Vocabulary in this Lesson with students.

⚡ FLIP IT!

Assign the Flipped Video for this lesson.

■ STUDENT EDITION PRINT PAGES: 242–250

■ INVESTIGATE

DIGITAL TEXT 1

Structure of the Executive Office of the President

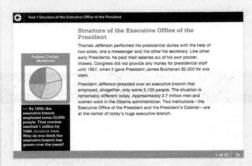

Objectives 1: Analyze the structure and function of the executive branch of government; 2: Describe the Executive Office of the President; 3: Explain the duties of the White House, the National Security Council, and the Office of Management and Budget; 4: Identify other agencies that make up the Executive Office of the President.

Quick Instruction

The executive branch of the Federal Government is composed of a huge number of agencies. The Executive Office of the President (the EOP) and the President's Cabinet are at the center of today's huge executive branch. The President's right arm is the EOP. The EOP's nerve center, in fact, the nerve center of the entire executive branch, is an agency called the White House. Most of the President's key personal and political aides work there. EOP agencies have a wide variety of functions, including, for example, the Office of the United States Trade Representative, which plays an important role in setting international trade policy, or the Council on Environmental Quality, which helps ensure that federal agencies comply with the nation's environmental laws.

Interactive 3-D Model: The White House West Wing Step through the interactive model with students. Point out that it shows structure of the White House building and provides information about the Oval Office, the Cabinet Room, and Vice President's office.

INTERACTIVE 3-D MODEL

The White House West Wing

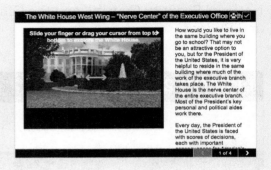

🔊 ACTIVE CLASSROOM

Have students do an Audio Tour activity. Pair students. Have the first student give the second student a verbal tour of the White House West Wing, using the interactive 3D model as an aid. The tour will describe what the model shows. The second student will explain what happens in the various areas in the White House West Wing.

D Differentiate: **Challenge/Gifted** Pair students. Have pairs act out a conversation between the President and the director of the Office of Management and Budget. The dialogue should deal with putting together the next fiscal year's budget.

ELL Use the ELL activity described in the ELL chart.

Further Instruction

Editable Presentation Use the Editable Presentation to present the main ideas for this Core Reading.

Structure of the Executive Office of the President: Core Reading and Interactive Reading Notepad Project and discuss the Interactive Reading Notepad questions, including the chart showing the functions of some of the agencies and advisors that are part of the Executive Office of the President. Review the functions with the class and fill in the chart on the whiteboard as you go.

DIGITAL TEXT 2

The Executive Departments

INTERACTIVE TIMELINE

The Executive Departments

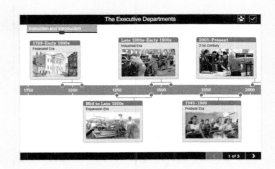

For further discussion, ask the following questions:

Compare and Contrast How is the Office of Management and Budget and the Office of the U.S. Trade Representative similar and different? *(Possible answer: Both agencies deal with economic matters. However, the Office of Management and Budget focuses on the government's budget. On the other hand, the Office of the U.S. Trade Representative focuses on advising the chief executive in all matters of foreign trade.)*

Draw Conclusions If the President faced a sudden crisis in the Middle East, with which unit of the Executive Office of the President would the President meet? Why would the President meet with this unit? *(Possible answer: The President would meet with the National Security Council. This agency deals with foreign affairs and military matters.)*

Objective 5: Describe the role of the Cabinet and executive departments in the executive branch.

Quick Instruction

Each historical era brought about new challenges to the United States and its people. In order to address these new issues, additional executive departments were created. The departments are structured with a secretary at the head and subunits below that carry out specialized functions. They are one of the primary means by which the Federal Government carries out its major responsibilities for domestic policy. As a way to introduce the topic, write the following names on the board: George Washington, Thomas Jefferson, Andrew Jackson, Abraham Lincoln, Franklin Roosevelt, and Ronald Reagan. Then tell students that these men were significant individuals in the field of government and politics for many reasons, some of which they will learn about in this text.

Interactive Timeline: The Executive Departments Project the timeline. Ask students to click the five eras to learn about the executive departments established during each era. Help students use the timeline as a tool to analyze the functions of the executive departments. Ask: Are there any aspects of life in the United States that are NOT covered by one of the executive departments? How do they help the Federal Government carry out the nation's domestic policies?

Analyze Information Does government regulation sometimes serve as a restriction to private enterprise? What role do the executive departments and their subunits play in this regard? *(Some agencies of the executive departments, such as the Occupational Safety and Health Administration in the Department of Labor, have regulatory functions that can be seen as restrictive to private enterprise. The rules and regulations they impose can be confusing or overly burdensome.)*

Cause and Effect Analyze the growth of presidential power in terms of the size of the Executive Office of the President. How are the two related? *(More departments are added to handle increasing responsibilities and work. As the Executive Office grows, so do the responsibilities of the President, who with Congress, crafts and carries out domestic and foreign policies through these departments.)*

⬛ ACTIVE CLASSROOM

Have students do a PMI activity in groups. Give each group a 3-column organizer with headings "Plus," "Minus," and "Interesting" for recording responses to the following three questions about the Occupational Safety and Health Administration (OSHA).

What are the positive views of the OSHA? What are the negative views about this agency? What is interesting about the OSHA?

The EOP and the Executive Departments

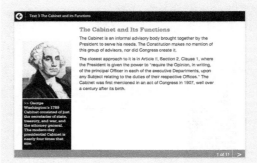

DIGITAL TEXT 3
The Cabinet and Its Function

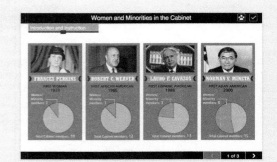

INTERACTIVE GALLERY
Women and Minorities in the Cabinet

ELL Use the ELL activity described in the ELL chart.

Further Instruction

The Executive Departments: Core Reading and Interactive Reading Notepad Go through the Interactive Reading Notepad questions and discuss the answers with the class. For further discussion, ask the following question:

Evaluate Sources Alexander Hamilton stated that "the true test of a good government is its aptitude and tendency to produce a good administration." How did the Framers of the Constitution give each President the freedom to produce a good administration? *(Possible answer: The Framers of the Constitution spent little time on the organization of the executive branch of the government. They left this organization loose and undefined. As a result, each President could change and adapt the executive branch to best deal with the needs and problems that he faced.)*

Objective 4: Describe the role of the Cabinet and executive departments in the executive branch.

Quick Instruction

As the head of the executive branch of the Federal Government, the President has the constitutional power to appoint the heads of the 15 executive departments. These department heads then form a group known as the Cabinet. The Cabinet's role has changed from administration to administration, but it generally serves as an advisory body to the President.

Interactive Gallery: Women and Minorities in the Cabinet Ask students to select each image to learn more about the first woman and the first minorities in the Cabinet.

Analyze Graphs What trend you see in the pie graphs? *(Possible answer: The number of women and minorities in the Cabinet was very low for many years during the 1900s. Then in the 1980s, this number started to increase. Recently, the number of women and minorities in the Cabinet has increased significantly.)*

Draw Conclusions Analyze the constitutional power of the President to name the heads of the executive departments.How might this power affect the implementation of the nation's foreign and domestic policies? *(Possible answer: The President often names heads of the executive department that have similar political views to the President. As a result, the implementation of the nation's foreign and domestic policies will reflect the President's political approach.)* How does the way the Cabinet secretary posts are filled compare to the way other public posts are filled—for

example, the post of President or a member of Congress? *(The Cabinet secretary posts are filled by an appointment by the president and confirmation by the Senate. Most other public posts are elected by U.S. citizens.)*

ACTIVE CLASSROOM

Have students use the Take a Stand activity on the following question: Should the Cabinet be eliminated? Yes or no? Tell students to divide into two groups based on their answer. If one group has only a few members, then assign other students to this group. Have students talk to each other to compare their reasons for answering yes or no. Then ask a representative from each side to present and defend the group's point of view.

D Differentiate: Extra Support Help students to understand why a woman was not appointed as a member of the Cabinet until 1933. Remind students that women were not allowed to vote until 1920. Ask students: Why do you think women were not allowed to vote for so long? Then ask: Do you think similar reasons could have delayed the appointment of a woman to the Cabinet? Why or why not?

Further Instruction

Go through the Interactive Reading Notepad questions and discuss the answers with the class. For further discussion, ask the following questions:

Hypothesize What do you think are two of the major reasons why Cabinet appointments have been rejected by the Senate? *(Possible answer: The person seeking appointment*

SYNTHESIZE

DIGITAL SYNTHESIZE ACTIVITY
Revisit Your Cabinet Pick

DEMONSTRATE

DIGITAL QUIZ
Lesson Quiz and Class Discussion Board

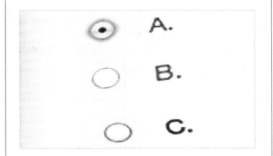

might have controversial views about certain issues or be too liberal or too conservative. Also, the person might have personal problems that cause him or her to be rejected.)

Check Understanding Analyze the role of the Cabinet. For example, what are the main factors that influence that role within the executive branch? *(The role of each Cabinet member is to serve as the head on one of the executive departments and to advise the president. However, the advisory role can vary depending on the President. Today, many Presidents rely more on advice from the Executive Office staff, instead of from Cabinet members.)*

Ask students to look at the personal attributes, practical experience, and professional credentials that they wrote down at the beginning of the lesson. Tell students to compare these qualities to what they now know about the job responsibilities of the President's chief of staff. Have students revisit their list and add or delete attributes based on new knowledge. Students should explain why they added or deleted items.

Discuss Ask students: Do you think the job qualifications of the President's chief of staff has changed over the years? If so, how? If not, why not?

Assign the online Lesson Quiz for this lesson if you haven't already done so. Students will be offered automatic remediation or enrichment based on their score.

Pose these questions to the class on the Discussion Board:

Make Generalizations What overall trends do you see in the development of the Executive Office of the President throughout the history of the United States? *(Possible answer: The Executive Office of the President has grown in size and in importance.)*

Make Predictions How do you think the Executive Office of the President will change in the future? *(Possible answer: I think it will continue to grow in importance and eventually will replace the Cabinet.)*

Topic Inquiry
Have students continue their investigations for the Topic Inquiry.

The Independent Agencies

Supporting English Language Learners

Use with the lesson 3 readings.

Listening
Have students listen as you read aloud the sections of the text with the key terms: *independent agencies*, *civil service*, *patronage*, *spoils system*, *draft*, and *government corporations*. Guide students to use context clues to understand these words or phrases, which will, in turn, help them better understand the purpose of selected independent executive agencies.

Beginning Have students listen as you read aloud. Display the sentences containing the key terms. Underline words that serve as context clues as you describe how they are related to the key terms.

Intermediate Read aloud as students listen and follow along in the text. Point out the words that serve as context clues. Have students complete a word web with the key term in the middle and the context clues on the branches.

Advanced Have partners take turns listening and reading aloud the text. The partner who is listening should note any context clues for the key terms that he or she hears. Have students compare and discuss their lists with another set of partners.

Advanced High Have partners take turns listening and reading aloud the text. Have students identify the context clues for the key terms and then write a definition for each term using the context clues.

Use with Digital Text 2, **Independent Executive Agencies.**

Writing
Guide students to read the text, focusing on the independent executive agencies. Review or teach the words *explain*, *identify*, and *describe*. Have students practice writing using these words by completing the following activities.

Beginning Have students copy and complete the following sentence stems based on the independent executive agencies. *I can explain _____. I can identify _____. I can describe ____ _____.*

Intermediate Have students copy and complete the following sentence stems based on the independent executive agencies: *I can explain why _____. I can explain how _____. I can identify who _____. I can identify what _____. I can describe _____.*

Advanced Explain to students that the words can be used when telling someone what to do. Have them write commands based on the independent executive agencies by completing the following sentence stems: *Explain why _____. Explain how _____. Identify the _____. Identify the person who _____. Describe what _____.*

Advanced High Have students use the words *explain*, *identify*, and *describe* as they write sentences about the independent executive agencies.

▣ Differentiate Instruction

Use the Differentiated Instruction notes throughout the lesson plan to support the varied skill sets, levels of readiness, and interests in the mixed-ability classroom.

Challenge These notes include suggestions for expanding the activity for advanced students.

On-Level These notes include suggestions for modifying the activity to address different interests or learning styles.

Extra Support These notes include ideas for providing more scaffolding or reading spuport.

Special Needs These notes provide ideas for adapting instruction to support the needs of various special needs students.

◼ NOTES

PEARSON
realize™
www.PearsonRealize.com

Go online to access additional resources including:
Primary Sources • Biographies • Supreme Court cases •
21st Century Skill Tutorials • Maps • Graphic Organizers.

Objectives

Objective 1: Explain why Congress created the independent agencies.

Objective 2: Identify the characteristics of independent executive agencies.

Objective 3: Describe the history, purpose, and effect on private enterprise of selected independent executive agencies and regulatory commissions, including NASA and the EPA.

Objective 4: Explain the structure and function of government corporations.

LESSON 3 ORGANIZER	PACING: APPROX. 1 PERIOD, .5 BLOCKS			
			RESOURCES	
	OBJECTIVES	**PACING**	**Online**	**Print**
Connect				
DIGITAL START UP ACTIVITY **Is a Federal Government Job Right for You?**		10 min.	●	
Investigate				
DIGITAL TEXT 1 **The Purpose of Independent Agencies**	Objective 1	10 min.	●	●
DIGITAL TEXT 2 **Independent Executive Agencies**	Objectives 2, 3	10 min.	●	●
INTERACTIVE ILLUSTRATION **The Application of NASA Research to Consumer Products**		10 min.	●	
DIGITAL TEXT 3 **Independent Regulatory Commissions**	Objective 3	10 min.	●	●
INTERACTIVE GALLERY **Independent Agencies: A Closer Look**		10 min.	●	
DIGITAL TEXT 4 **Government Corporations**	Objective 4	10 min.	●	●
Synthesize				
DIGITAL SYNTHESIZE ACTIVITY **Design Your Own Independent Agency**		10 min.	●	
Demonstrate				
DIGITAL QUIZ **Lesson Quiz and Class Discussion Board**		10 min.	●	

The Independent Agencies

■ CONNECT

DIGITAL START UP ACTIVITY
Is a Federal Government Job Right for You?

Project the Start Up Activity Ask students to answer the questions as they enter and get settled. Then have them share their ideas with another student.

Inform students that the Federal Government is the largest employer in the United States, with more than two million employees.

Ask students: What types of jobs do you think the Federal Government offers? Have students make a list of careers that might be within the Federal Government. Then have students tell which jobs might interest them and why.

Tell students that in this lesson they will be learning about the independent executive agencies and government corporations.

Aa Vocabulary Development: Use the Interactive Reading Notepad to preview the Key Terms and Academic Vocabulary in this Lesson with students.

⇌ FLIP IT!
Assign the Flipped Video for this lesson.

■ STUDENT EDITION PRINT
PAGES: 251–260

■ INVESTIGATE

DIGITAL TEXT 1
The Purpose of Independent Agencies

Objective 1: Explain why Congress created the independent agencies.

Quick Instruction
Inform students that Congress has created a large number of independent executive agencies, including National Aeronautics and Space Administration (NASA), and regulatory commissions, including the Environmental Protection Agency (EPA), the Food and Drug Administration (FDA), and the Federal Communications Commission (FCC). Ask students: Why do you think Congress calls these agencies "independent"? In what ways do you think these agencies are different from Cabinet agencies? What are the advantages of making an agency "independent"? What purposes might these agencies serve?

ELL Use the ELL activity described in the ELL chart.

Further Instruction
The Purpose of Independent Agencies: Core Reading ain Interactive Reading Notepad Go through the Interactive Reading Notepad questions and discuss the answers with the class. For further discussion, ask the following:

Infer Why do you think Congress wanted the U.S. Commission on Civil Rights to be non-partisan? *(Possible answer: Congress did not want party politics to influence decisions on civil rights. These decisions should be based on protecting the rights of the people and should not be based on a political party's agenda.)*

Identify Central Ideas Independent executive agencies include many different types of entities. What do all of these agencies have in common? *(They are not located within any of the 15 Cabinet departments.)*

DIGITAL TEXT 2
Independent Executive Agencies

Objectives 2: Identify the characteristics of independent executive agencies; 3: Describe the history, purpose, and effect on private enterprise of selected independent executive agencies and regulatory commissions, including NASA and the SEC.

Quick Instruction
The independent executive agenices include most non-Cabinet agencies of the executive branch. Some have had a strong impact on American culture and society. A prime example of this type of agency is the National Aeronautics and Space Administration (NASA), which has conducted research that, when shared with the private sector, has resulted in improved consumer products and communications. Others, such as the National Science Foundation, have had an impact on society through their support for recent scientific discoveries and technological innovations. Still others, such as the Office of Personnel Management, were born out of particular events in the nation's history. Significant individuals in government and politics were involved in the events leading to the creation of the OPM, such as Andrew Jackson, who made wide use of the spoils system, and later, Theodore Roosevelt, who championed the merit system.

Interactive Gallery: NASA Inventions in Consumer Products Project the interactive gallery on the whiteboard and click through the hot spots. Ask students: Which of these technologies have you used? Which has been the most helpful to you?

INTERACTIVE ILLUSTRATION

The Application of NASA Research to Consumer Products

DIGITAL TEXT 3

Independent Regulatory Commissions

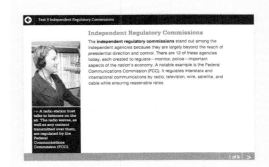

Support a Point of View with Evidence Do you think the technological innovations developed by NASA justify the existence of this agency? *(Possible answer: Yes; through their research for space exploration, NASA has improved the daily lives of people and has even saved lives. For example, the protective clothing developed by NASA has probably saved the lives of firefighters.)*

📷 ACTIVE CLASSROOM

Use the Sequence It activity to have students place the main events in the history of the military draft and Selected Service System in chronological order. Give students the following list of events: the first peacetime draft, Congress rejects national compulsory military service, the Selective Service Act, the President's power to order induction expires, and the first national draft. Have students organize the list in chronological order. Then ask students to form groups of five. Have students in each group compare their lists and decide the correct chronological order of the events. Each group should then create a "Human Order" line. Each member of a group should represent an event. The member should arrange themselves in chronological order, with the student representing the earliest event at the front of the line.

D Differentiate: Challenge/Gifted Ask students to draw a poster that promotes NASA. The poster should include contributions that NASA has made to society.

ELL Use the ELL activity described in the ELL chart.

Further Instruction

Editable Presentation Use the Editable Presentation to present the main ideas for this Core Reading.

Independent Executive Agencies: Core Reading and Interactive Reading Notepad Project and discuss the Interactive Reading Notepad questions, including the Venn diagram asking students to compare and contrast the three types of independent agencies. Review these agencies with the class and fill in the Venn diagram on the whiteboard as you go.

For further discussion, ask the following questions:

Check Understanding What are the purposes of the Food and Drug Administration (FDA) and the Environmental Protection Agency (EPA)? *(The FDA protects citizens by regulating safety standards for food, drugs, medical devices, vaccines, veterinary supplies, tobacco, and cosmetics. The EPA establishes and enforces pollution and other standards in order to protect the environment.)*

Summarize What was the spoils system and under which President was its use expanded? *(Possible answer: It was a system in which people were appointed to government positions or fired from government positions based on patronage-based rewards and punishments. As a result, inefficiency and corruption became widespread in the government. Its use became more entrenched during the presidency of Andrew Jackson.)*

Objective 3: Describe the history, purpose, and effect on private enterprise of selected regulatory commissions, including NASA and the SEC.

Quick Instruction

Interactive Gallery: Independent Agencies: A Closer Look Project the interactive on the whiteboard and click through images with students. Introduce the gallery activity by telling students that there are many different types of independent agencies. Some of these agencies are called regulatory agencies.

Discuss Which agency in the gallery is a regulatory agency? Explain the reasons for your choice. *(Possible answer: The EPA is a regulatory agency because it has legislative-like and judicial-like powers unlike the other agencies featured in the gallery.)*

Compare and Contrast How are the FCC and CPB similar and different? *(Possible answer: Both the FCC and CPB deal with the media and communications. However, the FCC focuses on regulating interstate and foreign communications by radio, television, wire, satellite, and cable. On the other hand, the CPB focuses on funding radio, television, and other programming.)*

The Independent Agencies

INTERACTIVE GALLERY

Independent Agencies: A Closer Look

DIGITAL TEXT 4

Government Corporations

🎥 ACTIVE CLASSROOM

Have students do a Take a Stand activity. Ask students to take a stand on the following questions: Do regulatory agencies have too much control over private enterprise? Yes or no? Tell students to divide into two groups based on their answers and move to separate areas of the classroom. If one group has only a few members, assign more students to this group. Ask students to talk to each other to compare their reasons for answering yes or no. Then ask a representative from each side to present and defend the group's point of view.

D Differentiate: Extra Support Tell students that regulatory agencies deal with thousands of cases each year. Ask students: How much time would be required to do all this work? How large of a workforce would be required? Do you think Congress has enough time and a large enough workforce to handle this workload? Why do you think Congress allowed regulatory agencies to have executive, legislative, and judicial powers?

ELL Use the ELL activity described in the ELL chart.

Further Instruction
Go through the Interactive Reading Notepad questions and discuss the answers with the class. For further discussion, ask the following:

Identify Central Issues Consider agenices such as the Federal Reserve System and the Consumer Product Safety Commission. Choose one regulatory commission and explain how its regulatory policies influence the economy at the national, State, and local levels.

(Possible answer: The Consumer Product Safety Commission influences the economy by setting safety and other standards for products. This can increase the cost of a product and may make it more difficult for small companies to be able to survive in a competitive market. This lack of competition can affect the economy at all levels. OR The CPSC raises consumer confidence in products by ensuring that companies abide by safety and other regulations. This can affect the economy at all levels by increasing sales and making it possible for businesses to make a profit.)

Identify Steps in a Process How are the leaders of regulatory agencies determined and what role do the constitutional powers of the President play in this process? *(The President chooses the members of the agency's board or commission. The Senate then approves these choices.)*

Objective 4: **Explain the structure and function of government corporations.**

Quick Instruction
Congress has set up special independent agencies called government corporations, which are located in the executive branch. Since these entities conduct businesslike activities, they are different from other independent agencies.

Discuss Tell students that the U.S. Postal Service is a government corporation. Ask students: Why do you think Congress made the U.S. Postal Service a government corporation instead of a regulatory agency? *(Possible answer: because it produces income that is plowed back into the agency's programs)*

Further Instruction
Go through the Interactive Reading Notepad questions and discuss the answers with the class. For further discussion, ask the following:

Draw Conclusions Why do you think Congress often forms government corporations to handle emergency situations? *(Possible answer: Government corporations are probably easier to set up than other types of independent agencies. Also, government corporations are flexible, thereby allowing them to adapt to the needs of various emergency situations.)*

Infer The TVA is a government corporation that improves navigation and living standards and produces electrical power along the Tennessee River. Why do you think Congress gave this government corporation

■ SYNTHESIZE

DIGITAL SYNTHESIZE ACTIVITY
Design Your Own Independent Agency

■ DEMONSTRATE

DIGITAL QUIZ
Lesson Quiz and Class Discussion Board

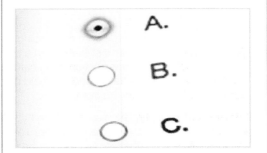

a large degree of independence? *(Possible answer: The function of the TVA is focused in a specific region. Since the leaders of the TVA have considerable knowledge about the Tennessee River region, they would have the best idea of how to use their income for their operations. Having the TVA attached to a larger, national agency would interfere with the efficiency of TVA.)*

Ask students to identify a segment of American life that might be better handled through an independent agency. Could our schools benefit from the guidance of an independent agency? What about medical research? How do independent agencies help to carry out the Federal Government's major responsibilities for domestic policy?

Integrate Information Ask students to design their own independent agency to handle any part of American life. In doing so, they should answer the following questions:

• What is the name of your agency?

• What does your agency do?

• Why can the country benefit from this new agency?

• Which type of agency would work best to perform the function of your agency? For example, should it be an independent executive agency, an independent regulatory commission, or a government corporation?

• Explain why this agency type would work best for your agency.

Assign the online Lesson Quiz for this lesson if you haven't already done so. Students will be offered automatic remediation or enrichment based on their score.

Pose these questions to the class on the Discussion Board:

Generate Explanations Why do you think the executive branch has grown so much larger than the legislative branch of the U.S. government? *(Possible answer: The purpose of the executive branch is to put into effect the laws and responsibilities of the government. Since these laws and responsibilities cover many areas, many independent agencies operated by thousands of workers needed to be established. On the other hand, the legislative branch makes specific laws that are then applied to millions of people. The creation of these laws does not require numerous agencies and thousands of people.)*

Express Problems Clearly What types of problems have the independent agencies of the executive branch attempted to solve? Give a specific example for each type of problem. *(Possible answer: Problems include standards that need to be established, such as for the environment; regulations that need to be developed, such as regulations for investments; and research that needs to be conducted, such as the research to enable space exploration.)*

Topic Inquiry
Have students continue their investigations for the Topic Inquiry.

Foreign Policy Overview

Supporting English Language Learners

Use with the Lesson 4 readings.

Listening

Have students listen as you read aloud the text and emphasize the words that are hyperlinked to the glossary: *domestic affairs, foreign affairs, isolationism* and *Isthmus of Panama.*

Beginning Write the words from the reading that are hyperlinked to the glossary on the board. Have students fold a piece of paper into fourths and write each word in one section, then cut the sections apart. Ask them to listen as you read the text aloud and hold up the paper with the correct word on it when that word is read.

Intermediate Display the words that are hyperlinked to the glossary. Tell students to listen for the words as you read aloud. Guide the students to find the definitions of the words. Discuss the meanings of the words.

Advanced Have students listen as a partner reads aloud the text. Guide them to create a list of words that are hyperlinked to the glossary and then find the definitions of those words. Have small groups discuss the meanings of the words.

Advanced High Have students listen as a partner reads aloud the text. Next, they should find the definitions for the words that are hyperlinked to the glossary. Finally, guide partners to write the definitions in their own words.

Use with the Lesson 4 readings.

Writing

Depending on the language levels of your students, provide a list of content-based vocabulary that fouses on the foreign policy of the United States, such as: *foreign affairs, isolationism, cold war,* and *deterrence.* Guide students to use the words in their writing by completing the following activities.

Beginning Discuss the meanings of the words. Display short definitions for each word or phrase. Help students match the content-based vocabulary to its definition. Have students copy the vocabulary and definitions.

Intermediate Discuss the meanings of the words. Guide the class to write a short phrase defining each word or phrase. Have students copy the vocabulary and the definitions.

Advanced Have partners read the text and find the vocabulary. Discuss the meanings and have students write short sentences with the words.

Advanced High Have students read the text and find the vocabulary. Have them write two sentences explaining the meaning of each word or phrase. Have them read their sentences to a partner.

▣ Differentiate Instruction

Use the Differentiated Instruction notes throughout the lesson plan to support the varied skill sets, levels of readiness, and interests in the mixed-ability classroom.

Challenge These notes include suggestions for expanding the activity for advanced students.

On-Level These notes include suggestions for modifying the activity to address different interests or learning styles.

Extra Support These notes include ideas for providing more scaffolding or reading spuport.

Special Needs These notes provide ideas for adapting instruction to support the needs of various special needs students.

■ NOTES

Objectives

Objective 1: Explain the major responsibilities of the Federal Government for foreign policy.

Objective 2: Summarize U.S. foreign policy during the first 150 years of its history, including its adherence to isolationism.

Objective 3: Show how World War II finally ended America's traditional policy of isolationism, giving way to internationalism and the principles of collective security and deterrence.

Objective 4: Analyze how today's U.S. foreign policy affects selected places and regions, as well as the significance to the United States of the location and key natural resources of selected global places or regions.

LESSON 4 ORGANIZER		PACING: APPROX. 1 PERIOD, .5 BLOCKS			
				RESOURCES	
		OBJECTIVES	PACING	Online	Print
Connect					
	DIGITAL START UP ACTIVITY **Isolationism or Internationalism?**		10 min.	●	
Investigate					
	DIGITAL TEXT 1 **What Is Foreign Policy?**	Objective 1	10 min.	●	●
	DIGITAL TEXT 2 **Beginnings Through World War I**		10 min.	●	●
	DIGITAL TEXT 3 **World War II to the End of the Cold War**	Objectives 2, 3	10 min.	●	●
	INTERACTIVE TIMELINE **Isolationism to Internationalism**		10 min.	●	
	DIGITAL TEXT 4 **Today's Foreign Policy Challenges**	Objective 4	10 min.	●	●
	INTERACTIVE MAP **Major Diplomatic Hotspots**		10 min.	●	
Synthesize					
	DIGITAL ACTIVITY **Revisiting Isolationism or Internationalism**		10 min.	●	
Demonstrate					
	DIGITAL QUIZ **Lesson Quiz and Class Discussion Board**		10 min.	●	

Foreign Policy Overview

■ **CONNECT**

■ **INVESTIGATE**

DIGITAL START UP ACTIVITY

Isolationism or Internationalism?

DIGITAL TEXT 1

What Is Foreign Policy?

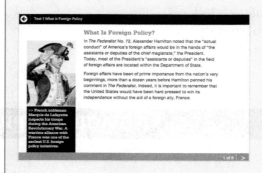

Project the Start Up Activity Have students think about the meanings of the words "isolationist" and "internationalist." Then tell students to describe, in a few sentences, the difference between the terms as they apply to United States foreign policy. Ask students to copy the list of foreign events. Students should then categorize each as an example of isolationism or internationalism. Tell students to save their lists. They will use them again at the end of the lesson.

Tell students that in this lesson they will be learning about the history of U.S. foreign policy and how today's U.S. foreign policy affects various places and regions throughout the world.

Aa Vocabulary Development: Use the Interactive Reading Notepad to preview the Key Terms and Academic Vocabulary in this Lesson with students.

⚑ FLIP IT!

Assign the Flipped Video for this lesson.

■ STUDENT EDITION PRINT PAGES: 261–272

Objective 1: Explain the major responsibilities of the Federal Government for foreign policy.

Quick Instruction

Tell students that the major responsibilities of the Federal Government for foreign policy cover many different areas. Have students think of possible responsibilities that fall under the foreign policy umbrella. Then ask volunteers to share their ideas and list them on the board. After this, list the topics covered in this section, including national defense, climate change, and space exploration. Examine how the U.S. government uses economic resources in foreign policy, including its role in the conduct of international trade and the use of economic sanctions and foreign economic aid.

Identify Why are the location and key natural resources of selected regions of significance to the United States? Give one example. *(Possible answer: It is important to maintain good relationships with countries that are geographically close to the U.S., for both trade and national security reasons. The natural resources of certain areas are important to the U.S. because they are necessary to the American economy. One example is oil from the Middle East.)*

ELL Use the ELL activity described in the ELL chart.

Further Instruction

What Is Foreign Policy?: Core Reading and Interactive Reading Notepad Go through the Interactive Reading Notepad questions and discuss the answers with the class. Be sure students understand the bedrock principles of

U.S. foreign policy: freedom of seas and staying on good terms with neighboring countries, for example. Remind students that because the United States is the world's only "superpower," American foreign policy has a dramatic effect on global places and regions.

Draw Conclusions Why do you think American sanctions can have a crippling effect on the economies of other nations? *(Possible answer: The United States has the largest economy in the world and provides many exports to other countries. When the United States imposes a sanction, it stops or limits trade with a country, which prevents that country from getting many needed resources. Also, this country is not able to sell many of its resources or products to the United States, which causes the economy of the sanctioned country to suffer.)*

Hypothesize Why might the United States want to maintain good relations with a country that has a harsh dictatorship? *(Possible answer: This country might have resources that the United States needs, such as oil. Because of this, the United States might want to stay on good terms with this country, even though the country's government is repressive.)*

DIGITAL TEXT 2

Beginnings Through World War I

DIGITAL TEXT 3

World War II to the End of the Cold War

INTERACTIVE TIMELINE

Isolationism to Internationalism

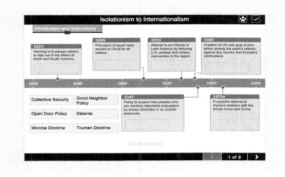

Objectives 2: Summarize U.S. foreign policy during the first 150 years of its history, including its adherence to isolationism; 3: Show how World War II finally ended America's traditional policy of isolationism, giving way to internationalism and the principles of collective security and deterrence.

Quick Instruction

In his Farewell Address in 1796, George Washington declared that "our true policy" was "to steer clear of permanent alliances with any portion of the foreign world." By the 1900s, Theodore Roosevelt's Corollary began to police Latin America. U.S. policies toward Latin America changed in the 1930s as Franklin D. Roosevelt's Good Neighbor Policy replaced the Roosevelt Corollary. The United States has gradually moved from a foreign policy of isolationism to one of internationalism.

Interactive Timeline: Isolationism to Internationalism Project the timeline. Have students place the policy titles in their appropriate location on the timeline according to the descriptions.

📷 ACTIVE CLASSROOM

Have students use the Sequence It activity. Ask students to form groups of six. Provide students with the following lists of events: the Cold War ends, United States purchases the Virgin Islands, Perry opens Japan to U.S. trade, the United States cuts ties with China, the Cuban missile crisis, the Korean War, and the Louisiana Purchase. Have each student write this list in chronological order

on a piece of paper. Then have students in each group compare their lists and decide what is the correct order of events. After this, each group forms a "Human Order" line, in which students represents an event. The students stand in chronological order with the earliest event at the front of the line and the last event at the end of the line. Groups can compare their orders to see if they got the right order.

D Differentiate: Challenge/Gifted Have students form groups of three. Then have each group act out one of the following events: the United States backing Mexico when France invaded Mexico or the attempt by the United States to implement détente with China and the Soviet Union.

Further Instruction

Editable Presentation Use the Editable Presentation to present the main ideas for this Core Reading.

Beginnings Through World War I and World War II to the End of the Cold War: Core Reading and Interactive Reading Notepad Project and discuss the Interactive Reading Notepad questions, including the timeline asking students to show how U.S. relations with China have changed. Review the changes in relations between the United States and China with the class and fill in the graphic organizer on the whiteboard as you go.

The Cold War Ends Relations with mainland China have improved since the 1970s. Efforts at détente with the Soviets proved less successful as Moscow continued its efforts to provide military and economic aid to revolutionary

movements around the world. Beginning in the 1980s, Reagan and Gorbachev met in a series of summit conferences that would eventually bring about the end of the Cold War.

Interpret Graphs Look at the American Troops in Vietnam & Other Wars graph. About how many troops were in Vietnam during 1964 compared to 1966? What can you infer about this data? *(There were less than 100,000 troops in 1964, but by 1966 there were nearly 500,000 troops. The number of troops increased more than four times, which indicates a rapid escalation occurred during these years.)*

Support Ideas with Evidence How do you think "Manifest Destiny" influenced U.S. isolationism? *(Possible answer: Following the idea of "Manifest Destiny" the United States focused on expanding westwards. As a result, the government was concerned about creating domestic policies that dealt with adding new territories. "Manifest Destiny," therefore, increased isolationism. The United States wanted to build up its own strength and wasn't as concerned about interacting on the international stage.)*

Support Point of View with Evidence Do you think the Korean War or the Vietnam War is a better example of internationalism? *(Possible answer: I think the Korean War is a better example of internationalism. In the Korean War, the United States military joined with the forces of many other nations to stop the spread of communism into southern Korea. In the Vietnam War, the United States interacted with other countries, such as France and South Vietnam, but did not successfully put together a coalition of international forces.)*

Foreign Policy Overview

Today's Foreign Policy Challenges

Major Diplomatic Hotspots

Objective 4: Analyze how today's U.S. foreign policy affects selected places and regions, as well as the significance to the United States of the location and key natural resources of selected global places or regions.

Quick Instruction

Interactive Map: Major Diplomatic Hotspots Project the map on the whiteboard and click through the hot spots on the map. Introduce the map activity by telling students that there are many troubled regions in the world today. The reasons for these conflicts vary, but often involve conflicting interests between countries. These conflicts often shape U.S. foreign policy, including the Federal Government's national defense, in these regions.

Analyze Maps All of the hotspot areas have conflicts with other countries. Which of these conflicts do you think is most strongly influenced by economic factors? *(Possible answer: I think economic concerns are the major cause for conflict between China and other countries. China has a huge economy, and it is seeking to expand this economy. Because of this, China poses as a major competitor and threat to the U.S. economy.)*

Evaluate Data Have students use the scale of miles to compare the distance from the United States to Panama versus the distance from the U.S. to Afghanistan. *(U.S. (Florida) to Panama: approximately 1,000 miles; U.S. to Afghanistan: approximately 10,000 miles)* How might these distances affect U.S. foreign policy with these countries? *(Possible answer: The U.S. would want to ensure friendly relations with a country*

that is as close to its borders as Panama. In addition, in the event of a conflict, U.S. foreign policy might be influenced by the amount of time it would take to get troops and supplies to a country.)

📷 ACTIVE CLASSROOM

Have students use the Rank It activity. List the following on the board: terrorism, key natural resources, international treaties, and dictatorships. Ask students to rank these factors based on which has the greatest impact on U.S. foreign policy to the least impact on U.S. foreign policy. Have students provide a justification for the ranking decisions. Then ask students to work in pairs to share their rankings and justifications. Poll the class to see if there is agreement on the ranking.

D Differentiate: **Extra Support** To help students better understand U.S. foreign policy in the Middle East, ask the following questions: What does the Middle East have that the United States wants? What does the United States want to happen in the Middle East? What could prevent U.S. goals in the Middle East from happening?

ELL Use the ELL activity described in the ELL chart.

Further Instruction

Go through the Interactive Reading Notepad questions and discuss the answers with the class. For further discussion, ask the following questions:

Compare and Contrast How does U.S. relations with the Middle East differ from U.S.

relations with Afghanistan? *(Possible answer: U.S. relations with the Middle East involve strong economic factors that include key natural resources. There relations also involve political concerns, especially with Israel and the surrounding Arab nations. However, with Afghanistan, the United States mostly has political concerns, especially with terrorism.)*

Infer In today's world, the U.S. government often uses coalitions to settle disputes with other countries. Why do you think the United States does this? *(Possible answer: The U.S. government realizes that in today's world all countries are interconnected through trade and communication systems. If the United States acted alone, it would be ignoring its interconnectedness with other countries. Such action could offend other nations. Also, coalitions emphasize that many countries are opposed to something instead of just the United States.)*

SYNTHESIZE

DIGITAL SYNTHESIZE ACTIVITY

Revisit Isolationism or Internationalism

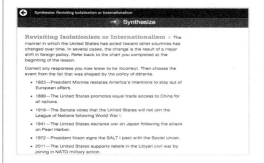

The manner in which the United States has acted towards other countries has changed over time. In several cases, the change in is the result of a change in policy. Tell students to refer back to the chart they completed at the beginning of the lesson. Ask them to change any changes they now know to be incorrect. Then have them to choose one event and tell how a policy of collective security, deterrence, containment, or détente, shaped U.S. actions and foreign policy.

Discuss Use the following question to start a class discussion. Ask students: Which of the policies of collective security, deterrence, containment, or détente do you think had the strongest effect on U.S. history? Have students provide examples to support their opinion.

DEMONSTRATE

DIGITAL QUIZ

Lesson Quiz and Class Discussion Board

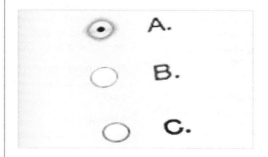

Assign the online Lesson Quiz for this lesson if you haven't already done so. Students will be offered automatic remediation or enrichment based on their score.

Pose these questions to the class on the Discussion Board:

Support Point of View with Evidence Do you think the U.S. government hung on to an isolationist approach for too long? *(Possible answers: Yes; by the early 1900s, countries throughout the world were interacting in important ways. World War I showed this. At that time, the United States should have realized that isolationism was no longer a practical or ethical approach. OR No; the United States was justified to stay out of conflicts in Europe and other areas of the world before World War II. These conflicts did not directly concern the United States. Getting involved would mean the loss of American lives and the use of American resources and money.)*

Make Predictions How do you think U.S. foreign policy will change in the future? *(Possible answer: U.S. foreign policy will move more toward internationalism as communication networks develop. Eventually, the primary goal of supporting U.S. interests will be replaced by the goal of supporting the world's interests.)*

Topic Inquiry
Have students continue their investigations for the Topic Inquiry.

Diplomacy

Supporting English Language Learners

Use with Digital Text 4, **The United Nations.**

Listening

Have students listen to an audio file on a topic related to U.S. diplomacy, such as President Carter's speech on the failed rescue of the Iranian hostages, which can be found online. Provide students with a list of important words, concepts, or questions that help them relate the audio file to the Federal Government's responsibility for foreign policy. Have students build and reinforce their understanding of the topic by completing the following activities.

Beginning Have students listen as you read aloud the list of important words or concepts. Have students focus on these words or concepts as you replay the audio file.

Intermediate Have partners read the list of questions. Tell students to listen for the answers to the questions as the audio file is replayed. Discuss the answers with the class.

Advanced Have partners predict the answers to the questions. Replay the audio file. Have partners discuss the answers to the questions and decide whether or not their predictions were correct.

Advanced High After students predict the answers to the questions, replay the audio file. Have students decide whether or not their predictions were correct.

Use with Digital Text 1, **America's Representatives to the World.**

Writing

Read and discuss the section *The Secretary of State*. Have students pay close attention to the spelling of the names of significant individuals mentioned in this section, such as Thomas Jefferson and Condoleezza Rice. Have students write about these people, taking care to spell these names and other words correctly.

Beginning Provide pictures of the people mentioned. Ask students to write the names of each person and several words that describe him or her.

Intermediate Provide pictures of the people mentioned. Ask students to write a sentence about each person. Have them check their spelling.

Advanced Have students write a short paragraph describing the accomplishments of two or three of the people mentioned. Have partners check each other's work for correct spelling.

Advanced High Have students write a summary of this section including the accomplishments of some of the people mentioned. Have partners check each other's work for correct spelling.

⊡ Differentiate Instruction

Use the Differentiated Instruction notes throughout the lesson plan to support the varied skill sets, levels of readiness, and interests in the mixed-ability classroom.

Challenge These notes include suggestions for expanding the activity for advanced students.

On-Level These notes include suggestions for modifying the activity to address different interests or learning styles.

Extra Support These notes include ideas for providing more scaffolding or reading spuport.

Special Needs These notes provide ideas for adapting instruction to support the needs of various special needs students.

■ NOTES

PEARSON
realize ™
www.PearsonRealize.com

Go online to access additional resources including:
Primary Sources • Biographies • Supreme Court cases • 21st Century Skill Tutorials • Maps • Graphic Organizers.

Objectives

Objective 1: Describe the functions, components, and organization of the State Department and its overseas representatives.

Objective 2: Examine how the U.S. government uses economic resources in foreign policy, including foreign aid.

Objective 3: Describe the major regional security alliances developed by the United States.

Objective 4: Examine the history, structure, and work of the United Nations and its relationship with the United States.

LESSON 5 ORGANIZER		PACING: APPROX. 1 PERIOD, .5 BLOCKS			
				RESOURCES	
		OBJECTIVES	**PACING**	**Online**	**Print**
Connect					
DIGITAL START UP ACTIVITY **What Does the State Department Do?**			10 min.	●	
Investigate					
DIGITAL TEXT 1 **America's Representatives to the World**		Objective 1	10 min.	●	●
INTERACTIVE MAP **U.S. Embassies Around the World**			10 min.	●	
DIGITAL TEXT 2 **American Foreign Aid**		Objective 2	10 min.	●	●
INTERACTIVE GALLERY **U.S. Foreign Aid Through the Years**			10 min.	●	
DIGITAL TEXT 3 **NATO**		Objective 3	10 min.	●	●
DIGITAL TEXT 4 **The United Nations**		Objective 4	10 min.	●	●
DIGITAL TEXT 5 **The UN's Work**		Objective 4	10 min.	●	●
Synthesize					
DIGITAL SYNTHESIZE ACTIVITY **Dollars and Diplomacy**			10 min.	●	
Demonstrate					
DIGITAL QUIZ **Lesson Quiz and Class Discussion Board**			10 min.	●	

Diplomacy

■ CONNECT

DIGITAL START UP ACTIVITY
What Does the State Department Do?

Project the Start Up Activity Ask students to answer the questions as they enter and get settled. Then have them share their ideas with another student, either in class or through a chat or blog space.

The State Department handles the major responsibilities of the Federal Government for foreign policy and is also in charge of American diplomatic activities around the world. The secretary of state is the head of the State Department.

Discuss Write three examples of major international events that occurred during the past 10 years that you think would have been handled by the State Department.

Aa Vocabulary Development: Use the Interactive Reading Notepad to preview the Key Terms and Academic Vocabulary in this Lesson with students.

⇪ FLIP IT!
Assign the Flipped Video for this lesson.

■ STUDENT EDITION PRINT
PAGES: 273–283

■ INVESTIGATE

DIGITAL TEXT 1
America's Representatives to the World

INTERACTIVE MAP
U.S. Embassies Around the World

Objective 1: Describe the functions, components, and organization of the State Department and its overseas representatives.

Quick Instruction
An ambassador is the highest ranking diplomat sent by a nation as its official representative in a foreign country, and an embassy is the diplomatic office where an ambassador is stationed. The U.S. recognizes more than 180 foreign countries and has an embassy in each. Embassies sometimes gain worldwide attention, such as in 1980 when militants seized the American embassy in Iran. The Iran hostages were released only moments after President Ronald Reagan had taken the oath of office.

Interactive Map: U.S. Embassies Around the World Project the map on the whiteboard and click through the hot spots on the map.

Analyze Maps Which region of the world has the highest concentration of U.S. embassies? Why do you think this is the case? *(Southeastern Europe in the Balkan area has the highest concentration of U.S. embassies. This region includes many small countries in a small geographic area. Since the United States recognizes these countries, there is a high concentration of U.S. embassies in this region.)*

Analyze Information Analyze the constitutional powers of the President with regard to the State Department and ambassadors, and the role of the secretary of state and the State Department with regard to foreign affairs. *(The President names the secretary of state and all ambassadors, who then must be confirmed by the Senate. As a result, he or she has significant influence over*

the State Department. The secretary of state and the State Department are most directly responsible for the conduct of the nation's foreign affairs.)

▐▶ ACTIVE CLASSROOM
Use a Conversation with History activity to have students analyze how a President relates to his or her secretary of state. Have students imagine that they are having a conversation with President Franklin Roosevelt. Tell students to ask: Why did you tend to ignore your secretaries of state? Then have students write Roosevelt's response and what they would say to this response. The same type of activity can be done for President George W. Bush. However, with this President, the question should be: Why did you rely heavily on your secretary of state?

■ ELL Use the ELL activity described in the ELL chart.

Further Instruction
Go through the Interactive Reading Notepad questions and discuss the answers with the class. For further discussion, ask the following questions:

Summarize What are the major responsibilities of the secretary of state for foreign policy? *(The secretary of state focuses on making and conducting the policy of the department and on the management of the department. This management includes the department's many overseas posts and its large workforce.)*

DIGITAL TEXT 2

American Foreign Aid

INTERACTIVE GALLERY

U.S. Foreign Aid Through the Years

Infer Why do you think ambassadors are often granted diplomatic immunity? *(Possible answers: An ambassador needs to be protected in the nation where he or she is stationed. If a political conflict happens in this nation, the ambassador should be protected from being arrested or having his or her residence searched. Also, the laws of countries are often quite different. An ambassador should not be expected to follows laws in a country that contradict the laws of his or her homeland.)*

Compare and Contrast How does the method of filling the offices of secretary of state and ambassadors differ from that of governor? *(The secretary of state and all ambassadors are appointed to office by the President, whereas a governor is elected to office by the people.)*

Objective 2: Examine how the U.S. government uses economic resources in foreign policy, including foreign aid.

Quick Instruction

U.S. foreign aid began in the early 1940s with economic and military assistance to the Allied nations. The United States' economic foreign aid priorities have changed over the years.

Interactive Gallery: U.S. Foreign Aid Through the Years Project the interactive gallery and ask students to click an image to learn more about the U.S. economic aid priorities of that era.

Contrast How was U.S. foreign aid in the 1960s different from U.S. foreign aid in the 1970s? How might these differences have reflected U.S. foreign policy at these times? *(In the 1960s, U.S. foreign aid helped to rebuild Europe as a way to stabilize the region and contain communism. In the 1970s, U.S. foreign aid shifted away from technical and capital assistance programs and toward addressing basic human needs. This might have reflected the U.S. foreign policy of détente, which involved a purposeful attempt to avoid conflict and relax tensions.)*

ACTIVE CLASSROOM

Use a Quick Write activity about U.S. foreign aid. Tell students to write in 30 seconds what they know about the purposes of U.S. foreign aid and how it affects other places and regions of the world. Ask volunteers to share their writing with the class.

Further Instruction

Go through the Interactive Reading Notepad questions and discuss the answers with the class. For further discussion, ask the following question:

Identify Central Issues How does the U.S. government use foreign aid to benefit the United States? *(Possible answer: The U.S. government uses foreign aid to support and protect U.S. interests throughout the world. For example, U.S. foreign aid is often giving to countries that have a strategic importance to the United States. In addition, U.S. aid monies must generally be used to purchase American goods and services, thereby providing a boost to the U.S. economy.)*

Diplomacy

DIGITAL TEXT 3
NATO

DIGITAL TEXT 4
The United Nations

Objective 3: Describe the major regional security alliances developed by the United States

Quick Instruction

Inform students that the North Atlantic Treaty Organization (NATO) was initially established to promote the defense of Western Europe. Ask students: Do you think the purpose of NATO has changed since then? Why or why not?

D Differentiate: Extra Support To help students understand the purpose of regional security alliances give them the following example: Let's say an explorer wants to build a house in a region that is next to a hostile region. The people in the hostile region might attack the explorer. Ask students: Do you think the explorer would have a better chance of success if he or she joined a group of friendly people who wanted to settle the region? Or would the explorer be more successful if he or she settled the area alone? Why? Tell students that countries make alliances for similar reasons.

Further Instruction

Go through the Interactive Reading Notepad questions and discuss the answers with the class. For further discussion, ask the following questions:

Draw Conclusions How has the U.S. foreign policy of forming large alliances, such as NATO, affected various places of the world? *(Possible answer: By forming large alliances, such as NATO, the United States has helped to put an end to ethnic cleansing in the Balkans and ousted the Taliban in Afghanistan.)*

Analyze Charts According to the chart "ISAF Top Troop-Contributing Nations," which region(s) of the world contributed the most troops to the war in Afghanistan? *(North America and Europe)*

Support Point of View with Evidence As part of its carrying out of its major responsibilities for foreign policy, including national defense, the United States often provides most of the military support for NATO forces. Do you think this is fair? *(Possible answers: Yes; the United States is the most powerful nation in the world and has the most powerful military. In addition, by providing the bulk of the forces, the United States ensures that it also has the greatest say in NATO interventions. Because of these reasons, it makes sense for the United States to provide the bulk of NATO forces.)*

Objective 4: Examine the history and structure of the United Nations.

Quick Instruction

Have the class divide into five groups. Ask students in group one to write about the purpose of the UN General Assembly. Group two writes about the purpose of the Security Council. Groups three to five write about the purpose of the Economic and Social Council, the International Court of Justice, and the Secretariat respectively. Students in each group can share information about their assigned section of the UN. After this, the members of each group visit other groups and gather information about the other five sections. Ask volunteers to share the information they have gathered.

D Differentiate: Challenge/Gifted Ask students to write a letter to the UN asking for help for a particular country. Students can make up a country and the problems in that country. Students must decide to which department of the UN they will address the letter and the type of assistance needed. Also, in the letter, students can refer to NGOs associated with the UN that might be able to help.

Further Instruction

Editable Presentation Use the Editable Presentation to present the main ideas for this Core Reading.

The United Nations: Core Reading and Interactive Reading Notepad Project and discuss the Interactive Reading Notepad questions, including the chart asking students to summarize the purpose and work of the UN

DIGITAL TEXT 5

The UN's Work

General Assembly and Security Council. Review the purposes and work of these departments of the UN with the class and fill in the graphic organizer on the whiteboard as you go.

For further discussion, ask the following questions:

Apply Concepts A person has committed war crimes to people from various countries. After the war, these countries want the war criminal to be tried and convicted. What department of the UN would these countries contact to reach this goal? Why? *(The countries would contact the International Court of Justice. This department handles cases brought to it by both members and nonmembers of the UN.)*

Identify Steps in a Process How is the budget of the UN formed? *(The secretary-general prepares the UN's two-year budget. Then this budget goes before the General Assembly to be approved.)*

Objective 4: Examine the work of the United Nations and its relationship with the United States.

Quick Instruction

The UN has many functions including peacekeeping, health, environment, and human rights. Have student form pairs. Ask them: Which of these functions of the UN do you think is the most important? Have pairs discuss possibilities, make a choice, and provide reasons for the choice. Then ask volunteers to share their answer.

ELL Use the ELL activity described in the ELL chart.

Further Instruction

The UN's Work: Core Reading and Interactive Reading Notepad Go through the Interactive Reading Notepad questions and discuss the answers with the class. For further discussion, ask the following questions:

Infer Why do you think the UN works closely with nongovernmental organizations (NGOs)? *(Possible answer: The UN tries to help countries throughout the world in many ways. However, the UN does not have a large enough staff or resources to accomplish all this on its own. As a result, the UN works closely with NGOs that have similar goals. Together, they have a better chance of achieving their goals.)*

Identify Main Ideas Why has the United States withheld payment of funds to the UN? *(The United States has not always agreed with some formal policy positions taken by the UN. Because of this, the United States has at times withdrawn its support of the UN.)*

Diplomacy

SYNTHESIZE

DIGITAL SYNTHESIZE ACTIVITY

Dollars and Diplomacy

The U.S. government has used foreign aid extensively for the past seventy years. During this time, the type of foreign aid has changed to meet the demands of the times. However, the government has always used foreign aid to benefit U.S. interests.

Discuss Ask students to identify and describe two types of foreign aid that help the American economy to thrive. Give examples of each type. Do these examples benefit other countries? If so, how? Do they further U.S. foreign policy goals? If so, how?

DEMONSTRATE

DIGITAL QUIZ

Lesson Quiz and Class Discussion Board

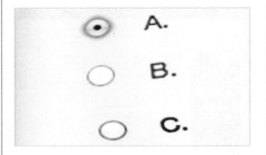

Assign the online Lesson Quiz for this lesson if you haven't already done so. Students will be offered automatic remediation or enrichment based on their score.

Pose these questions to the class on the Discussion Board:

Predict Consequences How did U.S. foreign policy after World War II affect Europe? What might have happened if the United States had not provided aid to European countries? *(Possible answer: U.S. aid helped Europe rebuild following the devastation of World War II. Without this aid, the Soviet Union might have attempted to take over all of Europe and might have succeeded.)*

Make Predictions How do you think U.S. foreign aid will change in the future? *(Possible answers: U.S. foreign aid might start to focus more on the environmental concerns of other countries. These concerns seem to be growing. They include water shortages, pollution, and deforestation. People are realizing that environmental concerns in one country affects all countries. Also, U.S. foreign aid might provide more military assistance to countries to stop terrorism.)*

Topic Inquiry

Have students continue their investigations for the Topic Inquiry.

National Security

Supporting English Language Learners

Use with Digital Text 1, **The Department of Defense.**

Listening

Have students listen to new or challenging words or phrases from the reading, such as *present-day successor, two historic Cabinet-level agencies, inherent,* and *studded with provisions.* Have students build and reinforce their understanding of English by completing the following activities.

Beginning Read and discuss the meanings of the new and challenging words and phrases. Read aloud the text and have students mark each word on the list when they hear it.

Intermediate Have partners read the list of words and phrases together and listen for them as you read the text aloud. Guide the group in discussing the meanings of the words and phrases.

Advanced Have partners read the list of words and phrases together. Ask them to predict their meanings. Read the text aloud as students listen, then have the group discuss the meanings of the words and phrases.

Advanced High Have students read the list of words phrases and predict their meanings. Read the text aloud as students listen, then have students decide whether or not their predictions were correct.

Use with Digital Text 2, **Branches of the Military.**

Writing

Explain to students that the spelling patterns *–ence* and *–ance* are usually pronounced the same. Because of this, it is important to become familiar with words that use these patterns and memorize how they are spelled. Read the text and have the students look for words with these patterns as they learn about national defense.

Beginning Guide the class to make a list of *–ence* words and a list of *–ance* words from the text. Discuss the meaning of each word. Have the students copy the lists and practice reading the words to each other.

Intermediate Have partners make a list of *–ence* words and a list of *–ance* words from the text. Discuss the meaning of each word. Have partners write short sentences using the words.

Advanced Have partners make a list of *–ence* words and a list of *–ance* words from the text. Have them think of other words with the same endings. Ask them to write sentences using the words.

Advanced High Ask partners to find and discuss the *–ence* and *–ance* words in the text. Have them write a paragraph using the words.

▣ Differentiate Instruction

Use the Differentiated Instruction notes throughout the lesson plan to support the varied skill sets, levels of readiness, and interests in the mixed-ability classroom.

Challenge These notes include suggestions for expanding the activity for advanced students.

On-Level These notes include suggestions for modifying the activity to address different interests or learning styles.

Extra Support These notes include ideas for providing more scaffolding or reading spuport.

Special Needs These notes provide ideas for adapting instruction to support the needs of various special needs students.

▮ NOTES

National Security

Objectives

Objective 1: Summarize the functions, components, and organization of the Defense Department and its military departments.

Objective 2: Explain how the Director of National Intelligence and the Department of Homeland Security contribute to national security.

LESSON 6 ORGANIZER		PACING: APPROX. 1 PERIOD, .5 BLOCKS			
				RESORCES	
		OBJECTIVES	PACING	Online	Print
Connect					
DIGITAL START UP ACTIVITY **Who Commands the U.S. Military?**			10 min.	●	
Investigate					
DIGITAL TEXT 1 **The Department of Defense**		Objective 1	10 min.	●	●
DIGITAL TEXT 2 **Branches of the Military**		Objective 1	10 min.	●	●
INTERACTIVE ILLUSTRATION **The Department of Defense: Mottoes and Missions**				●	
DIGITAL TEXT 3 **The Director of National Intelligence**		Objective 2	10 min.	●	●
DIGITAL TEXT 4 **The Department of Homeland Security**		Objective 2	10 min.	●	●
INTERACTIVE GALLERY **A Day at the Department of Homeland Security**				●	
Synthesize					
DIGITAL SYNTHESIZE ACTIVITY **Organization of the U.S. Military**			10 min.	●	
Demonstrate					
DIGITAL QUIZ **Lesson Quiz and Class Discussion Board**			10 min.	●	

PEARSON
realize™
www.PearsonRealize.com

Go online to access additional resources including:
Primary Sources • Biographies • Supreme Court cases •
21st Century Skill Tutorials • Maps • Graphic Organizers.

▪ CONNECT

DIGITAL START UP ACTIVITY
Who Commands the U.S. Military?

Project the Start Up Activity Ask students to answer the questions as they enter and get settled. Then have them share their ideas with another student, either in class or through a chat or blog space.

The United States military includes more than 1,400,000 people on active duty. These people serve around the world, in the Army, Navy, Marines, Air Force, and Coast Guard. As part of the Defense Department, they help put into action the foreign policy of the United States.

Discuss Ask students: Who do you think commands U.S. forces? Why do you think the Framers structured the command of the military as they did?

Aa Vocabulary Development: Use the Interactive Reading Notepad to preview the Key Terms and Academic Vocabulary in this Lesson with students.

⇱ FLIP IT!
Assign the Flipped Video for this lesson.

▪ STUDENT EDITION PRINT PAGES: 284–290

▪ INVESTIGATE

DIGITAL TEXT 1
The Department of Defense

Objective 1: Summarize the functions, components, and organization of the Defense Department.

Quick Instruction
Inform students that the structure and function of the Defense Department was created by Congress with the goal of unifying the nation's armed forces. Have students pair off. Ask pairs: What benefit would unifying the armed forces into one department have? Do you think there is any danger from unifying the armed forces in this way? Why or why not? Have pairs decide on answers to these questions. Ask volunteers to share their answers.

ELL Use the ELL activity described in the ELL chart.

Further Instruction
Go through the Interactive Reading Notepad questions and discuss the answers with the class. For further discussion, ask the following question:

Infer The structure of the Defense Department within the executive branch provides for civilian control of the military. Why is this principle of civilian control important? *(Civilian control is a safeguard that helps to prevent the U.S. military from taking control of the government.)*

Check Understanding What is the role of the Cabinet in terms of national defense? *(The secretary of defense heads the Defense Department, which is charged with protecting national security.)*

DIGITAL TEXT 2
Branches of the Military

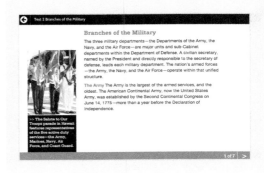

Objective 1: Summarize the functions, components, and organization of the military departments of the Defense Department.

Quick Instruction
Interactive Gallery: The Department of Defense Project the interactive on the whiteboard and click through the hot spots on the gallery. Ask students to select the different areas of the main Department seal to learn more about its symbols and meanings and how they reflect the major responsibilities of the department. Then tell them to select the seals of the various military branches for a description of each branch.

Analyze Images What do the arrows and laurels represent in the Department of Defense seal? *(The three arrows represent the three component parts of the Department of Defense. The laurel stands for the honors received in combat.)*

▣ ACTIVE CLASSROOM
Use a Circle Write activity for the U.S. Army. Break the class into groups and provide the question: What is the structure and function of the U.S. Army? Have students write as much as they can for 1 minute then switch with the person on their right. The next person tries to improve or elaborate the response where the other person left off. Continue to switch until the paper comes back to the first person. The group then decides which is the best composition (or response) and shares that with the larger group.

National Security

INTERACTIVE ILLUSTRATION

The Department of Defense: Mottoes and Missions

DIGITAL TEXT 3

The Director of National Intelligence

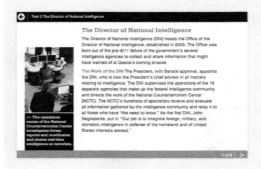

D Differentiate: Challenge/Gifted Ask students to draw posters that try to persuade people to join either the U.S. Navy or Air Force.

ELL Use the ELL activity described in the ELL chart.

Further Instruction

Editable Presentation Use the Editable Presentation to present the main ideas for this Core Reading.

Branches of the Military: Core Reading and Interactive Reading Notepad Project and discuss the Interactive Reading Notepad questions, including the chart asking students to explain how the three branches of the military differ. Review the three branches with the class and fill in the chart on the whiteboard as you go.

For further discussion, ask the following questions:

Hypothesize Do you think the number of women in the U.S. military has increased over the years? Explain your answer. *(Possible answer: Over the years, women have gained more rights. In the past, women were expected to do traditional roles, such as domestic chores and taking care of children. However, today, people realize that women can do more, including serving in the military.)*

Summarize How are the marines structured and what are their major responsibilities? *(The marines are a combat-ready land force for the navy. They have two major combat missions: (1) to seize or defend land bases from which the ships and air power of the navy can operate, and (2) to carry out other land operations essential to a naval campaign.)*

Objective 2: Explain how the Director of National Intelligence contributes to national security.

Quick Instruction

Review the structure of the Office of the Director of National Intelligence, which is headed by the Director of National Intelligence (DNI) who then supervises the operations of 16 separate agencies, which make up the federal intelligence community. Ask students: Which of these agencies have you heard of before you read this lesson? Which of these agencies did you not know about? How does the structure of the Office of the Director of National Intelligence facilitate the goal of protecting the nation's security? *(This office is headed by a director who reports directly to the President, thereby facilitating strong communication about security matters with the President. Also, this office controls many other security agencies, which supports communication between these agencies.)*

D Differentiate: Extra Support Help students analyze the function of the National Security Agency. Ask students: What does espionage or spying mean to you? What would happen if the information gathered by U.S. spies became public? The National Security Agency uses spies. Do you think is the function of this agency?

Further Instruction

Go through the Interactive Reading Notepad questions and discuss the answers with the class. For further discussion, ask the following question:

Support Point of View with Evidence As the Federal Government carries out its major responsibilities for foreign policy, should government leaders be more concerned about supporting the operations of the NSA or the privacy of individuals? *(Possible answers: The U.S government should be more concerned about supporting the NSA. Intelligence is of vital importance to keep Americans safe and to protect our nation. Because of this, the U.S. government needs to support and keep secret the operations of the NSA. The U.S. government should be more concerned about supporting the privacy of individuals. If the privacy of individuals is violated, then the rights of individuals guaranteed by the Constitution are also violated. The NSA would end up committing crimes that it is trying to protect American from. Because of this, the privacy of individuals must be upheld.)*

DIGITAL TEXT 4

The Department of Homeland Security

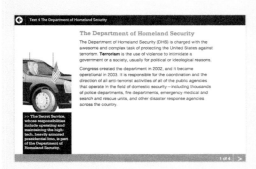

INTERACTIVE GALLERY

A Day at the Department of Homeland Security

Objective 2: Explain how the Department of Homeland Security contributes to national security.

Quick Instruction

The Department of Homeland Security (DHS) is charged with the awesome and complex task of protecting the United States against terrorism. The department consists mostly of agencies transferred to it from other Cabinet departments.

Interactive Gallery: Department of Homeland Security Project the gallery. Have students select each category to learn more about the responsibilities of the Department of Homeland Security.

Analyze Gallery What are some ways that the Department of Homeland Security helps to protect lives? *(Possible answer: The Department of Homeland Security helps to protect lives by pre-screening passenger in airports, lead search and rescue cases at sea, and provide secret service protection of government officials and their families.)*

🖳 ACTIVE CLASSROOM

Use the Wallpaper activity for the Department of Homeland Security. Ask students to review information they have learned about this department. Then tell each student to design a piece of "wallpaper" that encapsulates key learnings about this topic, including the structure and functions of the Department of Homeland Security. The wallpaper should include writing and illustrations. After this, have students post their wallpapers. Students take a "wisdom" walk and note what others have written and illustrated. Students can jot down ideas as they occur.

Further Instruction

Go through the Interactive Reading Notepad questions and discuss the answers with the class. For further discussion, ask the following question:

Support Point of View with Evidence What activity of the Department of Homeland Security do you think could most likely invade people's privacy? *(Possible answer: I think the department's work with computers could most likely invade people's privacy. In an attempt to secure computer's against terrorist attacks or to find terrorist activity on the Internet, the department might feel that learning private information about people is justified.)*

Identify Cause and Effect What responsibility were Congress and President Bush fulfilling when they created the Department of Homeland Security? *(Possible answer: The responsibility to protect the security and well-being of the United States.)*

National Security

■ SYNTHESIZE

DIGITAL SYNTHESIZE ACTIVITY
Organization of the U.S. Military

Ask students to recall the Topic Essential Question, "What Should Governments Do?" Have them use the Think Pair Share strategy to complete the Department of Defense activity. Ask them to take five minutes to fill out the flow chart. Then have students share their responses with a talking partner. For further discussion about this activity, ask the following question:

Draw Conclusions Why do you think the Joint Chiefs of Staff is separate from the other military branches? *(Possible answer: The role of the Joint Chiefs of Staff is to serve as the principal military advisers to the secretary of defense. Since it consists of the chiefs of the various military branches, this department has to be separate from the military branches. Also, by being a separate department, the Joint Chiefs of Staff can better provide objective advise.)*

Discuss Ask students to think about the questions they answered at the beginning of this Topic. Ask if they would change any of their responses now that they have learned more about the Department of Defense.

■ DEMONSTRATE

DIGITAL QUIZ
Lesson Quiz and Class Discussion Board

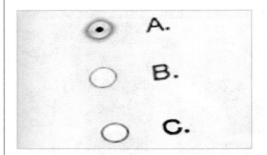

Assign the online Lesson Quiz for this lesson if you haven't already done so. Students will be offered automatic remediation or enrichment based on their score.

Pose these questions to the class on the Discussion Board:

Make Predictions In recent years, the Department of Defense has gone through many changes. How do you think it will change in the future? Think about the major responsibilities of the Federal Government for foreign policy, including national defense, as you formulate your answer. *(Possible answers: I think it will create a separate branch of the military that focuses on cyber defense. I think the CIA, NSA, and other intelligence agencies will combine into one department.)*

Hypothesize Do you think the 9/11 terrorist attacks would have happened if the Department of Homeland Security had existed at that time? Why or why not? *(Possible answers: No; because of the extensive work that the department does to protect the security of U.S. airports, the department would have identified and stopped the terrorists before the attack. Yes; even if this department existed, it would not have been on the alert for this attack because this type of attack was never attempted before. As a result, the 9/11 terrorist attacks might have still happened.)*

Topic Inquiry
Have students continue their investigations for the Topic Inquiry.

The Executive Branch at Work

SYNTHESIZE

DIGITAL ACTIVITY
Reflect on the Essential Question

First ask students to reconsider the Essential Question for the Topic: What Should Governments Do? Tell students that at the beginning of their study of the executive branch, they were asked to consider when the Federal Government should become involved in various issues.

Ask students to consider the list again in light of what they have learned about the executive branch.

One of the bulleted items notes aid for help in the transition of a nation to a democracy. Ask students: "Do you think the United States has an obligation to provide this kind of help?" Ask them to give at least three reasons supporting their position.

Have students take a few minutes to reflect on all that they have learned about the structure and functions of the executive branch. Ask them to write down three important questions they have thought about during the Topic and their answers to those questions. Share these examples if students need help getting started:

- What is the purpose of American foreign aid to other nations?
- Does U.S. foreign aid always prove successful?
- Does the government have an obligation to help out its citizens who have suffered from a natural disaster?

You may ask students to share their questions and answers on the Class Discussion Board.

Have students complete Step 3 of the Topic Inquiry.

DEMONSTRATE

DIGITAL TOPIC REVIEW AND ASSESSMENT
The Executive Branch at Work

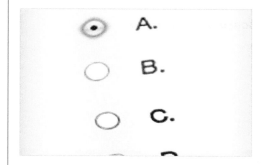

Students can prepare for the Topic Test by answering the questions in the Topic Review and Assessment online or the Assessment questions in the Print Student text. They can also prepare by reviewing their answers to the Interactive Reading Notepad questions or reviewing their notes in the Reading and Notetaking Study Guide.

DIGITAL TOPIC TEST
The Executive Branch at Work

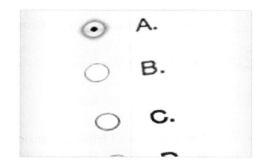

TOPIC TEST

Assign the Topic Test to assess students' understanding of topic content.

BENCHMARK TESTS

Assign these benchmark tests as you complete the relevant topics to monitor student progress toward mastering the course content and as preparation for the End-of-Course Test.

Benchmark Test 1: Topics 1–4

Benchmark Test 2: Topics 5–8

Benchmark Test 3: Topics 9–11

Benchmark Test 4: Topics 12–14

The Judicial Branch

	PACING
Connect	1 period
MY STORY VIDEO **Thurgood Marshall and *Brown v. Board of Education***	10 min.
DIGITAL ESSENTIAL QUESTION ACTIVITY **How Should We Handle Conflict?**	10 min.
DIGITAL OVERVIEW ACTIVITY **The Judicial Branch**	10 min.
TOPIC INQUIRY: CIVIC ACTION PROJECT **Constitutional Rights Foundation**	20 min.
Investigate	1–3 periods
TOPIC INQUIRY: CIVIC ACTION PROJECT **Constitutional Rights Foundation**	Ongoing
LESSON 1 The National Judiciary	30–40 min.
LESSON 2 The Supreme Court	30–40 min.
LESSON 3 The Inferior Courts and the Special Courts	30–40 min.
Synthesize	1 period
DIGITAL ACTIVITY **Reflect on the Essential Question**	10 min.
TOPIC INQUIRY: CIVIC ACTION PROJECT **Constitutional Rights Foundation**	20 min.
Demonstrate	1–2 periods
DIGITAL TOPIC REVIEW AND ASSESSMENT **The Judicial Branch**	10 min.
TOPIC INQUIRY: CIVIC ACTION PROJECT **Constitutional Rights Foundation**	20 min.

 **TOPIC INQUIRY:**

Civic Action Project

For this topic's Inquiry, you may choose to do a Civic Action Project with your students by using the materials found at the Constitutional Rights Foundation's CAP website: http://www.crfcap.org. Civic Action Project (CAP) is a project-based learning model for government and economics courses. It offers a practicum for high school students in effective and engaged citizenship and uses blended learning to engage students in civic activities both in the traditional U.S. government and economics classrooms.

Constitutional Rights Foundation
Educate. Participate.

THE TEACHER'S ROLE

THE CAP TEACHER coaches and guides students through the civic action process as they select a problem or issue, research it, determine and take civic actions, and report and document the experience. The teacher motivates, challenges, critiques, and assesses student progress. Through a blended learning approach, teachers can let students take the reins of their civic learning, guiding them along the way.

You can create your CAP classroom in three easy steps

STEP 1

Register yourself for the CAP website

STEP 2

Enroll your students

STEP 3

Engage your students in the CAP process and its many resources

THE STUDENT'S ROLE

CAP ALLOWS STUDENTS to create projects on issues they care about for their school or community. They see the connection between their civic actions and public policy and can share ideas for civics projects with each other and other CAP students nationwide. Students also see how the content of government and economics courses can apply to the real world. By taking civic actions, they practice what real citizens do when they go about trying to solve real policy-related problems. CAP fulfills best-practices in service-learning with an emphasis on public policy.

The CAP student is accountable for completing the civic action process, just as with a science project or term paper. The CAP Planner, a set of documents that guide students through the process, provides teachers with assessment information as well as a way to manage multiple student projects. While the teacher introduces and monitors the CAP, it is important that students take the lead in completing their civic actions. By using web-based technology and civics-based instruction and activities, students exercise important 21st century skills in digital literacy, critical thinking, collaboration, self-direction, and learning to be engaged and effective citizens.

CIVIC ACTIONS CAP challenges students to work on an actual problem, issue, or policy by taking civic actions. Civic actions build upon classroom civics issues, service-learning, and other proven practices of effective civic education. These actions can be many and varied, including:

- getting informed about a public issue or problem
- thinking critically about the issue or problem
- discovering how government is involved with the problem
- learning how government makes decisions
- developing a position
- engaging in civic dialogue
- building constituencies
- working together toward a common goal
- doing civic writing
- making presentations
- advocating for and defending positions
- meeting with officials

Brainstorming

Brainstorming is a method for generating ideas. It can be done by individuals or in small or large

Rules for Brainst

Pose a question to a

Set a time limit on th more ideas out.

Work as fast as you

Handout Lesson 5B
Civic Action Project

GRADE
CAP Policy Analysis Tool

AS CITIZENS IN A DEMOCRACY, YOU'LL BE CONFRONTED WITH POLICY QUESTIONS. IS A TAX PROPOSAL A GOOD IDEA? SHOULD YOU VOTE FOR A PARTICULAR BALLOT INITIATIVE? GOVERNMENT POLICIES CAN PROFOUNDLY AFFECT OUR NATION AND YOUR LIFE. IN A DEMOCRACY, YOU HAVE A SAY ON GOVERNMENT POLICIES AND PROPOSED POLICIES. IT'S IMPORTANT THAT YOU TAKE A CRITICAL LOOK AT THEM. USE THE FOLLOWING GRADE TESTS TO EVALUATE A POLICY:

GOAL. WHAT IS THE GOAL OF THE POLICY? IF YOU DON'T KNOW WHAT IT'S SUPPOSED TO DO, YOU CAN'T MEASURE ITS SUCCESS OR FAILURE. POLICIES ARE DESIGNED TO ADDRESS PROBLEMS. WHAT PROBLEM OR PROBLEMS IS

POLICY? WHO MIGHT (OR DOES) YOU UNDERSTAND WHO THE ICY FAVORS SPECIAL ES FOR INFORMATION, BUT

ITS? WHAT IS GOOD ABOUT THE ES OR EFFECTS OF THE VED) ITS GOAL? WILL IT NSIVE? DOES IT PROTECT E'S LIBERTIES?

OSTS? WHAT IS BAD ABOUT THE THE CAUSES OR EFFECTS OF THE ? DOES IT CAUSE HARM? DOES RE ANY POTENTIAL

 DISADVANTAGES. ARE THERE DO NOTHING. MOST SERIOUS EVALUATE THEM. LOOK AT ES.

© 2012 Constitutional Rights Foundation

Conducting Meetings

Your meetings should be organized, to-the-point, and fun.

Decide how you're going to make decisions. If you are a small group, try deciding by whole-group consensus or by a two-thirds vote. A simple-majority decision may lead to bad feelings and resentment.

Understand everyone's role at the meeting. At most meetings, people need to fill the following roles, which may change from meeting to meeting:

- Leader or facilitator runs the meeting, follows the agenda item by item, and watches the time allotted for each. The leader helps participants focus on the task and makes sure everyone has a chance to participate.
- Recorder takes minutes, which include date and time of meeting, the persons attending, and notes on each agenda item.
- Treasurer.
- Group members contribute agenda items, discuss topics, make decisions, and take responsibility for various tasks.
- Adviser is an adult whose role is to give advice—not to run the group.
- Guests may participate in group discussions, but usually do not participate in final decision making.

Have an agenda. This is a list of things to be dealt with at a meeting. All members should be encouraged to put topics on the agenda. After the recorder reads the minutes of the previous meeting and they are approved, the members approve the agenda. Agenda items are considered in the following order:

- Old business—ongoing and follow-up items.

© 2012, Constitutional Rights Foundation
and Close Up Foundation

Constitutional Rights Foundation
Educate. Participate.

Guardian of Democracy: The Civic Mission of Schools
Released September, 2011, *Guardian of Democracy: The Civic Mission of Schools report* builds on the findings of the seminal 2003 Civic Mission of Schools report. CAP has been designed to support the promising approaches described in these reports.

INTRODUCTION

The Judicial Branch

Outlined in the Constitution, the judicial branch consists mostly of the Supreme Court. The federal courts came later through various acts of Congress. Cases end up at the Supreme Court in a variety of ways. In some ways, the court's decisions whether federal district courts or the Supreme Court, are a form of enacted law. The judicial branch serves as more than just a check on the power of the other branches.

CONNECT

MY STORY VIDEO

Thurgood Marshall and *Brown* v. *Board of Education*

Watch a video that introduces students to an early leader in the fight for civil rights and equality.

Determine Point of View What did Thurgood Marshall think was the best way to end segregation? *(Through legal means and court cases)*

Trace Cause and Effect Why was the case of *Brown* v. *Board of Education* significant? *(Because it set an example for later cases about school segregation)*

⇧ FLIP IT!

Assign the My Story video.

DIGITAL ESSENTIAL QUESTION ACTIVITY

How Should We Handle Conflict?

Ask students to think about the Essential Question for this Topic: How Should We Handle Conflict? How is conflict handled between people? States? countries? Why is how people handle conflict determined by the type of government they subscribe to?

If students have not already done so, ask them to respond to the question. Then go over the results as a class.

Support Reasons with Evidence Why did you rate the 8th pillar as you did?

Make Connections What are the elements of democracy? *(Possible answer: compromise, rights of the minority, individual worth, equality.)* How do the pillars listed support those ideas of democracy? *(Possible answer: Each pillar is directly related to an important idea. For example, civil rights and rights of the minority are similar.)*

Make Judgments Is the judicial branch more or less important than the legislative or executive branch? Why? *(Possible answer: Equally important; they serve as an oversight for the other branches.)*

DIGITAL OVERVIEW ACTIVITY

The Judicial Branch

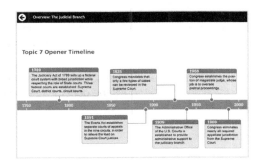

Display the timeline showing the actions taken by Congress which helped to build the judiciary system to its current form. Throughout this Topic, students will learn about all of these events and many more, but this timeline will provide a framework into which they can place the events they learn about.

D Differentiate: Extra Support Who makes most of the decisions regarding the structure of the judicial system? *(Congress)*

Check Understanding What common threads do you see binding together the actions taken by Congress when it comes to the judiciary system? *(Congress has consistently taken action to be sure the federal judiciary system can run smoothly, without placing too much of a burden on any one entity within the system. The actions also represent a desire to make the system fair and accessible for all citizens.)*

Topic Inquiry

Launch the Topic Inquiry with students after introducing the Topic.

The National Judiciary

Supporting English Language Learners

Use with Digital Texts 2 and 4, **Creation of a National Judiciary** and **Types of Jurisdiction.**

Listening
Read aloud the text *The National Judiciary*. Support students to analyze the structure and functions of the judicial branch of government, including the types of jurisdiction by completing the following activities:

Beginning Preview the text with students by looking at the images and reading the captions. Read aloud one section of the text at a time. Provide two statements—one that gives the general meaning of the section and one that does not. Guide students to choose the statement that gives the general meaning.

Intermediate After previewing the text with students, read aloud one section at a time. Provide a list of important words in the text. Have partners use the word list for support as they determine the general meaning of the section.

Advanced Have one partner read aloud a section of the text. Have the other partner tell the general meaning of the section. Then have them switch tasks.

Advanced High Read aloud several sections at a time. Have students take notes and then discuss the general meaning of the text.

Use with the lesson 1 readings.

Writing
As students analyze issues raised by judicial activism and restraint, model and review this spelling rule: When adding *-ing* to a word that ends in *e*, drop the *e*. Use words from the text such as *issuing, facing, advocating, arguing, arising, including, suing, determining, involving, nominating, increasing, settling,* and *citing*.

Beginning After explaining the rule, have students look in the text for the words above. Have them copy the words.

Intermediate Provide a list of the root words for the words above. Have students apply the spelling rule to the root words. Have them look in the text for the words.

Advanced Provide a list of the root words for the words above. Have students look in the text for the words with the *-ing* ending. Guide students to write sentences with the words.

Advanced High Provide a list of words where some of the words have been misspelled. Have students apply the spelling rule above in order to correct the words. Have students look in the text for the words. Ask them to write sentences using the words.

▣ Differentiate Instruction

Use the Differentiated Instruction notes throughout the lesson plan to support the varied skill sets, levels of readiness, and interests in the mixed-ability classroom.

Challenge These notes include suggestions for expanding the activity for advanced students.

On-Level These notes include suggestions for modifying the activity to address different interests or learning styles.

Extra Support These notes include ideas for providing more scaffolding or reading spuport.

Special Needs These notes provide ideas for adapting instruction to support the needs of various special needs students.

■ NOTES

Objectives

Objective 1: Explain why the Constitution created a national judiciary, and analyze its structure and functions.

Objective 2: Identify the criteria that determine whether a case is within the jurisdiction of a federal court, and compare the types of jurisdiction.

Objective 3: Outline the process for appointing federal judges, and list their terms of office.

Objective 4: Understand the impact of judicial philosophy, and analyze issues raised by judicial activism and judicial restraint.

Objective 5: Examine the roles of court officers.

LESSON 1 ORGANIZER		PACING: APPROX. 1 PERIOD, .5 BLOCKS		
			RESOURCES	
	OBJECTIVES	PACING	Online	Print
Connect				
DIGITAL START UP ACTIVITY **The Function of the Judicial Branch**		5 min.	●	
Investigate				
DIGITAL TEXT 1 **The Courts and Democracy**	Objective 1	10 min.	●	●
DIGITAL TEXT 2 **Creation of a National Judiciary**	Objective 1	10 min.	●	●
INTERACTIVE CHART **Constitutional Courts and Special Courts**		10 min.	●	
DIGITAL TEXT 3 **Jurisdiction in the Federal Court System**	Objective 2	10 min.	●	●
INTERACTIVE ILLUSTRATION **What Does a Judge Do?**		10 min.	●	
DIGITAL TEXT 4 **Types of Jurisdiction**	Objective 2	10 min.	●	●
DIGITAL TEXT 5 **Federal Judges and Court Officers**	Objectives 3, 4, 5	10 min.	●	●
Synthesize				
DIGITAL SYNTHESIZE ACTIVITY **Revisit the Function of the Judicial Branch**		5 min.	●	
Demonstrate				
DIGITAL QUIZ **Lesson Quiz and Class Discussion Board**		10 min.	●	

Topic 7 Lesson 1

The National Judiciary

DIGITAL START UP ACTIVITY

The Function of the Judicial Branch

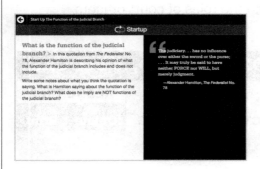

Project the Start Up Activity Ask students to read the quotation by Hamilton from the *The Federalist* No. 78 and answer the questions as they enter and get settled. Then have them share their ideas with another student, either in class or through a chat or blog space.

Discuss Share background information about the structure and functions of the judicial branch. What elements do students know? What do they want to find out? Collect responses in a chart.

Tell students that in this lesson they will be learning about the national judiciary.

Aa **Vocabulary Development:** Use the Interactive Reading Notepad to preview the Key Terms and Academic Vocabulary in this Lesson with students.

⇅ FLIP IT!

Assign the Flipped Video for this lesson.

■ **STUDENT EDITION PRINT PAGES: 298–305**

■ **INVESTIGATE**

DIGITAL TEXT 1

The Courts and Democracy

Objective 1: Explain why the Constitution created a national judiciary, and analyze its structure and functions.

Quick Instruction

The Framers knew that corrupt, tyrannical leaders throughout history used the courts to control the public. To promote self-government and protect civil liberties, the Framers wanted a separate judicial branch. To further separate judges from public pressure, the Constitution stipulated that federal judges should be appointed, not elected, and serve for life. The Framers expected that judges would make decisions based on their best judgment, without facing the prospect of removal for issuing an unpopular decision.

The Bill of Rights outlines citizen's rights. The 4th Amendment confronts illegal searches and the need for probable cause. The 6th Amendment speaks to jury trials.

ELL Use the ELL activity described in the ELL chart.

Further Instruction

Editable Presentation Use the Editable Presentation to present the main ideas for this Core Reading.

The Courts and Democracy: Core Reading and Interactive Reading Notepad Project and discuss the Interactive Reading Notepad questions.

In 1733, the governor of New York, William Crosby, replaced a popular judge with a friend who was both corrupt and incompetent. When a newspaper began running a series of articles critical of the governor, Crosby put the editor of the paper, Peter Zenger, in jail. The following trial established a precedent for freedom of the press and an impartial federal court system.

Identify Central Issues What are the most important functions of the judicial branch according to the Framers? *(The judicial branch should be independent and impartial.)*

Creation of a National Judiciary

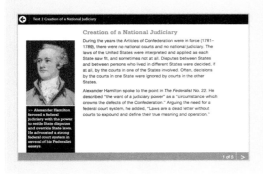

Constitutional Courts and Special Courts

Objective 1: Explain why the Constitution created a national judiciary, and analyze its structure and functions.

Quick Instruction

There are two separate court systems in the United States. They vary both in structure and function. The federal court system spans the country with its more than 100 courts. Each of the 50 States has its own system of courts. Their numbers run well into the thousands, and most of the cases that are heard in court today are heard in those State, not the federal, courts.

Further, there are two types of federal court. The Constitution establishes the Supreme Court and leaves to Congress the creation of the inferior courts—the lower federal courts. Constitutional courts are federal courts that Congress has formed under Article III to exercise "the judicial Power of the United States." The second type is special courts that are not connected to Article III. Rather, they have been created by Congress to hear cases arising out of some of the expressed powers given to Congress in Article I, Section 8. The special courts hear a much narrower range of cases than those that may come before the constitutional courts.

Interactive Chart: Constitutional Courts and Special Courts Project the Interactive Chart. Discuss the Constitutional and Special Courts with students. Have students give an example of or define each type.

ACTIVE CLASSROOM

Have students complete the activity. Then have them choose one type of court and the case suggested. Using a Headline strategy, have students create a headline for that case. They should also write a teaser that includes the type of court. Students should share their headlines and teasers.

D Differentiate: Extra Support Have students use a Sticky Note strategy as they define each court type. On the sticky notes, they should write whether the court is Constitutional or Special. Then they should write notes about what type of cases are heard in each type. For example, questions of tax law are heard in the special tax court.

ELL Use the ELL activity described in the ELL chart.

Further Instruction

Editable Presentation Use the Editable Presentation to present the main ideas for this Core Reading.

Creation of a National Judiciary: Core Reading and Interactive Reading Notepad Project and discuss the Interactive Reading Notepad questions.

Students should know that today the constitutional courts now include the courts of appeals, the district courts, and the U.S. Court of International Trade. These constitutional courts are also called the regular courts and, sometimes, Article III courts. Special courts, on the other hand, are also called the legislative courts and, sometimes, Article I courts. Today, they include the U.S. Court of Appeals for the Armed Forces, the U.S. Court of Appeals for Veterans Claims, the U.S. Court of Federal Claims, the U.S. Tax Court, the various territorial courts, and the courts of the District of Columbia.

Identify Central Ideas Why are constitutional courts called Article III courts? *(They are defined by Article III of the Constitution.)*

Draw Conclusions Why might the Framers have given the power to create special courts to the legislative branch instead of keeping it within the judicial branch? *(Possible answer: This is an example of checks and balances. They wanted to give the country room to grow and change in ways they couldn't expect.)*

The National Judiciary

DIGITAL TEXT 3

Jurisdiction in the Federal Court System

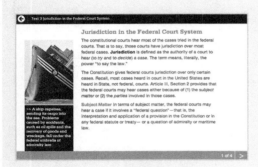

INTERACTIVE ILLUSTRATION

What Does a Judge Do?

Objective 2: **Identify the criteria that determine whether a case is within the jurisdiction of a federal court, and compare the types of jurisdiction.**

Quick Instruction

Jurisdiction is the power "to say the law." The Constitution gives federal courts jurisdiction over only certain cases. Article III, Section 2 provides that the federal courts may hear cases either because of the subject matter or the parties involved in those cases.

Subject Matters and Parties The federal courts may hear a case if it involves a "federal question"—that is, the subject matter involves the interpretation and application of a provision in the Constitution or in any federal statute or treaty. A case falls within the jurisdiction of the federal courts if one of the parties involved in the case is (1) the United States or one of its officers or agencies; (2) an ambassador, consul, or other official representative of a foreign government; (3) one of the 50 States suing another State, a resident of another State, or a foreign government or one of its subjects; (4) a citizen of one State suing a citizen of another State; (5) an American citizen suing a foreign government or one of its subjects; or (6) a citizen of a State suing another citizen of that same State where both claim title to land under grants from different States.

Interactive Illustration: What Does a Judge Do? Click through the hotspots with the students and discuss the various responsibilities of the judge.

ACTIVE CLASSROOM

Using a Write 1 Get 3 strategy, answer the question of the activity: What is a judge? Students should define the following terms as they write: *precedent*, *overruling*, *sustaining*, *voir dire*, *penalty*, *contempt*.

D **Differentiate:** **Extra Support** Have students work together and act out the different roles of being a judge using what they learned. Then have them continue with the activity.

ELL Use the ELL activity described in the ELL chart.

Further Instruction

Editable Presentation Use the Editable Presentation to present the main ideas for this Core Reading.

Jurisdiction in the Federal Court System: Core Reading and Interactive Reading Notepad Project and discuss the Interactive Reading Notepad questions.

Students should understand that the cases not heard in federal courts because they do not meet the subject or party criteria are heard in State courts.

Draw Conclusions Why are the separate State and federal courts a reflection of federalism? *(Possible answer: The Constitution balanced the rights of the States and Federal Government.)*

Compare Recall If an American citizen sues a citizen of another country, would the case be heard in a State or federal court? *(a federal court)*

Identify Central Ideas What is a "federal question"? *(a question that involves the interpretation and application of a provision in the Constitution or in any federal statute or treaty)*

DIGITAL TEXT 4

Types of Jurisdiction

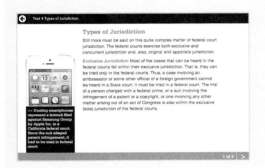

DIGITAL TEXT 5

Federal Judges and Court Officers

Objective 2: Identify the criteria that determine whether a case is within the jurisdiction of a federal court, and compare the types of jurisdiction.

Quick Instruction

The federal courts exercise serveral types of jurisdiction: both exclusive and concurrent jurisdiction and, also, original and appellate jurisdiction. Exclusive jurisdiction means that only federal courts can hear the case. Federal and State courts can also have concurrent jurisdiction, meaning they share the power to hear these cases. A court in which a case is first heard is said to have original jurisdiction over that case. That court, the trial court, is often described as "the court of first instance." A court that hears a case on appeal from a lower court exercises appellate jurisdiction over that case. Appellate courts do not retry cases. Rather, they determine whether a trial court has acted in accord with applicable law. The higher court—the appellate court—may uphold, overrule or in some way modify the decision appealed from the lower court.

ELL Use the ELL activity described in the ELL chart.

Further Instruction

Editable Presentation Use the Editable Presentation to present the main ideas for this Core Reading.

Types of Jurisdiction: Core Reading and Interactive Reading Notepad Project and discuss the Interactive Reading Notepad questions.

In the federal judiciary, the district courts have only original jurisdiction, and the courts of appeals have only appellate jurisdiction. The Supreme Court exercises both original and (most often) appellate jurisdiction.

Explain Describe how a court case travels through the federal court system from the first district court to the Supreme Court with exclusive jurisdiction. *(The case is first heard in the district court. Then it moves to an appellate court. It is finally decided at the Supreme Court.)*

Draw Conclusions Why might the Supreme Court exercise original jurisdiction? *(when the legislative branch sues the executive branch)*

Objectives 3: Outline the process for appointing federal judges, and list their terms of office; 4: Understand the impact of judicial philosophy, and analyze issues raised by judicial activism and judicial restraint; 5: Examine the roles of court officers.

Quick Instruction

Selection of Judges The Constitution says that the President can appoint to the federal bench anyone whom the Senate will confirm. Influential senators, especially those from the nominee's home State, and members of the Judiciary Committee, the President's allies and supporters in the legal profession, and various other personalities in the President's political party also play a major role in selecting judges.

The Judicial Philosophy of Judicial Restraint All federal judges make decisions in which they must interpret and apply provisions in the Constitution and acts of Congress. The judicial restraint philosophy is that judges should decide cases on the basis of (1) the original intent of the Framers or those who enacted the statute(s) involved in a case, and (2) precedent—a judicial decision that serves as a guide for settling later cases of a similar nature. The judicial activism philosophy indicates that provisions in the Constitution and in statute law should be interpreted and applied in the light of ongoing changes in conditions and values.

The National Judiciary

Terms of Judges This means that the judges of the constitutional courts are appointed for life; they serve until they resign, retire, or die in office.

Court Officers Today, federal judges have little involvement in the day-to-day administrative operations of the courts over which they preside. Their primary mission is to hear and decide cases. A clerk, several deputy clerks, bailiffs, court reporters and stenographers probation officers, and others provide support services.

ELL Use the ELL activity described in the ELL chart.

Further Instruction

Editable Presentation Use the Editable Presentation to present the main ideas for this Core Reading.

Federal Judges and Court Officers: Core Reading and Interactive Reading Notepad Project and discuss the Interactive Reading Notepad questions.

Image: Judicial Philosophy Timeline Project and step through the timeline with students. Define judicial restraint and judicial activism. Then have students choose an example and create a political cartoon from one of the incidents showing its judicial philosophy and making a comment on whether or not the philosophy was applied correctly.

Article III Read and discuss Article III with students. Ask students to describe which parts of how the judicial branch functions today were left out and why that might be. Students could discuss the individual special courts, retirement plans, judical philosophy, court officers, or preferential appointments.

Make Connections How does a judge's appointment show that the Framers were concerned with an independent judiciary? *(They don't have to be elected and they have a job for life. That means they can use their own judgment without fear of losing their position.)*

Make Judgments Which judicial philosophy would most likely be favored by Thomas Jefferson and other strict constructionists? *(judicial restraint)*

SYNTHESIZE

Revisit the Function of the Judicial Branch

Ask students to recall the Topic Essential Question, "How Should We Handle Conflict?" Have them use the Think Pair Share strategy to review the opinions they had before the lesson and any new ideas. Ask them to take five minutes to write down some brief answers to the questions below, then share their answers with a talking partner.

Have partners think about the following questions. Think about a recent Supreme Court decision or federal court case that you heard about. In your example, did the judiciary function as Hamilton described in this quotation? Was there simply a judgment rendered, or did the court step outside the boundaries Hamilton envisioned? Have pairs share their answers with the class.

Discuss Review the background chart from the beginning of the lesson. Discuss what students have learned and what they still want to know.

DEMONSTRATE

Lesson Quiz and Class Discussion Board

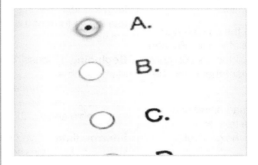

Assign the online Lesson Quiz for this lesson if you haven't already done so. Students will be offered automatic remediation or enrichment based on their score.

Pose these questions to the class on the Discussion Board: In "The National Judiciary" you read about federal courts, their jurisdictions, and the responsibilities of judges.

Make Judgments Which is a better philosophy for a modern country: judicial philosophy or judicial restraint?

Compare Why don't all court cases end up in federal court?

Explain What kinds of cases are heard by federal courts?

Topic Inquiry

Have students continue their investigations for the Topic Inquiry.

The Supreme Court

Supporting English Language Learners

Use with Digital Text 1, **What Is Judicial Review?**

Listening
Read aloud the text. Support students to understand the general meaning of the structure and functions of the judicial branch of government, including judicial review by completing the following activities:

Beginning Preview the text with students by looking at the images and reading the captions. Read aloud one section of the text at a time. Provide two statements—one which gives the general meaning of the section and one that does not. Guide students to choose the statement that gives the general meaning.

Intermediate After previewing the text with students, read aloud one section at a time. Provide a list of important words in the text. Have partners use the word list for support as they determine the general meaning of the section.

Advanced Have one partner read aloud a section of the text. Have the other partner tell the general meaning of the section. Then have them switch tasks.

Advanced High Read aloud several sections at a time. Have students take notes and then discuss the general meaning of the text.

Use with Digital Text 2, **Jurisdiction of the Supreme Court.**

Writing
As students learn about the structure and functions of the federal court system, explain subject-verb agreement using present tense sentences from the text. Teach students the following rule: If the subject is singular, use the *–s* form of the verb. If the subject is plural, use the base form of the verb.

Beginning Discuss, then have students copy and complete sentence stems such as: _____ *take an oath.* _____ *takes an oath.* _____ *announce a decision.* _____ *announces a decision.* _____ *resolve a case.* _____ *resolves a case.* (Accept any reasonable answer that has subject-verb agreement.)

Intermediate Have partners copy and complete the sentence stems such as: *The Supreme Court* _____. *The Justices* _____. *The solicitor general* _____.

Advanced Provide students with a list of verbs from the text such as: *provide*, *instruct*, *deliver*, and *refuse*. Have partners write sentences with singular and plural forms of each verb.

Advanced High Ask students to write a summary of the text. Have partners work together to check for subject-verb agreement.

▶ Differentiate Instruction

Use the Differentiated Instruction notes throughout the lesson plan to support the varied skill sets, levels of readiness, and interests in the mixed-ability classroom.

Challenge These notes include suggestions for expanding the activity for advanced students.

On-Level These notes include suggestions for modifying the activity to address different interests or learning styles.

Extra Support These notes include ideas for providing more scaffolding or reading spuport.

Special Needs These notes provide ideas for adapting instruction to support the needs of various special needs students.

■ NOTES

PEARSON
realize™
www.PearsonRealize.com

Go online to access additional resources including:
Primary Sources • Biographies • Supreme Court cases •
21st Century Skill Tutorials • Maps • Graphic Organizers.

Objectives

Objective 1: Define the concept of judicial review, and identify the roles played by Thomas Jefferson, James Madison, and John Marshall in the case in which the Court first asserted its power of judicial review.

Objective 2: Outline the types of jurisdiction that apply to the Supreme Court.

Objective 3: Explain how cases reach the Supreme Court.

Objective 4: Summarize the way the Supreme Court operates.

LESSON 2 ORGANIZER — PACING: APPROX. 1 PERIOD, .5 BLOCKS

	OBJECTIVES	PACING	RESOURCES Online	RESOURCES Print
Connect				
DIGITAL START UP ACTIVITY **Judicial Checks and Balances**		5 min.	●	
Investigate				
DIGITAL TEXT 1 **What Is Judicial Review?**	Objective 1	10 min.	●	●
DIGITAL TEXT 2 **Jurisdiction of the Supreme Court**	Objective 2	10 min.	●	●
DIGITAL TEXT 3 **Appealing to the Supreme Court**	Objective 3	10 min.	●	●
INTERACTIVE CHART **How a Case Reaches the Supreme Court**		10 min.	●	
DIGITAL TEXT 4 **Hearing a Supreme Court Case**	Objective 4	10 min.	●	●
INTERACTIVE TIMELINE **Key Supreme Court Cases**		10 min.	●	
Synthesize				
DIGITAL SYNTHESIZE ACTIVITY **Judicial Review of State Laws**		5 min.	●	
Demonstrate				
LESSON QUIZ **Lesson Quiz and Discussion Board**		10 min.	●	

The Supreme Court

■ CONNECT

DIGITAL START UP ACTIVITY
Judicial Checks and Balances

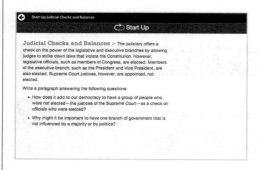

Project the Start Up Activity Ask students to answer the questions as they enter and get settled. Then have them share their ideas with another student, either in class or through a chat or blog space.

Discuss Some judges at the State level are elected. How do you think that changes their ability to be impartial? *(Possible answer: These judges might feel beholden to those who helped them win office, which might impair their impartiality.)*

Tell students that in this lesson they will be learning about the Supreme Court.

Aa Vocabulary Development: Use the Interactive Reading Notepad to preview the Key Terms and Academic Vocabulary in this Lesson with students.

ℕ FLIP IT!
Assign the Flipped Video for this lesson.

■ STUDENT EDITION PRINT PAGES: 306–312

■ INVESTIGATE

DIGITAL TEXT 1
What Is Judicial Review?

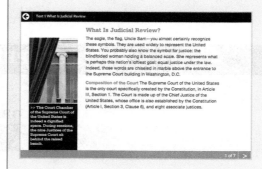

Objective 1: **Define the concept of judicial review.**

Quick Instruction
The Court first asserted its power of judicial review in *Marbury* v. *Madison* in 1803, in the aftermath of Thomas Jefferson having won the presidency and control of both houses of Congress. William Marbury went to the Supreme Court, seeking a writ of mandamus to force delivery of his commission as justice of the peace. A writ of mandamus is a court order compelling an officer of government to perform an act that the officer has a clear legal duty to perform. Marbury based his suit on the Judiciary Act of 1789, which gave the Supreme Court the right to hear such suits in its original jurisdiction. In a unanimous opinion written by Chief Justice John Marshall, the Court refused Marbury's request because it found the section of the Judiciary Act on which Marbury had based his case to be in conflict with Article III of the Constitution and, therefore, void.

Today With the Court's decision, Chief Justice Marshall claimed for the Supreme Court the right to declare acts of Congress unconstitutional, and so laid the foundation for the judicial branch's key role in the development of the American system of government. The power of judicial review can overshadow much of its other work. Each year, it hears dozens of cases in which questions of constitutionality are not raised, but in which federal law is interpreted and applied. Thus, many of the more important statutes that Congress has passed have been brought to the Supreme Court for review.

ELL Use the ELL activity described in the ELL chart.

Further Instruction
Editable Presentation Use the Editable Presentation to present the main ideas for this Core Reading.

What Is Judicial Review: Core Reading and Interactive Reading Notepad Project and discuss the Interactive Reading Notepad questions.

Marbury* v. *Madison Read and discuss the case materials with students. Link the judicial review instruction to the text. Discuss how Chief Justice Marshall came to the decision he did.

Predict Consequences How might the Federal Government have been affected if the Court had not asserted its power of judicial review? *(The judicial branch would not be able to check the power of the legislative and executive branches. As a result, those branches might have become overly powerful.)*

DIGITAL TEXT 2

Jurisdiction of the Supreme Court

Text 2 Jurisdiction of the Supreme Court

Jurisdiction of the Supreme Court

The Supreme Court has both original and appellate jurisdiction. Most of its cases, however, come on appeal—from the lower federal courts and from the highest State courts. Article III, Section 2 of the Constitution spells out two classes of cases that may be heard by the High Court in its original jurisdiction: (1) those to which a State is a party, and (2) those affecting ambassadors, other public ministers, and consuls.

>> The U.S. Ambassador to Colombia, William Brownfield (center left, pointing), was reprimanded by the Supreme Court in 2009 for interfering in Colombia's civil matters.

1 of 5 >

Objective 2: Outline the scope of Supreme Court's jurisdiction.

Quick Instruction

Explain that the Supreme Court has both original and appellate jurisdiction. Review the meaning of these terms: A court in which a case is first heard has original jurisdiction over that case; a court that hears a case on appeal from a lower court exercises appellate jurisdiction over that case. Give students the following examples and have them identify whether the Court is exercising original or appellate jurisdiction in each: 1) the State of Delaware sues the Federal Government over certain parts of the Affordable Care Act (original); 2) the plaintiff in a case believes he did not receive a fair trial and appeals the case to the Supreme Court (appellate); 3) the U.S. ambassador to the United Nations is accused of using government funds for personal expenses (original).

ELL Use the ELL activity described in the ELL chart.

Further Instruction

Editable Presentation Use the Editable Presentation to present the main ideas for this Core Reading.

Jurisdiction of the Supreme Court: Core Reading and Interactive Reading Notepad Project and discuss the Interactive Reading Notepad questions.

Discuss with students the fact that most cases that fall under original jurisdiction are tried in the lower courts. The Supreme Court hears only a case or two each term in its original jurisdiction, while it hears a few hundred in its

appellate jurisdiction. Ask: Why do you think Congress has provided that the Supreme Court has original jurisdiction over cases involving two or more States? *(It makes more sense for the Federal Government to hear these cases than for another State to be involved.)*

Draw Conclusions Why might the Supreme Court hear only a few cases in its original jurisdiction? *(Possible answer: The types of cases over which the Court exercises its original jurisdiction do not happen very often. In addition, the Court is too busy to hear other cases that might fall under Article III, Section 2 of the Constitution and instead leaves those cases to the lower courts.)*

Cause and Effect What would happen if Congress enlarged the Constitution's definition of original jurisdiction? *(It would be rewriting the Constitution.)*

Identify Central Ideas What kinds of cases does the Supreme Court mostly hear? Why? *(appellate cases because through these cases it can focus on significant points of law and act as a check against other federal courts as well as the legislative and executive branches)*

DIGITAL TEXT 3

Appealing to the Supreme Court

Text 3 Appealing to the Supreme Court

Appealing to the Supreme Court

More than 8,000 cases are now appealed to the Supreme Court each term. Of these, the Court accepts only a few hundred for decision. In most cases, petitions for review are denied, usually because most of the justices agree with the decision of the lower court or believe that the case involves no significant point of law.

In short, the High Court is in the somewhat enviable position of being able to set its own agenda. It decides what it wants to decide. The Court selects those cases that it does hear according to "the rule of four": At least four of its nine justices must agree that a case should be put on the Court's docket.

More than half the cases decided by the Court are disposed of in brief orders. For example, an order may remand (return) a case to a lower court for reconsideration in light of some other recent and related case decided by the High Court. All told, the Court now decides, after hearing arguments and with full opinions, fewer than 80 cases per term.

>> Justices can excuse themselves from cases. In 2010, Justice Elena Kagan (top right) sat out on a case involving former U.S. Attorney General John D. Ashcroft, with whom she had once worked.

1 of 4 >

Objective 3: Examine how cases reach the Supreme Court.

Quick Instruction

Ask students to explain what is meant by the statement that the Supreme Court can "set its own agenda." *(The Court decides which cases it will hear each term.)* Discuss the two main ways that cases can reach the Court: 1) by writ of certiorari or 2) by certificate.

Interactive Chart: How a Case Reaches the Supreme Court Project and step through the map. With students, define brief orders, writ of certiorari, and remanded before beginning. Then ask: How could each of the options on the chart be shown on the diagram? *(Possible answer: For Option 1, an arrow could be drawn leading from the Supreme Court back to the lower court; for Option 2, an arrow can go forward from the Supreme Court to a final decision; for Option 3, a short arrow can stop just after the Supreme Court)*

The Supreme Court

INTERACTIVE CHART

How a Case Reaches the Supreme Court

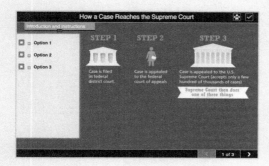

DIGITAL TEXT 4

Hearing a Supreme Court Case

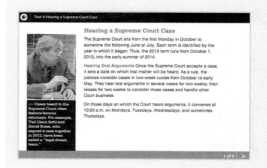

ACTIVE CLASSROOM

In pairs, have students create a timeline for a case. Students should identify the court with original jurisdiction, parties to the case, and how it got to the Supreme Court. Then they should choose one path and explain what happens next. For example, a case could be sent to the court via writ of certiorari or appealed to the court and not get past the rule of four. Explain what would happen in each case. Students should share their timelines with the class.

D Differentiate: **Extra Support** Have students create a decision tree or a timeline for what happens if a case is reviewed to the Supreme Court. They should define the terms they show in their decision tree.

ELL Use the ELL activity described in the ELL chart.

Further Instruction

Editable Presentation Use the Editable Presentation to present the main ideas for this Core Reading.

Appealing to the Supreme Court: Core Reading and Interactive Reading Notepad Project and discuss the Interactive Reading Notepad questions.

Remind students that most cases that reach the Court do so from the highest State courts and the federal courts of appeals. Ask: Under what circumstances is "cert" usually granted? *(typically, only when a petition raises some important constitutional question or a serious problem in the interpretation of a statute)*

Make Generalizations What is unique about the Supreme Court and the way it chooses cases? *(It chooses its own docket, or what it hears.)*

Identify Central Ideas Why are most cases denied hearing before the Supreme Court? *(usually because the Court agrees with the lower court's ruling or because the case does not raise significant constitutional issues)*

Cause and Effect What happens when a case is denied review? *(The lower court decision stands.)*

Compare How is the certificate process different from an appeals process? *(The Court is asked by a lower court to explain a particular point of law, not look at the ruling itself.)*

Objective 4: Summarize the way the Supreme Court operates.

Quick Instruction

Have students describe what happens during oral arguments before the Court. Then ask: What is the role of briefs in the process of appealing a case to the Supreme Court? *(Briefs explain the positions of both sides in a case and present relevant facts and precedents.)* Why does the Court often render split decisions? *(because the cases it hears are concerned with controversial legal questions that cause sharply differing opinions)*

Interactive Timeline: Key Supreme Court Cases Project and step through the timeline with students. Review with students the constitutional basis on which each case was decided. Then have students choose a case not on the timeline and write up their own summary of that case.

ACTIVE CLASSROOM

Have students take a poll to show which court case they think is most important to the rights of the majority. Then have students take a poll to show which court case they think is most important to the rights of the minority. Have students discuss the cases in pairs and then make their decision. *(Possible answers:* United States v. Darby *because it regulated child labor;* Brown v. Board of Education *because it disallowed separate but equal)*

INTERACTIVE TIMELINE

Key Supreme Court Cases

D Differentiate: **Challenge** Have students choose a case that was not chosen in the poll. Have them take sides and debate the merits of the case.

Further Instruction

Editable Presentation Use the Editable Presentation to present the main ideas for this Core Reading.

Hearing a Supreme Court Case: Core Reading and Interactive Reading Notepad Project and discuss the Interactive Reading Notepad questions. Have students summarize what happens when the Court is in conference. *(At the conference, the Chief Justice leads the discussion of each case to be considered—stating the facts, summarizing the questions of law involved, and usually indicating how he thinks the Court should dispose of that case. Then each of the associate justices, in order of seniority, presents their views and conclusions.)*

Ask students to define majority opinion, concurring opinion, and dissenting opinion. Then ask: If Justice Kagan disagrees with the majority opinion, what type of opinion would she write? *(a dissenting opinion)*

Explain The doctrine of precedent is often identified as *stare decisis* —Latin for "let the decision stand." Why is that an apt name? *(Possible answer: Precedent is considered the law of the land, so the decision stands as settled law.)*

Draw Conclusions Chief Justice Charles Evans Hughes once described dissenting opinions as "an appeal to the brooding spirit of the law, to the intelligence of a future day." What does he mean? Has this ever happened? *(The High Court does reverse itself, rarely, and so minority opinion of today could become the Court's majority position on some distant tomorrow. This happened in* Plessy *v* Fergusson *and then* Brow *v* Board of Education. *First the Court declared that separate but equal was the law of the land, and then they decided it was unconstitutional.)*

The Supreme Court

■ SYNTHESIZE

DIGITAL SYNTHESIZE ACTIVITY
Judicial Review of State Laws

Ask students to recall the Topic Essential Question, "How Should We Handle Conflict?" Have them use the Think Pair Share strategy to review the quotation and their interpretations. Ask them to take five minutes to write down some brief answers to the questions below, then share their answers with a talking partner.

Have partners think about the following questions. Why do you think Justice Holmes thought it was more important for the Supreme Court to review State laws than it was to review acts of Congress? Do you agree or disagree with him? Have pairs share their answers with the class.

Discuss Ask students to think about judicial elections. Have opinions changed?

■ DEMONSTRATE

LESSON QUIZ
Lesson Quiz and Discussion Board

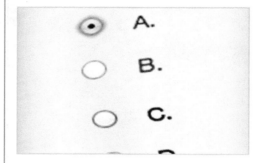

Assign the online Lesson Quiz for this lesson if you haven't already done so. Students will be offered automatic remediation or enrichment based on their score.

Pose these questions to the class on the Discussion Board: In "The Supreme Court" you read about how the Supreme Court operates.

Draw Conclusions What impact did *Marbury* v. *Madison* have on how the Supreme Court operates?

Predict Consequences Why is it important that justices write dissenting opinions instead of staying silent?

Explain What are three ways that cases arrive at the Supreme Court?

Topic Inquiry
Have students continue their investigations for the Topic Inquiry.

PEARSON realize.™
www.PearsonRealize.com
Access your Digital Lesson

The Inferior Courts and the Special Courts

Supporting English Language Learners

Use with Digital Text 1, **The Structure and Role of the Federal District Courts.**

Listening

Explain the role of context in understanding English by reading the first paragraph of the text which begins: *You know that the particular meaning of a word often depends on the context...* To help students better understand the structure and functions of the federal court system, read the text and guide students to use context to understand other words such as: *court, judges, expel,* and *record.*

Beginning Display the list of words. Read aloud the text to the students and have them listen for the words. Reread the sentences with the words and discuss their meanings in the text and in other contexts. Have students draw pictures to show the multiple meanings of the words.

Intermediate Read aloud the text to students while they look for the words that have been displayed. Have partners reread the sentences with the words. Discuss the meanings of the words in the text and in other contexts. Guide the class to write short phrases showing the multiple meanings of the words.

Advanced Read aloud the text to students. Provide several examples, then guide them to find words that have different meanings based on the context. Have partners write short sentences showing the multiple meanings of the words.

Advanced High After reading aloud, guide students to find words that have different meanings in different contexts. Have students write sentences showing the multiple meanings of the words. Have students share their sentences with each other.

Use with Digital Text 2, **The Structure and Role of the Federal Courts of Appeals.**

Writing

As students continue to learn about the structure and functions of the federal court system, remind them that the personal pronouns are: *I, you, he, she, it, we,* and *they.* Demonstrate how the pronoun agrees in number and person with the noun it replaces. Use sentences from the text when possible.

Beginning Provide sentences with nouns and have the students replace the nouns with pronouns. Example: *The Court of Federal Claims holds trials throughout the country. _____ holds trials throughout the country.*

Intermediate Provide two related sentences related to the same noun. Have students write the pronoun to replace the noun. Have them identify the noun it replaces. Example: *Congress created the United States Tax Court. _____ (It) is not a part of the federal court system. (United States Tax Court)*

Advanced Provide students with a list of nouns from the text such as: *federal judicial districts, judges, jurisdiction, docket,* and *cases.* Have partners write two related sentences for each word—one sentence using the noun and one sentence using a pronoun.

Advanced High Have students write a brief summary of the text. Have partners check each other's work for pronoun agreement.

⚠ Differentiate Instruction

Use the Differentiated Instruction notes throughout the lesson plan to support the varied skill sets, levels of readiness, and interests in the mixed-ability classroom.

Challenge These notes include suggestions for expanding the activity for advanced students.

On-Level These notes include suggestions for modifying the activity to address different interests or learning styles.

Extra Support These notes include ideas for providing more scaffolding or reading spuport.

Special Needs These notes provide ideas for adapting instruction to support the needs of various special needs students.

■ NOTES

The Inferior Courts and the Special Courts

Objectives

Objective 1: Describe the structure and jurisdiction of the federal district courts, the federal courts of appeals, and other constitutional courts.

Objective 2: Contrast the jurisdiction of the Court of Appeals for the Armed Forces and the Court of Appeals for Veterans Claims.

Objective 3: Explain how a citizen may sue the United States government in the Court of Federal Claims.

Objective 4: Examine the roles of the territorial courts and those of the District of Columbia courts.

Objective 5: Explain what types of cases are brought to the Tax Court.

LESSON 3 ORGANIZER		PACING: APPROX. 1 PERIOD, .5 BLOCKS		
	OBJECTIVES	**PACING**	**RESOURCES**	
			Online	**Print**
Connect				
DIGITAL START UP ACTIVITY **Create a Special Court**		5 min.	●	
Investigate				
DIGITAL TEXT 1 **The Structure and Role of the Federal District Courts**	Objective 1	10 min.	●	●
INTERACTIVE CHART **Civil and Criminal Cases**		10 min.	●	
DIGITAL TEXT 2 **The Structure and Role of the Federal Courts of Appeals**	Objective 2	10 min.	●	●
DIGITAL TEXT 3 **The Court of International Trade**		10 min.	●	●
DIGITAL TEXT 4 **Military Justice—Special Courts and Commissions**	Objective 4	10 min.	●	●
DIGITAL TEXT 5 **Other Special Courts**	Objectives 3, 5	10 min.	●	●
INTERACTIVE GALLERY **U.S. Special Courts**		10 min.	●	
Synthesize				
DIGITAL SYNTHESIZE ACTIVITY **Analyze Your Special Court**		5 min.	●	
Demonstrate				
LESSON QUIZ **Lesson Quiz and Discussion Board**		10 min.	●	

PEARSON realize™
www.PearsonRealize.com

Go online to access additional resources including:
Primary Sources • Biographies • Supreme Court cases •
21st Century Skill Tutorials • Maps • Graphic Organizers.

CONNECT

DIGITAL START UP ACTIVITY

Create a Special Court

Project the Start Up Activity Ask students to answer the questions as they enter and get settled. Then have them share their ideas with another student, either in class or through a chat or blog space.

Discuss Use a Think Pair Share strategy to come up with the scenario in the activity. In coming up with the scenario, consider groups of people that might require special attention or parts of the federal system that might engender a high case load. Then share their scenario with the class.

Tell students that in this lesson they will be learning about other federal courts set up by Congress and the Constitution.

Aa Vocabulary Development: Use the Interactive Reading Notepad to preview the Key Terms and Academic Vocabulary in this Lesson with students.

⚡ FLIP IT!

Assign the Flipped Video for this lesson.

■ STUDENT EDITION PRINT
PAGES: 313–319

INVESTIGATE

DIGITAL TEXT 1

The Structure and Role of the Federal District Courts

Objective 1: Describe the structure and jurisdiciton of the federal district courts, the federal courts of appeals, and other constitutional courts.

Quick Instruction

The States are divided into 89 federal judicial districts. Most cases are heard by a single judge, but some are heard by three-judge panels. District courts are the courts of first instance in the federal judiciary. They hear criminal and civil cases. In criminal cases, the United States is always a party as the prosecutor. It also can be a party in a civil case, but is not always. Most of these decisions are final and not appealed. Have students analyze the map to determine what the States with multiple districts have in common.

Interactive Chart: Civil and Criminal Cases Project and step through the chart with students.

📖 ACTIVE CLASSROOM

Have students read through and complete the activity, having them use their sticky notes. Then using a Circle Note strategy, have students define civil and criminal trials in a federal court. Students should use examples in their writing. Have students share their writing and post it.

INTERACTIVE CHART

Civil and Criminal Cases

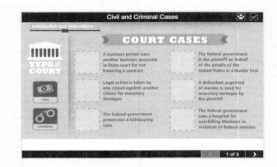

D Differentiate: Extra Support Discuss the differences between a criminal and a civil trial. Ask questions such as: What happens when someone is convicted in a criminal trial? a civil trial? How does the government act in a criminal trial? in a civil trial? Help students find the answers on the chart. Then continue with the activity.

ELL Use the ELL activity described in the ELL chart.

Further Instruction

Editable Presentation Use the Editable Presentation to present the main ideas for this Core Reading.

The Structure and Role of the Federal District Courts: Core Reading and Interactive Reading Notepad Project and discuss the Interactive Reading Notepad questions.

Multi-judge Panels Certain cases may be heard by a three-judge panel. These are cases that involve congressional districting or State legislative apportionment questions; those arising under the Civil Rights Act of 1964 or the Voting Rights Acts of 1965, 1970, 1975, and 1982; and certain antitrust actions. Two little-known multi-judge panels—made up entirely of judges drawn from the district courts—play a key role in ongoing efforts to combat terrorism in this country and abroad. One is the Foreign Intelligence Surveillance Court (FISA court), created by Congress in 1978. It is composed of 11 federal district court judges, who are appointed to seven-year terms by the Chief Justice of the United States. The court, which meets in secret, has the power to issue secret search

The Inferior Courts and the Special Courts

DIGITAL TEXT 2

The Structure and Role of the Federal Courts of Appeals

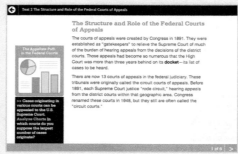

DIGITAL TEXT 3

The Court of International Trade

warrants—court orders that allow the FBI and other federal law enforcement agencies to conduct covert surveillance of individuals suspected of being spies or members of terrorist organizations. The other is the Alien Terrorist Removal Court, created by Congress in 1996. It is made up of five district court judges, appointed by the Chief Justice to five-year terms. This court has the power to decide whether those persons identified as "alien terrorists" by the Attorney General of the United States should be expelled from this country.

District Court Jurisdiction The district courts have original jurisdiction over more than 80 percent of the cases that are heard in the federal court system. The only federal cases that do not begin in the district courts are those few that fall within the original jurisdiction of the Supreme Court, as well as those cases heard by the Court of International Trade or by one of the special courts.

Make Judgments Why do you think that most cases are settled in district court and don't go on to the appeals courts? *(Most cases are settled in district court because the questions they ask are simple and based on existing law or previous precedent.)*

Objective 2: Contrast the jurisdiction of the Court of Appeals for the Armed Forces and the Court of Appeals for Veterans Claims.

Quick Instruction

The courts of appeals were created by Congress in 1891. They were established as "gatekeepers" to relieve the Supreme Court of much of the burden of hearing appeals from the decisions of the district courts. Those appeals had become so numerous that the High Court was more than three years behind its docket—its list of cases to be heard. There are now 13 courts of appeals in the federal judiciary. The country is divided into 12 judicial circuits, including the District of Columbia. There is one court of appeals for each of those circuits, and they hear cases on appeal from the various district courts within their circuit. The Court of Appeals for the Federal Circuit is the thirteenth of these appellate tribunals. It sits in the District of Columbia, but its jurisdiction is nationwide and it is mostly concerned with appeals of decisions in patent, copyright, and international trade cases.

Court of International Trade Congress has established one other Article III court, the Court of International Trade. It is a federal trial court, a court of first instance. It tries all civil (but not criminal) cases that arise out of the nation's customs and other trade-related laws.

ELL Use the ELL activity described in the ELL chart.

Further Instruction

Editable Presentation Use the Editable Presentation to present the main ideas for this Core Reading.

The Structure and Role of the Federal Courts of Appeals: Core Reading and Interactive Reading Notepad Project and discuss the Interactive Reading Notepad questions. Each of federal appeals courts is structured with 6 to 28 judges and a justice of the Supreme Court. Each court of appeals usually sits in three-judge panels. The appellate courts only review the record, the transcript of proceedings made in the trial court, and ponder the oral and written arguments (the briefs) submitted by attorneys representing parties to a case. Less than one percent of their decisions are appealed to the Supreme Court.

Jurisdiction The 13 courts of appeals have only appellate jurisdiction. For the 12 circuit-based courts, most cases come to them from the district courts within their circuit, but some are appealed from the Tax Court and some from the territorial courts. They are also empowered to hear appeals from the decisions of several federal regulatory agencies—for example, the Federal Trade Commission and the National Labor Relations Board. Unlike the 12 circuit-based courts, the jurisdiction of the thirteenth, the Court of Appeals for the Federal Circuit, is nationwide in scope. It handles appeals in certain types of federal civil cases.

DIGITAL TEXT 4

Military Justice—Special Courts and Commissions

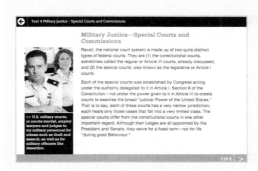

Military Justice—Special Courts and Commissions

Recall, the national court system is made up of two quite distinct types of federal courts. They are (1) the constitutional courts, sometimes called the regular or Article III courts, already discussed, and (2) the special courts, also known as the legislative or Article I courts.

Each of the special courts was established by Congress acting under the authority delegated to it in Article I, Section 8 of the Constitution—not under the power given to it in Article III to create courts to exercise the broad "judicial Power of the United States." That is to say, each of these courts has a very narrow jurisdiction; each hears only those cases that fall into a very limited class. The special courts differ from the constitutional courts in one other important regard. Although their judges are all appointed by the President and Senate, they serve for a fixed term—not for life "during good Behaviour."

>> U.S. military courts, or courts-martial, employ lawyers and judges to try military personnel for crimes such as theft and assault, as well as for military offenses like desertion.

1 of 6 >

Make Inferences Sometimes appeals courts sit *en banc*, that is with all the judges presiding. Why might that happen? *(Possible answer: It is a particularly difficult case with important or murky questions and more opinions are needed.)*

Make Inferences Before 1891, each Supreme Court justice "rode circuit," hearing appeals from the district courts within that geographic area. Why are these courts today still called circuit courts? *(It comes from the justice riding around to each court within their area.)*

Make Judgments Do you think having a Supreme Court justice hear appeals is beneficial for the federal appeals courts or not? Explain your answer. *(Possible answer: No, they should concentrate on the few cases that come before the court because those are the stickiest and require the most consideration. Going out to supervise or hear appeals takes time away from that important job.)*

Objective 4: Examine the roles of the territorial courts and those of the District of Columbia courts.

Quick Instruction

Like constitutional courts, judges for special courts are appointed by the president and Senate, but serve for a fixed term. Beginning in 1789, Congress has created a system of military courts for each branch of the nation's armed forces, as an exercise of its expressed power to "make Rules for the Government and Regulation of the land and naval Forces." (Article I, Section 8, Clause 14.) These military courts—courts-martial—serve the special disciplinary needs of the armed forces and are not a part of the federal court system. Their judges, prosecutors, defense attorneys, court reporters, and other personnel are all members of the military.

Further Instruction

Editable Presentation Use the Editable Presentation to present the main ideas for this Core Reading.

Military Justice—Special Courts and Commissions: Core Reading and Interactive Reading Notepad Project and discuss the Interactive Reading Notepad questions.

The Courts of Appeals In 1950, Congress created the Court of Military Appeals, now titled the Court of Appeals for the Armed Forces, to review the more serious court-martial convictions of military personnel. This appellate court is a civilian tribunal, a part of the judicial branch, entirely separate from the military establishment. Appeals from the court's decisions can be taken to the Supreme Court. Congress created the Court of Veterans Appeals in 1988. This court has the power to hear appeals from the decisions of the Board of Veterans' Appeals in the Department of Veterans Affairs. Appeals from the decisions of the Court of Appeals for Veterans Claims can be taken to the Court of Appeals for the Federal Circuit. In 2001, President Bush issued a controversial executive order creating several military commissions. These court-like bodies were set up, outside the regular courts-martial system, to try "unlawful enemy combatants"—suspected terrorists captured by American forces in Iraq and Afghanistan.

Cause and Effect In 2006, the Supreme Court found that those military commissions had been improperly established. The Court held that a chief executive could create such tribunals, but only if authorized to do so by an act of Congress. What might the chief executive do because of the ruling? *(try to get Congress to authorize the tribunals)*

The Inferior Courts and the Special Courts

DIGITAL TEXT 5
Other Special Courts

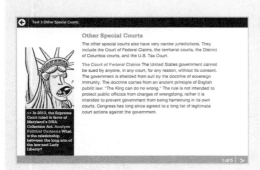

INTERACTIVE GALLERY
U.S. Special Courts

Objectives 3: **Explain how a citizen may sue the United States government in the Court of Federal Claims; 5:** **Explain what types of cases are brought to the Tax Court.**

Quick Instruction

The other special courts also have very narrow jurisdictions. They include the Court of Federal Claims, the territorial courts, the District of Columbia courts, and the U.S. Tax Court.

Interactive Gallery: U.S. Special Courts
Project and click through the gallery with students.

🎥 ACTIVE CLASSROOM

Using a Cartoon It strategy, have students choose one example of a case in a special court. Then have them illustrate it to show why the court is important to the Federal Government. Have students explain their cartoons. Publish the cartoons online.

🅳 **Differentiate: Extra Support** Click through the gallery with students and review each type of court. Have students use a Sticky Note strategy if necessary to remind themselves of they what happens in each court. Then continue with the activity.

Further Instruction

Editable Presentation Use the Editable Presentation to present the main ideas for this Core Reading.

Other Special Courts: Core Reading and Interactive Reading Notepad Project and discuss the Interactive Reading Notepad questions.

Court of Federal Claims The government may be taken to court only in cases in which Congress has declared the United States to be open to suit. In 1855, however, acting under its expressed power to pay the debts of the United States (Article I, Section 8, Clause 1), Congress set up the Court of Claims to hear money claims against the United States. The Court of Federal Claims holds trials throughout the country, hearing claims for damages against the Federal Government. Those claims it upholds cannot in fact be paid until Congress appropriates the money, which it does almost as a matter of standard procedure. Appeals from the court's decisions may be carried to the Court of Appeals for the Federal Circuit.

The Territorial Courts The territorial courts function much like the local courts in the 50 States. Show students the locations of the territories covered by these courts on a map: the Virgin Islands, Guam, and the Northern Mariana Islands.

The District of Columbia Courts Acting under its power to "exercise exclusive Legislation in all Cases whatsoever, over such District . . . as may . . . become the Seat of the Government of the United States" (Article I, Section 8, Clause 17), Congress has set up a judicial system for the nation's capital. Both the federal district court and the federal Court of Appeals for the District of Columbia hear cases as constitutional courts. Congress has also established two local courts, much like the courts in the States: a superior court, which is the general trial court, and a court of appeals.

The United States Tax Court Acting under its power to tax (Article I, Section 8, Clause 1), Congress created the United States Tax Court in 1969 as "an independent judicial body" in the legislative branch. It is not, in fact, a part of the federal court system. The Tax Court hears civil but not criminal cases involving disputes over the application of the tax laws. Its decisions may be appealed to the federal courts of appeals.

Draw Conclusions The government is shielded from suit by the doctrine of sovereign immunity, which comes from an ancient principle of English public law: "The King can do no wrong." Why is this an important idea in setting up federal courts? *(It ensures that the courts cannot so interfere with the government that it can no longer function.)*

Identify Central Ideas What gives Congress the power to set up courts to address debts owed by the government? *(Congress has the power to set up special courts in and outside the judicial branch. It also has the power to pay the debts of the United States.)*

SYNTHESIZE

DIGITAL SYNTHESIZE ACTIVITY

Analyze Your Special Court

Ask students to recall the Topic Essential Question, "How Should We Handle Conflict?" Have them use the Think Pair Share strategy to review the scenario that had at the beginning. Ask them to take five minutes to write down some brief answers to the questions below, then share their answers with a talking partner.

Have partners think about the following questions. How does your proposed area of need compare with the types of situations that have led Congress to establish special courts? What argument about your scenario could you present that would be compelling enough to move Congress to take this action? Have pairs share their answers with the class.

Discuss Ask students to compare and contrast the special courts and the Supreme Court. Discuss the important role they have in keeping the government functional.

DEMONSTRATE

LESSON QUIZ

Lesson Quiz and Discussion Board

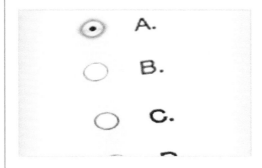

Assign the online Lesson Quiz for this lesson if you haven't already done so. Students will be offered automatic remediation or enrichment based on their score.

Pose these questions to the class on the Discussion Board: In "The Inferior Courts and the Special Courts" you read about inferior and special courts.

Make Judgments Why were the special courts set up by Congress under Article I of the Constitution, rather than Article III?

Compare Compare the military courts with the other special courts, including the types of cases heard in each.

Topic Inquiry

Have students continue their investigations for the Topic Inquiry.

The Judicial Branch

SYNTHESIZE

Reflect on the Essential Question

First ask students to reconsider the Essential Question for the Topic: How Should We Handle Conflict? Remind students how the judiciary system has been artfully set up to balance many things, including States' and federal jurisdiction, citizens' rights to a fair process, equalization of power among the governments' three branches, and even different perspectives on judicial decision-making.

Project the quotation and ask students "Would you agree that how we handle conflict must involve conflict, or do you think the judicial process should be designed as 100% consistent without allowance for disagreement?" Ask them to give at least 3 reasons to support their position. Discuss their answers as a class or ask students to post their answers on the Class Discussion Board.

Next ask students to reflect on the Topic as a whole and jot down 1–3 questions they've thought about during the Topic. Share these examples if students need help getting started:

- What is the benefit of concurring and dissenting opinions?
- What impact does the Supreme Court have on the day-to-day running of the federal courts?
- What is the most important court case in terms of ensuring the survival of democracy in the United States?

You may ask students to share their questions and answers on the Class Discussion Board.

Topic Inquiry

Have students complete the Topic Inquiry.

DEMONSTRATE

The Judicial Branch

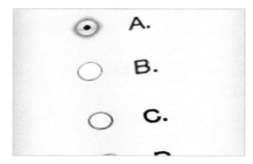

Students can prepare for the Topic Test by answering the questions in the Topic Review and Assessment online or the Assessment questions in the Print Student text. They can also prepare by reviewing their answers to the Interactive Reading Notepad questions or reviewing their notes in the Reading and Notetaking Study Guide.

The Judicial Branch

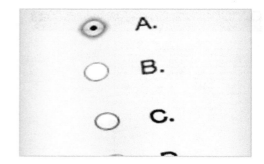

TOPIC TEST

Assign the Topic Test to assess students' understanding of topic content.

BENCHMARK TESTS

Assign these benchmark tests as you complete the relevant topics to monitor student progress toward mastering the course content and as preparation for the End-of-Course Test.

Benchmark Test 1: Topics 1–4

Benchmark Test 2: Topics 5–8

Benchmark Test 3: Topics 9–11

Benchmark Test 4: Topics 12–14

Protecting Civil Liberties

TOPIC 8 ORGANIZER	PACING: APPROX. 1 PERIOD, .5 BLOCKS	
		PACING
Connect		1 period
MY STORY VIDEO **Surveillance and Security**		10 min.
DIGITAL ESSENTIAL QUESTION ACTIVITY **How Much Power Should a Government Have?**		10 min.
DIGITAL OVERVIEW ACTIVITY **Protecting Civil Liberties**		10 min.
TOPIC INQUIRY: CIVIC ACTION PROJECT **Constitutional Rights Foundation**		20 min.
Investigate		3–7 periods
TOPIC INQUIRY: CIVIC ACTION PROJECT **Constitutional Rights Foundation**		Ongoing
LESSON 1 The Unalienable Rights		30–40 min.
LESSON 2 Freedom of Religion		30–40 min.
LESSON 3 Freedom of Speech and Press		30–40 min.
LESSON 4 Freedom of Assembly and Petition		30–40 min.
LESSON 5 Due Process of Law		30–40 min.
LESSON 6 Freedom and Security of the Person		30–40 min.
LESSON 7 Rights of the Accused		30–40 min.
Synthesize		1 period
DIGITAL ACTIVITY **Reflect on the Essential Question and Topic**		10 min.
TOPIC INQUIRY: CIVIC ACTION PROJECT **Constitutional Rights Foundation**		20 min.
Demonstrate		1–2 periods
DIGITAL TOPIC REVIEW AND ASSESSMENT **Protecting Civil Liberties**		10 min.
TOPIC INQUIRY: CIVIC ACTION PROJECT **Constitutional Rights Foundation**		20 min.

 **TOPIC INQUIRY:**

Civic Action Project

For this topic's Inquiry, you may choose to do a Civic Action Project with your students by using the materials found at the Constitutional Rights Foundation's CAP website: http://www.crfcap.org. Civic Action Project (CAP) is a project-based learning model for government and economics courses. It offers a practicum for high school students in effective and engaged citizenship and uses blended learning to engage students in civic activities both in the traditional U.S. government and economics classrooms.

Constitutional Rights Foundation
Educate. Participate.

THE TEACHER'S ROLE

THE CAP TEACHER coaches and guides students through the civic action process as they select a problem or issue, research it, determine and take civic actions, and report and document the experience. The teacher motivates, challenges, critiques, and assesses student progress. Through a blended learning approach, teachers can let students take the reins of their civic learning, guiding them along the way.

You can create your CAP classroom in three easy steps

STEP 1
Register yourself for the CAP website

STEP 2
Enroll your students

STEP 3
Engage your students in the CAP process and its many resources

Constitutional Rights Foundation

Pearson Magruder's American Government Students
Welcome to the Civic Action Project site

All of the information you're learning in your Government course will help you understand important Government policy issues that will be discussed and debated at the local, state, and national level throughout your lifetime.

Participating in a Civic Action Project (CAP) of your choosing will show you how you can use that knowledge as an engaged citizen in a democracy.

This CAP website will show you how to plan and carry out your project and give you lots of help along the way. Good luck!

Click on the logo to get started on your CAP!

THE STUDENT'S ROLE

CAP ALLOWS STUDENTS to create projects on issues they care about for their school or community. They see the connection between their civic actions and public policy and can share ideas for civics projects with each other and other CAP students nationwide. Students also see how the content of government and economics courses can apply to the real world. By taking civic actions, they practice what real citizens do when they go about trying to solve real policy-related problems. CAP fulfills best-practices in service-learning with an emphasis on public policy.

The CAP student is accountable for completing the civic action process, just as with a science project or term paper. The CAP Planner, a set of documents that guide students through the process, provides teachers with assessment information as well as a way to manage multiple student projects. While the teacher introduces and monitors the CAP, it is important that students take the lead in completing their civic actions. By using web-based technology and civics-based instruction and activities, students exercise important 21st century skills in digital literacy, critical thinking, collaboration, self-direction, and learning to be engaged and effective citizens.

CIVIC ACTIONS CAP challenges students to work on an actual problem, issue, or policy by taking civic actions. Civic actions build upon classroom civics issues, service-learning, and other proven practices of effective civic education. These actions can be many and varied, including:

· getting informed about a public issue or problem

· thinking critically about the issue or problem

· discovering how government is involved with the problem

· learning how government makes decisions

· developing a position

· engaging in civic dialogue

· building constituencies

· working together toward a common goal

· doing civic writing

· making presentations

· advocating for and defending positions

· meeting with officials

Brainstorming

Brainstorming is a method for generating ideas. It can be done by individuals or in small or large

Rules for Brainst

Pose a question to a

Set a time limit on th
more ideas out.

Work as fast as you

Handout Lesson 5B
Civic Action Project

GRADE
CAP Policy Analysis Tool

As citizens in a democracy, you'll be confronted with policy questions. Is a tax proposal a good idea? Should you vote for a particular ballot initiative? Government policies can profoundly affect our nation and your life. In a democracy, you have a say on government policies and proposed policies. It's important that you take a critical look at them. Use the following GRADE tests to evaluate a policy:

GOAL. What is the goal of the policy? If you don't know what it's supposed to do, you can't measure its success or failure. Policies are designed to address problems. What problem or problems is

...OLICY? Who might (or does)
...YOU understand who the
...LICY favors special
...CES for information, but

...ITS? What is good about the
...SES or effects of the
...VED) its goal? Will it
...NSIVE? Does it protect
...E'S liberties?

...OSTS? What is bad about the
...HE causes or effects of the
...T? Does it cause harm? Does
...RE any potential

...E disadvantages. Are there
...TO DO NOTHING. Most serious
...Evaluate them. Look at
...ES.

© 2012 Constitutional Rights Foundation

Conducting Meetings

Your meetings should be organized, to-the-point, and fun.

Decide how you're going to make decisions. If you are a small group, try deciding by whole-group consensus or by a two-thirds vote. A simple-majority decision may lead to bad feelings and resentment.

Understand everyone's role at the meeting. At most meetings, people need to fill the following roles, which may change from meeting to meeting:

· **Leader or facilitator** runs the meeting, follows the agenda item by item, and watches the time allotted for each. The leader helps participants focus on the task and makes sure everyone has a chance to participate.

· **Recorder** takes minutes, which include date and time of meeting, the persons attending, and notes on each agenda item.

· **Treasurer.**

· **Group members** contribute agenda items, discuss topics, make decisions, and take responsibility for various tasks.

· **Adviser** is an adult whose role is to give advice—not to run the group.

· **Guests** may participate in group discussions, but usually do not participate in final decision making.

Have an agenda. This is a list of things to be dealt with at a meeting. All members should be encouraged to put topics on the agenda. After the recorder reads the minutes of the previous meeting and they are approved, the members approve the agenda. Agenda items are considered in the following order:

· Old business—ongoing and follow-up items.

© 2012, Constitutional Rights Foundation
and Close Up Foundation

Constitutional
Rights
Foundation
Educate. Participate.

Guardian of Democracy: The Civic Mission of Schools
Released September, 2011, *Guardian of Democracy: The Civic Mission of Schools report* builds on the findings of the seminal 2003 Civic Mission of Schools report. CAP has been designed to support the promising approaches described in these reports.

Protecting Civil Liberties

The Bill of Rights was created to make sure that individual freedoms would be protected. The document was added after several Framers of the Constitution expressed concern that there was nothing specific to protect individual freedoms. The first ten amendments outline constitutional rights and freedoms guaranteed to every citizen.

■ CONNECT

MY STORY VIDEO
Surveillance and Security

Watch a video that introduces students to the many ways in which Americans are being watched.

Compare Points of View What are the competing points of view in the arguments about surveillance, privacy, and security? *(Those in favor of surveillance programs say they help prevent acts of terrorism and other crimes; others say that government and others violate the right to privacy.)*

Evaluate Sources Do you accept the arguments in favor of Prism and other information-gathering programs? Why or why not? *(Answers will vary but students should present reasoned ideas.)*

⇅ FLIP IT!

Assign the My Story video.

DIGITAL ESSENTIAL QUESTION ACTIVITY
How Much Power Should a Government Have?

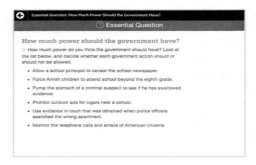

Ask students to think about the Essential Question for this Topic: How much power should the government have?

If students have not already done so, have them respond to the activity asking them to decide whether the examples of government action should or should not be allowed. Then go over their answers as a class.

Support a Point of View with Evidence Choose one government action and explain why you decided it should or should not be allowed. What was your reasoning?

Evaluate What are the pros and cons of limiting the role of government?

D Differentiate: Challenge Ask students to pick one of the examples of government actions and write a speech that argues for allowing or not allowing this action to be legal.

DIGITAL OVERVIEW ACTIVITY
Protecting Civil Liberties

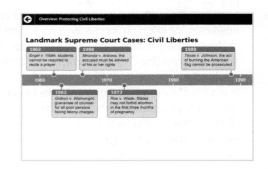

Display the timeline showing the major Supreme Court cases that have protected the civil liberties of United States citizens. During this Topic, students will learn about all of these cases and several more, but this timeline will provide a framework into which they can place the events they learn about.

D Differentiate: Extra Support How many years are there between the cases of *Gideon* v. *Wainwright* and *Texas* v. *Johnson*? (26 years)

Analyze Why do you think so many of these landmark Supreme Court cases took place in the 1960s? *(Sample answer: The 1960s were a time of great change in the United States, including many government actions that increased rights for different racial and ethnic groups. These cases reflect this overall movement at this time in our nation.)*

Topic Inquiry
Launch the Topic Inquiry with students after introducing the Topic.

The Unalienable Rights

Supporting English Language Learners

Use with Digital Text 3, **The 14th Amendment, Fundamental Rights, and Federalism.**

Listening
Read the section on the 9th Amendment. Help students identify the freedoms and rights guaranteed by this amendment by discussing the following sentence: *The enumeration in the Constitution, of certain rights, shall not be construed to deny or disparage others retained by the people.*

Beginning Read aloud the section to the students. Explain the meaning of the sentence, using visuals as support. For example, to illustrate the meaning of *enumeration,* draw a numbered list on the board. For *deny,* make a large "X." Rephrase the sentence in simple terms; for example, *The Constitution lists certain rights, but they are not the only ones the people have.* Then have students copy the sentence and read it to each other.

Intermediate Read aloud the section as the students follow along in the text. Explain the meaning of the sentence. Focus on the words *enumeration, construed, deny, disparage,* and *retained.* Have students listen to the sentence again.

Advanced Have one student read the section aloud while the others listen. Guide the group to discuss the meaning of the sentence. Ask partners to name possible freedoms and rights that are implicit in the 9th Amendment.

Advanced High Have students read the section and discuss the meaning of the sentence, listening to one another's interpretations of its meaning. Have the group list possible freedoms and rights that are implicit in the 9th Amendment.

Use with Digital Text 3, **The 14th Amendment, Fundamental Rights, and Federalism.**

Writing
Read the section on the Blaine Amendment and how it extends some of the Bill of Rights to the States. Guide students to write about the relationship between the Establishment Clause of the 1st Amendment and the Blaine Amendment.

Beginning Read aloud the section to students. Discuss the first sentences of the first two paragraphs in the section. Have students copy the sentences and then write a list of any words in the sentences that they do not know. Ask students to look up the words in a dictionary and write their meanings.

Intermediate Read aloud and discuss the section with students. Guide partners to rewrite the first sentences of the first two paragraphs in their own words. Have partners read their sentences to one another.

Advanced Have partners read the section. Ask them to write one sentence explaining the Establishment Clause of the 1st Amendment and one sentence explaining the Blaine Amendment. Then have them write a third sentence that explains how the two are related.

Advanced High Have students read the section. Ask them to write about how the Blaine Amendment extends some of the 1st Amendment to the States. Have students share their writing with the group.

▣ Differentiate Instruction

Use the Differentiated Instruction notes throughout the lesson plan to support the varied skill sets, levels of readiness, and interests in the mixed-ability classroom.

Challenge These notes include suggestions for expanding the activity for advanced students.

On-Level These notes include suggestions for modifying the activity to address different interests or learning styles.

Extra Support These notes include ideas for providing more scaffolding or reading spuport.

Special Needs These notes provide ideas for adapting instruction to support the needs of various special needs students.

▮ NOTES

The Unalienable Rights

Objectives

Objective 1: Explain how Americans' commitment to freedom led to the creation of the Bill of Rights.

Objective 2: Understand that the obligation of citizenship requires that personal desires and interests be subordinated to the public good.

Objective 3: Describe efforts to extend some of the protections of the Bill of Rights to the States and analyze the impact of that process on the scope of fundamental rights and federalism.

Objective 4: Describe how the 9th Amendment helps protect individual rights.

LESSON 1 ORGANIZER		PACING: APPROX. 1 PERIOD, .5 BLOCKS			
				RESOURCES	
		OBJECTIVES	PACING	Online	Print
Connect					
DIGITAL START UP ACTIVITY **List Your Rights**			5 min.	●	
Investigate					
DIGITAL TEXT 1 **A Commitment to Individual Rights**		Objective 1	10 min.	●	●
INTERACTIVE GALLERY **The Founding of American Rights and Freedoms**			10 min.	●	
DIGITAL TEXT 2 **Limited Government**		Objective 2	10 min.	●	●
DIGITAL TEXT 3 **The 14th Amendment, Fundamental Rights, and Federalism**		Objectives 3, 4	10 min.	●	●
INTERACTIVE GALLERY **Examples of the Incorporation of the Bill of Rights**			10 min.	●	
Synthesize					
DIGITAL SYNTHESIZE ACTIVITY **Tough Choices**			5 min.	●	
Demonstrate					
DIGITAL QUIZ **Lesson Quiz and Class Discussion Board**			10 min.	●	

PEARSON realize™
www.PearsonRealize.com

Go online to access additional resources including:
Primary Sources • Biographies • Supreme Court cases •
21st Century Skill Tutorials • Maps • Graphic Organizers.

CONNECT

DIGITAL START UP ACTIVITY
List Your Rights

Project the Start Up Activity Ask students to complete the chart as they enter and get settled.

Analyze Ask students to think about what they know about how the Constitution protects individual rights and freedoms. For each constitutional basis in the chart, have students list something they have the right to do without government interference. *(Possible answer: Freedom to write what I want. Freedom of speech.)*

Tell students that in this lesson they will be learning about the creation of the Bill of Rights and the extension of the Bill of Rights to the States.

Aa Vocabulary Development: Use the Interactive Reading Notepad to preview the Key Terms and Academic Vocabulary in this Lesson with students.

⇅ FLIP IT!
Assign the Flipped Video for this lesson.

■ STUDENT EDITION PRINT
PAGES: 326–332

INVESTIGATE

DIGITAL TEXT 1
A Commitment to Individual Rights

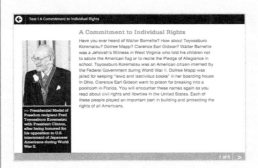

Objective 1: Explain how Americans' commitment to freedom led to the creation of the Bill of Rights.

Quick Instruction
Interactive Gallery: The Founding of American Rights and Freedoms Project the slideshow. Look at each image individually and then the collection of images as a whole. Tell students that the events shown in this gallery embody how Americans' commitment to freedom led to the creation of the Bill of Rights.

Analyze Images How are the colonists depicted in the second image? *(Possible answer: determined, brave, resolute, defiant)*

🗪 ACTIVE CLASSROOM
Have students make the picture of the ratification of the Constitution come to life. Students complete an Act It Out activity, in which they imitate the characters in the painting and become a living tapestry. Then the students state what their characters are thinking.

D Differentiate: Extra Support Ask students to explain the definition of *liberty*. Can the government constrain liberties? Why or why not? What does *rights* mean? Can the government guarantee rights? What is the difference between civil liberties and civil rights?

INTERACTIVE GALLERY
The Founding of American Rights and Freedoms

Further Instruction
Go through the Interactive Reading Notepad questions and discuss the answers with the class.

Remind students that the original Constitution did not include a general listing of the rights of the people. Many Americans objected to this. As a result, Congress added a series of amendments to the Constitution, ten of which became known as the Bill of Rights. The Bill of Rights guarantees many freedoms and rights, including the right to a trial by jury and the right to petition the government. Ask students to add to this list by identifying the rights guaranteed by each amendment in the Bill of Rights.

Draw Conclusions How do you think the American conflict with Great Britain influenced American understanding that limited government plays an important role in the protection of individual rights? *(Possible answer: When Great Britain controlled the American colonies, it denied many of the colonists' rights. After Americans gained their freedom from Great Britain, they wanted to make sure that no government took away their rights again. As a result, they made sure that the Constitution included a Bill of Rights.)*

Define Write a definition in your own words of the term *unalienable rights*. Do not refer to the lesson or a dictionary. *(Possible answer: the rights of people that cannot be taken away or destroyed by anything, including governments)*

The Unalienable Rights

DIGITAL TEXT 2

Limited Government

Text 2 Limited Government

Limited Government

Remember, government in the United States is limited. The Constitution is filled with examples of this fact. Chief among them are its many guarantees of personal freedom. Each of those guarantees is either an outright prohibition or a restriction on the power of government to do something.

All governments have and use authority over individuals. The all-important difference between a democratic government and a dictatorial one lies in the extent of that authority. In a dictatorial regime, the government's powers are practically unlimited. The government regularly suppresses dissent, often harshly. In the United States, however, governmental authority is strictly limited. As Justice **Robert H. Jackson** once put the point:

>> North Korean leader Kim Jong-un runs a dictatorial regime, as did his father, Kim Jong-il, whom he succeeded in 2011. Here, he stands authoritatively with members of his military.

1 of 8   >

Discuss Identify the unalienable rights. *(life, liberty, and the pursuit of happiness)* Discuss what is meant by each of these rights. "Life" is fairly easily understood, but what things might be included in "liberty" and the "pursuit of happiness"? *(Possible answer: "Liberty" might include many of the freedoms guaranteed in the Bill of Rights, such as freedom of speech and religion.)*

Check Understanding Using the definition of *civil rights*, explain how the Civil Rights Act of 1964 affected particular groups. *(The Civil Rights Act of 1964 was a positive act of government that sought to extend to minority groups constitutional guarantees against discrimination on the basis of race, sex, religious belief, or national origin.)*

Objective 2: **Understand that the obligation of citizenship requires that personal desires and interests be subordinated to the public good.**

Quick Instruction

Have students form pairs. Help them to evaluate constitutional provisions for limiting the role of government, including the protection of individual rights, by looking at each amendment in the Bill of Rights and answering the question: How does this amendment limit the role of government and protect individual rights? *(Possible answer: The 10th Amendment limits government to only those powers given to it in the Constitution; it protects individual rights by reserving all other powers to the people.)*

D **Differentiate:** **Challenge** Ask students to draw or describe a political cartoon that expresses a point of view about Japanese internment during World War II. Tell students that these cartoons can use characters, words, and symbols to convey meaning.

Further Instruction

Go through the Interactive Reading Notepad questions and discuss the answers with the class.

Write the following on the board: Each person's rights are relative to the rights of every other person. Ask students to find synonyms that could be used in place of the word *relative*. *(Possible answers: connected, related, comparative)*

Discuss The healthcare reform law passed in 2010 requires all citizens to have health insurance. This requirement is meant to help cover the cost of providing low-cost health insurance to those who cannot otherwise afford it. Discuss this issue in terms of whether and/or when the obligation of citizenship requires that personal desires and interests be subordinated to the public good. *(Points to raise during the discussion include whether or not government should become involved in providing healthcare to citizens; whether or not healthcare coverage can reasonably be considered a critical component of "the public good"; and whether the benefit of achieving universal coverage balances the loss of liberty for those who would choose not to have health insurance.)*

DIGITAL TEXT 3

The 14th Amendment, Fundamental Rights, and Federalism

INTERACTIVE GALLERY

Examples of the Incorporation of the Bill of Rights

Objectives 3: Describe efforts to extend some of the protections of the Bill of Rights to the States and analyze the impact of that process on the scope of fundamental rights and federalism; 4: Describe how the 9th Amendment helps protect individual rights.

Quick Instruction

Interactive Hotspot: Examples of the Incorporation of the Bill of Rights Project the hotspot on the whiteboard and click through the images. Introduce the activity by telling students that the process of incorporation is the judicial process that has extended most of the Bill of Rights guarantees to the 14th Amendment's Due Process Clause. Incorporating these guarantees makes them applicable at the State, as well as the national, level. Have students select each amendment to find out more about how it was incorporated.

🗪 ACTIVE CLASSROOM

Have students complete a Quick Write activity about the Blaine Amendment, in which they write all they know about this amendment in 30 seconds.

ELL Use the ELL activity described in the ELL chart.

Further Instruction

Editable Presentation Use the Editable Presentation to present the main ideas for this Core Reading.

The 14th Amendment, Fundamental Rights, and Federalism Project and discuss the Interactive Reading Notepad questions, including the graphic organizer asking students to record their thoughts on questions about the 9th and 14th Amendments.

Be sure students understand that the efforts to extend the Bill of Rights to the States is often noncontroversial. In some cases, however, such as banning prayer in schools, the Federal Government has broadened its control to areas traditionally left to the States, which has led to some controversy.

Summarize Describe efforts to selectively extend some of the Bill of Rights to the States, including the Blaine Amendment and U.S. Supreme Court rulings. *(Possible answer: In a long series of rulings stretching over many years, the Supreme Court has held that most of the protections in the Bill of Rights also apply to the States. Prior to the incorporation of the Establishment Clause of the 1st Amendment, Blaine amendments were passed by many States to prevent State funds from being used to support religious schools.)*

Analyze Analyze the impact of the efforts to selectively extend some of the Bill of Rights to the States on the scope of fundamental rights and federalism. *(The efforts to selectively extend the Bill of Rights to the States have expanded fundamental rights by ensuring that protections guaranteed at the federal level are also guaranteed at the State level. Those efforts have impacted federalism by requiring States to alter some of their policies and practices based on incorporation, such as prayer in public schools or federal protections for those accused of crimes.)*

The Unalienable Rights

■ SYNTHESIZE

DIGITAL SYNTHESIZE ACTIVITY
Tough Choices

Remind students that in this lesson they learned about protecting individual rights and freedoms, and balancing those with the public good. Then ask students to consider the following proposal for government action:

"The government should pass a law limiting the use of cell phones in public places."

Analyze Ask students to think about how two sides might debate this issue. What are some of the arguments that could be used for and against this measure? *(Possible answer: For: Cell phones annoy other people in public places; Against: People have the right to freedom of speech in public places.)* How can you balance individual rights and freedoms and the public good in this instance? *(Possible answer: Allow the use of cell phones in public places, except in areas that require a quiet environment, such as libraries, classrooms, and theaters.)* Tell students to complete a table, listing the conflicting issues that should be considered when debating this issue.

Debate Ask students to divide into two groups based on their viewpoint on the issue. One group will be for government restrictions on cell phones in public places and the other will be against it. Have students in each group talk with each other to compare reasons for their stance. Ask a representative from each side to present and defend the group's point of view.

■ DEMONSTRATE

DIGITAL QUIZ
Lesson Quiz and Class Discussion Board

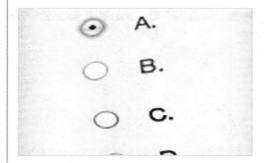

Assign the online Lesson Quiz for this lesson if you haven't already done so. Students will be offered automatic remediation or enrichment based on their score.

Remind students that in "The Unalienable Rights" they read about the creation of the Bill of Rights, some obligations of citizenship, efforts to extend the Bill of Rights to the States, and the 9th Amendment.

Pose these questions to the class on the Discussion Board:

Predict Consequences What might be the consequences if citizens refused to subordinate their desires to the public good? *(Possible answer: The consequences would be a much more chaotic society. Crime rates would skyrocket, and public services, such as transportation, would suffer.)*

Hypothesize Do you think the authors of the Bill of Rights would be surprised to learn about the difficulty the Federal Government has had in incorporating some of these rights to the States? *(Possible answer: No; during the early history of the United States, the States had a good deal of influence and independence. Because of this, the authors would not be surprised that some of the States have resisted incorporating some of the Bill of Rights.)*

Topic Inquiry
Have students continue their investigations for the Topic Inquiry.

PEARSON
realize™
www.PearsonRealize.com
Access your Digital Lesson

Freedom of Religion

Supporting English Language Learners

Use with Digital Text 1, **Religious Liberty.**

Learning Strategies
Guide students to list what they know about *religious freedom.* Read the section *Protecting Religious Freedom.* Guide students to examine the reason(s) the Founding Fathers protected religious freedom in America.

Beginning Have students write one or two words or short phrases to describe what they know about religious freedom. Read aloud the section while students follow along in the text. Provide simple sentences giving reasons the Founding Fathers protected religious freedom, such as "Some colonial governments set up churches, which many colonists did not like. They thought the government should not be involved in religion." Have students connect these sentences to their prior knowledge.

Intermediate Have the group create a list of what they know about religious freedom. Read aloud the section while students follow along. Have students complete the following sentence frame: *The Founding Fathers protected religious freedom in America because _____.* Have students connect this sentence to their prior knowledge.

Advanced Have partners list what they know about religious freedom. Ask them to read the section. Have small groups examine the reasons the Founding Fathers protected religious freedom and connect these reasons to their prior knowledge about religious freedom.

Advanced High Have students hold a discussion about religious freedom, focusing on what they think it means, what role it has in American life, and if (or how) it is related to American government. Have students read the section and compare their original ideas to the section content.

Use with Digital Text 2, **Religion and Education.**

Listening
Read the section *Prayers and the Bible.* Guide students to analyze the U.S. Supreme Court's interpretation of religious rights guaranteed by the U.S. Constitution by having them follow directions to complete graphic organizers.

Beginning Read aloud the section and discuss the cases. Provide a basic web graphic organizer to students, with the center circle labeled "Prayers and the Bible," and each of the Supreme Court cases from the reading surrounding it. Guide them to add a note for each case telling whether the law or policy was found constitutional or unconstitutional. Have students listen as you review the cases, using the completed graphic organizer to support your discussion.

Intermediate Read aloud the section and discuss the cases. Provide a basic web graphic organizer to students, with the center circle labeled "Prayers and the Bible." Have students add the cases from the section to the organizer, including adding a note for each case telling whether the law or policy was found constitutional or unconstitutional. Have students listen as members of the group review each case.

Advanced Have partners read the section and discuss the cases. Guide students to complete a web graphic organizer for the content in the reading. Have students listen to one another as they take turns summarizing each case.

Advanced High Have students read the section and discuss the cases. Direct students to complete a graphic organizer for the content in the reading. Have students listen as one member of the group re-reads the section aloud, marking off each case on their graphic organizers as it is mentioned.

⊡ Differentiate Instruction

Use the Differentiated Instruction notes throughout the lesson plan to support the varied skill sets, levels of readiness, and interests in the mixed-ability classroom.

Challenge These notes include suggestions for expanding the activity for advanced students.

On-Level These notes include suggestions for modifying the activity to address different interests or learning styles.

Extra Support These notes include ideas for providing more scaffolding or reading spuport.

Special Needs These notes provide ideas for adapting instruction to support the needs of various special needs students.

▮ NOTES

Freedom of Religion

Objectives

Objective 1: Examine the reasons the Founding Fathers protected religious freedom and guaranteed its free exercise.

Objective 2: Understand the meaning of the phrase "separation of church and state."

Objective 3: Analyze Supreme Court interpretations of religious rights guaranteed by the Constitution in selected cases relating to education, including *Engel* v. *Vitale*.

Objective 4: Summarize Establishment Clause rulings in other areas, such as seasonal religious displays and public displays of the Ten Commandments.

Objective 5: Evaluate Supreme Court decisions that have affected a particular religious group, in particular those related to the Free Exercise Clause.

LESSON 2 ORGANIZER		PACING: APPROX. 1 PERIOD, .5 BLOCKS			
		OBJECTIVES	PACING	Online	Print
Connect					
DIGITAL START UP ACTIVITY **Is it Constitutional or Not?**			5 min.	●	
Investigate					
DIGITAL TEXT 1 **Religious Liberty**		Objectives 1, 2	10 min.	●	●
INTERACTIVE CHART **The Establishment Clause**			10 min.	●	
DIGITAL TEXT 2 **Religion and Education**		Objective 3	10 min.	●	●
DIGITAL TEXT 3 **Other Establishment Clause Cases**		Objective 4	10 min.	●	●
DIGITAL TEXT 4 **The Free Exercise Clause**		Objective 5	10 min.	●	●
INTERACTIVE CHART **Understanding the Free Exercise Clause**			10 min.	●	
Synthesize					
DIGITAL SYNTHESIZE ACTIVITY **Balancing Rights with the Common Good**			5 min.	●	
Demonstrate					
DIGITAL QUIZ **Lesson Quiz and Class Discussion Board**			10 min.	●	

PEARSON
realize.
www.PearsonRealize.com

Go online to access additional resources including:
Primary Sources • Biographies • Supreme Court cases •
21st Century Skill Tutorials • Maps • Graphic Organizers.

■ CONNECT

DIGITAL START UP ACTIVITY
Is It Constitutional or Not?

Project the Start Up Activity Ask students to study the quotation from the 1st Amendment as they enter and get settled.

Analyze Information Students should write their responses below each scenario. *(Students leading a prayer before a game: unconstitutional; display at a county courthouse: constitutional; posting the Ten Commandments: unconstitutional; leading a moment of silence: unconstitutional; studying the Bible in a historical or literary context: constitutional)*

Tell students that in this lesson they will be learning about the reasons why the Founding Fathers protected religious freedom.

Aa Vocabulary Development: Use the Interactive Reading Notepad to preview the Key Terms and Academic Vocabulary in this Lesson with students.

⇅ FLIP IT!
Assign the Flipped Video for this lesson.

■ STUDENT EDITION PRINT
PAGES: 333–339

■ INVESTIGATE

DIGITAL TEXT 1
Religious Liberty

Objectives 1: **Examine the reasons the Founding Fathers protected religious freedom and guaranteed its free exercise;**
2: **Understand the meaning of the phrase "separation of church and state."**

Quick Instruction
Interactive Chart: The Establishment Clause Remind students that the Establishment Clause is a constitutional provision that limits the role of government by guaranteeing religious liberty to individuals. It says that the government may not pass any laws that establish a state or national religion or favor one religion over another. Identify the contributions of the political philosophies of Thomas Jefferson on the development of the U.S. government by pointing out to students that he wrote the Virginia Statute for Religious Freedom on which the 1st Amendment guarantee of religious freedom is based. According to Thomas Jefferson, the Establishment Clause creates a "wall of separation between church and state." Past Supreme Court rulings have helped shape how high that wall stands in regards to certain issues. During past rulings, a high wall has reflected the greatest separation between Church and State, while a low wall has reflected the least separation between Church and State.

In the examples in this interactive, ask students to drag the wall icons that best describe the situation as a high or low "wall of separation." *(School-sponsored prayer: high wall; Chaplains in the military: low wall; Group*

INTERACTIVE CHART
The Establishment Clause

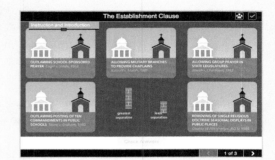

prayer in State legislatures: low wall; Posting of Ten Commandments in public schools: high wall; Single doctrine religious displays in public places: high wall)

▣ ACTIVE CLASSROOM
Ask students to complete a Conversation with Thomas Jefferson activity. Have students imagine they are having a talk with Thomas Jefferson. The students inform President Jefferson that the Federal Government eventually developed a high wall of separation between church and state for some cases and a low wall of separation between church and state for other cases. Then students ask him: Do you think the Federal Government should ever allow a low wall of separation between church and state? Does this sufficiently limit the role of government in religious matters? Why or why not? Students should write how they think President Jefferson would respond.

ELL Use the ELL activity described in the ELL chart.

Further Instruction
Editable Presentation Use the Editable Presentation to present the main ideas for this Core Reading.

Freedom of Religion

DIGITAL TEXT 2

Religion and Education

Religious Liberty: Core Reading and Interactive Reading Notepad Project and discuss the Interactive Reading Notepad questions, including the graphic organizer asking students to record information about Supreme Court cases that protect freedom of religion. Review these cases with the class and fill in the graphic organizer on the whiteboard as you go.

Discuss the fact that the constitutional guarantees of religious freedom were born out of decades of colonial oppression to established churches—to official government-sponsored churches in the colonies. Be sure that students understand the role of limited government in the protection of individual rights, a concept that prompted the addition of the Bill of Rights to the Constitution, including its guarantees of religious freedom.

Compare and Contrast Have students identify the religious freedoms and rights guaranteed by the 1st Amendment. How do you think the statement "Congress shall make no law respecting an establishment of religion, or prohibiting the free exercise thereof . . ." is similar to and different from the phrase "separation of church and state"? *(Possible answer: Both phrases advocate that the government should not be involved in religious matters. The second phrase, however, is more broad than the first. The first one deals specifically with the establishment of religion and free expression of religion. The second phrase states that the government should not be involved in any way with religious matters.)*

Objective 3: **Analyze Supreme Court interpretations of religious rights guaranteed by the Constitution in selected cases relating to education, including *Engel* v. *Vitale*.**

Quick Instruction

Have students form pairs. Remind students that conflicts between religion and government are found in educational settings far more than in any other areas. Ask students: Why do you think this type of conflict is found much more often in educational settings, such as schools, than in other areas? *(Possible answer: Religions deal with education. Because of this, there is an overlap between religions and schools, which often causes conflict.)* Have pairs discuss answers to this question. Tell pairs that they should think of at least two reasons for this situation. Then ask volunteers to share their reasons. Write these answers on the board.

D **Differentiate: Extra Support** In 1962, the Court ruled on *Engel* v. *Vitale*. The constitutionality of what practice by the New York public school was at issue? Use the three standards of the *Lemon* test to analyze the U.S. Supreme Court interpretations of rights guaranteed by the U.S. Constitution in this case. Do you think the New York public schools violated any of these standards? If so, which one(s)? What was the ruling of the Court in *Engel* v. *Vitale*?

ELL Use the ELL activity described in the ELL chart.

Further Instruction

Go through the Interactive Reading Notepad questions and discuss the answers with the class.

Apply Concepts In *Stone* v. *Graham*, the Supreme Court ruled that a Kentucky law was unconstitutional. What standard(s) of the *Lemon* test do you think this law violated? *(Sample answer: This law violated all three standards of the Lemon test. The Kentucky law ordered the posting of the Ten Commandments in all public classrooms. It therefore promoted a religious purpose, advanced a religion, and fostered an "excessive entanglement" of government and religion.)*

DIGITAL TEXT 3

Other Establishment Clause Cases

Other Establishment Clause Cases

Most church-state controversies have involved public education, as noted above. Some Establishment Clause cases have arisen in other policy areas, however.

Seasonal Displays Many public organizations sponsor celebrations of the holiday season with street decorations, programs in public schools, and the like. Can these publicly sponsored observances properly include expressions of religious belief?

In 1984, the Court held that the city of Pawtucket, Rhode Island, could include the Christian nativity scene in its holiday display, which also featured nonreligious objects such as candy canes and Santa's sleigh and reindeer. That ruling, however, left open this question: What about a public display made up *only* of a religious symbol?

>> This Hanukkah display and a Nativity scene adorned city hall in Jersey City, New Jersey. A federal judge ruled that they could stay if nonreligious items like Santa and a snowman were added.

1 of 4 >

Objective 4: Summarize Establishment Clause rulings in other areas, such as seasonal religious displays and public displays of the Ten Commandments.

Quick Instruction

Have students form pairs. Tell students that the Supreme Court has ruled that some State holiday displays that include religious elements are constitutional and others are unconstitutional. Ask students: Why do you think the Supreme Court has banned some holiday displays but has allowed others? *(Possible answer: If a holiday display includes a religious element along with secular elements or elements from many religions, then the display is not promoting a particular religion. The Supreme Court would be more likely to accept such a display, as opposed to a display that promotes only one religion.)* Ask pairs to discuss possible answers to this question. Then ask volunteers to share their answers. Write the responses on the board.

D Differentiate: **Challenge** Ask students to create a model of a holiday display that they think the Supreme Court would find unconstitutional. Then ask them to change this model so that the Court would find it constitutional.

Further Instruction

Go through the Interactive Reading Notepad questions and discuss the answers with the class.

Many American holidays have a religious basis besides Christmas and Easter. Other examples include Halloween, St. Valentine's Day, and St. Patrick's Day. Because of this, State displays that celebrate these holidays often include religious elements. The Supreme Court has found some of these displays to be constitutional and others to be unconstitutional.

Support Point of View with Evidence What religion do you think Supreme Court rulings on religious freedom has impacted the most? Why? *(Possible answer: Supreme Court rulings on religious freedom has impacted the Christian religion the most. The reason is because the majority religion in the United States is Christianity. Because of this, Christian beliefs have influenced many aspects of American culture, including education and holiday celebrations.)*

DIGITAL TEXT 4

The Free Exercise Clause

The Free Exercise Clause

The second part of the constitutional guarantee of religious freedom is set out in the Constitution's Free Exercise Clause, which guarantees to each person the right to believe whatever he or she chooses to believe in matters of religion. No law and no other action by any government can violate that absolute constitutional right. It is protected by both the 1st and the 14th amendments.

No person has an absolute right to act as he or she chooses, however. The Free Exercise Clause does not give anyone the right to violate criminal laws, offend public morals, or threaten community safety simply because it might be done in the name of religion. The Supreme Court laid down the basic shape of the Free Exercise Clause in the first case it heard on the issue, *Reynolds v. United States*, 1879. Reynolds, a Mormon, had two wives. That practice, polygamy, was allowed by his church, but it was prohibited by federal law in any territory of the United States.

>> Demonstrators supported construction of an Islamic cultural center and mosque near Ground Zero in New York after other demonstrators opposed building the Islamic center there.

1 of 5 >

Objective 5: Evaluate Supreme Court decisions that have affected a particular religious group, in particular those related to the Free Exercise Clause.

Quick Instruction

Interactive Chart: Understanding the Free Exercise Clause Remind students that the Free Exercise Clause of the 1st Amendment says the government may not restrict citizens' free exercise of their own religious beliefs. Citizens have an unlimited right to religious *belief*, but their rights to religious *practice* may be limited to be balanced with social values. Based on the information in the cases shown in the interactivity, ask students to decide whether the belief or practice is protected or prohibited by the Free Exercise Clause in the 1st Amendment. Students should click on the gavel to check their answers.

📖 ACTIVE CLASSROOM

Have students complete a Make Headlines activity concerning the Free Exercise Clause. Ask students to write a headline for the Supreme Court ruling on the *Welsh v. United States* case. Ask: If you were to write a headline for this ruling that captured the most important aspect that should be remembered, what would that headline be?

Further Instruction

Editable Presentation Use the Editable Presentation to present the main ideas for this Core Reading.

Freedom of Religion

INTERACTIVE CHART
Understanding the Free Exercise Clause

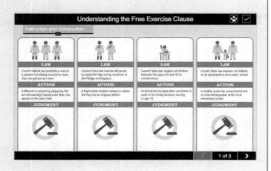

SYNTHESIZE

DIGITAL SYNTHESIZE ACTIVITY
Balancing Rights with the Common Good

DEMONSTRATE

DIGITAL QUIZ
Lesson Quiz and Class Discussion Board

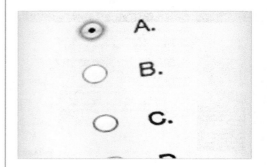

The Free Exercise Clause: Core Reading and Interactive Reading Notepad Project and discuss the Interactive Reading Notepad questions, including the graphic organizer asking students to record information about how the Supreme Court has ruled on cases involving the Free Exercise Clause. Review the information about this clause with the class and fill in the graphic organizer on the whiteboard as you go.

Synthesize The Supreme Court upheld a law that forbid the use of poisonous snakes in religious rites. How does this law relate to the obligation of good citizenship? *(Possible answer: By forbidding this use of poisonous snakes, the law is enforcing the obligation of good citizenship, which requires that personal desires and interests at times be subordinated to the public good. Since poisonous snakes can harm and kill people, it is for the public good to ban their use in religious ceremonies.)*

Summarize Have students evaluate a U.S. government policy or court decision that has affected a particular religious group, in this case, the Amish. Ask: How have the Amish been affected by the Free Exercise Clause and Court decisions? *(Possible answer: The Supreme Court ruled that the Free Exercise Clause prohibits the government from forcing the Amish to send their children to school beyond the 8th grade. The Court stated that this sect's self-sufficient agrarian lifestyle is essential to their religious faith. Requiring Amish children to attend school beyond the 8th grade would threaten this lifestyle.)*

Ask students to recall the Essential Question: "How much power should the government have?" Tell students to think about what they have learned about freedom of religion: the ways in which the Constitution both protects and limits religious freedom and the ways in which the Supreme Court has ruled on issues related to religion.

Then ask students to write a paragraph in response to this question: How has the judiciary balanced individual rights with the common good? *(Paragraphs will vary but should be supported by solid evidence. Possible examples include allowing public holiday displays if they do not promote one religion, allowing student religious groups to meet in public schools but not allowing school prayer in public schools, and allowing free religious expression as long as this expression is not harmful.)* Ask volunteers to read their paragraph with the class.

Critical Thinking Ask students to review the Supreme Court rulings studied in this Topic. Tell them to pick out one ruling that they disagreed with. Ask: Why do you disagree with this ruling? Support your answer with constitutional principles.

Assign the online Lesson Quiz for this lesson if you haven't already done so. Students will be offered automatic remediation or enrichment based on their score.

Remind students that in "Freedom of Religion" they read about the reasons the Founding Fathers protected religious freedom, the meaning of "separation of church and state," and Supreme Court interpretations of religious rights guaranteed by the Constitution. Also, students learned about Establishment Clause and Free Exercise Clause rulings.

Pose these questions to the class on the Discussion Board:

Infer Why do you think the Supreme Court supported the Equal Access Act of 1984?

Infer Why do you think the Supreme Court struck down a State law forbidding the teaching of evolution?

Topic Inquiry
Have students continue their investigations for the Topic Inquiry.

Freedom of Speech and Press

Supporting English Language Learners

Use with Digital Text 1, **The Right of Free Expression.**

Learning Strategies

Read the section *The Right of Free Expression.* Discuss the children's verse mentioned in the first sentence, connecting it to students' prior experiences with this verse or a similar verse or situation. Use this as a foundation to help students understand the importance of the 1st Amendment right of free speech and limitations on that right.

Beginning Read the verse aloud and discuss it with students. Tell them to draw on prior experience to think of a situation to which it might apply. Explain that the right of free expression allows each person to express an opinion, but that right also comes with reasonable restrictions.

Intermediate Read the verse aloud and discuss it with students. Tell them to draw on prior experience to think of a situation to which it might apply. Have students complete the following sentence frame: *Because words can be harmful, the law _____.*

Advanced Read the verse aloud and discuss it with students. Tell them to write about a prior experience to which it might apply and then to write an answer to the following question: What sort of restrictions are placed on the right of free speech?

Advanced High Have students read the verse and discuss it in a small group. Tell them to write about a prior experience to which it might apply and then to write an answer to the following question: How does this verse relate to the 1st Amendment right of free speech?

Use with Digital Texts 2 and 3, **Seditious Speech** and **The 1st Amendment and Symbolic Speech.**

Listening

Read aloud the sections *Sedition Law of 1917* and *Flag Burning.* Guide students to retell or summarize the cases of *Schenck* v. *United States* and *Texas* v. *Johnson* in order to analyze U.S. Supreme Court interpretations of rights guaranteed by the U.S. Constitution.

Beginning Read aloud the section while students listen. Display a list of key words and phrases for each case. Guide students to use these words and phrases as they retell the basic facts of the case. Have students take turns listening and retelling.

Intermediate Read aloud the section while students listen. Provide phrases and short sentences describing each case. Guide students to use the phrases and sentences as they retell the main points of each case. Have students take turns listening and retelling.

Advanced Read aloud the section while students listen and take notes. Have small groups verbally summarize the main points of each case. Have them share their summaries aloud as the others in the group listen.

Advanced High Read aloud the section while students listen and take notes. Have partners summarize the main points of each case in writing. Ask volunteers to read their summaries aloud while the rest of the group listens.

▣ Differentiate Instruction

Use the Differentiated Instruction notes throughout the lesson plan to support the varied skill sets, levels of readiness, and interests in the mixed-ability classroom.

Challenge These notes include suggestions for expanding the activity for advanced students.

On-Level These notes include suggestions for modifying the activity to address different interests or learning styles.

Extra Support These notes include ideas for providing more scaffolding or reading spuport.

Special Needs These notes provide ideas for adapting instruction to support the needs of various special needs students.

■ NOTES

Freedom of Speech and Press

Objectives

Objective 1: Analyze the purpose and importance of the 1st Amendment rights of free speech and press.

Objective 2: Analyze Supreme Court interpretations of rights guaranteed by the Constitution in *Schenck* v. *U.S.*, and other rulings related to seditious and obscene speech.

Objective 3: Define symbolic and commercial speech and describe the limits on their exercise, including Supreme Court interpretations of rights guaranteed by the Constitution in *Texas* v. *Johnson*.

Objective 4: Examine the issues of prior restraint and press confidentiality, and describe the limits the Court has placed on the media.

LESSON 3 ORGANIZER		PACING: APPROX. 1 PERIOD, .5 BLOCKS		
			RESOURCES	
	OBJECTIVES	**PACING**	**Online**	**Print**
Connect				
DIGITAL START UP ACTIVITY **Free Speech for Students**		5 min.	●	
Investigate				
DIGITAL TEXT 1 **The Right of Free Expression**	Objective 1	10 min.	●	●
INTERACTIVE GALLERY **Freedom of Speech in the United States and Around the World**		10 min.	●	
DIGITAL TEXT 2 **Seditious Speech**	Objective 2	10 min.	●	●
DIGITAL TEXT 3 **The 1st Amendment and Symbolic Speech**	Objective 3	10 min.	●	●
DIGITAL TEXT 4 **Prior Restraint on Expression**		10 min.	●	●
DIGITAL TEXT 5 **The Media in a Free Society**	Objectives 2, 3, 4	10 min.	●	●
INTERACTIVE CHART **The Limits of Free Speech and Press**		10 min.	●	
Synthesize				
DIGITAL SYNTHESIZE ACTIVITY **Free Thought**		5 min.	●	
Demonstrate				
DIGITAL QUIZ **Lesson Quiz and Class Discussion Board**		10 min.	●	

PEARSON **realize.**
www.PearsonRealize.com

Go online to access additional resources including:
Primary Sources • Biographies • Supreme Court cases •
21st Century Skill Tutorials • Maps • Graphic Organizers.

■ CONNECT

DIGITAL START UP ACTIVITY

Free Speech for Students

Tell students that although an individual's rights are guaranteed by the Constitution, no one has the right to do anything he or she wants.

Discuss Have students think of one example in which the obligation of citizenship requires that a student's individual rights be subordinated to the common good of other students. *(Possible answer: Students should not be allowed to disrupt the educational process.)*

Tell students that in this lesson they will be learning about the purpose and importance of free speech and press.

Aa **Vocabulary Development:** Use the Interactive Reading Notepad to preview the Key Terms and Academic Vocabulary in this Lesson with students.

⇪ FLIP IT!

Assign the Flipped Video for this lesson.

■ STUDENT EDITION PRINT PAGES: 340–349

■ INVESTIGATE

DIGITAL TEXT 1

The Right of Free Expression

Objective 1: Analyze the purpose and importance of the 1st Amendment rights of free speech and press.

Quick Instruction

The 1st Amendment of the Bill of Rights guarantees the freedom of speech and the press. In the United States, people often take these rights for granted. However, they are strongly limited or completely denied in many other countries. How do constitutional provisions related to individuals' right of freedom of speech limit the role of government?

Interactive Gallery: Freedom of Speech in the United States and Around the World Project the slideshow. Look at each image individually and then compare and contrast images that focus on the same type of speech.

Analyze Images How are the images showing Internet use in the United States and Cuba similar and different? *(Possible answer: Both images focus on Internet use. The image showing Internet use in the United States emphasizes that Americans can use the Internet whenever and wherever they have access. However, the images showing Internet use in Cuba shows that this use is restricted by the government.)*

INTERACTIVE GALLERY

Freedom of Speech in the United States and Around the World

🖳 ACTIVE CLASSROOM

Have students complete a Circle Write activity about free speech and press. Tell students to break into groups of four. Then provide the following prompt: The guarantees of free speech and press in the 1st and 14th Amendments limit the role of government by. . . .

Ask one student in each group to write as much as he or she can for one minute about this topic. Then the first student should switch with the student to his or her right. The next person tries to improve or elaborate the response. Students continue to switch until the paper comes back to the first person. The group then decides which is the best response and shares it with the class.

ELL Use the ELL activity described in the ELL chart.

Freedom of Speech and Press

DIGITAL TEXT 2

Seditious Speech

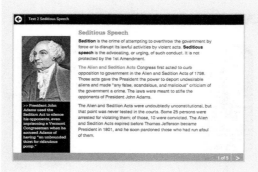

Seditious Speech

Sedition is the crime of attempting to overthrow the government by force or to disrupt its lawful activities by violent acts. **Seditious speech** is the advocating, or urging, of such conduct. It is not protected by the 1st Amendment.

The Alien and Sedition Acts Congress first acted to curb opposition to government in the Alien and Sedition Acts of 1798. Those acts gave the President the power to deport undesirable aliens and made "any false, scandalous, and malicious" criticism of the government a crime. The laws were meant to stifle the opponents of President John Adams.

The Alien and Sedition Acts were undoubtedly unconstitutional, but that point was never tested in the courts. Some 25 persons were arrested for violating them; of those, 10 were convicted. The Alien and Sedition Acts expired before Thomas Jefferson became President in 1801, and he soon pardoned those who had run afoul of them.

>> President John Adams used the Sedition Act to silence his opponents, even imprisoning a Vermont Congressman when he accused Adams of having "an unbounded thirst for ridiculous pomp."

1 of 5 >

Further Instruction

Go through the Interactive Reading Notepad questions and discuss the answers with the class.

Infer Why do you think the law does not protect public officials against libel or slander as much as private persons? *(Possible answer: By accepting the position of a public figure, people allow their actions to be evaluated and criticized by the public. As a result, these people should expect to receive some exaggerated or even false criticism. It "comes with the territory.")*

Support Point of View with Evidence
Analyze the importance of the 1st Amendment rights of free speech and press. Why are these important rights to have? *(Possible answer: Freedom of speech and press allows for a mix of ideas and debate, which can help a country grow. Also, these freedoms can be used to check people in power and to expose corruption.)*

Objective 2: Analyze Supreme Court interpretations of rights guaranteed by the Constitution in *Schenck* v. *United States* and other rulings related to seditious and obscene speech.

Quick Instruction

Tell students that seditious speech is the advocating, or urging, of the overthrow of government by force. Have students form pairs. Then ask: Why do you think seditious speech is not protected by the 1st Amendment? Do you think this lack of protection could ever be misused? *(Possible answer: If seditious speech was protected by the 1st Amendment, then the government could constantly be threatened by a violent takeover. If our government started to use oppressive tactics, such as a dictatorship often does, then not having the right of sedition could potentially make overthrowing the government more difficult.)*

Have students discuss answers with their partner and then write down their response. Ask volunteers to share their responses with the class.

D **Differentiate: Challenge** Have students form groups of five. Assign each group a case from the text on seditious speech. Ask each group to research its case and create a timeline of events in the case.

ELL Use the ELL activity described in the ELL chart.

Further Instruction

Identify the contributions of the political philosophies of Thomas Jefferson on the development of the U.S. government by explaining to students that he showed his view of the Alien and Sedition Acts by pardoning those who had been arrested for violating them. Then go through the Interactive Reading Notepad questions and discuss the answers with the class.

Identify Cause and Effect What do you think caused Congress to pass the Espionage Act of 1917? *(Possible answer: In 1917, the United States was embroiled in World War I. Congress passed this act to prevent any hindrance of the war effort.)*

DIGITAL TEXT 3

The 1st Amendment and Symbolic Speech

DIGITAL TEXT 4

Prior Restraint on Expression

Objective 3: Define symbolic speech and describe the limits on its exercise, including Supreme Court interpretations of rights guaranteed by the Constitution in *Texas* v. *Johnson*.

Quick Instruction

Provide the following example for students. Employees are picketing a corporation for their low wages and lack of benefits. As part of the protest, the picketers burn a straw figure of the corporation's CEO. The corporation sues the protesters, claiming that such symbolic speech is a crime. Ask students: Do you think the Supreme Court would uphold this lawsuit? Why or why not? *(Possible answer: Yes; the burning of the figure could be seen as a threat against an individual, which would make it a crime.)*

Ask for volunteers to share their answers. Write responses on the board and discuss them with the class.

D Differentiate: **Extra Support** Help students understand symbolic speech. Ask: What is a symbol? What is an example of expressing a symbol? What is symbolic speech?

ELL Use the ELL activity described in the ELL chart.

Further Instruction

Editable Presentation Use the Editable Presentation to present the main ideas for this Core Reading.

The 1st Amendment and Symbolic Speech: Core Reading and Interactive Reading Notepad Project and discuss the Interactive Reading Notepad questions, including the graphic organizer asking students to identify at least six rulings and to explain how those rulings affected Americans' rights to use symbolic speech. Review the rulings with the class and fill in the graphic organizer on the whiteboard as you go.

Recall Why did the Supreme Court strike down a State law in *Thornhill* v. *Alabama*? *(The law made picketing a business a crime if it influenced others not to trade or work at the business. The Court stated that picketing, if peaceful, is protected by the 1st and 14th Amendments.)*

Objectives 2: Analyze Supreme Court interpretations of rights guaranteed by the Constitution in *Schenck* v. *United States* and other rulings related to seditious and obscene speech; 3: Define symbolic and commercial speech and describe the limits on their exercise, including Supreme Court interpretations of rights guaranteed by the Constitution in *Texas* v. *Johnson*; 4: Examine the issues of prior restraint and press confidentiality, and describe the limits the Court has placed on the media.

Quick Instruction

Interactive Chart: The Limits of Free Speech and Press Project the graphic organizer on the whiteboard. Remind students that the 1st and 14th Amendments guarantee people the right to have their say and the right to hear what others have to say. While most expressions of free speech are covered in those amendments, there are also limitations.

Tell students to complete the boxes by typing an answer that matches the type of speech to its landmark case and limiting factor. Then students should type their own example of a limiting situation for each type of speech. Ask students: Which types of speech listed in this interactive are sometimes protected by the 1st and 14th Amendments? *(symbolic speech, commercial speech)*

Freedom of Speech and Press

DIGITAL TEXT 5

The Media in a Free Society

INTERACTIVE CHART

The Limits of Free Speech and Press

Have students complete a Sticky Note activity for prior constraint on expression. Ask students to spend one minute jotting down their response to the following question: In what type of circumstances does the Supreme Court often approve prior restraint? After students write down their answers, have them pair up and share their responses with their partner. Then ask pairs to post their sticky notes on the board. Have students look at all the various responses and discuss.

Further Instruction

Go through the Interactive Reading Notepad questions and discuss the answers with the class.

In general, the 1st Amendment grants the media freedom of speech. However, in certain situations, the government has determined that placing limits on freedom of speech for the media is necessary.

Infer Why do you think the Supreme Court ruled that the Constitution does not protect the film industry against prior restraint? *(Possible answer: Motion pictures are often shown to a mass audience. All of these people cannot determine whether a film has content that they find objectionable. As a result, the government has required that films be submitted to official censors.)*

Categorize What type of commercial speech is not protected by the government? Provide an example. *(The government does not protect commercial speech that presents false or misleading information, such as an advertisement for cold cereal that claims it reduces cholesterol when it doesn't.)*

Identify Cause and Effect What caused the Supreme Court to strike down a law that prohibited the sale of violent video games to minors? *(The Court ruled that video games are a form of expression and therefore should be granted freedom of speech. Also, the Court noted that a link has not been established between playing violent video games and violent behavior.)*

SYNTHESIZE

DIGITAL SYNTHESIZE ACTIVITY
Free Thought

Ask students to recall the Topic Essential Question: "How much power should the government have?" Have them use the Think Pair Share strategy to answer the following question: Do you think the U.S. government has too much power in limiting free speech? Why or why not? *(Possible answer: No; the government usually allows ideas that are critical of the government and other institutions. They limit free speech only when government security is at stake or when ideas endanger the public good.)* Ask them to take five minutes to write down a brief answer to the question and then share their answer with a talking partner.

Project the quotation presented in this activity. Ask students to consider this quotation and what they have learned in this lesson.

Discuss Ask students: Do you agree with Justice Holmes? Does the Constitution adequately guard the principle of free thought? Write several sentences to explain your thoughts. *(Possible answer: Student answers will vary as to whether or not they agree with Justice Holmes. The guarantee of free speech and press are intended to protect the expression of unpopular views.)*

DEMONSTRATE

DIGITAL QUIZ
Lesson Quiz and Class Discussion Board

Assign the online Lesson Quiz for this lesson if you haven't already done so. Students will be offered automatic remediation or enrichment based on their score.

Remind students that in "Freedom of Speech and Press" they read about the purpose and importance of free speech and press and analyzed Supreme Court rulings dealing with seditious, obscene, symbolic and commercial speech. In addition, they analyzed issues of prior constraint, press confidentiality, and limits on the media. Finally, they saw further examples of how individuals, political parties, interest groups, or the media challenge laws in court as a way to affect public policy.

Pose these questions to the class on the Discussion Board:

Make Predictions In the future, do you think the Supreme Court will place more or fewer limits on free speech? Support your answer with evidence.

Identify Central Issues What is the role of limited government in the protection of individual rights? Give one example from the lesson to support your answer.

Topic Inquiry
Have students continue their investigations for the Topic Inquiry.

Freedom of Assembly and Petition

Supporting English Language Learners

Use with Digital Text 1, **Constitutional Provisions.**

Learning Strategies

Read the section *Rights of Assembly and Petition*. Discuss the images in the text in order to guide students to analyze the importance of the 1st Amendment rights of petition and assembly. Provide students with opportunities to monitor and self-correct their oral language production during discussion. Whenever possible, provide feedback by modeling correct speech rather than pointing out student errors.

Beginning Using the images, ask students to complete the following sentence frame: *The people in these images are _____.* Model more sophisticated answers and encourage students to repeat after you.

Intermediate Ask students simple questions about the images that require short answers. Help students monitor their oral language with prompts such as *Tell me more* or *Can you say it another way?* Rather than explicitly correcting student errors, model correct grammar and pronunciation and encourage students to repeat after you.

Advanced Have students select several images. Ask them open-ended questions such as *What are the pictures about? What do the pictures tell us about the rights of assembly and petition?* As students make errors, provide opportunities to self-correct by using prompts such as *Can you explain that again?* Use the following or a similar sentence stem to model correct oral language: *Let me make sure I understand. What you are saying is _____.*

Advanced High Have students prepare brief oral presentations based on several images. Encourage students to self-correct their oral language while they practice with a partner. After the presentation, ask students to self-evaluate their presentations.

Use with Digital Text 3, **Assemblies on Public and Private Property.**

Listening

Read aloud the section *Assemblies on Public and Private Property*. Guide students to analyze the importance of the First Amendment right of assembly by asking them questions about the text.

Beginning Read aloud the section as students listen. Then ask them to listen and respond to questions that can be answered with a gesture, yes or no, or a one- or two-word response.

Intermediate Have students listen as you read aloud. Then ask them to listen and respond to questions about the text that can be answered with phrases or short sentences.

Advanced Before reading aloud, tell students you will be asking them questions about the text. Guide them to listen carefully and take notes as you read. Then ask them to listen and respond to questions with the 5Ws: *Who? What? Where? When? Why?*

Advanced High Have students listen and take notes as you read aloud. Ask students open-ended questions such as *Tell me an important fact about the right of assembly.* Guide students to use academic vocabulary in their responses.

▣ Differentiate Instruction

Use the Differentiated Instruction notes throughout the lesson plan to support the varied skill sets, levels of readiness, and interests in the mixed-ability classroom.

Challenge These notes include suggestions for expanding the activity for advanced students.

On-Level These notes include suggestions for modifying the activity to address different interests or learning styles.

Extra Support These notes include ideas for providing more scaffolding or reading spuport.

Special Needs These notes provide ideas for adapting instruction to support the needs of various special needs students.

▮ NOTES

PEARSON
realize™
www.PearsonRealize.com

Go online to access additional resources including:
Primary Sources • Biographies • Supreme Court cases •
21st Century Skill Tutorials • Maps • Graphic Organizers.

Objectives

Objective 1: Analyze the importance of the 1st Amendment rights of petition and assembly.

Objective 2: Analyze Supreme Court interpretations of rights guaranteed by the Constitution, including limits on the time, place, and manner of assembly.

Objective 3: Compare and contrast the freedom-of-assembly issues that arise on public versus private property.

Objective 4: Explore how the Supreme Court has interpreted freedom of association.

LESSON 4 ORGANIZER		PACING: APPROX. 1 PERIOD, .5 BLOCKS		RESOURCES	
	OBJECTIVES	PACING	Online	Print
Connect					
DIGITAL START UP ACTIVITY **The Occupy Movement**		5 min.	●	
Investigate					
DIGITAL TEXT 1 **Constitutional Provisions**	Objective 1	10 min.	●	●
INTERACTIVE TIMELINE **Protests That Made a Difference**		10 min.	●	
DIGITAL TEXT 2 **Time, Place, and Manner Rules**	Objectives 1, 2	10 min.	●	●
INTERACTIVE GALLERY **Freedom of Assembly in *Edwards v. South Carolina*, 1963**		10 min.	●	
DIGITAL TEXT 3 **Assemblies on Public and Private Property**	Objective 3	10 min.	●	●
DIGITAL TEXT 4 **Freedom of Association**	Objective 4	10 min.	●	●
Synthesize					
DIGITAL SYNTHESIZE ACTIVITY **How Important is Freedom of Assembly and Petition?**		5 min.	●	
Demonstrate					
DIGITAL QUIZ **Lesson Quiz and Class Discussion Board**		10 min.	●	

Freedom of Assembly and Petition

■ CONNECT

DIGITAL START UP ACTIVITY
The Occupy Movement

Tell students that the 1st Amendment protects the people's right to assemble and protest peaceably.

Discuss Ask: Under what circumstances do you think government should be able to regulate demonstrations? *(Possible answers: advance notice and permits can be required for demonstrations; demonstrations near schools prohibited if they are disruptive)*

Tell students that in this lesson they will be learning about the rights of petition and assembly and will compare and contrast freedom-of-assembly issues that arise on public versus private property.

Aa Vocabulary Development: Use the Interactive Reading Notepad to preview the Key Terms and Academic Vocabulary in this Lesson with students.

⮉ FLIP IT!

Assign the Flipped Video for this lesson.

■ STUDENT EDITION PRINT
PAGES: 350–354

■ INVESTIGATE

DIGITAL TEXT 1
Constitutional Provisions

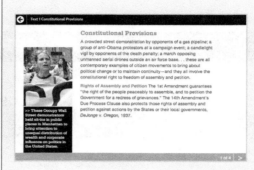

Objective 1: Analyze the importance of the 1st Amendment rights of petition and assembly.

Quick Instruction
Interactive Gallery: Protests That Made a Difference Project the interactive gallery. Introduce the activity by telling students that the 1st Amendment guarantees "the right of the people peaceably to assemble, and to petition the Government for a redress of grievances." Throughout our nation's history, people have used the freedom of assembly to express their views, bring attention to issues, or influence public policy.

Tell students to move the slider to explore four examples of people exercising their right to assemble and the outcome from each situation. Ask students: Why is the right to assemble important in a free society? *(The right to assemble is essential in a free society because it allows people to gather together to express their views and pressure the government to make changes.)*

INTERACTIVE TIMELINE
Protests That Made a Difference

👥 ACTIVE CLASSROOM
Have students complete a Take a Stand activity about civil disobedience. Ask students to take a stand on the following question: Do you think the 1st and 14th Amendments should include a right of civil disobedience? Tell students to divide into two groups based on their answer and move to separate areas of the classroom. If one group has a small number of students, assign more students to this group. Ask students in each group to talk with each other to compare reasons for answering yes or no. Have a representative from each side present and defend the group's point of view.

ELL Use the ELL activity described in the ELL chart.

Further Instruction
Go through the Interactive Reading Notepad questions and discuss the answers with the class.

Remind students that the 1st and 14th Amendments protect the rights of assembly and petition against actions by States or local governments, except under certain conditions. Both of these rights are important because they allow citizens to express their views and bring about political change.

DIGITAL TEXT 2

Time, Place, and Manner Rules

INTERACTIVE GALLERY

Freedom of Assembly in *Edwards v. South Carolina*, 1963

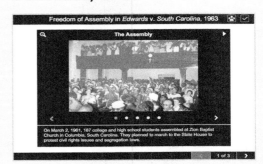

Paraphrase Define the right to assemble and the right to petition in your own words without using a dictionary or text. *(Possible answer: right to assemble: the right to come together as a group to influence policies made by the government and other public organizations; right to petition: the right to use written materials, such as petitions and letters, to bring views to the attention of public officials)*

Evaluate Information How do the 1st Amendment rights of assembly and petition limit the role of government? Does the protection of individual rights require that the role of government be limited? *(Possible answer: The rights of assembly and petition limit the role of government by prohibiting it from interfering with peaceful assemblies or with people's right to bring their views to the attention of public officials. The United States was founded on the belief that government should be limited in order to protect the rights of its citizens.)*

Summarize According to the information in the interactivity, what impact have political changes brought about by individuals, political parties, interest groups, or the media had? *(Possible answer: The political changes brought about by individuals, political parties, interest groups, or the media have impacted the nation in many ways. Some have led to a newly independent country, while others have led to expanded rights for large groups of people.)*

Objectives 1: **Analyze the importance of the 1st Amendment rights of petition and assembly; 2:** **Analyze Supreme Court interpretations of rights guaranteed by the Constitution, including limits on the time, place, and manner of assembly.**

Quick Instruction

Interactive Gallery: Free Assembly in *Edwards v. South Carolina,* 1963 Project the slideshow. Look at each image individually and then the collection of images as a whole. Tell students that this interactive takes an in-depth look at a landmark Supreme Court case, *Edwards* v. *South Carolina* (1963).

Analyze Images How are images two and three similar and different? What caused the difference? *(Possible answer: Both images show a group protesting. Image two shows a peaceful protest group. Image three shows a violent scene, in which protestors are being arrested. The difference is caused by the police, who decided to arrest the protestors.)*

📹 ACTIVE CLASSROOM

Ask students to complete a Quick Write activity, in which they write in 30 seconds all they know about "free speech zone."

🅳 **Differentiate: Challenge** Ask students to write a police report that describes how a protest group violated the limits of place and time placed on them by the government. The report should also include how the police responded to these violations.

Further Instruction

Editable Presentation Use the Editable Presentation to present the main ideas for this Core Reading.

Time, Place, and Manner Rules: Core Reading and Interactive Reading Notepad Project and discuss the Interactive Reading Notepad questions, including the graphic organizer asking students to review the issue and ruling for various cases. Review the cases with the class and fill in the graphic organizer on the whiteboard as you go.

Be sure that students understand that the government can make and enforce reasonable rules covering the time, place, and manner of assemblies. Point out that the reason underlying these rules is that the obligation of citizenship at times requires that personal desires and interests be subordinated to the public good. For example, a group might be denied the right to hold a protest on a busy street during rush hour, because such a desire would subvert the public good. At the same time, however, the government's rules must be precisely drawn and fairly administered.

Freedom of Assembly and Petition

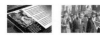

DIGITAL TEXT 3

Assemblies on Public and Private Property

Text 3 Assemblies on Public and Private Property

Assemblies on Public and Private Property

Over the past several years, most of the Court's freedom of assembly cases have involved organized demonstrations. Demonstrations are, of course, assemblies. Most demonstrations take place in public places—on streets and sidewalks, in parks or public buildings, and so on. This is the case because it is the *public* the demonstrators want to reach.

Demonstrations almost always involve some degree of conflict. Most often, they are held to protest something, and so there is an inherent clash of ideas. Many times there is also a conflict with the normal use of streets or other public facilities. It is hardly surprising, then, that the tension can sometimes rise to a serious level.

Given all this, the Supreme Court has often upheld laws that require advance notice and permits for demonstrations in public places. In an early leading case, *Cox v. New Hampshire*, 1941, it unanimously approved a State law that required a license to hold a parade or procession on a public street.

>> The Supreme Court has outlined different rules for demonstrations, depending in part on whether they take place on public or private property.

1 of 6 | >

Apply Concepts What are some examples of instances in which protesters have had to subordinate their desires to obey time, place, and manner rules? *(Possible answer: An angry protester might want to protest close to the offending organization's building, which is outside of the "free speech zone." Also, a protester might want to physically stop people from going to work at a particular business, which violates the manner rule. A protester might want to demonstrate during rush hour, which would disrupt traffic and violate the time rule. In all of these examples, protesters need to subordinate their desires to obey time, place, or manner rules.)*

Objective 3: Compare and contrast the freedom-of-assembly issues that arise on public versus private property.

Quick Instruction

Tell students that the workers at a retail store are very upset at the store's management because of low pay. As a result, the workers plan to picket the store. The store is located in the downtown area, but is also close to a residential area. Ask students to imagine they are the mayor of this town. Ask students: What guidelines would you require the picketers to follow? How would you prepare for the picket? Ask students to think about the location of the picket for their guidelines. *(Possible answer: The picketers would need to stay on public property, specifically a sidewalk area near the store. However, the strikers should not block access to the stores. Because of this, the picketing area would not be directly in front of the store's entrance. Also, the strikers should not wander onto private property in the nearby residential area. I would require advanced notice to prepare for the picket. Also, I would notify the police department to make sure they provide enough officers to patrol the area.)*

Have students write down their guidelines, and ask volunteers to share them with the class.

ELL Use the ELL activity described in the ELL chart.

Further Instruction

Go through the Interactive Reading Notepad questions and discuss the answers with the class.

Identify Cause and Effect What caused the State of Colorado to pass a law that limits "sidewalk counseling" by creating a buffer zone? *(The State of Colorado wanted to prevent demonstrators from coming in contact or interfering with people entering or exiting abortion clinics.)*

DIGITAL TEXT 4

Freedom of Association

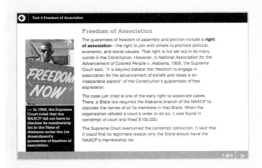

>> In 1958, the Supreme Court ruled that the NAACP did not have to disclose its membership list to the State of Alabama under the 1st Amendment's guarantee of freedom of association.

Objective 4: Explore how the Supreme Court has interpreted freedom of association.

Quick Instruction

Tell students that the U.S. government guarantees the right of association, which includes the right to join with others to promote political, economic, and social causes. Even so, some States have violated this right. Have students form pairs and answer the following question: Why do you think some States would not uphold the right of association? *(Possible answer: States might want to prevent a group from forming that would criticize or protest certain State laws.)* Student pairs should write down their answers. Then ask volunteers to share their answer with the class.

D Differentiate: **Extra Support** Help students understand the Court ruling for *Christian Legal Society* v. *Martinez*. Ask students: Was the Christian Legal Society an independent organization? Was this society supported by the University of California Hastings Law School? What do you think this support involved? Do you think this society should be allowed to require a "Statement of Faith" as a condition of membership even if the university is against such a condition? Why or why not?

Further Instruction

Go through the Interactive Reading Notepad questions and discuss the answers with the class.

Analyze Information Why do you think it is important for the freedom of assembly and petition to include the right of association? *(Possible answer: If people did not have the right of association, they could be prevented from assembling into groups to protest and petition issues.)*

Freedom of Assembly and Petition

▮ SYNTHESIZE

▮ DEMONSTRATE

DIGITAL SYNTHESIZE ACTIVITY
How Important is Freedom of Assembly and Petition?

DIGITAL QUIZ
Lesson Quiz and Class Discussion Board

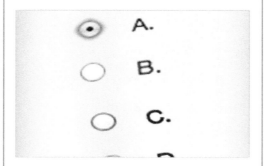

Project the two survey questions for this activity and ask students to create two separate pie graphs that show the text in a graphic format. Have students use their pie graphs to answer the following questions.

According to the survey results, on what freedom do Americans place the most importance? *(freedom of speech)* Why do you think that is the case? *(Possible answer: Many Americans believe that freedom of speech is paramount to being a democracy and that without it the United States would not be the democratic country that it is today, therefore, freedom of speech is considered the most important freedom to Americans.)*

Based on the results from both surveys, how important are the rights of assembly and petition to most Americans? *(Possible answer: Considering that in the first survey the rights to assembly and petition are not mentioned and in the second survey they have very low percentages, it suggests that Americans do not consider these rights to be very important.)* What reasons can you give for this attitude? *(Possible answer: Americans might not know that these rights are guaranteed by the Constitution.)*

How would life in the United States change if the rights of assembly and petition were no longer protected? *(Possible answer: Americans would lose their ability to make their concerns known to the government and the nation as a whole and the government would have more power to restrict the ideas and actions of Americans.)*

Assign the online Lesson Quiz for this lesson if you haven't already done so. Students will be offered automatic remediation or enrichment based on their scores.

Remind students that in *Freedom of Assembly and Petition* they read about the importance of the rights of petition and assembly and the limits of time, place, and manner of assembly. Also, they compared and contrasted the freedom-of-assembly issues that arise on public versus private property and explored how the Supreme Court has interpreted freedom of association.

Pose these questions to the class on the Discussion Board:

Summarize How does the Constitution allow the government to limit the right of assembly and petition?

Apply Concepts In the case of *Gregory* v. *Chicago*, who violated individual rights? What rights were violated? How were these rights violated?

Topic Inquiry
Have students continue their investigations for the Topic Inquiry.

PEARSON realize

www.PearsonRealize.com
Access your Digital Lesson

Due Process of Law

Supporting English Language Learners

Use with Digital Text 1, **Understanding Due Process.**

Listening
Guide students to create a graphic organizer summarizing the importance of due process rights to the protection of individual rights and in limiting the powers of government. Write *Due Process* in the middle of a web graphic organizer. Have students fill in the graphic organizer with important details about due process as they listen to you read aloud the section *Understanding Due Process*.

Beginning Pause to complete the graphic organizer as you read each section aloud. Have students copy the graphic organizer and read it aloud while a partner listens.

Intermediate Have students listen and create a list of important details as you read aloud. Have students use the list to complete the graphic organizer.

Advanced Have students listen and take notes on the graphic organizer as you read aloud. Have partners compare their notes and discuss the important details of what was read aloud.

Advanced High Have students use the graphic organizer as a note-taking tool as you read aloud. Ask students to share at least one important detail from the reading as the rest of the group listens.

Use with Digital Text 2, **Individual Rights and the Public Good.**

Writing
Read the sections *The Police Power and Civil Liberties* and *Protecting the Public*. Discuss the reading in order to help students evaluate whether and/or when the obligation of citizenship requires that personal desires and interests be subordinated to the public good. Use sentences 1–4 from the section *Protecting the Public* as a reference. Guide students to write using connecting words such as: *and, but, so, since, or*.

Beginning Display sentences 1–4. Model how to rewrite the sentences using the connecting words. Have students copy the sentences and read them to a classmate. Example: *States want to promote health, so they limit the sale of alcoholic beverages*.

Intermediate Provide cloze sentences for students to complete such as: *States can provide help to the medically needy in order to _____.* Provide a list of connecting words and phrases as a reference.

Advanced Guide partners to use information from sentences 1–4 to write their own sentences. Provide a list of connecting words and phrases for them to use.

Advanced High Have students use information from sentences 1–4 to write their own sentences using connecting words and phrases.

▣ Differentiate Instruction

Use the Differentiated Instruction notes throughout the lesson plan to support the varied skill sets, levels of readiness, and interests in the mixed-ability classroom.

Challenge These notes include suggestions for expanding the activity for advanced students.

On-Level These notes include suggestions for modifying the activity to address different interests or learning styles.

Extra Support These notes include ideas for providing more scaffolding or reading spuport.

Special Needs These notes provide ideas for adapting instruction to support the needs of various special needs students.

■ NOTES

Due Process of Law

Objectives

Objective 1: Explain the importance of due process rights to the protection of individual rights and in limiting the powers of government.

Objective 2: Define the police power and understand its relationship to the subordination of personal desires and interests to the public good.

LESSON 5 ORGANIZER		PACING: APPROX. 1 PERIOD, .5 BLOCKS			
				RESOURCES	
		OBJECTIVES	PACING	Online	Print
Connect					
	DIGITAL START UP ACTIVITY **What Is Due Process?**		5 min.	●	
Investigate					
	DIGITAL TEXT 1 **Understanding Due Process**	Objective 1	10 min.	●	●
	INTERACTIVE CHART **Procedural and Substantive Due Process**		10 min.	●	
	DIGITAL TEXT 2 **Individual Rights and the Public Good**	Objective 2	10 min.	●	●
	INTERACTIVE GALLERY **Protecting the Public through the Police Power**		10 min.	●	
Synthesize					
	DIGITAL SYNTHESIZE ACTIVITY **The Public Good and Due Process**		5 min.	●	
Demonstrate					
	DIGITAL QUIZ **Lesson Quiz and Class Discussion Board**		10 min.	●	

PEARSON
realize™
www.PearsonRealize.com

Go online to access additional resources including:
Primary Sources • Biographies • Supreme Court cases •
21st Century Skill Tutorials • Maps • Graphic Organizers.

■ CONNECT

DIGITAL START UP ACTIVITY
What Is Due Process?

Project the Start Up Activity Ask students to answer the questions as they enter and get settled. Then have them share their ideas with another student, either in class or through a chat or blog space.

Discuss What do you think due process is? *(rules that govern how suspects are treated during and after their arrests)*

Tell students that in this lesson they will be learning how the Constitution protects a person's right to due process.

Aa Vocabulary Development: Use the Interactive Reading Notepad to preview the Key Terms and Academic Vocabulary in this Lesson with students.

⚑ FLIP IT!

Assign the Flipped Video for this lesson.

■ STUDENT EDITION PRINT PAGES: 355–359

■ INVESTIGATE

DIGITAL TEXT 1
Understanding Due Process

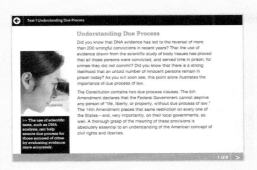

INTERACTIVE CHART
Procedural and Substantive Due Process

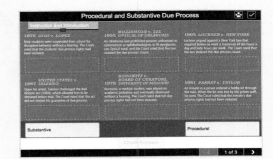

Objective 1: Explain the importance of due process rights to the protection of individual rights and in limiting the powers of government.

Quick Instruction

The Constitution has two due process clauses that limit the role of government. The 5th Amendment declares that the Federal Government cannot deprive any person of "life, liberty, or property, without due process of law." The 14th Amendment places that same restriction on every one of the States—and, very importantly, on their local governments, as well.

Interactive Chart: Procedural and Substantive Due Process Project and read through the introduction with students. Step through each Court case and then have students complete the activity. Have students work in pairs to discuss each case. You may wish to have students use the following questions in their discussions: Why did the Court rule the way that it did? Do you agree with the Court's ruling? Why or why not? Have students make generalizations about why the Court does not rule in favor of all due process cases.

▣ ACTIVE CLASSROOM

Have students choose one of the Court cases from the interactivity and complete a Make Headlines activity. Ask students to write a headline that captures the importance of due process rights to the protection of individual rights in the Court case. Then have them pass their headlines to a partner for them to review.

D Differentiate: Extra Support Ask: What is procedural due process? *(laws will be enforced in a fair and equal manner)* What is substantive due process? *(laws will be fair)* You may wish to have students write down the definitions in their own words and have them available as students complete the activity.

ELL Use the ELL activity described in the ELL chart.

Further Instruction

Go through the Interactive Reading Notepad questions and discuss the answers with the class. Students should understand that due process is a component of the concept of the rule of law, which holds that government is never above the law. In the words of patriot Thomas Paine, "In America THE LAW IS KING." Limited government is important in the protection of individual rights, because it prevents government from becoming too powerful.

Due Process of Law

Individual Rights and the Public Good

Protecting the Public through the Police Power

Due Process and Limited Government
Students should know that the Supreme Court has extended the protections of the Bill of Rights against the States through the 14th Amendment's Due Process Clause. Provisions of the Bill of Rights incorporated into the 14th Amendment's Due Process Clause include the 1st, 2nd, 4th, 6th, 8th, and portions of the 5th amendments.

Compare Define procedural and substantive due process. What is the difference between the two? *(Possible answer: Procedural due process guarantees that laws will be enforced in a fair and equal manner. Substantive due process guarantees that laws will be fair. One involves how laws are enforced and the other involves the laws themselves.)*

Draw Conclusions What is the role of due process in limiting the power of the government? *(Possible answer: Due process is a check on the power of the government, balancing the rights of citizens with the role of government in protecting its citizens.)*

Objective 2: Define police power and understand its relationship to the subordination of personal desires and interests to the public good.

Quick Instruction
Police power is the authority of each State to act to protect and promote the public health, safety, morals, and general welfare. Courts have often found that the right of a society to protect itself trumps the individual rights of citizens.

Interactive Gallery: Protecting the Public through the Police Power Project and step through the images with students. Discuss each caption and guide students to think about how each scenario might raise conflicts with civil liberty protections while also protecting the public.

▶ ACTIVE CLASSROOM
In groups, have students think and write about the following question from the interactive using a Circle Write strategy: What does it mean that State Governments must balance the use of police power and the needs of society with the individual freedoms of citizens? Have each group present their thinking to the whole class.

D **Differentiate: Challenge** Have students choose one of the elements of State power that trumps individual rights. Then have them research how that power has changed. For example, seat belt or car seat requirements have changed over time. Have students create a blog post explaining how the reach of State power has changed and share their opinion of whether the state has overreached or not.

ELL Use the ELL activity described in the ELL chart.

Further Instruction
Go through the Interactive Reading Notepad questions and discuss the answers with the class.

Eminent Domain Part of the state's power is the ability to take property from private citizens for public use. Citizens must be fairly compensated for their property. The Supreme Court recently ruled that "public use" can be expanded to mean "a public goal" in *Kelo* v. *City of New London*, 2005.

Make Judgments Many states are making laws against texting and driving. Do you think the state has an appropriate interest in restricting this behavior? Why or why not? *(Possible answer: Yes, because accidents have been linked to texting and driving. Protecting citizens is an important role of the government.)*

SYNTHESIZE

DIGITAL SYNTHESIZE ACTIVITY

The Public Good and Due Process

Have students use the Think Pair Share strategy to answer the questions in the activity. Ask them to take five minutes to write down some brief answers to the questions below, then share their answers with a talking partner. Have partners think about the following question: How do the 5th and 14th Amendments work together to guarantee due process rights in the United States? Have pairs share their answers with the class.

Discuss You learned that the Supreme Court takes a case-by-case approach to defining due process. After all you've learned about the protections that due process provides citizens and the overarching State interest in protecting citizens, do you think this case-by-case approach is justified? Why or why not?

DEMONSTRATE

DIGITAL QUIZ

Lesson Quiz and Class Discussion Board

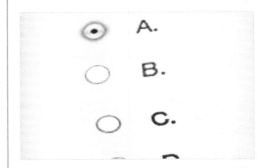

Assign the online Lesson Quiz for this lesson if you haven't already done so. Students will be offered automatic remediation or enrichment based on their scores.

In *Due Process of Law* you read about the Constitution's due process protections and the balance between the interests of the State in protecting its citizens with the individual rights of those citizens.

Pose these questions to the class on the Discussion Board:

Summarize Give examples that show how the due process provisions limit the power of the government and protect the rights of citizens.

Apply Concepts How does police power balance personal desire and the interests of the public?

Topic Inquiry
Have students continue their investigations for the Topic Inquiry.

Evaluate When do you think the obligation of citizenship requires that personal desires and interests be subordinated to the public good? Give an example. *(Possible answer: When citizens can't protect themselves, the State should step in. For example, providing a security net such as food stamps and social security to protect and provide for people who can't do it themselves.)*

Freedom and Security of the Person

Supporting English Language Learners

Use with Digital Text 2, **Right to Keep and Bear Arms.**

Listening

Guide students to identify the freedoms and rights guaranteed by the 2nd Amendment by listening as you read aloud the section *Right to Keep and Bear Arms*. Create a list of important details and discuss the context of the section in order to enhance understanding.

Beginning Preview the section with the students using visuals as support. Display a list of important details and discuss these with the students. Have students listen for these details as you read aloud.

Intermediate Display a list of important details and discuss these with the students. Read aloud while students listen and follow along in the text. Ask small groups to discuss the important details.

Advanced Read aloud while students listen and follow along in the text. Have partners create a list of important details. Have them compare and discuss their lists with another set of partners.

Advanced High Read aloud while students listen and take notes. Ask students to create a list of important details. Have students read and discuss their lists with the group.

Use with Digital Text 1, **Slavery and Involuntary Servitude.**

Writing

Read *The 13th Amendment: Section 2*. Guide students to evaluate a U.S. government policy or court decision that has affected a particular racial, ethnic, or religious group such as the Civil Rights Act of 1964 by writing a brief narrative about one of the cases described in this section.

Beginning Read and discuss the section. Provide visuals as support. Use a narrative graphic organizer to guide the class to write about one of the cases.

Intermediate Use a *Somebody Wanted But So* graphic organizer to guide small groups to write a narrative about one of the cases.

Advanced After reading and discussing the section, have partners write a narrative about one of the cases.

Advanced High Have students write a narrative about one of the cases. Have students read their narratives to each other.

▷ Differentiate Instruction

Use the Differentiated Instruction notes throughout the lesson plan to support the varied skill sets, levels of readiness, and interests in the mixed-ability classroom.

Challenge These notes include suggestions for expanding the activity for advanced students.

On-Level These notes include suggestions for modifying the activity to address different interests or learning styles.

Extra Support These notes include ideas for providing more scaffolding or reading spuport.

Special Needs These notes provide ideas for adapting instruction to support the needs of various special needs students.

■ NOTES

PEARSON
realize™
www.PearsonRealize.com

Go online to access additional resources including:
Primary Sources • Biographies • Supreme Court cases •
21st Century Skill Tutorials • Maps • Graphic Organizers.

Objectives

Objective 1: Evaluate how Supreme Court decisions regarding slavery and involuntary servitude have affected a particular racial group.

Objective 2: Analyze the importance of the 2nd Amendment's protection of the right to keep and bear arms.

Objective 3: Evaluate constitutional provisions for limiting the role of government, including those designed to guarantee the security of home and person.

Objective 4: Understand the Supreme Court's ongoing refinement of the exclusionary rule, including its ruling in *Mapp* v. *Ohio*.

Objective 5: Describe the right to privacy and its origins in constitutional law, and Supreme Court interpretations of rights guaranteed by the Constitution in selected cases, including *Roe* v. *Wade*.

LESSON 6 ORGANIZER		PACING: APPROX. 1 PERIOD, .5 BLOCKS			
		OBJECTIVES	PACING	RESOURCES	
				Online	Print
Connect					
DIGITAL START UP ACTIVITY **Drug Testing in Schools–Yes or No?**			5 min.	●	
Investigate					
DIGITAL TEXT 1 **Slavery and Involuntary Servitude**		Objective 1	10 min.	●	●
DIGITAL TEXT 2 **Right to Keep and Bear Arms**			10 min.	●	●
DIGITAL TEXT 3 **Security of Home and Person**		Objectives 2, 3	10 min.	●	●
INTERACTIVE GALLERY **Personal Privacy–Communication and the 4th Amendment**			10 min.	●	
DIGITAL TEXT 4 **The Exclusionary Rule**			10 min.	●	●
INTERACTIVE CHART **Exceptions to the Exclusionary Rule**		Objective 4	10 min.	●	
DIGITAL TEXT 5 **The Right of Privacy**		Objective 5	10 min.	●	●
Synthesize					
DIGITAL SYNTHESIZE ACTIVITY **Analyze a Political Cartoon**			5 min.	●	
Demonstrate					
DIGITAL QUIZ **Lesson Quiz and Discussion Board**			10 min.	●	

Freedom and Security of the Person

CONNECT

DIGITAL START UP ACTIVITY

Drug Testing in Schools–Yes or No?

Project the Start Up Activity Ask students to think about the quotes as they enter and get settled. Then have them jot down and share their opinions with another student, either in class or through a chat or blog space.

Discuss What do these quotes say about drug testing in schools? Do you think drug testing should be allowed in school? Why or why not? *(Possible answer: Drug testing should be allowed in schools because it promotes a healthy environment.)*

Tell students that in this lesson they will be learning about the 2nd, 3rd, and 4th Amendments which provide for of personal freedom and security.

Aa Vocabulary Development: Use the Interactive Reading Notepad to preview the Key Terms and Academic Vocabulary in this Lesson with students.

⇡ FLIP IT!

Assign the Flipped Video for this lesson.

STUDENT EDITION PRINT PAGES: 360–371

INVESTIGATE

DIGITAL TEXT 1

Slavery and Involuntary Servitude

Objective 1: Evaluate how Supreme Court decisions regarding slavery and involuntary servitude have affected a particular racial group.

Quick Instruction

The 13th Amendment declares that "Neither slavery nor involuntary servitude, . . . shall exist within the United States, or any place subject to their jurisdiction." It further gives Congress the expressed power "to enforce this article by appropriate legislation." It took a century before Congress and the courts began to enforce the article with court cases and Civil Rights Acts, especially the Civil Rights Act of 1964.

ELL Use the ELL activity described in the ELL chart.

Further Instruction

Editable Presentation Use the Editable Presentation to present the main ideas for this Core Reading.

Slavery and Involuntary Servitude: Core Reading and Interactive Reading Notepad Project and discuss the Interactive Reading Notepad questions. Several court cases affirmed the reach of the 13th Amendment. For example, *Runyon* v. *McCrary*, 1976, declared that because admissions contracts are public, denying one to a group of people based on race is illegal. Additionally, all classes of people are protected from discrimination solely because of their ancestry or ethnic characteristics.

Evaluate How effective was the 13th Amendment immediately after its passage? What Supreme Court decision changed that situation? *(Possible answer: The 13th Amendment outlawed slavery, but it did not end racial discrimination in the United States. It was generally thought that the 13th Amendment did not give Congress the power to act against discrimination. The case of Jones v. Mayer, 1968, changed that attitude. There, the Court held that the 13th Amendment gave Congress the power to abolish "the badges and incidents of slavery.")*

Analyze Give an example of something that the courts or Congress might declare a badge or incident of slavery. *(Possible answer: discrimination at a store or refusing service to someone because of his or her family name)*

DIGITAL TEXT 2

Right to Keep and Bear Arms

DIGITAL TEXT 3

Security of Home and Person

INTERACTIVE GALLERY

Personal Privacy–Communication and the 4th Amendment

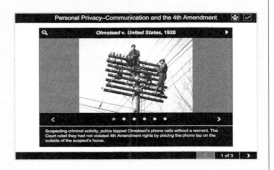

Objectives 2: Analyze the importance of the 2nd Amendment's protection of the right to keep and bear arms; **3:** Evaluate constitutional provisions for limiting the role of government, including those designed to guarantee the security of home and person.

Quick Instruction

The 2nd Amendment protects the rights of people to keep and bear arms. Recent court cases have interpreted the protection to include not only a State's right to form a militia, but also an individual's right to bear arms for self-defense.

The 3rd and 4th Amendments say that government cannot violate the home or person of anyone in this country without just cause. Probable cause is the reasonable suspicion of a crime. The 4th Amendment has governed how police arrest people, search vehicles, and gain evidence for conviction.

Interactive Gallery: Personal Privacy–Communication and the 4th Amendment Project the slideshow. Look at each image individually and then the collection of images as a whole. Tell students that this interactive takes an in-depth look at several examples of government intrusions into public privacy.

📖 ACTIVE CLASSROOM

Using a Cartoon It strategy, have students create a quick copy of one compelling image from this lesson on a piece of paper. Turn it into a political cartoon that illustrates a key concept or main idea. Share ideas and have students discuss their cartoons.

D Differentiate: **Challenge** Have students research one of the court cases presented in the interactive gallery. What implications did that particular case have on other privacy or 4th Amendment law? Students can present their findings in a blogpost.

ELL Use the ELL activity described in the ELL chart.

Further Instruction

Editable Presentation Use the Editable Presentation to present the main ideas for this Core Reading.

Right to Keep and Bear Arms: Core Reading and Interactive Reading Notepad Project and discuss the Interactive Reading Notepad questions. Students should know that the 2nd Amendment is now folded into the 14th Amendment's due process clause.

Security of Home and Person: Core Reading and Interactive Reading Notepad Project and discuss the Interactive Reading Notepad questions. Students should understand that the 2nd, 3rd, and 4th Amendments represent constitutional provisions limiting the role of government and protecting for individual rights.

Analyze Why is the 2nd Amendment's protection to keep and bear arms important? *(Possible answer: It prevents the government from taking personal arms, something the British often did to the colonists before and during the Revolution.)*

Cause and Effect What events in colonial days helped ensure that the authors of the Bill of Rights would include the 2nd, 3rd, and 4th Amendments? *(The British often violated colonists' rights in these ways before and during the Revolution.)*

Draw Conclusions Why is limiting the role of the Federal Government important when guaranteeing the security of person and home? *(Possible answer: The rights of the individual should not be sacrificed for the rights of the government. Clear restrictions on the government allow for more personal security.)*

Freedom and Security of the Person

DIGITAL TEXT 4

The Exclusionary Rule

INTERACTIVE CHART

Exceptions to the Exclusionary Rule

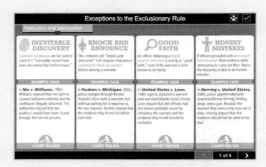

Objective 4: Understand the Supreme Court's ongoing refinement of the exclusionary rule, including its ruling in *Mapp* v. *Ohio*.

Quick Instruction

The exclusionary rule says that evidence gained as the result of an illegal act by police cannot be used at the trial of the person from whom it was seized. The rule represents a protection of individual rights. This rule has been refined by the Supreme Court, which weighs whether or not the government has a legitimate interest in allowing the search to go forth. The exclusionary rule thereby protects individual rights by limiting the role of government in the gathering of evidence in criminal cases.

Interactive Chart: Exceptions to the Exclusionary Rule Project the interactive, and step through each of the Court cases with students. Tell students that they focus on ways in which the scope of the exclusionary rule has been narrowed by the Supreme Court in recent years.

🖳 ACTIVE CLASSROOM

Use a Write 1 Get 3 strategy to answer the following question: What are the limits to the 4th Amendment as defined by the exclusionary rule? Students should use the information in the interactive as they work. Then discuss their findings. If time, put the decisions in chronological order and generalize about why the exclusionary rule has been narrowed.

D Differentiate: Extra Support Pair students with a more knowledgeable student and have the student needing extra support interview the other. Students should use the cases presented in their interviews. They do not need to acquire more information, just use the information provided.

Further Instruction

Editable Presentation Use the Editable Presentation to present the main ideas for this Core Reading.

The Exclusionary Rule: Core Reading and Interactive Reading Notepad Project and discuss the Interactive Reading Notepad questions. Present *Mapp* v. *Ohio* and walk through the decision, analyzing with students how the Supreme Court interpreted the rights guaranteed by the Constitution in this case (the Court interpreted the 4th Amendment's prohibition against unreasonable searches and seizures to mean that police officers must have a warrant to search a home). Discuss how *Mapp* expanded the rule set forth in *Weeks* v. *United States*. Then discuss how the courts have limited the rule in further decisions, such as the USA Patriot Act.

Privacy Rights Today Soon after September 11, President George W. Bush directed the National Security Agency (NSA), acting in secret and without court-approved warrants, to monitor the international telephone calls and e-mails of Americans with suspected ties to terrorists. The public did not become aware of that monitoring program until late 2005, and its disclosure brought a storm of protest. Many insisted that this NSA activity was illegal. Despite this, the Bush administration defended it as an appropriate exercise of the President's power as commander in chief and the practice was continued under the Obama administration. Balancing national security and American freedom remains a challenging task today and continues to be debated.

Make Judgments Does it make sense for individual rights to be subordinated to the public good in the case of national security? Explain your answer. *(Possible answer: No, because we are strongest as a country when we focus on our democratic principles as laid out in the Constitution.)*

DIGITAL TEXT 5

The Right of Privacy

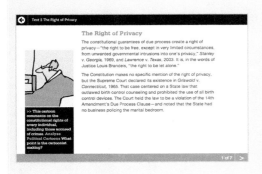

Text 5 The Right of Privacy

The Right of Privacy

The constitutional guarantees of due process create a right of privacy—"the right to be free, except in very limited circumstances, from unwanted governmental intrusions into one's privacy," *Stanley v. Georgia*, 1969, and *Lawrence v. Texas*, 2003. It is, in the words of Justice Louis Brandeis, "the right to be let alone."

The Constitution makes no specific mention of the right of privacy, but the Supreme Court declared its existence in *Griswold v. Connecticut*, 1965. That case centered on a State law that outlawed birth control counseling and prohibited the use of all birth control devices. The Court held the law to be a violation of the 14th Amendment's Due Process Clause—and noted that the State had no business policing the marital bedroom.

>> This cartoon comments on the constitutional rights of every individual, including those accused of crimes. Analyze Political Cartoons What point is the cartoonist making?

1 of 7 >

Objective 5: Describe the right of privacy and its origins in constitutional law, and Supreme Court interpretations of rights guaranteed by the Constitution in selected cases, including *Roe* v. *Wade*.

Quick Instruction

A right to privacy is not written into the Constitution. Instead the Supreme Court has ruled that the guarantees of due process create a right of privacy. There is, in the words of Justice Louis Brandeis, "the right to be left alone."

Further Instruction

Editable Presentation Use the Editable Presentation to present the main ideas for this Core Reading.

The Right of Privacy: Core Reading and Interactive Reading Notepad Project and discuss the Interactive Reading Notepad questions.

Roe v. *Wade* The balance between the government's interest in protecting its citizens and an individual's right to privacy has been challenged by the issue of whether or not a woman has a right to an abortion. Students should understand that several different, more recent, court cases have determined that the government has a broader interest than originally outlined in that case. Read through the annotated court case with students to see how the Court applied the constitutional guarantees of a right of privacy contained in the 5th Amendment's Due Process Clause to the facts of this case.

Make Inferences The right to privacy is not in the Constitution. Why do you think the Founders left it out? *(Possible answer: They thought that life, liberty, and the pursuit of happiness as enabled by the limited government set out in the Bill of Rights would be enough. They did not anticipate a unique right to privacy.)*

Freedom and Security of the Person

SYNTHESIZE

DIGITAL SYNTHESIZE ACTIVITY
Analyze a Political Cartoon

Have students use the Think Pair Share strategy to complete the activity. Ask them to take five minutes to write down some brief answers to the questions below, then share their answers with a talking partner.

Have partners think about the following questions. Which amendment is involved in the events described in the cartoon? What is the basic rule laid down by that amendment? Have pairs share their answers with the class.

Discuss Ask students to discuss the balance between personal liberty and government responsibility. How does the Constitution balance these two? What has the court response been? *(Possible answer: The Constitution lays out specific prohibitions for the government and rights for citizens that the government can't infringe. The courts have worked to define how far the government can infringe.)*

DEMONSTRATE

DIGITAL QUIZ
Lesson Quiz and Discussion Board

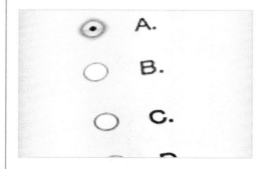

Assign the online Lesson Quiz for this lesson if you haven't already done so. Students will be offered automatic remediation or enrichment based on their scores.

In *Freedom and Security of the Person* you read about the 2nd, 3rd, and 4th Amendments. Taken together, these amendments guarantee the right to bear arms and bar the government from conducting unreasonable searches and seizures. The courts have limited and expanded the government's role related to all of these amendments. They have also created a right not in the Constitution called the right to privacy.

Pose these questions to the class on the Discussion Board:

Evaluate How has the Supreme Court treated the government's interest in searches over time? *(It has been expanded as the exclusionary rule has been curtailed. Government is seen to have a much more pertinent interest due to the fear of terrorism.)*

Evaluate Analyze the importance of the 2nd Amendment right to keep and bear arms. *(Possible answer: The 2nd Amendment is important because it guarantees the right of each State to keep a militia, which is a critical protection against encroachments by the Federal Government. It is also important for citizens to keep and bear arms for self-defense.)* How has the Court treated citizens' 2nd Amendment rights over time? (It has been expanded after a period of curtailing. There is now a right to bear arms that applies to the person, not just the state's interest in gaining a militia.)

Compare How did *Mapp* v. *Ohio* and *Roe* v. *Wade* expand or clarify the rights of citizens? What is one constitutional difference between the two cases? *(Possible answer: They both expanded rights to the States and interpreted the 4th and 5th amendments to include rights not specifically stated in the Constitution. The exclusionary rule was explicitly noted to apply to the States as well as the Federal Government. The right to privacy was created in Griswald v. Connecticut and expanded in Roe v Wade, but is not found in the Constitution.)*

Topic Inquiry
Have students continue their investigations for the Topic Inquiry.

Rights of the Accused

Supporting English Language Learners

Use with Digital Text 3, **Going to Trial.**

Listening

Help students identify the freedoms and rights guaranteed by the 6th Amendment by reading aloud the sections *Speedy Trial* and *Public Trial*. Discuss the implicit ideas suggested by this sentence: A trial must not be *too* speedy or *too* public, however. Have students answer the question: What might make a trial *too* speedy or *too* public?

Beginning Read aloud the sections as students listen. Help the class create a list of characteristics that would make a trial too speedy or too public. Have them copy the list.

Intermediate Have students listen and follow along in the text as you read aloud. Ask small groups to answer the question. Have them give the reasons for their answers.

Advanced Allow partners to refer to the text as they list answers to the question. Ask them to listen while another set of partners shares their answers. Pairs should then trade roles.

Advanced High Have students jot down their answers to the question after you read aloud. Have students share their answers during a group discussion, during which they should listen carefully to the answers formulated by others in the group.

Use with Digital Text 4, **Guarantee Against Self-Incrimination.**

Writing

Guide students to analyze U.S. Supreme Court interpretations of rights guaranteed by the U.S. Constitution by reading the section *Miranda* v. *Arizona*. Have them write answers to the 5 Ws (Who? What? Where? When? Why?).

Beginning After reading the section, provide a list of key words or phrases. Guide the class to use this list to write answers to the 5 Ws.

Intermediate Provide a list of key words or phrases as a resource. Guide small groups to write short sentences as answers to the 5 Ws.

Advanced Have partners use complete sentences to answer the 5 Ws. Remind them to give as many details as possible.

Advanced High Guide students to answer the 5 Ws in paragraph form. Remind them to use as many descriptive words and details as possible.

▣ Differentiate Instruction

Use the Differentiated Instruction notes throughout the lesson plan to support the varied skill sets, levels of readiness, and interests in the mixed-ability classroom.

Challenge These notes include suggestions for expanding the activity for advanced students.

On-Level These notes include suggestions for modifying the activity to address different interests or learning styles.

Extra Support These notes include ideas for providing more scaffolding or reading spuport.

Special Needs These notes provide ideas for adapting instruction to support the needs of various special needs students.

▮ NOTES

Rights of the Accused

Objectives

Objective 1: Understand the role of limited government in the protection of individual rights, including protections relating to the writ of habeas corpus, bills of attainder, and ex post facto laws.

Objective 2: Outline how the right to a grand jury and the guarantee against double jeopardy help safeguard the rights of the accused.

Objective 3: Describe issues that arise from guarantees of speedy and public trials.

Objective 4: Identify the freedoms and rights guaranteed by the Bill of Rights, including the right to a fair trial by jury.

Objective 5: Examine Supreme Court interpretations in selected cases of the right to an adequate defense, the guarantee against self-incrimination, and other rights.

LESSON 7 ORGANIZER		PACING: APPROX. 1 PERIOD, .5 BLOCKS		
			RESOURCES	
	OBJECTIVES	PACING	Online	Print
Connect				
DIGITAL START UP ACTIVITY **Miranda Rights**		5 min.	●	
Investigate				
DIGITAL TEXT 1 **Article I Protections**	Objectives 1, 2	10 min.	●	●
INTERACTIVE CHART **Protection of Individual Rights–Limits on Government**		10 min.	●	
DIGITAL TEXT 2 **Grand Jury and Double Jeopardy**		10 min.	●	●
DIGITAL TEXT 3 **Going to Trial**	Objectives 3, 4, 5	10 min.	●	●
INTERACTIVE CHART **The Steps of Justice**		10 min.	●	
DIGITAL TEXT 4 **Guarantee Against Self-Incrimination**	Objective 5	10 min.	●	●
DIGITAL TEXT 5 **Bail and Preventive Detention**	Objective 5	10 min.	●	●
DIGITAL TEXTS 6 AND 7 **Cruel and Unusual Punishments, Capital Punishment and Treason**		10 min.	●	●
Synthesize				
DIGITAL SYNTHESIZE ACTIVITY **The Right to Trial By Jury**		5 min.	●	
Demonstrate				
DIGITAL QUIZ **Lesson Quiz and Discussion Board**		10 min.	●	

PEARSON
realize™
www.PearsonRealize.com

Go online to access additional resources including:
Primary Sources • Biographies • Supreme Court cases •
21st Century Skill Tutorials • Maps • Graphic Organizers.

CONNECT

DIGITAL START UP ACTIVITY

Miranda Rights

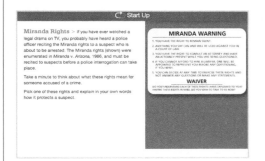

Project the Start Up Activity Ask students to think about the elements of the Miranda rights as they enter and get settled.

Discuss How do these rights protect a suspect? *(Sample answers: 1. right to remain silent—talking to police might lead to self-incrimination 2. Anything you say can and will be used against you—the police can use any statement as evidence in a trial.)*

Tell students that in this lesson they will be learning about the 5th, 6th, and 7th Amendments, which provide protections for those accused of a crime.

Aa Vocabulary Development: Use the Interactive Reading Notepad to preview the Key Terms and Academic Vocabulary in this Lesson with students.

⇅ FLIP IT!

Assign the Flipped Video for this lesson.

■ STUDENT EDITION PRINT PAGES: 372–384

INVESTIGATE

DIGITAL TEXT 1

Article I Protections

Objectives 1: Understand the role of limited government in the protection of individual rights, including protections relating to the writ of habeas corpus, bills of attainder, and ex post facto laws; 2: Outline how the right to a grand jury and the guarantee against double jeopardy help safeguard the rights of the accused.

Quick Instruction

Article I of the Constitution establishes several limits on the Federal Government, including several protections of individual rights. These include the command that an officer holding a prisoner must show cause why the prisoner should not be released (writ of habeus corpus); the prohibition against legislative acts that provide for the punishment of a person without a trial (no bills of attainder); and the prohibition against laws that apply to actions taken before the law was written (no ex post facto laws). These limits on government play an important part in preventing the abuse of power.

The 5th Amendment guarantees the right to a grand jury indictment before trial. This limits the government's power by requiring them to convince a group of citizens that there is reasonable evidence that might result in a conviction before arresting a suspect for a capital crime. The 5th Amendment also protects the accused from being tried twice for the same crime, or double jeopardy.

INTERACTIVE CHART

Protection of Individual Rights–Limits on Government

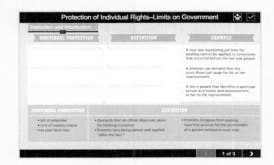

Interactive Chart: Protection of Individual Rights–Limits on Government Project the graphic organizer on the whiteboard. Introduce the activity by telling students that the Constitution limits some powers of Government that pertain to individual rights under the writ of habeus corpus, bills of attainder, and ex post facto laws. Explain to students that they will match the examples to the appropriate definitions and individual protections listed on the graphic organizer.

📷 ACTIVE CLASSROOM

Using a Sticky Note strategy, have students use the information and questions from the activity to generalize about the Framers' intent to limit the government with regard to trials. Generalize about why the Framers chose only those few rights to ennumerate. Share generalizations with the class.

D Differentiate: Extra Support Step through the questions with students. For each question, generate discussion by asking what the Constitution says about the issue. Then have students continue with the activity.

Rights of the Accused

DIGITAL TEXT 2
Grand Jury and Double Jeopardy

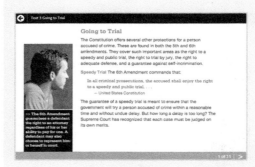

DIGITAL TEXT 3
Going to Trial

INTERACTIVE CHART
The Steps of Justice

Further Instruction

Editable Presentation Use the Editable Presentation to present the main ideas for this Core Reading.

Article I Protections: Core Reading and Interactive Reading Notepad Project and discuss the Interactive Reading Notepad questions. Students should understand that these protections are not amendments, but rather were written as part of the restrictions placed on Congress in the Constitution.

Grand Jury and Double Jeopardy: Core Reading and Interactive Reading Notepad Project and discuss the Interactive Reading Notepad questions. Students should understand that these protections are part of the amendments and were written to ennumerate individual rights and freedoms.

Draw Conclusions Why is the right against double jeopardy an important individual protection? *(It prevents the state from targeting one person, repeatedly arresting him or her until that person is finally found guilty of a crime.)*

Identify Central Issues What significant role did Abraham Lincoln play in shaping the government's approach to the writ of habeas corpus? *(Abraham Lincoln suspended the writ during the Civil War, but the Supreme Court found his action unconstitutional. Congress then passed the Habeas Corpus Act of 1863, giving the President the right to suspend the writ when he judged it necessary.)*

Objectives 3: **Describe issues that arise from guarantees of speedy and public trials; 4: Identify the freedoms and rights guaranteed by the Bill of Rights, including the right to a fair trial by jury; 5: Examine Supreme Court interpretations in selected cases of the right to an adequate defense and the guarantee against self-incrimination, including** *Gideon* v. *Wainwright* **and** *Miranda* v. *Arizona*.

Quick Instruction

The 6th Amendment guarantees the right to a speedy and public trial with an impartial jury. Additionally, it says that a defendant has the right (1) "to be informed of the nature and cause of the accusation," (2) "to be confronted with the witnesses against him" and question them in open court, (3) "to have compulsory process for obtaining witnesses in his favor" (that is, favorable witnesses can be subpoenaed), and (4) "to have the Assistance of Counsel for his defense."

Interactive Gallery: The Steps of Justice Project and step through the interactive with students. Read the introduction and explain that students will drag each constitutional guarantee to the stage in the judicial process to which it applies.

📷 ACTIVE CLASSROOM

Using a Ranking strategy, have students order the steps of a trial in order from most important to protecting the rights of the accused, to most important to limiting the role of the government. Some steps might do both. Discuss rankings as a class.

D Differentiate: Challenge Have students choose one of the steps and research which Court case cements or clarifies the right. Then have them create a short message, 40 characters or less, explaining what the case says. It could be similar to what a court reporter might report on the steps of the Supreme Court.

ELL Use the ELL activity described in the ELL chart.

Further Instruction

Editable Presentation Use the Editable Presentation to present the main ideas for this Core Reading.

Going to Trial: Core Reading and Interactive Reading Notepad Project and discuss the Interactive Reading Notepad questions.

Gideon v. Wainwright Project and discuss the court case *Gideon* v. *Wainwright*. This case protected the right of the accused to be represented at trial by an attorney and established that to not be so represented would violate the accused's due process rights under the 14th Amendment. The Court said that the community must furnish

DIGITAL TEXT 4

Guarantee Against Self-Incrimination

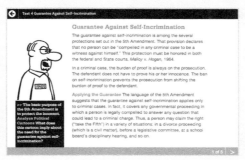

a representative if the accused cannot afford one. Ask: On what constitutional right did the Court base its opinion? *(the 6th Amendment right to counsel)*

Hernandez v. Texas Project and discuss the court case *Hernandez v. Texas*. This case tested the definition of "fair cross section" when it considered whether Pete Hernandez, a Mexican, had received a fair trial in a murder case when no one on the jury was Mexican American or had an Hispanic surname. The court ruled in Hernandez' favor, stating that the exclusion of Hispanics from jury service had denied him equal protection under the law. Ask: How might this ruling have affected Hispanics in the United States? *(Possible answer: It gave Hispanics more equal protection under the law and may have also led to an overall decrease in discrimination towards Hispanics in the United States.)*

Evaluate How do the protections of the 6th Amendment work together to guarantee a fair trial? *(Possible answer: The amendment lists elements that apply to all defendants, such as the right to an attorney, the right to confront the accuser, and the right to a hearing before one's peers.)*

Analyze Why is a speedy and public trial a limit on the government? *(Possible answer: Defendents can't languish in prison. They must be brought to trial. Nothing can happen behind closed doors. The government must declare why they arrested someone and prove it before a court of peers.)*

Objective 5: **Examine Supreme Court interpretations in selected cases of the right to an adequate defense and the guarantee against self-incrimination, including *Gideon* v. *Wainwright* and *Miranda* v. *Arizona*.**

Quick Instruction

The 5th Amendment guarantees the right against self-incrimination in any governmental proceeding in which a person is legally compelled to answer any question that could lead to a criminal charge, including trials and hearings.

ELL Use the ELL activity described in the ELL chart.

Further Instruction

Editable Presentation Use the Editable Presentation to present the main ideas for this Core Reading.

Guarantee Against Self-Recrimination: Core Reading and Interactive Reading Notepad Project and discuss the Interactive Reading Notepad questions.

Miranda v. Arizona Project and discuss the court case *Miranda v. Arizona*. Students should understand why the court struck down Miranda's conviction and the result of the findings in that case. They should also understand that today's listing of Miranda rights comes directly from this case, as well as the requirement that arresting officers must advise suspects of their rights before questioning. The Supreme Court is still refining the rule, but generally it has been upheld.

Draw Conclusions How do the Miranda rights protect suspects against self-incrimination? How do the rights support the protections in the 5th and 6th Amendments? *(They specify that suspects have the right to remain silent. They list the rights a suspect has that come from the amendments, including right to an attorney.)*

Make Judgments Miranda is somewhat controversial. Some people believe that it sends criminals back to the streets. Do you agree or disagree? *(Possible answer: I disagree because police still have the right to question and arrest suspects, they just have to do it carefully and within the law.)*

Rights of the Accused

DIGITAL TEXT 5

Bail and Preventive Detention

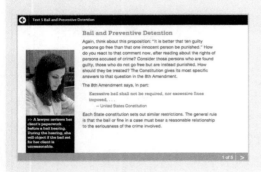

DIGITAL TEXT 6

Cruel and Unusual Punishments

DIGITAL TEXT 7

Capital Punishment and Treason

Objective 5: Examine Supreme Court interpretations in selected cases of the right to an adequate defense, the guarantee against self-incrimination, and other rights.

Quick Instruction

The 8th Amendment provides several protections for defendants. Bail cannot be excessive and must match the crime the defendant stands accused of. Cruel and unusual punishments are outlawed.

Further Instruction

Editable Presentation Use the Editable Presentation to present the main ideas for this Core Reading.

Bail and Preventive Detention: Core Reading and Interactive Reading Notepad Project and discuss the Interactive Reading Notepad questions. Preventive detention has been held by the Supreme Court to be in the state's interest and not as technically a punishment nor a violation of an accused's presumption of innocence.

Cruel and Unusual Punishment: Core Reading and Interactive Reading Notepad Project and discuss the Interactive Reading Notepad questions. The Supreme Court has found that most punishments imposed by the States and federal government are not cruel or unusual.

Capital Punishment: Core Reading and Interactive Reading Notepad Project and discuss the Interactive Reading Notepad questions. Capital punishment has not been found by the Supreme Court to be cruel or unusual punishment. However, the Court determined that judges or juries could not have wide discretion to impose the penalty, nor could it be applied capriciously. The Court is still refining its stance on the death penalty, though most cases focus on the application rather than the imposition of the penalty.

Analyze Treason is the only crime defined in the Constitution. Why might the Framers have chosen to only explain this one crime? *(Possible answer: Treason has often been used by tyrants to seize power. Defining treason and how one can be accused is a limit on the Federal Government's power.)*

▇ SYNTHESIZE

DIGITAL SYNTHESIZE ACTIVITY

The Right to Trial By Jury

Have students use the Think Pair Share strategy to complete the activity. Ask them to take five minutes to write down their answers, then share their answers with a talking partner.

Discuss Ask students to reflect on the statement and answer the following questions. Why does each person accused of a federal crime have the right to an attorney? What might happen if they did not have this right? *(Possible answer: The right to a jury trial comes from the 6th Amendment. This right protects a suspect from the decision of only one person—the judge. A jury represents the community as part of the judgment of a person's innocence or guilt. Without a jury trial, a judge would have too much power.)*

▇ DEMONSTRATE

DIGITAL QUIZ

Lesson Quiz and Discussion Board

Assign the online Lesson Quiz for this lesson if you haven't already done so. Students will be offered automatic remediation or enrichment based on their score.

In "Rights of the Accused" you read about the protections provided in the 5th, 6th, and 8th Amendments. You learned about the various court cases that have expanded and clarified those rights, providing protections for suspects and defendants at trial.

Pose these questions to the class on the Discussion Board:

Make Judgments "It is better that ten guilty persons go free than that one innocent person be punished." How do the protections found in the 5th, 6th, and 8th amendments support this idea? *(Possible answer: Defendants are given lawyers, thought to be innocent until proven guilty, given a jury of their peers, all in an effort to ensure that only the guilty go to prison.)*

Analyze How do the protections of the accused rely on a limited role of government? *(Possible answer: The protections purposely limit the role of the government to ensure that suspects and defendants remain innocent until proven guilty. They work to ensure that the deck is not stacked in the government's favor.)*

Topic Inquiry
Have students continue their investigations for the Topic Inquiry.

Protecting Civil Liberties

▮ SYNTHESIZE

DIGITAL ACTIVITY
Reflect on the Essential Question and Topic

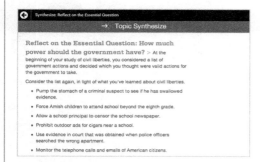

Remind students that at the beginning of their study of civil liberties, they considered a list of government actions and decided which they thought were valid actions for the government to take. Ask students to consider the list again, in light of what they've learned about civil liberties.

As students complete their study of civil liberties in the United States, ask them to take a few minutes to reflect on what they have learned. Have them write down three important questions they thought about as they read the lessons and their answers to those questions.

Here are some examples to get students thinking:

- What amendments reflect the experiences of the colonists under English rule? *(Sample answer: Amendments 1, 2, 3, and 4 were certainly written with thoughts of British acts such as the Stamp Act, the Quartering Act and the Intolerable Acts.)*

- What would life be like without the Bill of Rights? *(Sample answer: Citizens might be subject to actions by the government without cause and might not be able to speak freely, petition the government, or question actions of the government.)*

Topic Inquiry
Have students complete Step 3 of the Topic Inquiry.

▮ DEMONSTRATE

DIGITAL TOPIC REVIEW AND ASSESSMENT
Protecting Civil Liberties

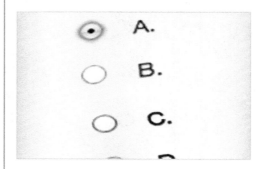

Students can prepare for the Topic Test by answering the questions in the Topic Review and Assessment online or the Assessment questions in the Print Student text. They can also prepare by reviewing their answers to the Interactive Reading Notepad questions or reviewing their notes in the Reading and Notetaking Study Guide.

TOPIC TEST
Assign the Topic Test to assess students' understanding of topic content.

DIGITAL TOPIC TEST
Protecting Civil Liberties

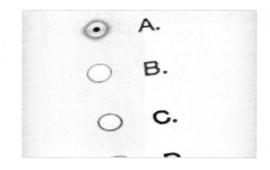

BENCHMARK TESTS
Assign these benchmark tests as you complete the relevant topics to monitor student progress toward mastering the course content and as preparation for the End-of-Course Test.

Benchmark Test 1: Topics 1–4

Benchmark Test 2: Topics 5–8

Benchmark Test 3: Topics 9–11

Benchmark Test 4: Topics 12–14

Topic 9

Citizenship and Civil Rights

TOPIC 9 ORGANIZER	PACING: APPROX. 1 PERIOD, .5 BLOCKS	
		PACING
Connect		1 period
MY STORY VIDEO Minniejean Brown-Trickey, A Sojourn to the Past		10 min.
DIGITAL ESSENTIAL QUESTION ACTIVITY What Are the Challenges of Diversity?		10 min.
DIGITAL OVERVIEW ACTIVITY Citizenship and Civil Rights		10 min.
TOPIC INQUIRY: CIVIC ACTION PROJECT Constitutional Rights Foundation		20 min.
Investigate		2–4 periods
TOPIC INQUIRY: CIVIC ACTION PROJECT Constitutional Rights Foundation		Ongoing
LESSON 1 American Citizenship		30–40 min.
LESSON 2 Diversity and Discrimination		30–40 min.
LESSON 3 Equality Before the Law		30–40 min.
LESSON 4 Federal Civil Rights Laws		30–40 min.
Synthesize		1 period
DIGITAL ACTIVITY History and Diversity		10 min.
TOPIC INQUIRY: CIVIC ACTION PROJECT Constitutional Rights Foundation		20 min.
Demonstrate		1–2 periods
DIGITAL TOPIC REVIEW AND ASSESSMENT Citizenship and Civil Rights		10 min.
TOPIC INQUIRY: CIVIC ACTION PROJECT Constitutional Rights Foundation		20 min.

 TOPIC INQUIRY:

Civic Action Project

For this topic's Inquiry, you may choose to do a Civic Action Project with your students by using the materials found at the Constitutional Rights Foundation's CAP website: http://www.crfcap.org. Civic Action Project (CAP) is a project-based learning model for government and economics courses. It offers a practicum for high school students in effective and engaged citizenship and uses blended learning to engage students in civic activities both in the traditional U.S. government and economics classrooms.

Constitutional
Rights
Foundation
Educate. Participate.

THE TEACHER'S ROLE

THE CAP TEACHER coaches and guides students through the civic action process as they select a problem or issue, research it, determine and take civic actions, and report and document the experience. The teacher motivates, challenges, critiques, and assesses student progress. Through a blended learning approach, teachers can let students take the reins of their civic learning, guiding them along the way.

You can create your CAP classroom in three easy steps

STEP 1
Register yourself for the CAP website

STEP 2
Enroll your students

STEP 3
Engage your students in the CAP process and its many resources

Constitutional Rights Foundation

Pearson Magruder's American Government Students
Welcome to the Civic Action Project site

All of the information you're learning in your Government course will help you understand important Government policy issues that will be discussed and debated at the local, state, and national level throughout your lifetime.

Participating in a Civic Action Project (CAP) of your choosing will show you how you can use that knowledge as an engaged citizen in a democracy.

This CAP website will show you how to plan and carry out your project and give you lots of help along the way. Good luck!

Click on the logo to get started on your CAP!

THE STUDENT'S ROLE

CAP ALLOWS STUDENTS to create projects on issues they care about for their school or community. They see the connection between their civic actions and public policy and can share ideas for civics projects with each other and other CAP students nationwide. Students also see how the content of government and economics courses can apply to the real world. By taking civic actions, they practice what real citizens do when they go about trying to solve real policy-related problems. CAP fulfills best-practices in service-learning with an emphasis on public policy.

The CAP student is accountable for completing the civic action process, just as with a science project or term paper. The CAP Planner, a set of documents that guide students through the process, provides teachers with assessment information as well as a way to manage multiple student projects. While the teacher introduces and monitors the CAP, it is important that students take the lead in completing their civic actions. By using web-based technology and civics-based instruction and activities, students exercise important 21st century skills in digital literacy, critical thinking, collaboration, self-direction, and learning to be engaged and effective citizens.

CIVIC ACTIONS CAP challenges students to work on an actual problem, issue, or policy by taking civic actions. Civic actions build upon classroom civics issues, service-learning, and other proven practices of effective civic education. These actions can be many and varied, including:

- getting informed about a public issue or problem
- thinking critically about the issue or problem
- discovering how government is involved with the problem
- learning how government makes decisions
- developing a position
- engaging in civic dialogue
- building constituencies
- working together toward a common goal
- doing civic writing
- making presentations
- advocating for and defending positions
- meeting with officials

Brainstorming

Brainstorming is a method for generating ideas. It can be done by individuals or in small or large

Rules for Brainst

Pose a question to a

Set a time limit on th more ideas out.

Work as fast as you

Handout Lesson 5B
Civic Action Project

GRADE
CAP Policy Analysis Tool

As citizens in a democracy, you'll be confronted with policy questions. Is a tax proposal a good idea? Should you vote for a particular ballot initiative? Government policies can profoundly affect our nation and your life. In a democracy, you have a say on government policies and proposed policies. It's important that you take a critical look at them. Use the following GRADE tests to evaluate a policy:

GOAL. What is the goal of the policy? If you don't know what it's supposed to do, you can't measure its success or failure. Policies are designed to address problems. What problem or problems is this policy supposed to address?

...policy? Who might (or does) ...you understand who the ...icy favors special ...ces for information, but

...its? What is good about the ...es or effects of the ...ved) its goal? Will it ...nsive? Does it protect ...e's liberties?

...osts? What is bad about the ...the causes or effects of the ...e? Does it cause harm? Does ...re any potential

...e disadvantages. Are there ...to do nothing. Most serious ...Evaluate them. Look at ...es.

© 2012 Constitutional Rights Foundation

Conducting Meetings

Your meetings should be organized, to-the-point, and fun.

Decide how you're going to make decisions. If you are a small group, try deciding by whole-group consensus or by a two-thirds vote. A simple-majority decision may lead to bad feelings and resentment.

Understand everyone's role at the meeting. At most meetings, people need to fill the following roles, which may change from meeting to meeting:

- Leader or facilitator runs the meeting, follows the agenda item by item, and watches the time allotted for each. The leader helps participants focus on the task and makes sure everyone has a chance to participate.
- Recorder takes minutes, which include date and time of meeting, the persons attending, and notes on each agenda item.
- Treasurer.
- Group members contribute agenda items, discuss topics, make decisions, and take responsibility for various tasks.
- Adviser is an adult whose role is to give advice—not to run the group.
- Guests may participate in group discussions, but usually do not participate in final decision making.

Have an agenda. This is a list of things to be dealt with at a meeting. All members should be encouraged to put topics on the agenda. After the recorder reads the minutes of the previous meeting and they are approved, the members approve the agenda. Agenda items are considered in the following order:

- Old business—ongoing and follow-up items.

© 2012. Constitutional Rights Foundation and Close Up Foundation

Constitutional Rights Foundation
Educate. Participate.

Guardian of Democracy: The Civic Mission of Schools
Released September, 2011, *Guardian of Democracy: The Civic Mission of Schools report* builds on the findings of the seminal 2003 Civic Mission of Schools report. CAP has been designed to support the promising approaches described in these reports.

INTRODUCTION

Citizenship and Civil Rights

The Constitution guarantees certain unalienable rights for every U.S. citizen, including freedom of religion, freedom of speech and the press, freedom of assembly and petition, due process of law, freedom and security of the person, and rights of the accused. However, saying that U.S. citizens have these rights and implementing them are two different matters. Throughout American history, groups of people have been denied many or all rights. To make sure all American citizens have these rights, civil rights laws have been established.

◼ CONNECT

MY STORY VIDEO

Minniejean Brown-Trickey, A Sojourn to the Past

Watch a video about the lessons Minniejean Brown-Trickey teaches to students today about a historical event in which she participated.

Check Understanding What was Minniejean Brown-Trickey's brush with history? *(She was one of the "Little Rock Nine," the nine black students who desegregated Little Rock's schools in 1957.)*

Identify Patterns What was the importance of Brown-Trickey's actions in 1957? *(She and her fellow students provided inspiration for many of the participants in the civil rights movement in the decade that followed. She continues to teach lessons about the civil rights movement today.)*

⇅ FLIP IT!

Assign the My Story Video.

DIGITAL ESSENTIAL QUESTION ACTIVITY

What Are the Challenges of Diversity?

Ask students to think about the Essential Question for this Topic: What Are the Challenges of Diversity? Think about the political changes brought about by individuals, past and present. What were the challenges they faced?

As students prepare to analyze historical and contemporary examples of citizen movements in America, ask them to think about the different civil rights these movements stood for. Have students make a list of rights that they believe belong to every citizen of the United States.

Ⓓ Differentiate: Challenge Have students draw a poster, in which they express in visual form the rights they believe every citizen of the United States should have.

Support a Point of View with Evidence Why do you think these rights belong to every citizen?

Infer Why do you think J. Elizabeth Jones believed it was necessary to emphasize that all human beings are entitled to the rights that belong to humanity? *(Answers will vary)*

Identify Central Issues What rights do you think J. Elizabeth Jones believed were being denied? *(Answers will vary)*

DIGITAL OVERVIEW ACTIVITY

Citizenship and Civil Rights

Tell students that this photograph shows the March on Washington for Jobs and Freedom. Goals included a comprehensive civil rights bill to do away with segregated public accommodations; that the right to vote would be protected; there would be a clear system for seeking redress of violations of constitutional rights; there would be a huge federal works program to train and place unemployed workers; and there would be a Federal Fair Employment Practices Act barring discrimination in all employment. The March on Washington helped push the Kennedy-Johnson administration toward sponsoring the Civil Rights Act of 1964 and the Voting Rights Act of 1965.

Ask students:

- Do you think this type of major event could happen in the United States today?
- Do you think that the March on Washington was a success? Explain.
- What new goals, if any, for civil rights do you think need to be stated?

Topic Inquiry

Launch the Topic Inquiry with students after introducing the Topic.

American Citizenship

Supporting English Language Learners

Use with Digital Text 5, **Government Immigration Policies.**

Listening
Read the sections *The Quota System* and *Quota System Changes*. Help students explain the changes in American culture brought by the Immigration and Nationality Act of 1965. Discuss the meaning of the word *quota*.

Beginning Read aloud the sections to the students. Discuss, using visuals as support. Have students draw a visual representation of the quota system.

Intermediate Read aloud the section as the students follow along in the text. Discuss the meaning of the quota system. Have students draw and label a visual representation of the quota system.

Advanced Have partners read the sections to each other. Guide the class to list the changes made to the quota system.

Advanced High Have students read the sections and discuss the significance of the quota system. Have the class discuss possible reasons why changes to the system were made.

Use with Digital Text 6, **Government Policies on Undocumented Aliens.**

Writing
Read the section *Current Law*. Guide students to explain the changes in American culture brought by the Immigration Reform and Control Act of 1986. Provide students with a list of key words to use in their writing such as: *undocumented, amnesty, aliens, hire,* and *deportation*.

Beginning Read aloud the section to students. Using the list of key words, guide the class to write two sentences explaining the two major effects of the 1986 law. Have students copy the sentences and read them to each other.

Intermediate Read aloud and discuss the section with students. Guide partners to use the list of key words to write two sentences explaining the two major effects of the 1986 law. Have partners read their sentences to other students.

Advanced Have partners read the section. Have them use the list of key words to explain the two major effects of the law. Then have them write a third sentence which explains why the law was created.

Advanced High Have students read the section. Then have them write a paragraph about the effects law of 1986.

Ⅾ Differentiate Instruction

Use the Differentiated Instruction notes throughout the lesson plan to support the varied skill sets, levels of readiness, and interests in the mixed-ability classroom.

Challenge These notes include suggestions for expanding the activity for advanced students.

On-Level These notes include suggestions for modifying the activity to address different interests or learning styles.

Extra Support These notes include ideas for providing more scaffolding or reading spuport.

Special Needs These notes provide ideas for adapting instruction to support the needs of various special needs students.

■ NOTES

American Citizenship

Objectives

Objective 1: Describe how people become American citizens by birth and by naturalization.

Objective 2: Explain how an American can lose his or her citizenship.

Objective 3: Illustrate how the United States is a nation of immigrants.

Objective 4: Compare and contrast the status of undocumented aliens and legal immigrants.

LESSON 1 ORGANIZER		PACING: APPROX. 1 PERIOD, .5 BLOCKS			
				RESOURCES	
		OBJECTIVES	PACING	Online	Print
Connect					
DIGITAL START UP ACTIVITY **What Does Citizenship Mean?**			10 min.	●	
Investigate					
DIGITAL TEXTS 1 AND 2 **Citizenship in the United States/Natural-Born Citizens**		Objective 1	10 min.	●	●
DIGITAL TEXTS 3 AND 4 **Naturalized Citizens/Losing One's Citizenship**		Objectives 1, 2	10 min.	●	●
DIGITAL TEXT 5 **Government Immigration Policies**		Objective 3	10 min.	●	●
INTERACTIVE MAP **Foreign-Born Population**			10 min.	●	
DIGITAL TEXT 6 **Government Policies on Undocumented Aliens**		Objective 4	10 min.	●	●
INTERACTIVE CARTOON **Immigration Reform**			10 min.	●	
Synthesize					
DIGITAL SYNTHESIZE ACTIVITY **Good Citizenship**			10 min.	●	
Demonstrate					
DIGITAL QUIZ **Lesson Quiz and Class Discussion Board**			10 min.	●	

PEARSON
realize™
www.PearsonRealize.com

Go online to access additional resources including:
Primary Sources • Biographies • Supreme Court cases •
21st Century Skill Tutorials • Maps • Graphic Organizers.

■ CONNECT

DIGITAL START UP ACTIVITY
What Does Citizenship Mean?

Project the Start Up Activity Ask students to answer the questions as they enter and get settled. Then have them share their ideas with another student.

Discuss Based on the quotation, did President Eisenhower believe that Americans needed to take their citizenship more seriously? What do you think about this issue? *(Possible answer: The fact that Eisenhower made this statement indicates that he thought many Americans needed to be reminded of the importance of citizenship. I think that many U.S. citizens take their citizenship for granted.)*

Tell students that in this lesson they will be learning about citizenship and immigration.

Aa Vocabulary Development: Use the Interactive Reading Notepad to preview the Key Terms and Academic Vocabulary in this Lesson with students.

⇅ FLIP IT!

Assign the Flipped Video for this lesson.

■ STUDENT EDITION PRINT PAGES: 390–397

■ INVESTIGATE

DIGITAL TEXT 1
Citizenship in the United States

Objective 1: Describe how people become American citizens by birth and by naturalization.

Quick Instruction

Inform students a person can acquire U.S. citizenship through two methods: *jus soli* and *jus sanguinis*. Tell students that *jus soli* means the law of the soil, and *jus sanguinis* means the law of the blood.

Ask students to define the two ways of acquiring citizenship in their own words without using a dictionary or without referring to the text. Have students give an example for each term. Ask volunteers to share their definitions and examples and write them on the board. *(Possible answer: Jus soli means that citizenship is determined by where a person is born. For example, if a person is born in the United States, he or she is granted U.S. citizenship. Jus sanguinis means that citizenship is determined by who a person's parents are. For example, if a person is born in England but his or her parents are U.S. citizens, then this person is granted U.S. citizenship.)*

D Differentiate: Extra Support Help students to understand the difference between *jus soli* and *jus sanguinis* by providing the following example. Juan was born in France. Both of his parents are U.S. citizens. Is Juan a U.S. citizen? Why? Does this example show *jus soli* or *jus sanguinis*? Explain your answer.

DIGITAL TEXT 2
Natural-Born Citizens

Further Instruction

Project and discuss the Interactive Reading Notepad questions, including the graphic organizer asking students to record details of the two ways of acquiring citizenship by birth. Review *jus soli* and *jus sanguinis* with the class and fill in the graphic organizer on the whiteboard as you go. Then ask students to revise their definitions of *jus soli* and *jus sanguinis* based on what they learned.

Support Point of View with Evidence Do you think the Supreme Court ruling on the Wong Kim Ark case changed American culture through government policy? *(Possible answer: Yes, this ruling probably broadened many people's ideas about who qualified as a U.S. citizen. Even though the 14th Amendment already existed in 1882, the ruling emphasized that U.S. citizenship is not based on race or language, but instead on being born in the United States.)*

American Citizenship

DIGITAL TEXT 3
Naturalized Citizens

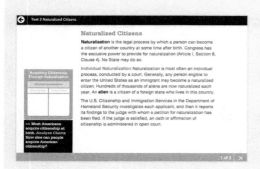

DIGITAL TEXT 4
Losing One's Citizenship

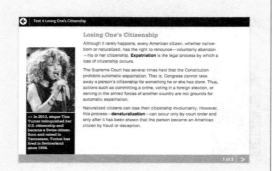

DIGITAL TEXT 5
Government Immigration Policies

Objectives 1: Describe how people become American citizens by birth and by naturalization; 2: Explain how an American can lose his or her citizenship.

Quick Instruction

Conduct a class discussion about naturalization. Have students form pairs. Then tell students to answer the following questions based on their own opinion, not on what they think the Constitution states. Ask students: How long do you think an alien needs to live within the United States to become a U.S. citizen? Why? What other qualifications do you think an alien should have to become a U.S. citizen? Why? (Possible answers: I think an alien should live in the United States for 10 years before he or she can become a U.S. citizen. If an alien lives in the United States for 10 years, that means he or she has established a permanent residence in this country. Also, an alien should not have a criminal record and should be employed. These qualifications help to ensure that the alien will contribute to U.S. society and will not engage in destructive behavior.)

Have pairs discuss these questions and then write down their answers. Ask volunteers to share their answers, and have the class discuss them.

D **Differentiate:** **Challenge** Ask students to imagine they are attorneys attempting to denaturalize a U.S. citizen. Have students create a scenario about the person they are prosecuting. Then have them form arguments to convince a judge that the denaturalization of this person should be done. Ask volunteers to present their scenarios and arguments before the class.

Further Instruction

Go through the Interactive Reading Notepad questions and discuss the answers with the class.

Hypothesize How do you think American culture would be different if the naturalization process did not exist in the United States? (Possible answer: There would be many more non-citizens living in the United States, and those non-citizens would not have be invested in the country in the same way that citizens are.)

Objective 3: Illustrate how the United States is a nation of immigrants.

Quick Instruction

Interactive Map: Foreign-Born Population Project the map on the whiteboard. Introduce the map activity by telling students that the first map shows percentages of foreign-born citizens by State for 2005. Then move the slider to show current 2012 increases or decreases.

Analyze Maps How did the foreign-born population of Texas change from 2005 to 2012? Why do you think this change happened? (Possible answer: The foreign-born population of Texas increased from 15.9 percent in 2005 to 16.4 percent in 2012. Since this State is close to Mexico, it probably has a high number of aliens from this country. Perhaps many of these aliens were granted U.S. citizenship from 2005 to 2012.)

📷 ACTIVE CLASSROOM

Have the class form groups of seven. Tell each group to list what they think are the seven most important immigration laws passed by Congress. Then have each group assign one of these laws to each member of the group. After this, each group should form a "Human Order" line, in which members arrange themselves in chronological order with the first person representing the earliest immigration law, the second person representing the second earliest law and so on.

INTERACTIVE MAP
Foreign-Born Population

DIGITAL TEXT 6
Government Policies on Undocumented Aliens

INTERACTIVE CARTOON
Immigration Reform

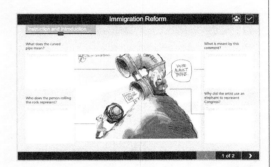

Further Instruction

Editable Presentation Use the Editable Presentation to present the main ideas for this Core Reading.

Government Immigration Policies: Core Reading and Interactive Reading Notepad Go through the Interactive Reading Notepad questions and discuss the answers with the class.

The Immigration and Nationality Act of 1965 eliminated the country-based quota system for U.S. immigration. However, the law still gave preference to certain types of people seeking residency in the United States.

ELL Use the ELL activity described in the ELL chart.

Compare Do you think the Immigration and Nationality Act of 1965 was more or less fair than the National Origins Act of 1929? Explain your answer. *(Possible answer: Yes, the 1965 law eliminated the quota system enforced by the 1929 law. This system did not allow immigrants from certain nations. Such a policy was totally unfair to people in these countries.)*

Support a Point of View with Evidence Explain how you think the Immigration and Nationality Act of 1965 changed American culture. *(Possible answer: I think this act allowed more cultural diversity in the United States, which enriched American culture. Also, this law promoted family unity by giving preference to immediate relatives of American citizens or of aliens legally residing in this country.)*

Objective 4: Compare and contrast the status of undocumented aliens and legal immigrants.

Quick Instruction

Interactive Graphic Organizer: Immigration Reform Project the graphic organizer. Inform students that the cartoon is a commentary on immigration reform. For each of the text input boxes, tell students to type in what they think that piece of the cartoon means or what opinion is being expressed.

Analyze Cartoons What type of immigration reform do you think the creator of this cartoon would support? *(Possible answer: The creator of the cartoon would probably support reform that made the naturalization process easier and more accessible for illegal aliens.)*

📷 ACTIVE CLASSROOM

Have students complete a Wallpaper activity about undocumented aliens. Students should review information they have learned about this topic. Each student then designs a piece of "wallpaper" that encapsulates key learnings about undocumented aliens in the United States. Post the Wallpaper and have students take a "wisdom" walk and note what others have written and illustrated. Students can jot down ideas as they occur.

Further Instruction

Editable Presentation Use the Editable Presentation to present the main ideas for this Core Reading.

Government Policies on Undocumented Aliens: Core Reading and Interactive Reading Notepad Project and discuss the Interactive Reading Notepad questions.

The Immigration Reform and Control Act of 1986 established a one-year amnesty program under which many undocumented aliens could become legal residents. Also, this act made it a crime to hire any person who is in the United States illegally.

ELL Use the ELL activity described in the ELL chart.

Identify Cause and Effect What issues led Congress to pass the Immigration Reform and Control Act of 1986? *(Possible answer: the problems posed by undocumented aliens, which included increasing the burdens of the public school systems and welfare systems of many States)*

Summarize In 1996, how did Congress change the Immigration Reform and Control Act of 1986? *(Possible answer: The 1996 law made it easier to deport illegal aliens, toughened the penalties for smuggling aliens into this country, prevented undocumented aliens from claiming Social Security or public housing, and doubled the size of the Border Patrol.)*

American Citizenship

■ SYNTHESIZE

Good Citizenship

■ DEMONSTRATE

Lesson Quiz and Class Discussion Board

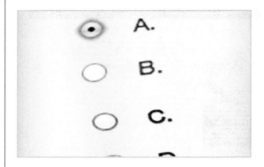

Have students reread the Dwight D. Eisenhower quotation from the Connect activity at the beginning of the Lesson, and then review the notes they made right after reading the quotation. Now, divide the class into small groups and have each group discuss the quotation. Tell groups to brainstorm ways that each of them could be "part-time politicians." Ask students: Can you think of ways that you could "protect the rights and privileges of free people"? *(participating in elections, getting involved in civic activities that promote the rights of citizens)* Are there any ways that you could "preserve what is good and fruitful in our national heritage"? *(getting involved in organizations that support good aspects of American culture, such as promoting the arts, supporting education, and helping the underprivileged)* Ask volunteers to share their group's thoughts with the rest of the class.

Discuss As volunteers share their thoughts, write their ideas on the board. Then have the class discuss pros and cons of these ideas. Conduct a class poll, in which students vote on the two best ideas. *(The pros and cons will vary depending on the ideas. However, all pros and cons should be supported by well thought out reasons.)*

Assign the online Lesson Quiz for this lesson if you haven't already done so. Students will be offered automatic remediation or enrichment based on their score.

Pose these questions to the class on the Discussion Board:

In "American Citizenship" you read about how U.S. government policy changed concerning citizenship, immigration, and undocumented aliens.

Identify Cause and Effect What effects do you think America's changing culture over time has had on U.S. laws dealing with immigration and undocumented aliens? *(Possible answer: When more people immigrated to the United States from southern and eastern Europe, they began to change American culture. This culture became less centered on northern and western European traditions. In an attempt to preserve these traditions, many Americans wanted to limit immigrants from areas outside of northern and western Europe. As a result, the U.S. government set up a quota system that favored immigration from northern and western Europe.)*

Make Predictions How do you think U.S. laws dealing with immigration and undocumented aliens will continue to change in the future? *(Possible answer: Even though the U.S. government has attempted to crackdown on allowing undocumented aliens to enter the country, these aliens continue to be a problem. Because of this, the government will realize that the law needs to allow more people to enter the country legally. Since undocumented aliens continue to be a problem, the punishment for people illegally entering the country will become more severe.)*

Topic Inquiry
Have students continue their investigation for the Topic Inquiry.

Diversity and Discrimination

Supporting English Language Learners

Use with Digital Text 2, **Discrimination in America.**

Learning Strategies
Guide students to list what they know about Native American reservations. Read the sections *White Settlers Bring Discrimination* and *Continued Discrimination Against Native Americans*. Guide students to analyze the political changes brought about by the Indian Education Act of 1972.

Beginning Briefly describe what Native Reservations are. Have students draw an image or write a few words that describe knowledge or experience they have about reservation-type places.

Intermediate Have the class create a list of what they know about Native American reservations. Read aloud the sections while students follow along. Discuss the goals of the Indian Education Act of 1972.

Advanced Have partners list what they know about Native American reservations. Ask them to read the sections. Then have small groups discuss the goals of the Indian Education Act of 1972.

Advanced High Have students jot down what they know about Native American reservations and share with a partner. Have students read the sections and jot down the goals of the Indian Education Act of 1972. Have the class discuss the relationship between the reservations and the policy.

Use with Digital Text 2, **Discrimination in America.**

Listening
Read aloud the section *Government Actions Against Asian Americans*. Guide students to evaluate how two government policies affected Asian Americans. Have students follow directions to complete a graphic organizer.

Beginning Read aloud the section and discuss the policies that are described. Use visuals for support. Give directions to partners to draw and label illustrations for both policies.

Intermediate Read aloud the section and discuss the two policies. Give directions to partners to complete a web graphic organizer with information for one of the policies.

Advanced Have partners read the section and discuss the policies. Guide students to follow directions to complete a Venn diagram using information for both policies.

Advanced High Have students read the section and discuss the policies. Have students follow directions for completing a compare and contrast graphic organizer for the two policies.

◨ Differentiate Instruction

Use the Differentiated Instruction notes throughout the lesson plan to support the varied skill sets, levels of readiness, and interests in the mixed-ability classroom.

Challenge These notes include suggestions for expanding the activity for advanced students.

On-Level These notes include suggestions for modifying the activity to address different interests or learning styles.

Extra Support These notes include ideas for providing more scaffolding or reading spuport.

Special Needs These notes provide ideas for adapting instruction to support the needs of various special needs students.

■ NOTES

Topic 9 Lesson 2

Diversity and Discrimination

Objectives

Objective 1: Understand what it means to live in a heterogeneous society.

Objective 2: Summarize the history of race-based discrimination in the United States.

Objective 3: Examine discrimination against women in the past and present.

LESSON 2 ORGANIZER		OBJECTIVES	PACING	RESOURCES	
				Online	Print
Connect					
DIGITAL START UP ACTIVITY **The Country's Vision**			10 min.	●	
Investigate					
DIGITAL TEXT 1 **A Changing American Culture**		Objective 1	10 min.	●	●
INTERACTIVE CHART **Changing Minority Demographics**			10 min.	●	
DIGITAL TEXT 2 **Discrimination in America**		Objective 2	10 min.	●	●
DIGITAL TEXT 3 **Discrimination Against Women**		Objective 3	10 min.	●	●
INTERACTIVE GALLERY **Women's Rights**			10 min.	●	
Synthesize					
DIGITAL SYNTHESIZE ACTIVITY **Strategies to End Discrimination**			10 min.	●	
Demonstrate					
DIGITAL QUIZ **Lesson Quiz and Class Discussion Board**			10 min.	●	

PEARSON
realize™
www.PearsonRealize.com

Go online to access additional resources including:
Primary Sources • Biographies • Supreme Court cases •
21st Century Skill Tutorials • Maps • Graphic Organizers.

▮ CONNECT

DIGITAL START UP ACTIVITY
The Country's Vision

Project the Start Up Activity Ask students to answer the questions as they enter and get settled. Then have them share their ideas with another student.

Discuss Which image reflects a healthier ideal for the country and its citizens? Why? *(Students should give examples and explanations to support their opinion.)* What new image would best describe the United States today? *(Answers will vary)*

Tell students that in this lesson they will be learning about the ethnic makeup of U.S. society, raced-based discrimination, and discrimination against women.

Aa Vocabulary Development: Use the Interactive Reading Notepad to preview the Key Terms and Academic Vocabulary in this Lesson with students.

⇪ FLIP IT!
Assign the Flipped Video for this lesson.

▮ STUDENT EDITION PRINT
PAGES: 398–404

▮ INVESTIGATE

DIGITAL TEXT 1
A Changing American Culture

Objective 1: Understand what it means to live in a heterogeneous society.

Quick Instruction
Interactive Chart: Changing Minority Demographics Project the chart on the whiteboard. Introduce the graphic organizer activity by telling students that the demographics of the United States have changed throughout its history. In this activity, students will be focusing on demographic data from 2009 to 2012 for persons born in Mexico or South America. For each category, have students type in their observations about the data. Ask students: Is there a notable change in the data for each demographic category for any or all of the groups? *(Possible answer: There is a notable change in the date for each demographic category for all of the groups.)*

🖳 ACTIVE CLASSROOM
Have students use a Graffiti Concepts activity to compare and contrast the changing demographics in the United States. Ask students to reflect on how the demographics of the United States have changed from 1790 to the present day. Then tell students to draw an image that shows U.S. demographics in 1790 and another image that shows present-day U.S. demographics.

Ask students to post their "graffiti" on the board or on chart paper. Have students look at all the various responses, then discuss similarities and differences in the responses as a group.

INTERACTIVE CHART
Changing Minority Demographics

Further Instruction
Editable Presentation Use the Editable Presentation to present the main ideas for this Core Reading.

A Changing American Culture: Core Reading and Interactive Reading Notepad Go through the Interactive Reading Notepad questions and discuss the answers with the class.

The changing demographics in the United States were partially caused by changes in immigration law. For example, a new immigration law in 1965 abolished the quota system that severely limited immigration from many countries. Since then, our nation's African American, Hispanic, and Asian populations have increased significantly.

Infer Citizen movements helped bring about many changes to immigration law. What type of citizen movements do you think helped change U.S. immigration law in 1965? *(Possible answer: Ethnic minorities, such as Hispanics and Asians, probably protested the restrictions placed on immigration as being unconstitutional. Also, many whites probably became aware of the injustice of this system and supported these protests.)*

Diversity and Discrimination

DIGITAL TEXT 2

Discrimination in America

DIGITAL TEXT 3

Discrimination Against Women

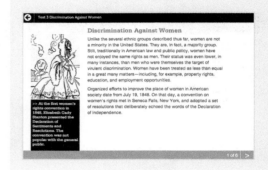

Objective 2: Summarize the history of race-based discrimination in the United States.

Quick Instruction

Tell students that throughout the history of the United States many ethnic minority groups have been discriminated against. Much of this discrimination has come from white-male Americans. Ask students: Why do you think white-male Americans discriminated against minority-groups? *(Possible answer: White-male Americans have historically held most of the power in the United States and have been reluctant to give up power to minority groups.)* List answers on the board. Then conduct a class discussion about these answers.

D Differentiate: **Challenge** Have students form groups of four. Have each group create a skit that shows an example of discrimination against a particular minority group. Students will need to write dialogue. Also, encourage them to use props and costumes.

ELL Use the ELL activity described in the ELL chart.

Further Instruction

Project and discuss the Interactive Reading Notepad questions, including the graphic organizer asking students to compare and contrast the types of discrimination against minority groups. Ask volunteers to share their comparison-contrast paragraphs.

Identify Cause and Effect How did the movement led by Martin Luther King, Jr., and others affect U.S. law? *(This movement resulted in the Civil Rights Act of 1964 and the Voting Rights Act of 1965.)*

Evaluate Sources Review the quotation by Thomas E. Patterson. What does the sentence "The only good Indian is a dead Indian" reveal about how many European Americans viewed Native Americans? *(Possible answer: This sentence shows that many European Americans viewed Native Americans as being the enemy and subhuman. Because of this, these European Americans thought that Native Americans should be wiped out completely.)*

Objective 3: Examine discrimination against women in the past and present.

Quick Instruction

The history of the women's rights movement in the United States dates back to the 1840s and continues to this day. This movement strove to gain equal rights for women in many areas, including voting, ownership of property, employment, and pay.

Interactive Gallery: Women's Rights Project the sideshow. Look at each image individually and then the collection of images as a whole.

Analyze Images How does the third image in the gallery, a woman in a factory, differ from the traditional view of women? *(Possible answer: The third image shows women working in a factory. Traditionally, women were supposed to focus on domestic chores and raising children. If they did work outside of the home, it would be in low-paying clerical or service jobs. However, working in a factory was probably considered to be men's work. Also, since this work involved helping the war effort, it was considered to be important and probably had high pay.)*

INTERACTIVE GALLERY
Women's Rights

Women's Rights

Seneca Falls Convention ▶

The 1848 Seneca Falls Convention on women's rights was the idea of Elizabeth Cady Stanton and Lucretia Mott. Stanton listed sixteen "injuries and usurpations on the part of man toward woman."

< ● ● ● ● ● ●   1 of 3   >

⬛ ACTIVE CLASSROOM

Have students do an If Images Could Talk activity about the women's rights movement. Ask students to study the image of the Seneca Falls convention. Then ask: If the people in this image knew about women's rights in today's world, what might they say about these rights and the women's movement? What's your evidence?

D Differentiate: **Extra Support** Help students to analyze discrimination against women in today's world. Remind students that very few of the fifty State governors are women. Then ask the following: Why do you think there are much fewer women governors than men governors? Do you think these reasons are just? Why or why not? Do you think there is discrimination against women as governors? Explain your answer.

Further Instruction

Go through the Interactive Reading Notepad questions and discuss the answers with the class.

People who fought for women's suffrage thought that women would achieve many basic rights soon after they achieved the right to vote. However, this result did not happen.

Draw Conclusions Why do you think women did not achieve many other rights soon after they won the right to vote? *(Possible answer: Even though women gained the right to vote, men still held the positions of power in politics and business. Many of these men probably still held traditional views on the roles of women. Because of this, they were not willing to support women gaining more rights.)*

Infer Why do you think women earn less than men? *(Possible answers: The white-male-dominated power structure is reluctant to allow equal pay because it feels threatened by it OR Women are underrepresented at the upper levels of corporate management where wages are determined.)*

Diversity and Discrimination

SYNTHESIZE

DIGITAL ACTIVITY

Strategies to End Discrimination

Tell students that the impetus for reversing discrimination usually comes from those who are discriminated against rather than from the government. Groups have learned from each other effective ways to bring about change.

Discuss Ask students: If you were working to end discrimination of any type, what strategies would you try? Make a list of ideas. Tell students that they might consider methods of raising awareness, getting people to support the cause, or pushing politicians to act. After students make their lists, have them choose the strategy they would try first because they think it would be the most effective in bringing about change. Advise students to use clear language for giving an explanation and rationale, while also employing a convincing tone in presenting the positives of the strategy. *(Students' lists might include strategies they have read about as well as ideas of their own. In describing what they believe to be the most effective strategy, the reasons should show how they might share the ideas with those who could employ it.)*

DEMONSTRATE

DIGITAL QUIZ

Lesson Quiz and Class Discussion Board

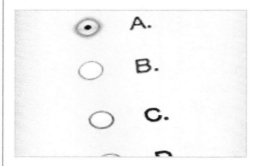

Assign the online Lesson Quiz for this lesson if you haven't already done so. Students will be offered automatic remediation or enrichment based on their score.

Tell students that in "Diversity and Discrimination" they learned about the changing demographics in the United States, various types of discrimination, and the movements that attempted to end this discrimination.

Pose these questions to the class on the Discussion Board:

Make Predictions Why types of movements might develop in the future to end discrimination? *(Possible answer: Since the Hispanic American population is rapidly growing in the United States, more Hispanic movements might develop to end discrimination against this group. Also, the technology gap is growing between the haves and have nots. People who cannot afford new technology may claim they are being discriminated against and demand more access to this technology.)*

Contrast What are some of the differences between the discrimination against women and the discrimination against ethnic groups? *(Possible answer: Ethnic groups are minority groups; women are a majority group. Discrimination against ethnic groups is based on race. Discrimination against women is based on gender. The U.S. government supports the equal rights of ethnic groups. However, by rejecting the ERA, the U.S. government does not support the equal rights of men and women.)*

Topic Inquiry
Have students continue their investigation for the Topic Inquiry.

Equality Before the Law

Supporting English Language Learners

Use with Digital Text 3, **Gender, Sexual Orientation, and Equality.**

Learning Strategies

Guide the class to create a KWL chart for the topic of gender and sex discrimination. Use this chart to record prior experiences to enhance students' understanding of the role of limited government in the protection of individual rights. Focus on the following sections of the text: *Gender, Sexual Orientation, and Equality*; *Challenging Sex Discrimination*; and *A Closer Look at Sex Discrimination*.

Beginning Help the class fill in the K and W sections of the chart. Divide the class into four groups, and have each group read aloud and discuss one section of the text. Guide the class to fill in the L section of the chart.

Intermediate Guide small groups to fill in the K and W sections of the chart. Read aloud the sections of the text as the students follow along. After discussion, guide the groups to fill in the L section of the chart using single words or short phrases.

Advanced Have partners fill in the K and W sections of the chart then read the sections of the text. After a class discussion, guide partners to fill in the L section of the chart.

Advanced High Have individual students fill in the K and W sections of the chart. Guide them to read and discuss the sections of the text. Have students fill in the L section of the chart and share with a classmate.

Use with Digital Text 2, **A History of Segregation.**

Listening

Read aloud the section *Brown* v. *Board of Education*. Guide students to retell or summarize this case in order to evaluate a court decision that has affected a particular racial group. Support students by providing a list of key words and phrases such as: *white*, *word*, *separate*, *public schools*, *segregation*, *race*, *equal*, and *minority*.

Beginning Have students choose several of the key words to illustrate. Have them summarize using their illustration.

Intermediate Use the visuals in the text as support as you read aloud. Guide students to use the key words and phrases as they summarize the case.

Advanced Guide students to listen and take notes using the key words and phrases for support. Have small groups share their notes with one another and summarize the main points of the case. Have them share their summaries with the class.

Advanced High Have students listen and take notes. Have partners summarize the main points of the case in writing using the key words and phrases as needed. Have the partner groups share their summaries with the class.

▣ Differentiate Instruction

Use the Differentiated Instruction notes throughout the lesson plan to support the varied skill sets, levels of readiness, and interests in the mixed-ability classroom.

Challenge These notes include suggestions for expanding the activity for advanced students.

On-Level These notes include suggestions for modifying the activity to address different interests or learning styles.

Extra Support These notes include ideas for providing more scaffolding or reading spuport.

Special Needs These notes provide ideas for adapting instruction to support the needs of various special needs students.

■ NOTES

Equality Before the Law

Objectives

Objective 1: Explain the importance of the Equal Protection Clause in safeguarding individual rights.

Objective 2: Describe the history of segregation in America.

Objective 3: Examine how classification by gender relates to discrimination.

LESSON 3 ORGANIZER		PACING: APPROX. 1 PERIOD, .5 BLOCKS			
				RESOURCES	
		OBJECTIVES	**PACING**	**Online**	**Print**
Connect					
DIGITAL START UP ACTIVITY **Equal Protection Under the Law**			10 min.	●	
Investigate					
DIGITAL TEXT 1 **Equal Protection and Individual Rights**		Objective 1	10 min.	●	●
DIGITAL TEXT 2 **A History of Segregation**		Objective 2	10 min.	●	●
INTERACTIVE TIMELINE **Events in the History of Inequality**			10 min.	●	
DIGITAL TEXT 3 **Gender, Sexual Orientation, and Equality**		Objective 3	10 min.	●	●
INTERACTIVE CHART **Constitutionality in Gender Discrimination**			10 min.	●	
Synthesize					
DIGITAL SYNTHESIZE ACTIVITY **Disagreement on the Supreme Court**			10 min.	●	
Demonstrate					
DIGITAL QUIZ **Lesson Quiz and Class Discussion Board**			10 min.	●	

PEARSON
realize™
www.PearsonRealize.com

Go online to access additional resources including:
Primary Sources • Biographies • Supreme Court cases •
21st Century Skill Tutorials • Maps • Graphic Organizers.

■ CONNECT

DIGITAL START UP ACTIVITY

Equal Protection Under the Law

Project the Start Up Activity Ask students to review the quotation from the 14th Amendment and answer the questions as they enter and get settled. Then have them share their ideas with another student, either in class or through a chat or blog space.

Discuss Have students review the list of situations dealing with equal protection under the law. Ask: Do any of the situations deny a person the equal protection of individual rights under the law? What classifications seem reasonable?

Tell students that in this lesson they will be learning about the Equal Protection Clause, segregation in America, and how classification by gender relates to discrimination.

Aa **Vocabulary Development:** Use the Interactive Reading Notepad to preview the Key Terms and Academic Vocabulary in this Lesson with students.

↻ FLIP IT!

Assign the Flipped Video for this lesson.

■ STUDENT EDITION PRINT PAGES: 405–411

■ INVESTIGATE

DIGITAL TEXT 1

Equal Protection and Individual Rights

Objective 1: Explain the importance of the Equal Protection Clause in safeguarding individual rights.

Quick Instruction

Have students form pairs. Read aloud the Equal Protection Clause from the text. Ask students: How do you think this clause protects individual rights? *(Possible answer: This clause allows all citizens to have the same rights within reason. However, it allows States to draw reasonable distinctions between classes of people.)* Do you think this clause puts a limit on government? *(Possible answer: Yes, the clause limits the government by prohibiting it from unreasonably discriminating against people.)* Have students discuss their answers with their partner. Each pair should then write down their answer. Ask volunteers to share their answers and discuss them with the class.

D Differentiate: **Extra Support** Help students understand the strict scrutiny test. First read the definition of this test. Then give the following example: A State denied the right to vote to all Americans living in that State who were born in Mexico. Does this example deal with a fundamental right? If so, what is the right? Would the Court use the strict scrutiny test for this example? Why or why not? Then give an example of a State that denies a fishing permit to residents that have violated littering laws. Would the Court use the strict scrutiny test for this example? Why or why not?

Further Instruction

Go through the Interactive Reading Notepad questions and discuss the answers with the class.

The government must have the power to draw distinctions between persons and groups. In other words, the government must be able to discriminate. If the government did not have this power, then it could not regulate human behavior.

Apply Concepts Give an example of the government discriminating reasonably. *(Possible answers: Students might give examples of denying driver's licences to people who are blind, allowing people over 65 to use handicapped parking, and fining people who drive over the speed limit.)*

Equality Before the Law

A History of Segregation

Events in the History of Inequality

Gender, Sexual Orientation, and Equality

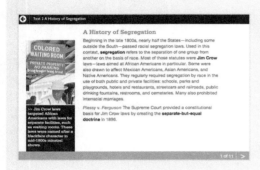

Objective 2: Describe the history of segregation in America.

Quick Instruction

Interactive Chart: Events in the History of Inequality Project the chart on the whiteboard and click through each of the events. Tell students that many cases or events in U.S. history represented movement away from or towards equality. The topics presented in this interactive look at different aspects of the fight towards equality such as civil rights, desegregation, and women's rights. Have students choose one of these events to learn more about why it was a key issue in the quest for equality in the United States.

📹 ACTIVE CLASSROOM

Have students complete a Rank It activity for court decisions dealing with racial discrimination. List the following court decisions: *Alexander* v. *Holmes County Board of Education*, *Swann* v. *Charlotte-Mecklenburg*, *Brown* v. *Board of Education of Topeka* and *Baltimore* v. *Dawson*. Ask students to rank these court decisions based on which had the greatest impact on ending racial discrimination. Tell students to provide a justification for the ranking decisions they made. Then ask students to work in pairs to share their rankings and justifications. Poll the class to see if there is agreement on the ranking.

D **Differentiate: Challenge** Have students write a proposal to end de facto segregation in a city's neighborhood. The proposal should describe several possible methods of ending this segregation, and then promote one of these methods as being the best to bring about political change or to maintain community. The proposal should be backed by evidence.

ELL Use the ELL activity described in the ELL chart.

Further Instruction

Editable Presentation Use the Editable Presentation to present the main ideas for this Core Reading.

Racial Segregation: Core Reading and Interactive Reading Notepad Project and discuss the Interactive Reading Notepad questions. Many times, a law comes about after years of citizen movements and court decisions show the need for the law.

Identify Cause and Effect What Court decisions led to the passing of the Civil Rights Act of 1964? *(Possible answers:* Missouri ex rel. Gaines *v.* Canada, Sweatt *v.* Painter, McLaurin *v.* Oklahoma, *and* Brown *v.* Board of Education of Topeka*)*

Draw Conclusions How do you think the Civil Rights Act of 1964 changed American culture? *(Possible answer: The Civil Rights Act of 1964 quickened the desegregation process in the United States. Also, since this act showed that the Federal Government strongly opposed segregation, more people began to view segregation in a negative way and the separate but equal doctrine as unfair.)*

Objective 3: Examine how classification by gender relates to discrimination.

Quick Instruction

Interactive Chart: Constitutionality in Gender Discrimination Project the chart. Tell students that these cases were either upheld or deemed unconstitutional by the Supreme Court. Have students type in reasons why the Court may have made those decisions. Evaluate with students how constitutional provisions limit the role of government in these specific rulings regarding individual rights.

Support Point of View with Evidence Do you agree with the U.S. Court of Appeals ruling on the *Flores-Villar* v. *United States* case? Why or why not? *(Possible answers: I agree with the ruling. Since mothers are often the primary caregivers for their children, the different residency requirements for fathers and mothers is justified by the rational basis test. OR I do not agree with the ruling. Fathers are needed just as much as mothers in the raising of their children. Because of this, the residency requirement for fathers and mothers should be the same.)*

📹 ACTIVE CLASSROOM

Have students complete a Quick Write activity, in which they write in one minute what they know about discrimination based on gender and discrimination based on sexual orientation.

ELL Use the ELL activity described in the ELL chart.

INTERACTIVE CHART

Constitutionality in Gender Discrimination

Further Instruction

Go through the Interactive Reading Notepad questions and discuss the answers with the class.

Changes in American culture have strongly affected laws dealing with gender discrimination. Even though the Constitution does not make its guarantees only to "men" and separately to "women," U.S. law used gender as a basis for classification for many years. Only after the view of women changed in American culture, did the use of gender classification lessen.

Paraphrase Read the Concurring Opinion about the role of women. Paraphrase this quotation in your own words. How has this quotation been proven inaccurate? *(Possible answer: Nature and civil law shows that there are wide differences between men and women. Men are stronger than women, and therefore should protect and defend them. Women are weak and scared, which makes them unfit for working at many jobs. In today's world, women excel at many jobs once held almost entirely by men, such as politicians, doctors, lawyers, and athletes.)*

Summarize Summarize government policy that has affected gay and lesbian marriage over the past 40 years. *(Possible answer: In the early 1970s, the State Supreme Court ruled that the Constitution does not protect "a fundamental right" for marriage between same-sex couples. In the 1990s, many States passed laws defining marriage as the union of a man and woman and, in 1996, the Federal Government implemented the Defense of Marriage Act. However, a few States began to rule that a ban on gay marriage violated State constitutions. Since then, the Supreme Court has struck down a key provision in the Defense of Marriage Act, and about three fourths of the States have legalized same-sex marriage.)*

Equality Before the Law

■ SYNTHESIZE

DIGITAL SYNTHESIZE ACTIVITY
Disagreement on the Supreme Court

Ask students to recall the Topic Essential Question, "What Are the Challenges of Diversity?" Tell students that some of the Supreme Court's decisions are made unanimously, while others are split decisions—cases about which "reasonable people can disagree." The quotations from *Rostker* v. *Goldberg* show Justice Rehnquist and Justice Marshall each expressing a different viewpoint about the same evidence—congressional hearings on the question of whether to require women to register for the draft.

Discuss Have students compare and contrast the two opinions. Ask students: Why does it matter what evidence was heard before Congress? *(Possible answer: The justices want to determine if Congress was given enough evidence and accurate evidence to make a good decision.)* Why do justices so closely examine the reasoning that went into the passing of a law? *(Possible answer: The justices want to determine if Congress used sound reasons based on the Constitution in passing a law. By examining Congress's reasoning, justices can find flaws in this reasoning if any exist.)* What differences do you see in the level of scrutiny given to the law by each justice? *(Possible answer: The first justice gives a general response, which claims that Congress did the due diligence in passing the law. The second justice provides more specific information of the contribution of women in the military.)*

■ DEMONSTRATE

DIGITAL QUIZ
Lesson Quiz and Class Discussion Board

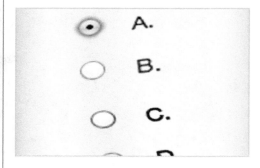

Assign the online Lesson Quiz for this lesson if you haven't already done so. Students will be offered automatic remediation or enrichment based on their score.

Tell students that in "Equality Before the Law" they read about the Equal Protection Clause and how it is decided in Court decisions. They also learned about Court decisions dealing with racial discrimination and the various types of discrimination and segregation. Finally, they studied Court decision dealing with sex discrimination and how views of gender roles and sexual orientation have changed in American society.

Support Point of View with Evidence
Which do you think changed American culture more: laws dealing with racial discrimination or laws dealing with sex discrimination? *(Possible answer: Laws dealing with racial discrimination changed American culture more. De jure segregation has been abolished. De facto segregation still exists, but many advances are being made to lessen it. However, despite the many laws against sex discrimination, women still often face discrimination in the workplace. For example, the number of women in leadership roles in the government and in business is much less than the number of men. Also, women receive less pay for doing the same work as men. Another answer is acceptable if supported by evidence.)*

Make Predictions How do you think U.S. laws will develop concerning same-sex marriage? *(Possible answer: The trend seems to be that more and more States are recognizing same-sex marriage. Since American culture is becoming more accepting of same-sex marriage, I expect this trend will continue. Another answer is acceptable if supported by evidence.)*

Topic Inquiry
Have students continue their investigations for the Topic Inquiry.

Federal Civil Rights Laws

Supporting English Language Learners

Use with Digital Text 1, **The History of Civil Rights Laws.**

Learning Strategies

Read *The History of Civil Rights Laws* and discuss the images in the text in order to guide students to explain changes in American culture brought about by government policies. Provide students with opportunities to monitor and self-correct their oral language production during discussion. Whenever possible, provide feedback by modeling correct speech.

Beginning Using the images, ask students simple questions about what they see and what they believe is happening. Model more sophisticated answers and encourage students to repeat after you.

Intermediate Ask students simple questions about the images that require short answers. Help students to monitor their oral language with prompts such as *Tell me more* or *Can you say it another way?* Model correct grammar and pronunciation and encourage students to repeat after you.

Advanced Have students select several images. Ask them open-ended questions such as *What are the pictures about? What do the pictures tell us about the civil rights?* As students make errors, provide opportunities to self-correct by using prompts such as *Can you explain that again?* Use the following sentence frame to model correct oral language: *Let me make sure I understand. What you are saying is _____.*

Advanced High Have students prepare brief oral presentations based on several images. Encourage students to self-correct their oral language while they practice with a partner. After the presentation, ask students to self-evaluate their presentations.

Use with Digital Text 1, **The History of Civil Rights Laws.**

Listening

Have students listen as you read aloud the sections *The Civil Rights Act of 1964*, *The Civil Rights Act of 1968*, and *Title IX*. Guide students to evaluate a U.S. government policy or court decision that has affected a particular racial, ethnic, or religious group by asking them questions about the text.

Beginning Have students listen as you read the text aloud and provide visuals as support. Ask students questions that can be answered with a gesture or a one- or two-word response.

Intermediate Have students listen and follow along in the text as you read aloud. Ask students questions about the text that can be answered with phrases or short sentences.

Advanced Before reading aloud, tell students you will be asking them questions about the text to encourage them to listen closely. Guide them to take notes as you read. Ask questions with the 5Ws: *Who? What? Where? When? Why?*

Advanced High Have students listen and take notes as you read aloud. Ask students open-ended questions such as *Tell me an important fact about civil rights laws.* Guide students to use academic vocabulary in their responses.

▣ Differentiate Instruction

Use the Differentiated Instruction notes throughout the lesson plan to support the varied skill sets, levels of readiness, and interests in the mixed-ability classroom.

Challenge These notes include suggestions for expanding the activity for advanced students.

On-Level These notes include suggestions for modifying the activity to address different interests or learning styles.

Extra Support These notes include ideas for providing more scaffolding or reading spuport.

Special Needs These notes provide ideas for adapting instruction to support the needs of various special needs students.

■ NOTES

Federal Civil Rights Laws

Objectives

Objective 1: Outline the history of civil rights legislation from Reconstruction to today.

Objective 2: Explore the issues surrounding affirmative action.

LESSON 4 ORGANIZER		PACING: APPROX. 1 PERIOD, .5 BLOCKS			
		OBJECTIVES	**PACING**	**Online**	**Print**
Connect					
DIGITAL START UP ACTIVITY **Which Is the Most Important Civil Right?**			10 min.	●	
Investigate					
DIGITAL TEXT 1 **The History of Civil Rights Laws**		Objectives 1, 2	10 min.	●	●
INTERACTIVE GALLERY **Struggle for Equal Rights**			10 min.	●	
DIGITAL TEXT 2 **Government Policies on Affirmative Action**		Objective 2	10 min.	●	●
INTERACTIVE CARTOON **Affirmative Action**			10 min.	●	
Synthesize					
DIGITAL SYNTHESIZE ACTIVITY **Following Precedents**			10 min.	●	
Demonstrate					
DIGITAL QUIZ **Lesson Quiz and Class Discussion Board**			10 min.	●	

PEARSON **realize**™
www.PearsonRealize.com

Go online to access additional resources including:
Primary Sources • Biographies • Supreme Court cases •
21st Century Skill Tutorials • Maps • Graphic Organizers.

■ CONNECT

DIGITAL START UP ACTIVITY
Which Is the Most Important Civil Right?

Project the Start Up Activity Ask students to answer the questions as they enter and get settled. Then have them share their ideas with another student.

Discuss Which of the groups listed in this activity do you think might be in danger of having their civil rights violated? Why? *(Possible answer: Illegal immigrants; since they are in the country illegally, people can take advantage of this and violate their rights.)*

Tell students that in this lesson they will learn about the history of civil rights legislation from Reconstruction to today and the issues surrounding affirmative action.

Aa Vocabulary Development: Use the Interactive Reading Notepad to preview the Key Terms and Academic Vocabulary in this Lesson with students.

⇡ FLIP IT!
Assign the Flipped Video for this lesson.

■ STUDENT EDITION PRINT PAGES: 412–417

■ INVESTIGATE

DIGITAL TEXT 1
The History of Civil Rights Laws

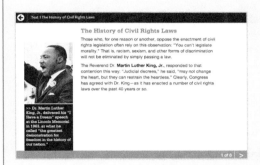

Objectives 1: Outline the history of civil rights legislation from Reconstruction to today; **2:** Explore the issues surrounding affirmative action.

Quick Instruction
From the late 1950s to the present day, individuals, political parties, and interest groups have helped to bring about a series of civil rights legislation that has changed the cultural and political landscape of the United States.

Interactive Gallery: Struggle for Equal Rights Project the gallery and click through the images. Introduce the activity by telling students that the gallery highlights important events in the struggle for equal rights and affirmative action.

Analyze Images What does the image of the Rosa Parks tell you about the impact she had on the civil rights movement? *(Possible answer: The image shows a determined Rosa Parks sitting in a seat in front of a white man. Her refusal to give up her seat to the white man sparked the beginning of the civil rights movement.)*

▣ ACTIVE CLASSROOM
Have students complete a See-Think-Wonder activity concerning the civil rights movement. Project the image of the sit-in at the whites-only lunch counter. Ask students to form pairs. Ask them: What do you see? What does that make you think? What are you wondering about now that you've seen this? Have pairs discuss answers to these questions. Ask volunteers to share insights with the class.

INTERACTIVE GALLERY
Struggle for Equal Rights

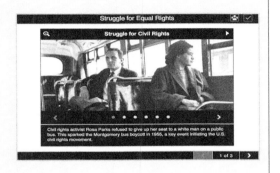

D Differentiate: Challenge Ask students to draw a picture that represents one of the following: the Civil Rights Act of 1964, the Civil Rights Act of 1968, or Title IX.

ELL Use the ELL activity described in the ELL chart.

Further Instruction
Go through the Interactive Reading Notepad questions and discuss the answers with the class.

Before the late 1950s, the U.S. government did not pass any civil rights legislation. However, after the Civil Rights Act of 1957, the floodgates were opened, and Congress passed numerous civil rights laws during the following decades.

Identify Cause and Effect What factors do you think caused Congress to begin passing civil rights legislation? *(Possible answer: Civil rights movements led by individuals such as Martin Luther King, Jr., and public protests by Rosa Parks and many others raised public awareness of the injustice of separate but equal policies and Jim Crow laws. Soon public pressure was placed on the government to pass civil rights laws.)*

Federal Civil Rights Laws

DIGITAL TEXT 2

Government Policies on Affirmative Action

INTERACTIVE CARTOON

Affirmative Action

Objective 2: Explore the issues surrounding affirmative action.

Quick Instruction

Interactive Cartoon: Affirmative Action
Project the cartoon on the whiteboard. Tell students to think about what this cartoon is saying about affirmative action. Ask students to type their comments about each part of the cartoon in the text boxes. Then review those questions and answers as a class. Ask: Whom do the people in this cartoon represent? *(the white and African American populations of the U.S.)* What are some possible meanings for the space between these two people? *(The space could be interpreted as a symbol of the lack of understanding between white Americans and African Americans in terms of race and civil rights; or, the space could be interpreted as a representation of the gap that still exists in terms of racial equality in the U.S. and an unwillingness or inability for white Americans and African Americans to communicate about that issue or to find common ground)* Why do you think the cartoonist shows both characters thinking the same thought? *(Possible answer: to show that there is a lack of understanding and resentment between the races)* What message do you think this cartoonist is trying to communicate? *(Possible answer: that white Americans and African Americans need to come together to bridge the gap in understanding between the races, a gap that is unnecessary and based on misconceptions)*

Analyze Cartoons Ask students: Do you think this cartoon is critical or supportive of affirmative action, or is it neutral? *(Possible answer: I think the cartoon is neutral, because*

it shows both sides of the issue. The African American character in the cartoon is shown as thinking that white Americans "get all the breaks." This reflects the fact that white Americans have historically been in positions of power in the U.S., which is the original reason that affirmative action programs were put in place. At the same time, the second character reflects criticisms of affirmative action programs by some white Americans and others, who believe that those programs amount to reverse discrimination and give minorities unfair advantages.)

📽 ACTIVE CLASSROOM

Ask students to Take a Stand on the following question: Should affirmative action policies be eliminated? Tell students to divide into two groups based on their answers and move to separate areas of the classroom. If one area has few students, assign more students to this area. Have students talk to each other to compare their reasons for answering yes or no. Then ask a representative from each side to present and defend the group's point of view.

D **Differentiate: Extra Support** Even though Benito is an excellent chess player, he is passed over for membership to a chess club because the club needs one more girl member to meet a quota. As a result, the club accepts a girl who is perhaps not as good a chess player as Benito. Ask students: Is there anything you don't understand about this example? Do you think it is fair for the club to deny membership to Benito? Why or why

not? Do you think this example is similar to affirmative action?

Further Instruction

Editable Presentation Use the Editable Presentation to present the main ideas for this Core Reading.

Government Policies on Affirmative Action: Core Reading and Interactive Reading Notepad Project and discuss the Interactive Reading Notepad questions.

By 1965, the Federal Government began to demand the adoption of affirmative action programs. Critics of affirmative action programs claim that these programs promote reverse discrimination, or discrimination against the majority group. Affirmative action cases have come under strict scrutiny, and by the twenty-first century Michigan cases such as *Grutter* v. *Bollinger* have signaled a continuation of the move away from this policy. However, the government uses discrimination all the time. If it didn't discriminate, then the government could not regulate people's actions.

Support Ideas with Examples Do you think the type of government discrimination involved in affirmative action programs is justified? *(Possible answer: All answers, whether pro or con, should be supported by examples from the text, including Court decisions, statements by justices, and legislation.)*

■ SYNTHESIZE

DIGITAL SYNTHESIZE ACTIVITY
Following Precedents

Ask students to recall the Topic Essential Question, "What Are the Challenges of Diversity?" Have them use the Think Pair Share strategy to answer the questions in the Federal Civil Rights Activity.

Analyze Ask students to read the quotations about affirmative action. Then have them write a paragraph explaining what guidelines they think the Court should follow in making decisions about affirmative action cases in the future. Ask volunteers to share their paragraphs. *(Possible answers: Guidelines will vary but should all be supported by well thought out reasons. Guidelines could include the following: make sure that no group whether majority or minority is being discriminated against; make sure that affirmative action quotas do not discriminate against qualified people; make sure that affirmative action quotas are still needed and if so are continually adjusted according the need.)*

■ DEMONSTRATE

DIGITAL QUIZ
Lesson Quiz and Class Discussion Board

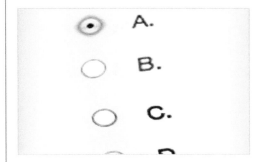

Assign the online Lesson Quiz for this lesson if you haven't already done so. Students will be offered automatic remediation or enrichment based on their score.

Tell students that in "Federal Civil Rights Laws" they read about the history of civil rights laws and the issues concerning affirmative action policies.

Pose these questions to the class on the Discussion Board:

Synthesize Do you think Title IX has affected how well the United States has done in the Olympics? *(Possible answer: Yes; Title IX has required schools to have equal funding and opportunities for athletic programs. As a result, more and more women developed their skills as athletes. The United States, therefore, developed strong female Olympic teams, which often excelled.)*

Predict Consequences What would be the consequences if all affirmative action policies were abolished? *(Possible answers: The opportunities for minorities and women would be reduced. Because of this, minorities would have a more difficult time getting the education needed to get well-paying jobs. Also, women would have more difficulty getting ahead in businesses. The quality of education might improve, since educational institutions could accept applicants based solely on academic merit instead of on meeting a quota.)*

Topic Inquiry
Have students continue their investigations for the Topic Inquiry.

Citizenship and Civil Rights

SYNTHESIZE

DIGITAL ACTIVITY
Reflect on the Essential Question and Topic

First ask students to reconsider the Essential Question for the Topic: What Are the Challenges of Diversity? Tell students that at the beginning of their study of citizenship and civil rights, they analyzed why the 1963 March on Washington occurred and whether or not a protest of this magnitude might occur today.

Now that they have studied this topic more deeply, do they think the nation's diversity still presents large scale challenges such as those that led to the March on Washington? Students should give at least three reasons to support their opinion. *(Students should clearly express their opinion: they either agree that an event like the March on Washington might still occur, or they do not believe such big challenges exist today. The reasons they give in support of their opinion should be relevant.)*

Reflect on the Topic As students complete their study of citizenship and civil rights, have them take a few minutes to reflect on all that they have learned. Students should write down three important questions they have thought about during the Topic and their answers to those questions. For example, perhaps students thought about the people who have risen to leadership positions in various civil rights movements and wondered what qualities they have in common. Or students might have considered why changes to the Constitution or to the judicial review process are necessary to ensure equal rights for all. As they answer the questions they pose, students should use evidence from what they have learned while studying the Topic.

Topic Inquiry
Have students complete Step 3 of the Topic Inquiry.

DEMONSTRATE

DIGITAL TOPIC REVIEW AND ASSESSMENT
Citizenship and Civil Rights

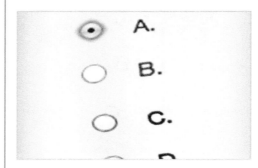

Students can prepare for the Topic Test by answering the questions in the Topic Review and Assessment online or the Assessment questions in the Print Student text. They can also prepare by reviewing their answers to the Interactive Reading Notepad questions or reviewing their notes in the Reading and Notetaking Study Guide.

TOPIC TEST
Assign the Topic Test to assess students' understanding of topic content.

DIGITAL TOPIC TEST
Citizenship and Civil Rights

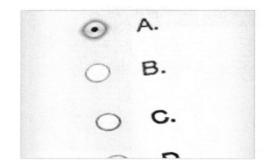

BENCHMARK TESTS
Assign these benchmark tests as you complete the relevant topics to monitor student progress toward mastering the course content and as preparation for the End-of-Course Test.

Benchmark Test 1: Topics 1–4
Benchmark Test 2: Topics 5–8
Benchmark Test 3: Topics 9–11
Benchmark Test 4: Topics 12–14

Government by the People

TOPIC 10 ORGANIZER	PACING: APPROX. 1 PERIOD, .5 BLOCKS
	PACING
Connect	**1 period**
MY STORY VIDEO **Politics and the New Media**	10 min.
DIGITAL ESSENTIAL QUESTION ACTIVITY **What Is the Role of the People in Government?**	10 min.
DIGITAL OVERVIEW ACTIVITY **The Five Stages of Expanding Suffrage**	10 min.
TOPIC INQUIRY: DOCUMENT-BASED QUESTION **Regulating Special Interests and Earmarks**	20 min.
Investigate	**3–7 periods**
TOPIC INQUIRY: DOCUMENT-BASED QUESTION **Regulating Special Interests and Earmarks**	Ongoing
LESSON 1 The History of Voting Rights	30–40 min.
LESSON 2 Your Right to Vote	30–40 min.
LESSON 3 Voting Trends	30–40 min.
LESSON 4 The Voting Process	30–40 min.
LESSON 5 Public Opinion and Polling	30–40 min.
LESSON 6 Influencing Public Opinion: The Mass Media	30–40 min.
LESSON 7 Understanding Interest Groups	30–40 min.
Synthesize	**1 period**
DIGITAL ACTIVITY **Reflect on the Essential Question and Topic**	10 min.
TOPIC INQUIRY: DOCUMENT-BASED QUESTION **Regulating Special Interests and Earmarks**	20 min.
Demonstrate	**1–2 periods**
DIGITAL TOPIC REVIEW AND ASSESSMENT **Government by the People**	10 min.
TOPIC INQUIRY: DOCUMENT-BASED QUESTION **Regulating Special Interests and Earmarks**	20 min.

Regulating Special Interests and Earmarks

In this Document Based Question activity, students work independently to analyze and evaluate the validity of information, arguments, and counterarguments from primary and secondary sources for bias, propaganda, point of view, and frame of reference. Their goal in doing so is to answer the question: Are interest groups, lobbyists, and earmarks beneficial or are they a threat to the American political system? Examining the primary and secondary sources will contribute to students' understanding of the Topic Essential Question: What Is the Role of People in Government?

STEP 1: CONNECT
Develop Questions and Plan the Investigation

Launch the DBQ Writing Activity

Display the graphs showing lobbying spending and the number of lobbyists and discuss the information they present. Define the difference between special interest groups and lobbyists (lobbyists work for special interest groups).

Explain to students that evaluating the validity of a source means determining how reliable it is and how much bias is present. Bias is the extent to which an author expresses his or her own point of view. Point out that point of view and frame of reference are different than bias. Point of view is the ideas and personal feelings that influence how a person sees the facts and events in a particular situation. Frame of reference is the context that a person brings to a situation. For example, a child has a different frame of reference than an adult. Propaganda, a persuasive technique aimed at creating a particular belief, is another factor that can affect the validity of a source.

Suggestion: To support instruction on bias, have students research the opensecrets.org website and the mission statement of the group that sponsors it, the Center for Responsive Politics. This mission statement can be found under "About Us." Students should share their thoughts with the class, such as how the statement that CRP "accepts no contributions from businesses, labor unions, or trade associations." Why do students think the group makes it a point to note this on their website? What is the group's point of view about interest groups and lobbyists? What is its frame of reference?

Generate Questions

Provide the Need to Know Questions document and have students work together to list questions about the topic.

Resources
- Project Launch
- Project Contract
- Need to Know Questions
- Student Instructions
- Lobbying Chart

STEP 2: INVESTIGATE
Apply Disciplinary Concepts and Tools

Analyze the Documents

Discuss the difference between primary and secondary sources. Primary sources are documents that were written at the time. They are first-hand information, and include speeches, diary entries, eyewitness accounts, and the like. Secondary sources were written after the fact, and they often analyze or interpret primary sources.

List questions students can use as they read and evaluate the documents, such as *What argument is presented? What, if any, counterarguements are presented? Is the information valid? How do I know?*

Encourage students to think about the point of view of the author and his or her frame of reference to determine the author's potential biases. Remind students that understanding bias is important to evaluating information and arguments.

Have students analyze each of the six documents. Students will use these documents in their essays, so encourage them to carefully summarize arguments, bias, point of view, and frame of reference. Have students answer the questions at the end of each document.

Suggestion: To save time, you may wish to form the class into small groups and assign each group one document. The groups can then present their findings to the class. However, students will need to be familiar with all documents to write their final essays.

Resources
- Student Instructions
- Document A Top Lobbying Industries for 2013
- Document B Ex-Congressman Lobbyist cartoon
- Document C Requested Earmarks for Texas, 2011
- Document D Speech by President Barack Obama
- Document E "We Should Be Done with Earmarks" by Alexandra Booze
- Document F "Some want earmarks back to help Congress pass bills," USA Today, October 29, 2013

⏻ PROFESSIONAL DEVELOPMENT

Document-Based Question
Be sure to view the Document-Based Question Professional Development resources in the online course.

STEP 3: SYNTHESIZE
Evaluate Sources and Use
Evidence to Formulate Conclusions

Write Your Essay

Remind students of the question they are to answer in their essays: Are interest groups, lobbyists, and earmarks beneficial or are they a threat to the American political system? Students will be making an argument, so they should include relevant and valid details from the documents to support their opinions. Students may answer each part of the question separately as noted on the Student Instruction sheet.

Edit Your Essay

Remind students that they should edit their essays based on the rubric. Encourage students to work on one element at a time as they revise.

After students have edited the content of their paper, have them edit to ensure they have used standard grammar, spelling, sentence structure, and punctuation.

Suggestion: Allow time for peer editing of essays. Have peers summarize the arguments and evidence they find in their partners' papers. Have editors discuss their findings with writers so that writers can evaluate the effectiveness of their arguments.

Resources
• Essay Rubric

STEP 4: DEMONSTRATE
Communicate Conclusions
and Take Informed Action

Present Your Paper

Ask volunteers to read their essays aloud, choosing those who took opposing positions on the thesis. Discuss some of the analysis done by students, using information they wrote in their papers. Discuss how bias, point of view, and frame of reference affect the validity of a source. Discuss propaganda, including its purpose and how to recognize it.

Reflect on the Activity

Evaluate the effectiveness of the activity. Discuss how students' research will help them become better consumers of political and other information and help them make more informed decisions.

Suggestion: As an extension activity, encourage students to study news articles over the next few days or weeks to identify the influence lobbying groups have on current issues.

Resources
• Essay Rubric   • Self-Assessment

Government by the People

Voting is one of the most effective tools that citizens have to make their voices heard in government. People throughout American history have fought to win voting rights and today, that right is held by every citizen aged 18 and over. The media, public opinion polls, and interest groups play a dual role in a democracy. They not only help give the people a say in government, they also play a role in keeping citizens informed.

■ CONNECT

MY STORY VIDEO
Politics and the New Media

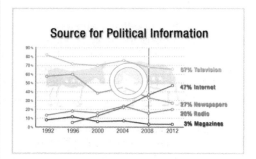

Watch a video that introduces students to the new ways that politicians are using social media to reach voters.

Identify Patterns What changes are taking place in the way that people get political information? *(More and more are getting that information from Internet sources, not television.)*

Make Generalizations How are changes in the media affecting how politicians connect with voters? *(They are using social media such as Twitter and Facebook to make personal connections. Their staffs use media to explain policies.)*

🔄 FLIP IT!

Assign the My Story video.

DIGITAL ESSENTIAL QUESTION ACTIVITY
What Is the Role of the People in Government?

Ask students to think about the Essential Question for this Topic: What Is the Role of the People in Government? People are vital to a democracy, but what should be their exact role in the government?

If students have not already done so, ask them to read the list of roles of people in government. Then have them use an Opinion Line to show which one they think is most important. Review the results as a class.

Support a Point of View with Evidence Why did you rate this reason as most valid? *(Possible answer: I think the role of voter is the most important because this is how people can truly shape their government and public policy.)*

Draw Conclusions What might happen if not all the people in a democracy were allowed to share their opinions? *(Possible answer: The government would not be a true democracy in which the equality of all people was safeguarded and respected.)* What if an election were held and no one showed up? *(Possible answers: Democracy would be threatened, because if the people do not participate in government, then a decision-making void is created; Individuals would have to step up to make decisions and those individuals may not reflect the opinion of the majority.)*

DIGITAL OVERVIEW ACTIVITY
The Five Stages of Expanding Suffrage

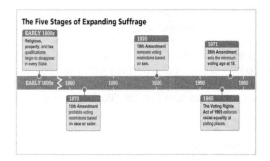

Display the timeline. During this Topic, students will learn about government by the people, and this image can serve as a jumping-off point for students' entry into the content. Remind students that *suffrage* means "the right to vote." Point out that the timeline begins in the early 1800s, not long after the Revolutionary War was won, and ends in 1965. What does this tell students about the right to vote in the United States? Why is the right to vote central to a government by the people?

🅳 Differentiate: Extra Support Ask students: What sort of religious or property qualifications might have existed in the nation's early days? *(People had to belong to a certain church or own property in order to be allowed to vote.)*

Check Understanding What main mechanism was used to achieve the expansion of voting rights? *(constitutional amendment)*

Topic Inquiry
Launch the Topic Inquiry with students after introducing the Topic.

The History of Voting Rights

Supporting English Language Learners

Use with Digital Text 1, **Voting Rights in the United States.**

Learning Strategies

Read the section *The Struggle to Extend Voting Rights* with students. Have students write about the changes in American culture that might have been brought about by government policies on voting rights. Guide students to monitor and self-correct their writing.

Beginning Read aloud, using the visuals in the reading as support. For each of the five stages of expanding suffrage, have students write a short summary sentence. Then write your own summary sentences on the board and model how to monitor and self-correct by comparing what students have written to what is on the board.

Intermediate After reading, guide students to write short sentences about each of the five stages. Have them read their sentences to themselves as a way to monitor their work. Guide them to make corrections and read their work again.

Advanced Have students write a short description of each stage. Guide students to read their work to themselves and to a partner in order to make their writing clear. Have them self-correct their work.

Advanced High Have students write about each of the five stages. Have them monitor their work for clarity and punctuation. After they self-correct, have them share their work with a partner.

Use with Digital Text 3, **Civil Rights Acts of 1957, 1960, and 1964.**

Listening

Read aloud the section *The Civil Rights Act of 1964* in order to guide students to evaluate a U.S. government policy that has affected a particular racial or ethnic group. Have students demonstrate listening comprehension by working together to respond to the reading.

Beginning Have students listen as you read each paragraph aloud, pointing out the visuals in the reading as you proceed through the text. Provide a list of questions, such as *What is discrimination? What are racial barriers?* Have students work together to provide one- or two-word responses to these questions.

Intermediate Have students listen as you read the text aloud. Then provide question stems using the words *who, what, where, when,* and *why.* Have students work together to complete these stems. Have them pose the questions to the others in the group.

Advanced Have partners create questions based on the reading. Have students listen to and then answer their partner's questions. Then have them switch roles so they are asking questions and then listening to the answers.

Advanced High Pose questions about the reading to the students. Have small groups work together to answer the questions by creating a presentation. Groups should listen to one another's presentations.

▣ Differentiate Instruction

Use the Differentiated Instruction notes throughout the lesson plan to support the varied skill sets, levels of readiness, and interests in the mixed-ability classroom.

Challenge These notes include suggestions for expanding the activity for advanced students.

On-Level These notes include suggestions for modifying the activity to address different interests or learning styles.

Extra Support These notes include ideas for providing more scaffolding or reading spuport.

Special Needs These notes provide ideas for adapting instruction to support the needs of various special needs students.

■ NOTES

The History of Voting Rights

Objectives

Objective 1: Summarize the history of voting rights in the United States.

Objective 2: Identify the main intention of the 15th Amendment, and describe the results of its lack of enforcement.

Objective 3: Analyze the impact of political changes brought about by individuals with regard to the civil rights laws enacted in 1957, 1960, and 1964.

Objective 4: Analyze the provisions and effects of the Voting Rights Act of 1965.

LESSON 1 ORGANIZER		PACING: APPROX. 1 PERIOD, .5 BLOCKS		
			RESOURCES	
	OBJECTIVES	PACING	Online	Print
Connect				
DIGITAL START UP ACTIVITY **Do 18-Year-Olds Vote?**		5 min.	●	
Investigate				
DIGITAL TEXT 1 **Voting Rights in the United States**	Objective 1	10 min.	●	●
INTERACTIVE TIMELINE **An Expanding Electorate**		10 min.	●	
DIGITAL TEXT 2 **The 15th Amendment**	Objective 2	10 min.	●	●
DIGITAL TEXT 3 **Civil Rights Acts of 1957, 1960, and 1964**	Objective 3	10 min.	●	●
INTERACTIVE GALLERY **Poll Taxes and the 24th Amendment**		10 min.	●	
DIGITAL TEXT 4 **Voting Rights Act of 1965—Then and Now**	Objective 4	10 min.	●	●
Synthesize				
DIGITAL SYNTHESIZE ACTIVITY **Important Dates in Voting Rights**		5 min.	●	
Demonstrate				
DIGITAL QUIZ **Lesson Quiz and Discussion Board**		10 min.	●	

PEARSON
realize™
www.PearsonRealize.com

Go online to access additional resources including:
Primary Sources • Biographies • Supreme Court cases •
21st Century Skill Tutorials • Maps • Graphic Organizers.

■ CONNECT

DIGITAL START UP ACTIVITY
Do 18-Year-Olds Vote?

Project the Start Up Activity Ask students to review the chart and answer the questions as they enter and get settled. Then have them share their ideas with another student, either in class or through a chat or blog space.

Discuss If you were a high school student in 1971 instead of today, how would you have felt about the possibility of voting earlier? *(Possible answers: excited, nonplussed)* Would you have supported the amendment? *(Possible answers: Yes, because I want to vote and I feel I would have had enough knowledge and experience to do so at an earlier age.)*

Tell students that in this lesson they will be learning about the history of voting rights.

Aa Vocabulary Development: Use the Interactive Reading Notepad to preview the Key Terms and Academic Vocabulary in this Lesson with students.

⇅ FLIP IT!
Assign the Flipped Video for this lesson.

■ STUDENT EDITION PRINT
PAGES: 424–431

■ INVESTIGATE

DIGITAL TEXT 1
Voting Rights in the United States

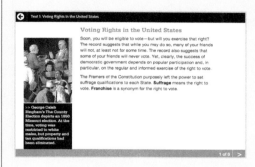

Objective 1: Summarize the history of voting rights in the United States.

Quick Instruction

Point out to students that voting is one of the responsibilities of citizenship, because democracy cannot survive if the people do not participate at the ballot box. Ask students to imagine a situation in which no one showed up at the polls on election day. Guide them to the realization that lack of participation could lead to autocratic forms of government.

Explain that Americans have always valued the right to vote. For this reason, citizens have struggled to secure this right throughout history.

Interactive Timeline: An Expanding Electorate Project and step through the timeline with students. Explain that the timeline shows important milestones in the expansion of suffrage in the United States.

🎥 ACTIVE CLASSROOM

Use the Ranking strategy to have students go through the amendments shown in the activity, and rank which ones had the greatest impact on increasing suffrage in the United States.

D Differentiate: Extra Support Students may benefit from using a Sticky Note strategy to write down the description of each amendment from the reading with teacher support. Then have them continue with the activity.

INTERACTIVE TIMELINE
An Expanding Electorate

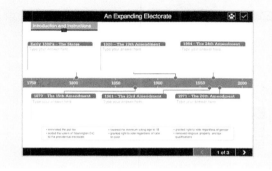

ELL Use the ELL activity described in the ELL chart.

Further Instruction

Editable Presentation Use the Editable Presentation to present the main ideas for this Core Reading.

Voting Rights in the United States: Core Reading and Interactive Reading Notepad Project and discuss the Interactive Reading Notepad questions. Discuss changes in American culture brought about by government policies such as voting rights. Students may discuss what happened after African Americans, women, and young people got the right to vote. How might the fact that these groups now had political power and input into public policy have changed American culture?

Evaluate Data Look at the map "Women's Suffrage in 1919." According to the data shown, which region of the country would you have chosen to live in, had you been a woman who wished to have a say in public policy in the early 1900s? Why? *(Possible answer: States in the western portion of the country allowed women to vote in all elections. Therefore, this would have been the best area in which to live for a woman who wished to have a voice in public policy.)* What percentage of the States did not allow women to vote in any elections in 1919? *(Seventeen of fifty States, or 34 percent, did not allow women to vote at this time.)*

The History of Voting Rights

DIGITAL TEXT 2

The 15th Amendment

The 15th Amendment

How important is the right to vote? For those who do not have it, that right can seem as important as life itself. Indeed, in the Deep South of the 1960s, civil rights workers suffered arrest, beatings, shocks with electric cattle prods, even death—all in the name of the right to vote. Their efforts inspired the nation and led to large-scale federal efforts to secure that right for African Americans and other minority groups in the United States.

The effort to extend the franchise to African Americans began with the 15th Amendment, which was ratified in 1870. It declares that the right to vote cannot be denied to any citizen of the United States because of "race, color, or previous condition of servitude." The amendment was plainly intended to ensure that African American men, nearly all of them former slaves and nearly all of them living in the South, could vote.

>> Dr. Martin Luther King, Jr. and Coretta Scott King vote in the presidential election of 1964, the same year the Civil Rights Act of 1964 outlawed discriminatory voting practices.

Objective 2: **Identify the main intention of the 15th Amendment and describe the results of its lack of enforcement.**

Quick Instruction

The 15th Amendment explains that the right to vote cannot be denied to any citizen of the United States because of "race, color, or previous condition of servitude." Meant to extend the franchise to African American men, the amendment included no means of enforcement. Lack of enforcement allowed for the continued disenfranchisement of African American men using a variety of tactics.

Further Instruction

Editable Presentation Use the Editable Presentation to present the main ideas for this Core Reading.

The 15th Amendment: Core Reading and Interactive Reading Notepad Project and discuss the Interactive Reading Notepad questions.

The 15th Amendment of the Constitution Project and read through the amendment with commentary. Students should evaluate why the Federal Government's lack of enforcement of the 15th Amendment affected a particular racial group. Point out that this policy made it easy for States to disenfranchise people based on race. Then examine the two Court cases from the reading: *Smith* v. *Allwright*, 1944, and *Gomillion* v. *Lightfoot*, 1960. Discuss how those two cases used the language of the 15th Amendment to extend voting rights.

Make Predictions White primaries and gerrymandering were outlawed by the courts. Why did this not stop all disenfranchisement? *(Possible answer: This case-by-case method was too slow. There were legal methods, such as poll taxes and literary tests, that were still in effect.)*

Analyze What is the intention of the 15th Amendment? Why did the amendment not live up to the intention? *(It was meant to provide suffrage to all men, regardless of race or previous servitude. The amendment was not followed with congressional action establishing consequences if the law was not followed.)*

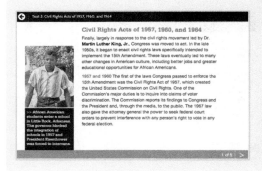

DIGITAL TEXT 3

Civil Rights Acts of 1957, 1960, and 1964

Civil Rights Acts of 1957, 1960, and 1964

Finally, largely in response to the civil rights movement led by Dr. **Martin Luther King, Jr.**, Congress was moved to act. In the late 1960s, it began to enact civil rights laws specifically intended to implement the 15th Amendment. These laws eventually led to many other changes in American culture, including better jobs and greater educational opportunities for African Americans.

1957 and 1960 The first of the laws Congress passed to enforce the 15th Amendment was the Civil Rights Act of 1957, which created the United States Commission on Civil Rights. One of the Commission's major duties is to inquire into claims of voter discrimination. The Commission reports its findings to Congress and the President and, through the media, to the public. The 1957 law also gave the attorney general the power to seek federal court orders to prevent interference with any person's right to vote in any federal election.

>> African American students enter a school in Little Rock, Arkansas. The governor blocked the integration of schools in 1957 and President Eisenhower was forced to intervene.

Objective 3: **Analyze the impact of political changes brought about by individuals with regard to the civil rights laws enacted in 1957, 1960, and 1964.**

Quick Instruction

Congress, through civil rights laws in the 1950s and 1960s, began to fully implement the 15th Amendment. The Civil Rights Acts of 1957, 1960, and 1964 are examples of U.S. government policies that affected a particular racial, ethnic, or religious group. Each of these laws played an important role in expanding voting rights to ethnic and racial minorities. Ask: What do you think were the likely effects of the provisions of the Civil Rights Acts?

Interactive Gallery: Poll Taxes and the 24th Amendment Project and step through the gallery with students. Look at each image individually and then the collection of images as a whole.

Analyze Images Describe the expressions of the men in the last image showing the signing of the 24th Amendment. Why was this event important? *(Possible answer: They look pleased and proud. It was important because it eliminated the poll tax, which prevented African Americans from voting.)*

🖵 ACTIVE CLASSROOM

Using a Headline strategy, have students create headlines about events that led to the 24th Amendment. Assign groups one event from the gallery to write their headlines about and then gather all the class headlines. Discuss the evolution of this amendment.

INTERACTIVE GALLERY
Poll Taxes and the 24th Amendment

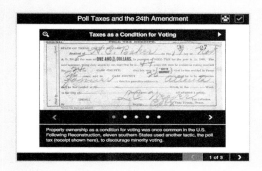

Property ownership as a condition for voting was once common in the U.S. Following Reconstruction, eleven southern States used another tactic, the poll tax (receipt shown here), to discourage minority voting.

D Differentiate: **Extra Support** What is a poll tax? *(a tax one pays before voting)* Which group of people did a poll tax mostly prevent from voting? *(African Americans)*

ELL Use the ELL activity described in the ELL chart.

Further Instruction

Editable Presentation Use the Editable Presentation to present the main ideas for this Core Reading.

Civil Rights Acts of 1957, 1960, and 1964: Core Reading and Interactive Reading Notepad Project and discuss the Interactive Reading Notepad questions.

Affecting Public Policy Have students use the information in the lesson to create a graphic organizer listing the various processes used by individuals, political parties, interest groups, or the media to bring about changes in the nation's voting laws throughout history. *(Government leaders at the State level used legal means to eliminate religious, property, and tax qualifications; legislators, urged by individuals, political parties, interest groups, and the media, used constitutional amendments; federal legislation and court decisions were also used.)*

Evaluate Impact The civil rights movement was a citizen movement initiated to bring about political change in the United States. It focused on minority rights, including voting rights. How effective was this movement in bringing about political change? Use evidence from the lesson to support your answer. *(Possible answer: The civil rights movement was quite effective. Its participants succeeded in bringing about fundamental political change in terms of the civil rights of African Americans. Evidence of their success can be seen in the Civil Rights Acts, the Voting Rights Act, and the 24th Amendment.)*

Compare Which Civil Rights Act had the greatest impact on increasing the right to vote for African Americans? Why? *(Possible answer: The Civil Rights Act of 1964 because it outlawed specific practices commonly used to disenfranchise people.)*

Analyze Why was an amendment to the Constitution needed to outlaw poll taxes? *(Possible answer: They were a legal method of disenfranchisement.)*

DIGITAL TEXT 4
Voting Rights Act of 1965—Then and Now

Objective 4: Analyze the provisions and effects of the Voting Rights Act of 1965.

Quick Instruction

Write the following statement on the board: The Voting Rights Act of 1965 made the 15th Amendment an effective part of the Constitution. Help students to evaluate the Voting Rights Act and this statement by reviewing its provisions. How did it differ from earlier civil rights legislation?

Further Instruction

Editable Presentation Use the Editable Presentation to present the main ideas for this Core Reading.

Voting Rights Act of 1965—Then and Now: Core Reading and Interactive Reading Notepad Project and discuss the Interactive Reading Notepad questions. Students should understand the elements of preclearance and why they were invalidated recently.

Make Predictions What is a possible result of invalidating preclearance? *(Possible answer: Congress will have to pass another law that reflects current issues in voting. There may be an increase in disenfranchisement.)*

Analyze Which provision of the Voting Rights Act was most effective in extending the right to vote? Why? *(Possible answer: Giving the Federal Government oversight over local and State elections allows for all people to be treated equally regardless of the State in which they reside.)*

The History of Voting Rights

■ SYNTHESIZE

DIGITAL SYNTHESIZE ACTIVITY
Important Dates in Voting Rights

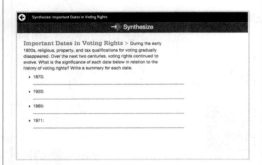

Have students use the Think Pair Share strategy to complete the activity. Ask them to take five minutes to write down some brief answers to the questions below, then share their answers with a talking partner.

Have partners think about the following question. How have voting rights changed? Have pairs share their answers with the class.

Discuss Ask students to think about the most important change to voting rights and discuss with a partner why they think as they do.

■ DEMONSTRATE

DIGITAL QUIZ
Lesson Quiz and Discussion Board

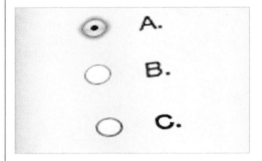

Assign the online Lesson Quiz for this lesson if you haven't already done so. Students will be offered automatic remediation or enrichment based on their score.

In "The History of Voting Rights" you read about how America has changed the Constitution in an effort to expand and clarify voting rights.

Pose these questions to the class on the Discussion Board:

Analyze How have individual actions influenced changes to expand voting rights?

Draw Conclusions How have the Voting Rights Acts supported the goal of the 15th Amendment?

Topic Inquiry

Have students continue their investigations for the Topic Inquiry.

Your Right to Vote

Supporting English Language Learners

Use with Digital Text 3, **The Voter Registration Process.**

Learning Strategies
Guide students to understand the voter registration process and the criteria for voting in elections by focusing on the lesson vocabulary words, including *registration, purging,* and *poll books.* Have students complete a concept map to help them acquire this vocabulary.

Beginning After discussing each word, have students complete a concept map for each, with the word in the center of the map. Around the word, students should draw an illustration that reflects its meaning and also write a definition in their own words.

Intermediate Guide students to complete a concept map by drawing illustrations and writing simple phrases for each word. Have them share their work with a classmate.

Advanced Have partners complete a concept map for each word. Concept maps should include the word, the definition, a sentence using the word, and a synonym or example.

Advanced High Guide students to complete a concept map using all the words. Concept maps should include the word, the definition, a synonym or example, and sentences that use two or more words each.

Use with Digital Text 2, **Universal Criteria for Voting.**

Listening
Read aloud and discuss the sections *Citizenship Criteria, Residence Criteria,* and *Age Criteria*. Model note-taking by emphasizing the important information and writing it in an outline. Have students listen again as you reread the sections. Monitor students as they take notes to support their understanding of voting criteria.

Beginning Provide students with a note-taking outline that contains the titles of the sections. Have students listen as you model how to take notes using words or short phrases. Have students copy the notes and add additional information (single words or illustrations), as they are able.

Intermediate Using a note-taking outline, have students listen as you model how to take notes with the first section. Guide students to take notes on the remaining sections using words or short phrases.

Advanced Provide students with a note-taking outline. Guide students to listen and take notes on each section as a partner reads it aloud. Have students share their notes and switch roles before moving on to the next section.

Advanced High Provide a note-taking outline to the students. Guide students to listen and take notes on each section as a partner reads it aloud. Then have students compare their notes with students in other groups so they can add and/or delete information.

▣ Differentiate Instruction

Use the Differentiated Instruction notes throughout the lesson plan to support the varied skill sets, levels of readiness, and interests in the mixed-ability classroom.

Challenge These notes include suggestions for expanding the activity for advanced students.

On-Level These notes include suggestions for modifying the activity to address different interests or learning styles.

Extra Support These notes include ideas for providing more scaffolding or reading spuport.

Special Needs These notes provide ideas for adapting instruction to support the needs of various special needs students.

■ NOTES

Your Right to Vote

Objectives

Objective 1: Identify and explain constitutional restrictions on the States' power to set voting qualifications.

Objective 2: Understand the criteria for voting in elections.

Objective 3: Understand the voter registration process and the controversies surrounding voter registration.

Objective 4: Explain the other requirements that States use or have used as voting qualifications.

LESSON 2 ORGANIZER		PACING: APPROX. 1 PERIOD, .5 BLOCKS			
				RESOURCES	
		OBJECTIVES	PACING	Online	Print
Connect					
	DIGITAL START UP ACTIVITY **Are You Qualified to Vote?**		5 min.	●	
Investigate					
	DIGITAL TEXT 1 **Voting Qualifications and the Federal Government**	Objective 1	10 min.	●	●
	DIGITAL TEXT 2 **Universal Criteria for Voting**	Objective 2	10 min.	●	●
	INTERACTIVE CHART **Universal Voting Qualifications**		10 min.	●	
	DIGITAL TEXT 3 **The Voter Registration Process**	Objective 3	10 min.	●	●
	INTERACTIVE GALLERY **Voter ID Laws**		10 min.	●	
	DIGITAL TEXT 4 **Historical Criteria for Voting**	Objective 4	10 min.	●	●
Synthesize					
	DIGITAL SYNTHESIZE ACTIVITY **Should Voter Qualifications Exist?**		5 min.	●	
Demonstrate					
	DIGITAL QUIZ **Lesson Quiz and Discussion Board**		10 min.	●	

PEARSON
realize™
www.PearsonRealize.com

Go online to access additional resources including:
Primary Sources • Biographies • Supreme Court cases •
21st Century Skill Tutorials • Maps • Graphic Organizers.

■ CONNECT

DIGITAL START UP ACTIVITY
Are You Qualified to Vote?

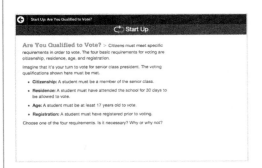

Project the Start Up Activity Ask students to answer the questions as they enter and get settled. Then have them share their opinions with another student, either in class or through a chat or blog space.

Discuss Why are there requirements for voting? *(Possible answer: to help prevent voter fraud)*

Tell students that in this lesson they will be learning about voting qualifications.

Aa Vocabulary Development: Use the Interactive Reading Notepad to preview the Key Terms and Academic Vocabulary in this Lesson with students.

> **⇅ FLIP IT!**
>
> Assign the Flipped Video for this lesson.

■ STUDENT EDITION PRINT PAGES: 432–439

■ INVESTIGATE

DIGITAL TEXT 1
Voting Qualifications and the Federal Government

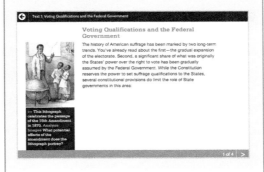

Objective 1: Identify and explain constitutional restrictions on the States' power to set voting qualifications.

Quick Instruction
The Constitution places five restrictions on the ability of the States to set suffrage qualifications. Review these five limitations and then ask students to evaluate these constitutional provisions in terms of how they limit the role of government.

> **ELL** Use the ELL activity described in the ELL chart.

Further Instruction
Editable Presentation Use the Editable Presentation to present the main ideas for this Core Reading.

Voting Qualifications and the Federal Government: Core Reading and Interactive Reading Notepad Project and discuss the Interactive Reading Notepad questions.

Make Connections How does the Equal Protection Clause apply to the States and their voting rules? *(No voting rule can violate the Equal Protection Clause; all people should have the equal opportunity to vote, with a few exceptions.)*

DIGITAL TEXT 2
Universal Criteria for Voting

Objective 2: Understand the criteria for voting in elections.

Quick Instruction
There are three criteria for voting: voters must be citizens; voters must be residents of the State or community in which they would like to cast a ballot; and voters must be older than 18. States differ in how they set the terms for the first two, but are constitutionally mandated not to set the minimum age higher than 18.

Interactive Chart: Universal Voting Qualifications Project the graphic organizer and ensure that students understand how to fill in the organizer.

> **🗒 ACTIVE CLASSROOM**
>
> Using a Sticky Note strategy, have students complete the organizer. Discuss the different universal voting qualifications.

D Differentiate: Extra Support What are the three factors on which a person's ability to vote is based? *(citizenship, residency, age)*

> **ELL** Use the ELL activity described in the ELL chart.

Further Instruction
Editable Presentation Use the Editable Presentation to present the main ideas for this Core Reading.

Your Right to Vote

Universal Voting Qualifications

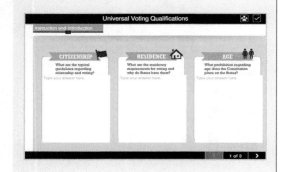

The Voter Registration Process

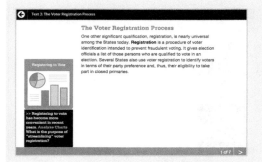

Voter ID Laws

Universal Criteria for Voting: Core Reading and Interactive Reading Notepad Project and discuss the Interactive Reading Notepad questions. Students should understand that the States have different criteria for voting, but that all requirements are overseen by the Federal Government to ensure they don't run afoul of the Constitution. Discuss *Dunn* v. *Blumstein* 1972, in which the Supreme Court found that a residency requirement of longer than 30 days discriminated against residents. Explain changes in American culture brought about by government policies, such as the effect of larger numbers of people having a voice in government due to shortened residency requirements (leading to more people registering and voting) and the adoption of the 26th Amendment.

Draw Conclusions Why might western States have encouraged voting by people who had applied for citizenship? *(They wanted to encourage more people to settle in their States.)*

Check Understanding Give examples of the processes used by individuals to affect public policy regarding the voting age. *(Possible answer: Individuals lobbied members of Congress, conducted State-by-State grassroots campaigns, and held marches and demonstrations across the country in order to bring about the passage of the 26th Amendment, which lowered the voting age to 18.)*

Objective 3: **Understand the voter registration process and the controversies surrounding voter registration.**

Quick Instruction

Registration is a nearly universal requirement for voting. Ask students to describe the typical voter registration process. *(Possible answer: Typically, a prospective voter must register his or her name, age, place of birth, present address, length of residence, and similar facts. The information is logged by a local official, usually a registrar of elections or the county clerk. A person can register to vote by mail, while getting a driver's license, and at many events, such as concerts, fairs, and shopping centers.)*

Interactive Gallery: Voter ID Laws Project and step through the gallery with students. Look at each image individually and then the collection of images as a whole.

📹 ACTIVE CLASSROOM

Have students form an Opinion Line to answer the following question: Should voters have to prove their identity with a photo ID before they vote? Why or why not? *(Possible answer: No, it can discriminate against certain populations, and there is no voting fraud that it will prevent.)*

D Differentiate: **Challenge** Have students research the different kinds of voter ID presented in the gallery. Create a graphic organizer that compares the different state requirements.

ELL Use the ELL activity described in the ELL chart.

Further Instruction

Editable Presentation Use the Editable Presentation to present the main ideas for this Core Reading.

The Voter Registration Process: Core Reading and Interactive Reading Notepad Project and discuss the Interactive Reading Notepad questions. Discuss controversies surrounding the voter registration process, such as how to increase registration while preventing voter fraud.

Check Understanding Why do some critics think the United States should not have any registration requirements? *(They think the requirements prevent people from voting. In other countries, voter registration is the law and thus voter turnout is much higher in those places.)*

Draw Conclusions What makes the Motor Voter Law successful in terms of registration? *(Possible answer: It makes it easier for people to sign up to vote. It also provides for a way to keep voting rolls current.)*

SYNTHESIZE

DEMONSTRATE

DIGITAL TEXT 4
Historical Criteria for Voting

DIGITAL SYNTHESIZE ACTIVITY
Should Voter Qualifications Exist?

DIGITAL QUIZ
Lesson Quiz and Discussion Board

Objective 4: Explain the other requirements that States use or have used as voting qualifications.

Quick Instruction
Ask students to identify historical voting criteria that discriminated against a particular group and the group against which it discriminated. Then have them evaluate the following government actions or court decisions in terms of their effect on African Americans: the congressional ban on literacy tests, the Supreme Court ruling in *Oregon* v. *Mitchell* and *Harper* v. *Virginia Board of Education*, and the 24th Amendment.

Further Instruction
Editable Presentation Use the Editable Presentation to present the main ideas for this Core Reading.

Historical Criteria for Voting: Core Reading and Interactive Reading Notepad Project and discuss the Interactive Reading Notepad questions.

24th Amendment Read this amendment with commentary with students. Discuss Justice William O. Douglas's opinion: "Once the franchise is granted to the electorate, lines may not be drawn which are inconsistent with the Equal Protection Clause. . . . Voter qualifications have no relation to wealth nor to paying this or any other tax. . . . Wealth, like race, creed, or color, is not germane to one's ability to participate intelligently in the electoral process."

Draw Conclusions Why do States disenfranchise some voters? *(Possible answer: They feel that it is in the States' best interest to prevent certain people from voting.)*

Have students use the Think Pair Share strategy to complete the activity. Ask them to take five minutes to write down some brief answers to the questions below, then share their answers with a talking partner.

Have partners think about the following questions. How have voting rights changed? How are the States involved in creating qualifications and rules for voting? Have pairs share their answers with the class.

Discuss Ask students to discuss the balance between State and federal power in the voting process.

Assign the online Lesson Quiz for this lesson if you haven't already done so. Students will be offered automatic remediation or enrichment based on their score.

In "Your Right to Vote" you read about the criteria for voting: age, citizenship, and residency. The States set their own rules about voting, but they must ensure that the laws and procedures for voting that they write do not run counter to the Constitution and court rulings about voting.

Make Judgments What changes in American culture were the likely result of changes in government policies concerning voting rights? *(Possible answer: Changes in government voting rights policies led to a gradual increase in the size and diversity of the American electorate. This might have affected American culture in many ways as these newly enfranchised voters began to have a voice in public policy decisions.)*

Make Connections Evaluate each of the following constitutional provisions in terms of how much they limit the role of government in the area of voting rights: Article I, Section 2, Clause 1; the 15th, 19th, 24th, and 26th Amendments. *(Students can mention any of the following: Article I, Section 2, Clause 1; the 15th, 19th, 24th, and 26th Amendments; all of these provisions places significant limits on the government's ability to restrict voting rights and the passage of each amendment resulted in a major increase in the size of the electorate.)*

Topic Inquiry
Have students continue their investigations for the Topic Inquiry.

Voting Trends

Supporting English Language Learners

Use with the lesson 3 readings.

Speaking
Discuss the lesson vocabulary words in order to support students' understanding of the factors that influence an individual's political attitudes and actions.Provide opportunities for students to pronounce these words.

Beginning Read aloud and discuss each vocabulary word. Provide images to support understanding. Model correct pronunciation of each word and have students repeat.

Intermediate After reading aloud and discussing each word, highlight the words with -tion. Have students look for and read other words with -tion. Model correct pronunciation for all the vocabulary words and have students repeat.

Advanced Have partners read the words and their definitions. Ask them to identify words that have similar sounds or spellings. Model correct pronunciation as needed.

Advanced High Have students write sentences for each word and read them to a classmate. Ask them to identify words that have similar sounds or spellings. Have students help each other with pronunciation.

Use with Digital Text 3, **Influences on Voters and Voting Behavior.**

Learning Strategies
List on the board the following factors that influence an individual's political attitudes and actions: income, occupation, education, gender, age, religion, ethnic background, geography, family, party identification, candidates, and issues. As a class, create a list of synonyms and related words for these factors. This list can serve as a reference as students use synonyms to answer questions.

Beginning Guide students to use the list as they answer questions such as *What is age? What is a co-worker?* Encourage students to use synonyms in their one- or two-word responses.

Intermediate Have students refer to the list as they answer questions such as *What is another way to say occupation? What are some examples of religion?* Encourage students to use synonyms in their short-sentence responses.

Advanced Ask students questions such as *What are a voter's personal characteristics? What are a voter's group affiliations?* Encourage students to use synonyms for the factors as they craft full-sentence responses.

Advanced High Have students write short summaries of the factors that influence an individual's political attitudes and actions, using synonyms for the words in the list as often as possible.

▣ Differentiate Instruction

Use the Differentiated Instruction notes throughout the lesson plan to support the varied skill sets, levels of readiness, and interests in the mixed-ability classroom.

Challenge These notes include suggestions for expanding the activity for advanced students.

On-Level These notes include suggestions for modifying the activity to address different interests or learning styles.

Extra Support These notes include ideas for providing more scaffolding or reading spuport.

Special Needs These notes provide ideas for adapting instruction to support the needs of various special needs students.

▉ NOTES

Objectives

Objective 1: Examine the problem of nonvoting in the United States

Objective 2: Identify the reasons why some people do not vote and compare these attitudes to those of voters.

Objective 3: Recognize the sources of information about voter behavior.

Objective 4: Understand the factors that influence an individual's political attitudes and actions, including voting and voter behavior.

LESSON 3 ORGANIZER		PACING: APPROX. 1 PERIOD, .5 BLOCKS			
				RESOURCES	
		OBJECTIVES	**PACING**	**Online**	**Print**
Connect					
DIGITAL START UP ACTIVITY **What is Voter Apathy?**			5 min.	●	
Investigate					
DIGITAL TEXT 1 **Voter Turnout in the United States**		Objective 1	10 min.	●	●
DIGITAL TEXT 2 **Why People Do Not Vote**		Objective 2	10 min.	●	●
INTERACTIVE CHART **Voter Behavior Key Terms**			10 min.	●	
DIGITAL TEXT 3 **Influences on Voters and Voting Behavior**		Objective 3	10 min.	●	●
DIGITAL TEXT 4 **Sociological Factors and Political Attitudes**		Objective 4	10 min.	●	●
INTERACTIVE GRAPH **Party Identification—Then and Now**			10 min.	●	
DIGITAL TEXT 5 **Psychological Factors and Political Attitudes**			10 min.	●	●
Synthesize					
DIGITAL SYNTHESIZE ACTIVITY **Graphing Voter Turnout**			5 min.	●	
Demonstrate					
DIGITAL QUIZ **Lesson Quiz and Discussion Board**			10 min.	●	

Voting Trends

▊ CONNECT

DIGITAL START UP ACTIVITY
What Is Voter Apathy?

Project the Start Up Activity As students enter and get settled, ask them to study the cartoon and write down the message they think the cartoonist is trying to convey. Then have them share their ideas with another student, either in class or through a chat or blog space.

Discuss Why is voting considered an important responsibility of citizenship in a democracy? *(Possible answer: Democracy is based on the will of the people, and one way citizens express their will is through the ballot box.)*

Tell students that in this lesson they will be learning about voting trends.

Aa Vocabulary Development: Use the Interactive Reading Notepad to preview the Key Terms and Academic Vocabulary in this Lesson with students.

⇅ FLIP IT!
Assign the Flipped Video for this lesson.

▊ STUDENT EDITION PRINT PAGES: 440–449

▊ INVESTIGATE

DIGITAL TEXT 1
Voter Turnout in the United States

Objective 1: Examine the problem of nonvoting in the United States.

Quick Instruction
Explain that voting is one of the responsibilities of citizenship and is one of the processes used by individuals to affect public policy. By helping to choose public officials and decide ballot questions, citizens can have a real impact on public policy. By choosing not to do so, citizens abdicate their say in government to others. Point out that off-year elections and presidential elections have very different turn-out numbers. More people vote for the most publicized races than those that follow further down the ballot.

ELL Use the ELL activity described in the ELL chart.

Further Instruction
Editable Presentation Use the Editable Presentation to present the main ideas for this Core Reading.

Voter Turnout in the United States: Core Reading and Interactive Reading Notepad Project and discuss the Interactive Reading Notepad questions.

Make Predictions What might the government do to increase voter turnout? *(Possible answer: Mailing a ballot to every voter might increase turnout.)*

DIGITAL TEXT 2
Why People Do Not Vote

Objective 2: Identify the reasons why some people do not vote and compare these attitudes to those of voters.

Quick Instruction
Interactive Graphic Organizer: Voter Behavior Key Terms Review the key terms with students to identify those that describe factors that influence an individual's political attitudes and actions. Which factors do individuals have control over?

▊ ACTIVE CLASSROOM
Have students use a Write 1 Get 3 strategy to complete the activity. Ask the following question: What are four key characteristics of a voter? Have students take a piece of paper and fold it into quarters, write down one response in the first box, and then go around the room asking to hear other responses. If you think a response is correct, write it in one of your boxes until you have three more responses on your page. Share responses with class.

D Differentiate: Extra Support Step through the options with students and have them explain what is meant by each definition. Then as they complete the activity, have them ask themselves how that category might impact voting.

INTERACTIVE CHART

Voter Behavior Key Terms

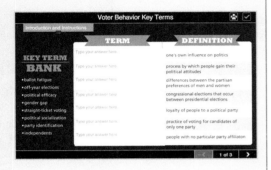

DIGITAL TEXT 3

Influences on Voters and Voting Behavior

DIGITAL TEXT 4

Sociological Factors and Political Attitudes

ELL Use the ELL activity described in the ELL chart.

Further Instruction

Editable Presentation Use the Editable Presentation to present the main ideas for this Core Reading.

Why People Do Not Vote: Core Reading and Interactive Reading Notepad Project and discuss the Interactive Reading Notepad questions. Students should be able to compare voters and nonvoters and understand that there are often several reasons why people make the choice not to vote.

Draw Conclusions Candidates running for office are often judged on their local voting records. For example, how many times they have turned out to the polls in federal or municipal elections? What might this prove? *(Voting is a responsiblity of citizenship. Showing that you've voted demonstrates a belief in democracy.)*

Compare How are voters different from non-voters? *(Possible answer: Voters tend to have higher levels of income and education, believe that voting is important, and have a strong party connection.)*

Make Predictions Once you turn 18, how might you stay informed about upcoming elections so that you can participate in as many as possible? *(Follow the news; connect with a political party or a local government organization.)*

Objective 3: Recognize the sources of information about voter behavior.

Quick Instruction

Most of what is known about voter behavior comes from three sources: the results of particular elections, especially how certain groups of people vote; the field of survey research, completed through polling public opinion; and studies of political socialization, or the process by which people gain their political attitudes and opinions.

ELL Use the ELL activity described in the ELL chart.

Further Instruction

Editable Presentation Use the Editable Presentation to present the main ideas for this Core Reading.

Influencing Voters and Voting Behavior: Core Reading and Interactive Reading Notepad Project and discuss the Interactive Reading Notepad questions.

Explain What are the sources of information about voter behavior? *(scientific polls, election results, and studies of political socialization)*

Objective 4: Understand the factors that influence an individual's political attitudes and actions, including voting and voter behavior.

Quick Instruction

Review the following factors that influence an individual's political attitudes and actions: income, occupation, education, gender, age, religion, ethnic background, geography, family, party identification, candidates, and issues. Point out to students that these factors are complex and interrelated. Being aware of them can help students in the future as they make their choices at the polls. For example, the knowledge that geography or co-workers can influence one's voting behavior allows individuals to evaluate their choices in that light: Are they voting based on their own values, or the values of those around them?

⚑ ACTIVE CLASSROOM

Use a Making Headline strategy as students complete the activity. Have students write a headline that captures the information in the graph. Ask: If you were to write a headline for this topic that captured the most important aspect that should be remembered, what would that headline be? Pass your headline to a partner for them to review—they can keep yours or ask for theirs back. Encourage students to make their headline address a generalization supported by both graphs.

Voting Trends

INTERACTIVE GRAPH

Party Identification— Then and Now

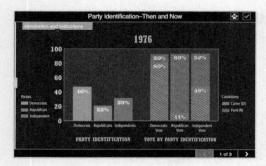

DIGITAL TEXT 5

Psychological Factors and Political Attitudes

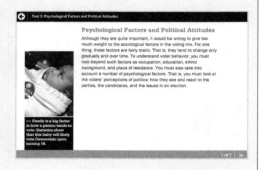

D Differentiate: Extra Support Ask questions to encourage students to make generalizations about the graphs before completing the activity. Help students understand that the number of people identifying themselves as independents differs between the two graphs.

ELL Use the ELL activity described in the ELL chart.

Further Instruction

Editable Presentation Use the Editable Presentation to present the main ideas for this Core Reading.

Sociological Factors and Political Attitudes: Core Reading and Interactive Reading Notepad Project and discuss the Interactive Reading Notepad questions. Discuss how population shifts affect voting patterns. For example, older Americans moving to the Sunbelt have given a slight advantage to Republicans in some States. African Americans migrating north in search of work in the nineteenth century changed the voting patterns in those communities.

Psychological Factors and Political Attitudes: Core Reading and Interactive Reading Notepad Project and discuss the Interactive Reading Notepad questions. Students should understand that party identification is a major factor influencing voter behavior.

Make Predictions How might political parties react to more people becoming independents? *(Parties might reach out to these voters by finding out what their concerns are and attempting to address them.)*

Make Judgments What do you think should be the most important factor when deciding which candidate to support in an election? *(Possible answer: the candidate's position on particular issues)*

SYNTHESIZE

DIGITAL SYNTHESIZE ACTIVITY

Graphing Voter Turnout

Have students create visual representations of the information provided. Ask volunteers to share their work with the class. If time allows, provide a similar activity that has students transfer written information into a graphic showing how sociological and psychological factors influence voting. Then, have partners think about the following questions: What influences on voter behavior are most important? Have partners share their answers with the class.

Discuss Discuss whether or not feelings about voting have changed. Are students more likely to vote now? *(Possible answer: No, I was always going to vote.)* Which reason for not voting do you think could be changed? How? *(Possible answer: Votes don't matter. Show evidence of races where a relatively small number of votes made a difference.)*

DEMONSTRATE

DIGITAL QUIZ

Lesson Quiz and Discussion Board

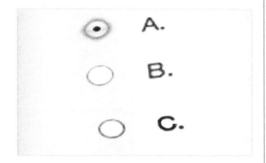

Assign the online Lesson Quiz for this lesson if you haven't already done so. Students will be offered automatic remediation or enrichment based on their score.

Pose these questions to the class on the Discussion Board:

In "Voting Trends" you read about why people vote: the sociological and psychological underpinnings of why some people tend to be voters or nonvoters.

Draw Conclusions What makes a voter? Is that a definitive list? Why? *(Possible answer: There are many reasons a person is a voter, though they are not definitive. Sometimes people are swept onto the bandwagon of voting. Generally, voters tend to be more educated, women, well integrated into their communities, and wealthier.)*

Topic Inquiry

Have students continue their investigations for the Topic Inquiry.

The Voting Process

Supporting English Language Learners

Use with Digital Text 1, **Filling Elected Public Offices.**

Speaking
Guide students to compare different methods of filling public offices at the local, State, and national levels by discussing and reading the captions of the images in the lesson. Have students retell the information in their own words.

Beginning Read aloud the captions and discuss the images in the lesson. Model how to retell what was written or discussed. Guide students to retell by using words or phrases to describe the images.

Intermediate Have students use phrases or short sentences to speak about the images.

Advanced Guide students to speak about what they learned from the captions and images by using one or more sentences.

Advanced High Have partners speak about what they learned from the images by using complex sentences in a conversation.

Use with the lesson 4 readings.

Learning Strategies
Display and discuss the following terms: *voting*, *public offices*, *election*, *polling place*, and *ballot*. Guide students as they learn examples of how individuals affect public policy by using these terms while speaking.

Beginning Provide visuals as support. Work with the group to write short sentences for each term. Have them practice reading the sentences.

Intermediate Have partners write short sentences for each term. Have them read their sentences to the group.

Advanced Guide partners to write a brief definition for each term. Have them read their definitions to the group.

Advanced High Guide students to write cloze sentences for each term. For example: *The place where voters go to vote is called a _____.* Have them read their sentences to the group for other students to provide the answers.

▶ Differentiate Instruction

Use the Differentiated Instruction notes throughout the lesson plan to support the varied skill sets, levels of readiness, and interests in the mixed-ability classroom.

Challenge These notes include suggestions for expanding the activity for advanced students.

On-Level These notes include suggestions for modifying the activity to address different interests or learning styles.

Extra Support These notes include ideas for providing more scaffolding or reading spuport.

Special Needs These notes provide ideas for adapting instruction to support the needs of various special needs students.

■ NOTES

Objectives

Objective 1: Analyze how the administration of elections in the United States helps make democracy work.

Objective 2: Compare different methods of filling public offices at the local, state, and national levels, including the role of local precincts and polling places in the election process

Objective 3: Describe the various ways in which voters can cast their ballots.

Objective 4: Outline the role that voting devices play in the election process.

LESSON 4 ORGANIZER		PACING: APPROX. 1 PERIOD, .5 BLOCKS			
		OBJECTIVES	**PACING**	**RESOURCES**	
				Online	**Print**
Connect					
	DIGITAL START UP ACTIVITY **How Many Elected Officials Are There?**		5 min.	●	
Investigate					
	DIGITAL TEXT 1 **Filling Elected Public Offices**	Objective 1	10 min.	●	●
	INTERACTIVE GALLERY ***Bush* v. *Gore***		10 min.	●	
	DIGITAL TEXT 2 **Precincts, Polling Places, and Ballots**	Objectives 2, 3	10 min.	●	●
	DIGITAL TEXT 3 **Casting and Counting Ballots**	Objective 4	10 min.	●	●
	INTERACTIVE CHART **Counting Your Vote**		10 min.	●	
Synthesize					
	DIGITAL SYNTHESIZE ACTIVITY **A Day in the Life of a Voter**		5 min.	●	
Demonstrate					
	DIGITAL QUIZ **Lesson Quiz and Discussion Board**		10 min.	●	

The Voting Process

■ CONNECT

DIGITAL START UP ACTIVITY
How Many Elected Officials Are There?

Project the Start Up Activity Ask students to answer the questions as they enter and get settled. Then have each student share his or her guess with another student, either in class or through a chat or blog space.

Discuss List examples of federal, State, and local offices. *(Possible answers: senator (State and federal), mayor, governor, judge, treasurer)* Have students share experiences of voting. If no one has an experience, share yours. Tell about the type of machine used, and the process from sign-in to ballot collection.

Tell students that in this lesson they will be learning about the process of voting.

Aa Vocabulary Development: Use the Interactive Reading Notepad to preview the Key Terms and Academic Vocabulary in this Lesson with students.

↑↓ FLIP IT!
Assign the Flipped Video for this lesson.

■ STUDENT EDITION PRINT PAGES: 450–457

■ INVESTIGATE

DIGITAL TEXT 1
Filling Elected Public Offices

Objective 1: Analyze how the administration of elections in the United States helps make democracy work.

Quick Instruction
Compare the different methods of filling public elected offices at the local, State, and national levels by reviewing the following information. Most election law in the U.S. is State, not federal, law. However, the Constitution sets broad parameters for the election of public officials, such as providing for the election of members of the House of Representatives every two years and creating and defining the electoral college. In addition, Congress sets the date for national elections, sets the policies for federal elections per the Constitution, and ensures a safe, equal, and secret elections process. At the State and local levels, States can create their own rules for elections, including allowing early or absentee voting and setting the dates on which State and local elections are held.

Interactive Gallery: *Bush* v. *Gore* — The Contested 2000 Election
Project and step through the gallery with students. After students have completed the activity, project the two quotations from Justice Kennedy and Justice Stevens.

▶ ACTIVE CLASSROOM
Using an Opinion strategy, have students agree or disagree with the two quotations. Discuss why students think as they do. Then discuss the Help America Vote Act and whether or not the act addressed the concerns expressed by the justices.

INTERACTIVE GALLERY
Bush v. *Gore*

D Differentiate: Extra Support Review the 2000 election. Students should know that there was no incumbent. Vice President Al Gore was the Democratic candidate and George W. Bush was the Republican candidate. Then complete the activity.

ELL Use the ELL activity described in the ELL chart.

Further Instruction
Editable Presentation Use the Editable Presentation to present the main ideas for this Core Reading.

Filling Elected Public Offices: Core Reading and Interactive Reading Notepad Project and discuss the Interactive Reading Notepad questions. Link the information about the Help America Vote Act and the information about *Gore* v. *Bush*. Discuss how the Federal Government impacts the filling of public offices at the State level.

Draw Conclusions Why does the Federal Government have a wide reach in overseeing elections? *(The Constitution gives specific duties to Congress. Congress has expanded the Federal Government's reach to ensure safe, equal, and secret elections.)*

DIGITAL TEXT 2

Precincts, Polling Places, and Ballots

DIGITAL TEXT 3

Casting and Counting Ballots

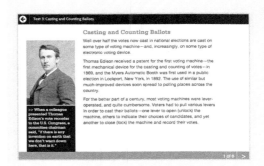

Objectives 2: Compare different methods of filling public offices at the local, state, and national levels, including the role of local precincts and polling places in the election process; 3: Describe the various ways in which voters can cast their ballots.

Quick Instruction
The filling of elected offices happens at the polls. While States use different methods of voting, they all use voting districts called precincts to make voting more orderly. A precinct is the smallest geographic unit for elections. Each precinct includes many polling places, where voters cast their ballots. State law requires that ballots be cast in secret, but they differ in other ways. Some States have paper ballots, while others have optical scanners or touch screens. States can provide sample ballots, some even mail them to each voter.

Further Instruction
Editable Presentation Use the Editable Presentation to present the main ideas for this Core Reading.

Precincts, Polling Places, and Ballots: Core Reading and Interactive Reading Notepad Project and discuss the Interactive Reading Notepad questions. Students should be able to compare the different ways that voters cast their ballots. Point out that voting is one of the hallmarks of democracy. If the process does not work smoothly, democratic government itself is threatened, because voting is one of the main ways for individuals to affect public policy and to have a voice in government.

Make Predictions Do you think voting by mail would increase voter participation? Why? *(Possible answer: Yes, because voting by mail allows voters to fill out a ballot at his or her convenience and eliminates the need to travel to a polling place.)*

Draw Conclusions Why might it be important for States or localities to determine their own election rules instead of the Federal Government handling this? *(Possible answer: States differ in what their citizens need. For example, States might need different plans for weather emergencies, or they might need to allocate precincts in a different way because of their population densities.)*

Objective 4: Outline the role that voting devices play in the election process.

Quick Instruction
Filling public elected offices, whether at the local, State, or national level, is done through elections. As they administer elections, State election officials must balance the need to do quick, accurate counting of ballots with the need to safeguard individual votes. Have students evaluate the impact of electronic technology on the political process by discussing how ballots are cast. *(Today, most ballots are cast on electronic voting devices instead of paper.)* Only two States, Washington and Oregon, have switched all ballots to mail. Some States have stopped using direct response voting machines, most use either optical scanners or paper ballots.

Interactive Chart: Counting Your Vote Step through the chart with students. Point out the various ways that votes are kept secure.

🎥 ACTIVE CLASSROOM
In groups, have students step through the flow chart. Have students use a Sticky Note strategy to answer the following question: What happens to the votes cast by voters? Have groups present their ideas.

D Differentiate: **Extra Support** Walk through each step of the flow chart with students. Clarify any term or phrase relating to the security measures taken during an election with which students are unfamiliar, such as *tamper-resistant ballot* and *certified*. Then discuss why these security measures are important in a democracy.

The Voting Process

SYNTHESIZE

DEMONSTRATE

INTERACTIVE CHART
Counting Your Vote

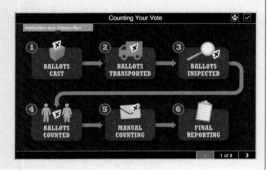

DIGITAL SYNTHESIZE ACTIVITY
A Day in the Life of a Voter

DIGITAL QUIZ
Lesson Quiz and Discussion Board

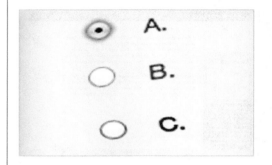

Further Instruction

Editable Presentation Use the Editable Presentation to present the main ideas for this Core Reading.

Casting and Counting Ballots: Core Reading and Interactive Reading Notepad Project and discuss the Interactive Reading Notepad questions. Point out that the overriding concerns related to the counting of ballots are fraud and protecting secrecy. Given these concerns, have students evaluate the impact of the Internet on the voting process and the reasons behind that impact. *(The impact has been minimal thus far due to concerns about the electronic infrastructure, fraud, and secrecy.)*

Compare Which ballot-casting and counting methods do you think prevent the most fraud while also increasing voter turnout? Why? *(Possible answer: hand-counted paper ballots cast in person at conveniently located polling places, because they decrease the opportunities for tampering with ballots)*

Make Predictions How might Internet technology improve the voting process in the future? *(More people might vote if ballots are available on the Internet.)*

Have students use the Think Pair Share strategy to complete the activity. Ask them to take five minutes to write down some brief answers to the questions below, then share their answers with a talking partner.

Have partners think about the following questions. What is the best way to prepare to vote? Which element of the voting process could take the longest? Why? Have pairs share their answers with the class.

Discuss Have students compare and contrast the major differences among methods for voting in the States. If they were to create a voting process for a local election, how would it work? *(Students should explain where people will vote, what kind of ballot they will use, and how the votes will be counted.)*

Assign the online Lesson Quiz for this lesson if you haven't already done so. Students will be offered automatic remediation or enrichment based on their score.

Pose these questions to the class on the Discussion Board:

In "The Voting Process" you read about how America votes, including where people vote and how ballots are counted.

Compare Compare how candidates are elected to State and federal office. What elements of elections are determined by the Constitution? *(State and federal candidates are elected in a similar way, but State elections can be held on different days than federal as determined by the States. The Constitution gives Congress the power to set the dates for federal elections.)*

Topic Inquiry

Have students continue their investigations for the Topic Inquiry.

Public Opinion and Polling

Supporting English Language Learners

Use with the readings **Family, School, and Political Attitudes** and **Other Factors That Influence Political Attitudes and Actions.**

Speaking
Help students to understand the factors that influence an individual's political attitudes and actions by discussing and reading the captions of the images in the lesson. Have students retell the information and ask them to identify whether the image is showing a political attitude or a political action.

Beginning Choose one reading in the lesson. Read aloud the captions and discuss the images in the reading. Model how to retell what was written or discussed by using words or phrases to describe the images. Then provide sentence frames in relation to each picture, such as *This picture is about _____. It represents political _____ [attitude/action].*

Intermediate Have students use phrases or short sentences to retell the information in the image captions. Then have them review the images and identify whether each is showing a political attitude or a political action.

Advanced Guide students to use one or more sentences to retell the information in the image captions, including identifying whether each is showing a political attitude or a political action.

Advanced High Have partners use complex sentences to retell the information in the image captions, including identifying whether each is showing a political attitude or a political action.

Use with the lesson 5 readings.

Learning Strategies
Display and discuss the following terms: *public opinion, polling, peer group, mass media,* and *sample.* Guide students to use these terms in their writing in order to understand the factors that influence an individual's political attitudes and actions.

Beginning Provide visuals as support. Work with the group to write short sentences for each term. Have each student copy the sentences and practice reading them.

Intermediate Have partners write short sentences for each term. Have them read their sentences to the group.

Advanced Guide partners to write a brief definition for each term. Have them read their definitions to the group.

Advanced High Guide students to write cloze sentences for each term. For example: *Television and radio are examples of _____.* Have them read their sentences to the group for other students to provide the answers.

▣ Differentiate Instruction

Use the Differentiated Instruction notes throughout the lesson plan to support the varied skill sets, levels of readiness, and interests in the mixed-ability classroom.

Challenge These notes include suggestions for expanding the activity for advanced students.

On-Level These notes include suggestions for modifying the activity to address different interests or learning styles.

Extra Support These notes include ideas for providing more scaffolding or reading spuport.

Special Needs These notes provide ideas for adapting instruction to support the needs of various special needs students.

■ NOTES

Public Opinion and Polling

Objectives

Objective 1: Examine the term *public opinion* and understand why it is so difficult to define.

Objective 2: Understand the factors that influence an individual's political attitudes and actions.

Objective 3: Recognize how polls are used by individuals, political parties, interest groups, or the media to affect public policy and describe the challenges involved in measuring public opinion.

Objective 4: Identify the steps in the polling process, evaluate the role of the Internet and other electronic information on the polling process, and understand the challenges involved in evaluating polls.

Objective 5: Recognize the limits on the impact of public opinion in a democracy.

LESSON 5 ORGANIZER				PACING: APPROX. 1 PERIOD, .5 BLOCKS	
				RESOURCES	
		OBJECTIVES	PACING	Online	Print
Connect					
DIGITAL START UP ACTIVITY **According to a Recent Survey . . .**			5 min.	●	
Investigate					
DIGITAL TEXT 1 **What Is Public Opinion?**		Objective 1	10 min.	●	●
DIGITAL TEXT 2 **Family, School, and Political Attitudes**		Objective 2	10 min.	●	●
DIGITAL TEXT 3 **Other Factors That Influence Political Attitudes and Actions**			10 min.	●	●
DIGITAL TEXT 4 **Ways to Measure Public Opinion**		Objective 3	10 min.	●	●
DIGITAL TEXT 5 **Public Opinion Polls**			10 min.	●	●
INTERACTIVE GALLERY **George Gallup, Pioneer Pollster**			10 min.	●	
DIGITAL TEXT 6 **How Polls Are Designed and Administered**		Objectives 4, 5	10 min.	●	●
INTERACTIVE GRAPH **The Politics of Public Opinion**			10 min.	●	
DIGITAL TEXT 7 **Poll Reliability**			10 min.	●	●
Synthesize					
DIGITAL SYNTHESIZE ACTIVITY **Evaluating Polls**			5 min.	●	
Demonstrate					
DIGITAL QUIZ **Lesson Quiz and Discussion Board**			10 min.	●	

PEARSON
realize.™
www.PearsonRealize.com

Go online to access additional resources including:
Primary Sources • Biographies • Supreme Court cases •
21st Century Skill Tutorials • Maps • Graphic Organizers.

■ CONNECT

According to a Recent Survey . . .

Project the Start Up Activity Ask students to answer the questions as they enter and get settled. Then have them share their ideas with another student, either in class or through a chat or blog space.

Discuss Discuss polls students have taken. Ask: Was the poll reliable? Why or why not? *(Students might talk about online polls, which are not reliable because people can vote more than once, or phone polls, which are more reliable because they represent a random sample.)*

Tell students that in this lesson they will be learning about public opinion and the ways it is measured.

Aa Vocabulary Development: Use the Interactive Reading Notepad to preview the Key Terms and Academic Vocabulary in this Lesson with students.

⇅ FLIP IT!

Assign the Flipped Video for this lesson.

■ STUDENT EDITION PRINT PAGES: 458–470

■ INVESTIGATE

What Is Public Opinion?

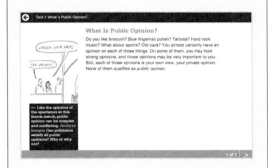

Objective 1: Examine the term *public opinion* and understand why it is so difficult to define.

Quick Instruction
Public opinion can be described this way: those attitudes held by a significant number of people on matters of government and politics. Public opinion is made up of expressed group attitudes. A view must be expressed in order to be an opinion in the public sense.

ELL Use the ELL activity described in the ELL chart.

Further Instruction
Editable Presentation Use the Editable Presentation to present the main ideas for this Core Reading.

What Is Public Opinion?: Core Reading and Interactive Reading Notepad Project and discuss the Interactive Reading Notepad questions.

Draw Conclusions Why is whether or not someone likes broccoli NOT a public opinion? *(It applies only to one person and does not have a bearing on government or politics.)*

Make Inferences Why is public opinion so difficult to define? *(There are many different opinions that people have, though not all are expressed in a public venue, shared by a lot of people, or related to government or politics.)*

Family, School, and Political Attitudes

Objective 2: Understand the factors that influence an individual's political attitudes and actions.

Quick Instruction
The factors that influence an individual's political attitudes are gleaned from his or her surroundings. Early on, parents and family members influence political attitudes. School and other group interactions can cement or change these early influences. These factors influence political actions later in life, such as which candidates or political party a voter supports and whether or not they become involved in public affairs. Additionally, pundits and the mass media try to influence public opinion (and thus affect public policy) by presenting information in a particular way or offering opinions on public policy issues.

ELL Use the ELL activity described in the ELL chart.

Further Instruction
Editable Presentation Use the Editable Presentation to present the main ideas for these Core Readings.

Family, School, and Political Attitudes and Other Factors That Influence Political Attitudes and Actions: Core Reading and Interactive Reading Notepad Project and discuss the Interactive Reading Notepad questions. Students should understand that the factors that influence a person's political attitudes are not set in stone and may change as people acquire new information.

Public Opinion and Polling

DIGITAL TEXT 3

Other Factors That Influence Political Attitudes and Actions

DIGITAL TEXT 4

Ways to Measure Public Opinion

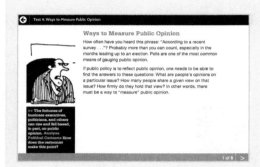

DIGITAL TEXT 5

Public Opinion Polls

Make Predictions How might the Great Recession of 2007–2009 change political attitudes for those who grew up during that time? *(Possible answer: The economic downturn and government response may influence individuals' attitudes about whether and how much the government should be involved in the economy.)*

Draw Conclusions How might reciting the Pledge of Allegiance at school influence political attitudes? *(It teaches students the values of the American political system.)*

Objective 3: Recognize how polls are used by individuals, political parties, interest groups, or the media to affect public policy and describe the challenges involved in measuring public opinion.

Quick Instruction

In a democracy, understanding public opinion is key to governing. Polls are the most accurate means we have to measure the general shape of public opinion on an issue. Polls are then often used by candidates running for office, political parties, interest groups, and the media to affect public policy. The most accurate polls are based on scientific polling techniques.

Interactive Gallery: George Gallup, Pioneer Pollster Project and step through the gallery with students.

⚏ ACTIVE CLASSROOM

Use a Conversation with History strategy to imagine that you are having a conversation with George Gallup. Write down a question you'd like to ask, then what that person would say to you, and what you would say in response. Share your ideas with the class and create a class interview.

D **Differentiate: Challenge** Have students look at primary source material available online about Gallup, including interviews with his son, George Gallup, Jr., and his biographers. Use this information to prepare an interview about how Gallup introduced polling into different areas of life, such as the movies or youth studies.

ELL Use the ELL activity described in the ELL chart.

Further Instruction

Editable Presentation Use the Editable Presentation to present the main ideas for these Core Readings.

Ways to Measure Public Opinion: Core Reading and Interactive Reading Notepad Project and discuss the Interactive Reading Notepad questions. Students should understand that polls are used by political parties, interest groups, and the media to both identify public opinion and to affect public policy. Before relying on a particular poll, groups should first determine how many people are represented by a particular political opinion and how strongly that opinion is held. To illustrate this point, ask students if they have every heard the phrase, "According to a recent poll"? Point out that candidates for office, political parties, interest groups, and the media have all used this strategy to convince people to support a particular public policy.

INTERACTIVE GALLERY

George Gallup, Pioneer Pollster

Public Opinion Polls: Core Reading and Interactive Reading Notepad Project and discuss the Interactive Reading Notepad questions. Students should understand the difference between straw polls and scientific polling. Polls today are often done by news organizations using the scientific methods developed by pollsters.

Make Inferences Why is it better to call an election a "direction" for public policy rather than a mandate? *(People cast ballots for a candidate for a wide variety of reasons.)*

Draw Conclusions Why are straw poll results not reliable as a survey of public opinion? *(They are self-selected and do not inherently represent a cross-section of the country.)*

DIGITAL TEXT 6

How Polls Are Designed and Administered

Objectives 4: Identify the steps in the polling process, evaluate the role of the Internet and other electronic information on the polling process, and understand the challenges involved in evaluating polls;
5: Recognize the limits on the impact of public opinion in a democracy.

Quick Instruction

Interactive Graph: The Politics of Public Opinion Project the graph and click through the hot spots with students. Introduce the activity by telling students that scientific poll-taking is an extremely complex process that can best be described in five basic steps. Pollsters must (1) define the universe to be surveyed; (2) construct a sample; (3) prepare valid questions; (4) select and control how the poll will be taken; and (5) analyze and report their findings to the public.

> **📷 ACTIVE CLASSROOM**
>
> Using a Sticky Note strategy, have students determine how a poll might have helped affect public policy. Then have them use the information to create a generalization about the limits of the impact of public opinion in a democracy. Share generalizations and have students explain the data they used to arrive at their generalizations.

INTERACTIVE GRAPH

The Politics of Public Opinion

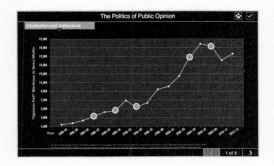

D Differentiate: Extra Support Ask: What makes a valid public opinion? What are the five steps of polling?

ELL Use the ELL activity described in the ELL chart.

Further Instruction

Editable Presentation Use the Editable Presentation to present the main ideas for these Core Readings.

How Polls are Designed and Administered: Core Reading and Interactive Reading Notepad Project and discuss the Interactive Reading Notepad questions. Evaluate with students how cell phone use has impacted polling and the difficulties that cell phones have created for pollsters.

Poll Reliability: Core Reading and Interactive Reading Notepad Project and discuss the Interactive Reading Notepad questions. The "bandwagon effect" is the tendency of people to want to agree with the most popular opinion. This is used in advertising to great effect, but when conducting a scientific poll, it can skew results.

Public Opinion and Polling

SYNTHESIZE

DEMONSTRATE

DIGITAL TEXT 7
Poll Reliability

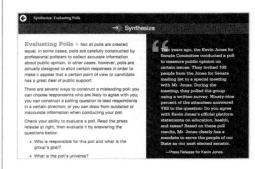

DIGITAL SYNTHESIZE ACTIVITY
Evaluating Polls

DIGITAL QUIZ
Lesson Quiz and Discussion Board

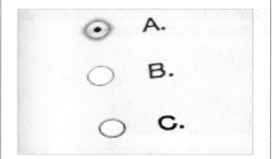

Analyze Information Remind students that Internet polls are usually not random, and thus their reliability is compromised. Ask: How might Internet polls be changed to address this problem? Explain your thinking. *(Possible answer: Currently, there is no widely available database of email addresses. People give their addresses to specific organizations, with whom they generally agree. By creating a database of emails similar to telephone directories, pollsters would be able to choose their samples to be both random and geographically balanced.)*

Have students use the Think Pair Share strategy to complete the activity. Ask them to take five minutes to write down the best practices for creating a poll, then share their answers with a talking partner.

Discuss Ask students to reflect on their political attitudes. What elements of their lives influenced how they think about particular politial topics? *(Students might discuss their family history, encounters with government, club memberships, etc. as they explain how they have been influenced about political topics. You might want to guide the discussion with particular topics that might be of interest to your students, or recently in the news.)*

Assign the online Lesson Quiz for this lesson if you haven't already done so. Students will be offered automatic remediation or enrichment based on their score.

Pose these questions to the class on the Discussion Board:

In "Public Opinion and Polling" you read about the definition of public opinion and how it is determined. You learned the elements of a scientific and straw polls.

Analyze Why is a random poll the best measure of how a large group of people think about a political policy? *(A random poll hopes to identify a representative sample, but the number of people must be large to achieve true randomness.)*

Evaluate What is the Internet's impact on polling and determining public opinion? Is this a positive or negative development? *(It is easier to reach people and poll them. However, the polls are not random because people self-select the sites they visit.)*

Topic Inquiry
Have students continue their investigations for the Topic Inquiry

Influencing Public Opinion: The Mass Media

Supporting English Language Learners

Use with Digital Text 1, **The Role of Mass Media.**

Speaking
Read the text, then have students use the information to discuss the similarities and differences among various types of media. Elicit or review words and phrases that are commonly used to compare and contrast, such as *both, similar, alike, different, but, however, compared to,* and *in contrast.* Help students to use these routine words as they discuss the role of the mass media.

Beginning Have beginning students use the following sentence frames in their discussion: *Both television and newspapers _____. Newspapers _____, but radio _____.*

Intermediate Have intermediate students discuss the similarities and differences of different types of media in a small group. They should use complete sentences and at least one of the words or phrases of comparison and contrast as they speak.

Advanced Have students discuss the similarities and differences of different types of media in a small group. Have them use connecting words in their discussions to make more complex sentences, such as *because, and,* and *but.* Ask them also to use comparison and contrast words and phrases as they speak.

Advanced High Have students use connecting words and words and phrases used for comparison and contrast as they discuss the various forms of media with a partner. Then have each student choose two forms of media and speak to group about their similarities and differences.

Use with the lesson 6 readings.

Learning Strategies
As they read the text, guide students to analyze the impact of political changes brought about by the media. Reread sections of the text that contain academic words such as: *medium, manipulate, participation, impact, alter, communicate,* and *demonstration.* Discuss the meaning and use of these words.

Beginning Choose three academic words from the text. Discuss these words using images as support. Guide students to use the words in short phrases as they speak.

Intermediate Choose five academic words from the text. Have small groups discuss the meaning of each word, using dictionaries, if necessary. Have the students write short sentences using the words and read them to the group.

Advanced Choose at least five academic words from the text. Have partners discuss the meaning of each word, then look up the words in the dictionary. Ask partners to write questions using the words and read them to the group. Have other students use the words when answering the questions.

Advanced High Choose up to seven academic words from the text. Support students to discuss the meaning of each word, then look up the words in the dictionary. Guide students to ask the group questions using the words. Remind students to use the academic words in their answers.

▣ Differentiate Instruction

Use the Differentiated Instruction notes throughout the lesson plan to support the varied skill sets, levels of readiness, and interests in the mixed-ability classroom.

Challenge These notes include suggestions for expanding the activity for advanced students.

On-Level These notes include suggestions for modifying the activity to address different interests or learning styles.

Extra Support These notes include ideas for providing more scaffolding or reading spuport.

Special Needs These notes provide ideas for adapting instruction to support the needs of various special needs students.

■ NOTES

Influencing Public Opinion: The Mass Media

Objectives

Objective 1: Examine the role of the mass media in providing the public with political information.

Objective 2: Understand the role played by the mass media in the U.S. political system and give examples of the processes used by the media to affect public policy.

Objective 3: Analyze the impact of political changes brought about by the media, including the Internet and other electronic information, and understand the factors that limit the influence of the media on the political process.

LESSON 6 ORGANIZER		PACING: APPROX. 1 PERIOD, .5 BLOCKS			
				RESOURCES	
		OBJECTIVES	PACING	Online	Print
Connect					
DIGITAL START UP ACTIVITY **Ranking Mass Media**			5 min.	●	
Investigate					
DIGITAL TEXT 1 **The Role of Mass Media**		Objective 1	10 min.	●	●
DIGITAL TEXT 2 **How the Media Affects Politics**		Objective 2	10 min.	●	●
INTERACTIVE GALLERY **The Transformation of the Mass Media**			10 min.	●	
DIGITAL TEXT 3 **The Media's Limited Influence**		Objective 3	10 min.	●	●
INTERACTIVE ILLUSTRATION **Social Media and the 2012 Election**			10 min	●	
Synthesize					
DIGITAL SYNTHESIZE ACTIVITY **Create a Campaign Web Site**			5 min.	●	
Demonstrate					
DIGITAL QUIZ **Lesson Quiz and Discussion Board**			10 min.	●	

PEARSON
realize™
www.PearsonRealize.com

Go online to access additional resources including:
Primary Sources • Biographies • Supreme Court cases •
21st Century Skill Tutorials • Maps • Graphic Organizers.

■ CONNECT

DIGITAL START UP ACTIVITY
Ranking Mass Media

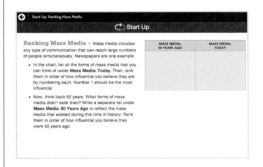

Project the Start Up Activity Ask students to complete the chart as they enter and get settled. Then have them share their ideas with another student, either in class or through a chat or blog space.

Discuss What forms of mass media do you consume regularly? *(Possible answers: television, Internet)* What forms of mass media do you use to get your news? *(Possible answers: television, Web sites)*

Tell students that in this lesson they will be learning about the various forms of mass media and how they influences the political process.

Aa **Vocabulary Development:** Use the Interactive Reading Notepad to preview the Key Terms and Academic Vocabulary in this Lesson with students.

⇑ FLIP IT!

Assign the Flipped Video for this lesson.

■ STUDENT EDITION PRINT PAGES: 471–479

■ INVESTIGATE

DIGITAL TEXT 1
The Role of Mass Media

Objective 1: Examine the role of the mass media in providing the public with political information.

Quick Instruction
Review Thomas Jefferson's comment about the importance of the press in a democracy with students, and how that viewpoint is reflected in the 1st Amendment. Point out that the mass media do not function as an arm of government in the United States. They are almost entirely privately owned and operated. Unlike political parties and interest groups, their prime goal is not that of influencing the course of public affairs. They are, nonetheless, an extremely potent force in American politics.

ELL Use the ELL activity described in the ELL chart.

Further Instruction
Editable Presentation Use the Editable Presentation to present the main ideas for this Core Reading.

The Role of Mass Media: Core Reading and Interactive Reading Notepad Project and discuss the Interactive Reading Notepad questions. Students should understand the processes used by the media to affect public policy, such as providing people with political information. Explain that consumers must be wary of bias that can influence them positively or negatively.

Identify Central Issues What is the connection between President Franklin Roosevelt and the use of the media by the government? *(President Roosevelt was the first major public figure to use the radio effectively through his fireside chats.)*

Check Understanding Identify examples of government-assisted research that has been shared with the private sector. What improved computer and communication technologies have resulted from this research? *(The Internet is an example of government-assisted (Defense Department) research that was shared with the private sector. It has resulted in the ability to send information around the world in a matter of seconds and the easy availability of an unprecedented amount of information. Social media networks have become important tools in the processes used to affect public policy, including fundraising, mobilizing supporters, uniting political activists worldwide, and humanitarian efforts.)*

Influencing Public Opinion: The Mass Media

DIGITAL TEXT 2
How the Media Affects Politics

INTERACTIVE GALLERY
The Transformation of the Mass Media

Objective 2: Understand the role played by the mass media in the U.S. political system and give examples of the processes used by the media to affect public policy.

Quick Instruction

Give examples of the processes used by the media to affect public policy, including focusing people's attention on particular issues and influencing the nation's leaders. Point out that the media is among the factors that influence an individual's political attitudes and actions. For example, media portrayal of a particular candidate can influence a person's decision at the ballot box. Similarly, media coverage of certain issues rather than others can influence an individual's decision to join a protest or contribute to a particular cause.

Interactive Gallery: Social Media and the 2012 Election Project and step through the gallery with students.

ACTIVE CLASSROOM

Using a Sticky Note strategy, have students analyze the images and write questions or comments that arise from the different images and text. Discuss the questions and comments in groups. Make generalizations about how effective social media was in the 2012 elections. Prompt with questions such as: Why might it be beneficial to candidates to use different media, even if it only appeals to a few people? What messages can be sent via social media that might not be sent via general media?

D **Differentiate: Extra Support** Introduce the 2012 elections. Ensure that students know the background: Barack Obama was the Democratic incumbant, vying for reelection against Mitt Romney, his Republican challenger. Obama was reelected for a second term.

ELL Use the ELL activity described in the ELL chart.

Further Instruction

Editable Presentation Use the Editable Presentation to present the main ideas for this Core Reading.

How the Media Affects Politics: Core Reading and Interactive Reading Notepad Project and discuss the Interactive Reading Notepad questions. Students should compare and contrast the role of the press throughout American history. What political changes might be brought about by the partisan press? What might be one impact of those changes?

Analyze Tell students that a newspaper has broken a story about improper use of political power by a particular presidential candidate. The story contributed to a push for new limits on presidential powers. Ask students to describe one possible impact of the political change brought about by the media in this case. *(Possible answer: One possible impact might be a rise in public confidence in government if the limits are perceived as necessary. Alternatively, the impact might be to limit the President's effectiveness and ability to respond to situations.)*

Make Judgments Is the echo chamber a positive or negative phenomenon? How might it influence an individual's political attitudes? *(Possible answer: It is negative because it narrows people's informational sources to only those that agree with their own ideas. This means that opposing arguments are rarely considered and individuals' political attitudes may become entrenched.)*

DIGITAL TEXT 3
The Media's Limited Influence

INTERACTIVE ILLUSTRATION
Social Media and the 2012 Election

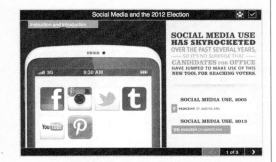

Objective 3: Analyze the impact of political changes brought about by the media, including the Internet and other electronic information, and understand the factors that limit the influence of the media on the political process.

Quick Instruction

Interactive Gallery: The Transformation of the Mass Media Project the gallery and click through the images with students. Analyze the impact of political changes brought about by the media by asking students how many of them watched the news in the past week (probably very few). Point out that this is a national trend and tends to limit the impact of the media in American politics. In addition, the fact that there are so many types of media available today also tends to limit the influence overall. Ask: Do you think this was true in the nation's early days? Why or why not? *(Possible answer: In the early days of the nation, the newspapers were the primary media and there were fewer things competing for people's attention, so the media may have had a larger impact.)*

⚎ ACTIVE CLASSROOM

Using a Ranking strategy, have students identify the most important form of media over time. Use the following general time spans: 1940s–1950s, 1960s–1970s, 1980s–1990s, 2000–today. Discuss why students decided as they did.

D Differentiate: **Extra Support** Have students do a Ranking strategy for the media they consume. Then have them generalize about how a candidate might best reach them.

ELL Use the ELL activity described in the ELL chart.

Further Instruction

Editable Presentation Use the Editable Presentation to present the main ideas for this Core Reading.

The Media's Limited Influence: Core Reading and Interactive Reading Notepad Project and discuss the Interactive Reading Notepad questions. Analyze the factors that influence an individual's political attitudes and actions. For example, people tend to consume only news with which they agree, even though 43 percent of people pay very close attention to news or choose to consume sports and entertainment over political news. Discuss how political parties or interest groups might take advantage of these tendencies.

Make Judgments Which had a larger impact on the political process—the Internet or television? Explain your reasoning. *(Possible answer: The Internet had a larger impact because it is cheap and widely available. It also has a variety of ways to connect people to politics.)*

Draw Conclusions Why is the media's impact limited if it can be widely consumed? *(People choose which media they consume, which limits its impact.)*

Influencing Public Opinion: The Mass Media

SYNTHESIZE

DEMONSTRATE

DIGITAL SYNTHESIZE ACTIVITY
Create a Campaign Web Site

DIGITAL QUIZ
Lesson Quiz and Discussion Board

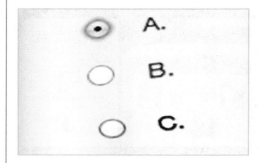

Have students complete the activity and share their Web sites with a partner. Have students critique the Web sites from the perspective of a voter.

Discuss How important is the media to the political process? Which element of mass media is most important to a political campaign? *(Possible answer: Media is very important because it is how a candidate can reach the most people. Social media is most important because it allows the candidate to react at a moment's notice and to fundraise effectively.)*

Assign the online Lesson Quiz for this lesson if you haven't already done so. Students will be offered automatic remediation or enrichment based on their scores.

Pose these questions to the class on the Discussion Board:

In "Influencing Public Opinion: The Mass Media" you read about mass media and the influence it has on the political process. In addition you compared how the media's influence has changed over time as media has changed.

Make Connections How have the media affected politics and public policy over the course of American history? Give specific examples for different kinds of media and show how the types of media influence have changed over the years. *(Possible answers: The televised presidential debates allowed Kennedy to win because he seemed more poised than Nixon. Fireside chats on the radio made FDR more popular. Political ads by interest groups have played a role in the defeat of ballot initiatives in different States.)* How important was the impact of these political changes? *(Students' should recognize that the political changes potentially have a large impact, for example, FDR might not have won another term had his popularity waned.)*

Topic Inquiry

Have students continue their investigations for the Topic Inquiry.

Understanding Interest Groups

Supporting English Language Learners

Use with Digital Text 1, **What Are Interest Groups?**

Speaking
Read the section *Interest Groups Shape Public Policy*. Have students use sentence stems while speaking about the impact of political changes brought about by interest groups.

Beginning Read aloud and discuss the section with students using images as support. Model use of sentence frames such as: _____ are _____. _____ are not _____. _____ can _____. Guide students to use sentence frames to speak about the text.

Intermediate Read aloud as students follow along in the text. Provide sentence frames such as: _____ are _____ and _____. _____ do not _____ because _____. Guide students to use sentence frames to speak about the text.

Advanced Have partners read the text. Provide sentence frames such as: *What do you think about _____? What does _____ mean? _____ and _____ are _____ because _____.* Guide partners to discuss the text using sentence frames.

Advanced High Have students read the text. Provide sentence frames such as: *What impact does _____ have on _____? What would happen if _____? How is _____ related to _____?* Guide students to discuss the text using sentence frames.

Use with Digital Text 1, **What Are Interest Groups?**

Learning Strategies
Read the section *Comparing and Contrasting Political Parties and Interest Groups*. Help students use academic words to write about the similarities and differences of political parties and interest groups. Focus on words such as: *significant, crucial, focus, scope, range,* and *functions*.

Beginning Read aloud and discuss the section. Display academic words from the text and discuss them. Have students copy the words and practice reading them.

Intermediate Read aloud as students follow along in the text. Display academic words from the text. Guide students to write short sentences using the words and read them aloud to the group.

Advanced Choose at least five academic words from the text. Have partners discuss the meaning of each word, then look up the words in the dictionary. Ask partners to write questions using the words. Have other students write the answers to the questions.

Advanced High Choose up to seven academic words from the text. Have students discuss the meaning of each word, then look up the words in the dictionary to see whether they were correct or incorrect. Guide students to write sentences using the words. Have them read their sentences to the group.

◗ Differentiate Instruction

Use the Differentiated Instruction notes throughout the lesson plan to support the varied skill sets, levels of readiness, and interests in the mixed-ability classroom.

Challenge These notes include suggestions for expanding the activity for advanced students.

On-Level These notes include suggestions for modifying the activity to address different interests or learning styles.

Extra Support These notes include ideas for providing more scaffolding or reading spuport.

Special Needs These notes provide ideas for adapting instruction to support the needs of various special needs students.

■ NOTES

Understanding Interest Groups

Objectives

Objective 1: Understand the role played by interest groups in the U.S. political system.

Objective 2: Analyze the impact of political changes brought about by interest groups and examine the viewpoints of those who see interest groups as both good and bad for American politics, including that of James Madison in the *Federalist Papers* Number 10.

Objective 3: Describe the various types of interest groups in the United States.

Objective 4: Give examples of the direct approach used by interest groups to affect public policy by influencing the legislative, executive, and judicial branches of government.

Objective 5: Examine the indirect lobbying approach and its use of grass-roots pressure, media, propaganda, and political campaigns to influence public opinion and policy.

LESSON 7 ORGANIZER		OBJECTIVES	PACING	RESOURCES	
				Online	**Print**
Connect					
DIGITAL START UP ACTIVITY **Which Interest Group Is Most Interested?**			5 min.	●	
Investigate					
DIGITAL TEXT 1 **What Are Interest Groups?**		Objective 1	10 min.	●	●
INTERACTIVE CHART **Interest Groups Lobby Congress**			10 min.	●	
DIGITAL TEXT 2 **Different Views of Interest Groups**		Objective 2	10 min.	●	●
DIGITAL TEXT 3 **Why Do Individuals Join Interest Groups?**		Objective 3	10 min.	●	●
INTERACTIVE GALLERY **Top Lobbyists and Spending**			10 min	●	
DIGITAL TEXT 4 **Processes Used by Interest Groups—The Direct Approach**		Objectives 4, 5	10 min	●	●
DIGITAL TEXT 5 **Processes Used by Interest Groups—The Indirect Approach**			10 min	●	●
Synthesize					
DIGITAL SYNTHESIZE ACTIVITY **Who, What, and Where of Lobbying**			5 min.	●	
Demonstrate					
DIGITAL QUIZ **Lesson Quiz and Discussion Board**			10 min.	●	

PEARSON
realize.™
www.PearsonRealize.com

Go online to access additional resources including:
Primary Sources • Biographies • Supreme Court cases •
21st Century Skill Tutorials • Maps • Graphic Organizers.

CONNECT

DIGITAL START UP ACTIVITY
Which Interest Group Is Most Interested?

Project the Start Up Activity Ask students to answer the questions as they enter and get settled. Then have them share their ideas with another student, either in class or through a chat or blog space.

Discuss What groups do you participate in at school and outside of it? *(Possible answers: sports, church groups, 4H, chess club)* What political influence might each of those groups have? *(Possible answers: the environment, lobbying members of Congress, land use)*

Tell students that in this lesson they will be learning about the influence of interest groups on voting.

Aa Vocabulary Development: Use the Interactive Reading Notepad to preview the Key Terms and Academic Vocabulary in this Lesson with students.

⇅ FLIP IT!
Assign the Flipped Video for this lesson.

◼ STUDENT EDITION PRINT
PAGES: 480–495

INVESTIGATE

DIGITAL TEXT 1
What Are Interest Groups?

Objective 1: Understand the role played by interest groups in the U.S. political system.

Quick Instruction
Interactive Chart: Interest Groups Lobby Congress Project the chart on the whiteboard. Introduce the activity by telling students that an interest group is a collection of people who share certain views on public matters and work to shape public policy to their benefit. They try to persuade public officials to respond to their positions favorably.

🗨 ACTIVE CLASSROOM

Post the following questions: With which public policies do interest groups concern themselves? Using a Circle Write strategy, have students work in groups to hypothesize about and analyze the impact interest groups have on public policy. For example, there has been an increase in digital product infringement due to a loophole in existing laws. As a result, Microsoft wants to change the national policy on intellectual property theft. The company forms an interest group and invests considerable amounts of money toward changing the law. The public benefits, because the new policy increases protection for the ideas and inventions of entrepreneurs in all businesses and industries.

D Differentiate: Challenge Have students think of an issue they are interested in and build a platform for their own interest group. Students can present their ideas to the class.

INTERACTIVE CHART
Interest Groups Lobby Congress

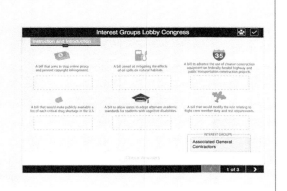

ELL Use the ELL activity described in the ELL chart.

Further Instruction
Editable Presentation Use the Editable Presentation to present the main ideas for this Core Reading.

What Are Interest Groups?: Core Reading and Interactive Reading Notepad Project and discuss the Interactive Reading Notepad questions. Students should understand the difference between interest groups and political parties: political parties nominate candidates, control government, and have an opinion on a wide-range of issues, whereas interest groups cannot nominate candidates, are interested in controlling policy, and have an opinion on a narrow range of issues.

Make Judgments Which are more powerful in the United States: interest groups or political parties? Explain your thinking. *(Possible answer: Political parties are more important because they can nominate candidates. OR Interest groups are more important because they control policy.)*

Understanding Interest Groups

DIGITAL TEXT 2
Different Views of Interest Groups

DIGITAL TEXT 3
Why Do Individuals Join Interest Groups?

Objective 2: Analyze the impact of political changes brought about by interest groups and examine the viewpoints of those who see interest groups as both good and bad for American politics, including that of James Madison in the *Federalist Papers* Number 10.

Quick Instruction
James Madison and Alexis de Tocqueville had different views of interest groups, and the split opinion continues to resonate with citizens today. Madison saw constitutional provisions for limiting the role of government, including checks and balances, as essential to controlling interest groups, or "factions," as he called them.

Further Instruction
Editable Presentation Use the Editable Presentation to present the main ideas for this Core Reading.

Different Views of Interest Groups: Core Reading and Interactive Reading Notepad Project and discuss the Interactive Reading Notepad questions. Students should understand the negative and positive aspects of interest groups.

Primary Sources In groups have students use a Sticky Note strategy to read the *Federalist Papers* Number 10. Have students write a paragraph analyzing how the essay explains a major principle of the American constitutional system of government.

Make Judgements Do you agree with Madison or de Tocqueville about interest groups? Why? *(Possible answer: De Toqueville's argument that interest groups bring people together is effective.)*

Analyze Which positive aspect of interest groups might have the most impact on the creation of policy? *(Possible answer: Interest groups can collect specific information and provide it to lawmakers.)*

Objective 3: Describe the various types of interest groups in the United States.

Quick Instruction
People join interest groups for a variety of reasons, including economics, geography, religion, or race. Interest groups can work on a local, State, or federal level. Analyze with students the following historical examples of citizen movements to bring about political change or to maintain continuity: role of business groups in the calling of the Constitution Convention in 1787 or in wining the protective tariff in the early 1800s; role of labor groups in winning a raise in the minimum wage; and the role of agricultural groups in pressing for a continuation of government crop subsidies.

Interactive Gallery: Top Lobbyists and Spending Project the gallery and step through each image with students.

⬛ ACTIVE CLASSROOM
Using a Ranking strategy, have students create a list of the most important issues they think Americans face today and rank that list by importance. Then, using a Ranking strategy, have students rank the companies listed in the Top Spenders chart according to their list of issues. Have students compare their rankings with the actual order of the companies shown in the Top Spenders chart.

INTERACTIVE GALLERY

Top Lobbyists and Spending

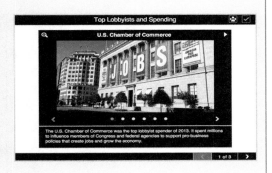

DIGITAL TEXT 4

Processes Used by Interest Groups—The Direct Approach

DIGITAL TEXT 5

Processes Used by Interest Groups—The Indirect Approach

D **Differentiate: Challenge** Have students think of an important contemporary issue they are passionate about, such as the environment. Then have them research two interest groups with different points of view related to that issue. Students should prepare a poster or presentation about the organizations and their viewpoints.

Further Instruction

Editable Presentation Use the Editable Presentation to present the main ideas for this Core Reading.

Why Do Individuals Join Interest Groups?: Core Reading and Interactive Reading Notepad Project and discuss the Interactive Reading Notepad questions. Discuss the connection between interest groups and policy. For example, unions work on economic policy, whereas the NAACP and LULAC work to eliminate barriers to equality for minorities. The NRA, on the other hand, supports gun rights for individuals.

Draw Conclusions When might two interest groups work together? Give an example. *(Possible answer: Interest groups might work together if the policy they are each trying to enact is the same. For example, a labor union might work with an environmental group to create a policy that increases manufacturing of solar energy parts.)*

Make Inferences Why might a company join an interest group instead of trying to change policy on its own? *(An interest group might have connections already, so the company can give money to promote its agenda while utilizing the infrastructure of the interest group.)*

Objectives 4: Give examples of the direct approach used by interest groups to affect public policy by influencing the legislative, executive, and judicial branches of government; 5: Examine the indirect lobbying approach and its use of grass-roots pressure, media, propaganda, and political campaigns to influence public opinion and policy.

Quick Instruction

Interest groups use both direct and indirect processes in their attempts to affect public policy. Their direct efforts involve immediate, face-to-face contacts with policymakers in the executive and legislative branches, as well as lawsuits. Their indirect efforts include letter-writing, phone calls, emails, demonstrations, and marches; helping candidates win public office; and attempts to mold public opinion through advertisements, press releases, propaganda, and the like.

Further Instruction

Editable Presentation Use the Editable Presentation to present the main ideas for these Core Readings.

Processes Used by Interest Groups— The Direct Approach: Core Reading and Interactive Reading Notepad Project and discuss the Interactive Reading Notepad questions. Students should understand that interest groups groups can lobby through the courts. Examine *Brown* v. *Board of Education* to analyze how interest groups can act to change policy through the courts and the impact of those political changes. Then ask students to think of a current example of the impact of political changes brought about by interest groups.

Processes Used by Interest Groups—The Indirect Approach: Core Reading and Interactive Reading Notepad Project and discuss the Interactive Reading Notepad questions. Students should understand the definition of grassroots lobbying and the influence of propaganda and electioneering. Evaluate the impact of the Internet and other electronic information on the way that interest groups conduct grassroots lobbying efforts, including appeals to government officials, mobilization of members, circulation of petitions, and fundraising.

Understanding Interest Groups

SYNTHESIZE

DIGITAL SYNTHESIZE ACTIVITY

Who, What, and Where of Lobbying

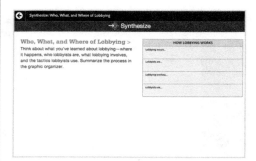

DEMONSTRATE

DIGITAL QUIZ

Lesson Quiz and Discussion Board

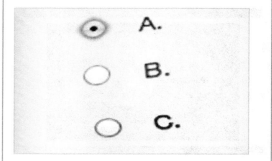

Examine Evidence Explain how direct lobbying can effect public policy. *(Possible answer: Lobbyists work with senior aides in the executive branch to effect the carrying out of legislative tasks.)*

Analyze Several laws at the federal and State level govern how much lobbyists can do in secret. They require political ads to state their funding source and lobbyists to register their name, business, and purpose. Should lobbying be regulated? *(Possible answer: No, freedom of speech is important. It is up to the individual voter to research the candidate or issue he or she will vote on and make up his or her own mind. OR Yes, people should know who or what organization is supplying their information. Requiring transparency gives the voting public a better understanding of who or what is trying to influence their point of view.)*

Ask students to recall the Topic Essential Question, "What Is the Role of the People in Government?" Have them use the Think Pair Share strategy to complete the activity. Ask them to take five minutes to write down some brief answers to the questions below, then share their answers with a talking partner.

Have partners think about the following questions. What influence do interest groups have on the political process? Is the influence generally positive or negative? Have pairs share their answers with the class.

Discuss Ask students to think about the poll they took at the beginning of this Topic. Ask if they would change any of their responses now that they have learned more about interest groups.

Assign the online Lesson Quiz for this lesson if you haven't already done so. Students will be offered automatic remediation or enrichment based on their score.

Pose these questions to the class on the Discussion Board:

In "Understanding Interest Groups" you read about the various interest groups that influence elections and how they attempt to do so.

Analyze What impact have interest groups had on the political process? What changes have they brought about? *(Possible answer: Interest groups put pressure on lawmakers to create or pass legislation on a specific topic. They have both defeated and championed legislation. They support court cases via briefs. They supported constitutional amendments and ballot initiatives.)*

Make Judgments Do you think interest groups have a positive or negative influence on the political process? *(Possible answer: They have a positive influence because they connect people and the political process around a specific issue.)*

Compare Compare the direct and indirect tactics used by interest groups. Which is more effective? *(Possible answer: Indirect is more effective because creating a group of grassroots activists allows the interest group to build a wider base.)*

Topic Inquiry

Have students continue their investigations for the Topic Inquiry.

Government by the People

SYNTHESIZE

DIGITAL ACTIVITY

Reflect on the Essential Question and Topic

First ask students to reconsider the Essential Question for the Topic: What Is the Role of the People in Government? Remind students of the roles they considered at the start of the Topic. For example:

- As voters, people help shape government and public policy.
- As consumers of mass media, people learn about issues and candidates in order to make informed decisions.
- As candidates for political office, people bring new ideas and energy to government.
- As members of interest groups, people influence the government on issues.

Have students share their instances where public opinion has made a difference and their three supporting reasons. Then ask students to give at least three reasons to support their position. Discuss their answers as a class.

Next ask students to reflect on the Topic as a whole and jot down 1–3 questions they've thought about during the Topic. Share these examples if students need help getting started:

- The Internet allows more people to participate in political discussions, but how can government leaders hear and respond to so many voices?
- What strategies could be pursued to eliminate obstacles to online voting?
- Should the government make voting mandatory?

You may ask students to share their questions and answers on the Class Discussion Board.

Topic Inquiry

Have students complete Step 3 of the Topic Inquiry.

DEMONSTRATE

DIGITAL TOPIC REVIEW AND ASSESSMENT

Government by the People

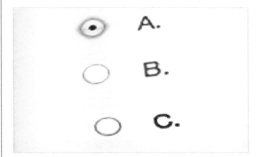

Students can prepare for the Topic Test by answering the questions in the Topic Review and Assessment online or the Assessment questions in the Print Student text. They can also prepare by reviewing their answers to the Interactive Reading Notepad questions or reviewing their notes in the Reading and Notetaking Study Guide.

DIGITAL TOPIC TEST

Government by the People

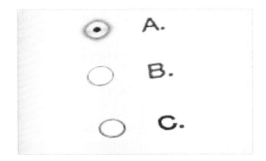

TOPIC TEST

Assign the Topic Test to assess students' understanding of topic content.

BENCHMARK TESTS

Assign these benchmark tests as you complete the relevant topics to monitor student progress toward mastering the course content and as preparation for the End-of-Course Test.

Benchmark Test 1: Topics 1–4

Benchmark Test 2: Topics 5–8

Benchmark Test 3: Topics 9–11

Benchmark Test 4: Topics 12–14

Elements

TOPIC 11 ORGANIZER	PACING: APPROX. 1 PERIOD, .5 BLOCKS	
		PACING
Connect		1 period
MY STORY VIDEO **Political Operatives and Spin Doctors**		10 min.
DIGITAL ESSENTIAL QUESTION ACTIVITY **Who Gets Elected?**		10 min.
DIGITAL OVERVIEW ACTIVITY **Who Gets Elected?**		10 min.
TOPIC INQUIRY: CIVIC DISCUSSION **The Electoral College**		20 min.
Investigate		2–4 periods
TOPIC INQUIRY: CIVIC DISCUSSION **The Electoral College**		Ongoing
LESSON 1 Political Parties and What They Do		30–40 min.
LESSON 2 Nominations		30–40 min.
LESSON 3 Electing the President		30–40 min.
LESSON 4 Money and Elections		30–40 min.
Synthesize		1 period
DIGITAL ACTIVITY **Reflect on the Essential Question and Topic**		10 min.
TOPIC INQUIRY: CIVIC DISCUSSION **The Electoral College**		20 min.
Demonstrate		1–2 periods
DIGITAL TOPIC REVIEW AND ASSESSMENT **Elections**		10 min.
TOPIC INQUIRY: CIVIC DISCUSSION **The Electoral College**		20 min.

TOPIC INQUIRY: CIVIC DISCUSSION

The Electoral College

In this Topic Inquiry, students work in teams to examine different perspectives on this issue by analyzing several sources, arguing both sides of a Yes/No question, then developing and discussing their own point of view on the question: **Should the electoral college be abolished?**

STEP 1: CONNECT
Develop Questions and Plan the Investigation

Launch the Civic Discussion

Divide the class into groups of four students. Students can access the materials they'll need in the online course or you can distribute copies to each student. Read the main question and introduction with the students.

Have students complete Step 1 by reading the Discussion Launch and filling in Step 1 of the Information Organizer. The Discussion Launch provides YES and NO arguments on the main question. Students should extract and paraphrase the arguments from the reading in Step 1 of their Information Organizers.

Next, students share within their groups the arguments and evidence they found to support the YES and NO positions. The group needs to agree on the major YES and NO points and each student should note those points in their Information Organizer.

Resources
- Student Instructions
- Discussion Launch
- Information Organizer

STEP 2: INVESTIGATE
Apply Disciplinary Concepts and Tools

Examine Sources and Perspectives

Students will examine sources with the goal of extracting information and perspectives on the main question. They analyze each source and describe the author's perspective on the main question and key evidence the author provides to support that viewpoint in Information Organizer Step 2.

Ask students to keep in mind:

- **Author/Creator:** Who created the source? An individual? Group? Government agency?
- **Audience:** For whom was the source created?
- **Date/Place:** Is there any information that reveals where and when the source was created?
- **Purpose:** Why was the source created? Discuss with students the importance of this question in identifying bias.
- **Relevance:** How does the source support one argument or another?

Suggestion: Reading the source documents and filling in Step 2 of the Information Organizer could be assigned as homework.

Resources
- Student Instructions
- Source documents
- Information Organizer

⏻ PROFESSIONAL DEVELOPMENT

Civic Discussion

Be sure to view the Civic Discussion Professional Development resources in the online course.

The Electoral College *(continued)*

STEP 3: SYNTHESIZE
Use Evidence to Formulate Conclusions

Formulate Compelling Arguments with Evidence

Now students will apply perspectives and evidence they extracted from the sources to think more deeply about the main question by first arguing one side of the issue, then the other. In this way students become more prepared to formulate an evidence-based conclusion on their own.

Within each student group, assign half of the students to take the position of YES on the main question and the others to take the position of NO. Students will work with their partners to identify the strongest arguments and evidence to support their assigned YES or NO position.

Present Yes/No Positions

Within each group, those assigned the YES position share arguments and evidence first. As the YES students speak, those assigned NO should listen carefully, take notes to fill in the rest of the Compelling Arguments Chart (Step 3 in Information Organizer) and ask clarifying questions.

When the YES side is finished, students assigned the NO position present while those assigned YES should listen, take notes, and ask clarifying questions. Examples of clarifyin questions are:

- I think you just said [x]. Am I understanding you correctly?
- Can you tell me more about [x]?
- Can you repeat [x]? I am not sure I understand, yet.

Suggestion: You may want to set a 5 minute time limit for each side to present. Provide a two-minute warning so that students make their most compelling arguments within the time frame.

Switch Sides

The students will switch sides to argue the opposite point of view. To prepare to present the other position, partners who first argued YES will use the notes they took during the NO side's presentation, plus add any additional arguments and evidence from the reading and sources. The same for students who first argued the NO position.

STEP 4: DEMONSTRATE
Communicate Conclusions and Take Informed Action

Individual Points of View

Now the students will have the opportunity to discuss the main question from their own points of view. To help students prepare for this discussion, have them reflect on the YES/NO discussions they have participated in thus far and fill in Step 4 of their Information Organizers.

After all of the students have shared their points of view, each group should list points of agreement, filling the last portion of Step 4 on their Information Organizers.

Reflect on the Discussion

Ask students to reflect on the civic discussion thinking about:

- The value of having to argue both the YES and NO positions.
- If their individual views changed over the course of the discussion and why.
- What they learned from participating in the discussion.

Resources
- Student Instructions
- Information Organizer

INTRODUCTION

Elections

Elections in the United States are controlled by several factors: the Constitution, State constitutions, and major party structures and conventions. There are different methods used to fill the many elected offices at the federal, State, and local levels, but all begin with nominations and all end with a form of election. Citizen participation through donations of time and money are important, as is becoming educated about the candidates' and parties' platforms.

■ CONNECT

MY STORY VIDEO

Political Operatives and Spin Doctors

Watch a video that introduces students to the methods that political operatives use to influence public opinion.

Assess Credibility How can you decide what to believe in political speeches? *(By trying to determine whether a speaker is giving you the whole picture or only the "good" or the "bad.")*

Draw Conclusions Do you think the work of "spin doctors" helps or harms the politcal process? *(Possible answers: It helps because it lets people listen and make their own choices. It is harmful because it can influence many people who haven't learned enough about real issues.)*

⇅ FLIP IT!

Assign the My Story Video.

DIGITAL ESSENTIAL QUESTION ACTIVITY

Who Gets Elected?

Ask students to think about the Essential Question for this Topic: Who Gets Elected? Leaders are important to ensure the government functions as it is supposed to and represents the citizens it serves. What qualities do you look for in a leader in general and why do you think each is important?

Display students' answers. Then use a Ranking Strategy to have students determine which quality is most important to them.

Support a Point of View with Evidence Why did you rate this reason as most valid? *(Answers will vary. Students should explain their thinking using what they know about leadership and qualities necessary in American democracy.)*

Generalize Think about what you know about the people in office. What qualities do they have? *(Answers will vary. Students should be able to list two or three elected officials and the qualities they share. Then they should use that evidence to create a generalization. For example, people in office may be attractive and passionate about certain issues.)*

DIGITAL OVERVIEW ACTIVITY

Who Gets Elected?

Project the image showing the Republican national convention in 2012. During this Topic, students will learn about the various factors that control and help decide elections.

D Differentiate: Challenge Have students describe the process by which George Washington was elected to office.

Discuss In deciding who will best represent their point of view, whether as a representative to Congress, a governor of a State, or the President of the United States, people look for certain qualities in their candidates. For example, is the candidate honest? Reliable? Can a candidate make good decisions under pressure? These are just a few qualities that people might take into consideration. What qualities should a candidate for political office have? Why is each quality important? *(Answers will vary. Students may list qualities such as honesty, reliability, trustworthiness, responsiveness to constituents, good fundraiser, etc. Students should have appropriate reasons for why each quality is important.)*

Political Parties and What They Do

Supporting English Language Learners

Use with Digital Text 2, **The Role of Political Parties.**

Reading
Using images as support, discuss the definition and functions of political parties at State and national levels. Model the use of different sentence lengths. Encourage students to speak using a variety of sentence lengths by completing the following activities:

Beginning Refer to the images. Write a short sentence and a longer sentence for each image. Read the sentences to the students and have them repeat. Have students copy the sentences and read them to a partner.

Intermediate Model how to make a short sentence longer by using the word *and* or adding descriptive phrases. Example: *There are signs in front of the house. There are signs from political parties in front of the house.* Have students describe the images to each other.

Advanced Have partners say a short sentence and a longer sentence for different images in the text.

Advanced High Have partners use a variety of sentence lengths to discuss images in the text and the functions of political parties.

Use with the lesson 1 readings.

Learning Strategies
To support the analysis of political changes brought about by individuals and political parties, past and present, review the list of glossary words in the text such as *political party*, *partisanship*, and *bipartisan* or choose words based on the language levels of your students. If possible, select words that can be supported by images. Guide students to use accessible words to learn these new words by completing vocabulary web graphic organizers.

Beginning Using visuals from the text as support, discuss the meaning of three to five of the new words with students. Display a short definition for each word. Help students identify the accessible words. Create a vocabulary web graphic organizer for each new word by completing it with accessible words. Example: ***bipartisan*** —*supported by* **two parties**

Intermediate Using visuals as support, discuss the meanings of the new words with students. Have partners create a vocabulary web graphic organizer for a new word. Ask them to write accessible words on the graphic organizer. Have them share their work with the class.

Advanced Have partners use the text to determine the meanings of the new words. Have them use accessible words to complete vocabulary web graphic organizers with related phrases for the new words.

Advanced High Have students use the text to determine the meanings of the new words. Have students use accessible words to write their own definitions for the words on the graphic organizer. Have them share their definitions with partners or students in the same group.

D Differentiate Instruction

Use the Differentiated Instruction notes throughout the lesson plan to support the varied skill sets, levels of readiness, and interests in the mixed-ability classroom.

Challenge These notes include suggestions for expanding the activity for advanced students.

On-Level These notes include suggestions for modifying the activity to address different interests or learning styles.

Extra Support These notes include ideas for providing more scaffolding or reading spuport.

Special Needs These notes provide ideas for adapting instruction to support the needs of various special needs students.

■ NOTES

PEARSON
realize™
www.PearsonRealize.com

Go online to access additional resources including:
Primary Sources • Biographies • Supreme Court cases •
21st Century Skill Tutorials • Maps • Graphic Organizers.

Objectives

Objective 1: Understand the origins of political parties in the United States and analyze their major functions.

Objective 2: Understand multiparty and one-party systems and how they a political system, and explain the two-party system of the United States.

Objective 3: Evaluate the role of minor parties in American politics and understand why they are important.

Objective 4: Understand why the major parties have a decentralized structure.

Objective 5: Describe the national party machinery and party organization at the State and local levels.

LESSON 1 ORGANIZER		OBJECTIVES	PACING	RESOURCES	
PACING: APPROX. 1 PERIOD, .5 BLOCKS				Online	Print
Connect					
DIGITAL START UP ACTIVITY **Why Do We Have Political Parties?**			5 min.	●	
Investigate					
DIGITAL TEXT 1 **What Is a Political Party?**		Objective 1	10 min.	●	●
DIGITAL TEXT 2 **The Role of Political Parties**			10 min.	●	●
DIGITAL TEXT 3 **The Two-Party System**		Objective 2	10 min.	●	●
INTERACTIVE MAP **Political Party Changes in the Southern States**			10 min.	●	
DIGITAL TEXTS 4 AND 5 **Multiparty and One-Party Politics, Third and Minor Parties in the United States**		Objective 3	10 min.	●	●
INTERACTIVE TIMELINE **History of the Two-Party System**			10 min.	●	
DIGITAL TEXT 6 **The Decentralized Nature of the Parties**		Objective 4	10 min.	●	●
DIGITAL TEXT 7 **National Party Functions**		Objective 5	10 min.	●	●
DIGITAL TEXT 8 **State and Local Party Functions**			10 min.	●	●
Synthesize					
DIGITAL SYNTHESIZE ACTIVITY **Reflect on Why We Have Political Parties**			5 min.	●	
Demonstrate					
DIGITAL QUIZ **Lesson Quiz and Class Discussion Board**			10 min.	●	

Political Parties and What They Do

CONNECT

DIGITAL START UP ACTIVITY
Why Do We Have Political Parties?

Project the Start Up Activity Ask students to answer the questions as they enter and get settled. Then have them share their ideas with another student, either in class or through a chat or blog space.

Discuss What do you think the quotation is saying about political parties in the United States? *(Possible response: I think the quotation says that political parties are a necessity for American politics, but that the parties need to be willing to compromise and take moderate positions on issues.)*

Tell students that in this lesson they will be learning about political parties in the United States and their impact on how government functions.

Aa Vocabulary Development: Use the Interactive Reading Notepad to preview the Key Terms and Academic Vocabulary in this Lesson with students.

⇅ FLIP IT!
Assign the Flipped Video for this lesson.

STUDENT EDITION PRINT PAGES: 502–517

INVESTIGATE

DIGITAL TEXT 1
What Is a Political Party?

DIGITAL TEXT 2
The Role of Political Parties

Objective 1: Understand the origins of political parties in the United States and analyze their major functions.

Quick Instruction
A political party is a group of persons who seek to control government through the winning of elections and the holding of public office. Political parties include three groups of party loyalists: the party organization, the party in government, and the party in the electorate.

ELL Use the ELL activity described in the ELL chart.

Further Instruction
What Is a Political Party? and The Role of Political Parties: Core Reading and Interactive Reading Notepad Project and discuss the Interactive Reading Notepad questions.

Parties are important because they are the principal means by which the will of the people is made known to government and by which government is held accountable to the people. They also work to blunt conflict, building unity between groups with disparate views.

Significant Functions of Parties In the electoral process, the parties nominate candidates and inspire and activate supporters. They also serve to ensure that their members perform well in office and provide channels to help government to function more smoothly.

The party that is out of power functions to convince voters that it is "the loyal opposition" — opposed to the party in power but loyal to the people and the nation. One example where this

backfired was in the case of *Marbury* v. *Madison* when an individual from the party out of power challenged a decision in the Supreme Court by the party in power. It affected the Supreme Court in a major way by establishing the power of judicial review.

Predict Consequences Why might the United States have grown into a two-party system instead of a three- or even ten-party system? *(Possible answer: This might have had its roots in the Federalist-Anti-Federalist fight. Two parties make it easy to understand who is for something and who is against it.)*

Evaluate Ideas The text explains that past important welfare functions provided by the parties have long since been taken over by a number of government programs put in place in the twentieth century. What is the impact of moving welfare functions away from the parties and into the government? What are the positive and negative impacts of that change? *(Possible answer: Parties can no longer use welfare as a way to recruit people to their cause. Instead they must create platforms that appeal to a wide audience. That allows for more freedom because people can decide whether to support a platform on its merits instead of whether or not the party will give them a job.)*

DIGITAL TEXT 3

The Two-Party System

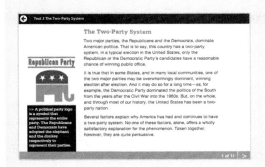

INTERACTIVE MAP

Political Party Changes in the Southern States

Objective 2: Understand multiparty and one-party systems and how they a political system, and explain the two-party system of the United States.

Quick Instruction

The Two-Party System The Federalist and Anti-Federalist parties were the first parties in the United States, and the legacy of a two-party system derives from them.John Adams first defeated Thomas Jefferson, who led the Anti-Federalists, in 1796, but by 1800 was in turn defeated by Jefferson and the Federalists never returned to power. Most of the Framers believed the parties were agents of disunity and George Washington warned of this in his Farewell Address in 1796. Election law also supports the current system, as does the ideology of the United States, which is based on certain shared beliefs. The political parties do differ on certain policy issues, such as abortion and social welfare programs.

Interactive Map: Political Party Changes in the Southern States Remind students that over time, the parties and their platforms have changed. Project the map and move the image slider from left to right to examine the two periods.

ACTIVE CLASSROOM

Using a Questioning strategy, have students jot down questions they have as they look at the two maps. Share the questions with the class and discuss answers.

D Differentiate: **Extra Support** What differences do you notice between the 1900 map and the 2012 map? *(The southern States have shifted from primarily Democratic to Republican.)*

Further Instruction

The Two-Party System and Multiparty and One-Party Politics: Core Reading and Interactive Reading Notepad Project and discuss the Interactive Reading Notepad questions.

Multiparty politics involve the creation of coalitions because it is difficult to win a majority. This kind of system is often used in European countries. One-party politics can be seen in dictatorships where there is only one accepted party. Modified one-party politics can occur in the United States when one party, Democrat or Republican, dominates the political landscape.

Predict Consequences What creates a situation where one party dominates the political landscape? How might the other party become competitive? *(Possible answers: The members of a community all share one viewpoint as supported by only one party. This may relate to common ideas of how government best functions, or what services government should provide. The other party might become competitive if the first party shifts farther away from the shared ideas of the community, leaving a space for the second party.)*

Compare Why is a two-party system more stable than a multiparty system? *(Possible answer: In an two-party system, one party wins and can govern. In a multiparty system, it is difficult to win outright so parties form coalitions, which may or may not be very stable or long lasting.)*

Political Parties and What They Do

Multiparty and One-Party Politics

Third and Minor Parties in the United States

History of the Two-Party System

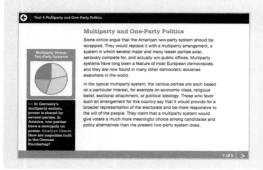

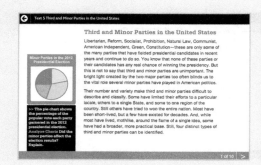

Objective 3: **Evaluate the role of minor parties in American politics and understand why they are important.**

Quick Instruction

Four distinct types of minor, or third, parties have existed in the United States. They have an impact on political change since they can play a spoiler role in elections, taking votes away from the two major parties. They also critique the two major parties, and are able to take quite clear-cut stands on controversial issues. Sometimes these platforms are then adopted by the major parties.

Interactive Timeline: History of the Two-Party System Project the timeline and click through the periods. Introduce the timeline by telling students that right from the start, the process of ratifying the Constitution (1787–1790) prompted the development of political parties, the first being the Federalist Pary, which was formed around Alexander Hamilton. Point out that the Era of the Republicans began with Abraham Lincoln and that this was the only time a third party became a major one. Through the first three periods after 1800, one of the major parties was dominant in holding the presidency and usually both houses of Congress. The present fourth period shows a divided government, where one party holds the presidency, but the other holds one or both houses of Congress.

ACTIVE CLASSROOM

Using a Think Pair Share strategy, have students compare and contrast the eras shown in the timeline.

Then have students use their comparisons to answer the following question about the effect two-party systems have: For a system rife with checks and balances, how does a two-party system in a divided government differ from a two-party system in the Democratic or Republican Era? Have students share their answers.

D **Differentiate:** **Challenge** Have pairs of students identify a politician who exemplifies one of the time periods and think of questions to ask him or her about the time period. Research the questions. Students can create interview skits to show what they learned.

Further Instruction

Third and Minor Parties in the United States: Core Reading and Interactive Reading Notepad Project and discuss the Interactive Reading Notepad questions.

Four Types of Parties The four types of third parties are ideological, economic protest, single-issues, and splinter. Third parties play several roles and encompass different points of view.Ideological parties encompass a comprehensive view of social, economic, and political matters. They are often short-lived. Examples of ideological parties are the Libertarian or Socialist parties. Economic protest parties have been rooted in periods of economic discontent and are often without ideology. These parties can be geographically

based, as economic downturns or issues affect regions. Single-issue parties focus on a single question and are often be short-lived, as events pass them by, as their themes fail to attract voters, or as one or both of the major parties take their key issues as their own. Parties often disappeared as the nation climbed out of the difficult economic period in which that party arose. Splinter parties are those that have split away from the main parties. Theodore Roosevelt's "Bull Moose" Progressive Party of 1912 is among the leading groups that have spit away from the Republicans.

Make Connections How do third parties influence the two-party system? Choose one type of party and give an example of how it might influence the major parties. *(Possible answer: Single-issue parties could force the major parties to focus on that issue and adopt it as part of their platform.)*

Hypothesize What would have to happen to third parties to transform the United States into a multiparty system? *(Possible answer: The parties would have to start winning elections.)*

DIGITAL TEXT 6

The Decentralized Nature of the Parties

Objective 4: Understand why the major parties have a decentralized structure.

Quick Instruction

The parties are highly decentralized, fragmented, and often plagued by factions and internal squabbling. There is no chain of command running from the national through the State to the local level. This is related to the enormous number of widely distributed offices that parties try to control by getting their people elected to those offices. Even so, in the electoral process, the State parties are loosely tied to the national parties and generally cooperate.

Further Instruction

The Decentralized Nature of the Parties: Core Reading and Interactive Reading Notepad Project and discuss the Interactive Reading Notepad questions.

Exceptions to Decentralization The one exception to the decentralized nature of the parties is the party that controls the presidency. The President's party is almost always more solidly united and better organized than the other major party. The President is automatically the party's leader, and asserts that leadership with such tools as ready access to the media, personal popularity, the power to make appointments to federal office, and the ability to dispense other favors.

Determine Cause and Effect Why does the fact that the nominations occur within each party create highly fractured parties? *(Possible answer: There can be only one person nominated for each position, but many people might apply. This creates tension since the party must choose the best candidate.)*

Hypothesize Is decentralization a good thing for the parties? Should the parties make more of an effort to centralize decision-making and other party functions? *(Possible answer: Decentralization is a good thing because it allows different States and localities to handle issues in their own ways.)*

DIGITAL TEXT 7

National Party Functions

Objective 5: Describe the national party machinery and party organization at the State and local levels.

Quick Instruction

At the national level, both major political parties function with five basic elements: a national convention, a national committee, a national chairperson, and two congressional campaign committees. At the State level, party structure is determined by State law. It usually consists of a State chairperson and a State committee. Local party structure is highly varied. Party structure is still marked at the local and State level by decentralization, fragmentation, and power struggles.

Further Instruction

National Party Functions: Core Reading and Interactive Reading Notepad Project and discuss the Interactive Reading Notepad questions.

Five Functions The National Convention meets every Presidential election year to choose the party's presidential and vice-presidential nominees. It also adopts the party's rules and the platform. Between conventions, the party's affairs are handled by the national committee and by the national chairperson. The chairperson leads the national committee. There are also two congressional campaign committees, one for the Senate and one for the House of Representatives.

Political Parties and What They Do

SYNTHESIZE

DEMONSTRATE

DIGITAL TEXT 8

State and Local Party Functions

DIGITAL SYNTHESIZE ACTIVITY

Reflect on Why We Have Political Parties

DIGITAL QUIZ

Lesson Quiz and Class Discussion Board

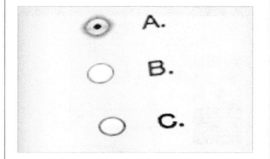

State and Local Party Functions: Core Reading and Interactive Reading Notepad Project and discuss the Interactive Reading Notepad questions.

Local Organization Generally, local parties follow the electoral map of the State, with a party unit for each district in which elective offices are to be filled: congressional and legislative districts, counties, cities and towns, wards, and precincts. Cities are often divided into wards, which elect city council members. A precinct is the smallest unit of election administration. Citizens in each precinct have the opportunity to participate in the voting process at local, State, and national levels by casting their ballots at one polling place located within the precinct.

Draw Conclusions Why is national party organization largely the product of custom and of rules adopted by the party's national conventions over time? *(Possible answer: National parties are very visible and so need to be consistant in their organization.)*

Evaluate Ideas How does decentralization contribute to the variation in local party structure? *(Possible answer: Local structures vary due to geography and State laws, thereby giving rise to decentralization.)*

Ask students to recall the quotation from Clinton Rossiter from the Connect activity at the beginning of the lesson. Have students revisit their notes and responses made right after reading the quotation, comparing them to what they have learned.

Discuss Have partners think about the following question: Are the thoughts about political parties that you wrote down after reading the quotation still valid after studying Lesson 1? If not, how have your thoughts about political parties changed? Have pairs share their answers with the class.

Assign the online Lesson Quiz for this lesson if you haven't already done so. Students will be offered automatic remediation or enrichment based on their score.

Pose these questions to the class on the Discussion Board: In "Political Parties and What They Do" you read about political parties in America.

Evaluate Ideas If you were to create your own political party, what would its platform be? How would it compete with the major parties?

Make Decisions Do you think the two-party structure is useful in governing the United States? What elements of the structure make it most useful?

Topic Inquiry
Have students continue their investigations for the Topic Inquiry.

Nominations

Supporting English Language Learners

Use with Digital Text 1, **Nominations: A Critical First Step.**

Speaking
Using images as support, compare different methods of filling public offices, including elected and appointed offices, with students. Model different sentence types for students: statement, question, command, exclamation. Tell students that using different types of sentences makes it easier for other people to understand them. Tell them they will practice using these sentence types while talking about the text.

Beginning Provide a list of different sentences types for the images in the text. Read each sentence with students, have them use a sentence frame in order to identify its type, and guide them to choose its corresponding image.

Intermediate Provide sentence starters for each type of sentence. Guide students to use the sentence starter to discuss images in the text. Examples: *This is _____. Why are _____? Do not _____! How interesting _____!*

Advanced Have partners choose an image from the text. Have them take turns saying at least one sentence of each type for the image. Have them choose another image and repeat the task.

Advanced High Have partners choose two images from the text. Have them practice saying at least one sentence of each type for each image. Have them share their sentences with a partner or other students in their group.

Use with Digital Texts 4–6, **The Direct Primary, The Evaluation of the Primary, Petition.**

Learning Strategies
As you discuss the process of filling public offices, explain the difference between formal and informal English. Tell students that most textbooks are written in formal English. Guide students to use the glossary or dictionary to find the definitions of the following words and rewrite them in informal English: *nomination*, *general election*, *runoff primary*, *platform*.

Beginning Provide formal and informal definitions for the words. Read them to the students and have them repeat. Guide students to realize that informal English is the way we would speak to a classmate.

Intermediate Provide formal and informal definitions for the words. Guide students to read the definitions. Help students to identify the formal and informal versions.

Advanced Guide partners to write informal definitions of the words. Have them share their definitions with the class.

Advanced High Have students write informal definitions of the words. Ask them to share their definitions with two other students.

▣ Differentiate Instruction

Use the Differentiated Instruction notes throughout the lesson plan to support the varied skill sets, levels of readiness, and interests in the mixed-ability classroom.

Challenge These notes include suggestions for expanding the activity for advanced students.

On-Level These notes include suggestions for modifying the activity to address different interests or learning styles.

Extra Support These notes include ideas for providing more scaffolding or reading spuport.

Special Needs These notes provide ideas for adapting instruction to support the needs of various special needs students.

▮ NOTES

Nominations

Objectives

Objective 1: Explain why the nominating process is a critical first step in the process for filling public offices.

Objective 2: Describe self-announcement, the caucus, and the convention as nominating methods.

Objective 3: Discuss the direct primary as the principle nominating method used in the United States today, and understand why some candidates use the petition as a nominating device.

LESSON 2 ORGANIZER		PACING: APPROX. 1 PERIOD, .5 BLOCKS			
				RESOURCES	
		OBJECTIVES	PACING	Online	Print
Connect					
DIGITAL START UP ACTIVITY **The Dangers of the Party System**			5 min.	●	
Investigate					
DIGITAL TEXT 1 **Nominations: A Critical First Step**		Objective 1	10 min.	●	●
DIGITAL TEXT 2 **The Caucus**		Objective 2	10 min.	●	●
DIGITAL TEXT 3 **The Convention**			10 min.	●	●
DIGITAL TEXT 4 **The Direct Primary**		Objective 3	10 min.	●	●
DIGITAL TEXT 5 **Evaluation of the Primary**			10 min.	●	●
DIGITAL TEXT 6 **Petition**			10 min.	●	●
INTERACTIVE MAP **Types of Primaries**			10 min.	●	
INTERACTIVE GALLERY **Political Appointees**			10 min.	●	
Synthesize					
DIGITAL SYNTHESIZE ACTIVITY **How Nominations Are Made**			5 min.	●	
Demonstrate					
DIGITAL QUIZ **Lesson Quiz and Classroom Discussion Board**			10 min.	●	

PEARSON
realize™
www.PearsonRealize.com

Go online to access additional resources including:
Primary Sources • Biographies • Supreme Court cases •
21st Century Skill Tutorials • Maps • Graphic Organizers.

■ CONNECT

DIGITAL START UP ACTIVITY
The Dangers of the Party System

Project the Start Up Activity Ask students to answer the questions as they enter and get settled. Then have them share their ideas with another student, either in class or through a chat or blog space.

Discuss In George Washington's Farewell Address of 1796, he warns of the dangers of a party system in the United States, and the destructive effects of the spirit of party. More than 200 years later, was he right? Are there problems with the party system in the United States today? Why or why not? *(Possible answers: I think it is still an issue today because most people care more about their party being right or in charge rather than being willing to reach across the aisle and do what's best for this country.)*

Aa Vocabulary Development: Use the Interactive Reading Notepad to preview the Key Terms and Academic Vocabulary in this Lesson with students.

⇅ FLIP IT!
Assign the Flipped Video for this lesson.

■ STUDENT EDITION PRINT
PAGES: 518–527

■ INVESTIGATE

DIGITAL TEXT 1
Nominations: A Critical First Step

Objective 1: **Explain why the nominating process is a critical first step in the process for filling public offices.**

Quick Instruction
Nomination—the naming of those who will seek public office—is a critically important step in the election and appointment process at the national, State, and local levels. Nominations to fill elective office are made in five different ways in this country. Candidates are named to the ballot by (1) self-announcement, (2) caucus, (3) convention, (4) direct primary, and (5) petition.

ELL Use the ELL activity described in the ELL chart.

Further Instruction
Nominations: A Critical First Step: Core Reading and Interactive Reading Notepad Project and discuss the Interactive Reading Notepad questions.

Nominations In a two-party system, the nominating stage is a critically important step in the electoral process. Those who make nominations place real, very practical limits on the choices that voters can make in the general election. In a one-party system, once the dominant party has made its nomination, the general election is little more than a formality.

Hypothesize What might happen in elections without nominations? *(Possible answer: Too many candidates would be on the ballot.)*

Make Inferences Why are there so many different ways to nominate people for public office? *(Possible answer: The State and local party structure is decentralized, meaning that they each can have their own way of nominating.)*

Nominations

DIGITAL TEXT 2
The Caucus

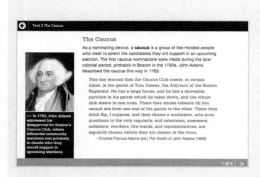

The Caucus

As a nominating device, a **caucus** is a group of like-minded people who meet to select the candidates they will support in an upcoming election. The first caucus nominations were made during the later colonial period, probably in Boston in the 1720s. John Adams described the caucus this way in 1763:

This day learned that the Caucus Club meets, at certain times, in the garret of Tom Dawes, the Adjutant of the Boston Regiment. He has a large house, and he has a moveable partition in his garret which he takes down, and the whole club meets in one room. There they smoke tobacco till you cannot see from one end of the garret to the other. There they drink flip. I suppose, and they choose a moderator, who puts questions to the vote regularly; and selectmen, assessors, collectors, wardens, fire-wards, and representatives, are regularly chosen before they are chosen in the town.

—Charles Francis Adams (ed.) *The Works of John Adams* (1856)

>> In 1763, John Adams expressed his disapproval for Boston's Caucus Club, where influential community members met privately to decide who they would support in upcoming elections.

1 of 5 >

DIGITAL TEXT 3
The Convention

The Convention

As the caucus method collapsed, the convention system took its place. The first national convention to nominate a presidential candidate was held by a minor party, the Anti-Masons, in Baltimore in 1831. The newly formed National Republican (soon to become Whig) Party also held a convention later that same year. The Democrats picked up the practice in 1832. All major-party presidential nominees have been chosen by conventions ever since. By the 1840s, conventions had become the principal means for making nominations at every level in American politics.

On paper, the convention process seems perfectly suited to representative government. A party's members meet in a local caucus to pick candidates for local offices and, at the same time, to select delegates to represent them at a county convention. (The meeting at which delegates to local conventions are chosen are still often called caucuses.)

>> The 1940 Republican National Convention was the first televised national political convention. Delegates nominated Wendell Willkie for President and Charles McNary for Vice President.

1 of 5 >

DIGITAL TEXT 4
The Direct Primary

The Direct Primary

A **direct primary** is an intraparty election. It is held within a party to pick that party's candidates for the general election. Wisconsin adopted the first Statewide direct primary law in 1903; several other States soon followed its lead. Every State now makes at least some provision for its use.

In most States, State law requires that the major parties use the primary to choose their candidates for the United States Senate and House of Representatives, for the governorship and all other Statewide offices, and for most local offices as well. In a few States, however, different combinations of convention and primary are used to pick candidates for the top offices.

>> In Newark, New Jersey, Mayor Cory Booker speaks after winning the Democratic primary for a vacated U.S. Senate seat. Booker went on to defeat the Republican candidate in a special election.

1 of 12 >

Objective 2: Describe self-announcement, the caucus, and the convention as nominating methods.

Quick Instruction

There are several different nominating methods of filling public office. Self-announcement is the oldest form used in the United States. It occurs when the candidate says that he or she is running for a particular office. The second oldest form is the caucus, where a group of like-minded people meet to select the candidates they will support in an upcoming election.

Conventions The newest form is the convention. A party's members meet in a local caucus to pick candidates for local offices and, at the same time, to select delegates to represent them at a county convention. At the county convention, the delegates nominate candidates for county offices and select delegates to the next rung on the convention ladder, usually the State convention. There, the delegates from the county conventions pick the party's nominees for governor and other Statewide offices. State conventions also send delegates to the party's national convention, where the party selects its presidential and vice-presidential candidates.

Further Instruction

The Caucus and The Convention: Core Reading and Interactive Reading Notepad Project and discuss the Interactive Reading Notepad questions.

Issues in Nominating Processes Conventions took the place of the caucus, but it soon became evident that they could be manipulated by party bosses. As a result, direct primaries have replaced conventions in most States, except at the presidential level.

Make Inferences How have direct primaries solved the problems in the nominating process? *(Possible answer: They reflect the ability of the voting public to make their choice known as opposed to having a choice foisted upon them.)*

Objective 3: Discuss the direct primary as the principle nominating method used in the United States today, and understand why some candidates use the petition as a nominating device.

Quick Instruction

The direct primary is the principle nominating method. It can be open or closed. Closed primaries allow only people registered with a particular party to vote. Open primaries allow any registered voter to cast a ballot. Candidates for public office are sometimes nominated by means of petitions signed by a certain number of qualified voters in the election district. The number of signatures required varies by office and State.

Interactive Map: Examples of Types of Primaries Click through the colored States to review the types of primaries with students.

> **◤◢ ACTIVE CLASSROOM**
>
> Use a Sticky Note strategy to compare the different kinds of primaries. What do they have in common? With a partner decide which primary is the most democratic. Have students support their ideas using their sticky notes.

D Differentiate: **Extra Support** Ask the following questions: What is a primary? How is it different than a general election?

DIGITAL TEXT 5

Evaluation of the Primary

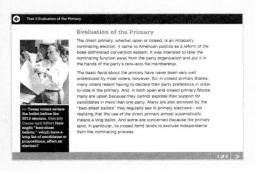

>> Texas voters review the ballot before the 2012 election. Identify Cause and Effect How might "bed-sheet ballots," which have a long list of candidates or propositions, affect an election?

Interactive Gallery: Political Appointees
Project the gallery and scroll through each image. Remind students that there are many processes for filling public offices.

ACTIVE CLASSROOM

Using a 3-1 strategy, have students use the images to answer the following question. What qualities make for a good political appointee?

D Differentiate: **Challenge** Choose a position for which people get appointed. Students can nominate someone they know and create a brief introduction. Share introductions with the class and have students give feedback on whether or not the person would be a good appointee.

Discuss Have students share their qualities. Then ask students to discuss how those qualities might differ from those needed to be nominated for an election. *(Possible answer: In both cases, people need to be trustworthy and have skills suited to the job. However, in order to be nominated to stand in an election, people might need to have more ability to talk to constituents.)*

ELL Use the ELL activity described in the ELL chart.

DIGITAL TEXT 6

Petition

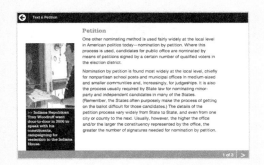

>> Indiana Republican Troy Woodruff went door-to-door in 2006 to speak with his constituents, campaigning for reelection to the Indiana House.

Further Instruction

The Direct Primary: Core Reading and Interactive Reading Notepad Project and discuss the Interactive Reading Notepad questions.

Evaluation of the Primary Primaries are intraparty, meaning that the process takes place within a party. Voters can get frustrated that they must declare a party or that the ballot is too long. Voter turnout for primaries is often very low. Name familiarity can give an edge to some contenders, even though this quality has little to do with whether or not that person would be suited for office. Finally, the nominating process, whatever its form, can have a very divisive effect on a party. A bitter fight in the primaries can so wound and divide a party that it cannot recover in time to present a united front for the general election.

INTERACTIVE MAP

Types of Primaries

Petition: Core Reading and Interactive Reading Notepad Project and discuss the Interactive Reading Notepad questions.

Explain Causes and Effects How does the increasing cost of primaries change politics at the local, State, and national levels? *(Possible answer: The more money needed to run a campaign, the fewer people will want to run for office. Unless the candidate has easy access to funds, he or she might spend more time raising money than meeting constituents. That may make it harder to recruit candidates.)*

Make Judgments Do you think the closed primary or the open primary represents a more democratic ideal? Why? *(Possible answer: An open primary represents a more democratic ideal because it allows any qualified voter to cast a ballot, whereas a closed primary is open only to party members.)*

Nominations

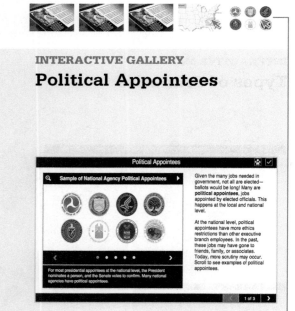

INTERACTIVE GALLERY
Political Appointees

Draw Conclusions Why is the petition nominating process used for judges instead of the party primary process? *(Judges are supposed to be impartial. Keeping away from partisan nominations, like a party primary process, is one way to ensure an impartial judiciary.)*

SYNTHESIZE

DIGITAL SYNTHESIZE ACTIVITY
How Nominations Are Made

Ask students to recall the methods of nomination used in the United States. Have them use the Sticky Note strategy to record what they know about methods of nomination and examples of each method. Then have them consider how to show that information in a graphic organizer.

Have students create a graphic organizer that shows the following information: The five ways in which nominations are made in this country, a brief summary of the nomination method, and examples of the nomination in use at the local, State, or national level. (Students' graphic organizers, such as a table, should include as methods of nomination: self-announcement, caucus, convention, direct primary, and petition. For each of the five methods of nomination, students should include a brief summary of the method and a suitable example at the State, local, or national level.)

DEMONSTRATE

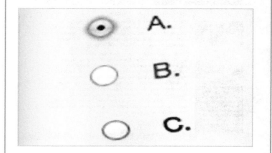

DIGITAL QUIZ
Lesson Quiz and Classroom Discussion Board

Assign the online Lesson Quiz for this lesson if you haven't already done so. Students will be offered automatic remediation or enrichment based on their scores.

In *Nominations*, students read that the process of nominating is a critical first step in filling public offices. Pose these questions to the class on the Discussion Board:

Explain Why is the nominating process important to fill public offices?

Make Inferences How is the process of nominating different for members of third parties than for the two majority parties?

Make Decisions Which method of nominating is most likely to produce strong candidates for public office? Why?

Topic Inquiry
Have students continue their investigations for the Topic Inquiry.

Electing the President

Supporting English Language Learners

Use with Digital Text 1, **Presidential Primaries.**

Speaking

Using images as support, discuss the process of electing the President while modeling the use of connecting words. Provide opportunities for students to speak using connecting words.

Beginning Write a list of connecting words on the board, such as *and*, *so*, *but*, *or*, and *because*. For each image, say at least one sentence using a connecting word. Have students repeat the sentences.

Intermediate Provide students with a list of sentence starters with connecting words. Guide students to use the sentence starters to talk about the images. Examples: *These people are voting because* _____. *This person is talking and* _____. *This map shows* _____ *and* _____.

Advanced Write a list of connecting words on the board such as *first*, *next*, *then*, *however*, and *also*. Guide students to discuss the election process and the images in the text using the words on the list.

Advanced High Provide a list of words such as *thus*, *otherwise*, *however*, *also*, *but*, *although*, and *whether*. Have partners discuss the election process and the images in the text using these words.

Use with the lesson 3 readings.

Reading Strategies

As you explain how national public offices are filled, discuss the use of formal and informal English. Model examples of each. Have students look at images in the text and consider whether the people in the images are using formal and informal English.

Beginning For each image, model two sentences—one in formal English, one in informal English. Have students repeat each sentence. Ask students which sentence they think is an example of how the people in the image are speaking.

Intermediate For each image, provide two sentences—one in formal English, one in informal English. Ask students which sentence they think is an example of how the people in the image are speaking. Ask students to explain their thinking.

Advanced Have students look at several images and sort them into two groups: situations where formal English would be used and situations where informal English would be used. Ask students to explain their thinking.

Advanced High Ask partners to look at the images and consider whether formal or informal English would be used in that situation. Have them explain their thinking. Ask them to write a sentence that might be used in each situation.

▣ Differentiate Instruction

Use the Differentiated Instruction notes throughout the lesson plan to support the varied skill sets, levels of readiness, and interests in the mixed-ability classroom.

Challenge These notes include suggestions for expanding the activity for advanced students.

On-Level These notes include suggestions for modifying the activity to address different interests or learning styles.

Extra Support These notes include ideas for providing more scaffolding or reading spuport.

Special Needs These notes provide ideas for adapting instruction to support the needs of various special needs students.

▮ NOTES

Electing the President

Objectives

Objective 1: Describe the role of conventions in the presidential nominating process, understand the caucus-convention process, and outline the events that take place during a national convention.

Objective 2: Evaluate the importance of primaries.

Objective 3: Examine the characteristics that determine who is nominated as a presidential candidate.

Objective 4: Describe the features of the presidential campaign.

Objective 5: Analyze how the electoral college provides for the election of the President.

Objective 6: Identify several flaws in the electoral college system and outline the advantages and disadvantages of proposed reforms of the electoral college.

LESSON 3 ORGANIZER		PACING: APPROX. 1 PERIOD, .5 BLOCKS		
			RESOURCES	
	OBJECTIVES	PACING	Online	Print
Connect				
DIGITAL START UP ACTIVITY **How Will You Vote?**		5 min.	●	
Investigate				
DIGITAL TEXTS 1 AND 2 **Presidential Primaries, Evaluation of the Presidential Primary**	Objective 2	10 min.	●	●
DIGITAL TEXT 3 **The National Convention**	Objective 1	10 min.	●	●
DIGITAL TEXT 4 **Who Is Nominated?**	Objective 3	10 min.	●	●
DIGITAL TEXT 5 **The Presidential Campaign**	Objective 4	10 min.	●	●
INTERACTIVE TIMELINE **The Race for the Presidency**		10 min.	●	
DIGITAL TEXT 6 **The Electoral College**	Objective 5	10 min.	●	●
INTERACTIVE MAP **The Presidential Election—Distribution of Electoral Votes**		10 min.	●	
DIGITAL TEXT 7 **Flaws in the Electoral College**	Objective 6	10 min.	●	●
DIGITAL TEXT 8 **Proposed Reforms and a Defense**		10 min.	●	●
Synthesize				
DIGITAL SYNTHESIZE ACTIVITY **Take a Stand**		5 min.	●	
Demonstrate				
DIGITAL QUIZ **Lesson Quiz and Class Discussion Board**		10 min.	●	

PEARSON **realize**™
www.PearsonRealize.com

Go online to access additional resources including:
Primary Sources • Biographies • Supreme Court cases •
21st Century Skill Tutorials • Maps • Graphic Organizers.

■ CONNECT

DIGITAL START UP ACTIVITY

How Will You Vote?

Project the Start Up Activity Ask students to answer the questions as they enter and get settled. Then have them share their ideas with another student, either in class or through a chat or blog space.

Discuss Some day you will get the opportunity to cast your first vote for the President. What will you look for in a candidate? *(Possible answer: Personality traits as well as factors such as age, gender, stance on particular issues, and experience.)*

Tell students that in this lesson they will learn about the process of electing the President of the United States.

Aa Vocabulary Development: Use the Interactive Reading Notepad to preview the Key Terms and Academic Vocabulary in this Lesson with students.

⚐ FLIP IT!

Assign the Flipped Video for this lesson.

■ STUDENT EDITION PRINT PAGES: 528–544

■ INVESTIGATE

DIGITAL TEXT 1

Presidential Primaries

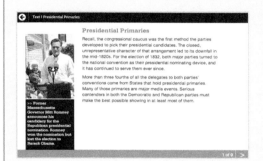

Objective 2: Evaluate the importance of primaries.

Quick Instruction

Presidential primaries select the major party candidates for the presidential election. They are held on a State-by-State basis using a variety of methods. At the national convention, delegates representing each State nominate their State's choice for the candidate.

ELL Use the ELL activity described in the ELL chart.

Further Instruction

Presidential Primaries: Core Reading and Interactive Reading Notepad Project and discuss the Interactive Reading Notepad questions.

Delegates for National Convention Candidates for President are nominated at the party's national convention. The delegates for this convention are selected in different ways. Proportional representation means that delegates are awarded to candidates in proportion to the number of votes each received. Preference primaries indicate a preference for a candidate, with the delegates chosen later. Hopefully those delegates will vote to support the preference of the State. A presidential primary is either or both of two things: a delegate-selection process and/or a candidate preference election.

DIGITAL TEXT 2

Evaluation of the Presidential Primary

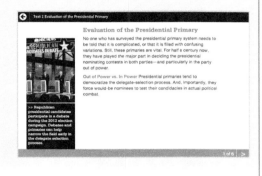

Evaluation of the Presidential Primary: Core Reading and Interactive Reading Notepad Project and discuss the Interactive Reading Notepad questions.

Make Inferences How would changing the schedule, for example making the primary shorter or longer, change the race? *(Possible answer: If the primary was shorter, the candidate might not be as tested. He or she might not be ready for a general election. If the primary is longer, there is more time to learn about the candidate, but campaign resources might be exhausted.)*

Make Decisions If the primary system was going to be reformed, would you rather see an open primary for the whole country or several open regional primaries? Why? *(Possible answer: Several regional primaries might make more sense because then a candidate would travel to all States, not just the ones with the greatest populations.)*

Electing the President

DIGITAL TEXT 3
The National Convention

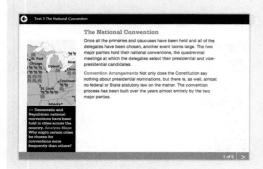

Objective 1: Describe the role of conventions in the presidential nominating process, understand the caucus-convention process, and outline the events that take place during a national convention.

Quick Instruction

To understand the processes for filling public offices, we need to compare the different methods of filling those offices at the national level. These comparisons are outlined in the text below.

Presidential Caucuses Caucuses occur only in States without primaries. A caucus is a closed meeting of members of a political party who gather to appoint delegates to the National Convention. The caucus-convention process is the oldest method for choosing national convention delegates. The Iowa caucuses generally get the most attention, largely because they are now the first delegate-selection event held in every presidential election season. The caucus-convention process is declining in popularity. By 2012, less than one-fourth of all delegates to either party's national convention came from States that still use this method of delegate choice.

The National Convention Conventions are held every four years for three major purposes: (1) naming the party's presidential and vice-presidential candidates, (2) bringing the various factions and the leading personalities in the party together in one place for a common purpose, and (3) adopting the party's platform.

Further Instruction

The National Convention: Core Reading and Interactive Reading Notepad Project and discuss the Interactive Reading Notepad questions.

Convention Schedule In three or four days, the parties attempt to achieve their purpose in meeting. The first day delegates are welcomed. The second day parties propose their platforms and a keynote speaker glorifies the party, its history, its leaders, and its programs, blisters the other party, and predicts a resounding victory for the party and its candidates in November. The third day is reserved for the nomination of the vice-presidential and the presidential candidates. The vice-presidential candidate usually accepts the nomination in a speech on the third day. The fourth day is reserved for the acceptance speech of the presidential candidate. This ends the convention and begins the party's general election campaign.

Predict Consequences The conventions are very staged affairs because the candidates are known well in advance. How might the convention be different if the candidates had yet to be decided? *(Possible answer: They would be more contentious as people argued over which candidate would best match the goals of the party and win in November.)*

Make Inferences People from American Somoa and Puerto Rico cannot vote in presidential elections because they are considered nationals and not citizens of the United States. They do, however, hold primary elections and send delegates to national conventions. Why is it important to be a part of the process even though they cannot vote for President? *(Possible answer: The President is responsible for carrying out laws that would affect those living on these islands. This is the way that these people can show a preference for who will make those decisions.)*

DIGITAL TEXT 4
Who Is Nominated?

DIGITAL TEXT 5
The Presidential Campaign

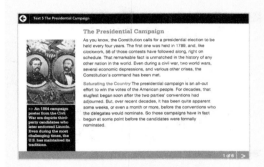

Objective 3: Examine the characteristics that determine who is nominated as a presidential candidate.

Quick Instruction
Presidential candidates tend to have a record of public service, usually as a governor or senator. They are usually men in their 50s or 60s, tend to come from larger States, and are often Protestant. Candidates have engaging speaking styles. In short, parties nominate people they think will appeal to a wide audience and who are likely to win.

Further Instruction
Who Is Nominated?: Core Reading and Interactive Reading Notepad Project and discuss the Interactive Reading Notepad questions.

Exceptions to the Norm Not all presidential candidates follow trends. Dwight Eisenhower came from a military background, a version of public service seldom seen in candidates. Bob Dole came from Kansas, instead of a large, populous State. John F. Kennedy was a Catholic.

Make Inferences What challenges do you think a candidate faces when they do not follow the general tendencies of presidential candidates? *(Possible answer: They may have to justify that their differences—age, religion, race, gender—will not interfere with their ability to carry out the responsibilities and duties of the office of the President.)*

Hypothesize Do you think a woman will ever be nominated as President? Why or why not? *(Possible answer: Yes, because women have gained more and more positions of power in the United States.)*

Objective 4: Describe the features of the presidential campaign.

Quick Instruction
There have been 56 presidential campaigns over the history of the United States. Every four years beginning in 1789, people gather to campaign and vote for an executive. The process of electing the President of the United States is complex. Candidates compete across the nation using social media, traditional media, and campaign stops. Campaigns focus on persuading swing voters, or those who haven't made up their minds, and encouraging their base voters to work on their campaigns. The two major party candidates meet for a series of three debates. The vice-presidential candidates also meet for a debate.

Interactive Timeline: Race for the Presidency Project the timeline and step through each element with students.

🎥 ACTIVE CLASSROOM
Using a Sequence strategy, have students evaluate the process of becoming a party nominee for public office.

Discuss the following question: What is advantageous about nominating candidates in this process? *(Possible answer: The candidate that is most viable will probably win. Viability having been tested by the amount of money the candidate is able to raise, the number of people the candidate can inspire to work on a campaign as well as come out to vote twice, and the number of party supporters the candidate can amass.)*

Electing the President

The Race for the Presidency

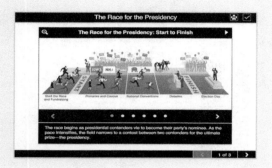

The Electoral College

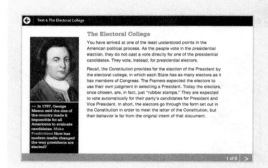

D Differentiate: **Extra Support** Have students ask questions about the nominating process before they look at the timeline. After looking at the timeline, have them work in pairs to see if they can answer their questions, then continue with the activity.

Further Instruction

The Presidential Campaign: Core Reading and Interactive Reading Notepad Project and discuss the Interactive Reading Notepad questions.

Debates Campaign debates are overseen by an independent, nonpartisan organization created by Congress in 1987, the Commission on Presidential Debates. The participants must be party-nominated candidates who are (1) supported by at least 15 percent of the respondents in five national polls and (2) listed on the ballot of States which, taken together, will cast at least a majority (270) of the electoral votes in the upcoming election. Therefore the rules exclude third-party candidates.

Televised Debates The first presidential debates, in 1960, featured then-Vice President Richard Nixon and his Democratic opponent, Senator John F. Kennedy. Many analysts credit John Kennedy's strong performance in them as one of the keys to his very narrow victory in the election that year. In all, an average of 64 million people watched each debate in 2012. Some 51 million viewers watched the single vice-presidential debate between Vice President Joe Biden and Congressman Paul Ryan of Wisconsin. The 1980 presidential debate between President Jimmy Carter and Ronald Reagan holds the record, with some 81 million viewers.

Connect How important are the base voters to a general campaign? *(Possible answer: They are very important because they can work on campaigns, freeing paid workers to spend time and effort elsewhere.)*

Determine Cause and Effect One important characteristic for a candidate is to be personable. With the emphasis on televised debates and campaign stops, why might this be even more important? *(Possible answer: Voters and viewers make judgments about a person's character based on that person's appearance and actions.)*

Make Inferences Why do you think more people watched the Carter-Reagan debates in 1980 than the Obama-Romney debates in 2012? *(Possible answer: People don't need to watch the debates when they happen now because they will be streamed later by the campaign or news organizations.)*

Objective 5: Analyze how the electoral college provides for the election of the President.

Quick Instruction

Choosing Electors The Constitution provides the process of electing the President by the electoral college, in which each State has as many electors as it has members of Congress. On Election Day, the Tuesday after the first Monday in November every four years, people vote for electors. Electors are chosen based on who wins each State, with the exception of Maine and Nebraska.

Counting the Electoral Votes The Constitution provides that the date Congress sets for the electors to meet "shall be the same throughout the United States." (Article II, Section 1, Clause 4) The 12th Amendment provides that "the Electors shall meet in their respective States." The electors meet at their State capital on the Monday after the second Wednesday in December. There they each cast their electoral votes, one for President and one for Vice President. The electors' ballots, signed and sealed, are sent by registered mail to the President of the Senate. The formal election of the President and Vice President finally takes place in early January. On that date, the president of the Senate opens the electoral votes from each State and counts them before a joint session of Congress. The candidate who receives a majority of the electors' votes for President is declared elected, as is the candidate with a majority of the votes for Vice President.

INTERACTIVE MAP
The Presidential Election—Distribution of Electoral Votes

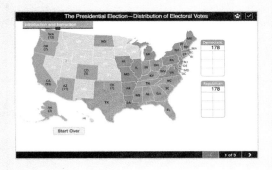

Interactive Map: The Presidential Election—Distribution of Electoral Votes Project the gallery and drag the abbreviations of the green States to the Republican or Democratic columns. Remind students that although the President and Vice President are not actually elected until January, the result of the election is known often on Election Day.

◆◆ ACTIVE CLASSROOM

Using a See-Think-Wonder strategy, have students explore the easiest way to 270 electoral votes. Have students examine political boundaries to make inferences about the distribution of political power.

Project the following question and have students use the same strategy to answer it: How would you spend your last few days as a candidate to end up with the most votes as early as possible?

D Differentiate: **Extra Support** Ask the following questions: What is the electoral college? What is it responsible for?

Further Instruction
The Electoral College: Core Reading and Interactive Reading Notepad Project and discuss the Interactive Reading Notepad questions.

Special Cases If no candidate has won a majority, the election is moved into the House of Representatives. This happened in 1800 and again in 1824. The House chooses a President from among the top three candidates voted for by the electoral college. Each State delegation has one vote, and it takes a majority of 26 to elect. If the House fails to choose a President by January 20, the 20th Amendment provides that the newly elected Vice President shall act as President until a choice is made. The 20th Amendment also says that "the Congress may by law provide for the case wherein neither a President elect nor a Vice President elect shall have qualified" by Inauguration Day. Congress has done so, in the Presidential Succession Act of 1947. The Speaker of the House would "act as President . . . until a President or Vice President shall have qualified."

Make Inferences Why did the Framers provide for an electoral college, rather than direct election of the President? *(Possible answer: They thought the nation was too large to allow voters to get to know the candidates well enough to make an informed decision.)*

Draw Conclusions The electoral college is one of the most misunderstood elements of the political process. Why do you think that might be? *(Possible answer: The process is complicated. People vote for candidates without realizing they are actually voting for electors.)*

DIGITAL TEXT 7
Flaws in the Electoral College

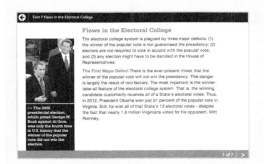

Objective 6: **Identify several flaws in the electoral college system and outline the advantages and disadvantages of proposed reforms of the electoral college.**

Quick Instruction
The electoral college system is plagued by three major defects: (1) the winner of the popular vote is not guaranteed the presidency; (2) electors are not required to vote in accord with the popular vote; and (3) any election might have to be decided in the House of Representatives. Most proposals to change the electoral college system fall under four headings: the district plan, the proportional plan, direct popular election, and the national popular vote plan.

Further Instruction
Flaws in the Electoral College: Core Reading and Interactive Reading Notepad Project and discuss the Interactive Reading Notepad questions.

Popular Votes The most consistent problem with the electoral college is the distortion of the popular vote. The popular vote winner has failed to win the presidency four times: in 1824, 1876, 1888, and 2000. Fifteen Presidents have won the White House with less than a majority of the popular votes cast in their elections.

Electing the President

SYNTHESIZE

DEMONSTRATE

DIGITAL TEXT 8

Proposed Reforms and a Defense

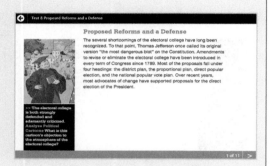

DIGITAL SYNTHESIZE ACTIVITY

Take a Stand

DIGITAL QUIZ

Lesson Quiz and Class Discussion Board

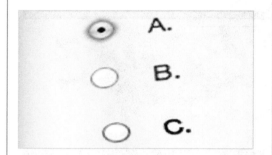

Proposed Reforms and a Defense: Core Reading and Interactive Reading Notepad Project and discuss the Interactive Reading Notepad questions.

The National Popular Vote Plan The plan asks each State's lawmaking body to (1) amend State election laws to provide that all of a State's electoral votes are to be awarded to the presidential candidate who wins the national popular vote and (2) enter into an interstate compact, the Agreement Among the States to Elect the President by National Popular Vote. That compact, and with it each State's election law changes, would come into force only if and when the compact has been agreed to by enough States to account for a majority (at least 270) of the 538 electoral votes.

Draw Conclusions To implement the direct popular election plan, the Constitution would need to be amended. Why does the national popular vote plan not need a constitutional amendment to succeed? *(Possible answer: It provides for the States to change their electoral vote process.)*

Evaluate Ideas Which defect in the electoral college is the worst? Why? *(Possible answer: The winner of the popular election is not guaranteed to become President. Everything else in this country works on majority rules. It seems out of place that this process does not reflect that tendency.)*

Ask students to analyze the electoral college and its role in the process of electing the president. Ask the following questions. What position do you take in the ongoing debate regarding the electoral college system? Should it be reformed, or should it remain intact? If the system should be reformed, what specific plan do you prefer? Have students freewrite for 10–15 minutes in response to the questions. Then have them use their freewrite to craft a letter to their senators explaining their position.

Remind students that their letters should include a clear statement of opinion and several reasons and explanations for their position.

Assign the online Lesson Quiz for this lesson if you haven't already done so. Students will be offered automatic remediation or enrichment based on their scores.

In *Electing the President*, students read about the process of electing the head of the executive branch. Pose these questions to the class on the Discussion Board:

Predict Consequences If the electoral college was eliminated and the national popular vote plan implemented, how might presidential campaigns change?

Make Decisions Which process is more democratic, taking into account the most people's preferences, the presidential primaries, or the general campaign?

Topic Inquiry

Have students continue their investigations for the Topic Inquiry.

Money and Elections

Supporting English Language Learners

Use with Digital Texts 2 and 5, **Where the Money Comes From** and **Loopholes in Finance Laws.**

Speaking

As you analyze the impact of political parties and interest groups, discuss the definitions of the following content area vocabulary words: *political action committee*, *subsidy*, *hard money*, and *soft money*.

Beginning Provide simple sentence frames for each of the words. Have students work with partners, using the sentence frames as a guide for authentic speaking with the content vocabulary.

Intermediate Ask students simple questions that require the vocabulary words as answers. Guide students to use complete sentences when answering.

Advanced Guide students to create word webs for each of the vocabulary words. Have students discuss their word webs with a partner. Remind them to use the vocabulary words when speaking.

Advanced High Have partners discuss and then write sentences for each of the vocabulary words. Have them read their sentences to a partner or other students in their group.

Use with the lesson 4 readings.

Reading Strategies

After you discuss the impact of political parties and interest groups, tell students that looking for patterns in words will help them understand English. Have students look in the text for related words that come from the same base word. Explain the meaning of the base words. Examples of base words: *elect*, *corrupt*, *contribute*, *subsidy*.

Beginning Write the base and related words on the board. Model the use of each word by using it in a sentence. Have students copy and repeat the sentences.

Intermediate Have partners make a list of the base and related words they find. Have them share their list with the class. Model the use of each word by using it in a sentence. Have students repeat the sentences and think of their own.

Advanced Ask students to make a list of the base and related words they find. Have students share their words with the class. Ask students to use the words in sentences.

Advanced High Ask students to make a list of the base and related words they find. Have the class sort the words into parts of speech such as verbs, nouns, and adjectives. Ask students to use the words in sentences.

◗ Differentiate Instruction

Use the Differentiated Instruction notes throughout the lesson plan to support the varied skill sets, levels of readiness, and interests in the mixed-ability classroom.

Challenge These notes include suggestions for expanding the activity for advanced students.

On-Level These notes include suggestions for modifying the activity to address different interests or learning styles.

Extra Support These notes include ideas for providing more scaffolding or reading spuport.

Special Needs These notes provide ideas for adapting instruction to support the needs of various special needs students.

■ NOTES

Money and Elections

Objectives

Objective 1: Analyze the impact of campaign spending on the media.

Objective 2: Explain how campaign contributions by individuals and organizations affect the political process.

Objective 3: Explain how public funding of candidates affects the political process.

Objective 4: Explain how campaign finance laws have changed over time.

Objective 5: Distinguish hard money from soft money.

LESSON 4 ORGANIZER		PACING: APPROX. 1 PERIOD, .5 BLOCKS			
				RESOURCES	
		OBJECTIVES	**PACING**	**Online**	**Print**
Connect					
	DIGITAL START UP ACTIVITY **Does Campaign Spending Affect Democracy?**		5 min.	●	
Investigate					
	DIGITAL TEXT 1 **The Price of an Election**	Objective 1	10 min.	●	●
	INTERACTIVE GRAPH **Campaign Finance**		10 min.	●	
	DIGITAL TEXT 2 **Where the Money Comes From**	Objective 2	10 min.	●	●
	INTERACTIVE CHART **Outside Sources of Campaign Funding**		10 min.	●	
	DIGITAL TEXT 3 **Federal Finance Laws**	Objective 3	10 min.	●	●
	DIGITAL TEXT 4 **FEC Requirements**	Objective 4	10 min.	●	●
	DIGITAL TEXT 5 **Loopholes in Finance Laws**	Objective 5	10 min.	●	●
Synthesize					
	DIGITAL SYNTHESIZE ACTIVITY **Campaign Money**		5 min.	●	
Demonstrate					
	DIGITAL QUIZ **Lesson Quiz and Class Discussion Board**		10 min.	●	

PEARSON
realize™
www.PearsonRealize.com

Go online to access additional resources including:
Primary Sources • Biographies • Supreme Court cases •
21st Century Skill Tutorials • Maps • Graphic Organizers.

CONNECT

DIGITAL START UP ACTIVITY

Does Campaign Spending Affect Democracy?

Project the Start Up Activity Ask students to answer the questions as they enter and get settled. Then have them share their ideas with another student, either in class or through a chat or blog space.

Evaluate Evidence Ask: How does campaign spending affect democracy? *(Sample answer: Students' paragraphs should contain clear reasoning about how campaign spending affects democracy. Students may decide the effect is positive, negative, or neither; however, they should support their opinion reasonably.)*

Tell students that in this lesson they will learn how money influences elections.

Aa Vocabulary Development: Use the Interactive Reading Notepad to preview the Key Terms and Academic Vocabulary in this Lesson with students.

⚡ FLIP IT!

Assign the Flipped Video for this lesson.

■ STUDENT EDITION PRINT PAGES: 545–554

INVESTIGATE

DIGITAL TEXT 1

The Price of an Election

Objective 1: Explain the issues raised by campaign spending.

Quick Instruction

Dollars are absolutely necessary campaign resources. How much depends on several things: the office involved, the candidate and whether he or she is the incumbent or the challenger, the nature of the opposition, and much more—including, not least, the availability of campaign funds. The getting and spending of campaign funds can corrupt the entire political process.

Interactive Graph: Campaign Finance Project the graph and select each date shown. Compare how the funding sources were created.

📖 ACTIVE CLASSROOM

Using a Headline strategy, have students write a headline for each date. Remind students that headlines summarize information and provide a hook for readers to get them to read more.

D Differentiate: Extra Support Have students use a Sticky Note strategy and work together to find the big ideas for each date. Students can then use their sticky notes as they write their headlines.

ELL Use the ELL activity described in the ELL chart.

INTERACTIVE GRAPH

Campaign Finance

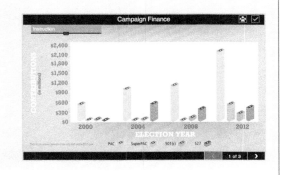

Further Instruction

The Price of an Election: Core Reading and Interactive Reading Notepad Project and discuss the Interactive Reading Notepad questions.

What Does Campaign Money Pay For? Radio and television time, professional campaign managers and consultants, newspaper advertisements, pamphlets, buttons, posters and bumper stickers, office rent, polls, data processing, mass mailings, Web sites, travel, and much more all make up the huge sums spent in campaigns. Television ads are far and away the largest item in most campaign budgets today, even at the local level. For 2012, total spending for all of the major and minor party presidential efforts exceeded $2.5 billion. Nearly $2 billion was spent on House and Senate contests in 2012.

Draw Conclusions Recall with students the impact of political changes brought about by the media.Why are television ads the largest item in most campaign budgets? *(Possible answer: Television ads are the best way to reach a wide variety of people.)*

Predict Consequences What are the consequences of having such costly campaigns? *(Possible answer: Only people with money will run. People with more money may be able to influence elections.)*

Money and Elections

DIGITAL TEXT 2

Where the Money Comes From

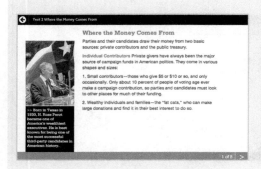

INTERACTIVE CHART

Outside Sources of Campaign Funding

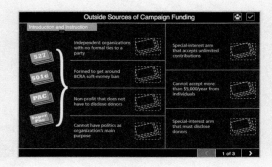

DIGITAL TEXT 3

Federal Finance Laws

Objective 2: **Describe the various sources of funding for campaign spending.**

Quick Instruction

Interactive Chart: Outside Sources of Campaign Funding Parties and their candidates draw their money from two basic sources: private contributors and the public treasury.

> **ACTIVE CLASSROOM**
>
> Have students complete the Drag and Drop activity. Then use a Ranking strategy to evaluate which source of funding seems to have the greatest impact on campaigns. Have students discuss their thinking.

D Differentiate: **Challenge** Have students use their ranks to write a letter to the editor arguing their position.

ELL Use the ELL activity described in the ELL chart.

Further Instruction

Where the Money Comes From: Core Reading and Interactive Reading Notepad Project and discuss the Interactive Reading Notepad questions.

Individual Contributors Individual contributions to candidates and political groups that support various issues or candidates and candidate fundraising are examples of private contributions.

Government Money Public financing is available in the form of subsidies for both State and national campaigns.

Make Inferences Political contributions are considered by the Supreme Court to be a form of free and protected speech. Why might the Supreme Court have held this to be true? *(Possible answer: Money is a way that voters can express their approval for a particular idea, similar to putting a campaign sign in your yard.)*

Identify Causes and Effects How might campaign contributions be corrupting? *(Possible answer: People may expect something in return for their money, especially if they give a lot of money to a candidate.)*

Objective 3: **Examine federal laws that regulate campaign finance.**

Quick Instruction

Congress first began to regulate campaign finance in 1907, but the rules were loosely drawn and rarely enforced. Several laws between 1971 and 2002 attempted to change that. The regulations are found in four detailed laws: FECA, the Federal Election Campaign Act of 1971; the FECA Amendments of 1974 and of 1976; and BCRA, the Bipartisan Campaign Reform Act of 2002. However, in 2010 the Supreme Court ruled that the government ban on political spending by corporations or labor unions violated the 1st Amendment right to free speech. That ruling overturned, or called into question, several key points of the campaign finance laws.

Further Instruction

Federal Finance Laws: Core Reading and Interactive Reading Notepad Project and discuss the Interactive Reading Notepad questions.

State and Local Elections Congress cannot regulate State and local elections. They make their own campaign finance rules. Some States have strong and effective laws, while others have weak or non-existent regulations.

Hypothesize Why might the Watergate scandal have brought about changes in campaign finance regulation? *(Possible answer: The scandal was related to paying for running for office.)*

DIGITAL TEXT 4

FEC Requirements

Draw Conclusions The first campaign finance law in 1907 made it unlawful for any corporation or national bank to make "a money contribution in any election" to candidates for federal office. Why might it have been a good thing to make that unlawful? *(Possible answer: Corporations and national banks might have more access to money and pay for certain favors from the government that would be unavailable to the rest of the population.)*

Objective 4: Outline the role of the Federal Election Commission in enforcing campaign finance laws.

Quick Instruction

The Federal Election Commission (FEC) administers all federal law dealing with campaign finance. Set up by Congress in 1974, the FEC is an independent agency in the executive branch. Its six members are appointed by the President, with Senate confirmation. The laws that the FEC is supposed to enforce cover four broad areas. They (1) require the timely disclosure of campaign finance data, (2) place limits on campaign contributions, (3) place limits on campaign expenditures, and (4) provide public financing for several parts of the presidential election process.

Further Instruction

FEC Requirements: Core Reading and Interactive Reading Notepad Project and discuss the Interactive Reading Notepad questions.

Disclosure Requirements Campaigns are required to report who has donated and how much they have given. The time requirements change depending on how much the person has given.

Limits on Individual Donations Today, no person can give more than $2,500 per election to any federal candidate. Also, no person can contribute more than $5,000 in any year to a political action committee (PAC), or $30,800 to a national party committee. The total of any person's contributions to federal candidates, political parties, and committees must be limited to no more than $117,000 in an election cycle (the two years from one general election to the next). The FEC adjusts these figures, to account for inflation, every two years.

Public Financing Public financing is overseen by the FEC. Taxpayers contribute to this fund if they choose to by marking a box on their tax forms each year. Accepting public subsidies, however, means that they can spend no more than the amount of the subsidy in the general election campaign, nor accept campaign funds from any other source. Public financing is available for the preconvention campaign, the conventions, and the general election. Minor party candidates are eligible for funding, but will receive it only after the campaign is finished.

Make Inferences Why is the relationship between Congress and the FEC sometimes described as the fox guarding the hen house? *(Possible answer: Congress, whose elections are governed by the FEC, must confirm appointees and set aside money for the FEC to do its job, which is to regulate how Congress gets elected.)*

Predict Consequences In 2008, Barack Obama became the first candidate in the history of the program to refuse public financing. Instead, he raised over $500 million on his own and won the presidency. What effect might that decision have on future campaigns? *(Possible answer: More candidates might refuse to accept public financing, preferring to raise money on their own.)*

Money and Elections

DIGITAL TEXT 5

Loopholes in Finance Laws

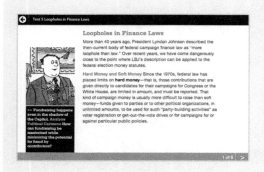

Loopholes in Finance Laws

More than 40 years ago, President Lyndon Johnson described the then-current body of federal campaign finance law as "more loophole than law." Over recent years, we have come dangerously close to the point where LBJ's description can be applied to the federal election money statutes.

Hard Money and Soft Money Since the 1970s, federal law has placed limits on **hard money**—that is, those contributions that are given directly to candidates for their campaigns for Congress or the White House, are limited in amount, and must be reported. That kind of campaign money is usually more difficult to raise than soft money—funds given to parties or to other political organizations, in unlimited amounts, to be used for such "party-building activities" as voter registration or get-out-the-vote drives or for campaigns for or against particular public policies.

>> Fundraising happens even in the shadow of the Capitol. Analyze Political Cartoons How can fundraising be maximized while minimizing the potential for fraud by contributors?

1 of 6 >

Objective 5: Distinguish hard money from soft money.

Quick Instruction

Hard money is given directly to candidates and their campaigns. It is regulated. Soft money is given to parties or to other political organizations, in unlimited amounts, to be used for such "party-building activities" as voter registration or get-out-the-vote drives or for campaigns for or against particular public policies.

ELL Use the ELL activity described in the ELL chart.

Further Instruction

Loopholes in Finance Laws: Core Reading and Interactive Reading Notepad Project and discuss the Interactive Reading Notepad questions.

Exploiting Soft Money Most 527s are advocacy groups that try to influence the outcome of elections through voter mobilization efforts and television advertisements that praise or criticize a candidate's record. They are allowed to raise unlimited sums of money. Super PACs are independent political action committees, unaffiliated with any political party. Unlike traditional PACs, Super PACs are allowed to raise and spend unlimited amounts, although they must reveal their donors and cannot work directly with a candidate's campaign.
501(c)s are nonprofit groups registered under the IRS tax code 501(c). 501(c)s, unlike 527s and Super PACs, do not have to disclose their donors. All three types of groups can raise and spend unlimited amounts, as long as those dollars are not given directly to a candidate or campaign.

Connect In the past, the first campaign finance laws regulated banks and corporations. How might those groups be able to contribute to present campaigns in ways they couldn't years ago? *(Possible answer: They could contribute to a Super PAC, which doesn't have to disclose its doners.)*

Evaluate Evidence More than forty years ago, President Lyndon Johnson described the then-current body of federal campaign finance law as "more loophole than law." Given what you know about campaign finance laws and spending in presidential campaigns, does his statement hold true today? *(Possible answer: Yes, because anyone can give money to a super PAC and no one would know.)*

SYNTHESIZE

DIGITAL SYNTHESIZE ACTIVITY

Campaign Money

Have students think about what they learned about the sources of money for political campaigns. Have them consider the potential influence of individuals and groups who contribute money to campaigns.

Have partners think about the following questions: What influence could the size of the contribution have on a campaign? Does it make a difference whether the contribution is made directly to the candidate or is spent on the candidate's behalf? Have pairs share their answers with the class.

Discuss Using a Think Pair Share strategy, have partners discuss their answers, explaining whether or not they believe politicians are too greatly influenced by donors to their campaigns. *(Answers will vary. Students should clearly express how the size of a contribution might influence a campaign and what differences there might be between a direct and indirect contribution.)*

DEMONSTRATE

DIGITAL QUIZ

Lesson Quiz and Class Discussion Board

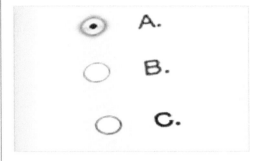

Assign the online Lesson Quiz for this lesson if you haven't already done so. Students will be offered automatic remediation or enrichment based on their scores.

In *Money and Elections*, students read about the relationship between money and elections. Pose these questions to the class on the Discussion Board:

Evaluate Ideas Several times in this lesson you read that the Supreme Court ruling in *Citizens United* sent shockwaves through the campaign regulation system. Do you agree? Why or why not?

Predict Consequences Public financing may not survive because it doesn't give candidates enough money to run a federal campaign. What do you think will happen next? Will something replace public financing?

Make Decisions You read about the explosion of money in the 2008, 2010, and 2012 federal campaigns. Do you think that the amount of money spent on campaigns has an upper hand? Explain your thinking.

Topic Inquiry

Have students continue their investigations for the Topic Inquiry.

Elections

◼ SYNTHESIZE

DIGITAL ACTIVITY
Reflect on the Essential Question and Topic

First ask students to reconsider the Essential Question for the Topic: Who Gets Elected?

Discuss what it takes for a political candidate to become elected to public office. Certainly one important consideration is thinking about what makes for a good candidate. In small groups, talk about the qualifications a good candidate possesses. Discuss similarities and differences among answers. Encourage students to add new answers.

Next ask students to reflect on the Topic as a whole and revisit the qualifications they chose. Have students write a brief paragraph stating why the qualification they chose is most important for a presidential candidate.

You may ask students to share their ideas on the Class Discussion Board.

Topic Inquiry
Have students complete Step 3 of the Topic Inquiry.

◼ DEMONSTRATE

DIGITAL TOPIC REVIEW AND ASSESSMENT
Elections

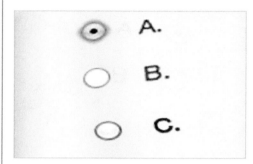

Students can prepare for the Topic Test by answering the questions in the Topic Review and Assessment online or the Assessment questions in the Print Student text. They can also prepare by reviewing their answers to the Interactive Reading Notepad questions or reviewing their notes in the Reading and Notetaking Study Guide.

DIGITAL TOPIC TEST
Elections

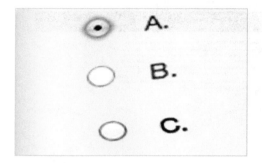

TOPIC TEST
Assign the Topic Test to assess students' understanding of topic content.

BENCHMARK TESTS
Assign these benchmark tests as you complete the relevant topics to monitor student progress toward mastering the course content and as preparation for the End-of-Course Test.

Benchmark Test 1: Topics 1–4
Benchmark Test 2: Topics 5–8
Benchmark Test 3: Topics 9–11
Benchmark Test 4: Topics 12–14

Government and the Economy

TOPIC 12 ORGANIZER	PACING: APPROX. 1 PERIOD, .5 BLOCKS

	PACING
Connect	1 period
MY STORY VIDEO **The United States Currency System**	10 min.
DIGITAL ESSENTIAL QUESTION ACTIVITY **What is the Proper Role of Government in the Economy?**	10 min.
DIGITAL OVERVIEW ACTIVITY **Government and the Economy**	10 min.
TOPIC INQUIRY: CIVIC ACTION PROJECT **Constitutional Rights Foundation**	20 min.
Investigate	2–5 periods
TOPIC INQUIRY: CIVIC ACTION PROJECT **Constitutional Rights Foundation**	Ongoing
LESSON 1 Types of Economic Systems	30–40 min.
LESSON 2 Fiscal and Monetary Policy	30–40 min.
LESSON 3 Financing Government	30–40 min.
LESSON 4 Spending and Borrowing	30–40 min.
LESSON 5 The U.S. in a Global Economy	30–40 min.
Synthesize	1 period
DIGITAL ACTIVITY **Reflect on the Essential Question and Topic**	10 min.
TOPIC INQUIRY: CIVIC ACTION PROJECT **Constitutional Rights Foundation**	20 min.
Demonstrate	1–2 periods
DIGITAL TOPIC REVIEW AND ASSESSMENT **Government and the Economy**	10 min.
TOPIC INQUIRY: CIVIC ACTION PROJECT **Constitutional Rights Foundation**	20 min.

 **TOPIC INQUIRY:**

Civic Action Project

For this topic's Inquiry, you may choose to do a Civic Action Project with your students by using the materials found at the Constitutional Rights Foundation's CAP website: http://www.crfcap.org. Civic Action Project (CAP) is a project-based learning model for government and economics courses. It offers a practicum for high school students in effective and engaged citizenship and uses blended learning to engage students in civic activities both in the traditional U.S. government and economics classrooms.

Constitutional
Rights
Foundation
Educate. Participate.

THE TEACHER'S ROLE

THE CAP TEACHER coaches and guides students through the civic action process as they select a problem or issue, research it, determine and take civic actions, and report and document the experience. The teacher motivates, challenges, critiques, and assesses student progress. Through a blended learning approach, teachers can let students take the reins of their civic learning, guiding them along the way.

[You can create your
CAP classroom in
three easy steps]

[**STEP 1**
Register yourself
for the CAP website]

[**STEP 2**
Enroll your
students]

[**STEP 3**
Engage your
students in the
CAP process and its
many resources]

Constitutional Rights Foundation

Pearson Magruder's American Government Students
Welcome to the Civic Action Project site

All of the information you're l... ...ur Government course will help you understand impor... ...t Govern... ...policy issues that will be discussed and debated at ...e lo... ...ate, ...d national level throughout your lifetime.

Participating in a Civic Action ... ...P) of your choosing will show you how you can use that knowledge as an engaged citizen in a democracy.

This CAP website will show you how to plan and carry out your project and give you lots of help along the way. Good luck!

Click on the logo to get started on your CAP!

THE STUDENT'S ROLE

CAP ALLOWS STUDENTS to create projects on issues they care about for their school or community. They see the connection between their civic actions and public policy and can share ideas for civics projects with each other and other CAP students nationwide. Students also see how the content of government and economics courses can apply to the real world. By taking civic actions, they practice what real citizens do when they go about trying to solve real policy-related problems. CAP fulfills best-practices in service-learning with an emphasis on public policy.

The CAP student is accountable for completing the civic action process, just as with a science project or term paper. The CAP Planner, a set of documents that guide students through the process, provides teachers with assessment information as well as a way to manage multiple student projects. While the teacher introduces and monitors the CAP, it is important that students take the lead in completing their civic actions. By using web-based technology and civics-based instruction and activities, students exercise important 21st century skills in digital literacy, critical thinking, collaboration, self-direction, and learning to be engaged and effective citizens.

CIVIC ACTIONS CAP challenges students to work on an actual problem, issue, or policy by taking civic actions. Civic actions build upon classroom civics issues, service-learning, and other proven practices of effective civic education. These actions can be many and varied, including:

- getting informed about a public issue or problem
- thinking critically about the issue or problem
- discovering how government is involved with the problem
- learning how government makes decisions
- developing a position
- engaging in civic dialogue
- building constituencies
- working together toward a common goal
- doing civic writing
- making presentations
- advocating for and defending positions
- meeting with officials

Brainstorming

Brainstorming is a method for generating ideas. It can be done by individuals or in small or large

Rules for Brainst

Pose a question to ar

Set a time limit on th more ideas out.

Work as fast as you

Handout Lesson 5B
Civic Action Project

GRADE
CAP Policy Analysis Tool

As citizens in a democracy, you'll be confronted with policy questions. Is a tax proposal a good idea? Should you vote for a particular ballot initiative? Government policies can profoundly affect our nation and your life. In a democracy, you have a say on government policies and proposed policies. It's important that you take a critical look at them. Use the following GRADE tests to evaluate a policy:

GOAL. What is the goal of the policy? If you don't know what it's supposed to do, you can't measure its success or failure. Policies are designed to address problems. What problem or problems is

POLICY? Who might (or does)
YOU UNDERSTAND WHO THE
ICY FAVORS SPECIAL
CES FOR INFORMATION, BUT

ITS? What is good about the
ES OR EFFECTS OF THE
VED) ITS GOAL? WILL IT
NSIVE? DOES IT PROTECT
E'S LIBERTIES?

OSTS? What is bad about the
THE CAUSES OR EFFECTS OF THE
E? DOES IT CAUSE HARM? DOES
RE ANY POTENTIAL

E DISADVANTAGES. Are there
TO DO NOTHING. MOST SERIOUS
EVALUATE THEM. LOOK AT
ES.

© 2012 Constitutional Rights Foundation

Conducting Meetings

Your meetings should be organized, to-the-point, and fun.

Decide how you're going to make decisions. If you are a small group, try deciding by whole-group consensus or by a two-thirds vote. A simple-majority decision may lead to bad feelings and resentment.

Understand everyone's role at the meeting. At most meetings, people need to fill the following roles, which may change from meeting to meeting:

- **Leader or facilitator** runs the meeting, follows the agenda item by item, and watches the time allotted for each. The leader helps participants focus on the task and makes sure everyone has a chance to participate.
- **Recorder** takes minutes, which include date and time of meeting, the persons attending, and notes on each agenda item.
- **Treasurer.**
- **Group members** contribute agenda items, discuss topics, make decisions, and take responsibility for various tasks.
- **Adviser** is an adult whose role is to give advice—not to run the group.
- **Guests** may participate in group discussions, but usually do not participate in final decision making.

Have an agenda. This is a list of things to be dealt with at a meeting. All members should be encouraged to put topics on the agenda. After the recorder reads the minutes of the previous meeting and they are approved, the members approve the agenda. Agenda items are considered in the following order:

- Old business—ongoing and follow-up items.

© 2012, Constitutional Rights Foundation
and Close Up Foundation

Constitutional
Rights
Foundation
Educate. Participate.

Guardian of Democracy: The Civic Mission of Schools Released September, 2011, *Guardian of Democracy: The Civic Mission of Schools report* builds on the findings of the seminal 2003 Civic Mission of Schools report. CAP has been designed to support the promising approaches described in these reports.

Government and the Economy

The Federal Government takes in huge amounts of money each year. The plan for how that money will be spent is called the budget. When the government spends more than it takes in, it must borrow to make up the difference. This is called deficit spending, and it has been the norm for most of the years since the Great Depression of the 1930s. What effect does government taxing and spending have on the economy as a whole?

CONNECT

MY STORY VIDEO

The United States Currency System

Watch a video that shows how the United States' supply of money is produced and distributed to the banks and people who spend it.

Identify Central Issues Why is it important for the US to have currency that is secure and hard to imitate or counterfeit? *(A safe money supply is necessary for a country to have a stable economy; people need to trust their money.)*

Hypothesize Do you think that virtual currencies and e-commerce might someday replace paper money? Would you welcome this change? *(Possible answers: Yes, because it would be fast and easy and secure. No, having actual coins and bills feels safer. Online currency would be easier to counterfeit.)*

⇆ FLIP IT!

Assign the My Story video.

DIGITAL ESSENTIAL QUESTION ACTIVITY

What is the Proper Role of Government in the Economy?

Ask students to think about the Essential Question for this Topic: "What is the proper role of government in the economy?" The economy is an important aspect of our nation. What role should the government play in this vital area? *(Possible answers: Some students might mention that the government should help to create jobs. Others might say that the government should be involved as little as possible in the economy. Instead, the government should allow businesses the freedom to operate without interference.)*

If students have not already done so, ask them to respond to the poll. Then go over the results as a class.

Discuss Read Vice President Joe Biden's quotation with students, then point out that the United States was founded on the belief that all people deserve equality, liberty, safety, and the right to pursue happiness. Ask students: Since these are our country's most basic values, should the government help every citizen achieve them? If so, how? If not, why not? *(Possible answer: Students who believe the government should help citizens achieve these goals might mention that the government could provide money for equal educational opportunities, incentives to help people start businesses, or national defense.)*

DIGITAL OVERVIEW ACTIVITY

Government and the Economy

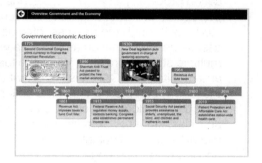

Display the timeline showing the major actions of the U.S. government concerning the economy. During this Topic students will learn about all of these events and many more, but this timeline will provide a framework into which they can place the events they learn about.

D Differentiate: Extra Support What event happened before the Federal Reserve Act? What event happened after this act? *(Sherman Antitrust Act; "New Deal" legislation)*

Check Understanding How many years after the Revenue Act did the Patient Protection and Affordable Care Act become established? *(46 years)*

Sequence Events Place the following events in chronological order: Social Security Act provides assistance; "New Deal" legislation is put into effect; the Revenue Act imposes taxes; and the Revenue Act creates significant tax cuts. *(Revenue Act imposes taxes; "New Deal" legislation is put into effect; Social Security Act provides assistance; Revenue Act creates significant tax cuts.)*

Topic Inquiry

Launch the Topic Inquiry with students after introducing the Topic.

Types of Economic Systems

Supporting English Language Learners

Use with Digital Text 7, **Comparing the Free Enterprise System with Other Economic Systems.**

Speaking
Use the following content area vocabulary from the text in order to help students compare the role of government in the U.S. free enterprise system and other economic systems: *capitalism, factors of production, capital, entrepreneur.* Guide students to speak the words aloud and then complete a four-section graphic organizer for each word. The graphic organizer should contain the word, the definition, a visual representation, and characteristics or personal associations.

Beginning Display one content area word at a time. Say the words and have the students repeat. Guide the group to complete graphic organizers for the words, then have students complete sentence frames for the words by speaking them aloud. For example, *An entrepreneur is a person who _____.*

Intermediate Say the words and have the students repeat. Have small groups complete graphic organizers for the words. Then have students verbalize a phrase or short sentence using each word.

Advanced Say the words and have the students repeat. Have pairs complete graphic organizers for the words. Ask them to use the words in complete sentences, then have them read their sentences to their partners.

Advanced High Have students complete graphic organizers for the words. Ask them to have a conversation within their group about the reading content, during which they use the words correctly.

Use with Digital Texts 2 and 3, **The American Free Enterprise System** and **What Is a Mixed Economy?**

Listening
To support students as they learn about different types of economic systems, choose words from the text that students have difficulty reading or pronouncing. Model correct pronunciation of the words. Have students repeat, and accept their attempts while continuing to model correct pronunciation.

Beginning Display the words. Read the words as students listen, emphasizing the letter sounds. Explain the meaning of the words. Provide visuals as support, if possible. Have students repeat and copy the words.

Intermediate Display phrases from the text and explain their meanings. Read each phrase one at a time as students listen. As you read each phrase have students repeat and copy the phrase.

Advanced Display sentences from the text. Read each sentence as students listen and have students repeat. Have students read each sentence to each other.

Advanced High Display a short paragraph from the text. Read the paragraph aloud as students listen. Have the students read the paragraph to a partner. Have them identify words they need to practice.

▣ Differentiate Instruction

Use the Differentiated Instruction notes throughout the lesson plan to support the varied skill sets, levels of readiness, and interests in the mixed-ability classroom.

Challenge These notes include suggestions for expanding the activity for advanced students.

On-Level These notes include suggestions for modifying the activity to address different interests or learning styles.

Extra Support These notes include ideas for providing more scaffolding or reading spuport.

Special Needs These notes provide ideas for adapting instruction to support the needs of various special needs students.

■ NOTES

Types of Economic Systems

Objectives

Objective 1: Identify the factors of production.

Objective 2: Understand the role played by the National Government in both the public and private sectors of the U.S. free enterprise system.

Objective 3: Understand the relationship between U.S. government policies and the economy in a mixed economy.

Objective 4: Describe the four fundamental factors in a free enterprise system and understand how the Federal Government fosters competition and entrepreneurship, as well as how government regulation can serve as a restriction to private enterprise.

Objective 5: Summarize the theories of Karl Marx and identify important characteristics of socialist and communist economies and describe socialism and communism in today's world.

Objective 6: Evaluate the strengths and weaknesses of capitalism versus socialism and communism.

LESSON 1 ORGANIZER		PACING: APPROX. 1 PERIOD, .5 BLOCKS			
				RESOURCES	
		OBJECTIVES	PACING	Online	Print
Connect					
DIGITAL START UP ACTIVITY **Running Your Own Business**			5 min.	●	
Investigate					
DIGITAL TEXT 1 **Capitalism and the Factors of Production**		Objective 1	10 min.	●	●
DIGITAL TEXT 2 **The American Free Enterprise System**		Objectives 2, 4	10 min.	●	●
DIGITAL TEXT 3 **What is a Mixed Economy?**		Objective 3	10 min.	●	●
DIGITAL TEXT 4 **Socialism, Communism, and Karl Marx**		Objective 5	10 min.	●	●
DIGITAL TEXTS 5 AND 6 **Communism, The Special Case of China**		Objective 5	10 min.	●	●
INTERACTIVE GALLERY **China's Economy, Past and Present**			10 min.	●	
DIGITAL TEXT 7 **Comparing the Free Enterprise System with Other Economic Systems**		Objective 6	10 min.	●	●
INTERACTIVE CHART **Three Types of Economic Systems**			10 min.	●	
Synthesize					
DIGITAL SYNTHESIZE ACTIVITY **Evaluating Economic Systems**			5 min.	●	
Demonstrate					
DIGITAL QUIZ **Lesson Quiz and Class Discussion Board**			10 min.	●	

PEARSON •••••
realize™
www.PearsonRealize.com

Go online to access additional resources including:
Primary Sources • Biographies • Supreme Court cases •
21st Century Skill Tutorials • Maps • Graphic Organizers.

CONNECT

DIGITAL START UP ACTIVITY
Running Your Own Business

Project the Start Up Activity After briefly describing their businesses, have students answer the questions.

Discuss What things would you need to start your business? *(land, buildings, equipment, money, and workers)* What would you need to do well? *(Students should describe particular skills, talents, knowledge, and traits.)* How might government policies influence your success? *(Students' answers should reflect their ideas about how much government should be involved in business.)*

Tell students that in this lesson they will be learning about various economic systems, including capitalism, socialism, and communism.

Aa **Vocabulary Development:** Use the Interactive Reading Notepad to preview the Key Terms and Academic Vocabulary in this Lesson with students.

⇅ FLIP IT!
Assign the Flipped Video for this lesson.

■ STUDENT EDITION PRINT
PAGES: 562–572

INVESTIGATE

DIGITAL TEXT 1
Capitalism and the Factors of Production

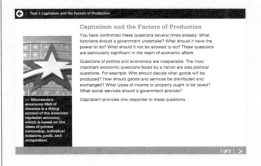

Objective 1: Identify the factors of production.

Quick Instruction
Tell students that many factors must work together in order for a business to produce goods. Have students form pairs. Then ask: What do you think is the most important factor of production? Why do you think this? Have pairs discuss their answers and write summaries of their responses. Ask volunteers to share their responses. *(Possible answers: Answers will vary. Students might say that land is the most important factor, because businesses need natural resources before any goods can be produced. Others might say labor is the most important, because it involves skills and knowledge that are critical to profitability.)*

Further Instruction
Go through the Interactive Reading Notepad questions and discuss the answers with the class.

Remind students that capitalism is an economic system in which individuals are free to own the means of production and maximize profits. Ask students to think of an example of a business in their area that shows capitalism working successfully. Who profits the most from the success of this business? *(Possible answer: The person who owns the business profits the most because he or she gets the most money from the business.)* Who profits the least? *(Possible answer: The low-level employees profit the least because they have low salaries.)*

Support Point of View with Evidence Do you think entrepreneurs want the government to own most of the land in a nation? *(Possible answer: No; entrepreneurs probably do not want to deal with government rules and restrictions dealing with land use. Such rules would limit how the land could be used and might result in expensive fees and regulations.)*

Types of Economic Systems

DIGITAL TEXT 2

The American Free Enterprise System

Text 2: The American Free Enterprise System

The American Free Enterprise System

Capitalism is frequently referred to as a **free enterprise system**, which is an economic system characterized by private ownership of capital and by investments that are determined by private decision, not by public authorities. This system needs a **free market**, a market in which buyers and sellers are free to buy and sell as they wish. A free market is most likely to exist in a democratic nation, such as the United States, where security and the rule of law are protected by the government.

A free enterprise system lets consumers, entrepreneurs, and workers enjoy freedom of choice. Consumers can choose from a variety of products and services. Entrepreneurs can switch from one business to another. Workers can quit their jobs and seek new ones, and they can choose to organize labor unions as a way to bargain for better working conditions or benefits.

>> Freedom of choice and competition mean that a vast variety of goods are available in a capitalist economy. Here, shoppers peruse wares at historic Charleston City Market in South Carolina.

1 of 12 | >

Objectives 2: Understand the role played by the National Government in both the public and private sectors of the U.S. free enterprise system; 4: Describe the four fundamental factors in a free enterprise system and understand how the Federal Government fosters competition and entrepreneurship, as well as how government regulation can serve as restrictions to private enterprise.

Quick Instruction

Tell students that a free enterprise system is based on private ownership, individual initiative, profit, and competition. Have students form pairs. Ask students: Do you think private ownership, profit, and competition can enhance individual initiative? Why or why not? *(Possible answer: Yes; having ownership over something and the possibility of making a profit will motivate people to try harder at making their business a success. Competition prevents people from getting complacent and motivates them to do better than their competitors.)* Do you think government regulation can serve as a restriction to private enterprise? Why or why not? *(Possible answer: Yes; by implementing heavy taxes and business restrictions or by taking away private ownership of businesses, governments can make individuals less motivated to achieve business success.)* Ask volunteers to share their answers.

D **Differentiate: Challenge** Have students choose an existing business, either one in the community or anywhere in the United States. Then ask them to research that business to find at least one government regulation with which it must comply. Then ask them to consider how that regulation does or does not serve to restrict private enterprise in this specific case and present their conclusions to the class.

ELL Use the ELL activity described in the ELL chart.

Further Instruction

Go through the Interactive Reading Notepad questions and discuss the answers with the class.

Point out to students that the U.S. Constitution includes various protections that foster competition and entrepreneurship. Some of those protections, such as the power of Congress to regulate commerce among the States, simply create an economic climate within which the free enterprise system can operate. Others are more specific, such as the Sherman Anti-Trust Act and the Anti-Trust Division of the Department of Justice, both of which act specifically to maintain competition in the U.S. marketplace.

Finally, point out that the power of Congress to issue patents also fosters competition and entrepreneurship. Tell students to suppose that they are an inventor who has just developed a new type of cell phone. Without a patent, anyone could copy the idea, which would limit their profits. Competition would

also be threatened, because big businesses with large resources would be able to dominate the marketplace.

Check Understanding How do government regulatory policies such as the 5th and 14th Amendments influence the economy at the national level? *(These amendments declare that no person may be deprived of life, liberty, or property without due process of law. They therefore protect and support the private ownership of business and enhance a capitalistic economy.)* How does the executive branch of government, especially the Department of Justice, function in terms of fostering competition and entrepreneurship? *(The DOJ has an Anti-Trust Division that monitors business acivities to determine whether competition is threatened. It can stop the sale or merger of a company or break up a monopoly to restore competition.)*

DIGITAL TEXT 3

What is a Mixed Economy?

DIGITAL TEXT 4

Socialism, Communism, and Karl Marx

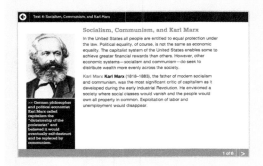

Objective 3: Understand the relationship between U.S. government policies and the economy in a mixed economy.

Quick Instruction

Remind students that government at the federal, State, and local levels regulates aspects of the U.S. economy. Conduct a class debate centered around this question: Do you think the government regulates the economy too much, too little, or just enough? Have students form groups depending on their answers to this question. Tell each group to discuss reasons for their answer. Then have a representative from each group summarize the group's argument for the class.

ELL Use the ELL activity described in the ELL chart.

Further Instruction

Go through the Interactive Reading Notepad questions and discuss the answers with the class.

Remind students that the U.S government not only restricts the economy, but also promotes it. Ask students to find examples of how the U.S. government promotes the economy. (constructs roads and highways; provides public health programs, weather reports, and census data; offers loan programs; operates insurance programs)

Infer Do you think government restrictions of the economy at the national level affect larger or smaller businesses more? Explain. *(Possible answer: At the national level, the government prohibits trusts and protects the environment.*

Large businesses are the most likely to form trusts. Also, large businesses potentially can do the most damage to the environment.)

Draw Conclusions In China, the government owns steel mills and factories. Do you think this government regulation serves as a restriction or an encouragement to economic growth? Explain. *(Possible answer: A restriction; by owning steel mills and factories, the government is limiting private enterprise. This restriction probably lessens individual initiative and thereby hinders economic growth.)*

Objective 5: Summarize the theories of Karl Marx and identify important characteristics of socialist and communist economies and describe socialism and communism in today's world.

Quick Instruction

Tell students that the economic theory of Karl Marx gave rise to two economic systems: socialism and communism. Have students use a Think Pair Share to complete the following activity. First, have pairs summarize the economic theory of Marx. Then ask: How does socialism attempt to achieve these goals? *(Socialist governments regulate the distribution of necessities and services to provide an equal distribution of these elements to the people. By doing this, these governments hope to establish a classless society.)* Have volunteers share their answers with the class.

D Differentiate: **Extra Support** Help students compare the U.S. constitutional republic to historical forms of government, such as socialist governments. Point out that one major difference between the two forms of government has centered around the role that government plays in the economy. Under the American free enterprise system, the government's role has historically been much more limited than it has been in socialist countries. This has often meant the nationalization of industries and central planning of the economy by government officials.

Types of Economic Systems

DIGITAL TEXT 5
Communism

DIGITAL TEXT 6
The Special Case of China

Further Instruction

Go through the Interactive Reading Notepad questions and discuss the answers with the class. To extend the teaching of this objective have students answer the following question.

Contrast Do you think the influence of the economic policies of a socialist government would differ from the influence of the economic policies of a communist government? Explain your answer. *(Possible answers: Answers will vary. Students might claim that the influence of these policies would be different. Socialist policies would allow democracy to exist. Communist policies would eliminate democracy. Others might state that there would be similarities and differences. Socialist policies would allow democracy and communist policies would not. However, both would attempt to achieve the same kind of changes, namely an economy controlled by the government and a classless society.)*

Objective 5: Summarize the theories of Karl Marx and identify important characteristics of socialist and communist economies and describe socialism and communism in today's world.

Quick Instruction

Tell students that the Soviet Union and China both implemented a communist system. However, the economic policies of these communist governments had some differences. Have students use a Think Pair Share to answer the following questions. How did the economic policies of communist China and the Soviet Union differ? How were they similar? *(The economic policies of the Soviet Union emphasized using labor for heavy industry. The economic policies of China emphasized training the peasantry to do skilled labor. Both economic policies supported the collectivization of agriculture.)* What was the influence of these policies on the people of China and the Soviet Union? *(Both economic policies brought great hardship to the people, including scarce resources and famine.)* Have volunteers share their responses with the class.

Interactive Gallery: China's Economy, Past and Present Project the slideshow. Look at each image individually and then the collection of images as a whole.

Analyze Graphs Review the bar graph on the last slide that compares the GDP of China and the United States by sector. Summarize the differences in GDP between these countries. *(Most of China's GDP comes from industry and services. In the United States, services dominate the GDP. China has a much higher agricultural GDP than the United States. The United States has a much higher services GDP than China.)*

ACTIVE CLASSROOM

Have students do a Graffiti Concepts activity to compare the role of government in the U.S. free enterprise system with China's economic system. Ask them to reflect on these systems and create a visual image that represents the role of government in each. Ask students to post their "graffiti" on the board or on chart paper. Have students look at all the responses and then discuss similarities and differences in the responses as a group.

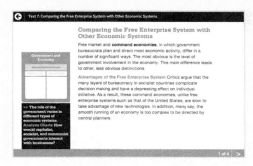

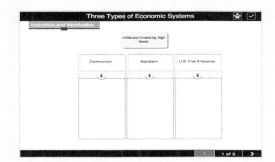

INTERACTIVE GALLERY

China's Economy, Past and Present

DIGITAL TEXT 7

Comparing the Free Enterprise System with Other Economic Systems

INTERACTIVE CHART

Three Types of Economic Systems

Further Instruction

Go through the Interactive Reading Notepad questions and discuss the answers with the class. To extend the teaching of this objective have students answer the following questions.

Identify Cause and Effect How did the economic policies of the Soviet Union contribute to its collapse? *(These economic policies caused scarce consumer goods, housing, and urban services. The services that were available were often poor quality. Also, economic policies created a privileged class which contradicted the basic goals of communism. Since these policies were not working, the Soviet Union became weaker and eventually collapsed.)*

Check Understanding How do the current government policies of China combine communism and private enterprise? *(The Communist Party remains in power and directs overall economic growth. However, the government also encouraged private enterprise and investment.)*

Objective 6: Evaluate the strengths and weaknesses of capitalism versus socialism and communism.

Quick Instruction

Tell students that both the free enterprise system and command economies have advantages and disadvantages. Have a class discussion about these systems. Ask students: If you had a choice, would you prefer that the United States have a free enterprise system, a command economy, or a mixture of both? Ask volunteers to give their responses, and encourage them to provide reasons for their responses, including the role government plays in each system. Write important points raised by students on the board. Review these points after the discussion.

Interactive Chart: Three Types of Economic Systems Project the tile sort on the whiteboard and explain how this interactive works. Introduce the activity by telling students that the writings of Karl Marx inspired two movements to improve the conditions of workers: communism and socialism. However, these government and economic systems have key differences from each other as well as from the free enterprise system of the United States. Ask students to drag each tile to the type of economic systems it describes.

◼◼ ACTIVE CLASSROOM

Ask student to use the Take a Stand strategy to answer this question: Is the free enterprise system better than command economies? Yes or no? Have students divide into two groups based on their answer and move to separate areas of the classroom. If one group does not have enough members, assign more students to this group. Ask students to talk to each other to compare their reasons for answering "yes" or "no." Have a representative from each side present and defend the group's point of view.

Compare Based on the chart and the text, how are the free enterprise system found in the U.S. constitutional republic and the type of economy found under socialism similar? *(Both include privately owned businesses and use a capitalistic system.)* How are they different? *(Unlike the U.S. free enterprise system, socialist economies usually involve high taxes to fund government social welfare programs and have some elements of central planning.)*

Further Instruction

Editable Presentation Use the Editable Presentation to present the main ideas for this Core Reading.

Types of Economic Systems

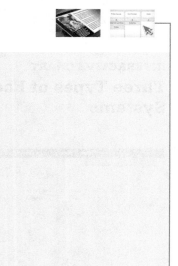

 SYNTHESIZE

DEMONSTRATE

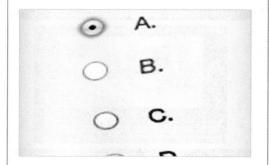

DIGITAL SYNTHESIZE ACTIVITY

Evaluating Economic Systems

DIGITAL QUIZ

Lesson Quiz and Class Discussion Board

Comparing the Free Enterprise System with Other Economic Systems: Core Reading and Interactive Reading Notepad Project and discuss the Interactive Reading Notepad questions, including the graphic organizer asking students to place the labels for the economic systems in the correct position on the scale. Review these economic systems with the class and fill in the graphic organizer on the whiteboard as you go.

Check Understanding Does the government have a larger role in the free enterprise system or in a command economy? Explain your answer. *(The government has a larger role in a command economy. In the free enterprise system, private individuals and companies own most of the factors of production and decide how to use them. In a command economy, the government controls the economy and many of the factors of production are owned by the government.)*

Ask students to recall the Topic Essential Question: "What is the proper role of government in the economy?" Remind students that they have read about capitalism, socialism, and communism in relation to the level of government involvement in a nation's economy.

Project the quotation from President Reagan. Have students use the Think Pair Share strategy to evaluate this quotation in terms of what they have learned and their opinions about government and the economy. Tell partners to answer the following questions. Which economic philosophy is reflected in his statement? Do you agree or disagree with President Reagan? Why? Be sure to address each part of his assurance: strong economy, abundant lives, and freedom. *(Possible answer: President Reagan's quotation reflects a laissez-faire approach to government involvement in the economy. Students should also clearly state whether they agree or disagree with President Reagan. Their reasons should include facts from the lesson. Students should also address whether the laissez-faire government suggested by Reagan will make the economy stronger, lead to abundance, and also enhance freedom.)* Have pairs share their answers with the class.

Hypothesize Do you think Reagan's economic approach is still used in today's U.S. economy? *(Possible answer: Answers will vary. Students might mention that the current government still encourages private enterprise and allows businesses a large amount of freedom. Because of this, Reagan's approach still applies. However, other students might mention that the government is applying more environmental and product safety restrictions on businesses. As a result, Reagan's approach has been modified.)*

Assign the online Lesson Quiz for this lesson if you haven't already done so. Students will be offered automatic remediation or enrichment based on their score.

Tell students that in "Types of Economic Systems" they read about various economic systems, including capitalism, socialism, and communism. Also, they studied mixed economies and compared the free enterprise system with other economic systems.

Pose these questions to the class on the Discussion Board:

Make Predictions Do you think Russia will develop more of a free enterprise economy or revert back to a complete command economy? *(Possible answer: Answers will vary. Students might point out that since most countries have a free market economy, Russia will have to develop more of a free market system to keep pace. Others might mention that since Russia is having problems establishing a free market system, it might revert to the more familiar command economy.)*

Support Ideas with Evidence Why do you think most countries have adopted a capitalistic system? *(Possible answer: Capitalism encourages rewards for hard work. Because of this, workers are motivated to work harder and better, which helps to improve a nation's economy.)*

Topic Inquiry

Have students continue their investigations for the Topic Inquiry

Fiscal and Monetary Policy

Supporting English Language Learners

Use with Digital Text 3, **How Fiscal Policy Influences the Economy.**

Speaking
Read the section *How Fiscal Policy Influences the Economy.* Have the students discuss the information in groups, then work together to create a graphic organizer on government fiscal policies. The graphic organizer should have three sections: *How Fiscal Policy Influences the Economy, Historical Use of Fiscal Policy,* and *Another Use for Fiscal Policy.*

Beginning Read aloud the text, using visuals as support, as students follow along. Divide the students into three groups. Each group will discuss what they have learned in order to complete one section of the graphic organizer. Allow students to use drawings, words, or phrases to complete the graphic organizer. Students should discuss the finished work with the other groups.

Intermediate Read aloud the text, using visuals as support, as students follow along. Have small groups discuss what they have learned in order to complete a section of the graphic organizer, using drawings, phrases, or short sentences. Guide students to discuss their graphic organizers with the larger group.

Advanced Have partners read the text and discuss what they have learned. Then assign one section of the graphic organizer to each group, to be completed using short sentences. Have the groups discuss the completed graphic organizer and the information that was gathered.

Advanced High Have students read the text, then assign one section of the graphic organizer to each student in the group. Have students write short paragraphs to complete the graphic organizer, then discuss their completed work and the information that was gathered.

Use with Digital Text 4, **How Monetary Policy Influences the Economy.**

Listening
Tell students that intonation patterns are different for statements and questions. Read aloud the third paragraph under the heading "Fiscal and Monetary Policies at the State and Local Levels." Point out the differences in the intonation of your voice for the various parts of the paragraph.

Beginning Guide students to repeat after you as you read aloud. Have students listen as a partner reads the paragraph aloud using proper intonation.

Intermediate Read the paragraph aloud as students listen. After students repeat after you, have partners read the statement and questions to each other using proper intonation.

Advanced Emphasize different words as you read aloud while the students listen. Discuss how this affects the meaning.

Advanced High Have one partner read a the paragraph, emphasizing different words while the other listens. Have the second partner tell how the intonation affected the meaning. Have partners switch roles.

▣ Differentiate Instruction

Use the Differentiated Instruction notes throughout the lesson plan to support the varied skill sets, levels of readiness, and interests in the mixed-ability classroom.

Challenge These notes include suggestions for expanding the activity for advanced students.

On-Level These notes include suggestions for modifying the activity to address different interests or learning styles.

Extra Support These notes include ideas for providing more scaffolding or reading spuport.

Special Needs These notes provide ideas for adapting instruction to support the needs of various special needs students.

■ NOTES

Fiscal and Monetary Policy

Objectives

Objective 1: Explain the major responsibilities of the federal government for domestic economic policy.

Objective 2: Describe the overall goals of the Federal Government's actions in the economy.

Objective 3: Explain how government fiscal policy influences the economy at the national level.

Objective 4: Explain how government monetary policy influences the economy at the national level.

LESSON 2 ORGANIZER		PACING: APPROX. 1 PERIOD, .5 BLOCKS			
				RESOURCES	
		OBJECTIVES	**PACING**	**Online**	**Print**
Connect					
DIGITAL START UP ACTIVITY **An Influential Economist**			5 min.	●	
Investigate					
DIGITAL TEXT 1 **Federal Government and the Domestic Economy**		Objective 1	10 min.	●	●
INTERACTIVE CHART **Setting Interest Rates**			10 min.	●	
DIGITAL TEXT 2 **Key Goals for the Economy**		Objective 2	10 min.	●	●
DIGITAL TEXT 3 **How Fiscal Policy Influences the Economy**		Objective 3	10 min.	●	●
DIGITAL TEXT 4 **How Monetary Policy Influences the Economy**		Objective 4	10 min.	●	●
INTERACTIVE CHART **Booms, Busts, and Fiscal and Monetary Policy**		Objectives 1, 3, 4	10 min.	●	
Synthesize					
DIGITAL SYNTHESIZE ACTIVITY **Government and the Economy**			5 min.	●	
Demonstrate					
DIGITAL QUIZ **Lesson Quiz and Class Discussion Board**			10 min.	●	

PEARSON
realize.™
www.PearsonRealize.com

Go online to access additional resources including:
Primary Sources • Biographies • Supreme Court cases •
21st Century Skill Tutorials • Maps • Graphic Organizers.

■ CONNECT

DIGITAL START UP ACTIVITY
An Influential Economist

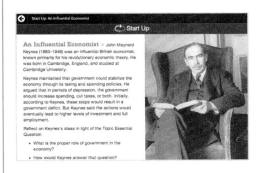

Project the Start Up Activity Have students share their ideas with another student, either in class or through a chat or blog space.

Discuss According to Keynes, what causes depressions? *(Depressions are caused when the "effective demand" drops.)* Why do you think this happens? *(People, businesses, and government spend less money; businesses earn less profit and close down or let employees go.)*

Tell students that in this lesson they will be learning the responsibilities of the Federal Government for domestic policy and how government fiscal and monetary policies influence the economy at all levels.

Aa Vocabulary Development: Use the Interactive Reading Notepad to preview the Key Terms and Academic Vocabulary in this Lesson with students.

⇅ FLIP IT!
Assign the Flipped Video for this lesson.

■ STUDENT EDITION PRINT
PAGES: 573–579

■ INVESTIGATE

DIGITAL TEXT 1
Federal Government and the Domestic Economy

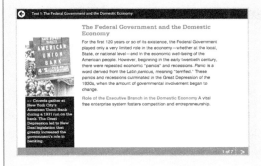

Objective 1: **Explain the major responsibilities of the Federal Government for domestic economic policy.**

Quick Instruction
Tell students that the Federal Government has responsibilities concerning domestic economic policy. Ask students: What are the main agencies within the executive branch that regulate economic policy? Have students take a piece of paper and fold it into thirds. Students should write down the name of the agency in the first box and explain that agency's role in regulating economic activities. Then students should go around the room asking for other responses. If students think a response is correct, then they should write it in one of their boxes. Have volunteers share their responses with the class.

Help students analyze the functions of the executive branch of government, including the constitutional powers of the President, by asking what role the President plays in the Federal Reserve System. *(He or she appoints the members of the Board of Governors.)*

Interactive Drag and Drop: Setting Interest Rates Project the drag and drop on the whiteboard. Introduce the activity by telling students that the Federal Reserve System is known as "the Fed." It is part of the executive branch and functions as the central banking system for the U.S. The Fed sets

INTERACTIVE CHART
Setting Interest Rates

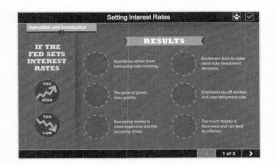

monetary policies that influence the economy at the local, State, and national levels. The Fed can expand the economy in a downturn or contract it in boom times if inflation is too high. It can do this by regulating the amount of money flowing into the economy through changing interest rates. How interest rates are set affects jobs, prices, and business decisions at the local, State, and national levels. Tell students to drag the Too High or Too Low icons to the description of the result.

📷 ACTIVE CLASSROOM
Have students use a Make Headlines activity for government involvement in domestic economic policy. Tell students to write a headline about a Federal Government action related to domestic economic policy. This action should attempt to correct a domestic economic problem and should involve one of the major responsibilities of the Federal Government concerning domestic economic policy. Also, the headline should capture the most important aspect of the action. Students should pass their headlines to partners for them to review.

Fiscal and Monetary Policy

DIGITAL TEXT 2

Key Goals for the Economy

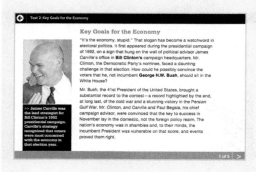

Text 2: Key Goals for the Economy

Key Goals for the Economy

"It's the economy, stupid." That slogan has become a watchword in electoral politics. It first appeared during the presidential campaign of 1992, on a sign that hung on the wall of political advisor James Carville's office in **Bill Clinton's** campaign headquarters. Mr. Clinton, the Democratic Party's nominee, faced a daunting challenge in that election: How could he possibly convince the voters that he, not incumbent **George H.W. Bush**, should sit in the White House?

Mr. Bush, the 41st President of the United States, brought a substantial record to the contest—a record highlighted by the end, at long last, of the cold war and a stunning victory in the Persian Gulf War. Mr. Clinton, and Carville and Paul Begala, his chief campaign advisor, were convinced that the key to success in November lay in the domestic, not the foreign policy realm. The nation's economy was in shambles and, to their minds, the incumbent President was vulnerable on that score, and events proved them right.

>> James Carville was the lead strategist for Bill Clinton's 1992 presidential campaign. Carville's strategy recognized that voters were most concerned with the economy in that election year.

1 of 5 >

Further Instruction

Go through the Interactive Reading Notepad questions and discuss the answers with the class. To extend the teaching of this objective have students answer the following question:

Support Point of View with Evidence What do you think is the most important responsibility of the government concerning domestic economic policy? *(Possible answer: The responsibility of the Labor Department is the most important because it deals with occupational safety and ensures fairness in contracts, benefits, and wages. These actions help to prevent workers from being exploited.)*

Remind students that government regulatory policies also influence the economy at the local, State, and national levels. Many independent agencies within the executive branch of the Federal Government have an important role in this regulation. Write *the Fed, SEC,* and *OSHA* on the board. Then have students review the narrative to find out how these agencies influence the economy. Point out that federal regulations have a major impact on citizens' everyday lives and that regulatory policies are also found at the State and local levels.

Objective 2: Describe the overall goals of the Federal Government's actions in the economy.

Quick Instruction

Tell students that the Federal Government has three key goals: full employment, price stability, and economic growth. Have students use a Think Pair Share to answer the following question. Can the government achieve one of these goals without achieving the other two? Why or why not? *(Possible answer: No; these goals are all dependent on each other. For example, for the United States to achieve full employment requires that it has a growing economy that offers enough jobs for people. A growing economy requires price stability, which curbs inflation and deflation.)* Ask volunteers to share their answers with the class.

D Differentiate: **Challenge** Have students write a speech for a presidential candidate seeking election. This candidate wants to stress that he or she will improve the economy. The speech should include the key economic goals of the government and explain how these goals will be achieved.

Further Instruction

Go through the Interactive Reading Notepad questions and discuss the answers with the class. To extend the teaching of this objective have students answer the question below.

Explain that one of the functions of the executive branch of government, including the executive departments, is to help the nation achieve its key economic goals. The Department of Labor plays a major role in this effort by compiling reports that are used to measure the nation's economic health, tracking trends in the prices of consumer goods, and many other activities.

Infer How can the executive branch of the government be used to help achieve the economic goals of the Federal Government? *(Possible answer: Answers will vary. Students might mention that the President and executive branch should implement legislation and policies that curb inflation and deflation, increase hiring, and raise the standard of living.)*

DIGITAL TEXT 3

How Fiscal Policy Influences the Economy

Text 3: How Fiscal Policy Influences the Economy

How Fiscal Policy Influences the Economy

Fiscal policy is a major tool with which both the executive and legislative branches of the Federal Government seek to achieve broad economic goals. Fiscal policy consists of the government's powers to tax and spend to influence the economy. The President, aided by agencies such as the Council of Economic Advisors, often makes specific recommendations with regard to the economy, while the legislative branch enacts laws to put fiscal policy into action. The executive branch then carries out those laws through its various executive departments and independent agencies.

In addition to deciding how to raise money through taxation and how to spend money, policymakers in both the executive and legislative branches must consider what effects their taxing and spending decisions will have on the overall economy. Federal spending represents about 20 percent of the nation's GDP. How money is taxed and spent can have a real effect throughout the domestic economy—on private enterprise, on employment, on prices, and on growth. In fact, the effects of taxing and spending may be felt well beyond the economy.

>> President Obama signs the American Recovery and Reinvestment Act in 2009. At the time, he noted that "Our American story is . . . about converting crisis into opportunity. . . ."

1 of 5 >

Objective 3: Explain how government fiscal policy influences the economy at the national level.

Quick Instruction

Tell students that both the executive and legislative branches of government have a role in setting fiscal policy. The President often recommends economic actions such as tax cuts or government spending. He is advised on matters of fiscal policy by various departments and agencies in the executive branch, such as the Council of Economic Advisers. It is the legislative branch which then enacts the laws that accomplish these goals.

Explain that government fiscal policy influences the economy at the State and local levels, as well as the national level. For example, if the legislative branch (Congress) raises taxes, people get to keep less of their pay. That means Mike on Main Street won't be able to buy the new car he was considering, and the local car dealership might have to downsize or even close. Or, if State governments cut spending, schools may not have enough funds to buy new textbooks for their students.

ACTIVE CLASSROOM

Have students use a Quick Write activity to share all they know about the setting of fiscal policy by the executive and legislative branches of the Federal Government and its effect on the national economy. Give students about one minute to write their responses.

ELL Use the ELL activity described in the ELL chart.

Further Instruction

Editable Presentation Use the Editable Presentation to present the main ideas for this Core Reading.

How Fiscal Policy Influences the Economy: Core Reading and Interactive Reading Notepad Project and discuss the Interactive Reading Notepad questions, including the graphic organizer asking students to write details about how the executive and legislative branches use fiscal policy to control economic growth and to slow inflation. Point out that government revenue comes mainly from taxes. This revenue impacts the U.S. economy dramatically, because higher taxes (more government revenue) tend to slow economic growth, while tax cuts (less government revenue) tend to boost the economy. Help students to understand this by showing how government taxation can serve as a restriction to private enterprise: If Julita owns a small design firm, her profits will decrease as taxes increase. Shrinking profits can cause people to refrain from starting new businesses.

Finally, explain that government expenditures are those things on which the government spends its revenue, including such things as national **defense and social programs. Point out** that these expenditures also impact the U.S. economy—more spending can cause the economy to grow, while spending cuts can shrink the economy.

Check Understanding In what way is the Servicemen's Readjustment Act of 1944 (GI Bill of Rights) an example of a change in American culture brought about by government policies? *(During the late 1940s and 1950s, the government's fiscal policy called for increased spending on education, including through the GI Bill of Rights. As a result, more people received a college education, which contributed to the prosperity and cultural changes of the era.)*

Fiscal and Monetary Policy

DIGITAL TEXT 4

How Monetary Policy Influences the Economy

INTERACTIVE CHART

Booms, Busts, and Fiscal and Monetary Policy

Objective 4: Explain how government monetary policy influences the economy at the national level.

Quick Instruction

Tell students that the Federal Government uses several types of monetary policies to influence the nation's economy. Break students into groups of four. Then ask: How does the Fed use monetary policy to influence the nation's economy? Have students write as much as they can about this topic for one minute and then switch to the person on their right. The next person should attempt to improve or elaborate the response where the other person left off. Students in each group should continue to switch until the paper comes back to the first person. Then the group decides which is the best composition and shares that with the class.

D Differentiate: Extra Support To help students understand open market operations, have them answer the following questions. When the government buys back bonds from banks, does the amount of money that banks have increase or decrease? Why? When banks have more money, how does this affect their loans to individuals and businesses? When people have more money from loans, how does this affect the economy?

ELL Use the ELL activity described in the ELL chart.

Further Instruction

Go through the Interactive Reading Notepad questions and discuss the answers with the class. To extend the teaching of this objective have students answer the following question.

Support Ideas with Examples Why is the balance between spending and taxes difficult for State and local governments to achieve? Provide at least one example. *(Possible answer: The balance is difficult to achieve because State and local governments cannot predict how people will respond. For example, if taxes and spending are increased to help fund a new sports stadium, will people respond by staying in their community and paying the tax increase, or will they move out because taxes are too high? If many people move, the economy of the area will suffer.)*

Objectives 1: Explain the major responsibilities of the federal government for domestic economic policy; 3: Explain how government fiscal policy influences the economy at the national level; 4: Explain how government monetary policy influences the economy at the national level.

Quick Instruction

Interactive Chart: Booms, Busts, and Fiscal and Monetary Policy Project the chart on the whiteboard. Introduce the activity by telling students that the government acts in different ways depending on whether the economy is booming (growing) or contracting. Boom economies can result in inflation that is too high. In downturns, the economy needs to be stimulated. Tell students that the statements on the tiles are possible government actions, depending on whether the goal is to expand or contract the economy. Ask them to drag the tile to the appropriate column.

SYNTHESIZE

DIGITAL SYNTHESIZE ACTIVITY
Government and the Economy

DEMONSTRATE

DIGITAL QUIZ
Lesson Quiz and Class Discussion Board

Further Instruction

To extend the teaching of this objective have students answer the following questions.

Draw Conclusions One example of a fiscal policy is the raising of bank reserve requirements during a boom. This approach tends to reduce inflation. Why? *(By raising bank reserve requirements, the money supply is decreased. As a result, there is less money in circulation and banks have less money to loan or invest. This tends to slow business activity and reduce inflation.)*

Apply Concepts During an economic downturn, a city government decides to build a waterfront area for restaurants, hotels, and shops. How could the city pay for this project? Identify sources of revenue that could be used. *(Possible answer: The city could pay for this project by imposing a hotel occupancy tax, restaurant consumption tax, or a sales tax.)*

Ask students to recall the Topic Essential Question: "What is the proper role of government in the economy?" Now that students have studied this lesson, ask them how would they answer that question? Tell students to consider taxes, employment, spending, and borrowing for their responses. Have them use the Think Pair Share strategy to answer. Students should write a few sentences for their answers.

Have partners think about the following question. Do you think the Federal Government was justified in increasing the use of fiscal policy during the 1930s? *(Possible answer: Yes, during the 1930s the United States was dealing with the Great Depression. Because of this, it needed to take more control of the economy to end the depression.)* Why do you think the extensive use of fiscal policy by the Fed continued after the 1930s? *(Possible answer: Answers will vary. Students might mention that the Fed realized that by using Keynes' theory, it could benefit the economy significantly by using fiscal policy. As a result, the Fed wanted to continue to use this constructive tool.)* Have pairs share their answers with the class.

Discuss Ask students to think about the poll they took at the beginning of this Topic. Ask if they would change any of their responses now that they have learned more about the government's involvement in economic policy.

Assign the online Lesson Quiz for this lesson if you haven't already done so. Students will be offered automatic remediation or enrichment based on their score.

Remind students that in "Fiscal and Monetary Policy" students read about major responsibilities and goals of the Federal Government concerning fiscal policy. Also, students learned how the government's fiscal and monetary policies influence the economy at the local, State, and national levels.

Pose these questions to the class on the Discussion Board:

Predict Consequences What do you think would happen if the Federal Government stopped making use of fiscal policy, as it did before the 1930s? *(Possible answer: The economy might have more severe booms and downturns without the moderating influence of the Fed's fiscal policy.)*

Compare and Contrast How is the federal funds rate similar to and different from the discount rate? *(Possible answer: Both involve interest on money borrowed by banks. The federal funds rate deals with interest on money that banks lend to other banks on a daily basis. On the other hand, the discount rate deals with the interest rate a bank must pay when it borrows money from a Federal Reserve Bank.)*

Topic Inquiry
Have students continue their investigations for the Topic Inquiry.

Financing Government

Supporting English Language Learners

Use with Digital Text 2, **Federal Taxes Today.**

Speaking
Guide students to read the captions and headings of the visuals in the text in order to gather information about the sources of revenue of the U.S. government. Have partners discuss and ask for information as they preview the lesson.

Beginning Using visuals and captions from the lesson, model *who, what, where, when, why,* and *how* questions. Provide sentences with the question word missing and have students speak the question word that completes the sentence. Explain that they can use similar formats to ask for information about other lesson content.

Intermediate Prepare cards with the words *who, what, where, when, why,* and *how*. After guiding students to discuss the visuals and captions in the text, have students select a card and use the word on the card to ask aloud a question about the visuals.

Advanced Prompt students to ask questions aloud about the visuals and captions using the following sentence stems: *What does _____ mean? Why is _____ important? How is _____ like _____? How are _____ and _____ different?*

Advanced High Have student pairs take turns asking each other questions about the visuals and captions. Prompt students to use academic and content-based vocabulary. Encourage open-ended discussion.

Use with Digital Text 2, **Federal Taxes Today.**

Speaking
Read aloud the section titled "Taxes on Income." As the text is being read, ask students to form ideas about the benefits or drawbacks of a progressive tax. Demonstrate for the students the concept of progressive taxes. Distribute 5 index cards with dollar signs on them to one student and 3 index cards to another student. Tell the students you are the Federal Government and take two cards from the student holding 5 cards and one card from the student holding 3 cards. Explain to the students that progressive taxing is based on the ability to pay. Ask students to share their ideas about progressive taxes with partners.

Beginning Read the selection to the students. Reread the information and ask students to whisper read it along with you. Remind students that progressive taxes are based on the ability to pay. Ask the students to talk to a partner about the benefits or drawbacks of progressive taxes. Students may use single words in their "conversations."

Intermediate Read the selection with students. Ask them to think about the benefits or drawbacks of progressive taxes before turning and sharing their ideas with partners. Students should use short phrases in their discussions.

Advanced Have students read the selection with partners. Ask them to develop ideas about the benefits or drawbacks of progressive taxing before sharing their ideas with partners. Students should use complete sentences in their discussions.

Advanced High Have students read the selection independently and then pair each student with a partner. Ask one partner to develop ideas about the benefits of progressive taxing and the other partner to develop ideas about the drawbacks. Students should then participate in an extended discussion, using a variety of simple and complex sentences to convey their ideas.

◻ Differentiate Instruction

Use the Differentiated Instruction notes throughout the lesson plan to support the varied skill sets, levels of readiness, and interests in the mixed-ability classroom.

Challenge These notes include suggestions for expanding the activity for advanced students.

On-Level These notes include suggestions for modifying the activity to address different interests or learning styles.

Extra Support These notes include ideas for providing more scaffolding or reading spuport.

Special Needs These notes provide ideas for adapting instruction to support the needs of various special needs students.

▮ NOTES

Objectives

Objective 1: Explain how the Constitution gives Congress the power to tax and at the same time places limits on that power, as well as, how government taxation and regulation can serve as restrictions to private enterprise.

Objective 2: Identify the sources of revenue of the U.S. government today, including both tax and non-tax revenues.

LESSON 3 ORGANIZER		OBJECTIVES	PACING	RESOURCES Online	RESOURCES Print
Connect					
DIGITAL START UP ACTIVITY **How Much Goes for Taxes?**			5 min.	●	
Investigate					
DIGITAL TEXT 1 **The Power to Tax**		Objective 1	10 min.	●	●
DIGITAL TEXT 2 **Federal Taxes Today**		Objective 2	10 min.	●	●
INTERACTIVE GRAPH **Comparing Federal Taxes**			10 min.	●	
INTERACTIVE ILLUSTRATION **Federal Tax Dollars at Work**		Objectives 1, 2	10 min.	●	
Synthesize					
DIGITAL SYNTHESIZE ACTIVITY **Calculate Your Federal Taxes**			5 min.	●	
Demonstrate					
DIGITAL QUIZ **Lesson Quiz and Class Discussion Board**			10 min.	●	

PACING: APPROX. 1 PERIOD, .5 BLOCKS

Financing Government

DIGITAL START UP ACTIVITY

How Much Goes for Taxes?

Project the Start Up Activity Inform students that taxes are the major source of revenue of the U.S. government.

Discuss Have students review the statistics. Ask students: What do you find surprising about these statistics? *(Possible answer: Students might be surprised about the amount of days the average American has to work to pay his or her taxes, or the large amount that has to be paid for federal social insurance taxes.)*

Tell students that in this lesson they will be learning how the Constitution gives Congress the power to tax and places limits on that power and about the sources of revenue of the U.S. government.

Aa Vocabulary Development: Use the Interactive Reading Notepad to preview the Key Terms and Academic Vocabulary in this Lesson with students.

⚡ FLIP IT!

Assign the Flipped Video for this lesson.

■ STUDENT EDITION PRINT PAGES: 580–588

INVESTIGATE

DIGITAL TEXT 1

The Power to Tax

Objective 1: **Explain how the Constitution gives Congress the power to tax and at the same time places limits on that power, as well as how government taxation and regulation can serve as restrictions to private enterprise.**

Quick Instruction

Tell students that much of the nation's domestic policy involves the economy. The Federal Government has many responsibilities related to the economy, including the laying and collecting of taxes. Taxes are the main source of revenue for the U.S. government and those taxes have a major impact on the U.S. economy. They can also serve as a restriction to private enterprise. List the following generalizations on the board: 1) Tax cuts stimulate the economy; tax increases slow the economy. 2) Taxes can be used to regulate certain activities, such as the sale of narcotics. 3) Taxes can be used to eliminate industries or other aspects of the economy.

D Differentiate: **Extra Support** To help students understand the difference between direct and indirect taxes, give the following examples. Example 1: Sarah owns an apartment building. She must pay a tax on this building to the government. Is this an example of a direct or indirect tax? Why? *(direct tax; the tax is borne by the person upon whom it is levied)* Example 2: Sarah owns a retail store that sells shirts. A person buys a shirt and pays a sales tax for the item to the store's owner (Sarah). Sarah in turn files a tax return which forwards the proceeds of this sales tax to the government. Is this an example of a direct or

indirect tax? Why? *(indirect tax; the tax has been shifted to another–the consumer–for payment)*

Further Instruction

Editable Presentation Use the Editable Presentation to present the main ideas for this Core Reading.

The Power to Tax: Core Reading and Interactive Reading Notepad Project and discuss the Interactive Reading Notepad questions. To extend the teaching of this objective have students answer the following questions.

Support Point of View with Evidence How can government taxation serve as a restriction to private enterprise? *(Taxes take money out of people's hands, which means they have less to use for starting new businesses or other types of private enterprise. In addition, taxes have been used by the government to destroy certain industries.)*

Draw Inferences What are the major functions of the Treasury Department? *(to collect taxes and other revenues and to pay the bills of the United States)* Why do you think this was among the first executive departments created by Congress? *(The government needed a stable currency and a means to collect revenue. It had been without a uniform currency under the Articles of Confederation, which was one of the causes of economic turmoil in the nation following the Revolutionary War. The means to collect revenue is also critical to the functioning of the Federal Government.)*

Federal Taxes Today

Comparing Federal Taxes

Federal Tax Dollars at Work

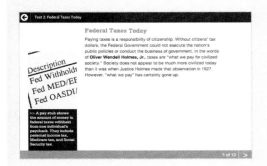

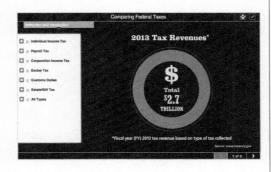

Objective 2: Identify the sources of revenue of the U.S. government today, including both tax and nontax revenues.

Quick Instruction

Tell students that there are many types of taxes, which serve as the major source of revenue of the U.S. government. Have students write a brief definition of each of the following taxes: individual income tax, corporate income tax, social insurance tax, excise tax, and estate tax. Students should write their definitions without referring to the text or using a dictionary. Ask volunteers to share their definitions with the class.

Interactive Graph: Comparing Federal Taxes Project the chart on the whiteboard. Introduce the interactive by telling students that this pie chart shows a breakdown of the different types of taxes in the United States shown as a percentage of total tax revenue. The Federal Government (Congress) enacts tax laws. The Internal Revenue Service (IRS) is responsible for collecting those taxes. Ask students to select a type of tax to see its percentage and to learn more about what the tax is designed to address. Ask: Do you think the estate tax restricts private enterprise? *(Possible answer: No, because most estates are not subject to the federal estate tax.)*

▶ ACTIVE CLASSROOM

Have students use their definitions of various taxes for a Word Wall activity. Tell students to create a visual image for one of their definitions. Students should then post their definition and image on the board or on chart paper. Ask students to look at all the various responses and then discuss the similarities and differences as a group.

D Differentiate: **Challenge** Have students write a letter to a friend who has complained about paying taxes. In this letter, students should explain why paying taxes is an important responsibility of being a citizen.

ELL Use the ELL activity described in the ELL chart.

Further Instruction

Go through the Interactive Reading Notepad questions and discuss the answers with the class. To extend the teaching of this objective have students answer the following question.

Support Point of View with Evidence Collecting taxes is an important responsibility of the Federal Government. Which tax do you think is the most important for the government to collect? Why? *(Possible answer: Answers will vary. Some students might say the social insurance taxes are the most important because they provide much needed services. Others might say that the individual income tax is the most important because it produces the largest amount of federal revenue.)*

Objectives 1: Explain how the Constitution gives Congress the power to tax and at the same time places limits on that power, as well as how government taxation and regulation can serve as restrictions to private enterprise; 2: Identify the sources of revenue of the U.S. government today, including both tax and nontax revenues.

Quick Instruction

Interactive Illustration: Federal Tax Dollars at Work Project the illustration on the whiteboard and click through the hot spots. Introduce the activity by telling students that although the word *taxes* may make people cringe, taxes do play an important role in the daily life of a community. Specifically, federal taxes help fund a variety of services and projects that might not otherwise be addressed, and that people may take for granted. Ask students to choose a spot on the map to see how taxes work in the day-to-day life of communities. Then ask students to discuss why paying taxes is a responsibility of citizenship.

Financing Government

SYNTHESIZE

DEMONSTRATE

DIGITAL SYNTHESIZE ACTIVITY

Calculate Your Federal Taxes

DIGITAL QUIZ

Lesson Quiz and Class Discussion Board

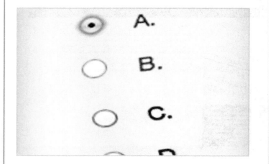

📷 ACTIVE CLASSROOM

Have students use a Rank It activity for this interactive. Ask students to rank the taxes described in this interactive according to their importance to the community shown in the illustration. Have students provide a justification for the ranking decisions they made. Then ask students to work in pairs to share their rankings and justifications. Poll the class to see if there is agreement on the ranking.

Further Instruction

To extend the teaching of this objective have students answer the following questions.

Infer How are the major responsibilities of the Federal Government being fulfilled by the taxes described in this interactive? *(Possible answer: Education is fulfilled by the student loan funded by income tax; caring for the aged is fulfilled by Medicare funded by payroll taxes; national defense is fulfilled by the federal tax revenue; scientific research is fulfilled by a grant funded by tax dollars; and NASA projects are fulfilled by federal tax dollars.)*

Ask students to recall the Topic Essential Question: "What is the proper role of government in the economy?" Inform students that the average high school graduate makes about $29,950 per year. In 2014, a single taxpayer making that amount could expect to pay a tax rate of $907.50 plus 15 percent of the amount earned over $9,075. The average graduate of a four-year college makes $44,970. In 2014, a single taxpayer making that amount could expect to pay a tax rate of $5,081.25 plus 25 percent of the amount earned over $36,900.

Have students use the Think Pair Share strategy to figure out what their take home income would be, after taxes, if they made the amounts listed above. Then have pairs consider that the above tax only includes federal individual income tax—they could expect to pay an additional 6.2 percent of their income for Social Security tax, as well as paying other social insurance taxes, and State and local taxes. Some employees also have health insurance costs deducted from their paychecks.

Discuss Remind students that paying taxes is a responsibility of citizenship. What would happen if people stopped paying taxes? Give a specific example. *(Possible answer: If people stopped paying taxes, the government would be unable to execute its public policies or conduct the government. Specific example: Without tax money, the government could not maintain a military or patrol the nation's borders.)*

Assign the online Lesson Quiz for this lesson if you haven't already done so. Students will be offered automatic remediation or enrichment based on their score.

Remind students that in "Financing Government" they read about how the Constitution gives Congress the power to tax and limits that power. Also, students learned about the sources of revenue of the U.S. government.

Pose these questions to the class on the Discussion Board:

Analyze Do you think President Obama pushing for legislation extending tax cuts was a justified use of presidential power? *(Possible answer: No; the President should allow the economy to adjust itself, without interference.)*

Make Predictions Do you think the amount of taxes paid to the Federal Government will increase or decrease in the future? Explain your answer. *(Possible answer: The amount of services provided by the government, such as health insurance, seems to be increasing. Because of this, taxes will continue to increase.)*

Topic Inquiry

Have students continue their investigations for the Topic Inquiry.

Spending and Borrowing

Supporting English Language Learners

Use with Digital Text 2, **Creating the Budget.**

Speaking

Use the following high-frequency, concrete, abstract, and/or content-based vocabulary from the text: *significant, financing, enormous, initiate, fiscal, execution, lengthy, dissect, binding.* Guide students to use these words to give information about the budget process.

Beginning Display the words. Read the words and have the students repeat. Discuss the meaning of the words and then use them to ask questions that require one- or two-word spoken responses from students.

Intermediate Display the words. Read the words and have the students repeat. Discuss the meaning of the words and ask students to verbalize information about the budget process using each of the words.

Advanced Display the words. Guide students in a discussion in which they provide information about the budget process using the words. Finally, have them verbalize a definition for each word based on the discussion, then have them check their definitions against a dictionary.

Advanced High Display the words. Have students explain or give information about each word based on prior knowledge and then guide students to look up the definitions of the words in the dictionary. Ask the students to write a short paragraph using the words and then read their paragraphs to the group.

Use with Digital Texts 1–3, **Federal Expenditures, Creating the Budget,** and **Borrowing and the Deficit.**

Listening

As students learn about government spending and the federal budget, use words from the text to help them learn new language structures related to singular and plural forms of words—for example *entitlement(s), expenditure(s), benefit(s).*

Beginning Have students listen as you read simple sentences to model the use of singular and plural words. For example: ***Entitlements*** *are benefits that must be paid to all who are eligible.* and *An* ***entitlement*** *is a benefit that must be paid to all who are eligible.*

Intermediate Have students listen as you read simple sentence stems and words from the text to model and explain the use of singular and plural words. For example: *Federal* ***expenditures*** *must be approved by Congress.* and *Any* ***expenditure*** *proposed by the President must be approved by Congress.*

Advanced Have students listen as a partner reads aloud sentence stems and words from the text to model the use of singular and plural verbs. For example: *Defense spending* ***is*** *by far the largest controllable item in the federal budget today.* and *Entitlements* ***are*** *benefits that federal law says must be paid to all those who meet the eligibility requirements.*

Advanced High Guide students to write two sentences using singular verbs and two using plural verbs, using words from the text. Have students take turns listening as a partner reads the sentences aloud.

ⅅ Differentiate Instruction

Use the Differentiated Instruction notes throughout the lesson plan to support the varied skill sets, levels of readiness, and interests in the mixed-ability classroom.

Challenge These notes include suggestions for expanding the activity for advanced students.

On-Level These notes include suggestions for modifying the activity to address different interests or learning styles.

Extra Support These notes include ideas for providing more scaffolding or reading spuport.

Special Needs These notes provide ideas for adapting instruction to support the needs of various special needs students.

▉ NOTES

Spending and Borrowing

Objectives

Objective 1: Identify the sources of expenditures of the U.S. government and define controllable and uncontrollable spending.

Objective 2: Analyze the executive branch function of creating the federal budget, in conjunction with Congress.

Objective 3: Understand the relationship between U.S. government policies as set out in the yearly federal budget and the economy.

Objective 4: Analyze the impact of Federal Government sources of revenue and expenditures on the U.S. economy.

Objective 5: Analyze the causes and effects of the public debt.

LESSON 4 ORGANIZER		PACING: APPROX. 1 PERIOD, .5 BLOCKS			
		OBJECTIVES	PACING	**RESOURCES**	
				Online	Print
Connect					
DIGITAL START UP ACTIVITY **In the Red**			5 min.	●	
Investigate					
DIGITAL TEXT 1 **Federal Expenditures**		Objective 1	10 min.	●	●
INTERACTIVE GRAPH **Federal Spending Comparison**			10 min.	●	
DIGITAL TEXT 2 **Creating the Budget**		Objective 2	10 min.	●	●
DIGITAL TEXT 3 **Borrowing and the Deficit**		Objectives 3 and 4	10 min.	●	●
INTERACTIVE CHART **Demand-side and Supply-side Economics**			10 min.	●	
DIGITAL TEXT 4 **Understanding the Public Debt**		Objective 5	10 min.	●	●
Synthesize					
DIGITAL SYNTHESIZE ACTIVITY **Federal Spending Priorities**			5 min.	●	
Demonstrate					
DIGITAL QUIZ **Lesson Quiz and Class Discussion Board**			10 min.	●	

PEARSON
realize.
www.PearsonRealize.com

Go online to access additional resources including:
Primary Sources • Biographies • Supreme Court cases •
21st Century Skill Tutorials • Maps • Graphic Organizers.

■ CONNECT

DIGITAL START UP ACTIVITY
In the Red

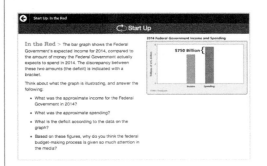

Project the Start Up Activity Ask students to answer the questions as they enter and get settled. Then have them share their ideas with other students, either in class or through a chat or blog space.

Analyze Graphs Inform students that in 2014, the Federal Government is planning to spend more than it takes in. *(Answers: income: $3 trillion; spending: $3.75 trillion; deficit: $750 billion; federal spending involves huge sums and has a major impact on the nation's economy)*

Tell students that in this lesson they will be learning about Federal Government spending and the process of creating a budget.

Aa Vocabulary Development: Use the Interactive Reading Notepad to preview the Key Terms and Academic Vocabulary in this Lesson with students.

⇅ FLIP IT!

Assign the Flipped Video for this lesson.

■ STUDENT EDITION PRINT PAGES: 589–597

■ INVESTIGATE

DIGITAL TEXT 1
Federal Expenditures

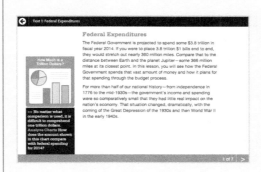

Objectives 1: Identify the sources of expenditures of the U.S. government and define controllable and uncontrollable spending; 4: Analyze the impact of Federal Government sources of revenue and expenditures on the U.S. economy.

Quick Instruction

Explain that the U.S. government has several sources of revenue, including tax monies, nontax revenues, and borrowing. Then identify for students the two types of Federal Government expenditures: controllable and uncontrollable expenditures. Have students write a definition of each type without using the text or a dictionary. Also, students should provide at least two examples of controllable spending and uncontrollable spending. Ask volunteers to share their definitions and examples with the class.

Interactive Graph: Federal Spending Comparison Project the interactive graph on the whiteboard. Introduce the activity by telling students that each year the government spends based on national and world events, and on the priorities set by the President and Congress. The first graph shows how revenues were spent in 1973. Ask students to move the slider to the right to see how spending changed in 2013. Tell students to examine what has changed between those two years.

INTERACTIVE GRAPH
Federal Spending Comparison

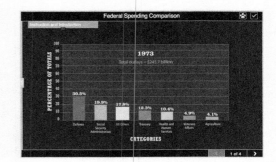

⬛ ACTIVE CLASSROOM

Have students use a Take a Stand activity to examine federal spending. Tell them to look at the second graph in the slider and identify the largest expenditures of the U.S. government in 2013. Ask students: Do you think the largest expenditures of the U.S. government make sense? Yes or no? Ask students to divide into two groups based on their answers and move to separate areas of the classroom. If one group has only a few members, then assign more students to this group. Then tell students to talk with each other to compare reasons for answering "yes" or "no." Ask a representative from each side to present and defend the group's point of view to the class.

Draw Conclusions In 2012, the percent of spending for health and human services increased significantly from 1970. Why do you think this happened? What impact do you think this change had on the economy? *(Possible answer: Answers will vary. Students might mention that people are living longer, and the "baby boomer" generation is reaching retirement age. Some may argue that the increased spending on health and human services is taking money away from businesses and is therefore harming the economy.)*

ELL Use the ELL activity described in the ELL chart.

Spending and Borrowing

DIGITAL TEXT 2
Creating the Budget

Further Instruction

Editable Presentation Use the Editable Presentation to present the main ideas for this Core Reading.

Federal Expenditures: Core Reading and Interactive Reading Notepad Project and discuss the Interactive Reading Notepad questions, including the graphic organizer asking students to record information about the top four federal spending priorities. Review the priorities with the class and fill in the graphic organizer on the whiteboard as you go.

Infer What impact do you think the huge public debt has on the U.S. economy? *(Possible answer: The huge public debt causes the government to raise taxes to pay for it, which slows down the economy.)*

Objective 2: Analyze the executive branch function of creating the federal budget, in conjunction with Congress.

Quick Instruction

Remind students that the federal budget is an extremely important document. Tell students to write as much as they know in one minute about why the budget is so important. Then have students form pairs. Ask students to share their response with their partner. Pairs should create one written answer based on the best elements of each response. Ask volunteers to share this answer with the class.

Explain that creating and helping to pass the federal budget is one of the functions of the executive branch of government and a critical part of the nation's domestic policy. The President's constitutional powers include the power to recommend legislation to Congress—in this case, by proposing a budget—and to sign bills passed by Congress—in this case, the appropriations bills passed by Congress as part of the budget process.

D **Differentiate: Extra Support** To help students understand the executive branch's involvement in creating the federal budget, ask the following questions. What executive branch agency gathers spending plans from all federal agencies? What does this agency do with the spending plans? What does the executive budget document sent to Congress consist of?

ELL Use the ELL activity described in the ELL chart.

Further Instruction

Go through the Interactive Reading Notepad questions and discuss the answers with the class. To extend the teaching of this objective have students answer the following questions.

Compare and Contrast How is the OMB similar to and different from the CBO? *(Both supply important budget information to branches of the federal government. The OMB reviews and revises spending plans and sends them to the President. The CBO acts independently of the OMB and provides both houses of Congress and their committees with basic budget information.)*

Identify What is the sequence of events that happens to the President's budget when it reaches Congress? *(The tax proposals in the President's budget are referred to the House Ways and Means Committee and the Senate's Finance Committee. Also, the President's budget is sent to both the House and the Senate Appropriations Committees. After reviewing and revising the budget, the two Budget Committees propose a concurrent resolution on the budget to their respective chambers. A second budget resolution is passed by the Budget Committees setting binding spending limits for all federal agencies. Finally, both houses must pass 13 appropriations bills.)*

DIGITAL TEXT 3

Borrowing and the Deficit

INTERACTIVE CHART

Demand-side and Supply-side Economics

Objectives 3: Understand the relationship between U.S. government policies as set out in the yearly federal budget and the economy; 4: Analyze the impact of Federal Government sources of revenue and expenditures on the U.S. economy.

Quick Instruction

Tell students that during the history of the United States, the Federal Government's approach toward borrowing money and deficit spending has changed significantly. Have students form pairs. Tell them to create a timeline that traces in chronological order the main events that affected the government's approach toward borrowing money and deficit spending. (Timelines should include at least the following entries: Federal Government first goes into debt during George Washington's presidency; government borrows to finance construction of the Panama Canal; government borrows to fund President Franklin Roosevelt's programs to alleviate the Great Depression; public debt reaches $1 trillion during Reagan administration; government borrows to fund economic stimulus plans in 2007–2009.)

Interactive Chart: Demand-side and Supply-side Economics Project the graphic organizer on the whiteboard. Introduce the activity by telling students that demand-side economics is also known as Keynesian economics, and proposes that the demands of households, government, and business drive the economy over free market dynamics. Increasing employment will result in higher

tax revenues. Ask students to type in which descriptions represent demand-side and supply-side economics.

Draw Conclusions What is Reagonomics? Why do you think this name was chosen? *(Reagonomics is another term for supply-side economics, which involves cutting taxes and increasing the supply of money in private hands. The name "Reagonomics" was used because President Reagan was the first president to strongly support this economic approach.)*

⏩ ACTIVE CLASSROOM

Using a Conversation with History activity, have students imagine they are having a conversation with Mr. Keynes about the current economy of the United States. Tell students to write one or two questions they would like to ask Keynes about the current economy. Then students should write what they think Keynes would say in response and how they would respond to Keynes.

ELL Use the ELL activity described in the ELL chart.

Further Instruction

Go through the Interactive Reading Notepad questions and discuss the answers with the class. To extend the teaching of this objective have students answer the following questions.

Point out that one of the functions of the executive branch of government is to borrow the money needed for the government to make up its deficit. This is done by the Treasury Department, by issuing securities to investors.

Check Understanding How did President Bush and President Obama attempt to stimulate the economy by using government expenditures? *(They attempted to shore up the loan-making capacities of the nation's banks and other financial institutions, overcome a decline in consumer spending, and combat a rising tide of unemployment.)*

Identify Main Ideas According to the theory of supply-side economics, what is a major economic responsibility of the Federal Government? *(to manage the nation's economy by cutting taxes during economic downturns to increase the supply of money in private hands and stimulate the economy)*

Spending and Borrowing

DIGITAL TEXT 4

Understanding the Public Debt

Objective 5: Analyze the causes and effects of the public debt.

Quick Instruction

Remind students that the public debt is the total outstanding indebtedness of the Federal Government. It includes all the money the government has borrowed and not yet repaid, plus the interest on that money. Have students use a Think Pair Share to answer the following question. Ask: Do you think demand-side economics or supply-side economics is more likely to increase the public debt? Explain your answer. *(Possible answers: Answers will vary. Some students might say demand-side economics because this approach increases government spending for programs, which would cause the government to borrow more money to pay for the programs. Others might say supply-side economics because this approach cuts taxes, which would cause the government to borrow more money to pay for programs.)*
Ask volunteers to share their responses with the class.

D Differentiate: **Challenge** Have students draw a political cartoon that makes a commentary or expresses a point of view on the public debt. Encourage students to use images, symbols, and words for this cartoon.

Further Instruction

Go through the Interactive Reading Notepad questions and discuss the answers with the class. To extend the teaching of this objective have students answer the following questions.

Cause and Effect What do you think is the cause of the public debt? *(Possible answer: The government borrows money to pay for various programs and services, such as national defense, welfare programs, and education.)*

Cause and Effect What do you think will be the long-term effect of the public debt? *(Possible answer: If the public debt keeps growing, it will probably have a major impact on future generations. U.S. citizens will have to pay high taxes to give the government enough money to just pay the interest on the debt. Also, there will be a shortage of money for much-needed services, such as social security and education.)*

■ SYNTHESIZE

Federal Spending Priorities

Ask students to recall the Topic Essential Question: "What is the proper role of government in the economy?" Now that students have learned about all of the spending and borrowing that the Federal Government does, tell them to take a look at this political cartoon. Have them use the Think Pair Share strategy to answer the questions about the cartoon.

Analyze Political Cartoons Tell students that this political cartoon about federal spending shows two pie charts. Ask: What point do you think this political cartoon is trying to get across concerning federal spending? Do you agree with the main point the cartoonist is making?

■ DEMONSTRATE

Lesson Quiz and Class Discussion Board

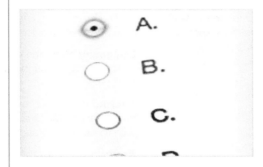

Assign the online Lesson Quiz for this lesson if you haven't already done so. Students will be offered automatic remediation or enrichment based on their score.

Remind students that in *Spending and Borrowing*, they read about sources of spending for the U.S. government and how the federal budget is created. Also, they learned about the impact of Federal Government sources of revenue and spending on the U.S. economy and the causes and effects of the public debt.

Pose these questions to the class on the Discussion Board:

Draw Conclusions Why do you think President Hoover was unable to get the United States out of the Great Depression? *(Possible answer: Hoover believed that the government should have very limited power to deal with problems in the economy. According to Hoover, the success or failure of businesses was a matter best left to the working of the free market. However, with the Great Depression, businesses had dug themselves such a deep financial hole that the free market was unable to correct the economy. The people's lack of faith in economic institutions, such as banks, only made this problem more difficult.)*

Hypothesize What do you think the Federal Government will need to do to decrease the public debt? *(Possible answer: Answers will vary. Some students might mention that the government will have to increase taxes significantly and also streamline government programs.)*

Topic Inquiry

Have students continue their investigations for the Topic Inquiry

The U.S. in a Global Economy

Supporting English Language Learners

Use with Digital Text 2, **U.S. Trade Policies.**

Speaking
Guide students to understand the role of the legislative and executive branches in setting international trade policy by reading aloud the section *U.S. Trade Policies.* Using visuals as appropriate, explain the terms *tariff, import quota,* and *trade embargo.* Provide a list of words that express opinions, such as *good, bad, fair, unfair, helpful,* and *harmful.* Have students express their opinions and ideas on these types of trade barriers.

Beginning Provide students with specific trade policies and have them express an opinion about each by using the words on the word list. For example, have students complete the following statement: *In my opinion, tariffs are _____ [good/bad/etc.]*

Intermediate Provide sentence stems for the students to use to express their opinions and ideas about U.S. trade policies, such as *I think _____. I feel _____.* Have students use the words from the list to complete the sentence stems.

Advanced Guide students to use the following sentence stems to express their opinions about U.S. trade policies: *In my opinion_____. I believe that_____.*

Advanced High Guide students to use the following sentence stems to express their opinions about U.S. trade policies: *Personally, I think _____. I agree that _____. I disagree that _____.*

Use with Digital Text 2, **U.S. Trade Policies.**

Reading
Provide the following basic sight vocabulary words from the text that students need to know in order to understand U.S. trade policies: *prices, profit, competition, imports, exports, foreign, domestic.* Guide students to focus on these words as they study this reading.

Beginning Write the vocabulary on the board and ask students to find the words in the text as they read. Reread the text aloud as students follow along. Have students copy the words.

Intermediate Read the text aloud as students follow along. Write the vocabulary on the board and ask students to find the words in the text. Have them copy the sentences with the words and read them to each other.

Advanced Write the vocabulary on the board. Have partners find the words in the text as they read together. Have partners write their own sentences using the words and read them to the other students in the group.

Advanced High Write the vocabulary on the board. Have students find the words in the text as they read independently. Guide them to write sentences using the words and read them to another student.

▣ Differentiate Instruction

Use the Differentiated Instruction notes throughout the lesson plan to support the varied skill sets, levels of readiness, and interests in the mixed-ability classroom.

Challenge These notes include suggestions for expanding the activity for advanced students.

On-Level These notes include suggestions for modifying the activity to address different interests or learning styles.

Extra Support These notes include ideas for providing more scaffolding or reading spuport.

Special Needs These notes provide ideas for adapting instruction to support the needs of various special needs students.

■ NOTES

PEARSON
realize™
www.PearsonRealize.com

Go online to access additional resources including:
Primary Sources • Biographies • Supreme Court cases •
21st Century Skill Tutorials • Maps • Graphic Organizers.

Objectives

Objective 1: Explain the causes of globalization, including recent scientific discoveries and technological innovations, and its effects on the American economy, including why certain places or regions are important to the United States.

Objective 2: Understand the roles of the executive and legislative branches in setting international trade and fiscal policies.

Objective 3: Identify international trade organizations and alliances to which the United States belongs.

Objective 4: Recognize the benefits and drawbacks of the global economy, including the significance to the United States of the location and key natural resources of selected global places or regions.

Objective 5: Understand world economic trends today.

LESSON 5 ORGANIZER		PACING: APPROX. 1 PERIOD, .5 BLOCKS		RESOURCES	
		OBJECTIVES	PACING	Online	Print
Connect					
DIGITAL START UP ACTIVITY **Texas Trade**			5 min.	●	
Investigate					
DIGITAL TEXT 1 **A Global Economy**		Objectives 1, 4	10 min.	●	●
INTERACTIVE CHART **Impact of Location and Natural Resources**			10 min.	●	
DIGITAL TEXT 2 **U.S. Trade Policies**		Objective 2	10 min.	●	●
INTERACTIVE GALLERY **Economic Sanctions: The Case of South Africa**			10 min.	●	
DIGITAL TEXT 3 **Trade Alliances and Organizations**		Objective 3	10 min.	●	●
DIGITAL TEXT 4 **The Consequences of the Global Economy**		Objectives 4, 5	10 min.	●	●
Synthesize					
DIGITAL SYNTHESIZE ACTIVITY **Pros and Cons of Globalization**			5 min.	●	
Demonstrate					
DIGITAL QUIZ **Lesson Quiz and Class Discussion Board**			10 min.	●	

The U.S. in a Global Economy

■ CONNECT

DIGITAL START UP ACTIVITY
Texas Trade

Project the Start Up Activity Ask students to answer the questions as they enter and get settled. Then have them share their ideas with other students, either in class or through a chat or blog space.

Discuss Answers: (*exports are a large part of the Texas economy; petroleum exports account for nearly double the value of any other exports, which implies that many people work for this industry; just as exports are vital to Texas, they are also vital to the U.S.*)

Tell students that in this lesson they learn about globalization and international trade policies and organizations.

Aa Vocabulary Development: Use the Interactive Reading Notepad to preview the Key Terms and Academic Vocabulary in this Lesson with students.

⚡ FLIP IT!

Assign the Flipped Video for this lesson.

■ STUDENT EDITION PRINT
PAGES: 598–606

■ INVESTIGATE

DIGITAL TEXT 1
A Global Economy

Objectives 1: Explain the causes of globalization, including recent scientific discoveries and technological innovations, and its effects on the American economy, including why certain places or regions are important to the United States; 4: Recognize the benefits and drawbacks of the global economy, including the significance to the United States of the location and key natural resources of selected global places or regions.

Quick Instruction

Tell students that during the past 20 years, globalization, or economic interdependence among nations, has soared. Have students use a Think Pair Share to answer the following question. What scientific and technological advances do you think have contributed to the rapid increase in globalization? (*computing power, the Internet, communications satellites, and better transportation vehicles*) Which do you think has contributed to globalization the most? Why? (*Possible answer: Answers will vary. Students might mention that the Internet has had the strongest effect because almost all businesses rely on it for communications and research.*) Ask volunteers to share their answers.

INTERACTIVE CHART
Impact of Location and Natural Resources

Interactive Chart: Impact of Location and Natural Resources Project the graphic organizer on the whiteboard. Introduce the activity by telling students that the U.S. is one of the largest importers and exporters of goods and services in the world. The physical location of a country can be an important factor when countries establish trade and other relationships with each other. Natural resources can also impact these relationships, regardless of physical location. Ask students to think about why the location or the natural resources of each of these countries might be important to the United States. Have students type in their responses in the text boxes for each country.

🖥 ACTIVE CLASSROOM

Have students use a Graffiti Concepts activity for globalization. Ask them to reflect on the meaning of globalization and create a visual image that represents this concept. Tell students to consider communications networks, natural resources, the location of these resources, and the location of various nations for their images.

Infer China and Mexico both have large deposits of petroleum. From which of these countries do you think the United States will import more petroleum? Why? (*Possible answer: The United States will likely import more petroleum from Mexico, because it is closer to the United States than China.*)

Further Instruction

Editable Presentations Use the Editable Presentation to present the main ideas for this Core Reading.

A Global Economy: Core Reading and Interactive Reading Notepad Project and discuss the Interactive Reading Notepad questions. To extend the teaching of this objective have students answer the following questions.

Check Understanding What are two reasons why Canada is the main trading partner of the United States? *(Canada is located close to the United States. Also, Canada relies on the United States as a source of fruits and vegetables.)*

Draw Conclusions There are many areas of the world that have large oil deposits, including Russia, Norway, China, and Libya. Why do you think the United States gets most of its oil from Canada, Saudi Arabia, Mexico, Venezuela, and Nigeria? Name at least two reasons. *(Possible answer: Answers will vary. Students might mention the close location of Canada, Mexico, and Venezuela; the huge amounts of oil in Saudi Arabia; friendly political relations; and the lack of accessibility to oil deposits in areas such as Russia.)*

DIGITAL TEXT 2

U.S. Trade Policies

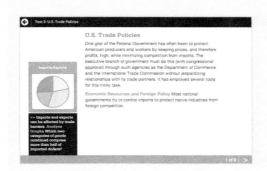

Objective 2: Understand the roles of the executive and legislative branches in setting international trade and fiscal policies.

Quick Instruction

Tell students that U.S. international trade and fiscal policies are part of this nation's foreign policy. One of the functions of the executive and legislative branches of the Federal Government is to carry out these policies. The President often negotiates agreements or recommends sanctions, for example, while Congress must approve those steps. Within the executive branch, a variety of agencies, including the State Department and the Department of Commerce, implement the laws passed by Congress and the nation's international trade and fiscal policies.

Introduce the concept of protectionism. Ask students to write all they know about protectionism in 30 seconds. Then have students form pairs. Tell partners to share their responses and create one response, combining the accurate elements of each response. Ask volunteers to share their answers. Then explain that protectionism is an example of a U.S. foreign policy. It affects other countries because it limits the amounts of certain goods those countries can sell in the United States. Discuss with students how protectionism differs from free trade agreements such as NAFTA.

Interactive Gallery: Economic Sanctions: The Case of South Africa Project the slideshow. Tell students that beginning in the 1950s, anti-apartheid activists within South Africa, such as Nelson Mandela, protested

INTERACTIVE GALLERY

Economic Sanctions: The Case of South Africa

apartheid. Later many countries, including the United States, imposed sanctions on South Africa to pressure the government to end apartheid. Explain that sanctions continue to be implemented by the U.S. government to counter threats to national security. Today, sanctions are imposed in several countries including Cuba, Iran, North Korea, and Sudan. Ask students to explore the images to see one example of the use of economic resources in foreign policy, and how American foreign policy can affect other nations.

📷 ACTIVE CLASSROOM

Have students use a Draw a Poster activity concerning NAFTA. Tell students to draw a propaganda poster that either supports NAFTA or criticizes NAFTA. For this activity, students should consider the pro or con aspects of NAFTA. For extra credit, students can draw another poster than shows the opposite view of NAFTA from the first poster.

Summarize Summarize how the use of sanctions against South Africa is an example of the U.S. government using economic resources in its foreign policy. *(The use of sanctions is an example of the U.S. using economic resources in its foreign policy because the refusal to buy or sell certain items to South Africa had an effect on its economy. Even more important, it signaled to the South African government that apartheid was not acceptable to the U.S.)*

ELL Use the ELL activity described in the ELL chart.

The U.S. in a Global Economy

DIGITAL TEXT 3

Trade Alliances and Organizations

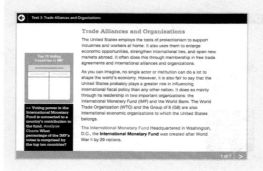

Further Instruction

Go through the Interactive Reading Notepad questions and discuss the answers with the class. To extend the teaching of this objective have students answer the following questions.

Point out that trade agreements such as NAFTA also affect other countries. The Mexican economy, for example, has both benefited and lost through this agreement. Increased trade has been a positive result, but the loss of agricultural jobs has been a drawback.

Check Understanding What is the role of the executive branch in setting international trade policies? *(The executive branch attempts to protect American producers and workers by keeping prices and profits high, while minimizing competition from imports. This should be done without jeopardizing relationships with its trade partners. To accomplish this, the executive branch uses agencies such as the Department of Commerce and the International Trade Commission.)* Explain that the legislative branch also has a role in setting international trade policies. Congress must approve any free trade agreements negotiated by the President, for example.

Infer How can a trade embargo placed by the U.S. government restrict private enterprise in the United States? *(A trade embargo can close a nation to U.S. businesses. Doing this restricts private enterprise in the United States.)*

Objective 3: Identify international trade organizations and alliances to which the United States belongs.

Quick Instruction

Inform students that the United States influences international fiscal policy through its involvement with the International Monetary Fund and the World Bank. Have students write a definition for each organization without using the text or a dictionary. Tell students to include the ways in which both the executive and legislative branches are involved in these groups. Ask volunteers to share their definitions.

D Differentiate: **Challenge** Have students create a timeline that shows the main events in the development of the European Union.

Further Instruction

Go through the Interactive Reading Notepad questions and discuss the answers with the class. To extend the teaching of this objective have students answer the following questions.

Compare and Contrast How are the World Trade Organization (WTO) and G8 similar and different? *(Possible answer: Both are trade organizations, in which the United States is a leading member. The WTO sets rules for international commerce, discusses new trade agreements, and resolves trade issues. The G8, though, does not have a rigid structure. This group meets to discuss world affairs and crises.)*

Draw Conclusions The U.S. government plays a leading role in the IMF and World Bank, which has been a source of controversy. What do you think is at the root of this controversy? *(Possible answers: Answers will vary. Students might mention that the U.S. government probably uses the IMF and World Bank to advance policies that favor the United States, perhaps at the expense of other countries. Other nations might resent how the U.S. government attempts to dominate the international economy through these groups.)*

DIGITAL TEXT 4

The Consequences of the Global Economy

Text 4: The Consequences of the Global Economy

The Consequences of the Global Economy

For the most part, a global economy seems to be a positive development. It means that more goods are available to more consumers, and that there are more markets in which producers can sell goods. Globalization and international partnerships also help developing nations expand their economies and raise their standards of living by enabling them to sell goods to more affluent countries.

And, clearly, competition in a global market lowers the price of goods. Goods made overseas, unblocked by tariffs, are less expensive and become more affordable for Americans. Increases in jobs and higher wages, in turn, allow consumers in developing nations to buy American goods and services, and this helps to increase or at least maintain American jobs.

>> Bhutan, a South Asian country, uses this hydroelectric plant to help fuel its economy by selling its excess power to India.

1 of 7 >

Objectives 4: Recognize the benefits and drawbacks of the global economy, including the significance to the United States of the location and key natural resources of selected global places or regions; 5: Understand world economic trends today.

Quick Instruction

Inform students that the global economy has both positive and negative effects. Ask students: Does the global economy have more positive or negative effects? Those that think the global economy has more positive effects form one group, and those that think it has more negative effects form another group. If one group has only a few members, assign more students to this group. Ask students to talk with each other to compare the reasons for their position. Have a representative from each side present and defend the group's viewpoint.

D Differentiate: **Extra Support** To help students understand how a crisis in a foreign nation can affect the U.S. economy, ask the following. How do you think war or a political crisis in a nation would affect its ability to produce natural resources? If a country produces fewer natural resources than normal, do you think this country will charge more for these resources? Why or why not? If a country increases the cost for resources, how do you think this affects Americans who buy products that use these resources?

Further Instruction

Go through the Interactive Reading Notepad questions and discuss the answers with the class. To extend the teaching of this objective have students answer the following question.

Identify Supporting Details The trend in the world economy is toward greater interdependence among nations. What are some important details that support this statement? *(The United States and other nations are joining more trade alliances. Developing nations are working toward diversifying their economies and opening their markets to more nations. The U.S. government is building international partnerships by establishing new trade agreements.)*

The U.S. in a Global Economy

SYNTHESIZE

DIGITAL SYNTHESIZE ACTIVITY
Pros and Cons of Globalization

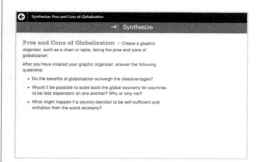

Ask students to recall the Topic Essential Question: "What is the proper role of government in the economy?" Have them use the Think Pair Share strategy to create a graphic organizer, such as a chart or table, listing the pros and cons of globalization.

Discuss After partners have created their graphic organizer, ask them to answer the following questions. Do the benefits of globalization outweigh the disadvantages? *(Possible answers: Answers will vary. For "yes" answers, students might point out increased goods, more markets, and more competition lowering the price of goods. For "no" answers, students might mention crises in nations that adversely affect the U.S. economy, the possible loss of sovereignty of some nations, and the exploitation of workers.)*

Infer Would it be possible to scale back the global economy, so that countries are less dependent on one another? Why or why not? *(Possible answer: No; globalization is being pushed forward by new technologies. Now that countries have become interconnected, it would be difficult to disentangle them without harming the global economy.)*

Hypothesize What would happen if a country decided to be self-sufficient and withdraw itself from the world economy? *(Possible answer: The country's economy would suffer. The nation would cut itself off from sources of income, services, and goods. This could lead to widespread famine and political turmoil. North Korea has to a certain extent economically isolated itself from other nations. As a result, the North Koreans have suffered from shortages of food and other resources.)*

DEMONSTRATE

DIGITAL QUIZ
Lesson Quiz and Class Discussion Board

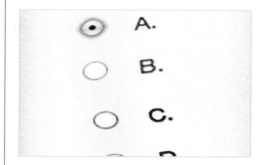

Assign the online Lesson Quiz for this lesson if you haven't already done so. Students will be offered automatic remediation or enrichment based on their score.

Remind students that in *The U.S. in the Global Economy*, they read about the causes of globalization and its effect on the U.S. economy. Also, they studied the roles of the U.S. government in setting international trade and fiscal policies and international trade alliances to which the United States belongs. In addition, they analyzed the benefits and drawbacks of the global economy.

Pose these questions to the class on the Discussion Board:

Hypothesize What qualities do you think a nation would need to have for the executive branch to attempt to eliminate tariffs with that nation? *(Possible answer: The nation would most likely have natural resources that the United States needs and need resources and services that the United States could provide. Also, the nation could be located close to the United States. If not, it probably would have transportation methods that could quickly and efficiently ship resources to the United States.)*

Make Predictions What do you think U.S. involvement in international trade will be like 20 years from now? *(Possible answer: I think that services in the United States will continue to soar, but manufacturing will continue to plummet. However, manufacturing in China will continue to increase. Because of this, the United States and China will become the major competitors and partners in world economics.)*

Topic Inquiry

Have students continue their investigations for the Topic Inquiry.

Topic 12

Government and the Economy

◼ SYNTHESIZE

DIGITAL ACTIVITY

Reflect on the Essential Question and Topic

First ask students to reconsider the Essential Question for the Topic: "What is the proper role of government in the economy?" Remind students of the budget items they considered at the start of the Topic. For example,

- funds for national defense
- grants to schools for computer technology
- money for veterans' health benefits
- money to build roads and bridges
- grants for scientific research
- funds to help farmers when crop prices drop

Ask students: What role should a government have in the nation's business endeavors, its citizens' financial well-being, and other economic areas? Ask them to present at least two reasons for their position. Discuss their answers as a class or ask students to post their answers on the Class Discussion Board.

As students complete their study of government and the economy, ask them to take a few minutes to reflect on all that they have learned. Tell students to write three important questions they have thought about during the Topic and their answers to those questions. Share these examples if students need help getting started:

- What are some advantages of government involvement in the economy?
- What are some drawbacks of government involvement in the economy?

Topic Inquiry

Have students complete Step 3 of the Topic Inquiry.

◼ DEMONSTRATE

DIGITAL TOPIC REVIEW AND ASSESSMENT

Government and the Economy

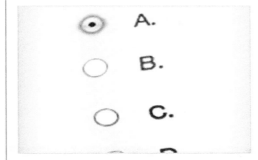

Students can prepare for the Topic Test by answering the questions in the Topic Review and Assessment online or the Assessment questions in the Print Student text. They can also prepare by reviewing their answers to the Interactive Reading Notepad questions or reviewing their notes in the Reading and Notetaking Study Guide.

TOPIC TEST

Assign the Topic Test to assess students' understanding of topic content.

DIGITAL TOPIC TEST

Government and the Economy

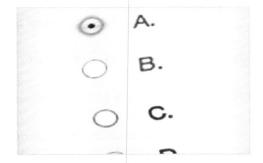

BENCHMARK TESTS

Assign these benchmark tests as you complete the relevant topics to monitor student progress toward mastering the course content and as preparation for the End-of-Course Test.

Benchmark Test 1: Topics 1–4
Benchmark Test 2: Topics 5–8
Benchmark Test 3: Topics 9–11
Benchmark Test 4: Topics 12–14

State and Local Government

TOPIC 13 ORGANIZER	PACING: APPROX. 1 PERIOD, .5 BLOCKS
	PACING
Connect	1 period
MY STORY VIDEO **Governorship, A Stepping Stone to the Presidency**	10 min.
DIGITAL ESSENTIAL QUESTION ACTIVITY **What Should Governments Do?**	10 min.
DIGITAL OVERVIEW ACTIVITY **Organization of State Government**	10 min.
TOPIC INQUIRY: CIVIC ACTION PROJECT **Constitutional Rights Foundation**	20 min.
Investigate	3–6 periods
TOPIC INQUIRY: CIVIC ACTION PROJECT **Constitutional Rights Foundation**	Ongoing
LESSON 1 State Constitutions	30–40 min.
LESSON 2 State Legislatures	30–40 min.
LESSON 3 The Governor and State Administration	30–40 min.
LESSON 4 The State Courts	30–40 min.
LESSON 5 Local Governments—Structure and Function	30–40 min.
LESSON 6 State and Local Spending and Revenue	30–40 min.
Synthesize	1 period
DIGITAL SYNTHESIZE ACTIVITY **Reflect on the Essential Question**	10 min.
TOPIC INQUIRY: CIVIC ACTION PROJECT **Constitutional Rights Foundation**	20 min.
Demonstrate	1–2 periods
DIGITAL TOPIC REVIEW AND ASSESSMENT **State and Local Government**	10 min.
TOPIC INQUIRY: CIVIC ACTION PROJECT **Constitutional Rights Foundation**	20 min.

 **TOPIC INQUIRY:**

Civic Action Project

For this topic's Inquiry, you may choose to do a Civic Action Project with your students by using the materials found at the Constitutional Rights Foundation's CAP website: http://www.crfcap.org. Civic Action Project (CAP) is a project-based learning model for government and economics courses. It offers a practicum for high school students in effective and engaged citizenship and uses blended learning to engage students in civic activities both in the traditional U.S. government and economics classrooms.

Constitutional Rights Foundation
Educate. Participate.

THE TEACHER'S ROLE

THE CAP TEACHER coaches and guides students through the civic action process as they select a problem or issue, research it, determine and take civic actions, and report and document the experience. The teacher motivates, challenges, critiques, and assesses student progress. Through a blended learning approach, teachers can let students take the reins of their civic learning, guiding them along the way.

You can create your CAP classroom in three easy steps

STEP 1
Register yourself for the CAP website

STEP 2
Enroll your students

STEP 3
Engage your students in the CAP process and its many resources

---

Constitutional Rights Foundation

Pearson Magruder's American Government Students
Welcome to the Civic Action Project site

All of the information you're learning in your Government course will help you understand important Government policy issues that will be discussed and debated at the local, state, and national level throughout your lifetime.

Participating in a Civic Action Project (CAP) of your choosing will show you how you can use that knowledge as an engaged citizen in a democracy.

This CAP website will show you how to plan and carry out your project and give you lots of help along the way. Good luck!

Click on the logo to get started on your CAP!

THE STUDENT'S ROLE

CAP ALLOWS STUDENTS to create projects on issues they care about for their school or community. They see the connection between their civic actions and public policy and can share ideas for civics projects with each other and other CAP students nationwide. Students also see how the content of government and economics courses can apply to the real world. By taking civic actions, they practice what real citizens do when they go about trying to solve real policy-related problems. CAP fulfills best-practices in service-learning with an emphasis on public policy.

The CAP student is accountable for completing the civic action process, just as with a science project or term paper. The CAP Planner, a set of documents that guide students through the process, provides teachers with assessment information as well as a way to manage multiple student projects. While the teacher introduces and monitors the CAP, it is important that students take the lead in completing their civic actions. By using web-based technology and civics-based instruction and activities, students exercise important 21st century skills in digital literacy, critical thinking, collaboration, self-direction, and learning to be engaged and effective citizens.

CIVIC ACTIONS CAP challenges students to work on an actual problem, issue, or policy by taking civic actions. Civic actions build upon classroom civics issues, service-learning, and other proven practices of effective civic education. These actions can be many and varied, including:

- getting informed about a public issue or problem
- thinking critically about the issue or problem
- discovering how government is involved with the problem
- learning how government makes decisions
- developing a position
- engaging in civic dialogue
- building constituencies
- working together toward a common goal
- doing civic writing
- making presentations
- advocating for and defending positions
- meeting with officials

Brainstorming

Brainstorming is a method for generating ideas. It can be done by individuals or in small or large

Rules for Brainst

Pose a question to an

Set a time limit on th more ideas out.

Work as fast as you

Handout Lesson 5B
Civic Action Project

GRADE
CAP Policy Analysis Tool

AS CITIZENS IN A DEMOCRACY, YOU'LL BE CONFRONTED WITH POLICY QUESTIONS. IS A TAX PROPOSAL A GOOD IDEA? SHOULD YOU VOTE FOR A PARTICULAR BALLOT INITIATIVE? GOVERNMENT POLICIES CAN PROFOUNDLY AFFECT OUR NATION AND YOUR LIFE. IN A DEMOCRACY, YOU HAVE A SAY ON GOVERNMENT POLICIES AND PROPOSED POLICIES. IT'S IMPORTANT THAT YOU TAKE A CRITICAL LOOK AT THEM. USE THE FOLLOWING GRADE TESTS TO EVALUATE A POLICY:

G OAL. WHAT IS THE GOAL OF THE POLICY? IF YOU DON'T KNOW WHAT IT'S SUPPOSED TO DO, YOU CAN'T MEASURE ITS SUCCESS OR FAILURE. POLICIES ARE DESIGNED TO ADDRESS PROBLEMS. WHAT PROBLEM OR PROBLEMS IS

POLICY? WHO MIGHT (OR DOES) YOU UNDERSTAND WHO THE ICY FAVORS SPECIAL CES FOR INFORMATION, BUT

ITS? WHAT IS GOOD ABOUT THE SES OR EFFECTS OF THE VED) ITS GOAL? WILL IT NSIVE? DOES IT PROTECT E'S LIBERTIES?

OSTS? WHAT IS BAD ABOUT THE THE CAUSES OR EFFECTS OF THE 7? DOES IT CAUSE HARM? DOES RE ANY POTENTIAL

E DISADVANTAGES. ARE THERE TO DO NOTHING. MOST SERIOUS EVALUATE THEM. LOOK AT ES.

© 2012 Constitutional Rights Foundation

Conducting Meetings

Your meetings should be organized, to-the-point, and fun.

Decide how you're going to make decisions. If you are a small group, try deciding by whole-group consensus or by a two-thirds vote. A simple-majority decision may lead to bad feelings and resentment.

Understand everyone's role at the meeting. At most meetings, people need to fill the following roles, which may change from meeting to meeting:

- Leader or facilitator runs the meeting, follows the agenda item by item, and watches the time allotted for each. The leader helps participants focus on the task and makes sure everyone has a chance to participate.
- Recorder takes minutes, which include date and time of meeting, the persons attending, and notes on each agenda item.
- Treasurer.
- Group members contribute agenda items, discuss topics, make decisions, and take responsibility for various tasks.
- Adviser is an adult whose role is to give advice—not to run the group.
- Guests may participate in group discussions, but usually do not participate in final decision making.

Have an agenda. This is a list of things to be dealt with at a meeting. All members should be encouraged to put topics on the agenda. After the recorder reads the minutes of the previous meeting and they are approved, the members approve the agenda. Agenda items are considered in the following order:

- Old business—ongoing and follow-up items.

© 2012, Constitutional Rights Foundation
and Close Up Foundation

Constitutional
Rights
Foundation
Educate. Participate.

Guardian of Democracy: The Civic Mission of Schools
Released September, 2011, *Guardian of Democracy: The Civic Mission of Schools report* builds on the findings of the seminal 2003 Civic Mission of Schools report. CAP has been designed to support the promising approaches described in these reports.

State and Local Government

The Constitution of the United States explains how the Federal Government should function. However, it leaves many roles and responsibilities to the States. The way these roles and responsibilities are to be handled is laid out in each State's constitution. The exact details of the organization of the executive, legislative, and judicial branches differs from State to State, but they are all based on certain basic principles. How do these principles and the way each State government is organized help the States meet the needs of their citizens and provide for public safety and welfare?

 **CONNECT**

MY STORY VIDEO

Governorship, A Stepping Stone to the Presidency

Watch a video that shows how the experience of being a governor can affect a politician's later career.

Compare and Contrast How do the powers of a governor compare and contrast with those of the President? *(They are alike in many ways; governors have power in all three branches but often have more influence on legislation and budgets. Some States do not have term limits for governors.)*

Hypothesize Why might a governor's experience influence his or her actions later, if elected President? *(Possible answer: He or she would be likely to keep the same ideas about economics, education, taxes, and so forth and apply the same policies nationally as in the State.)*

⇅ FLIP IT!

Assign the My Story video.

DIGITAL ESSENTIAL QUESTION ACTIVITY

What Should Governments Do?

Ask students to think about the Essential Question for this Topic: What Should Governments Do? Remind them that in their study of government they have learned that the Federal Government and the State governments have basic duties they perform. Some of these duties overlap, but many are the responsibility of State governments.

If students have not already done so, ask them to review the list of basic duties of State government and have them revise the list from the perspective of the National Government. Then go over the responses as a class.

Identify Central Ideas How does the list of basic duties for the National Government differ from that of the State government? *(Possible answer: The National Government's duties reflect those performed for the nation as a whole.)*

Draw Conclusions What types of services do you think are provided by State and/or local government? *(Possible answers: police and fire protection, waste management, education, public health and welfare services)* Do you think these services should be the responsibility of State government or should they be the

DIGITAL OVERVIEW ACTIVITY

Organization of State Government

Display the chart showing the different branches of State government. During this Topic, students will learn about the organization of State and local government. This chart will provide a framework into which they can place the elements they learn about.

D Differentiate: Extra Support How many branches of government are there in each State? *(three)*

Check Understanding How are State governments structured? Are they similar to or different from the Federal Government? *(The States each have three branches, similar to the Federal Government.)*

Topic Inquiry

Launch the Topic Inquiry with students after introducing the Topic.

State Constitutions

Supporting English Language Learners

Use with the reading, **The First State Constitutions**.

Speaking

Tell students that people often have strong feelings about the government. Read the sections *The First State Constitutions, Independence,* and *Principles of State Constitutions*. Have students discuss the emotions that people might have about the importance of a written constitution. Guide them to use the words *excited, angry, hopeful, disappointed, unsure, happy.*

Beginning Explain each word to the class and how they apply to the text. Have students repeat the words. Guide the class to sort the words into positive and negative feelings.

Intermediate Guide students to sort the words into positive and negative feelings. Help them use the words in short phrases as they discuss the text.

Advanced Have partners sort the words into positive and negative feelings. Guide them to add their own words to the lists. Have partners discuss the text using the words in short sentences.

Advanced High Have small groups discuss the positive and negative feelings people may have about the topic. Provide the list of words as a resource. Have them add their own words to the list.

Use with the reading, **State Constitutions Today**.

Listening

Display and discuss the following academic vocabulary words: *fundamental, guarantees, restrict, enhance, specific, transporting, committed.* Have students listen for the words as you read aloud the section *Protections of Civil Rights.* Use the words to discuss the role of limited government in the protection of individual rights.

Beginning Have students copy and repeat the academic words. Have students listen for the academic words as the teacher explains the meaning of each word using visuals as support.

Intermediate Guide the students to use the academic words in short sentences. Have students copy and repeat as other students use the academic words in short sentences.

Advanced Have partners write sentences with the academic words, one student listening as the other uses a dictionary as a resource, then alternating. Have them read their sentences to their classmates.

Advanced High Have partners write a summary of the section using the academic words, with partners alternating reading the text. Have them read their summary to their partner or the rest of the group.

▶ Differentiate Instruction

Use the Differentiated Instruction notes throughout the lesson plan to support the varied skill sets, levels of readiness, and interests in the mixed-ability classroom.

Challenge These notes include suggestions for expanding the activity for advanced students.

On-Level These notes include suggestions for modifying the activity to address different interests or learning styles.

Extra Support These notes include ideas for providing more scaffolding or reading spuport.

Special Needs These notes provide ideas for adapting instruction to support the needs of various special needs students.

■ NOTES

State Constitutions

Objectives

Objective 1: Examine the history, content, and significance of the first State constitutions.

Objective 2: Describe the basic principles common to all State constitutions today.

Objective 3: Explain the procedures used to change State constitutions.

Objective 4: Analyze why State constitutions are in need of reform.

LESSON 1 ORGANIZER		PACING: APPROX. 1 PERIOD, .5 BLOCKS			
				RESOURCES	
		OBJECTIVES	**PACING**	**Online**	**Print**
Connect					
DIGITAL START UP ACTIVITY **State Constitutions**			5 min.	●	
Investigate					
DIGITAL TEXTS 1 AND 2 **The First State Constitutions, State Constitutions Today**		Objectives 1, 2	10 min.	●	●
INTERACTIVE CHART **State Constitutions Today**			10 min.	●	
DIGITAL TEXTS 3 AND 4 **Constitutional Change, The Need for Reform**		Objectives 3, 4	10 min.	●	●
INTERACTIVE GALLERY **State Constitutional Change**			10 min.	●	
Synthesize					
DIGITAL ACTIVITY **Six Elements of State Constitutions**			5 min.	●	
Demonstrate					
DIGITAL QUIZ **Lesson Quiz and Class Discussion Board**			10 min.	●	

■ CONNECT

DIGITAL START UP ACTIVITY
State Constitutions

Project the Start Up Activity Ask students to answer the question as they enter and get settled. Then have them share their ideas with another student, either in class or through a chat or blog space.

Discuss What are some reasons for why it could be important to write down laws? *(Possible answers: so everyone knows what the laws are; promotes limited government)* What elements are found in State constitutions? *(Possible answer: those elements not found in the Federal Constitution, but not contrary to the Constitution)*

Tell students that in this lesson they will be learning about how the States govern themselves.

Aa Vocabulary Development: Use the Interactive Reading Notepad to preview the Key Terms and Academic Vocabulary in this Lesson with students.

⇗ FLIP IT!

Assign the Flipped Video for this lesson.

■ STUDENT EDITION PRINT PAGES: 614–619

■ INVESTIGATE

DIGITAL TEXT 1
The First State Constitutions

Objectives 1: **Examine the history, content, and significance of the first State constitutions; 2:** **Describe the basic principles common to all State consitutions today.**

Quick Instruction

The constitutions of the States are subservient to the Constitution of the United States, and can include no provision that takes power away from the Federal Government or restricts the rights in the Bill of Rights. Each State does have a constitution, some arising from their original charters, which the State uses to outline how it wants to govern itself. These State documents emphasize limited government, popular sovereignty, and the protection of individual rights.

Interactive Chart: State Constitutions Today Project the activity and work with students to place each constitutional category with its applicable example. Discuss the general elements of State constitutions: basic principles, civil rights, governmental structure, governmental powers, processes for change, and miscellaneous provisions.

INTERACTIVE CHART
State Constitutions Today

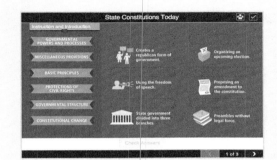

■ ACTIVE CLASSROOM

Have students use a Write 1 Get 3 strategy to answer the following question using information from the interactive chart: What are the most important elements of State constitutions today? Give examples of the elements to support your answer. *(Students might answer with different categories or decide one category is most important.)*

D Differentiate: Extra Support Step through the different elements of State constitutions and have students give a definition or example that explains each category.

ELL Use the ELL activities described in the ELL chart.

Further Instruction

Editable Presentation Use the Editable Presentation to present the main ideas for these Core Readings.

The First State Constitutions and State Constitutions Today: Core Reading and Interactive Reading Notepad Project and discuss the Interactive Reading Notepad questions, including the graphic organizer asking students to compare and contrast the United States Constitution and the State constitutions. Review the similarities and differences of the documents with the class and fill in the graphic organizer on the whiteboard as you go.

State Constitutions

DIGITAL TEXT 2
State Constitutions Today

DIGITAL TEXT 3
Constitutional Change

INTERACTIVE GALLERY
State Constitutional Change

Have students explain the importance of written constitutions. Discuss what might happen if constitutions were not written down. Remind students that State constitutions proclaim the principles of popular sovereignty and limited government.

Make Judgments Why is it important that the people are allowed to vote on whether or not to adopt their State's constitution? *(Possible answer: People should be able to approve their structure of government.)*

Draw Conclusions What is one reason that State constitutions have dead letter laws? *(Possible answer: Changing the document is difficult, so laws are not always removed, just added.)*

Objectives 3: Explain the procedures used to change State constitutions; 4: Analyze why State contitutions are in need of reform.

Quick Instruction

State constitutions can be changed through amendments, which deal with either one or a few smaller provisions in the constitution, or through revisions, which are large-scale changes. Constitutions need change and revision to address new problems faced by States, reduce their length, and excise contradictory material.

▣ ACTIVE CLASSROOM

Interactive Gallery: State Constitutional Change Project the activity and click through the images to explore the variety of amendment procedures available in Florida.

▣ ACTIVE CLASSROOM

Using the Cartoon It strategy, have students choose one of the ways Florida amends its constitution and create a cartoon that represents the process. Have students share their cartoons in small groups and discuss how creating the cartoon helped them compare and contrast other amendment procedures in Florida. You may wish to have students research a State not listed in the activity to see if its amendment process is similar to or different from Florida's.

D Differentiate: Extra Support Step through each of the examples of how Florida's constitution is changed.

Further Instruction

Editable Presentation Use the Editable Presentation to present the main ideas for these Core Readings.

Constitutional Change and The Need for Reform: Core Reading and Interactive Reading Notepad Project and discuss the Interactive Reading Notepad questions.

Students should understand that States have different procedures for constitututional change and revision. For example, some States provide for constitututional conventions to amend the document.

Evaluate Evaluate this statement: There are many provisions that clearly do not need to go in a State constitution. Do you agree or disagree? Why? *(Possible answer: I agree with the statement. The constitution should have only those elements necessary to set out the structure and function of the government. All other provisions can be part of the statutory law for each State. OR I disagree. The constitution should contain the list of laws and provisions important to the people of the State.)*

SYNTHESIZE

DEMONSTRATE

DIGITAL TEXT 4

The Need for Reform

DIGITAL ACTIVITY

Six Elements of State Constitutions

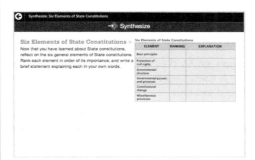

DIGITAL QUIZ

Lesson Quiz and Class Discussion Board

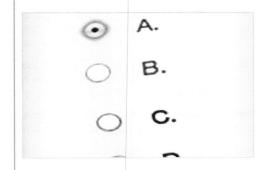

Draw Conclusions Why do you think some States might have more complicated processes for making changes to their constitution than others? *(Possible answer: States with more complicated processes in place might want to ensure that only important and necessary constitutional changes are allowed to move forward for consideration and ratification.)*

Ask students to recall the Topic Essential Question, What Should Governments Do? Have them use the Think Pair Share strategy to rank the elements in this activity. Ask them to take five minutes to write down some notes and rankings, then share their answers with a talking partner.

Have partners complete the activity. Students should rank each element in order of its importance, and write a brief statement explaining each element in their own words. Have pairs share their answers with the class.

Discuss Have students consider the question from the Start Up Activity: Why do we have State constitutions as well as a United States Constitution? Ask what other responses students have to that question now that they have completed the lesson.

Assign the online Lesson Quiz for this lesson if you haven't already done so. Students will be offered automatic remediation or enrichment based on their scores.

Pose these questions to the class on the Discussion Board:

In *State Constitutions,* you read that States wrote constitutions that are based on the principles of popular sovereignty and limited government, delineate the structure and function of their governments, and include methods for amendment.

Analyze Why does each State's constitution include different elements? Why are they not all the same? *(Possible answers: Each State has a different history, population, geography, and structure.)*

Make Judgments What is the purpose of a constitution? Should a constitution only include the structure and functions of government, or should it also include specific laws and amendments? *(Possible answer: Although a major purpose of a State constitution is to delineate the structure and function of a State's government, it is also important for it to establish limits on government, as well as protections of the rights of citizens. Therefore, it is equally important to include amendments and laws in the State constitution beyond those related to the structure and function of government.)*

Topic Inquiry

Have students continue their investigations for the Topic Inquiry.

State Legislatures

Supporting English Language Learners

Use with the reading, **The Legislature**.

Speaking
Read the sections *The Legislature, State Legislature Structure,* and *State Legislature Size.* Guide students to compare the structure and size of State legislatures by completing a graphic organizer with the following headings: *What is the same about all State legislatures? What characteristics of State legislatures vary?* Have students share their answers with each other.

Beginning Guide the class to complete the graphic organizer. Model how to use the graphic organizer as a resource in sharing the answers with a classmate. Have the students share the answers with a classmate.

Intermediate Have small groups complete the graphic organizer. Guide individual students to share the answers with a classmate.

Advanced Have partners complete the graphic organizer. Have them share their answers with another set of partners.

Advanced High Have individual students complete the graphic organizer. Have the students share their answers with another student.

Use with the reading, **State Legislators**.

Listening
Read and discuss the section *Legislature Districts,* focusing on the impact of *Baker* v. *Carr.* Teach vocabulary from the lesson such as *reapportioned, census, redistricting, urban,* and *rural* through listening activities. Guide students to monitor their understanding of spoken language as described below.

Beginning Have students copy the vocabulary words onto cards. During instruction, have students hold up the cards when they hear the word being used.

Intermediate Read aloud to students the list of the vocabulary words. As you discuss the words, have students put a mark next to each word according to their level of understanding. * = I understand it well. + = I have a general idea of what it means. ? = I need more explanation.

Advanced Have the students listen as you summarize the text, emphasizing the vocabulary words. Have them complete a two-column chart with the headings *Word,* filling in vocabulary words on the left side, and *Questions I Have,* entering questions they may have about individual words and their meaning or use. Discuss the charts with partners.

Advanced High Have the students listen as you summarize the text. Ask them to write two sentences telling what they have learned and two questions that they have about the topic. Have them discuss their work with a partner.

▶ Differentiate Instruction

Use the Differentiated Instruction notes throughout the lesson plan to support the varied skill sets, levels of readiness, and interests in the mixed-ability classroom.

Challenge These notes include suggestions for expanding the activity for advanced students.

On-Level These notes include suggestions for modifying the activity to address different interests or learning styles.

Extra Support These notes include ideas for providing more scaffolding or reading spuport.

Special Needs These notes provide ideas for adapting instruction to support the needs of various special needs students.

◼ NOTES

Objectives

Objective 1: Describe State legislatures.

Objective 2: Explain the election, terms, and compensation of legislators.

Objective 3: Examine the powers and organization of State legislatures.

Objective 4: Describe how voters may write and pass laws through direct legislation.

LESSON 2 ORGANIZER		PACING: APPROX. 1 PERIOD, .5 BLOCKS			
				RESOURCES	
		OBJECTIVES	**PACING**	**Online**	**Print**
Connect					
DIGITAL START UP ACTIVITY **State Police Power**			5 min.	●	
Investigate					
DIGITAL TEXT 1 **The Legislature**		Objectives 1, 2	10 min.	●	●
DIGITAL TEXT 2 **State Legislators**			10 min.	●	●
DIGITAL TEXT 3 **Powers of the Legislature**		Objective 3	10 min.	●	●
INTERACTIVE CHART **Powers of State Legislatures**			10 min.	●	
DIGITAL TEXT 4 **Organization of the Legislature**			10 min.	●	●
INTERACTIVE MAP **Comparing State Legislatures**			10 min.	●	
DIGITAL TEXT 5 **Direct Legislation**		Objective 4	10 min.	●	●
Synthesize					
DIGITAL ACTIVITY **Limiting State Power**			5 min.	●	
Demonstrate					
DIGITAL QUIZ **Lesson Quiz and Class Discussion Board**			10 min.	●	

State Legislatures

◼ CONNECT

DIGITAL START UP ACTIVITY
State Police Power

Project the Start Up Activity Ask students to write down their thoughts about the police power as they enter and get settled. Then have them share their ideas with another student, either in class or through a chat or blog space.

Discuss Why did the Framers of the Constitution reserve the police power to the States and not to the Federal Government? *(Possible answers: The Framers probably reserved this power to the States because they believed that each State could best handle local issues.)* Discuss student opinions about police power.

Tell students that in this lesson they will be learning about the State legislatures, their responsibilities, and their makeup.

Aa Vocabulary Development: Use the Interactive Reading Notepad to preview the Key Terms and Academic Vocabulary in this Lesson with students.

⇅ FLIP IT!
Assign the Flipped Video for this lesson.

◼ STUDENT EDITION PRINT
PAGES: 620–626

◼ INVESTIGATE

DIGITAL TEXT 1
The Legislature

DIGITAL TEXT 2
State Legislators

Objectives 1: Describe State legislatures; **2:** Explain the election, terms, and compensation of legislators.

Quick Instruction
The lawmaking branch of State government is the legislature; however, it can have many different names. With the single exception of Nebraska, all State legislatures are bicameral.

Legislators are chosen by popular vote, usually first nominated at party primaries. Each State has specific qualifications for representatives based on age, citizenship, and residence. Legislators are chosen from districts in the State, which are reapportioned every ten years. Gerrymandering is often used to protect legislators' districts.

ELL Use the ELL activities described in the ELL chart.

Further Instruction
Editable Presentation Use the Editable Presentation to present the main ideas for these Core Readings.

The Legislature and State Legislators: Core Reading and Interactive Reading Notepad Project and discuss the Interactive Reading Notepad questions. With students, compare the structures, functions, and processes of State legislatures in the U.S. federal system. Discuss details found in the Core Readings, such as qualifications, elections, terms, and sessions. Ensure that students understand the processes for filling public offices, including that of State legislator, in the U.S. system of government.

Baker v. Carr Explain to students how political divisions are crafted and how they are affected by Supreme Court decisions such as *Baker* v. *Carr*, which established that redistricting issues could be addressed by federal courts. Later cases established the one person, one vote standard, which now governs reapportionment. Discuss how this decision affects the way districts in the States are created every ten years, using information from the Core Reading.

Evaluate There is no ideal size for a legislature. What is more important than size? *(More important than size is the ability to represent the citizens of the State and effectively provide for their needs.)*

Make Judgments What is unique about the Nebraska legislature? Why might this be more effective? *(Possible answer: Nebraska's legislature is unicameral. The two houses of a bicameral body might contradict one another, whereas a unicameral body might work more effectively.)*

Compare Compare the compensation of legislators in California and Oregon. *(California pays just over $95,000 per year, while Oregon pays $22,000 per year. Both States provide expenses and benefits.)* What might be one reason for this wide discrepancy in legislators' pay? *(Possible answer: Perhaps legislators in California devote more of their time to legislative work than do legislators in Oregon. In addition, the cost of living in each State might contribute to the discrepancy.)*

<table>
<tr><td>

DIGITAL TEXT 3

Powers of the Legislature

</td><td>

INTERACTIVE CHART

Powers of State Legislatures

</td><td>

DIGITAL TEXT 4

Organization of the Legislature

</td></tr>
</table>

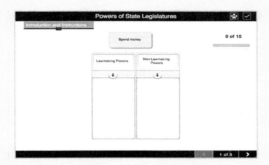

Objective 3: Examine the powers and organization of State legislatures.

Quick Instruction

Each State's constitution identifies the legislature's most important powers, including the power to tax, spend, borrow, establish crimes, and maintain public schools. Included is also a police power, which serves to protect and promote public safety, morality, and health and welfare.

Interactive Chart: Powers of State Legislatures
Project the interactive on the whiteboard. Remind students that most of the powers held by the State are vested in the legislature. As a class, categorize each legislative action as either an example of a lawmaking or non-lawmaking power.

🔲 ACTIVE CLASSROOM

Using a Sticky Note strategy, have students write why each individual power is important. Then use the information to summarize the powers of the State legislatures and compare those powers to those of the U.S. Congress. Have students use the information from the organizer in their summaries.

D Differentiate: Extra Support Discuss the elements of the State legislatures and the United States Congress. Note the differences students know and then have them add to this list as they complete the activity.

Further Instruction

Editable Presentation Use the Editable Presentation to present the main ideas for this Core Reading.

Powers of the Legislature: Core Reading and Interactive Reading Notepad Project and discuss the Interactive Reading Notepad questions. With students, compare the structures, functions, and processes of State legislatures in the U.S. federal system. Discuss examples of the similar functions of the federal legislative process found in the Core Reading.

Compare Which executive and judicial powers are similar in State legislatures and in the federal legislature? *(Both State and federal legislatures can approve some of the executive's appointments. The legislatures also can impeach the executive.)*

Quick Instruction

Interactive Map: Comparing State Legislatures Project the map on the whiteboard and step through the elements of legislatures that often differ from State to State. Point out to students that while the State legislatures are modeled after the U.S. Congress, there are differences in structure and function. Have students work in small groups to complete the activity. Then have them participate in the Active Classroom Activity.

🔲 ACTIVE CLASSROOM

Using a Quick Write strategy, have students answer the following questions: What are the benefits to citizens of our State of the way the State legislature is organized? Why might each State not have been willing or able to adopt the federal model in its entirety? *(Possible answers: Students might mention the difference in population or the part-time nature reflecting a more populist approach to governing.)* Use the information provided on the maps to compare the different legislatures.

D Differentiate: Extra Support Project and step through the map with students. Break the class into small groups and assign each group a State and have them summarize the way its legislature is organized and structured. Then bring the groups together to discuss similarities and differences.

State Legislatures

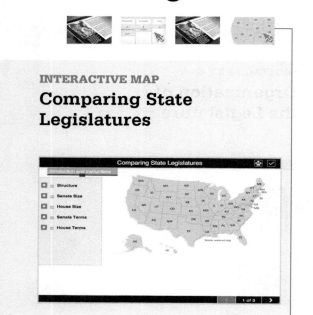

INTERACTIVE MAP

Comparing State Legislatures

DIGITAL TEXT 5

Direct Legislation

Objective 4: Describe how voters may write and pass laws through direct legislation.

Further Instruction

Editable Presentation Use the Editable Presentation to present the main ideas for these Core Readings.

Organization of the Legislature and Direct Legislation: Core Reading and Interactive Notepad Project and discuss the Interactive Reading Notepad questions.

Referendum Process Discuss the three different ways that a legislature can refer a measure to the voters for final approval or rejection. Define for students "hot potato issues" and discuss how they are dealt with in referendums.

Analyze Explain how important voters are in the creation of their State's constitutions. *(Voters can use the initiative process to propose amendments and laws. These can either be passed by legislators or the voters.)*

Draw Conclusions Why do most attempts to use the popular referendum fail? *(Voters do not often get the required number of signatures to force a popular vote.)*

▮ SYNTHESIZE

DIGITAL ACTIVITY
Limiting State Power

Ask students to recall the Topic Essential Question, What Should Governments Do? Have them use the Think Pair Share strategy to answer the questions in this activity. Ask them to take five minutes to write down some brief answers to the questions below, then share their answers with a talking partner.

Have partners think about the following questions. Consider what you know about the U.S. Congress and the different State legislatures. In what areas are they most alike? In what ways are they most different? *(Answers may vary.)*

Discuss Create a class Venn Diagram to compare and contrast two legislatures. Generalize about why they are different. Ask students to explain where the differences and similarities come from. *(Answers may vary.)*

▮ DEMONSTRATE

DIGITAL QUIZ
Lesson Quiz and Class Discussion Board

Assign the online Lesson Quiz for this lesson if you haven't already done so. Students will be offered automatic remediation or enrichment based on their scores.

Pose these questions to the class on the Discussion Board:

In *State Legislatures* you read about how different States organize their legislatures, including the qualifications and election processes for senators and representatives. You also compared different State legislatures to gain an understanding that each State has a similar organization, but differs in its specifics.

Draw Conclusions Why are some State legislatures part-time? What might change if each was a full-time body? *(Possible answer: Part-time legislatures support the idea of citizen-legislators, which is a way of limiting government. If a part-time legislature were to become full-time, more work might get done, but legislators would probably have to be paid more.)*

Topic Inquiry
Have students continue their investigations for the Topic Inquiry.

The Governor and State Administration

Supporting English Language Learners

Use with the reading, **The Governorship**.

Speaking
Read and discuss the section *Qualifications* and the different methods of filling public offices. Have students list and describe the formal and informal qualifications required to become governor of a State.

Beginning Guide students to copy the list of the formal and informal qualifications. Have them illustrate each one. Have students use their illustrations while describing the qualifications to a classmate.

Intermediate Guide students to copy the list of qualifications and jot down a description for each one. Have students share their descriptions in a small group.

Advanced Guide students to create the list of qualifications and write a sentence describing each one. Have students share their descriptions with at least two other students.

Advanced High Guide students to write a sentence describing each qualification and its importance. Have them discuss their work with the class.

Use with the reading, **The Governor's Powers**.

Listening
Read the sections *The Governor's Powers and Executive.* As you discuss the sections, have students ask and answer questions to clarify their understanding of the functions of State governments in the U.S. federal system.

Beginning Read aloud each section as students listen and follow along. Have students ask for clarification using sentence stems such as: *Please repeat that. What does _____ mean?*

Intermediate Guide partners to read the sections, taking turns reading and listening. During discussion, have students ask for clarification using sentence stems such as: *The part I don't understand is _____. Can you give an example of _____?*

Advanced Have partners read the sections. During discussion, provide sentence stems that require the students to repeat what they heard: *Did you mean _____? I heard you say _____.*

Advanced High Have partners read the sections taking turns reading and listening. During discussion, have students ask for clarification using sentence stems such as: *Can you tell me more about _____? How do these ideas fit together? I don't understand the use of the word _____.*

▣ Differentiate Instruction

Use the Differentiated Instruction notes throughout the lesson plan to support the varied skill sets, levels of readiness, and interests in the mixed-ability classroom.

Challenge These notes include suggestions for expanding the activity for advanced students.

On-Level These notes include suggestions for modifying the activity to address different interests or learning styles.

Extra Support These notes include ideas for providing more scaffolding or reading spuport.

Special Needs These notes provide ideas for adapting instruction to support the needs of various special needs students.

■ NOTES

Objectives

Objective 1: Describe the main features of the office of governor.

Objective 2: Summarize a governor's roles, powers, duties, and the limitations of the office.

Objective 3: List and describe the other executive offices at the State level.

LESSON 3 ORGANIZER		PACING: APPROX. 1 PERIOD, .5 BLOCKS			
				RESOURCES	
		OBJECTIVES	**PACING**	**Online**	**Print**
Connect					
DIGITAL START UP ACTIVITY **National v. State Executive Power**			5 min.	●	
Investigate					
DIGITAL TEXT 1 **The Governorship**		Objective 1	10 min.	●	●
DIGITAL TEXT 2 **The Governor's Powers**		Objective 2	10 min.	●	●
INTERACTIVE CHART **Powers of the Governor**			10 min.	●	
DIGITAL TEXT 3 **Other Executive Officers**		Objective 3	10 min.	●	●
INTERACTIVE GALLERY **State Government Executive Officers**			10 min.	●	
Synthesize					
DIGITAL ACTIVITY **Amending Executive Power**			5 min.	●	
Demonstrate					
DIGITAL QUIZ **Lesson Quiz and Class Discussion Board**			10 min.	●	

The Governor and State Administration

CONNECT

DIGITAL START UP ACTIVITY

National v. State Executive Power

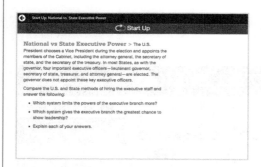

Project the Start Up Activity Ask students to answer the questions as they enter and get settled. Then have them share their ideas with another student.

Discuss Which system, U.S. or State, limits the powers of the executive branch more? Explain your answer. *(The States limit the powers of the executive branch more. Governors can only appoint board and commission members. The governor has no power to choose executive officers, who are usually directly elected by voters. By contrast, the President can choose the Vice President and all the members of the Cabinet, creating a unified and loyal executive team.)*

Tell students that, in this lesson, they will be learning about the roles of the governor and the executive officers.

Aa Vocabulary Development: Use the Interactive Reading Notepad to preview the Key Terms and Academic Vocabulary in this Lesson with students.

⇅ FLIP IT!

Assign the Flipped Video for this lesson.

◼ STUDENT EDITION PRINT PAGES: 627–634

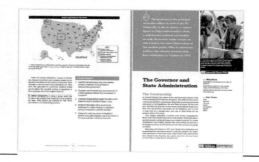

INVESTIGATE

DIGITAL TEXT 1

The Governorship

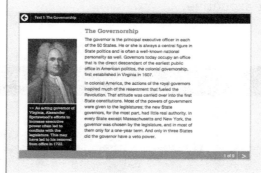

Objective 1: Describe the main features of the office of governor.

Quick Instruction

The governorship arises from the tradition of colonial governors, though today, governors are elected by the people instead of appointed by the legislature. The governor is unlike a President because executive powers in the State are shared by several people.

ELL Use the ELL activity described in the ELL chart.

Further Instruction

Editable Presentation Use the Editable Presentation to present the main ideas for this Core Reading.

The Governorship: Core Reading and Interactive Reading Notepad Project and discuss the Interactive Reading Notepad questions.

Students should know the qualifications, term, selection methods, and removal or resignation procedures. Compare with students how governors are elected and the lengths of their terms. Compare this with methods of succession and removal to get a complete picture of how each State fills the office of the governor.

Draw Conclusions What influence can a governor have over the State legislature? *(Possible answer: They can try to shape legislation and work to ensure their legislative vision is followed.)*

Explain How is a governor removed from office and what would happen next in most States? *(The governor can be removed from office if he or she is impeached and convicted. In most States, the lieutenant governor would succeed the impeached governor.)*

DIGITAL TEXT 2

The Governor's Powers

INTERACTIVE CHART

Powers of the Governor

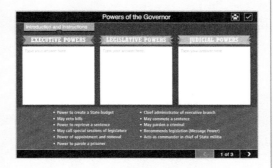

DIGITAL TEXT 3

Other Executive Officers

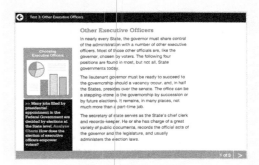

Objective 2: Summarize a governor's roles, powers, duties, and the limitations of the office.

Quick Instruction

Roles of the Governor Like the President, a governor plays a great many roles, including chief executive, chief administrator, commander in chief, and chief legislator. In order to fulfill these roles, the governor is vested with a variety of powers by the State constitution. However, each of the governor's powers are often restricted. For example, the governor can appoint a secretary of state, but the appointment must be approved by the legislature. In some States, the law requires the governor to appoint members of the opposing party to each board or commission so that one party isn't favored over the other.

Interactive Chart: Powers of the Governor Project the chart on the whiteboard. Introduce the activity by reminding students of the different roles of the governor: executive, administrator, legislator, party leader, opinion leader, and ceremonial figure. Continue with the activity.

📷 ACTIVE CLASSROOM

Have students use a Write 1 Get 3 strategy to answer the following question: Which power of the governor is most important to his or her office? Have students use the information in the Core Reading and the Interactive Chart to support their opinions. Share opinions with the class.

D Differentiate: **Extra Support** Ask the following question: To which branch of government does the governor belong? Continue with the activity.

ELL Use the ELL activity described in the ELL chart.

Further Instruction

Editable Presentation Use the Editable Presentation to present the main ideas for this Core Reading.

The Governor's Powers: Core Reading and Interactive Reading Notepad Project and discuss the Interactive Reading Notepad questions. Students should understand that the governor has many duties, and that he or she must rely on assistants, agency heads, or deputies. Discuss how the legislative branch influences the executive branch through its approval process. Continue the discussion by explaining how the executive branch influences the legislative branch through the governor's use of the veto power.

Draw Conclusions Why is the selection of assistants so important to the executive branch? *(Assistants carry out the vision of the governor and their effectiveness and loyalty are important to ensuring that his or her vision is carried out.)*

Analyze What does the budget represent to the people of the State? *(It represents the priorities of the executive branch and the struggle over who does or does not get resources.)*

Objective 3: List and describe the other executive offices at the State level.

Quick Instruction

Interactive Gallery: State Government Executive Officers Project the gallery on the whiteboard. Introduce the activity by reminding students that the governor must share power with a variety of officers. These officers are often chosen by the voters rather than appointed by the governor. Continue with the activity.

📷 ACTIVE CLASSROOM

Using a Sticky Note strategy, have students jot down questions, comments, or observations about the executive positions in the Interactive Gallery. Have students compare the offices, noting at least one similarity and one difference between a State executive office and a federal executive office. Post the questions on a wall. Sort and discuss in small groups or as a whole.

D Differentiate: **Challenge** Ask students to research an executive office not shown in the Interactive Gallery. Have them write a short biography about the person who holds the position in a particular State. Biographies should include interesting facts about what the person serving in the office has enacted, or plans to enact, during his or her tenure.

The Governor and State Administration

SYNTHESIZE

DEMONSTRATE

INTERACTIVE GALLERY
State Government Executive Officers

DIGITAL ACTIVITY
Amending Executive Power

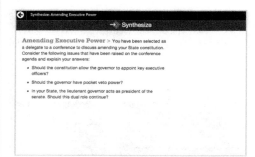

DIGITAL QUIZ
Lesson Quiz and Class Discussion Board

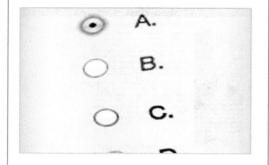

Further Instruction
Editable Presentation Use the Editable Presentation to present the main ideas for this Core Reading.

Other Executive Officers: Core Reading and Interactive Reading Notepad Project and discuss the Interactive Reading Notepad questions. With students, compare different methods of filling public offices, including elected and appointed offices, at State levels. Discuss responsibilities for each of the public offices found in the Core Reading.

Compare How does the lieutenant governor's power compare to that of the governor? *(In general, the governor has much more power. Although in some States the lieutenant governor presides over the senate, for the most part, a lieutenant governor has little responsibility, other than being available to take over the governorship should it become vacant.)*

Make Inferences What can the governor do to ensure that the elected executive offices carry out his or her vision? *(The governor can use his or her influence with the State party organization to put people he or she trusts on the ballot. Then, once in office, he or she could use personal persuasive powers to ensure the vision is carried out.)*

Ask students to recall the Topic Essential Question, What Should Governments Do? Have them use the Think Pair Share strategy to answer the questions in this activity. Ask them to take five minutes to write down some brief answers to the questions below, then share their answers with a talking partner.

Have partners think about the following questions. Should the constitution allow the governor to appoint key executive officers? *(Possible answers: Yes; the executive officers and the governor need to work together harmoniously. The current system has built-in conflict if the governor can't appoint the executive officers. OR No; the governor and executive officers best represent the interests of the citizens if each is directly elected by the voters.)* Should the governor have pocket veto power? *(Possible answers: Yes; a pocket veto gives the governor a chance to reject bills without having to face the legislature each time, creating more efficiency. It also parallels the power of the executive in the U.S. Constitution. OR No; the governor should have to justify each veto. A pocket veto does not require this step.)* In your State, the lieutenant governor acts as president of the senate. Should this dual role continue? *(Possible answers: Yes; the lieutenant governor can check and balance the power of the legislature by participating in the legislature. OR No; the lieutenant governor should advise the legislature but not participate, as participation gives too much power to this role.)*

Discuss Have students consider whether they think the office of governor is weak or strong. Discuss why they think as they do, using examples from the lesson. *(Answers will vary, but should include examples that support students' opinions.)*

Assign the online Lesson Quiz for this lesson if you haven't already done so. Students will be offered automatic remediation or enrichment based on their scores.

Pose this question to the class on the Discussion Board:

In *The Governor and State Administration*, you read about how the State executive branches are organized, including the responsibilites of each office and the qualifications. You compared how other States organized their executive branches.

Summarize Summarize the governor's many roles, including the powers, duties, and limitations of the office. *(Possible answer: The governor usually appoints assistants. He oversees the administration of funds and people, but shares oversight with various elected officials. The governor submits a budget that shows his or her priorities.)*

Topic Inquiry
Have students continue their investigations for the Topic Inquiry.

The State Courts

Supporting English Language Learners

Use with the reading, **State Courts and the Law**.

Listening
Guide students to preview the text by looking at all the visuals and reading the captions. Read aloud the text, then discuss how the visuals help students understand the State court systems and the functions, structures, and processes of State government in the U.S. federal system.

Beginning Read aloud one section of the text at a time. Ask the students questions about the visuals that can be answered with gestures, yes or no, or one- and two-word responses. Repeat with another section of the text.

Intermediate Have partners follow along as you read the text aloud. Ask students questions about the visuals that require short phrases as responses. Guide partners to find the answers to the questions.

Advanced Have partners read the text. Ask partners to select two visuals and discuss how the visuals help in understanding the content. Ask partners to share with another set of partners.

Advanced High Have partners read the text and select a visual that enhanced their understanding. Have them share the visual they selected and read aloud the portion of the text that is supported by the visual.

Use with the reading, **Understanding the Jury System**.

Speaking
Read the sections related to the jury system. Discuss the functions of the system and its place in the development of Anglo-American law. Provide a graphic organizer with the following sections: *Organization of the Jury System, The Grand Jury, The Information, The Petit Jury, Process of Juror Selection.* Support students as they explain the system in their own words.

Beginning Guide the class to complete the graphic organizer with words, short phrases or illustrations. Ask for volunteers to explain different topics on the graphic organizer using words or short phrases.

Intermediate Have small groups complete the graphic organizer. Encourage them to use phrases and short sentences. Have students take turns explaining the different topics on the graphic organizer.

Advanced Guide partners to complete the graphic organizer. Encourage them to use detailed sentences. Using the graphic organizer for support, have them explain the jury system to another set of partners.

Advanced High Have students complete the graphic organizer independently. Guide them to explain the jury system to other students using the graphic organizer for support.

Ⓓ Differentiate Instruction

Use the Differentiated Instruction notes throughout the lesson plan to support the varied skill sets, levels of readiness, and interests in the mixed-ability classroom.

Challenge These notes include suggestions for expanding the activity for advanced students.

On-Level These notes include suggestions for modifying the activity to address different interests or learning styles.

Extra Support These notes include ideas for providing more scaffolding or reading spuport.

Special Needs These notes provide ideas for adapting instruction to support the needs of various special needs students.

■ NOTES

The State Courts

Objectives

Objective 1: Identify and define the kinds of law applied in State courts.

Objective 2: Compare and contrast criminal law and civil law.

Objective 3: Describe the types and purposes of juries and juror selection.

Objective 4: Explain how State courts are organized and describe the work that each type of court does.

Objective 5: Examine and evaluate the different methods by which judges are selected among the States.

LESSON 4 ORGANIZER		PACING: APPROX. 1 PERIOD, .5 BLOCKS			
				RESOURCES	
		OBJECTIVES	**PACING**	**Online**	**Print**
Connect					
DIGITAL START UP ACTIVITY **Serving on a Jury**			5 min.	●	
Investigate					
DIGITAL TEXT 1 **State Courts and the Law**		Objectives 1, 2	10 min.	●	●
INTERACTIVE CHART **State Law**			10 min.	●	
DIGITAL TEXT 2 **Understanding the Jury System**		Objective 3	10 min.	●	●
DIGITAL TEXT 3 **How the State Courts Are Organized**		Objective 4	10 min.	●	●
INTERACTIVE CHART **The State Courts**			10 min.	●	
DIGITAL TEXT 4 **How Judges Are Selected**		Objective 5	10 min.	●	●
Synthesize					
DIGITAL ACTIVITY **Courts and Their Cases**			5 min.	●	
Demonstrate					
DIGITAL QUIZ **Lesson Quiz and Class Discussion Board**			10 min.	●	

PEARSON
realize™
www.PearsonRealize.com

Go online to access additional resources including:
Primary Sources • Biographies • Supreme Court cases •
21st Century Skill Tutorials • Maps • Graphic Organizers.

■ CONNECT

DIGITAL START UP ACTIVITY
Serving on a Jury

Project the Start Up Activity Ask students to answer the questions as they enter and get settled. Then have them share their ideas with another student.

Discuss Why must jurors follow all five of these rules? *(By following these rules, the defendant receives a fair trial.)* What would happen if a juror didn't follow a particular rule? *(Possible answer: Laws can be complex; if a juror did not follow these rules exactly, the defendant's right to a fair trial would be compromised.)*

Tell students that in this lesson they will be learning about how the State courts operate.

Aa Vocabulary Development: Use the Interactive Reading Notepad to preview the Key Terms and Academic Vocabulary in this Lesson with students.

↑↓ FLIP IT!
Assign the Flipped Video for this lesson.

■ STUDENT EDITION PRINT PAGES: 635–644

■ INVESTIGATE

DIGITAL TEXT 1
State Courts and the Law

Objectives 1: **Identify and define the kinds of law applied in State courts;** 2: **Compare and contrast criminal law and civil law.**

Quick Instruction
On the board, write the definition of each type of law in the interactivity: administrative, constitutional, statutory, equity, and common. Have students refer to these definitions as they complete the chart.

Interactive Chart: State Law Project and step through the chart with students. Link the forms of law they learned about with the examples.

📹 ACTIVE CLASSROOM
Using a Headline strategy, have students choose one of the cases and create a headline that summarizes the case and how it illustrates a particular type of law. Have students share their headlines in small groups and vote on the best.

D Differentiate: Extra Support Define each of the forms of law with students and then continue with the activity.

ELL Use the ELL activity described in the ELL chart.

INTERACTIVE CHART
State Law

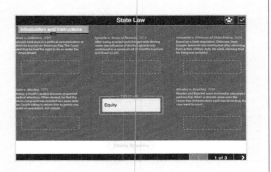

Further Instruction

Editable Presentation Use the Editable Presentation to present the main ideas for this Core Reading.

State Courts and the Law: Core Reading and Interactive Reading Notepad Project and discuss the Interactive Reading Notepad questions. With students, compare the structures, functions, and processes of State courts in the U.S. federal system. Discuss examples of differences among the State courts from the Core Reading, such as Louisiana and common law.

Make Inferences Why do State courts treat civil and criminal cases differently? *(Possible answer: Criminal cases deal with public wrongs damaging to society at large, whereas civil cases generally deal with conduct disputes. The two are treated differently in the courts because their resolutions are different. Criminal cases are punishable by fines, prison, or even death, whereas civil cases are resolved solely by monetary awards.)*

Apply Concepts In what way might legal precedents be important to legislators? *(Possible answer: Legislators can look to see how judges are generally ruling, or what precedents have been set. Then they can create or clarify legislation to overturn or support precedent.)*

The State Courts

DIGITAL TEXT 2

Understanding the Jury System

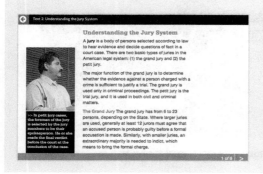

DIGITAL TEXT 3

How the State Courts Are Organized

INTERACTIVE CHART

The State Courts

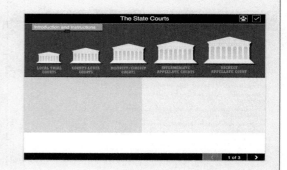

Objective 3: Describe the types and purposes of juries and juror selection.

Quick Instruction

Draw a chart on the board with two columns and have students complete it by listing the main features of the grand jury and the petit jury. For example, students might note the following: The grand jury must indict a person before he or she is tried for a crime. After the prosecuting attorney presents evidence, the grand jury meets in secret to deliberate. A petit jury hears both criminal and civil cases. It is also known as the trial jury.

ELL Use the ELL activity described in the ELL chart.

Further Instruction

Editable Presentation Use the Editable Presentation to present the main ideas for this Core Reading.

Understanding the Jury System: Core Reading and Interactive Reading Notepad Project and discuss the Interactive Reading Notepad questions. Discuss the process of juror selection. Discuss the role of the jury in the guarantee of the right to a fair trial. Ask students: Can justice be served without a jury trial?

Make Judgments Do you agree that the courts should move away from the use of the grand jury? *(Possible answers: Yes; it is too expensive and time consuming. OR No; the grand jury is an important check on the prosecutor and helps to ensure that only cases with strong evidence move forward through the system.)*

Objective 4: Explain how State courts are organized and describe the work that each type of court does.

Quick Instruction

Have students select each type of court and read the description of the types of cases heard by that court. Then go back through the courts and read the examples. Discuss as a class, rephrasing each example in "plain English."

Interactive Chart: The State Courts Project the chart on the whiteboard and click through each court on the chart with students. Point out that the chart shows how the court system is organized.

ACTIVE CLASSROOM

Using an Organizer strategy, assign students a different type of court case: civil, felony criminal, misdemeanor criminal. Then have them identify which court would hear the case, using what they learned in the interactive chart.

D Differentiate: Extra Support Provide sticky notes to students and have them note the important elements of each court system. Then continue with the activity.

Further Instruction

Editable Presentation Use the Editable Presentation to present the main ideas for this Core Reading.

How the State Courts Are Organized: Core Reading and Interactive Reading Notepad Project and discuss the Interactive Reading Notepad questions. Compare the structures, functions, and processes of the State courts described in the Core Reading.

Describe the difference between a unified court system and a geographical system. Students should understand the reasons why some States have moved to the unified system: it spreads out the workload and results in a more consistent interpretation of State law. Then ask: What might be the drawbacks of a unified court system? *(Possible answer: removal of local control might create problems)*

Draw Conclusions Why is it important for the appellate courts to be "gatekeepers" for the State's highest court? *(The process allows only the most important court cases to be heard by the highest courts, those that would impact the most people, clear up issues between the legislative and executive branches, or set important precedents. This helps keep the workload of the State supreme court from becoming unmanageable.)*

How Judges Are Selected

How Judges Are Selected

Clearly, the quality of any court system—indeed, the quality of justice itself—depends in large measure on the selection of competent, well-trained judges. More than 22,000 judges and another 9,000 judicial officers (magistrates, JPs, associate judges, and so on) now sit in the States' various trial and appellate courts. Nearly all of them came to office in one of three ways: (1) by popular election, (2) by appointment by the governor, or (3) by appointment by the legislature.

Popular election is by far the most widely used method of judicial selection. In fact, the only way to become a judge in about half of the States is by popular election. Midterm vacancies, caused by death or resignation, provide the only exception to that blanket rule; those vacancies are usually filled by gubernatorial appointment. Almost half of all judicial elections are nonpartisan contests today.

>> Voters show their support for Reaura Wawi for 49th district court judge before election day in Laredo, Texas.

1 of 6 >

Objective 5: Examine and evaluate the different methods by which judges are selected among the States.

Quick Instruction

With a show of hands, have students vote for the method of judicial selection that they think is most widely used: (1) popular election, (2) appointment by the governor, or (3) appointment by the legislature. After reading the text, return to students' responses to see how many of them chose the correct answer: popular election.

Further Instruction

Editable Presentation Use the Editable Presentation to present the main ideas for this Core Reading.

How Judges Are Selected: Core Reading and Interactive Reading Notepad Project and discuss the Interactive Reading Notepad questions. Discuss the Missouri Plan for appointing and electing judges. This method allows governors to appoint judges using a list created by a special judicial committee. The appointed judge appears on the ballot in the next election, but he or she runs unopposed. Voters decide whether or not they will keep the judge.

Make Judgments Do you think judges should be elected or appointed? Why? *(Possible answer: Appointed judges are less likely to have agendas or constituents to please, so they can more impartial, especially if they are appointed for long terms.)*

Cause and Effect What benefit does the Missouri Plan provide? *(It combines nomination by the governor with popular election and eliminates the drawbacks of gubernatorial selection by introducing a nominating commission to recommend candidates.)*

The State Courts

SYNTHESIZE

DIGITAL ACTIVITY
Courts and Their Cases

Ask students to recall the Topic Essential Question, What Should Governments Do? Have them use the Think Pair Share strategy to complete their tables. Ask them to take five minutes to write down some brief responses to the questions below, then share their answers with a talking partner.

Have partners think about the following questions: What are the different State courts and what types of cases do they generally hear? *(Local trial courts: traffic violations, small claims cases; county-level courts: minor criminal cases, wills and estates; general trial courts: important criminal and civil cases; intermediate appellate courts: case reviews, election disputes; State supreme court and court of criminal appeals: review appeals, final decisions)* What is the hierarchy of the State court systems? *(Possible answer: Local trial courts are at the bottom and the State supreme court is at the top.)*

Discuss Have students share the court cases they used to illustrate each different court.

DEMONSTRATE

DIGITAL QUIZ
Lesson Quiz and Class Discussion Board

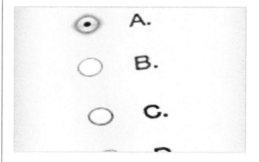

Assign the online Lesson Quiz for this lesson if you haven't already done so. Students will be offered automatic remediation or enrichment based on their score.

Pose these questions to the class on the Discussion Board: In *State Courts,* you read about the organization of the State courts. You also read how these organizations have changed over time.

Analyze What if the number of courts in a State had to be reduced by half? What would be the best way to organize them? *(Possible answer: The best way to organize them would be by unifying the court system instead of breaking it down geographically. That way, cases could be spread across several dockets.)*

Recall What are the kinds of law applied in the State courts? *(constitutional law, statutory law, administrative law, common law, and equity)*

Topic Inquiry
Have students continue their investigations for the Topic Inquiry.

Local Governments—Structure and Function

Supporting English Language Learners

Use with the reading, **Counties Across the United States**.

Speaking

Read the sections *Counties: Some Key Facts* and *How County Governments Are Structured.* Guide students to compare the structures of local governments by using formal spoken language. Tell students that one characteristic of formal spoken language is the use of complete sentences.

Beginning Guide the class to complete the following sentence stems: *A county is _____. A parish is _____. A township is _____.* Have them copy the sentences and read them aloud.

Intermediate Guide small groups to complete the sentence stems above. Have them read their sentences to the class.

Advanced Have partners write complete sentences using the words *county, parish, township, size.* Have them read their sentences to other students.

Advanced High Have individual students write complete sentences using the words above. Have them refer to these sentences during a discussion about the text.

Use with the reading, **Forms of City Government**.

Listening

Read aloud the sections of the text with the key terms *mayor-council government, strong-mayor government, weak-mayor government, commission government, council-manager government.* Tell the students that these terms are related to the structures of local governments. Guide students to use context clues to understand the terms by completing the following activities.

Beginning Display the sentences with the key terms as you read aloud. Underline words that serve as context clues as you describe how they are related to the key terms.

Intermediate Read aloud as students follow in the text. Discuss the words that serve as context clues. Have students complete a word web with the key term in the middle and the context clues on the branches.

Advanced Have partners read aloud. Guide them to list the context clues for the key terms. Have them compare and discuss their list with another set of partners.

Advanced High Have partners read aloud. Have students identify the context clues for the key terms. Have students write a definition for the key terms using the context clues.

▣ Differentiate Instruction

Use the Differentiated Instruction notes throughout the lesson plan to support the varied skill sets, levels of readiness, and interests in the mixed-ability classroom.

Challenge These notes include suggestions for expanding the activity for advanced students.

On-Level These notes include suggestions for modifying the activity to address different interests or learning styles.

Extra Support These notes include ideas for providing more scaffolding or reading spuport.

Special Needs These notes provide ideas for adapting instruction to support the needs of various special needs students.

■ NOTES

Local Governments—Structure and Function

Objectives

Objective 1: Describe the typical county, its governmental structure and functions, and the need for reform in county government.

Objective 2: Identify the responsibilities of tribal governments.

Objective 3: Examine the governments of towns, townships, and special districts.

Objective 4: Explain the process of incorporation and compare and contrast the major forms of city government.

Objective 5: Evaluate the need for city planning and list some major municipal functions.

Objective 6: Outline the challenges that face suburbs and metropolitan areas.

LESSON 5 ORGANIZER		PACING: APPROX. 1 PERIOD, .5 BLOCKS			
				RESOURCES	
		OBJECTIVES	PACING	Online	Print
Connect					
DIGITAL START UP ACTIVITY **My County, USA**			5 min.	●	
Investigate					
DIGITAL TEXT 1 **Counties Across the United States**		Objectives 1, 2	10 min.	●	●
DIGITAL TEXT 2 **Tribal Governments**			10 min.	●	●
DIGITAL TEXT 3 **Towns, Townships, and Special Districts**		Objective 3	10 min.	●	●
INTERACTIVE GALLERY **Special Districts**			10 min.	●	
DIGITAL TEXTS 4–6 **City Government, Forms of City Government, City Planning and Other Municipal Functions**		Objectives 4, 5	10 min.	●	●
INTERACTIVE GALLERY **Forms of City Government**			10 min.	●	
DIGITAL TEXT 7 **Suburbs and Metropolitan Areas**		Objective 6	10 min.	●	●
Synthesize					
DIGITAL ACTIVITY **Whose Job Is It?**			5 min.	●	
Demonstrate					
DIGITAL QUIZ **Lesson Quiz and Class Discussion Board**			10 min.	●	

PEARSON
realize.™
www.PearsonRealize.com

Go online to access additional resources including:
Primary Sources • Biographies • Supreme Court cases •
21st Century Skill Tutorials • Maps • Graphic Organizers.

CONNECT

DIGITAL START UP ACTIVITY
My County, USA

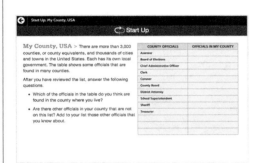

Project the Start Up Activity Ask students to answer the questions as they enter and get settled. Then have them share their ideas with another student.

Discuss Which of these officials do you think are found in the county where you live? *(Possible answer: My county has county board members, an assessor, a District Attorney, sheriff, and I think a coroner and a chief administrator.)*

Tell students that in this lesson they will be learning about local governments and how they govern with the support of the State and Federal governments.

Aa Vocabulary Development: Use the Interactive Reading Notepad to preview the Key Terms and Academic Vocabulary in this Lesson with students.

⚡ FLIP IT!
Assign the Flipped Video for this lesson.

▮ STUDENT EDITION PRINT PAGES: 645–659

INVESTIGATE

DIGITAL TEXT 1
Counties Across the United States

DIGITAL TEXT 2
Tribal Governments

Objectives 1: Describe the typical county, its governmental structure and functions, and the need for reform in county government; 2: Identify the responsibilities of tribal governments.

Quick Instruction
Ask students to name any types of local government they can think of. Then draw a simple chart to show the levels of government in a typical city or town: United States, State, County, Town/Township. Have students insert the particular names of their State, county, etc. Include tribal government on your chart if applicable. Then display a map showing counties and towns in your State and have students locate their own.

ELL Use the ELL activity described in the ELL chart.

Further Instruction

Editable Presentation Use the Editable Presentation to present the main ideas for these Core Readings.

Counties Across the United States and Tribal Governments: Core Reading and Interactive Reading Notepad Project and discuss the Interactive Reading Notepad questions. Compare the structures, functions, and processes of local governments in the U.S. federal system, including how local

governments organize themselves across the country. For example, Louisiana is divided into parishes, Alaska into boroughs, New England into towns, and the Mid-Atlantic and Midwest into townships. Some States, including Rhode Island and Connecticut, have no local government structure.

Discuss how tribal governments are similar to and different from State and local governments. For example, not all tribal governments have a written constitution. Native American tribes are considered sovereign nations and so are exempted from State or local control.

Make Judgments What reform, if any, might help reduce the chaos found in county government? Why? *(Possible answer: Reorganizing the counties to better reflect the realities of the modern world and the services people need would reduce the chaos and make the States function more efficiently.)*

Compare How are tribal governments similar to and different from State and county governments? *(Possible answer: Tribal governments are similar to State and county governments because they use federal funds and tax revenues to provide services. However, because they are recognized as sovereign nations, tribal governments have the right to govern their own people and in that sense are more similar to the Federal Government.)*

Local Governments—Structure and Function

DIGITAL TEXT 3
Towns, Townships, and Special Districts

INTERACTIVE GALLERY
Special Districts

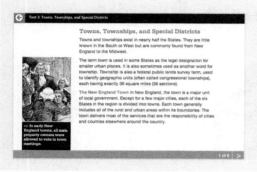

Objective 3: Examine the governments of towns, townships, and special districts.

Quick Instruction

Tell students that their county web site should provide information about any special districts in the local area. Have students locate this information on the county site or elsewhere online and summarize what they find. Students can also use the U.S. Census Bureau's Census of Governments, conducted every five years, to find this information.

Interactive Gallery: Special Districts

Project the gallery on the whiteboard and step through it with students. Introduce the activity by telling students that special districts are created to fulfill specific governmental functions. They can be created by the legislature, or voted into being by citizens.

📷 ACTIVE CLASSROOM

In pairs, have students review the special districts in the interactivity and decide on an organizer they think would best show the benefits of these special districts. Ask prompting questions, such as: What is the most important function of this district? Could it be done by another local or State government entity? Why or why not? Students should use the answers to these questions to create their chart or diagram. Share the organizers and discuss as a large group.

D **Differentiate: Extra Support** Ask: What is the main purpose of each district?

Further Instruction

Editable Presentation Use the Editable Presentation to present the main ideas for this Core Reading.

Towns, Townships, and Special Districts: Core Reading and Interactive Reading Notepad Project and discuss the Interactive Reading Notepad questions. Discuss how governmental organization is linked to rural and urban living. Students should understand that the needs of those living in rural and urban areas are different and local governments arose to address these differences.

Compare Compare the different methods of filling public offices, including elected and appointed offices, at the local level. Specifically, explain how those who run special districts are selected. *(The governing body of special districts is almost always an elected board.)*

Analyze Information Why might townships have outlived their usefulness? *(They are typically more rural in function. Much of their responsibility has been transferred to municipalities. Many States have abolished them without negative results.)*

Draw Conclusions Why is regulating water usage in a city an important local responsibility? *(Possible answer: Everyone, including businesses, uses and discards water. People expect that they will have access to clean water. Local government is responsible for protecting the public health and welfare.)*

DIGITAL TEXT 4

City Government

DIGITAL TEXT 5

Forms of City Government

INTERACTIVE GALLERY

Forms of City Government

Objectives 4: **Explain the process of incorporation and compare and contrast the major forms of city government; 5:** **Evaluate the need for city planning and list some major municipal functions.**

Quick Instruction

Interactive Gallery: Forms of City Government Project the gallery on the whiteboard. Introduce the activity by telling students that cities are governed by a mayor-council, commission, or council-manager form of government. Have students study the photographs, then ask: How do these three cities differ in terms of size and population? *(Possible answer: New York City is the largest, with many large businesses and buildings crowded together. Galveston is the smallest, with only a few large buildings and more space between buildings. Salt Lake City is medium-sized, with a good number of large buildings and some crowded areas, but also some less congested areas and smaller buildings.)* Then use the slider to highlight information about the governments of the example cities.

🎙 ACTIVE CLASSROOM

Have students use a Ranking strategy to explain which form of government they think is most effective. In small groups, have students share their ranks and reasons. Discuss whether or not one form of government would work for all cities.

D Differentiate: Challenge Have students research the form of government where they live and present their findings to the class.

ELL Use the ELL activity described in the ELL chart.

Further Instruction

Editable Presentation Use the Editable Presentation to present the main ideas for these Core Readings.

City Government, Forms of City Government, and City Planning and Other Municipal Functions: Core Reading and Interactive Reading Notepad Project and discuss the Interactive Reading Notepad questions. Compare the structures, functions, and processes of local governments in the U.S. federal system with students, focusing on the city governments explained in the Core Readings.

Discuss the different municipal functions of city government. Students should understand that the larger the size of the city, the more government functions the city must provide.

Draw Conclusions What questions should the courts ask when deciding whether a zoning ordinance is reasonable? *(Possible answers: Does the ordinance deny a person life, liberty, or property without due process of law? Is it reasonable?)*

Local Governments—Structure and Function

City Planning and Other Municipal Functions

Cause and Effect Why is it important to have one executive at the head of government, such as a mayor, instead of a group of commissioners? *(task delegation is easier, there is less empire-building, and accountability is more obvious)*

Suburbs and Metropolitan Areas

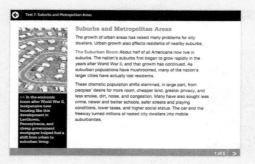

Objective 6: **Outline the challenges that face suburbs and metropolitan areas.**

Quick Instruction

Ask students to identify whether their school is located in a suburb, a metropolitan area, or a rural area. Explain that there were very few suburbs in the United States before World War II. People tended to live in either the city or the country. List the advantages and disadvantages associated with the growth of suburbs on the board.

Further Instruction

Editable Presentation Use the Editable Presentation to present the main ideas for this Core Reading.

Suburbs and Metropolitan Areas: Core Reading and Interactive Reading Notepad Project and discuss the Interactive Reading Notepad questions. Compare city and suburban governments, as explained in the Core Reading.

Cause and Effect What might cities do to make themselves more appealing and prevent "suburbanitis"? *(Possible answer: They can revitalize their center cities to attract businesses and set aside residential areas in specific parts of the city.)*

PEARSON
realize™

www.PearsonRealize.com
Access your Digital Lesson

○ A.
○ B.
○ C.

SYNTHESIZE

DIGITAL ACTIVITY

Whose Job Is It?

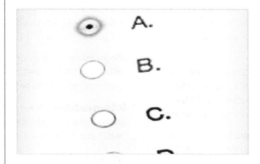

Ask students to recall the Topic Essential Question, What Should Governments Do? Have them use the Think Pair Share strategy to answer the questions in this activity. Ask them to take five minutes to write down some brief answers to the questions below, then share their answers with a talking partner.

Have partners think about the following questions. Suppose that you have an idea for a public works project—the construction of a footbridge over a busy street so that citizens can cross a highway safely to access public parks and facilities on either side. How could you, as a citizen, put this idea into action? *(Possible answer: A citizen could assemble a group of concerned citizens and send ideas to the county board.)* Which local and/or county government officials or departments would be involved in planning and carrying out the project? *(The officials and departments in my county that would be involved in planning and carrying out the project are: planning commission, public works department, zoning board, sheriff, treasurer, assessor.)* You might encourage students to use a graphic organizer to show answers.

Discuss Have students consider the chart from the Start Up Activity. Ask what other responsibilities local governments have that they did not add to the chart. Discuss why those responsibilities are best undertaken at the local level.

DEMONSTRATE

DIGITAL QUIZ

Lesson Quiz and Class Discussion Board

Assign the online Lesson Quiz for this lesson if you haven't already done so. Students will be offered automatic remediation or enrichment based on their scores.

Pose these questions to the class on the Discussion Board: In *Local Governments— Structure and Function* you read that States use local governments to provide services to their citizens, and that local governments have had to change to respond to population movement.

Compare What is the difference between a city and a suburb? *(Cities are more densely populated, and include residential, commercial, and sometimes industrial sections. Suburbs are largely residential, with much less crowding.)*

Draw Conclusions What challenges do local governments face regarding population densities? How are these addressed? Give an example. *(Possible answer: Sharing police protection between suburbs and cities; Some cities are annexing suburbs to provide those services and increase tax bases.)*

Topic Inquiry

Have students continue their investigations for the Topic Inquiry.

State and Local Spending and Revenue

Supporting English Language Learners

Use with the readings, **Education, Public Health, and Welfare** and **Public Safety, Highways, and Other Services**.

Listening

Read aloud the text and emphasize the words that are hyperlinked and/or found in the glossary. Tell the students that these words will help them understand how government fiscal policies influence State and local economies. Teach students how the hyperlinks and glossary can help them understand the text.

Beginning Display the words that are hyperlinked and/or found in the glossary. As you read aloud, have students listen and hold up a finger or otherwise indicate when each word is read. Have students use the hyperlinks and glossary with a partner. Discuss the meanings of the words.

Intermediate Display the words that are hyperlinked and/or found in the glossary. Tell students to listen for the words as you read the text aloud. Guide the students to find the definitions of the words. Discuss the meanings of the words.

Advanced Have partners take turns reading aloud the text and listening. Guide them to create a list of words that are hyperlinked and/or found in the glossary. Have them find the definitions of the words. Have small groups discuss the meanings of the words.

Advanced High Have partners take turns reading aloud the text and listening, and find the definitions for the words that are hyperlinked and/or found in the glossary. Guide partners to write the definitions in their own words.

Use with the reading, **Sources of State Revenue**.

Speaking

Read the text and discuss how government fiscal policies influence the local economy. Tell students that informal spoken language is the language we use with friends and family. Often phrases and simple sentences are used in informal language. Guide students to use informal spoken language by having them discuss the visuals in the text.

Beginning Based on the language levels of the students, choose 2–3 visuals from the text. Encourage students to use words, phrases, and gestures to describe the visuals.

Intermediate Have small groups use words, phrases, and short sentences to describe the visuals in the text. Ask groups to share what was said with the class.

Advanced Have partners discuss the visuals in the text. Have them share with other students.

Advanced High Guide partners to take turns asking and answering questions about the visuals.

▣ Differentiate Instruction

Use the Differentiated Instruction notes throughout the lesson plan to support the varied skill sets, levels of readiness, and interests in the mixed-ability classroom.

Challenge These notes include suggestions for expanding the activity for advanced students.

On-Level These notes include suggestions for modifying the activity to address different interests or learning styles.

Extra Support These notes include ideas for providing more scaffolding or reading spuport.

Special Needs These notes provide ideas for adapting instruction to support the needs of various special needs students.

■ NOTES

Objectives

Objective 1: Explain why State and local governments have a major role in providing important services.

Objective 2: Identify State and local services in the fields of education, public welfare, public safety, and highways.

Objective 3: Describe the major federal and State limits on raising revenue.

Objective 4: List the four principles of sound taxation.

Objective 5: Identify major tax and nontax sources of State and local revenues.

Objective 6: Explain the State budget process.

LESSON 6 ORGANIZER		PACING: APPROX. 1 PERIOD, .5 BLOCKS			
		OBJECTIVES	**PACING**	**RESOURCES**	
				Online	**Print**
Connect					
DIGITAL START UP ACTIVITY **You Are the Governor**			5 min.	●	
Investigate					
DIGITAL TEXT 1 **Education, Public Health, and Welfare**		Objectives 1, 2	10 min.	●	●
DIGITAL TEXT 2 **Public Safety, Highways, and Other Services**			10 min.	●	●
INTERACTIVE CHART **State and Local Spending**			10 min.	●	
DIGITAL TEXT 3 **Financing State and Local Government**		Objectives 3, 4	10 min.	●	●
DIGITAL TEXTS 4 AND 5 **Sources of State Revenue, State Budgets**		Objectives 5, 6	10 min.	●	●
INTERACTIVE ILLUSTRATION **State and Local Revenue**			10 min.	●	
Synthesize					
DIGITAL ACTIVITY **Services, Revenues, and Changing Economic Times**			5 min.	●	
Demonstrate					
DIGITAL QUIZ **Lesson Quiz and Class Discussion Board**			10 min.	●	

State and Local Spending and Revenue

■ CONNECT

DIGITAL START UP ACTIVITY
You Are the Governor

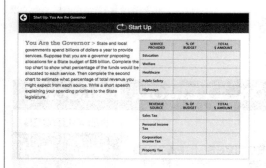

Project the Start Up Activity Ask students to complete the two charts as they enter and get settled. Then have them share their ideas with another student, either in class or through a chat or blog space.

Discuss What criteria did you use to decide how much of the budget to allocate to each service? *(Possible answers: I thought about how many people need the service, and how important it is to people's lives.)*

Tell students that in this lesson they will be learning about how the States spend money, including how they raise it and what they spend it on.

Aa Vocabulary Development: Use the Interactive Reading Notepad to preview the Key Terms and Academic Vocabulary in this Lesson with students.

↯ FLIP IT!

Assign the Flipped Video for this lesson.

■ STUDENT EDITION PRINT PAGES: 660–670

■ INVESTIGATE

DIGITAL TEXT 1
Education, Public Health, and Welfare

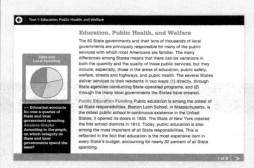

DIGITAL TEXT 2
Public Safety, Highways, and Other Services

Objectives 1: Explain why State and local governments have a major role in providing important services; **2:** Identify State and local services in the fields of education, public welfare, public safety, and highways.

Quick Instruction
Begin a class discussion by asking students who they think paid for their school building, books, desks, and other school equipment. Lead them to recognize that the funds come from the local government and that the local government, in turn, gets those monies from taxes. Explain that education is the largest item in every State's budget.

Interactive Chart: State and Local Spending Project the chart and step through it with students. Assign each spending category to an amount, based on how important the class thinks it is, relative to the other categories. Should States spend more on education or housing, for example?

📷 ACTIVE CLASSROOM

Have students use a Sticky Note strategy and the data in the chart to answer the following question: Why does spending differ at the State and local levels? Invite students to post their answers or additional questions they have about the comparison. Sort the notes. Make some general statements that answer the question. Then use the comments and questions to create a list of questions for further research. You might ask students to do this research in groups and present it to the class.

D Differentiate: Extra Support Ask: What are some services the State provides its citizens? What are some services a city or municipality provides its citizens? *(State: public health programs, welfare, police force, corrections system, road construction and maintenance, driver licensing; city or municipality: education, police and fire protection, street and sidewalk construction and maintenance, school and other facilities construction and maintenance, sewer and wastewater treatment, transportation system construction and operation)*

ELL Use the ELL activity described in the ELL chart.

Further Instruction

Editable Presentation Use the Editable Presentation to present the main ideas for these Core Readings.

Education, Public Health, and Welfare and Public Safety, Highways, and Other Services: Core Reading and Interactive Reading Notepad Project and discuss the Interactive Reading Notepad questions. Consider the various expenses and sources of revenue of State and local governments, as explained in the Core Readings. Discuss State budget priorities and review State sources of revenue. Identify the funds contributed by the Federal Government to the States as explained in the Core Reading, such as TANF block grants.

INTERACTIVE CHART
State and Local Spending

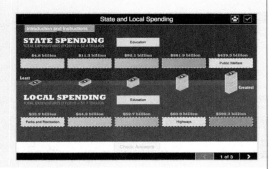

DIGITAL TEXT 3
Financing State and Local Government

Analyze Information You have read that the police power is the States' power to protect and promote the public health, safety, morals, and general welfare. How is the police power being exercised when States require drivers to be licensed? *(Possible answer: Requiring a driver's license to operate a motor vehicle is the State's way of ensuring that drivers understand traffic laws and regulations, which helps protect public safety.)*

Objectives 3: Describe the major federal and State limits on raising revenue; 4: List the four principles of sound taxation.

Quick Instruction
Write the following quotation on the board: "the power to tax involves the power to destroy." Ask whether anyone knows the source of this quotation. Then explain that it is from the Supreme Court's 1819 decision in *McCulloch* v. *Maryland.* Discuss the potential dangers for a people and a government inherent in the taxing power, including such points as the following: If a State were allowed to tax the Federal Government, it could tax it right out of existence. Similarly, an abuse of the taxing power could destroy an individual, a business, or a State. Explain that because of this type of concern, the Constitution limits the taxing power of State and local governments. In addition, each State's constitution limits that State's taxing powers.

Further Instruction
Editable Presentation Use the Editable Presentation to present the main ideas for this Core Reading.

Financing State and Local Government: Core Reading and Interactive Reading Notepad Project and discuss the Interactive Reading Notepad questions. With students, identify the sources of revenue of State and local governments. Note restrictions on the States' taxing abilities. For example, the Constitution forbids States from taxing interstate and foreign commerce.

Biography: Adam Smith Review the four principles of a sound tax system. Discuss how those basic principles should be at the heart of any tax system, whether federal, State, or local. Choose one tax, such as the sales tax, and discuss how well it meets each of Adam Smith's four criteria.

Draw Conclusions Suppose a county were to levy a 50 percent income tax on people who make more than $200,000 in order to build a private school. Is this legal under the United States Constitution? Why or why not? *(Possible answer: No; The Due Process clause requires that taxes be administered fairly and for a public purpose.)*

State and Local Spending and Revenue

DIGITAL TEXT 4

Sources of State Revenue

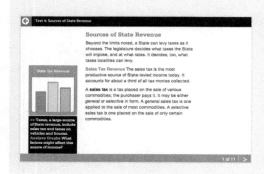

DIGITAL TEXT 5

State Budgets

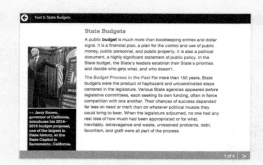

INTERACTIVE ILLUSTRATION

State and Local Revenue

Objectives 5: Identify major tax and nontax sources of State and local revenues; **6:** Explain the State budget process.

Quick Instruction

Create a two-column chart on the board, with the headings "Progressive" and "Regressive." Then have students categorize the following taxes as they read about them in the text: sales tax, income tax, property tax, tax on movie tickets, and drivers' licenses. Explain that progressive taxes rise along with ability to pay, while regressive taxes are the same for everyone. Point out to students that taxes are just one source of revenue for State and local governments. Ask them to list other sources. *(federal grants, publicly operated business enterprises, user fees, court fines, and lotteries)*

Interactive Illustration: State and Local Revenue Project the illustration and explore the hotspots with students. Remind students of the four elements of taxing as noted by Adam Smith. Then continue with the activity.

ACTIVE CLASSROOM

Have students use a Ranking strategy to explain which tax they think is most effective in raising revenue fairly. In small groups, have students share their ranks and reasons. Have students discuss their rankings, including how the regressive or progressive nature of the tax relates to its effectiveness.

D Differentiate: Extra Support Instead of the activity, have students list the different taxes and who is affected by each. Prompt with questions such as: Who might pay this tax? Does this tax apply to all people, or just a few? Then have students join the small groups and discuss which tax might be the most effective.

ELL Use the ELL activity described in the ELL chart.

Further Instruction

Editable Presentation Use the Editable Presentation to present the main ideas for these Core Readings.

Sources of State Revenue and State Budgets: Core Reading and Interactive Reading Notepad Project and discuss the Interactive Reading Notepad questions. Students should understand the budgeting process and its relationship to raising revenue. Be sure students understand that, in most States, the executive branch alone is responsible for preparing the intial budget, whereas in Mississippi, South Carolina, and Texas, both the executive and legislative branches are involved in this step.

Apply Concepts For what reason(s) might a State not levy any type of income tax? *(Possible answer: Putting income back into the economy supports other kinds of taxes, such as property or sales.)*

Analyze Why do States levy different kinds of taxes? *(Levying only one kind of tax would place a heavier burden on some citizens than others. Levying a variety of taxes spreads the burden out among more people, thus making the tax system more fair.)*

Make Judgments Do you think States should rely more heavily on nontax revenues, such as tolls and lotteries, for their funding, in order to reduce sales and property taxes? *(Possible answer: No; The amount of revenue that can be raised through tolls and lotteries is difficult to predict. This would make it difficult to prepare a budget, because it would be unclear how much revenue could be expected.)*

SYNTHESIZE

DIGITAL ACTIVITY

Services, Revenues, and Changing Economic Times

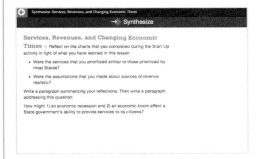

Ask students to recall the Topic Essential Question, What Should Governments Do? Have them use the Think Pair Share strategy to answer the questions in this activity. Ask them to take five minutes to write down some brief answers to the questions below, then share their answers with a talking partner.

Have partners think about the following question: How would an economic recession and, alternatively, an economic boom, affect government's ability to provide services to its citizens? *(An economic recession would mean a decrease in people's income, which would translate to a decrease in tax revenues and negatively affect government's ability to provide services. An economic boom would have the opposite effect: an increase in income and tax revenues, leading to an improvement in government's ability to provide services.)* Have pairs share their answers with the class.

Discuss Have students reconsider the chart from the Start Up Activity. Ask what they learned about State spending priorities and sources of revenue. Would they change their allocations based on that information?

DEMONSTRATE

DIGITAL QUIZ

Lesson Quiz and Class Discussion Board

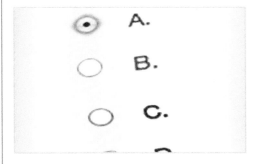

Assign the online Lesson Quiz for this lesson if you haven't already done so. Students will be offered automatic remediation or enrichment based on their score.

Pose these questions to the class on the Discussion Board:

In *State and Local Spending and Revenue*, you read about how States acquire and spend revenue, including budgeting procedures and restrictions on taxing imposed by State legislatures and the Federal Government. In addition, you learned how States try to balance providing services and keeping taxes to a minimum.

Analyze Recall the different services States provide for their citizens. How do these services reflect the priorities of each State? *(Possible answer: The government in each State is responsible for public safety and welfare. The services provided, such as police protection and education and the large amounts spent on each reflect a wish to provide a good education for children and protect those living in the State.)*

Discuss Ask students: Do you think progressive or regressive taxes are more fair? What are the benefits and drawbacks of each? *(Some students may believe that progressive taxes are more fair because they are based on ability to pay. Others may believe that regressive taxes are more fair because they affect only those who use the taxed items or services.)*

Topic Inquiry

Have students continue their investigations for the Topic Inquiry.

State and Local Government

SYNTHESIZE

DIGITAL ACTIVITY
Reflect on the Essential Question and Topic

First, ask students to reconsider the Essential Question for the Topic: What Should Governments Do? Remind students that at the beginning of their study of State government, they reviewed the following list of basic duties. The State government:

- makes laws for State residents to follow;
- settles disputes using the State court system;
- administers federal, State, and local elections;
- creates local governments;
- collects taxes to fund State and local programs.

Ask: "Do you think any of these items should be performed at *only* the State and local or *only* the national level?" *(Possible answer: I think that only State and local governments should administer elections, because 1) the vast majority of elected offices are at the State and local level, 2) polling places are located in local areas, and 3) votes are counted at the State and local level.)* Discuss answers as a class or ask students to post their answers on the Class Discussion Board.

Next ask students to reflect on the Topic as a whole and jot down 1–3 questions they've thought about during the Topic. Share these examples if students need help getting started:

- Who is my State representative?
- Why do voters often select former governors as Presidents?

Topic Inquiry
Have students complete Step 3 of the Topic Inquiry.

DEMONSTRATE

DIGITAL TOPIC REVIEW AND ASSESSMENT
State and Local Governments

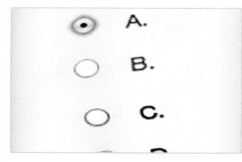

Students can prepare for the Topic Test by answering the questions in the Topic Review and Assessment online or the Assessment questions in the Print Student text. They can also prepare by reviewing their answers to the Interactive Reading Notepad questions or reviewing their notes in the Reading and Notetaking Study Guide.

DIGITAL TOPIC TEST
State and Local Governments

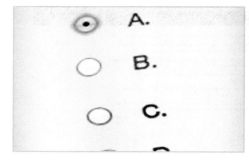

TOPIC TEST
Assign the Topic Test to assess students' understanding of topic content.

BENCHMARK TESTS
Assign these benchmark tests as you complete the relevant topics to monitor student progress toward mastering the course content and as preparation for the End-of-Course Test.

Benchmark Test 1: Topics 1–4
Benchmark Test 2: Topics 5–8
Benchmark Test 3: Topics 9–11
Benchmark Test 4: Topics 12–14

Comparative Political Systems

TOPIC 14 ORGANIZER	PACING: APPROX. 1 PERIOD, .5 BLOCKS	
		PACING
Connect		1 period
MY STORY VIDEO **Comparative Paths to Development**		10 min.
DIGITAL ESSENTIAL QUESTION ACTIVITY **What Makes a Government Successful?**		10 min.
DIGITAL OVERVIEW ACTIVITY **State of Democracy**		10 min.
TOPIC INQUIRY: CIVIC ACTION PROJECT **Constitutional Rights Foundation**		20 min.
Investigate		2–4 periods
TOPIC INQUIRY: CIVIC ACTION PROJECT **Constitutional Rights Foundation**		Ongoing
LESSON 1 Democracy and the Changing World		30–40 min.
LESSON 2 The United Kingdom		30–40 min.
LESSON 3 The Russian Federation		30–40 min.
LESSON 4 China		30–40 min.
Synthesize		1 period
DIGITAL ACTIVITY **Reflect on the Essential Question**		10 min.
TOPIC INQUIRY: CIVIC ACTION PROJECT **Constitutional Rights Foundation**		20 min.
Demonstrate		1–2 periods
DIGITAL TOPIC REVIEW AND ASSESSMENT **Comparative Political Systems**		10 min.
TOPIC INQUIRY: CIVIC ACTION PROJECT **Constitutional Rights Foundation**		20 min.

 **TOPIC INQUIRY:**

Civic Action Project

Constitutional Rights Foundation
Educate. Participate.

For this topic's Inquiry, you may choose to do a Civic Action Project with your students by using the materials found at the Constitutional Rights Foundation's CAP website: http://www.crfcap.org. Civic Action Project (CAP) is a project-based learning model for government and economics courses. It offers a practicum for high school students in effective and engaged citizenship and uses blended learning to engage students in civic activities both in the traditional U.S. government and economics classrooms.

THE TEACHER'S ROLE

THE CAP TEACHER coaches and guides students through the civic action process as they select a problem or issue, research it, determine and take civic actions, and report and document the experience. The teacher motivates, challenges, critiques, and assesses student progress. Through a blended learning approach, teachers can let students take the reins of their civic learning, guiding them along the way.

You can create your CAP classroom in three easy steps

STEP 1
Register yourself for the CAP website

STEP 2
Enroll your students

STEP 3
Engage your students in the CAP process and its many resources

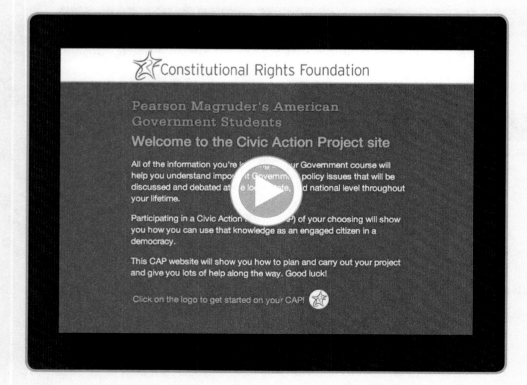

Constitutional Rights Foundation

Pearson Magruder's American Government Students
Welcome to the Civic Action Project site

All of the information you're l____ ___ ____ur Government course will help you understand impor___ __t Govern___ __ policy issues that will be discussed and debated at ___ e lo___ ___ te, ___ d national level throughout your lifetime.

Participating in a Civic Action ___ ___ __P) of your choosing will show you how you can use that knowledge as an engaged citizen in a democracy.

This CAP website will show you how to plan and carry out your project and give you lots of help along the way. Good luck!

Click on the logo to get started on your CAP!

THE STUDENT'S ROLE

CAP ALLOWS STUDENTS to create projects on issues they care about for their school or community. They see the connection between their civic actions and public policy and can share ideas for civics projects with each other and other CAP students nationwide. Students also see how the content of government and economics courses can apply to the real world. By taking civic actions, they practice what real citizens do when they go about trying to solve real policy-related problems. CAP fulfills best-practices in service-learning with an emphasis on public policy.

The CAP student is accountable for completing the civic action process, just as with a science project or term paper. The CAP Planner, a set of documents that guide students through the process, provides teachers with assessment information as well as a way to manage multiple student projects. While the teacher introduces and monitors the CAP, it is important that students take the lead in completing their civic actions. By using web-based technology and civics-based instruction and activities, students exercise important 21st century skills in digital literacy, critical thinking, collaboration, self-direction, and learning to be engaged and effective citizens.

CIVIC ACTIONS CAP challenges students to work on an actual problem, issue, or policy by taking civic actions. Civic actions build upon classroom civics issues, service-learning, and other proven practices of effective civic education. These actions can be many and varied, including:

- getting informed about a public issue or problem
- thinking critically about the issue or problem
- discovering how government is involved with the problem
- learning how government makes decisions
- developing a position
- engaging in civic dialogue
- building constituencies
- working together toward a common goal
- doing civic writing
- making presentations
- advocating for and defending positions
- meeting with officials

Brainstorming

Brainstorming is a method for generating ideas. It can be done by individuals or in small or large

Rules for Brainst

Pose a question to an

Set a time limit on th
more ideas out.

Work as fast as you

Handout Lesson 5B
Civic Action Project

GRADE
CAP Policy Analysis Tool

As citizens in a democracy, you'll be confronted with policy questions. Is a tax proposal a good idea? Should you vote for a particular ballot initiative? Government policies can profoundly affect our nation and your life. In a democracy, you have a say on government policies and proposed policies. It's important that you take a critical look at them. Use the following GRADE tests to evaluate a policy:

Goal. What is the goal of the policy? If you don't know what it's supposed to do, you can't measure its success or failure. Policies are designed to address problems. What problem or problems is this policy supposed to address?

... policy? Who might (or does)
... you understand who the
... icy favors special
... ces for information, but

... its? What is good about the
... ses or effects of the
... ved) its goal? Will it
... ensive? Does it protect
... e's liberties?

... osts? What is bad about the
... the causes or effects of the
... e? Does it cause harm? Does
... re any potential

... he disadvantages. Are there
... to do nothing. Most serious
... Evaluate them. Look at
... es.

© 2012 Constitutional Rights Foundation

Conducting Meetings

Your meetings should be organized, to-the-point, and fun.

Decide how you're going to make decisions. If you are a small group, try deciding by whole-group consensus or by a two-thirds vote. A simple-majority decision may lead to bad feelings and resentment.

Understand everyone's role at the meeting. At most meetings, people need to fill the following roles, which may change from meeting to meeting:

- Leader or facilitator runs the meeting, follows the agenda item by item, and watches the time allotted for each. The leader helps participants focus on the task and makes sure everyone has a chance to participate.
- Recorder takes minutes, which include date and time of meeting, the persons attending, and notes on each agenda item.
- Treasurer.
- Group members contribute agenda items, discuss topics, make decisions, and take responsibility for various tasks.
- Adviser is an adult whose role is to give advice—not to run the group.
- Guests may participate in group discussions, but usually do not participate in final decision making.

Have an agenda. This is a list of things to be dealt with at a meeting. All members should be encouraged to put topics on the agenda. After the recorder reads the minutes of the previous meeting and they are approved, the members approve the agenda. Agenda items are considered in the following order:

- Old business—ongoing and follow-up items.

© 2012. Constitutional Rights Foundation
and Close Up Foundation

Constitutional Rights Foundation
Educate. Participate.

Guardian of Democracy: The Civic Mission of Schools
Released September, 2011, *Guardian of Democracy: The Civic Mission of Schools report* builds on the findings of the seminal 2003 Civic Mission of Schools report. CAP has been designed to support the promising approaches described in these reports.

Comparative Political Systems

On the world stage, each country is unique with its own history and elements that shape it. As a result, even countries with democratic governments have differences from the U.S. government. Other countries do not follow the democratic model, and the structure and function of their governments reflect that fact. This topic will take a close look at the governments of the United Kingdom, Russia, and China. It will also analyze the democratization process and what makes a democracy successful.

CONNECT

MY STORY VIDEO

Comparative Paths to Development

Watch a video that compares economic development in North and South Korea.

Check Understanding What impact did the dissolution of the Soviet Union in 1991 have on North Korea? *(It was a blow to North Korea's economy because the Soviet Union had been its largest source of foreign aid.)*

Hypothesize How might the different economic systems help explain the difference in life expectancies in North Korea and South Korea? *(The command economy in North Korea has not resulted in economic growth or foreign trade, and the country has not been able to respond to natural disasters. Therefore, people have a low standard of living. South Korea, with its free market economy, has developed strong industries and has a successful foreign trade. This increases the standard of living, including life expectancy.)*

⇅ FLIP IT!

Assign the My Story Video.

DIGITAL ESSENTIAL QUESTION ACTIVITY

What Makes a Government Successful?

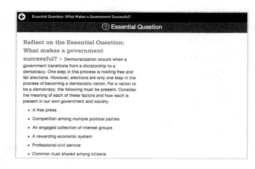

Ask students to think about the Essential Question for this Topic: What Makes a Government Successful? For a government to be successful, many elements need to be present. What are those elements?

Project the Essential Question Activity Inform students that democratization occurs when a government transitions from a dictatorship to a democracy. One step in this process is holding free and fair elections. However, elections are only one step in the process of becoming a democratic nation. For a nation to be a democracy, many factors must be present. Ask students to consider the meaning of each of the factors shown in this activity and how each is present in our own government and society.

Support Point of View with Evidence Which of these factors do you think is the most important for democratization to be successful?

Infer Why do you think a rewarding economic system is included as a factor?

DIGITAL OVERVIEW ACTIVITY

State of Democracy

Display the infographic, which shows the state of democracy around the world in 2012. Tell students that during this Topic they will learn about various types of democratic governments as well as other forms of government. This timeline will provide a framework into which they can place the governments they learn about.

Identify According to the pie chart, what is the most common type of government?

Infer Why do you think this type of government is the most common?

Paraphrase Write in your own words what you think Churchill is saying about democracy.

Ⓓ Differentiate: Challenge Tell students they have received a letter from a friend who has reviewed the list of Most Democratic Nations. The friend is outraged that the United States is so low on the list. Ask students to write a letter in response that explains why they think the position of the U.S. government on the list is justified.

Topic Inquiry
Launch the Topic Inquiry with students after introducing the Topic.

Democracy and the Changing World

Supporting English Language Learners

Use with Digital Text 2, **Examples of Transitions to Democracy.**

Listening
Display and discuss questions about the text. Tell students to listen for the answers as you read aloud. Read aloud the section *Examples of Transitions to Democracy*. Guide them to compare the U.S. constitutional republic to contemporary forms of government by having them respond to questions and requests.

Beginning Use questions about the text which require a gesture, yes or no, or a one- or two-word response. Read aloud focusing on the visuals and their captions. Ask students to answer the questions.

Intermediate Use questions about the text which require short answers or phrases as responses. Read aloud and discuss the text and visuals. Ask students to answer the questions.

Advanced Display *who*, *what*, *where*, *when*, and *why* questions. After reading aloud, have partners discuss and answer the questions.

Advanced High Display *who*, *what*, *where*, *when*, and *why* questions. After reading aloud, have partners discuss and answer the questions.

Use with Digital Text 1, **Transitions to Democracy.**

Reading
Find visuals in the text that are examples of environmental print such as words on signs, posters, and billboards. Discuss the use and purpose for each example of environmental print. After reading the section *Transitions to Democracy*, have students create their own posters using environmental print in order to compare the U.S. constitutional republic to contemporary forms of government.

Beginning After reading the section to the class, provide students with several examples of environmental print to use on their posters. Have small groups create posters and share with the class.

Intermediate After guiding the class through reading the section, provide the class with several examples of environmental print to use on their posters. Have partners create posters and share with the class.

Advanced Have partners read the text together, and then design and create posters using information from what they have just read. Ask them to explain to the class how the poster would be used.

Advanced High Have students independently read the section, and then guide them to individually create posters based on the content of the text. Have them share their posters in a small group.

▣ Differentiate Instruction

Use the Differentiated Instruction notes throughout the lesson plan to support the varied skill sets, levels of readiness, and interests in the mixed-ability classroom.

Challenge These notes include suggestions for expanding the activity for advanced students.

On-Level These notes include suggestions for modifying the activity to address different interests or learning styles.

Extra Support These notes include ideas for providing more scaffolding or reading spuport.

Special Needs These notes provide ideas for adapting instruction to support the needs of various special needs students.

■ NOTES

Democracy and the Changing World

Objectives

Objective 1: Examine how regimes can make transitions to democracy.

Objective 2: Analyze why some countries experience setbacks or failed transitions to democracy.

Objective 3: Explain the factors necessary for democratic consolidation to take place.

Objective 4: Describe democratic change and continuity in selected countries today.

LESSON 1 ORGANIZER		PACING: APPROX. 1 PERIOD, .5 BLOCKS		
			RESOURCES	
	OBJECTIVES	PACING	Online	Print
Connect				
DIGITAL START UP ACTIVITY **Democracy Requires Courage**		10 min.	●	
Investigate				
DIGITAL TEXT 1 **Transitions to Democracy**	Objective 1	10 min.	●	●
DIGITAL TEXT 2 **Examples of Transitions to Democracy**	Objective 2	10 min.	●	●
DIGITAL TEXT 3 **Outcomes of Transitions to Democracy**	Objectives 2, 3	10 min.	●	●
DIGITAL TEXT 4 **Democratic Change and Continuity Today**	Objective 4	10 min.	●	●
INTERACTIVE MAP **Comparing Governments Around the World**		10 min.	●	
Synthesize				
DIGITAL SYNTHESIZE ACTIVITY **Democracy Benefits and Challenges**		10 min.	●	
Demonstrate				
DIGITAL QUIZ **Lesson Quiz and Class Discussion Board**		10 min.	●	

PEARSON
realize™
www.PearsonRealize.com

Go online to access additional resources including:
Primary Sources • Biographies • Supreme Court cases •
21st Century Skill Tutorials • Maps • Graphic Organizers.

■ CONNECT

DIGITAL START UP ACTIVITY
Democracy Requires Courage

Project the Start Up Activity Tell students that Nobel Peace Prize winner Nelson Mandela spent twenty-seven years imprisoned by the country that would later elect him president in their first democratic election. Then read aloud the Mandela quote. Have students write short responses to the following questions.

Discuss How do Nelson Mandela's words reflect South Africa's long struggle and transition to democracy? What are some tactics that he may have tried to employ in order to persuade others?

Tell students that in this lesson they will study how nations transition to democracy and why some of these transitions fail. Also, they will be learning about democratic consolidation and democratic change in nations today.

Aa **Vocabulary Development:** Use the Interactive Reading Notepad to preview the Key Terms and Academic Vocabulary in this Lesson with students.

↻ FLIP IT!
Assign the Flipped Video for this lesson.

■ STUDENT EDITION PRINT PAGES: 676–681

■ INVESTIGATE

DIGITAL TEXT 1
Transitions to Democracy

Objective 1: Examine how regimes can make transitions to democracy.

Quick Instruction
Inform students that when nations attempt to transition to democracy, two types of groups often form, called *hard-liners* and *reformers*. Although these groups often conflict, they also have a few basic similarities. Have students do a Quick Write activity in which they write as much as they know in 30 seconds about the similarities and differences between hard-liners and reformers. Then have students form pairs and share their responses with their partners. Tell pairs to write a response that combines the accurate elements of each individual response. Ask volunteers to present these combined responses to the class.

D **Differentiate:** **Challenge** Have students write a letter from the point of view of a reformer in a country with a dictatorship. In this letter, the reformer is trying to convince a hard-liner to make democratic changes to the government. Students should keep in mind not only the changes they want to effect, but also concessions they are willing to make.

ELL Use the ELL activity described in the ELL chart.

Further Instruction
Go through the Interactive Reading Notepad questions and discuss the answers with the class. To extend the teaching of this objective, have students answer the following questions.

Support a Point of View with Evidence
The text states that recognizing an opposition leader or party is a significant step toward democracy. Why do you think this is true? *(Possible answers: This step may pressure governing institutions to reform without undermining the existing social order.)*

Democracy and the Changing World

DIGITAL TEXT 2

DIGITAL TEXT 2

Examples of Transitions to Democracy

DIGITAL TEXT 3

Outcomes of Transitions to Democracy

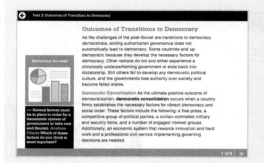

Objective 2: Analyze why some countries experience setbacks or failed transitions to democracy.

Quick Instruction

Inform students that there are many reasons why nations fail to democratize. Three of these reasons include: the failure of governing institutions to give up power; the onset of an economic crisis; and the failure to develop political parties and a free press. Have students use a Think Pair Share to rank the three reasons why nations fail to democratize, in the order of importance. Pairs should provide reasons for their rankings. Ask volunteers to orally present their responses to the class.

ELL Use the ELL activity described in the ELL chart.

Further Instruction

Go through the Interactive Reading Notepad questions and discuss the answers with the class. To extend the teaching of this objective have students answer the following questions.

Contrast How does the ongoing attempt to develop a democratic government in Russia differ from how a democratic government developed in the United States? *(Possible answer: The United States moved from a colony controlled by a monarchy to a democracy. Russia moved from a country controlled by an authoritarian (communist) government to a democracy. The United States did not have to change its economic*

system when it became a democracy. Russia did have to change its economic system. The United States established a democratic government through a revolution. Russia established an democratic government through the collapse of the Soviet Union. The United States made freedom of the press a constitutional right. Russia has had trouble establishing freedom of the press.)

Check Understanding What type of economic shift did Eastern European nations undergo after they attained independence from the Soviet Union? *(They shifted from centrally planned communist economies to more capitalistic economies.)*

Objectives 2: Analyze why some countries experience setbacks or failed transitions to democracy; **3:** Explain the factors necessary for democratic consolidation to take place.

Quick Instruction

Tell students that one of the most important factors needed for democratic consolation to happen in a country is trust among its citizens. In many countries, establishing this trust is very difficult. Have students use a Think Pair Share strategy to answer the following question. Why do you think establishing trust among citizens is so difficult to establish in many countries attempting to democratize? *(Answers may vary. Some students might mention that many countries have long standing feuds between various ethnic and religious groups. Because of this, these groups are hesitant to trust each other.)* Ask volunteers to share their answers.

D Differentiate: **Extra Support** Help students understand why terrorist groups often find havens in failed states. Ask: Do failed states have efficiently run central governments? Why or why not? Do you think terrorist groups want to form bases in countries with efficient governments? Why or why not? Why do you think terrorist groups often form bases in failed states?

DIGITAL TEXT 4

Democratic Change and Continuity Today

INTERACTIVE MAP

Comparing Governments Around the World

Further Instruction

Go through the Interactive Reading Notepad questions and discuss the answers with the class. To extend the teaching of this objective have students answer the following question.

Infer Why do you think the United States strongly supports state-building efforts in Afghanistan? *(Possible answer: Afghanistan has proven to be a haven for terrorist groups, especially the Taliban. One reason why the Taliban succeeded in forming a stronghold in this nation is because it had a weak government. Because of this, the United States supports the building of a strong state in Afghanistan to prevent the Taliban from once again gaining power there.)*

Objective 4: Describe democratic change and continuity in selected countries today.

Quick Instruction

Interactive Map: Comparing Governments Around the Word Project the map on the whiteboard and click through the hot spots. Introduce the map activity by telling students that countries around the world often take different approaches to governing their people. Discuss with students how the U.S. constitutional republic compares to contemporary forms of government, such as monarchy, authoritarian, theocracy, and other republics shown in the map. While many have made the transition to democratic governments through free and fair elections, many have not. Ask students to select the flags on the map to learn more about some examples of governments that are democratic, non-democratic, and working toward democracy.

💻 ACTIVE CLASSROOM

Have students use a Plus/Minus/Interesting activity for the recent political conflict in Egypt. Divide the class into groups. Give each group a three-column organizer with the headings Plus/Minus/Interesting for recording responses to the following questions. What is positive about the political changes in Egypt during the 2000s? What is negative about these changes? What is interesting about these changes? Have a representative from each group share the responses of his or her group.

Further Instruction

Editable Presentation Use the Editable Presentation to present the main ideas for this Core Reading.

Democratic Change and Continuity Today: Core Reading and Interactive Reading Notepad Project and discuss the Interactive Reading Notepad questions, including the graphic organizer asking students to cite evidence about how Egypt has moved farther away from a democracy instead of closer to it. Review the evidence with the class and fill in the graphic organizer on the whiteboard as you go.

Identify Cause and Effect What factors and events set the Arab Spring in motion? *(Possible answer: For many years in the Middle East, ruling parties, leaders, or families had suppressed political opposition. As a result, many people living in this region became frustrated and angered by the lack of representation in the government. In 2011, a merchant in Tunisia protested government indifference by setting himself on fire. This incident unleashed the suppressed frustrations of people in nations throughout the Middle East, thereby giving rise to the overthrow of governments.)*

Democracy and the Changing World

DIGITAL SYNTHESIZE ACTIVITY

Democracy Benefits and Challenges

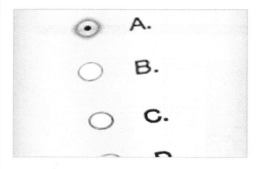

Ask students to recall the Topic Essential Question, "What Makes a Government Successful?" Tell students to consider what they have read about successful and unsuccessful democratizations. Have them use the Think Pair Share strategy to answer the following questions.

During the time of transition, what are some benefits of democracy that individuals experience? *(Possible answers: People can own private property. Police and the military are less controlling over the population. People experience the many forms of free press.)* In contrast, what new challenges does democracy bring? *(Possible answers: People who were relative economic equals become unequal. In capitalism, for example, some people profit more than others. Social order is disrupted in many ways, as it is a new way of living for citizens. Though people can freely express their opinions, this may lead to very different viewpoints and even violence.)* In conclusion, how might citizens feel about their new government in relation to their previous form of government? *(Possible answers: Some students might mention that citizens could have mixed feelings about the new government or might want to go back to the security of the old government.)*

Discuss Ask students to think about the poll they took at the beginning of this Topic. Ask if they would change any of their responses.

DIGITAL QUIZ

Lesson Quiz and Class Discussion Board

Assign the online Lesson Quiz for this lesson if you haven't already done so. Students will be offered automatic remediation or enrichment based on their scores.

Remind students that in "Democracy and the Changing World" they read about how regimes can make transitions to democracy and why some nations experience failed transitions to democracy. Also, they learned about the factors necessary for democratic consolidation. In addition, they studied about democratic change and continuity in selected countries today.

Pose this question to the class on the Discussion Board:

Make Predictions If the nations of the Middle East all successfully transitioned to democracy, what effects might this have on the United States? *(Answers may vary. Students might mention that such a change would greatly benefit the economy of the United States. The U.S. government could make better trade agreements with these nations that would provide important resources to the United States. Also, these countries would probably buy more U.S. exports. In addition, political tensions would ease between the United States and Middle Eastern nations. These nations might be more willing to pursue terrorists.)*

Topic Inquiry
Have students continue their investigations for the Topic Inquiry.

The United Kingdom

Supporting English Language Learners

Use with Digital Text 1, **A Legacy of Constitutionalism.**

Speaking
Model and explain the following sentence types: declarative (statement), interrogative (question), imperative (command), and exclamatory (exclamation). Read the section *A Legacy of Constitutionalism*. In order to compare the U.S. constitutional republic to contemporary forms of governments such as monarchy, have students practice using the different sentence types while speaking about the text.

Beginning Display each of the sentence types using content from the text. Read them and have the students repeat. Guide students to say sentences of their own.

Intermediate Display each of the sentence types using content from the text. Read the sentences. Have the students practice reading the sentences to each other. Guide them to say at least two different types of sentences to each other.

Advanced Have partners take turns saying at least one sentence of each type to each other.

Advanced High Have partners take turns saying at least two sentences of each type to each other.

Use with the lesson 2 readings.

Reading
Read the text in order to help students identify major intellectual, philosophical, political, and religious traditions that informed the American founding. Have students complete graphic organizers for the vocabulary words hyperlinked in the text. The graphic organizer should have five sections: the word, definition, illustration, sentence using the word, and example/non-example.

Beginning Guide the class to complete graphic organizers for the vocabulary words, using only the first four sections of the organizer—skip the section on example/non-example. Have students practice reading the words.

Intermediate Divide the class into small groups and guide them to complete graphic organizers for each word. Have them share their work with another group.

Advanced Have students work in partners to complete graphic organizers for each word. Have them share their work with others in their group.

Advanced High Have students independently complete graphic organizers for each vocabulary word. Guide them to share their work with a partner or others in their group.

▣ Differentiate Instruction

Use the Differentiated Instruction notes throughout the lesson plan to support the varied skill sets, levels of readiness, and interests in the mixed-ability classroom.

Challenge These notes include suggestions for expanding the activity for advanced students.

On-Level These notes include suggestions for modifying the activity to address different interests or learning styles.

Extra Support These notes include ideas for providing more scaffolding or reading spuport.

Special Needs These notes provide ideas for adapting instruction to support the needs of various special needs students.

■ NOTES

The United Kingdom

Objectives

Objective 1: Explain the United Kingdom's legacy of constitutionalism.

Objective 2: Outline the structure of government in the United Kingdom.

Objective 3: Examine public policy and elections in the United Kingdom.

Objective 4: Compare government in the United Kingdom with that of the United States.

LESSON 2 ORGANIZER		PACING: APPROX. 1 PERIOD, .5 BLOCKS		RESOURCES	
	OBJECTIVES		PACING	Online	Print
Connect					
DIGITAL START UP ACTIVITY **Shared Characteristics of Governments**			10 min.	●	
Investigate					
DIGITAL TEXT 1 **A Legacy of Constitutionalism**	Objective 1		10 min.	●	●
DIGITAL TEXT 2 **Government in the United Kingdom**	Objective 2		10 min.	●	●
DIGITAL TEXT 3 **Public Policy and Elections**	Objective 3		10 min.	●	●
DIGITAL TEXT 4 **Comparison to the United States**	Objective 4		10 min.	●	●
INTERACTIVE CHART **Comparing Governments—United States and United Kingdom**			10 min.	●	
Synthesize					
DIGITAL SYNTHESIZE ACTIVITY **The Magna Carta's Enduring Influence**			10 min.	●	
Demonstrate					
DIGITAL QUIZ **Lesson Quiz and Class Discussion Board**			10 min.	●	

CONNECT

DIGITAL START UP ACTIVITY
Shared Characteristics of Governments

Project the Start Up Activity Tell students that at this point, they have learned about how the Founders modeled some aspects of the new government off of Great Britain's government. Have pairs talk about features of the U.S. government that they believe were based on Great Britain's government and write them down.

Support a Point of View with Evidence
What aspect of Great Britain's government do you think influenced U.S. government the most?

Tell students that in this lesson they will be learning about the legacy of constitutionalism in the United Kingdom, the structure of the British government, and British public policy and elections.

Aa Vocabulary Development: Use the Interactive Reading Notepad to preview the Key Terms and Academic Vocabulary in this Lesson with students.

↳ FLIP IT!
Assign the Flipped Video for this lesson.

■ STUDENT EDITION PRINT PAGES: 682–688

INVESTIGATE

DIGITAL TEXT 1
A Legacy of Constitutionalism

Objective 1: Explain the UK's legacy of constitutionalism.

Quick Instruction
Tell students that the democratic governing institutions of the United Kingdom have been in place since the 1600s. Ask students to use the Think Pair Share strategy to answer the following question. Why do you think democracy has lasted so long in the United Kingdom? *(Answers may vary. Some students might mention that much of the British population shares an ethnic and religious heritage, which reduces conflict.)* Ask volunteers to share their responses.

ELL Use the ELL activity described in the ELL chart.

Further Instruction
Go through the Interactive Reading Notepad questions and discuss the answers with the class. To extend the teaching of this objective, have students answer the following questions.

Infer The United Kingdom is a monarchy, but the royalty lacks any governing power. Considering this, why do you think the monarchy still exists in this nation? *(Answers may vary. Some students might mention that the British want the continuity of having a monarchy; that a monarchy symbolizes the strength of the British people; and that the monarchy does have important functions other than governing.)*

Sequence Events List in chronological order the three main events in the development of democracy in the United Kingdom from the 1600s to the early 1900s. (Governing institutions are set (1600s). Political parties are established (1800s). Full voting rights are expanded to all Britons (early 1900s).)

The United Kingdom

DIGITAL TEXT 2
Government in the United Kingdom

DIGITAL TEXT 3
Public Policy and Elections

Objective 2: Outline the structure of government in the UK.

Quick Instruction
Remind students that the British government is a parliamentary system. Break the class into groups of four and have each group use a Circle Write activity to answer the following question. What is the structure of the British parliament? Have students write as much as they can for 1 minute and then switch with the person in their group to their right. The next student should try to improve or elaborate the response where the other person left off. Students in each group should continue to switch until the paper comes back to the first person. Then each group should decide which is the best response and share that with the class.

D Differentiate: Extra Support Help students understand the difference between the U.S. judicial system and the British judicial system. In the U.S. government, can the Supreme Court rule that legislation is unconstitutional? What U.S. government body has the power to determine the validity of legislation? In the British government, can the Supreme Court rule that legislation is unconstitutional? What British government body has the power to determine the validity of legislation?

ELL Use the ELL activity described in the ELL chart.

Further Instruction
Editable Presentation Use the Editable Presentation to present the main ideas for this Core Reading.

Government in the United Kingdom: Core Reading and Interactive Reading Notepad Project and discuss the Interactive Reading Notepad questions, including the graphic organizer asking students to show how the government of the United Kingdom is chosen and organized. Review the British government with the class and fill in the graphic organizer on the whiteboard as you go.

Support Ideas with Evidence What do you think are the advantages and disadvantages of the British parliamentary system of government? *(Answers will vary. All answers should be supported by evidence.)*

Objective 3: Examine public policy and elections in the UK.

Quick Instruction
Tell students that the House of Commons consists of the prime minister and the cabinet ministers, the party in power, the shadow cabinet, and the opposition party. Have students form pairs. Tell pairs to draw a diagram of the House of Commons, based on the text that describes where the above mentioned groups sit. The diagram should be labeled and should also provide a short description of the function of each group.

D Differentiate: Challenge Have students form groups of eight. Ask each group to recreate Question Time in the House of Commons. Four students should represent the prime minister and cabinet and four students should represent the opposition party. The prime minister and cabinet should present their policy on a certain issue. Then the opposition party should ask probing questions about this policy. Students should try to recreate the atmosphere of Question Time.

DIGITAL TEXT 4

Comparison to the United States

INTERACTIVE CHART

Comparing Governments— United States and United Kingdom

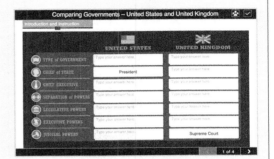

Further Instruction

Go through the Interactive Reading Notepad questions and discuss the answers with the class. To extend the teaching of this objective have students answer the following question.

Support Ideas with Evidence What do you think are the advantages and disadvantages of the British method of crafting legislation? *(Possible answer: The British method allows the party in power to craft and pass legislation without any veto or voting power by the opposition party. Because of this, legislation can be passed quickly and efficiently. However, the party in power does not have enough checks against the use of its power. Because of this, the party in power is probably more likely to pass legislation that favors that party, which could be unfair to people who belong to the opposition party.)*

Objective 4: Compare government in the British with that of the United States.

Quick Instruction

Interactive Chart: Comparing Governments—United States and United Kingdom Project the chart on the whiteboard. Tell students that while the United States and the United Kingdom are both constitutional governments, they have many differences in structure and function. Ask students to complete the graphic organizer about the United States and the United Kingdom by typing in the best answer for each open space.

ACTIVE CLASSROOM

Ask students to Take a Stand on the following question. Is the British government better than the U.S. government? Yes or no? Encourage students to consider the advantages and disadvantages for each system of government. Have students divide into two groups based on their answer and move to separate areas of the classroom. If a group has only a few members, assign more students to this group. Tell students to talk to each other to compare their reasons for answering yes or no. Ask a representative from each group to present and defend the group's point of view.

ELL Use the ELL activity described in the ELL chart.

Further Instruction

Editable Presentation Use the Editable Presentation to present the main ideas for this Core Reading.

Comparison to the United States: Core Reading and Interactive Reading Notepad Project and discuss the Close Reading Notepad question. To extend the teaching of this objective, have students answer the following questions.

Draw Conclusions Why do you think the Founding Fathers made the U.S. government different in some ways from the British government? *(Possible answer: The Founding Fathers had just finished dealing with the tyranny of the British monarchy. Because of this, they wanted to make sure to include a system of checks and balances that would prevent any one person or party from gaining too much power. This system of checks and balances is one of the major differences between the U.S. and British systems.)*

The United Kingdom

SYNTHESIZE

DIGITAL SYNTHESIZE ACTIVITY

The Magna Carta's Enduring Influence

Ask students to recall the Topic Essential Question, "What Makes a Government Successful?" Project the two quotations from the Magna Carta. Tell students that the Magna Carta was first signed by King John of England in 1215, and updated a number of times over the next several centuries. This document established the idea of limited governance and that Parliament would create laws that the monarchy would execute.

Inform students that there are two enduring principles of liberty in the Magna Carta that are described in the quotes. Ask students to study these quotes. Then tell them to explain how these two principles influenced the Founding Fathers when creating the Bill of Rights. *(The 5th and 6th Amendments portray these two principles of liberty found in the Magna Carta.)*

Discuss Ask students to think about the poll they took at the beginning of this Topic. Ask if they would change any of their responses now that they know more about the British government.

DEMONSTRATE

DIGITAL QUIZ

Lesson Quiz and Class Discussion Board

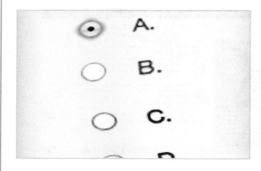

Assign the online Lesson Quiz for this lesson if you haven't already done so. Students will be offered automatic remediation or enrichment based on their scores.

Tell students that in *The United Kingdom* they read about the UK's legacy of constitutionalism and the structure of government in the United Kingdom. Also, they examined British public policy and elections and compared the British government with the U.S. government.

Pose these questions to the class on the Discussion Board:

Support Point of View with Evidence What do you think is the greatest disadvantage of the U.S. government? Do you think the British government shares this disadvantage? *(Possible answers: The U.S. system of checks and balances sometimes backfires and causes gridlock in Congress. As a result, legislation at times has difficulty passing. The British government does not share this disadvantage, since this government does not have a system of checks and balances.)*

Distinguish What are the differences between the U.S. President and the British prime minister? *(The prime minster has both legislative and executive powers. The President has only executive power, but can influence legislation through veto. The prime minister can dominate the legislative branch. The President can influence the legislative branch, but cannot dominate it. The President is head of state and, therefore must perform ceremonial functions. Since the prime minister is not head of state, he or she does not have to perform these functions.)*

Topic Inquiry

Have students continue their investigations for the Topic Inquiry.

The Russian Federation

Supporting English Language Learners

Use with the lesson 3 readings.

Speaking

After reading the text, guide students to summarize different sections of the text. Have students share these summaries with each other as they compare the U.S. constitutional republic to contemporary forms of government.

Beginning Divide students into three groups. Assign the groups the topic of V.I. Lenin, Josef Stalin, or Vladimir Putin. Guide students to create a word or picture web for their topic based to share with the class.

Intermediate Divide students into three groups. Assign the groups the topic of V.I. Lenin, Josef Stalin, or Vladimir Putin. Guide students to write short sentences about their topic to share with the class.

Advanced Divide the class into four groups. Assign each group one of the following sections of the text: *Russia and Its History*, *Government in the Russian Federation*, *Public Policy Creation*, or *Comparison to the United States*. Ask each group to write a short summary of key points to share with the class.

Advanced High Divide the class into four groups. Assign each group one of the following sections of the text: *Russia and Its History*, *Government in the Russian Federation*, *Public Policy Creation*, or *Comparison to the United States*. Have each student write a short summary of the key points to share with the group.

Use with the lesson 3 readings.

Reading

Before reading the text, point out and discuss the title, subheadings, captions, and visuals. In order to help students compare the U.S. constitutional republic to historical and contemporary forms of government, ask students what they think the text will be about.

Beginning Focus on the visuals. Guide the class to create and label illustrations about what they think the text will be about. Have them follow along as your read aloud. Point out any predictions that were correct.

Intermediate Have small groups create and label illustrations about what they think the text will be about. Have them follow along as your read aloud. Ask them to identify any predictions that were correct.

Advanced Guide partners to create a list of predictions about the text. Have them read together and identify any predications that were correct.

Advanced High Have students work independently to write what the text will be about. Have them read and identify their correct and incorrect predictions.

◗ Differentiate Instruction

Use the Differentiated Instruction notes throughout the lesson plan to support the varied skill sets, levels of readiness, and interests in the mixed-ability classroom.

Challenge These notes include suggestions for expanding the activity for advanced students.

On-Level These notes include suggestions for modifying the activity to address different interests or learning styles.

Extra Support These notes include ideas for providing more scaffolding or reading spuport.

Special Needs These notes provide ideas for adapting instruction to support the needs of various special needs students.

■ NOTES

The Russian Federation

Objectives

Objective 1: Examine Russia and its history since the Bolshevik Revolution.

Objective 2: Outline the structure of Russia's government.

Objective 3: Examine how public policy is created in Russia.

Objective 4: Compare government in Russia with that of the United States.

LESSON 3 ORGANIZER		PACING: APPROX. 1 PERIOD, .5 BLOCKS		
	OBJECTIVES	PACING	Online	Print
Connect				
DIGITAL START UP ACTIVITY **Russia's Leaders—Past and Present**		10 min.	●	
Investigate				
DIGITAL TEXT 1 **Russia and Its History**	Objective 1	10 min.	●	●
DIGITAL TEXT 2 **Government in the Russian Federation**	Objective 2	10 min.	●	●
DIGITAL TEXT 3 **Public Policy Creation**	Objective 3	10 min.	●	●
DIGITAL TEXT 4 **Comparison to the United States**	Objective 4	10 min.	●	●
INTERACTIVE GALLERY **Comparing Rights and Freedoms in Russia**		10 min.	●	
Synthesize				
DIGITAL SYNTHESIZE ACTIVITY **Revisiting Russia's Leaders**		10 min.	●	
Demonstrate				
DIGITAL QUIZ **Lesson Quiz and Class Discussion Board**		10 min.	●	

PEARSON **realize**™
www.PearsonRealize.com

Go online to access additional resources including:
Primary Sources • Biographies • Supreme Court cases •
21st Century Skill Tutorials • Maps • Graphic Organizers.

CONNECT

DIGITAL START UP ACTIVITY
Russia's Leaders—Past and Present

Project the Start Up Activity Ask students to answer the following questions as they enter and get settled. What do you know about Russia and its leaders? What would you like to know? Then have them share their ideas with another student.

Discuss Have students review the Russian leaders listed in the graphic organizer. They should record either a brief statement of what they know or a question for what they would like to know.

Tell students that in this lesson they will study an overview of Russia's history since the Bolshevik Revolution. They will also learn about the structure of Russia's government and how public policy is created in Russia.

Aa **Vocabulary Development:** Use the Interactive Reading Notepad to preview the Key Terms and Academic Vocabulary in this Lesson with students.

⇅ FLIP IT!
Assign the Flipped Video for this lesson.

■ STUDENT EDITION PRINT PAGES: 689–695

INVESTIGATE

DIGITAL TEXT 1
Russia and Its History

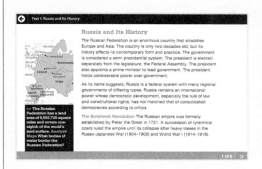

Objective 1: Examine Russia and its history since the Bolshevik Revolution.

Quick Instruction
Tell students that many political changes led to the establishment of the Russian Federation. Have students form groups of seven. Tell each group to decide what are the seven most significant events in Russian history from the early 1900s to the present day. For each event, students should write a brief explanation about why they consider it important. Then each group should form a "Human Order" timeline in which students arrange themselves in chronological order, with the first student representing the earliest event, the second student representing the second earliest event, and so on. Then each student in the timeline should state what event he or she represents and why it is important.

D Differentiate: **Challenge** Have students draw a picture of a major event in Russia's history that took place between the beginning of World War I and the ratification of a new Russian constitution in 1993.

ELL Use the ELL activity described in the ELL chart.

Further Instruction
Go through the Interactive Reading Notepad questions and discuss the answers with the class. To extend the teaching of this objective have students answer the following question.

Compare and Contrast How was the Bolshevik Revolution similar to and different from the American Revolution? *(Possible answer: In both revolutions, citizens were motivated by oppression. Both revolutions were violent and were led by strong leaders. The American Revolution led to the establishment of a democratic government and involved a colony breaking away from an imperialistic power. The Bolshevik Revolution led to the establishment of a communist government and did not involve a colony breaking away from an imperialistic power.)*

Topic (14) Lesson 3

The Russian Federation

DIGITAL TEXT 2

Government in the Russian Federation

Text 2: Government in the Russian Federation

Government in the Russian Federation

A new constitution was approved in a national referendum in late 1993. It proclaims the Russian Federation to be "a democratic federal legally-based state with a republican form of government." As constitutions do, it ensures an extensive list of individual rights, including guarantees of freedom of speech, press, association, and religious belief. The constitution also assures every citizen a right to freedom of movement within the federation, housing, and free medical care and education. Critics have questioned whether many of these liberties have been sufficiently protected from the state. The 1993 constitution also sets out a new government structure that provided significant power to the Russian presidency, which has grown based on the governing practices of Boris Yeltsin and **Vladimir Putin.**

>> A woman votes on a referendum in Moscow on April 25, 1993. Later the same year, Russians voted in favor of a new constitution.

1 of 8 >

Objective 2: Outline the structure of Russia's government.

Quick Instruction

Tell students that the Russian government is based on a federal system. Have students write what they know about the structure of the Russian government in one minute without referring to the text. Then ask students to form pairs and share their responses with their partners. Pairs should combine responses, including what they believe to be accurate information and deleting what they believe to be inaccurate information. Ask volunteers to share their combined responses.

D Differentiate: **Extra Support** Help students understand the difference between the president and prime minister in the Russian government. Ask: Which position is in command of the military and basic domestic and foreign policy? Which position appoints prime ministers? Which position administers policy goals? Does the president or prime minister have more power?

Further Instruction

Go through the Interactive Reading Notepad questions and discuss the answers with the class. To extend the teaching of this objective, have students answer the following questions.

Identify Main Ideas What do critics think is the main drawback of the Russian government? *(The president has too much power, which could lead to the development of a one-party system.)*

Infer In the Russian government, what checks are placed on the president's power? *(Presidential vetoes can be overridden by a two-thirds vote in both the Duma and Federation Council. The Constitutional Court can challenge the power of the presidency, but usually does not exercise this right.)*

DIGITAL TEXT 3

Public Policy Creation

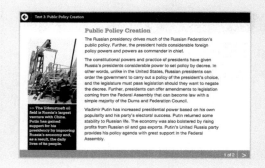

Text 3: Public Policy Creation

Public Policy Creation

The Russian presidency drives much of the Russian Federation's public policy. Further, the president holds considerable foreign policy powers and powers as commander in chief.

The constitutional powers and practice of presidents have given Russia's presidents considerable power to set policy by decree. In other words, unlike in the United States, Russian presidents can order the government to carry out a policy of the president's choice, and the legislature must pass legislation should they want to negate the decree. Further, presidents can offer amendments to legislation coming from the Federal Assembly that can become law with a simple majority of the Duma and Federation Council.

Vladimir Putin has increased presidential power based on his own popularity and his party's electoral success. Putin returned some stability to Russian life. The economy was also bolstered by rising profits from Russian oil and gas exports. Putin's United Russia party provides his policy agenda with great support in the Federal Assembly.

>> The Udmurtneft oil field is Russia's largest venture with China. Putin has gained support for his presidency by improving Russia's economy and, as a result, the daily lives of its people.

1 of 2 >

Objective 3: Examine how public policy is created in Russia.

Quick Instruction

Tell students that although Russia has a federal government, its public policy creation is different from public policy creation in the United States. Have students use the Think Pair Share strategy to answer the following question. What do you think are the advantages and disadvantages of the method of public policy creation in the Russian government? *(Possible answers: Since the president has a huge amount of control over public policy, policies can be implemented efficiently. Considering the recent political and economic troubles of Russia, this efficient policy-making can be helpful in restoring order to the country. However, the president can also use his or her power to enact oppressive and authoritarian policies.)* Ask volunteers to share their answers.

Further Instruction

Go through the Interactive Reading Notepad questions and discuss the answers with the class. To extend the teaching of this objective, have students answer the following questions.

Recall How can the policy decrees of the Russian president be negated? *(The legislature must pass legislation to negate the decree.)*

Check Understanding How did the presidential power of Putin benefit Russia? *(Putin restored stability to Russian life and bolstered the economy.)*

DIGITAL TEXT 4

Comparison to the United States

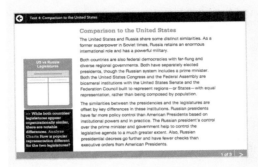

INTERACTIVE GALLERY

Comparing Rights and Freedoms in Russia

Identify Bias Do you think the author of the text has written an objective description of public policy creation in Russia's government? Why or why not? *(Possible answer: Yes; The author just states the facts about the way public policy is created. The author does not provide personal opinions, such as stating that policy creation in the Russian government is close to a dictatorship. A "no" answer is acceptable if supported by sound reasoning.)*

Objective 4: Compare government in Russia with that of the United States.

Quick Instruction

Interactive *Gallery*: Comparing Rights and Freedoms in Russia Project the gallery on the whiteboard. Introduce the activity by telling students that the Russian people endured a life with very limited freedoms until the early 1990s. The most recent constitution outlines many freedoms similar to those of the United States. While defined in their constitution, Russian people very rarely are allowed those freedoms in their daily lives. Tell students to use the gallery to explore some of the rights and freedoms related to past governments of Russia, as well as Russia and the United States today.

📖 ACTIVE CLASSROOM

Have students use a Conversation with Putin activity to compare the American and Russian governments. Ask students to imagine they are having a conversation with President Putin. Tell students to ask Putin the following question: Why do you think the Russian federal system is better for governing Russia than the American federal system? Then have students write Putin's response and how they would reply to it. Ask volunteers to share their work with the class.

Further Instruction

Editable Presentation Use the Editable Presentation to present the main ideas for this Core Reading.

Comparison to the United States: Core Reading and Interactive Reading Notepad Project and discuss the Interactive Reading Notepad questions, including the graphic organizer asking students to compare and contrast the governments of the United States and the Russian Federation. Review this comparison with the class and fill in the graphic organizer on the whiteboard as you go.

Infer Why do you think Russians tend to favor strong centralized leadership? *(Possible answer: Russia has had strong centralized leadership for hundreds of years. As a result, Russians are used to this type of leadership. Also, Russians might believe that strong centralized leadership is needed to run such a large country as Russia.)*

The Russian Federation

■ SYNTHESIZE

DIGITAL SYNTHESIZE ACTIVITY
Revisiting Russia's Leaders

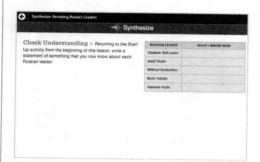

Ask students to recall the Topic Essential Question, "What Makes a Government Successful?" Ask students to review the Start Up activity from the beginning of this lesson. Have them write a statement of something that they now know about each Russian leader. *(Possible answers: V.I. Lenin: Led the Bolshevik Revolution and was the architect of the Communist party and its control over the Soviet Union. Joseph Stalin: Became Soviet leader after Lenin's death in 1924 and built the Soviet Union into a major industrial and military power. Mikhail Gorbachev: Became general secretary of the Communist Party in 1985 and led reforms that eroded the party's power. He was also president of the Soviet Union. Boris Yeltsin: Became president of Russian Republic in 1990. He guided the country through the tumultuous transition to a democratic Russian Federation. Vladimir Putin: The current president of the Russian Federation. Putin won elections in 2000, 2004, and 2012. Putin has also been Prime Minister.)* Have students share their answers with a talking partner.

Discuss Ask students to think about the poll they took at the beginning of this Topic. Ask if they would change any of their responses now that they have learned more about the Russian Federation.

■ DEMONSTRATE

DIGITAL QUIZ
Lesson Quiz and Class Discussion Board

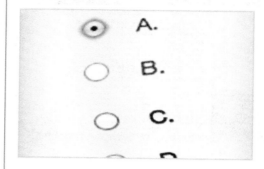

Assign the online Lesson Quiz for this lesson if you haven't already done so. Students will be offered automatic remediation or enrichment based on their scores.

Remind students that in *The Russian Federation* they read about the history of Russia since the Bolshevik Revolution. Also, they studied the structure of Russia's government and how public policy is created in Russia. In addition, they compared government in Russia with that of the United States.

Pose these questions to the class on the Discussion Board:

Identify Patterns What trends do you see happening in the Russian government since the collapse of the Soviet Union? *(Answers will vary. Students might mention that the Russian government seems to be moving from a government that lacked a strong central power base to one that has such a power base.)*

Make Predictions Do you think the Russian government will become more democratic or more totalitarian? Explain your answer. *(Answers will vary. Students who think the Russian government will become more democratic might argue that after tasting freedom following the collapse of the Soviet Union, the Russians will not want to go back to a totalitarian rule. Others might argue that the Russians feel more secure with strong central leadership. The political and economic problems suffered by Russians after the collapse of the Soviet Union might have convinced some Russians that such strong leadership is needed. Because of this, the Russian president may continue to gain more power until a totalitarian government is established.)*

Topic Inquiry
Have students continue their investigations for the Topic Inquiry.

www.PearsonRealize.com
Access your Digital Lesson

China

Supporting English Language Learners

Use with Digital Text 2, **Government in China.**

Speaking
Have students compare the U.S. constitutional republic to contemporary forms of government by reading the section *Government in China*. Create a chart with the title China's National Government. The chart should have two-columns with the headings National People's Congress and State Council. Guide students to complete and discuss the chart with information that explains each body of China's government.

Beginning Display a list of words related to the chart. Read the words and have the students repeat. Guide students to fill in the chart with the words. Allow them to illustrate the chart.

Intermediate Provide a list of words related to the chart. Read and discuss the words. Guide small groups to use the words to complete the chart.

Advanced Guide pairs to use the text to find information to complete the chart. Encourage them to use complete sentences. After the chart is complete, have pairs share their work with the class.

Advanced High Have students complete the chart using complete sentences. Guide students to read their charts to two other students.

Use with Digital Text 1, **China and Its History.**

Reading
Show students how a visual in the text supports a specific sentence or passage in the text. Examine and discuss each visual in the text as you guide students to compare the U.S. constitutional republic to contempory forms of government.

Beginning Read aloud the captions for the visuals. Ask students to describe what they see in each visual. Read the section of the text that is supported by the visual and explain how the visual helps students understand the text.

Intermediate Have small groups read the captions for each visual. Guide them to read the text and identify the section of the text supported by each visual. Have the students explain how the visual helps them understand the text.

Advanced Guide partners to read and discuss the visuals. Have them read the text and identify how each visual helps them understand the text.

Advanced High Have students independently jot notes about the visuals in the text. Have pairs share their notes and discuss how the visuals are related to the text.

▷ Differentiate Instruction

Use the Differentiated Instruction notes throughout the lesson plan to support the varied skill sets, levels of readiness, and interests in the mixed-ability classroom.

Challenge These notes include suggestions for expanding the activity for advanced students.

On-Level These notes include suggestions for modifying the activity to address different interests or learning styles.

Extra Support These notes include ideas for providing more scaffolding or reading spuport.

Special Needs These notes provide ideas for adapting instruction to support the needs of various special needs students.

■ NOTES

Topic 14 Lesson 4

China

Objectives

Objective 1: Examine China and its history starting with the birth of the People's Republic.

Objective 2: Outline the structure of China's government.

Objective 3: Examine how public policy is created in China.

Objective 4: Compare government in China with that of the United States.

LESSON 4 ORGANIZER		PACING: APPROX. 1 PERIOD, .5 BLOCKS			
				RESOURCES	
		OBJECTIVES	**PACING**	**Online**	**Print**
Connect					
DIGITAL START UP ACTIVITY **China—Myth or Fact?**			10 min.	●	
Investigate					
DIGITAL TEXT 1 **China and Its History**		Objective 1	10 min.	●	●
DIGITAL TEXT 2 **Government in China**		Objective 2	10 min.	●	●
DIGITAL TEXT 3 **Comparison to the United States**		Objectives 3, 4	10 min.	●	●
INTERACTIVE GALLERY **Analyzing Sources From China**			10 min.	●	
Synthesize					
DIGITAL SYNTHESIZE ACTIVITY **Government Policies and Constitutional Revision**			10 min.	●	
Demonstrate					
DIGITAL QUIZ **Lesson Quiz and Class Discussion Board**			10 min.	●	

PEARSON
realize™
www.PearsonRealize.com

Go online to access additional resources including:
Primary Sources • Biographies • Supreme Court cases •
21st Century Skill Tutorials • Maps • Graphic Organizers.

CONNECT

DIGITAL START UP ACTIVITY
China—Myth or Fact?

Project the Start Up Activity Ask students to read the statements about modern China and determine whether they are true or false.

Have students share their ideas with another student, either in class or through a chat or blog space.

Tell students that in this lesson they will be learning about the history of the People's Republic of China, the structure of its government, and how public policy is created in China.

Aa Vocabulary Development: Use the Interactive Reading Notepad to preview the Key Terms and Academic Vocabulary in this Lesson with students.

⇅ FLIP IT!

Assign the Flipped Video for this lesson.

▮ STUDENT EDITION PRINT PAGES: 696–700

INVESTIGATE

DIGITAL TEXT 1
China and Its History

Objective 1: Examine China and its history starting with the birth of the People's Republic.

Quick Instruction

Remind students that the People's Republic of China was established fairly recently compared to other countries. Ask students to use a Think Pair Share strategy to answer the following question. How was the establishment of the U.S. government different from the establishment of the People's Republic of China? *(Possible answer: The U.S. government was established by a revolution, during which colonies rebelled against an imperial power. The People's Republic of China was established by a civil war, during which the communists overthrew the Nationalist government. Americans established a democracy. The Chinese established a totalitarian, communist state.)* Ask volunteers to share their answers.

▯ Differentiate: Challenge Ask students to create an illustrated timeline of the history of China from the Chinese civil war in 1949 to the present. This timeline should include 4 or 5 important events. Students should write a brief description and draw an illustration for each event.

ELL Use the ELL activity described in the ELL chart.

Further Instruction

Go through the Interactive Reading Notepad questions and discuss the answers with the class. To extend the teaching of this objective have students answer the following questions.

Compare and Contrast How was the rule of Mao Zedong similar to and different from the rule of Deng Xiaoping? *(Mao Zedong had more of a strict communist approach, which applied to both politics and the economy. Deng Xiaoping also had a strict communist approach concerning politics. However, he was more open to capitalist reforms for the economy.)*

Recall What incident happened at Tiananmen Square in May 1989? *(About 100,000 students and workers staged a protest, demanding democratic reforms. China's military crushed the demonstration, killing hundreds of protestors.)*

China

DIGITAL TEXT 2
Government in China

Government in China

When the communists gained power, the People's Political Consultative Conference adopted a provisional constitution. That document became the basis for a new constitution adopted by the first session of the National People's Congress in 1954.

Unlike the Constitution of the United States and those of most other nations, China's constitution is not intended to be fundamental law. Instead, it is supposed to reflect current governmental policies. China has had four constitutions since its founding—in 1954, 1975, 1978, and 1982.

China's Communist Party China remains a communist state. The role of the Chinese Communist Party is not to mobilize people to vote; even though the Chinese Communist Party is the world's largest party with 82 million members, that translates to about six percent of the Chinese public. Rather, the role of the Communist Party is to govern. The top-ranking members of the party hold the highest positions in the government and the military. In short, the Communist Party is the government of China.

>> Censorship and propaganda are central to China's Communist Party. Colorful billboards and posters reflect a powerful government and bright future.

DIGITAL TEXT 3
Comparison to the United States

Comparison to the United States

The Communist Party dominates the policy process. Any policy coming from the National People's Congress or the State Council really reflects the policy leadership of the Communist Party. In fact, the Communist Party reviews legislation and can reject it before it can be voted upon. The Communist Party has officials throughout the country. The party holds authority over regional governments, controls their policies, and determines personnel decisions.

Other political actors, such as the media or interest groups seen in constitutional republics like the United States, do not influence governing decisions. In fact, the media is controlled and regulated by the government, which also imposes tight restrictions over the Internet.

>> In 2010, Google announced it would stop filtering search results in China. Analyze Political Cartoons Why would the Chinese government insist that Google comply with its censorship policies?

Objective 2: Outline the structure of China's government.

Quick Instruction
Remind students that the Communist Party dominates the government in China. Have students form groups of four. Then tell students to write for one minute as much as they can remember about the structure of China's government, without referring to the text. Students in each group should then pass their responses to the person to their right. The next person tries to improve or elaborate the response where the other person left off. Students should continue to switch responses until the papers come back to the original person. Each group then decides which is the best response and shares it with the class.

D Differentiate: **Extra Support** Help students understand the difference between the National People's Congress and the State Council. Ask: What is the main purpose of the National People's Council? What is the main purpose of the State Council? How are the two councils different?

ELL Use the ELL activity described in the ELL chart.

Further Instruction
Go through the Interactive Reading Notepad questions and discuss the answers with the class. To extend the teaching of this objective have students answer the following question.

Compare and Contrast How is the State Council of China's government similar to and different from the executive branch of the U.S. government? *(Both have major decision-making authority and make sure that laws are carried out. However, the State Council has much more control over the Chinese government than the executive branch has over the U.S. government. For example, the State Council can create and enforce laws that cannot be questioned. The U.S. executive branch does not have this power.)*

Objectives 3: Examine how public policy is created in China; 4: Compare government in China with that of the United States.

Quick Instruction
Interactive Gallery: Analyzing Sources From China Project the image gallery on the whiteboard. Look at each image individually and then the collection of images as a whole. Introduce the gallery activity by explaining to students the difference between primary and secondary sources. Tell students that sources often include bias. Bias is the favoring of one side or opinion over the others. A source may be reviewed for bias by looking at the author's point of view and the intended audience. Ask students to complete the graphic organizer by answering whether each is a primary or secondary source. Then, students should write whether there is bias in the source and why.

🗪 ACTIVE CLASSROOM

Have students use a Draw a Poster activity concerning propaganda in China. Ask students to form pairs. Then tell pairs to choose an issue for the Chinese government to promote. This issue should be something that the government would realistically want to support. Also, the issue should not repeat any of the issues in the interactive gallery. After pairs choose an issue, they should then draw a propaganda poster than promotes this issue. Ask volunteers to share their posters with the class.

SYNTHESIZE

DEMONSTRATE

INTERACTIVE GALLERY

Analyzing Sources From China

DIGITAL SYNTHESIZE ACTIVITY

Government Policies and Constitutional Revision

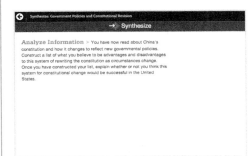

DIGITAL QUIZ

Lesson Quiz and Class Discussion Board

Further Instruction

Editable Presentation Use the Editable Presentation to present the main ideas for this Core Reading.

Comparison to the United States: Core Reading and Interactive Notepad Project and discuss the Interactive Reading Notepad questions, including the graphic organizer asking students to show how the role of the media has been the same and different in China under Mao Zedong and today. Also, students should add information about the role that media plays in the United States. Review the use of media in China and fill in the graphic organizer on the whiteboard as you go.

Support Ideas with Examples Do you think China and the United States have more political differences or more economic differences? *(Possible answer: China and the United States have more political differences than economic differences. The U.S. government is a democracy that has many checks and balances. The Chinese government is governed by a single party that has no checks and balances. However, the United States and China both have a privatized, market economy.)*

Ask students to recall the Topic Essential Question, "What Makes a Government Successful?" Have them use the Think Pair Share strategy to complete the following activity.

Analyze Information Remind students that they have read about China's constitution and how it changes to reflect new governmental policies. Tell partners to construct a list of what they believe to be advantages and disadvantages to this system of rewriting the constitution as circumstances change. Once partners have constructed their list, they should explain whether they think this system for constitutional change would be successful in the United States. *(Answers will vary, but should include several advantages and disadvantages. Advantages: As government policies change, the constitution is changed to reflect these policies; If the communist party ever loses power, the new party in charge could create a brand new constitution. Disadvantages: The government is not bound to its constitution; The government can create policies that completely disregard the constitution.)*

Discuss Ask students to think about the poll they took at the beginning of this Topic. Ask if they would change any of their responses now that they have learned more about China's government.

Assign the online Lesson Quiz for this lesson if you haven't already done so. Students will be offered automatic remediation or enrichment based on their scores.

Remind students that in *China* they read about the history of the People's Republic of China, the structure of China's government, and how public policy is created in China. Also, they compared government in China with government in the United States.

Pose these questions to the class on the Discussion Board:

Make Predictions Do you think the Chinese government will eventually become more democratic? Explain your answer. *(Answers will vary. Some students might response "yes," claiming that the free market system and the Internet will expose the Chinese to more and more democratic ideas. The Chinese government will find controlling these ideas to be increasingly difficult. As a result, the Chinese government will become more democratic. Others might say "no," claiming that the Chinese have never had a democracy and therefore would be uncomfortable with establishing such a government.)*

Identify Cause and Effect What caused the Chinese government to make economic reforms? *(The economic programs implemented by Mao Zedong had a disastrous effect on China's economy. The Chinese government probably realized that they had to move toward a market economy to prevent their economy from collapsing.)*

Topic Inquiry

Have students continue their investigations for the Topic Inquiry.

Comparative Political Systems

■ SYNTHESIZE

DIGITAL ACTIVITY
Reflect on the Essential Question

First, ask students to reconsider the Essential Question for the Topic: What Makes a Government Successful? Remind students that at the beginning of their study of democratization and democratic consolidation, they considered a list of what nations needed to obtain in order to transition to a true democracy. Ask students to consider the list again, in light of what they have learned about what is needed for a nation to become a democracy.

- A free press
- Competition among multiple political parties
- Civilian control of the military
- An engaged collection of interest groups
- A rewarding economic system
- Professional civil service
- Common trust shared among citizens

Point out to students that the second item on the list is "Competition among multiple political parties." Ask students: Why is this so important to a democracy? Give at least three reasons supporting your position.

Reflect on the Topic As students complete their study of democratization and democratic consolidation, ask them to take a few minutes to reflect on what they have learned. Ask them to write down three important questions they have thought about during the topic and their understanding of the answers to those questions.

You may ask students to share their questions and answers on the Class Discussion Board.

Topic Inquiry
Have students complete Step 3 of the Topic Inquiry.

■ DEMONSTRATE

DIGITAL TOPIC REVIEW AND ASSESSMENT
Comparative Political Systems

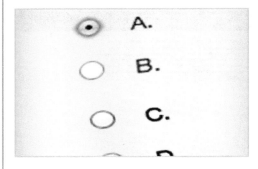

Students can prepare for the Topic Test by answering the questions in the Topic Review and Assessment online or the Assessment questions in the Print Student text. They can also prepare by reviewing their answers to the Interactive Reading Notepad questions or reviewing their notes in the Reading and Notetaking Study Guide.

TOPIC TEST
Assign the Topic Test to assess students' understanding of topic content.

DIGITAL TOPIC TEST
Comparative Political Systems

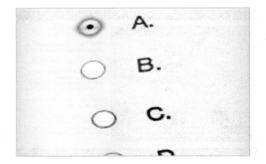

BENCHMARK TESTS
Assign these benchmark tests as you complete the relevant topics to monitor student progress toward mastering the course content and as preparation for the End-of-Course Test.

Benchmark Test 1: Topics 1–4

Benchmark Test 2: Topics 5–8

Benchmark Test 3: Topics 9–11

Benchmark Test 4: Topics 12–14

END-OF-COURSE TESTS
Assign End-Of-Course Test 1 or 2 to measure students' progress in mastering the course content.